Copyright © 2018 by Cláudio Rodrigues & Freek Berson

All rights reserved. No part of the contents of this b
transmitted in any form or by any means without the writter

Many of the designations used by the manufacturers and sellers to distinguish their products are claimed as trademarks. Where those designations appear in this book, and WTSLabs Inc. was aware of a trademark claim, the designations have been printed with initial capital letters or in all capitals.

This book expresses the authors' views and opinions. The information contained in this book is provided without any express, statutory, or implied warranties. Neither the authors, nor its resellers, or distributors, will be held liable for any damages caused or alleged to be caused either directly or indirectly by this book.

ISBN-13: 978-1718085251

RDS – The Complete Guide, First Edition

For additional content on this book, corrections or to contact the authors, please go to http://www.rdscomplete.com

Contents

Foreword 7
Preface 9
Getting Started 14
Environment 15
Active Directory Preparation 16
    Organizational Units (OUs) 16
Virtual Machine Preparation 17
The RDS Roles 18
    RD Session Host (RDSH) 18
    RD Web Access (RDWA) 19
    RD Gateway (RDGW) 19
    RD Connection Broker (RDCB) 20
    RD Licensing (RDLS) 20
The Deployment Types 21
    Role Based Deployment 21
    Scenario Based deployment 21
Performing a Quick Start deployment 24
    Using RDMS 31
Performing a Standard deployment 37
    Doing it 37
    Adding a Session Collection 45
    Publishing RemoteApps 63
    Adding RDSH Servers 74
    Setting up RDCB HA 82
    Adding Certificates 112
    Adding RDGW 136
    Setting up RDGW HA 154

Adding RDLS 171
  Fixing external access 184
Enhancing your Standard Deployment..196
  Configuring User Profile Disks 199
  Customizing RDWA 212
Performing a Role Based Deployment 220
Using the RemoteDesktop PowerShell Module 228
  Importing the RemoteDesktop module 228
  Installing a Session Based Desktop Deployment 228
  Creating a Session Collection 229
  Creating Remote Apps 230
  Configuring RD Gateway settings..231
  Configuring RD Licensing options..232
  Finding your favorite RemoteDesktop cmdlet..233
Troubleshooting the installation and configuration 234
  Enable tracing..234
  Troubleshooting using the debug log..236
  Troubleshooting sessions...237
  Troubleshooting RD Web Access...243
Accessing the environment..246
  RD Web Access 246
  Remote App and Desktop Connections 251
  Session Collection resource types 257
  Distributing RDP files...260
RemoteFX 263
  Single Sign-On, Email and web discovery of RemoteApps and Desktops..........263
  Adaptive Graphics...265
  Intelligent Transports 266
  Multi touch..267

Page 4 | RDS - The Complete Guide

  USB Redirection 267

Completing your RDS environment 268
  Basic GPO and GPP 268
  Customizing and locking down the 'Start' screen 278
  Installing applications 283
  Tricerat's Simplify Profiles - Managing the user environment, the right way..... 286

Printing 315
  Printer Types 315
  Drivers 316
  Flow 317
  Trying to fix the mess 321
  Tricerat's Simplify Printing - Fixing it for good 324
  The icing on the cake: 'Simplify Printing TX' 349

Connecting to the environment 386
  Setting up RDCMan 386
  Using RDCMan 389
  Devolutions Remote Desktop Manager 393
  Setting up Devolutions RDM 398
  Creating connections on Devolutions RDM 401
  Backing up and restoring your Devolutions RDM connections 407
  Setting up Devolutions RDM for multiple users 411

Monitoring the environment 433
  Creating an RDS dashboard with Performance Monitor 433
  Creating an RDS dashboard with PowerShell 435
  ControlUp Real-time 447
  ControlUp Insights 465
  Additional ControlUp Real-time Features 472

Foreword

By Brian Madden & Gabe Knuth

Let's be honest. We decided to write this forward for Cláudio and Freek because we wanted an early copy of this book.

There. We said it. That felt good.

It's not as bad as it sounds, though. You see, we *needed* this book because, well, we got rusty.

When we first became aware of Cláudio, it was sometime back in the 1900's on TheThin.net (an introduction to Freek came much later), and he was answering questions while occasionally promoting his own Terminal Server load balancing product. At the time, we really cared about this because we were up to our ears doing Terminal Server and Citrix MetaFrame installations, and Cláudio's stuff really helped.

When we had the first BriForum conference in 2005, Cláudio was one of the first people we invited to speak (we had to reach out to people back then). At that time, the entirety of desktop virtualization amounted to fewer than ten companies. You had Microsoft, Citrix, triCerat, ThinPrint, UniPrint (man, printing was really terrible back then), Lakeside Software, Softricity, and...uh...Kevsoft. That was it! We knew the space as well as anyone, and it made us into some really kickass bloggers.

Over time, though, desktop virtualization grew into End User Computing, and the ten companies grew to well over two hundred companies. As bloggers, we couldn't remain deeply technical, so we withdrew to a higher level. This was great—until we realized that we'd become so "high level" that the sight of a PowerShell prompt made us feel like our parents must feel when Windows wants to boot into Safe Mode (sort of an if-I-type-the-wrong-thing-I-could-erase-everything feeling).

We needed to get back in touch with the technology, and that's what we did. For the first time well over a decade, we found ourselves working for different companies, Brian for VMware and Gabe for FSLogix. In our new roles, we get to dig happily into some deep, dark corners of EUC, but we live in fear of someone asking us a question about a specific feature of Windows Server 2016 (or 2019—I smell a sequel!).

So, you see, we had to get this book early so we could look good at our jobs!

In reality, we feel very privileged to write this foreword, not for the half-true mea culpa (does that mean one of us stayed current, but the other didn't?), but because Cláudio and Freek have been friends of ours for many years. They are two of the sharpest Microsoft-minded people we've ever worked with, and this book will get you up to speed on RDS quickly and reliably, just like it did for us.

Happy reading,
Brian Madden & Gabe Knuth

Preface

Part I, by Cláudio Rodrigues

Here I am sitting at an apartment in Paris, France. The idea of writing a book about Remote Desktop Services as seen on Windows Server 2012, now 2016, haunted me since Microsoft announced the release date for it. At that point I approached fellow RDS MVP Freek Berson (by the way, one of the BEST RDS experts out there, trust me on this) and we decided to go for it.

After all, I had written pretty much the same about Windows Server 2003, years before 2012 was even at the horizon. So, it would be a walk in the park, right? Problem is I underestimated the impact a newborn can have on your writing abilities and time management skills and this simply postponed the book forever. Microsoft then released 2012 R2 and we are now deploying Windows Server 2016 RDS for some brave customers.

After coming back from BriForum 2015 in Denver and having a chat with both Brian and Gabe (from BrianMadden.com, now working for VMware and FSLogix respectively), Brian gave me his perspective on writing books at that time and how it was back in the day when he wrote his first Citrix one. Even though he had a point that a lot of information is now available on the internet, either in blog format or YouTube videos, the bottom line, at least for me, is the fact it is all scattered and not necessarily in a concise way. That and the fact Freek was indeed very eager to get this book out of the way, are the reasons why I did decide to move forward with the book, even with Brian telling me it sort of sucks to write them today.

If you, the reader, are like me, I do value being able to find everything I need about a certain topic in a single spot. Having to hunt for information, not necessarily written or recorded the same way (when you get it from multiple sources) is not only a chore in itself but also painful. Therefore, thank Brian (and Freek) for the fact you now have this book in your hands.

In addition, it was about time to sit down and put to words everything we learned the hard way over the years with Windows Server 2012 R2 Remote Desktop Services. It was not always smooth sailing in RDS 2012 R2 land. Many times it was actually frustrating. However, if you have someone to show you the quirks, the caveats and the pitfalls you may face with it, it is certainly much easier to get it going.

I think it is also worth mentioning a little thing about this book. The main idea behind it was to show you how to get RDS 2012 R2 going (keeping in mind that almost the whole book still applies for RDS 2016 and pretty certain to RDS 2019). Sure, that is why you bought this book. However, with a twist.

For every major topic you should be addressing on RDS, there is always the vendor way (in this case, Microsoft) and the other way. By other way I mean third party vendors and when you get to that, for certain topics there is a myriad of vendors to address that one task.

This is the twist on the book. I took the time to take a look at most vendors in this space, that address things like printing and monitoring and not only selected the best of the breed but also wrote complete start guides within each chapter on how to get that particular solution setup and working. So, by the end of each chapter you will not only know the Microsoft way of doing things but also how to do it with a proven and tested product in the industry.

For that reason, I must thank several people and companies in this industry. They understood the vision for this book and the approach we were taking even before I wrote a single page. Therefore, my big **THANK YOU** to these people:

- John Byrne, Tricerat (http://www.tricerat.com)
- Max Trottier, Devolutions (http://www.devolutions.net)
- Amir Harel, ControlUp, (http://www.controlup.com)

They are a big reason why this book was possible and I hope that by the end of it, you will agree these are indeed the best of the breed out there as of today.

Moreover, before you ask, why Paris? Well first, it inspires you to get it done. There is a reason why writers and artists chose the 'City of Light'. I simply went down the same path.

Finally, after having a kid at age forty I now understand I will be working until I am at least eighty. With that in mind, I can definitely afford two or three months of my long working life to write a book. What I did. Thing is three months turned into two years but hey, that is another story.

I do hope you enjoy this book as much as I enjoyed writing it. Next time you are in Paris, have a glass of wine on me and thank the French Gods for the book as they did have a big role on making this a reality.

And before you ask, the RDS 2016 companion is in the works and will be available shortly, covering all that is specific to that release. Same for RDS 2019 I must say.

Thank you for your support and for purchasing this awesome book.

Cláudio Rodrigues

Microsoft MVP, Remote Desktop Services

Twitter: @crod

Blog: blog.wtslabs.com

Part 2, by Freek Berson

First of all, thank you for your interest in this book!

Credit where credit is due, Cláudio is the brains behind this book! He contacted me back in 2012 if I was interested in co-authoring a new book on RDS, back then still RDS 2012 since R2 was not out yet. At that time, I had already written many TechNet Wiki articles because I too realized that documentation on RDS 2012 was missing. I jumped in on the book and as Cláudio explained in the first part of this preface, we started writing it with the plan to include a separate chapter covering everything new in 2012 R2 to be able to publish it shortly after the release of 2012 R2.

After a break in working on the book for reasons explained above, we picked up where we left of and modified it to cover RDS 2012 R2 right from the start. And now, in 2018, we are proud that our book is published and available!

It has been an honor and pleasure working with Cláudio on this book. Up until today, I have been part of the RDS MVP group for 6 years. Cláudio has been there since day one! He is the 1st, and up until today still the longest running RDS MVP out there! ☺. It is always fun to catch up and hang out with him during various IT conferences across the globe like MVP Summit, BriForum, E2EVC et cetera.

I would also like to take this opportunity to thank a few people. First of all, my family, and especially my wife Ingeborg, who has always supported me during these kinds of projects. Second, a big thank you to the authors of the Remote Desktop Services 2008 R2 Resource Kit, Christa Anderson and Kristin Griffin. In the meantime, we have become close friends and their book, probably without them knowing it, has been a big inspiration for my share on this book. Third, I would like to thank Wortell, my current employer, who provided time and hardware resources to build the necessary labs used in this book.

With Windows Server 2016 already out and 2019 looming in the horizon, we already have plans for companion books!

I hope you enjoy reading our book. If you have comments, feedback or questions on the contents of this book, feel free to reach out to either of us.

Thank you!

Freek Berson

Microsoft MVP, Remote Desktop Services

Blog: themicrosoftplatform.net

Twitter: @fberson

Getting Started

Before getting too far ahead, I just want to make one thing clear: it is NOT the idea of this book to show you how to use all the Virtual Desktop Infrastructure (VDI) features available on 2012 R2. We focus on the Terminal Services (TS)/Remote Desktop Services (RDS) side of it (now called "Session-Based Desktop Deployment" – thanks for another name change Microsoft) and may release another book down the road to cover the VDI side of things (yep, renamed as well to "Virtual-Machine Based Desktop Deployment"). It is important to mention that even though this book is indeed based on Windows Server 2012 R2 RDS, almost everything here does apply to Windows Server 2016. If you master what is given to you here, RDS 2016 will be a walk in the park. Trust us on that.

Another point is, we assume you have some knowledge of Windows Server 2008 R2/2012 R2 in general (Active Directory, Group Policies, Group Policy Preferences, etc.).

Finally, as mentioned before, you can do many of the things described here in different ways, all leading to the same results. This does not mean you are wrong and we are right or vice-versa. It just means there are many ways to perform different tasks so just use the one you feel more comfortable with.

Environment

The test environment setup for this book was based on Windows Server 2012 R2 with its latest patches (as of April 2018). We used a total of twelve virtual machines (VMs) running the Datacenter Edition (what should not matter) in two different environments. One on top of VMware ESXi 5.5 and the other on top of Hyper-V 2012 R2 (we are looking at you Freek). Keep in mind you can run these on many platforms – Citrix XenServer, VMware Workstation and even Parallels Desktop.

For the client VM we used Windows 8.1 Professional, joined to the same domain as the servers.

ⓘ **Note:** it is worth mentioning, in case you did not realize it so far, that Windows Server 2012 R2 is a 64-bit only platform (like 2008 R2) what means no support for 16-bit applications and/or installers. Make sure you clearly understand this AND that you test your apps under such platform before deciding to go for 2012 R2 RDS. If this seems obvious, our apologies but we have seen so many projects starting without even knowing if the apps would run on the target OS. Yes, this is not a joke.

The hostnames of the VMs used are as follows.

Name	Role / description
CRLAB-DC01	Domain Controller.
CRLAB-FS01	A simple 2012 R2 File Server. It will hold things like shared folders, redirected ones, profiles, User Profile Disks etc.
CRLAB-SQ01	Server running Microsoft SQL Server
CRLAB-LS01	Server running the Remote Desktop (RD) Licensing Role
CRLAB-CB01	Server running the RD Connection Broker Role
CRLAB-CB02	2nd Server running the RD Connection Broker Role
CRLAB-GW01	Server running the RD Gateway Role
CRLAB-GW02	2nd Server running the RD Gateway Role
CRLAB-WA01	Server running the RD Web Access Role
CRLAB-WA02	2nd Server running the RD Web Access Role
CRLAB-SH01	Server running the RD Session Host Role

Name	Role / description
CRLAB-SH02	2nd Server running the RD Session Host Role
CRLAB-CL01	Windows 8.1 client, part of the CRLAB domain

Do not worry too much at this stage about the RDS components and what they do. We will explain each of one in detail and show you how to set up these properly.

Active Directory Preparation

The active directory preparation for Windows Server 2012 R2 is pretty much the same as with Windows Server 2008 R2, or even Windows Server 2003.

In most environments, when Remote Desktop Services is deployed, settings that are applied to the regular computers (i.e. desktop wallpapers, themes, ability to shutdown the machine, etc.) are usually not applied to the RD Session Host Servers. This means a different set of rules should exist to deal only with the user experience when connected to an RD Session Host Server and these rules may not be the same ones that apply to the user's regular machine (i.e. his desktop on his desk).

This guide assumes you have a properly configured and working Windows Server 2012 R2 Active Directory environment but as you will see, many of the concepts/ideas here discussed will apply to pretty much any Active Directory version (2003, 2008, 2012 or 2016).

We also assume you have rights to perform such changes on your Active Directory. In case you do not have rights, you will need to discuss your requirements with the group that manages your Active Directory inside your organization (we do hope you will first do all this in a lab). In certain environments, getting approvals from all the relevant groups will be the hardest part of an RDS deployment.

Organizational Units (OUs)

To keep things easy to understand we created separate OUs with a name matching the different RDS roles. In our environment, we have used the following OU structure.

```
▲ 🖿 Servers
     🖿 Back End
     🖿 RD Connection Broker
     🖿 RD Gateway
     🖿 RD Licensing
     🖿 RD Session Host
     🖿 RD Web Access
```

After the OU structure is complete, we are able to move the servers hosting the different roles to the corresponding OUs. Another reason to put servers in corresponding OUs is the ability to easily create and link Group Policy Objects (GPOs) that contain specific settings for computers running these roles.

The names used are self-explanatory. Here we moved the file server and SQL server to the 'Back End' OU. Everything else goes to the corresponding OUs based on the RDS role the server runs.

Once you have your VMs up and running, patch all of them and make sure you have a snapshot ready, as we will be reverting them as we go along. Remember to disable machine password changes, otherwise, you may run into issues depending how old the snapshot is once you revert the VM. Do not ask me how we know that.

Virtual Machine Preparation

Before you start working on any RDS deployment, make sure all virtual machines that will hold any of the RDS roles are configured to allow remote management. Depending on the image or template you used to create your virtual machines, this may have been configured already but make sure you double-check it before starting.

There are various ways to check if remote management is enabled. The easiest way is to logon to each virtual machine and check if the remote management service is enabled. If not, set it to 'Enabled'. The reason for this is simple to understand. When performing an RDS deployment, we will be managing all the different RDS roles remotely, from a single 'Server Manager' console.

The RDS Roles

Now that we have our Active Directory environment in place we will take a look at the different RDS roles that come with Windows Server 2012 R2. In the first book I wrote, we discussed Terminal Services based on Windows Server 2003 (by the way, available for download at no cost at http://www.wtslabs.com). Since then Windows Server 2008/2008 R2/2012/2012 R2 have been released and we are now working with Windows Server 2016. Over the past decade, a lot has changed regarding the way RDS is installed. The most significant change since 2003 is the fact that RDS now comes with separate roles that make up the environment.

Let's take a look at the different RDS roles available for Windows Server 2012 R2. Note that you will get more in-depth knowledge of the different roles and the way they work together once we cover the setup process and guide you through several actual deployments.

> ⓘ **Note:** you may be asking why bother with RDS 2012 R2 if RDS 2016 is out and more than that, Windows Server 2019 is now on technical preview. The bottom line is actually quite simple. The vast majority is still on 2012 R2 and many, believe it or not, are still running 2008 R2 for their RDS deployments. On top of that, RDS 2016 is virtually identical to RDS 2012 so it makes sense to cover it as it will certainly lay down the foundation you will need to work with any RDS release, today or tomorrow.

RD Session Host (RDSH)

The RD Session Host (RDSH) role is what we called back in the day a 'Terminal Server'. It is the server that hosts the actual end users' sessions. Actually, one of the first chapters in the 2003 book called 'What is it?' still applies here. Multiple end-users logon to this server, each one getting his own session to perform their regular tasks just as they would on a local desktop or laptop. As users share most of the resources of the RD Session Host, this makes it highly scalable and easy to maintain. At the same time, special consideration has to be given regarding resources utilization, as we do not want a single user to slow down the whole server what would certainly affect all other users connected to the same session host. The same applies to locking down the RDSHs to prevent users from not only changing computers settings, or even worse, rebooting or shutting down these servers (this is addressed by using 'Group Policies', which we will cover later on in this book).

RD Web Access (RDWA)

Users can access their sessions in many different ways. Traditionally you would simply instruct your users to launch the 'Remote Desktop Client' software on their PCs (part of the Windows Operating System) and connect to a certain IP address or name. Alternatively, you could provide them with what we call a .RDP file, which contains all the information the RDP client needs to know in order to connect to the appropriate servers.

However, we can take all this to the next level and deliver the RDS environment using a website. This allows users to simply open their web browser and go to the website you provided (and guess what, you can even rebrand it to match your corporate image or needs). Once they authenticate, all the resources (applications or desktop – more details on this later) they are allowed to use will be shown to them as icons sitting on a web page. It is also possible to integrate all these with the local 'Start Menu' (or in Windows 8.x the 'Start Screen'), providing a complete seamless solution where users can barely distinguish between their own local applications and the ones you are providing through your RDS environment.

The RD Web Access (RDWA) is the component responsible for delivering this web portal to your users. It also handles the web feed used by Windows 7 or up clients to automatically add the RDSH applications to the 'Start Menu' or 'Start Screen' (this is done by configuring the 'Remote Access and Desktop Connection – RADC – applet seen under 'Control Panel' on Windows 7 or up, and yes, we will show you how to do that later on).

RD Gateway (RDGW)

When connecting to your RDS environment, by default the connection is established over a well-known protocol, RDP, on port 3389 (TCP). The protocol is indeed encrypted but unfortunately, it is not firewall friendly, meaning several places may block such port outbound. The other problem is if you have multiple RDS Session Hosts available to your outside users, you would need to open several ports on your firewall so all these servers can be reached from the outside.

That is where the RD Gateway (RDGW) comes to the picture. First, it uses a well-known port (443) and encryption mechanism (SSL) what makes it very firewall friendly. Secondly, as its name implies, it acts as a gateway between your users and your RDS Session Hosts so only a single port (TCP 443) needs to be open on your firewall (and directed to the RDGW). It will then extract the RDP traffic from the SSL one and send it to the correct RDSH (we will also explain why port UDP 3391 should be opened to the RDGW. Keep reading).

RD Connection Broker (RDCB)

One of the challenges when setting up an RDS environment is ensuring that connections are equally spread over multiple RD Session Host servers (what we call 'Load Balancing') and allowing users to reconnect to an existing session they may have running on your RDSHs (this can happen on purpose – they close the RDP client without logging off – or by accident - due to temporary network issues).

These are the two main tasks of the RD Connection Broker (RDCB). This role has evolved from what was called Session Directory on Windows Server 2003. At the time, the only thing it did was to reconnect users to their sessions. The TS Connection Broker in Windows Server 2008 added the load balancing part.
Finally, RD Connection Broker in Windows Server 2008 R2 brought support for VDI to the table.

With Windows Server 2012 R2, the RD Connection Broker plays an even more central and important part on any RDS environment. As we will discuss in more detail, the RD Connection Broker now also handles the initial connection (previously known as 'RD Dedicated Redirector') and finally has support for High Availability (HA).

RD Licensing (RDLS)

This role does exactly what its name implies. Users connecting to the RDS environment need a Remote Desktop Services Client Access License (RDS CAL) to connect. Once a user connects, the RD Session Hosts will try to retrieve a license from the RD Licensing Server (RDLS) and will act accordingly (denying or allowing the connection). This role has not changed much with Windows Server 2012 R2.

> ⓘ **Note:** RDS CALs are required on top of any other licenses you may need (i.e. Windows Client Access Licenses). It is also important to make it clear that RDS is not a licensing-saving miracle. The fact you only install an application once on your RDSHs (i.e. Office 2016) does not mean you only need one license. Make sure you contact the respective vendor before installing any application on your RDSHs to have these properly licensed.

The Deployment Types

Now that we have a basic understanding of the different roles that make up an RDS environment in Windows Server 2012 R2, we can finally start some hands-on work.

When it comes to deploying RDS environments there are two deployment types. We will briefly discuss both of them below. We will be guiding you through the process of using both of them but will focus on the Scenario Based Deployment since this was introduced with Windows Server 2012 (part of 2012 R2 and 2016 as well).

Role Based Deployment

In Windows Server 2008 Role Based Deployment was introduced. This simply meant you could install different roles (in our case the RDS ones explained above) separately on your servers, using the server manager console on each one of them (for the advanced readers, yes, you could also use PowerShell scripting and automate most of this).

Once the RDS roles were deployed you had to follow a fair amount of configuration guides to "glue" all the roles together and to create your RDS environment. It is still pretty much the same to this day. That means you need to have a good understanding of all the roles and how they are tied together in order to get your RDS environment fully up and running.

Scenario Based deployment

Windows Server 2012 introduced the ability to do what is called a "Scenario Based Deployment" renamed to "Remote Desktop Services Installation" on the Windows Server 2012 final release. The big difference there is that you run one single, simple server manager wizard to gather all the necessary information of all the roles you want to deploy. With that information available, the wizard installs all the different roles on all the different servers remotely and then performs the required "gluing" process for you.

After the wizard is completed, you have a basic operational RDS environment and, as we will see later on, it can be managed remotely from a central location.

ⓘ **Note:** Although we wrote a whole chapter about the Role Based Deployment, you will probably not be using it a lot with Windows Server 2012 R2 due to its own limitations as a deployment mode. More on that later.

Back to the "Remote Desktop Services Installation" in Windows Server 2012 R2, it comes in two different flavors. It is important to understand the difference between these two types before you proceed and choose a deployment type for your environment. That said, after reading what is next you will understand why we always go for one of the deployment types.

- **Quick Deployment**
The quick deployment is meant for a single server installation, installing all the required roles. Yes, it means you will end up with a single server running the RD Session Host, RD Web Access and the RD Connection Broker roles. Great for a lab or Proof of Concept setup but not really for production (all eggs in one basket is never a good idea). Even for small customers this is not recommended.

- **Standard Deployment**
The main difference with this deployment type is the fact you can select which servers will hold each role and everything required to get all working together will be done automatically for you. As the roles are installed on different servers, this does require more resources but does not give you a major single point of failure right out-of-the-box, what the "Quick Deployment" wizard really creates. Keep in mind even by using this deployment type you will still need to manually take care of HA for each component, with the exception of the RD SHs, assuming you install more than one of course.

Performing a Quick Start deployment

Now that we have some basic knowledge of the roles that make up RDS in Windows Server 2012 R2 and have seen the different deployment types available it is time to start working on your first RDS deployment.

Since this is the Quick Deployment, we only need a single server to host all the RDS roles. In our lab environment, we chose CRLAB-SH01 for this. After this scenario is finished, we will revert it back to its pristine state and reuse it for the Standard Scenario (the beauty of snapshots in virtualization).

The second server we will be using here is CRLAB-CB01, to show the remote management possibilities of Windows Server 2012 R2. In production environments, you should use a separate server (two for redundancy) for management purposes that would have other management tools and consoles installed. Even better, it would have session recording software installed so all actions, to manage anything off that server, from AD to Firewalls, would be recorded for later viewing. Neat eh?

1. Logon to CRLAB-CB01 and launch the server manager console since we will be using this server for management purposes.

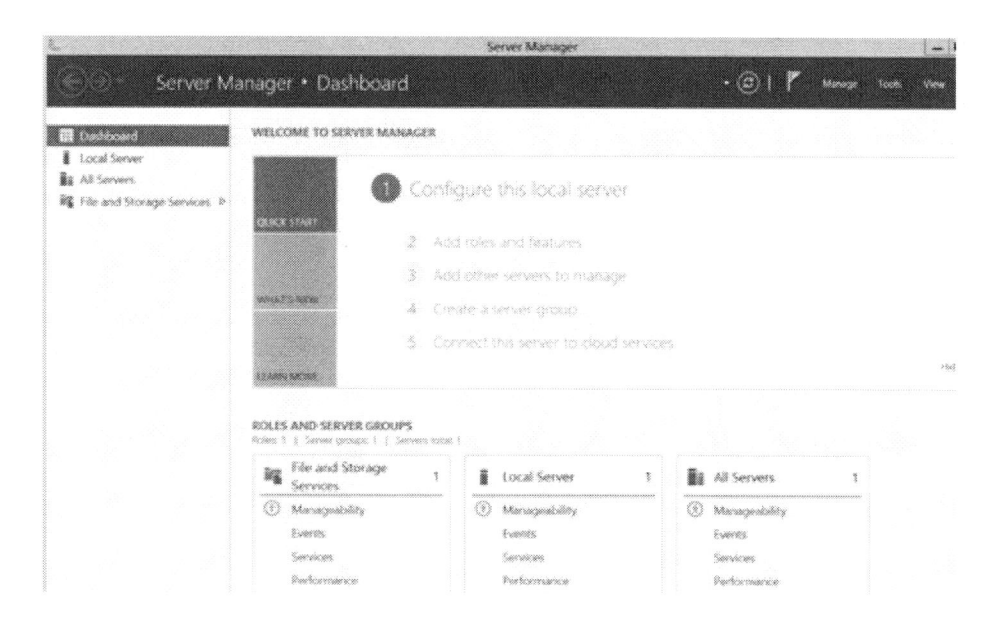

2. Before we can start our first RDS deployment, we must add all the servers we want to manage through this console so it is aware of these machines. Click '3. Add other servers to manage'.

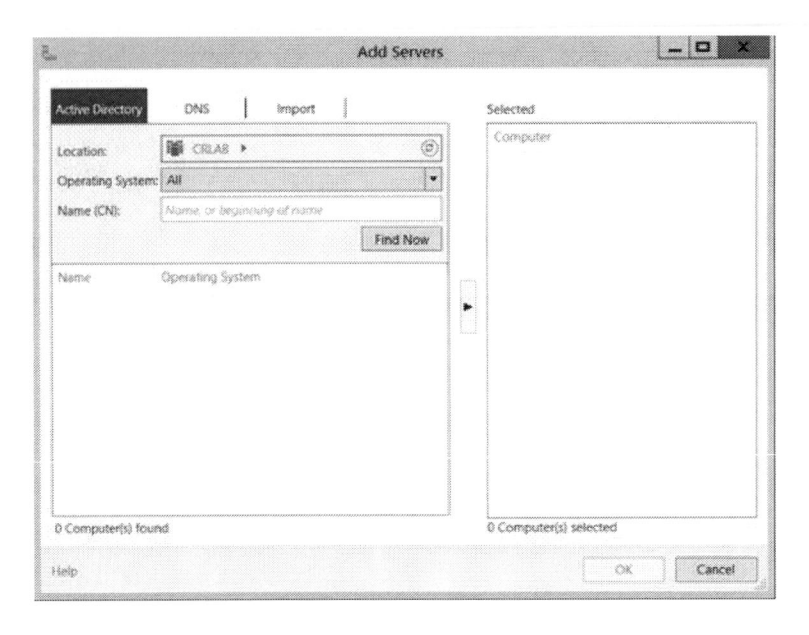

3. Leave the "Name (CN)" blank and click 'Find Now'. Select CRLAB-SH01 and click on the arrow button to add it to the 'Selected' pane and click 'Ok'.

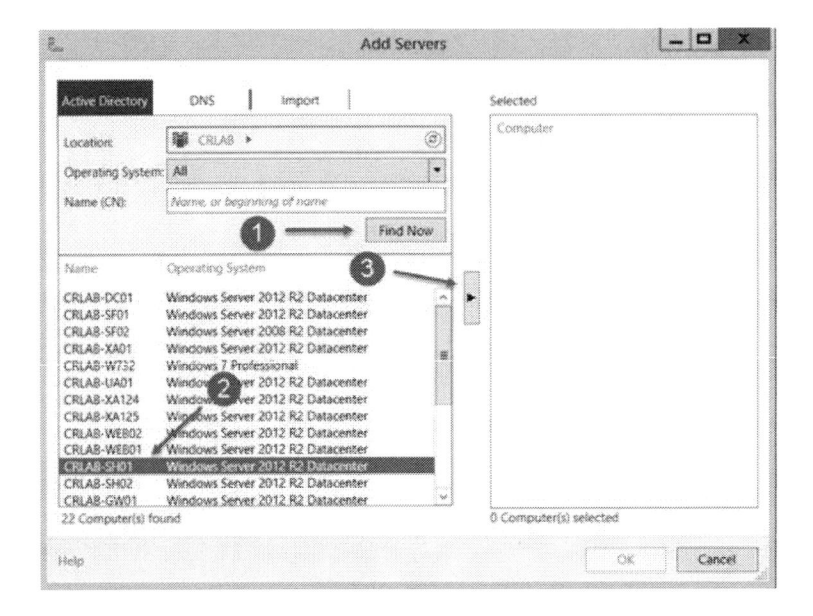

4. Now back to the server manager dashboard, click '2. Add roles and features'. The 'Add Roles and Features Wizard' launches, displaying some basic information about its features and showing a couple pre-requisites. Simply click 'Next'.

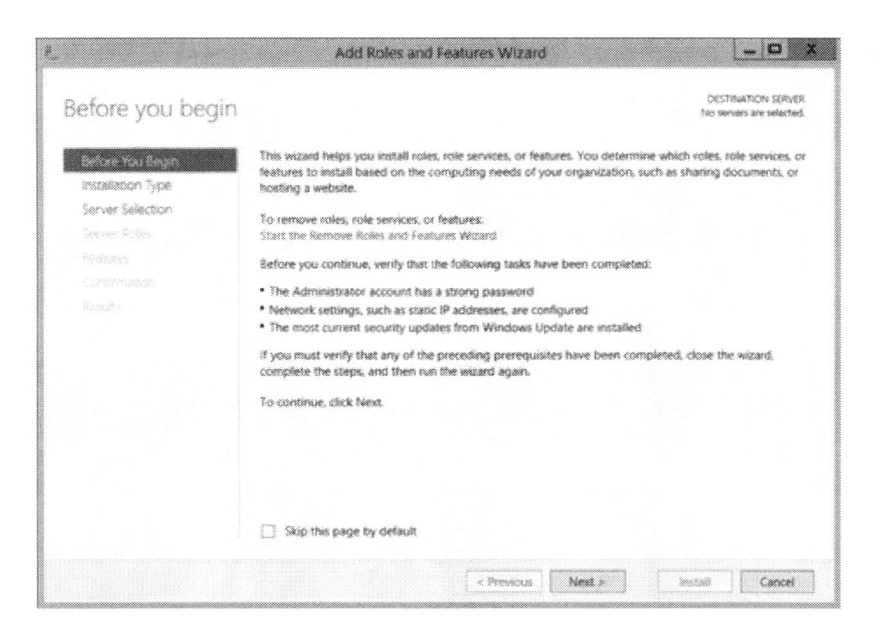

5. As we are deploying a full Microsoft RDS solution, select 'Remote Desktop Services installation' and click 'Next'.

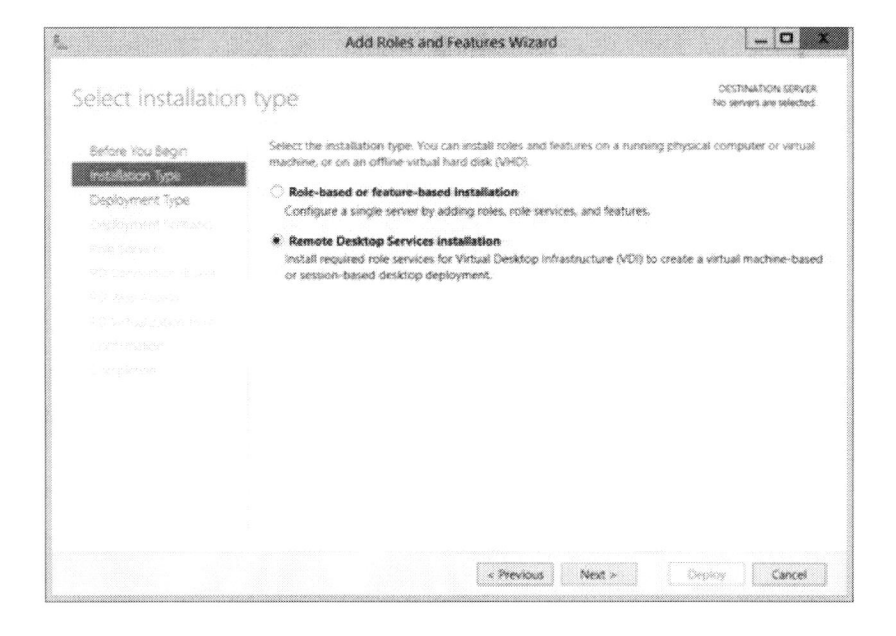

6. Now this is where the wizard asks you if you want to do a 'Standard deployment' (roles go to separate servers) or a 'Quick Start' one. As we are indeed performing an all-in-one deployment here, select 'Quick Start' and click 'Next'.

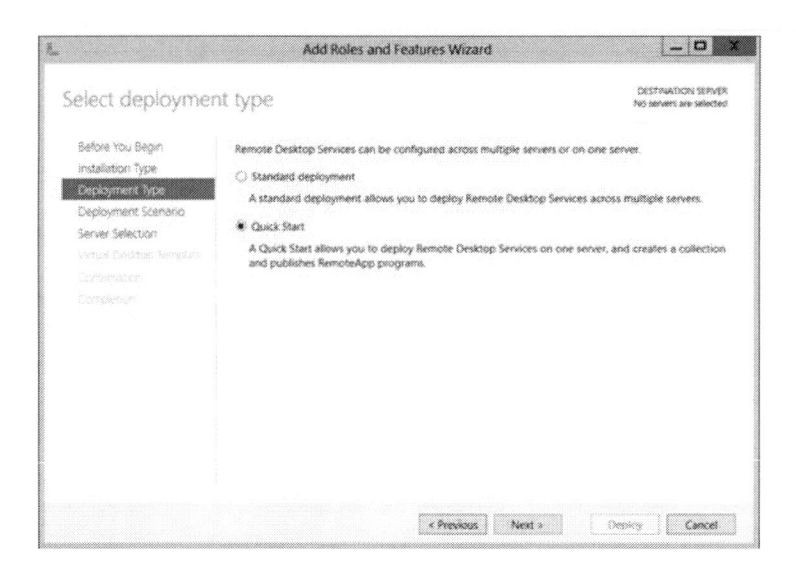

7. Now select 'Session-based desktop deployment' and click 'Next'. As mentioned previously this book is about RDS SH and not VDI. When doing a VDI deployment you would select 'Virtual machine-based desktop deployment'.

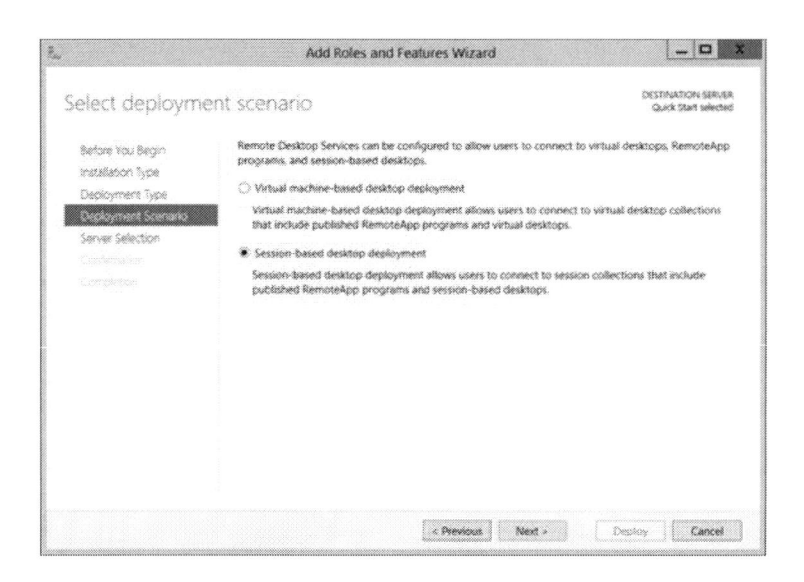

8. As we are going to use CRLAB-SH01 as the server holding all RDS roles (remember, this is the all-in-one 'Quick Start' deployment), select it and click the arrow button. You may need to right-click any other server and select 'Remove'. Once you see only CRLAB-SH01 under 'Selected', click 'Next'.

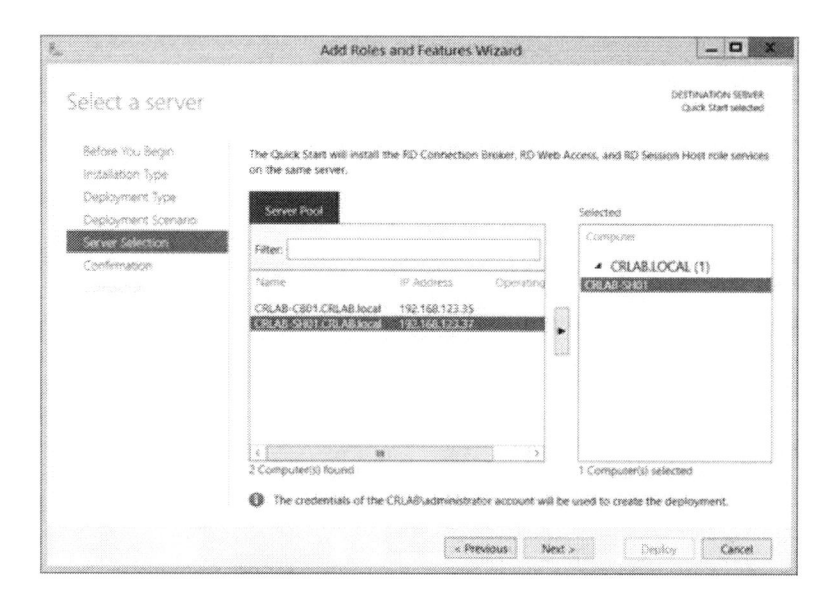

9. The wizard will display a quick summary. Please note the RDS Licensing and Gateway roles are not part of the 'Quick Start' deployment. More on that later. For now, make sure the check box to restart the server if needed is checked and click 'Deploy'.

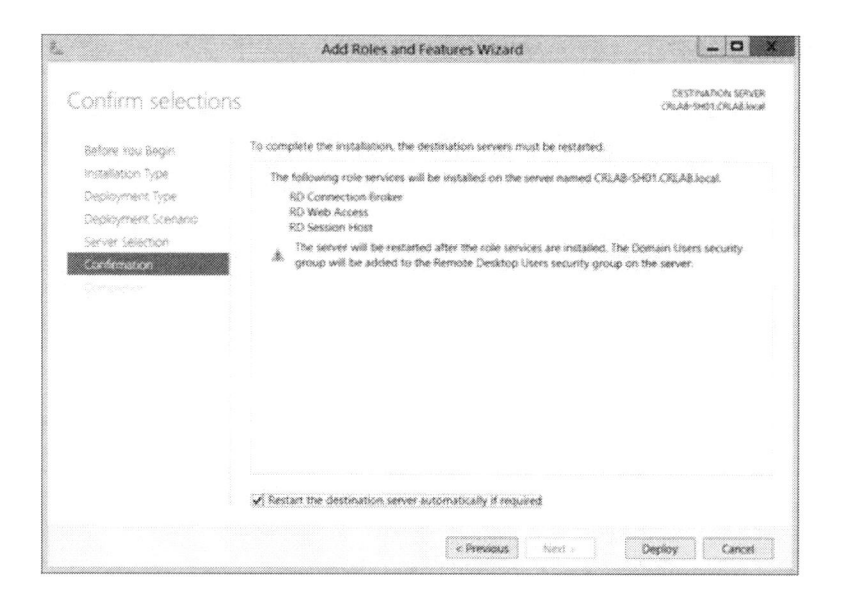

10. The wizard will then show you the status of the deployment. Simply wait and enjoy. You just finished your first RDS 2012 R2 'Quick Start' deployment.

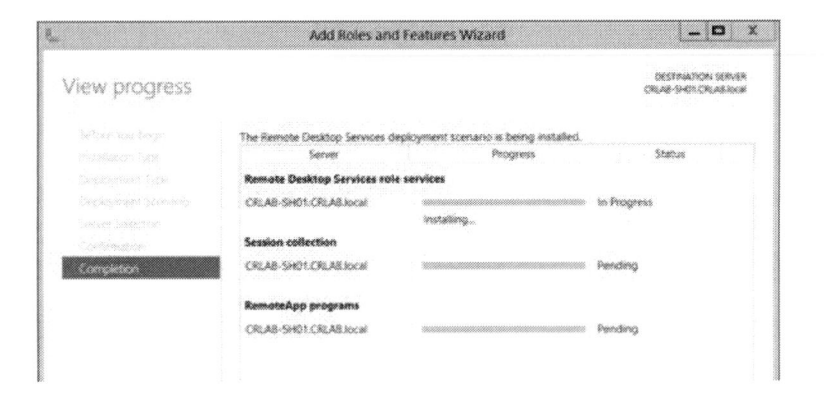

Note: If you get an error during the session collection phase, the issue is almost certainly a group policy that is somehow setting something related to RDS (i.e. timeouts for sessions, licensing, etc.). Make sure there are no policies applied to these servers that may enforce anything like that. Yes, another do-not-ask-me-how-we-know-that moment.

Assuming you do not experience the error mentioned above you will get a 'Succeeded' on all three tasks. Click 'Close'.

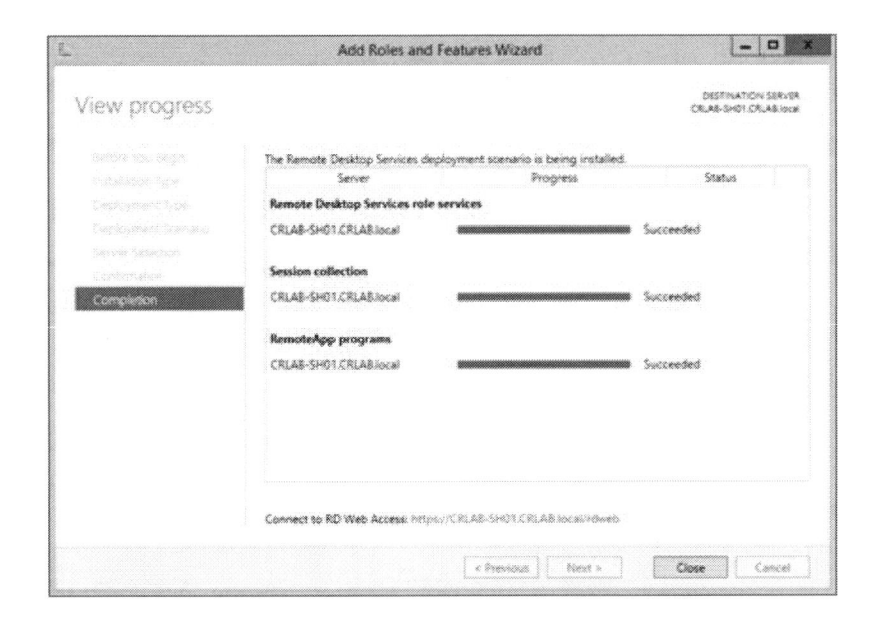

So, now you have a working RDS deployment. To test it, simply launch Internet Explorer (for example on a workstation) and go to the URL shown at the bottom of the progress screen, in our case, https://CRLAB-SH01.CRLAB.local/rdweb). Once you logon with valid credentials (in this case any domain account) you should see all the three RemoteApps created by the wizard – yes, it did create all that for you. Keep reading).

Let's take a look at what was created and configured by the wizard. As we did all this from the CRLAB-CB01 machine, its server manager is now aware of this deployment. You will notice it right on the server manager screen as shown below. This is what many people refer to as 'Remote Desktop Management Services', or RDMS for short and we will show you how to use it in the next chapter.

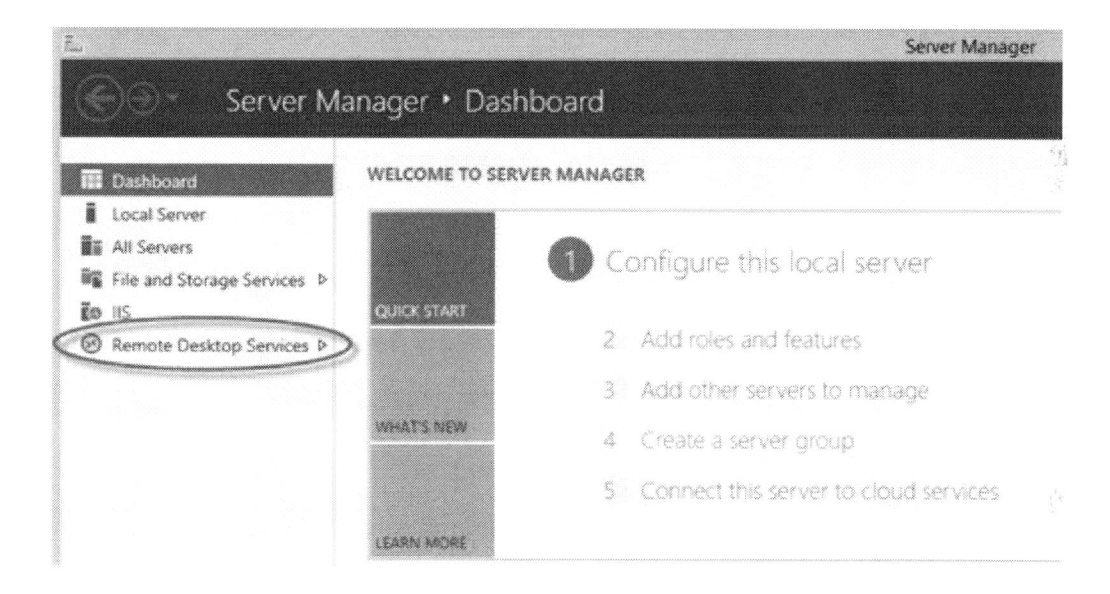

Using RDMS

Back to the CRLAB-CB01 server (you could do this on CRLAB-SH01, as it is the connection broker for the deployment) launch 'Server Manager' and click 'Remote Desktop Services' on the left.

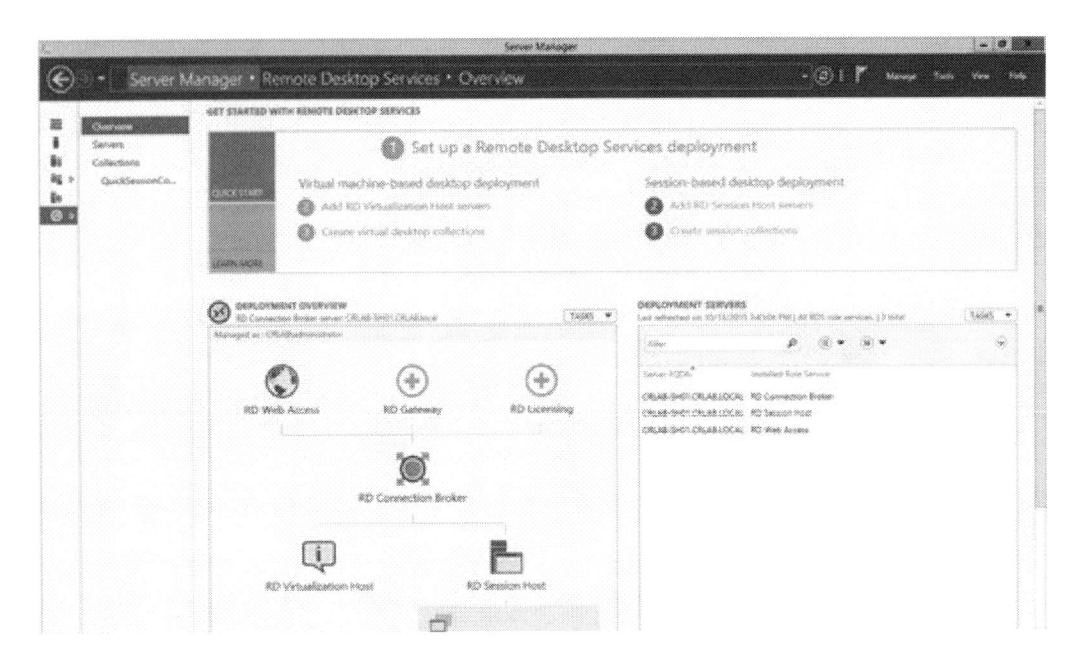

The first thing you probably noticed is the pretty diagram in the 'Deployment Overview' section. It shows a graphical representation of the 'Quick Start' deployment we just installed. The roles that were installed (RD Web Access, RD Connection Broker and RD Session Host) are displayed using a somewhat meaningful icon while roles not currently deployed (RD Gateway and RD Licensing) are shown as a green plus sign, indicating that we can add these roles to the deployment if we need them (licensing is mandatory, remember it?).

The cool thing is this diagram is interactive. That means if you want to add one of the remaining roles you simply click on one of the green plus signs and a wizard will start the process of adding such role to the deployment.

The pane on the right, 'Deployment Servers', shows all the servers that are part of this particular deployment. In this case, all we have is CRLAB-SH01 as we performed a 'Quick Start' deployment. Notice the 'Tasks' button on the upper right corners on both panes. These allow you to perform additional tasks for that particular section. Here for example, you can add more servers to the deployment, choosing which role they will perform on it.

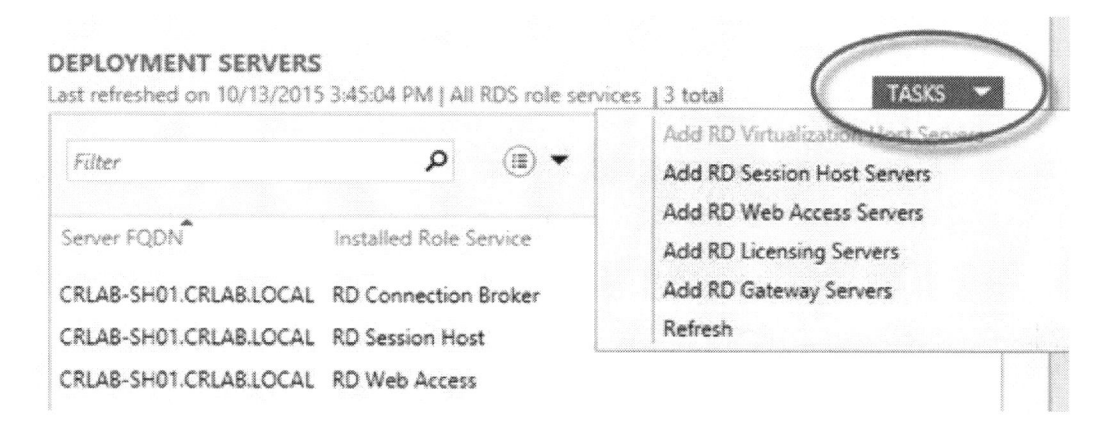

Now when we click on the 'Servers' section on the left, we can see the servers that are part of the deployment and the roles they perform. If you right-click any of the servers, you are then able to perform several tasks on that machine. This means there are several ways to work on these servers and in this case, Microsoft tried to add extra functionality to the management tool in use, so you can try to do most of it from a single place. You can even RDP to that server directly off RDMS!

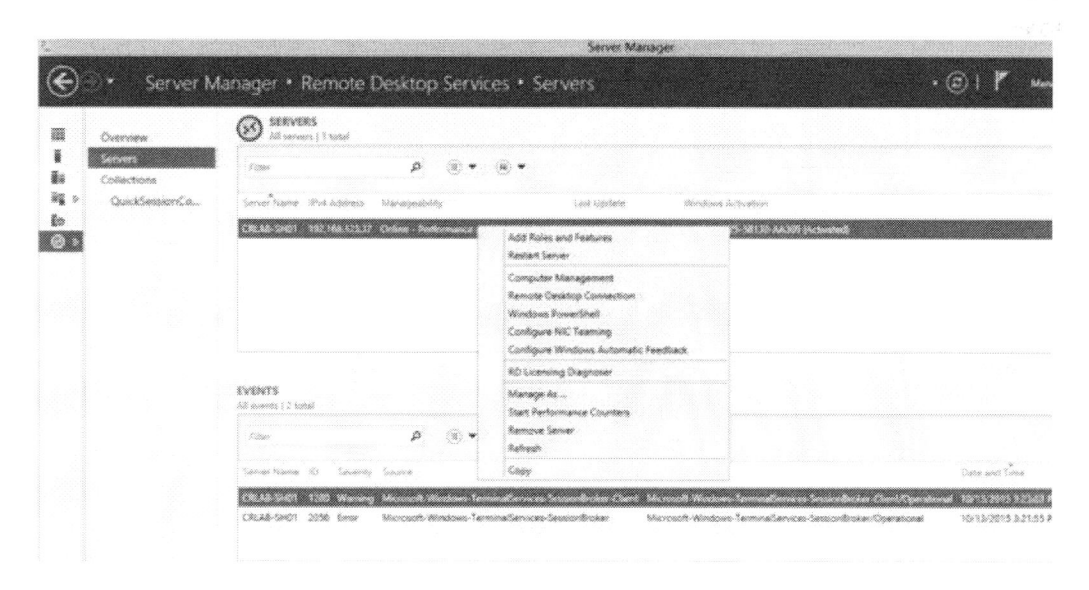

The next stop on the left is the 'Collections' section. Before we dig in too deep, let's clarify something and this will be very useful if you have a Citrix background. A collection, if you did not notice yet, is a logical group of RDSHs (most often referred as a farm in previous releases). Once in a collection, that particular RDSH cannot be part of any other collection. This is pretty much the same as what we call a 'silo' in the Citrix world. The difference is a server can belong to multiple silos if Citrix is in place but not to multiple collections in a pure Microsoft RDS solution. This is important as several companies are now looking at RDS 2012 R2 as a replacement to their existing Citrix XenApp 6.5 environments. So, consider this if you are thinking about going pure RDS.

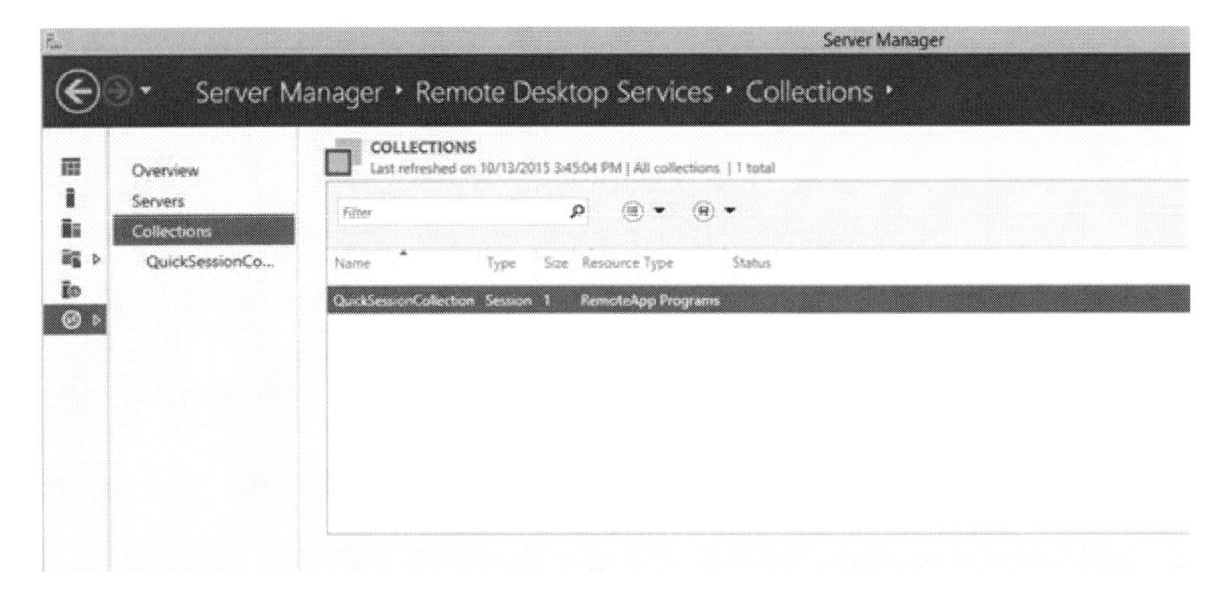

Of course, the collection is more than that. It has all the information about which applications or desktops are available to a particular user, which timeout settings are in use, the relative load balancing weights for each RDSH (to adjust for servers with more processing capabilities for example) and more.

As you can see this is quite different from what a deployment is. The deployment is at a higher level, dealing with things like which RD Licensing is in use, which certificates are in place and so on. That said a deployment could have more than one collection, each one with their own unique settings, serving multiple different purposes. A good example is to separate applications that cannot co-exist and cannot be virtualized (using something like Microsoft App-V) into different collections. Another scenario is when you want to provide both RemoteApps and full desktop access to your users (what is not officially supported – we will explain the reason behind this later on).

From here, you can use the tasks menu to edit an existing collection or to create a new one. We will get into that later in the book.

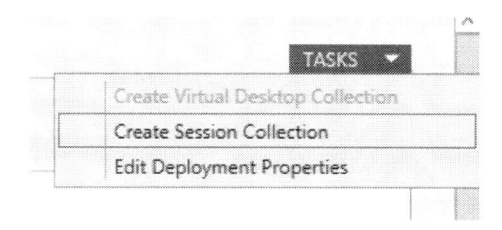

The connections pane shows you all the sessions running on every single collection that is part of your deployment. You can also interact with these by right clicking them.

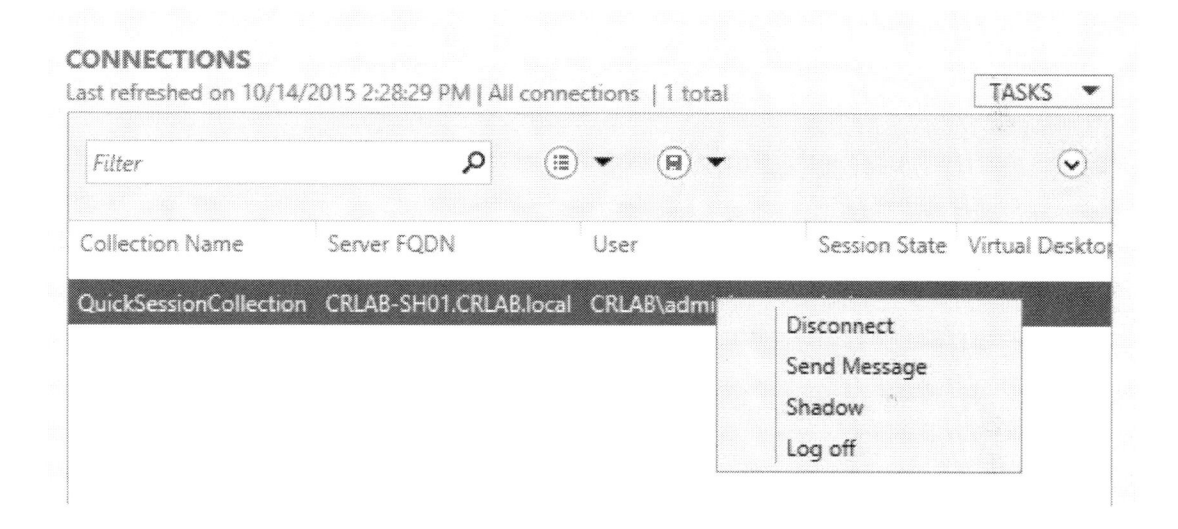

ⓘ In case you did not notice, 'Shadow' is back! This is what we call 'Remote Control' in an RDS world. 'Shadowing' is a well-known term in Citrix jargon and means the ability to see what a user is doing on his session, a very handy capability when troubleshooting RDS issues. Microsoft removed that on RDS 2012 to resurrect it within the R2 release after people promised to take matters on their own hands. Microsoft listened.

Finally, the last section on the deployment shows you the collections you have created. After performing a 'Quick Start' deployment, the wizard created our first and only collection, properly named 'QuickSessionCollection'.

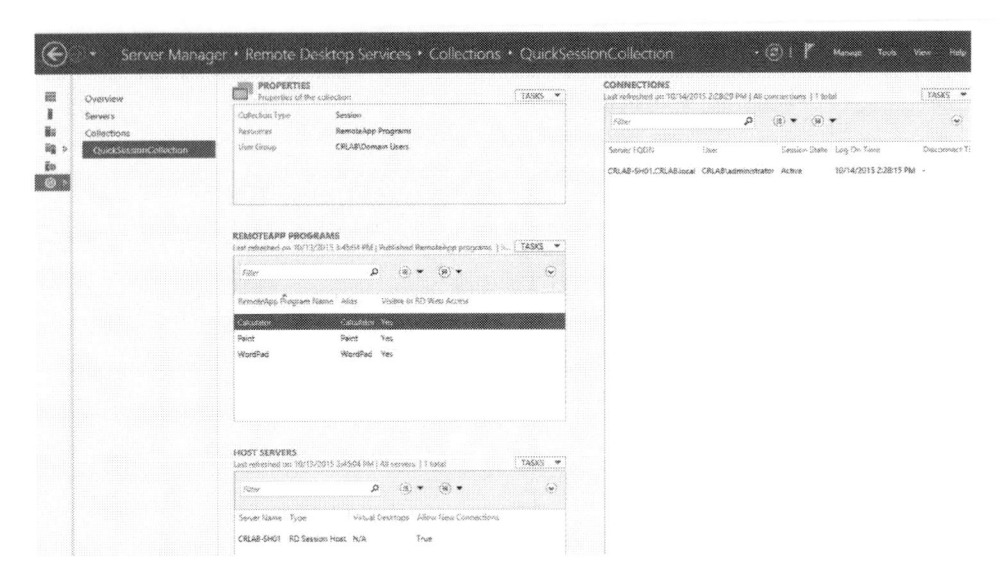

The properties of a collection can be accessed by clicking on 'Tasks' on the 'Properties' pane for the collection and then clicking on 'Edit Properties'. We will discuss all the options for a collection later in the book.

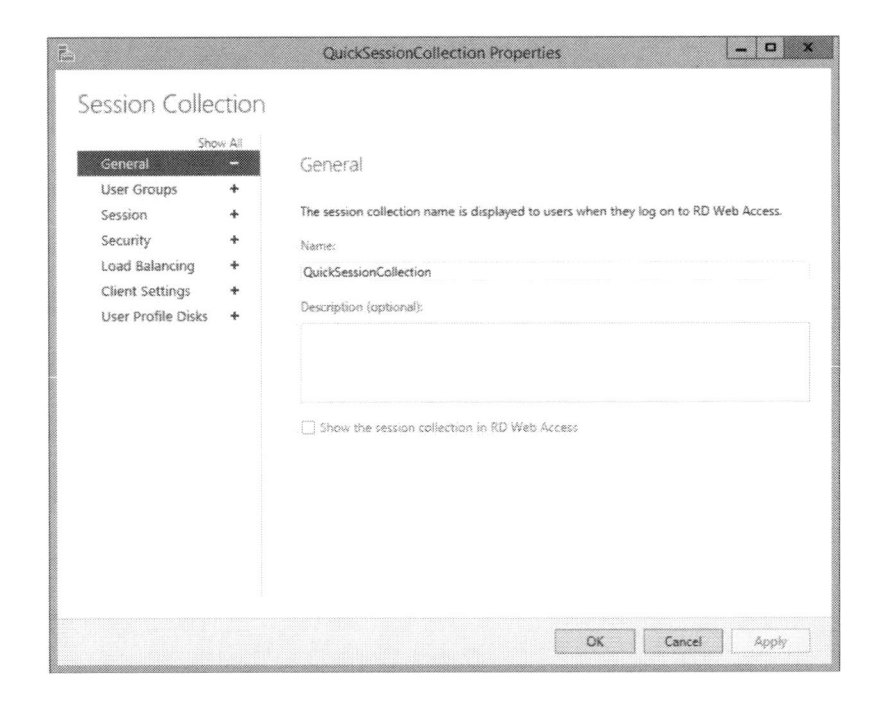

The 'RemoteApp Programs' pane contains the applications currently available to your users. As part of the 'Quick Start' deployment, the wizard creates three RemoteApps so you can test the deployment immediately.

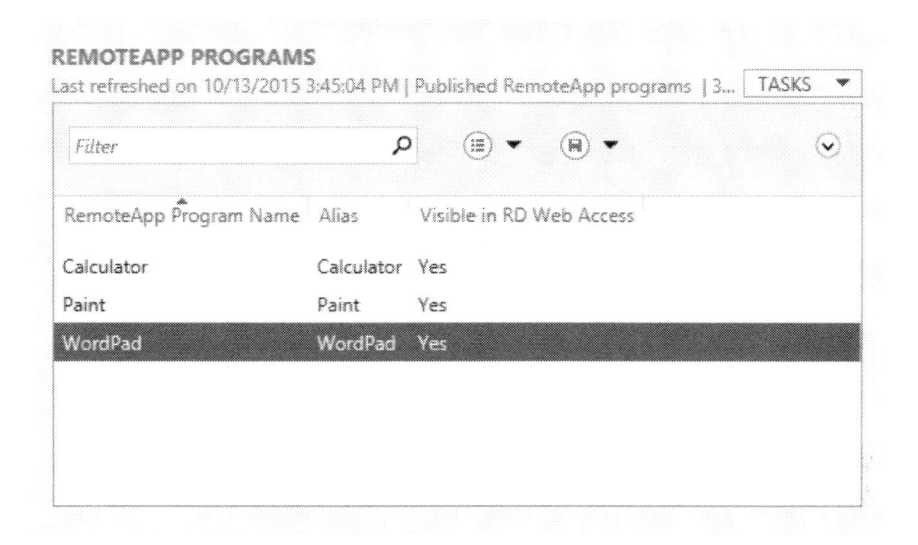

The 'Connections' pane shows the sessions connected to this particular collection, a little bit different from when at the 'Collections' section. There we could see all sessions on all collections. Here we are limited to the one collection we selected.

This is all you have to know about RDMS. It is far from perfect and cumbersome at times. However, if you worked with Windows Server 2003 or 2008 R2 RDS, this is indeed much better. That does not mean it is good. Keep that in mind.

From now on, we will be focusing on the 'Standard' deployment. You can certainly expand your 'Quick Start' deployment by adding an RD Gateway or RD Licensing server. As the steps to perform these are the same for both scenarios, and since most production environments will be based on the 'Standard' deployment, please check the sections under "Performing a Standard deployment".

Performing a Standard deployment

Now it is time to say goodbye to your first deployment. We know it is hard but we have to move on. Go ahead and revert the VMs used when doing the 'Quick start' deployment back to their original state.

As mentioned earlier, the main difference between the 'Standard' and 'Quick start' deployments is the fact we can install the roles we want on a different server to avoid the all eggs in one basket scenario. In addition, servers like RDLS will require far less resources than your RDSHs where users connect and run their applications from, making sense to have different settings for each server (i.e. RDLS will happily live with 2GB RAM where RDSH will struggle). This gives us the flexibility we need when designing a robust RDS environment.

For this deployment, we will be using separate servers for RDSH, RDCB and RDWA (CRLAB-SH01, CRLAB-CB01 and CRLAB-WA01) as described under 'Environment'.

Doing it

1. Launch 'Server Manager' on CRLAB-DC01. As mentioned earlier, we will use this server to manage the RDS deployment we are going to create.

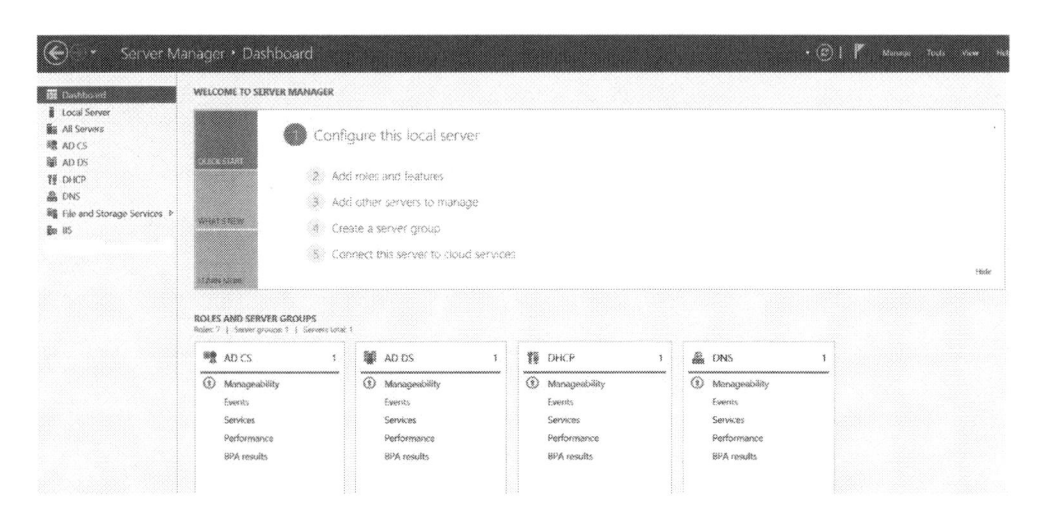

2. As we did previously, click '3. Add other servers to manage'.

3. Select CRLAB-CB01, CRLAB-SH01 and CRLAB-WA01 and click 'Ok'.

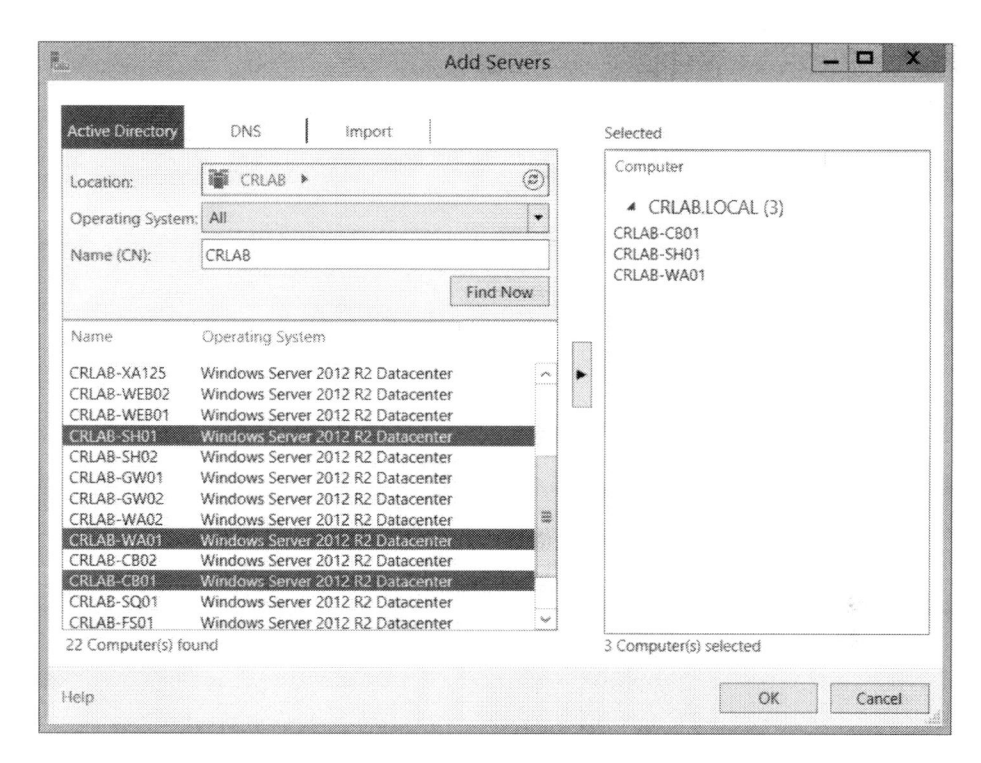

4. Now back to the main screen, click '2. Add roles and features' to launch the wizard. Click 'Next'.

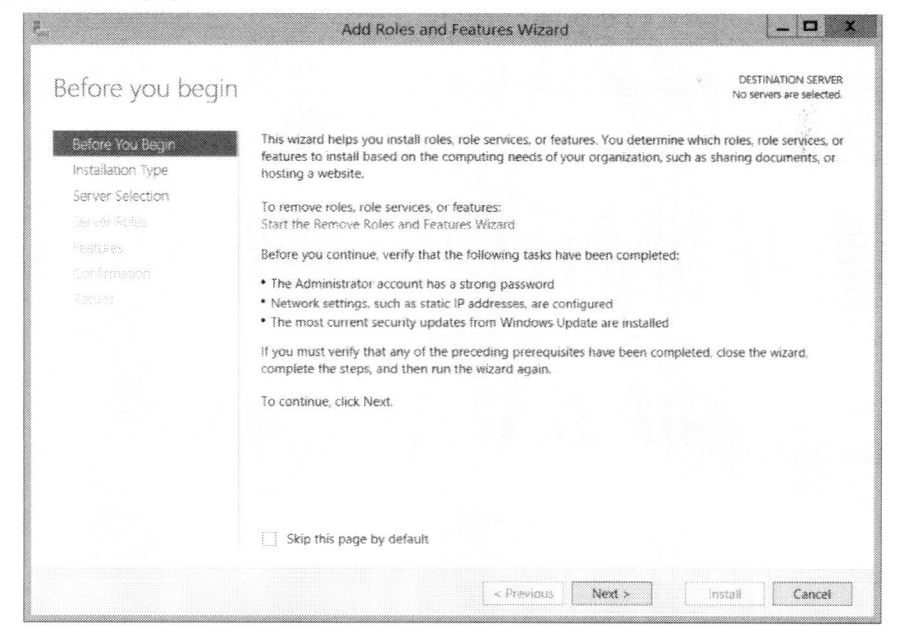

5. Select 'Remote Desktop Services Installation' and click 'Next'.

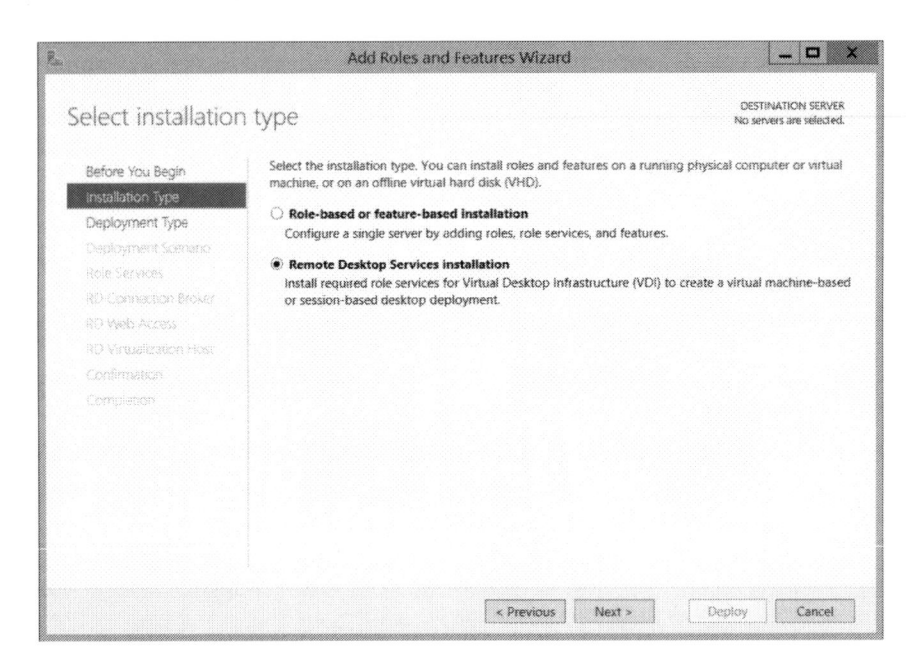

6. Now we are not doing the all-in-one 'Quick Start' anymore. The idea is to separate the roles needed into multiple servers so select 'Standard deployment' and click 'Next'.

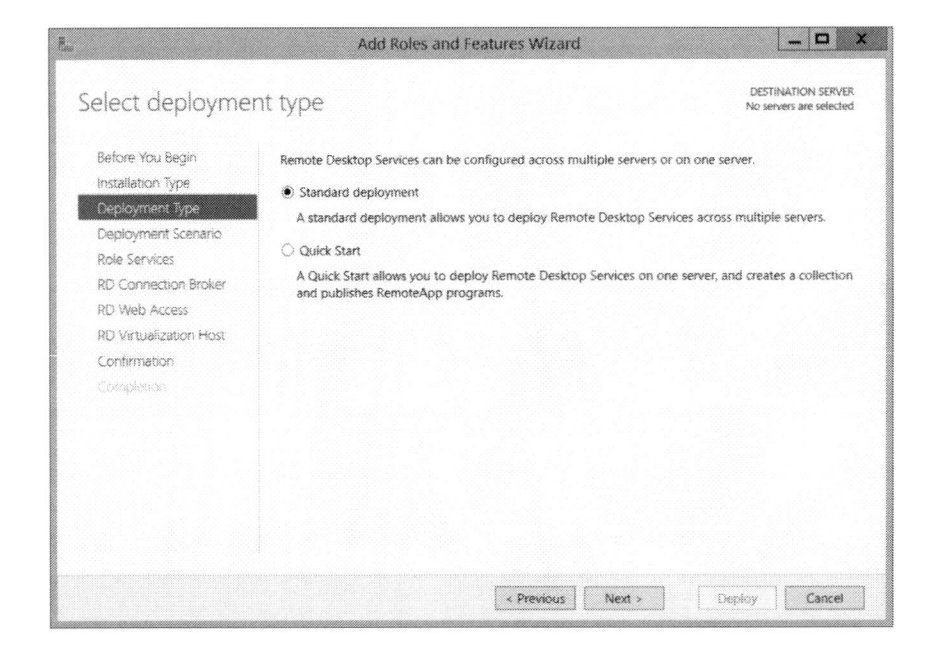

7. As we are not dealing with VDI (i.e. virtual machines running a desktop OS like Windows 8.1), select 'Session-based desktop deployment' and click 'Next'.

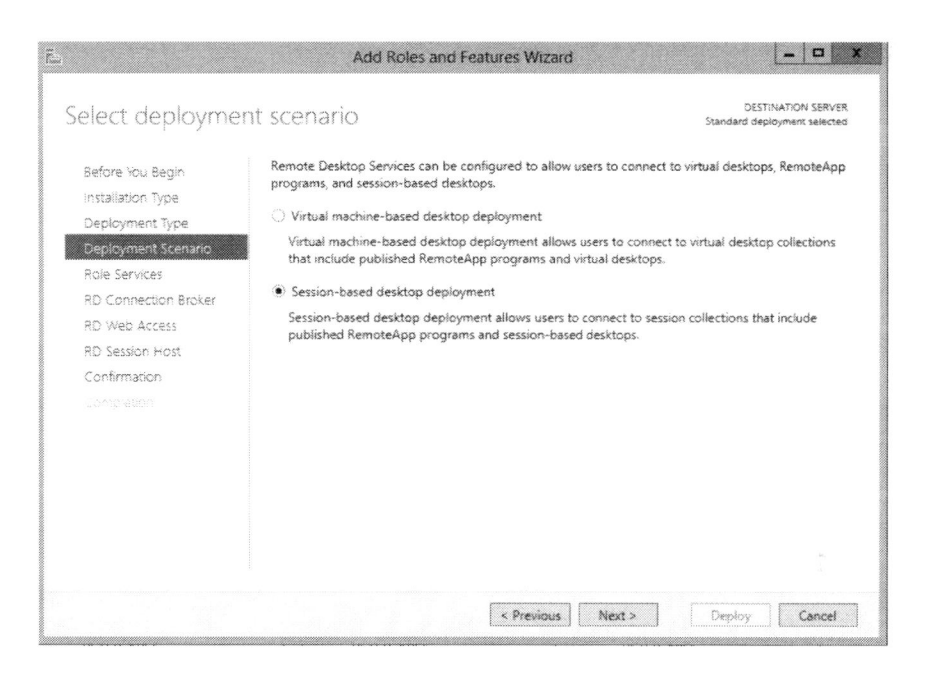

8. The wizard shows you the roles that will be installed and configured. Simply click 'Next'.

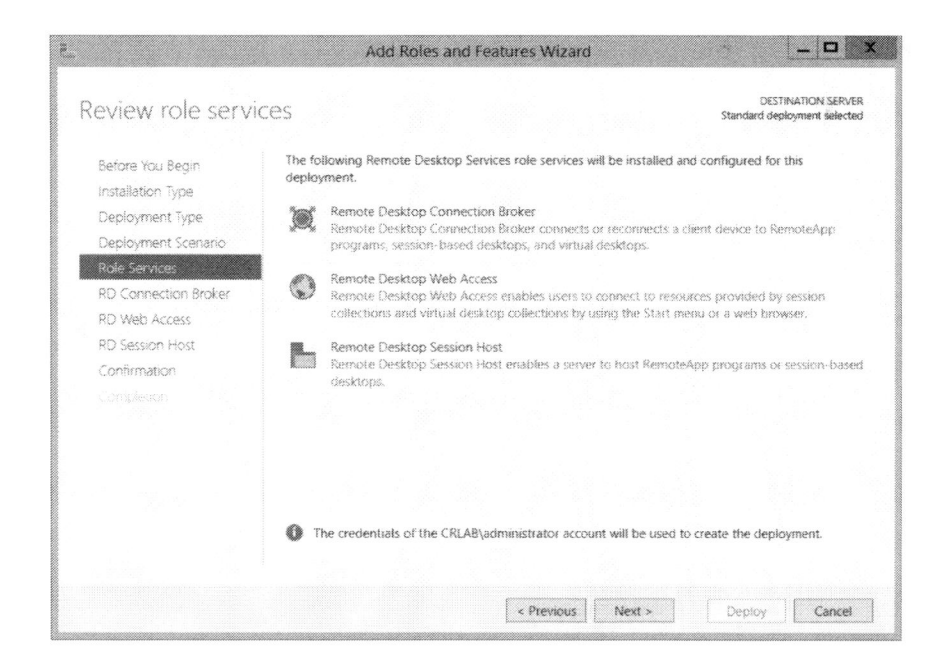

9. Now you must select which server will be the first connection broker for this deployment. Select 'CRLAB-CB01' and click the arrow button. Then click 'Next'.

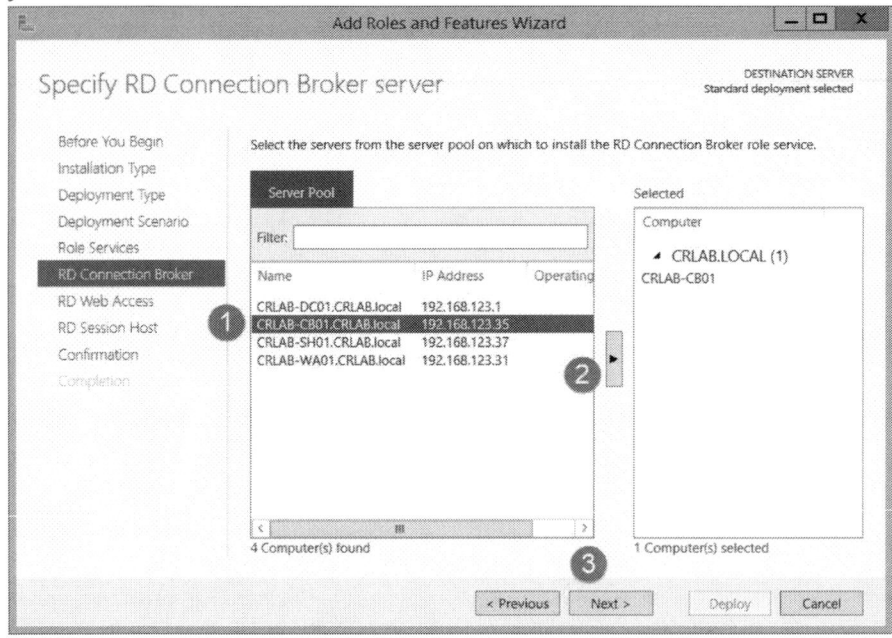

10. Now select the server that will hold the RDWA role, CRLAB-WA01 and click the arrow button. Then click 'Next'

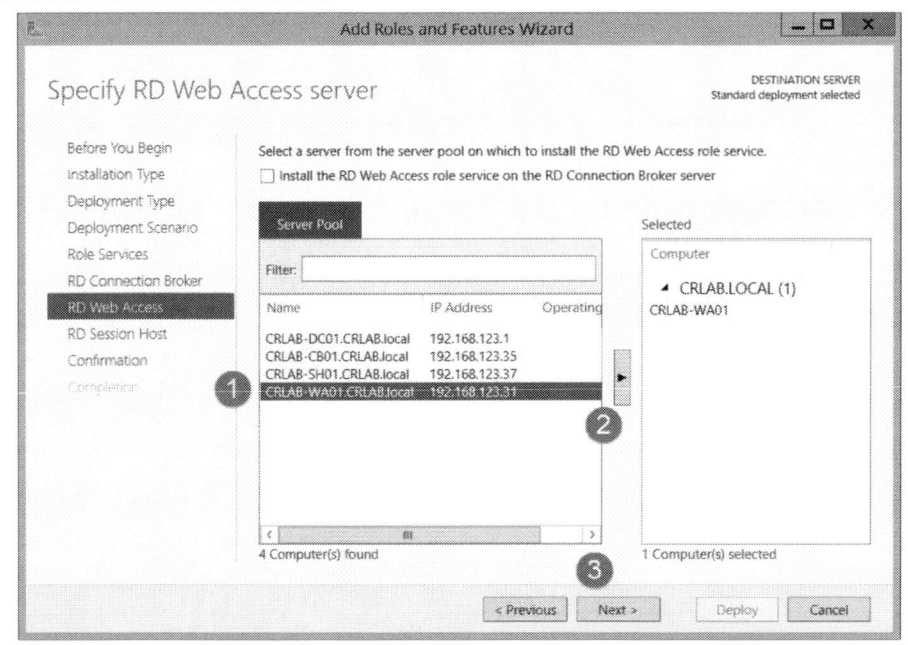

11. Finally select the server that will hold the RDSH role, in this case CRLAB-SH01 and click the arrow button. Then click 'Next'.

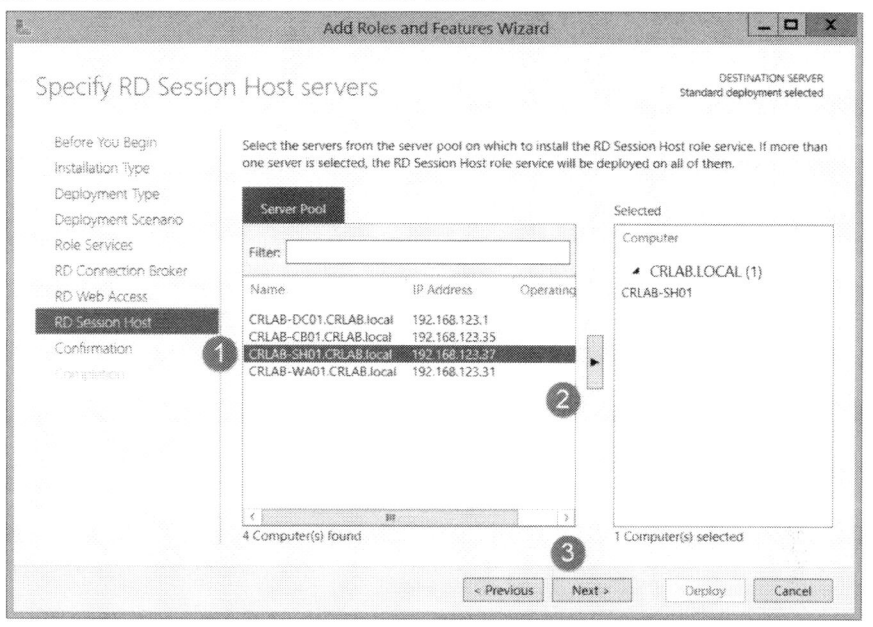

12. The wizard will show you a summary for the deployment. Select 'Restart the destination server automatically if required' (the RDSH role does require it) and click 'Deploy'.

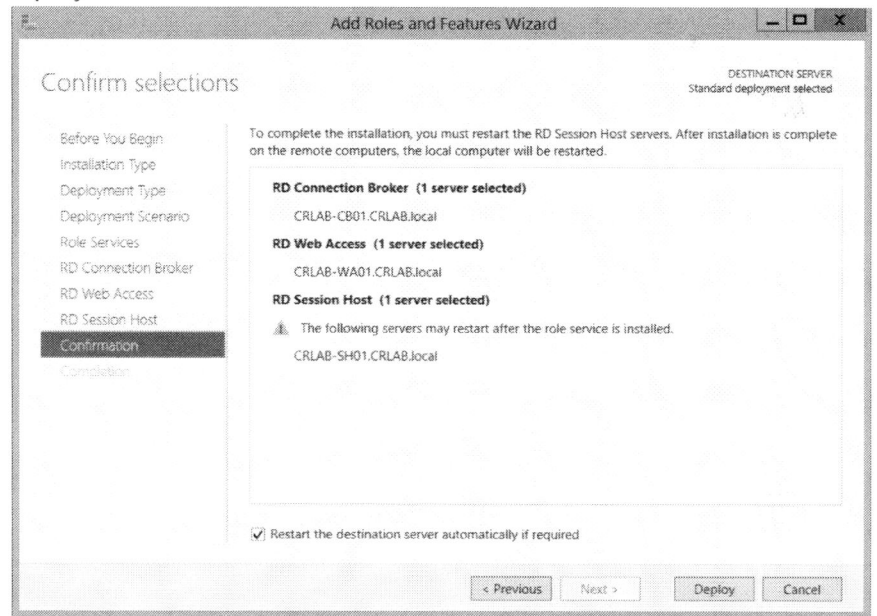

13. The wizard will show you the deployment progress. Just be patient as it may take a while depending on your hardware, etc.

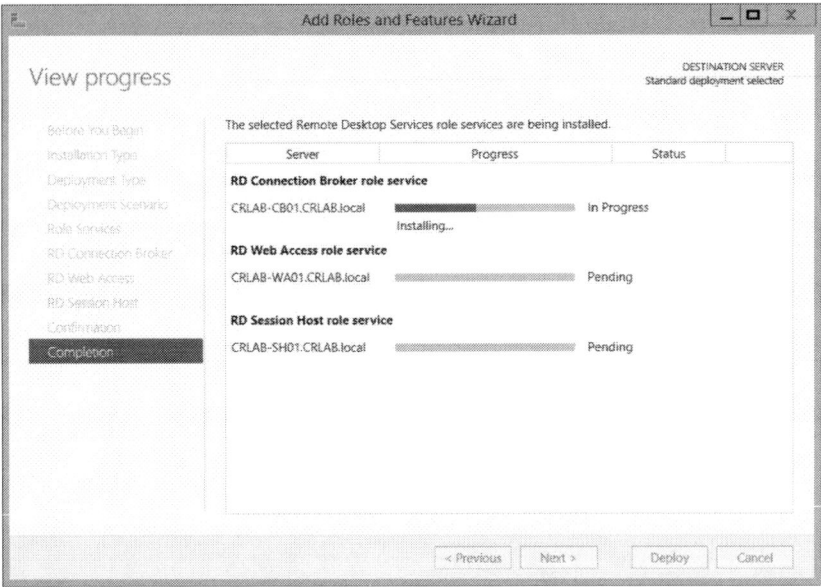

14. If everything works as expected you should see a 'Succeeded' status for each role deployed. Remember that as discussed when performing a 'Quick Start' deployment, if any policy interferes with anything RDS related the wizard will fail.

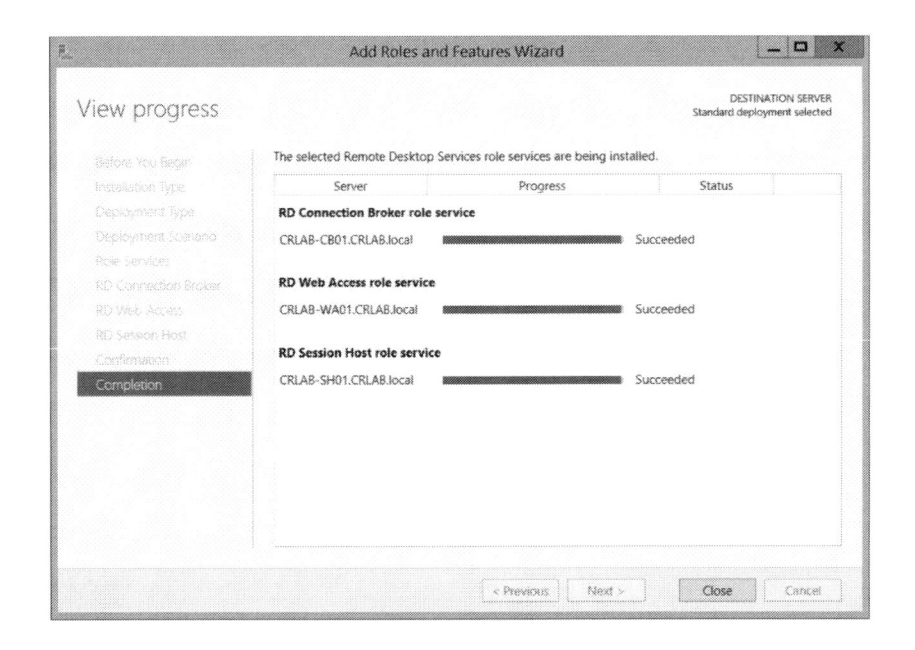

Resuming, this is what happened when we used the wizard to perform a 'Standard deployment':
- After selecting which servers we wanted to use the wizard asked us which roles would go on each server.
- RDCB was installed on CRLAB-CB01.
- RDWA was installed on CRLAB-WA01.
- Finally, RDSH was installed on CRLAB-SH01 and the server was rebooted (required).
- All the configuration required between roles was done for us and the deployment is ready to be used.

Now after launching Server Manager on CRLAB-DC01 you can see the Remote Desktop Services section. If you click on it, it will show us the overview diagram for the standard deployment we just performed.

The diagram now shows the three roles we deployed (RDWA, RDCB and RDSH) with the RDGW/RDLS roles still missing. Exactly the same you see after performing a 'Quick Start' deployment as we saw in the previous chapter. The difference is if we now look at the 'Deployment Servers' pane we can clearly see the three different servers we selected for each of the roles deployed.

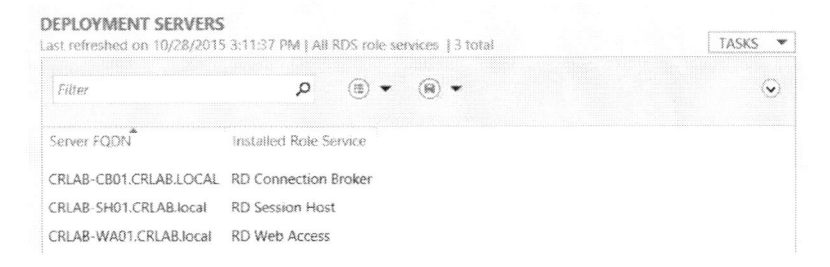

Now if you did not notice, under the 'Collections' pane, there is no collection at all.

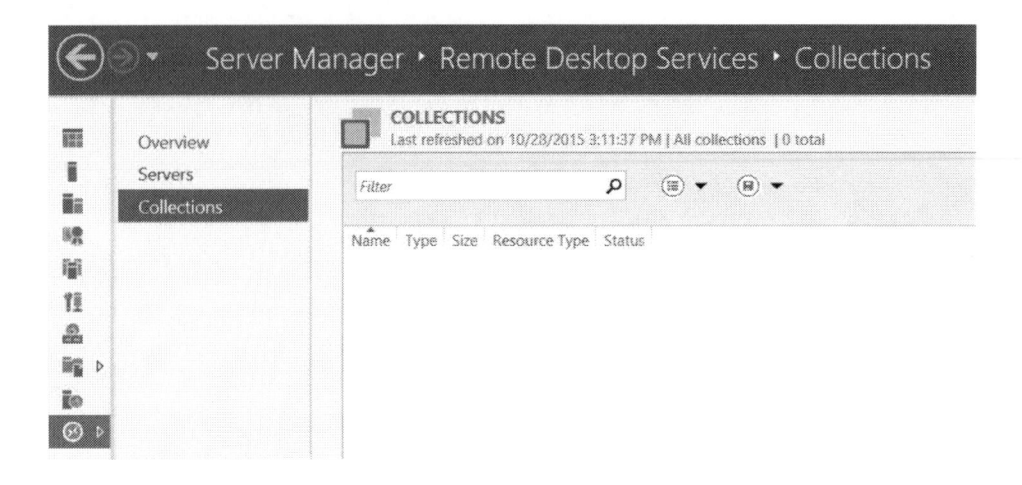

If you remember when performing a 'Quick Start' deployment, a basic collection is created as part of it; the 'Standard deployment' does not create one for us. That is what you will learn next.

Adding a Session Collection

Now that you have your first 'Standard deployment' ready to go, you are ready to add a session collection to it. Keep in mind you can follow the exact same steps to add additional collections to an existing deployment as you can indeed have multiple collections in a deployment.

Before moving ahead, in order to simulate in our lab what a potential production environment would be, we created two OUs under our 'location' one, that will hold the users and groups we want to use with this RDS environment. This is what we have:

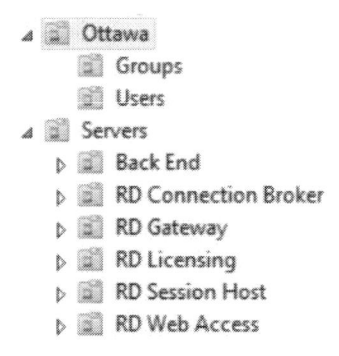

- Ottawa
  - Groups
  - Users
- Servers
  - Back End
  - RD Connection Broker
  - RD Gateway
  - RD Licensing
  - RD Session Host
  - RD Web Access

Page 44 | RDS - The Complete Guide

Under 'Ottawa' | 'Groups' we will have the groups we want to give access to a particular collection and under 'Ottawa' | 'Users', the real users that will be part of such groups. Of course, you can use any existing group, but we want to guide you through what we do believe would happen if deploying this in production (meaning chances are the groups you want to give access to would have to be created).

So, launch 'Active Directory Users and Computers' (ADUC) on your domain controller (in our case CRLAB-DC01) and create a new group under 'Ottawa' | 'Groups'.

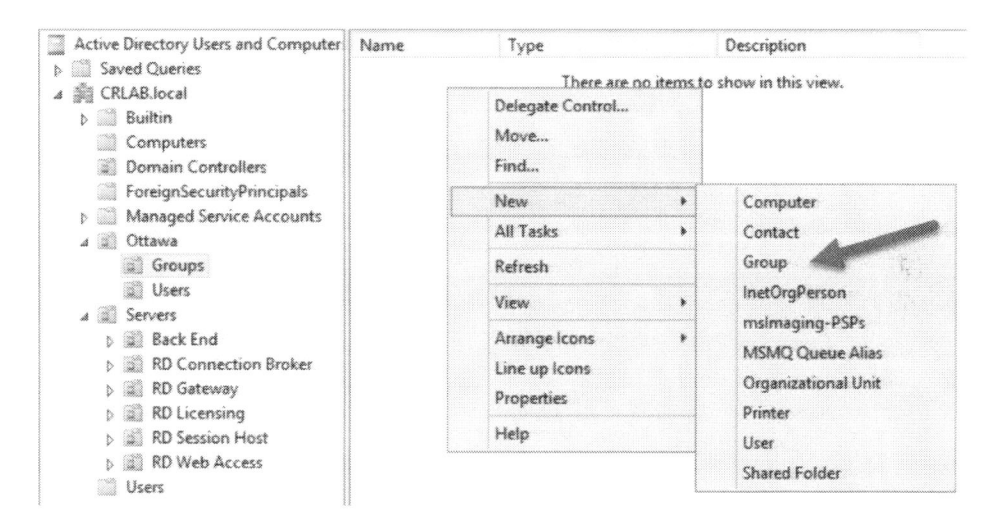

Enter 'RDS_SD_Collection' for the group name and click 'Ok'.

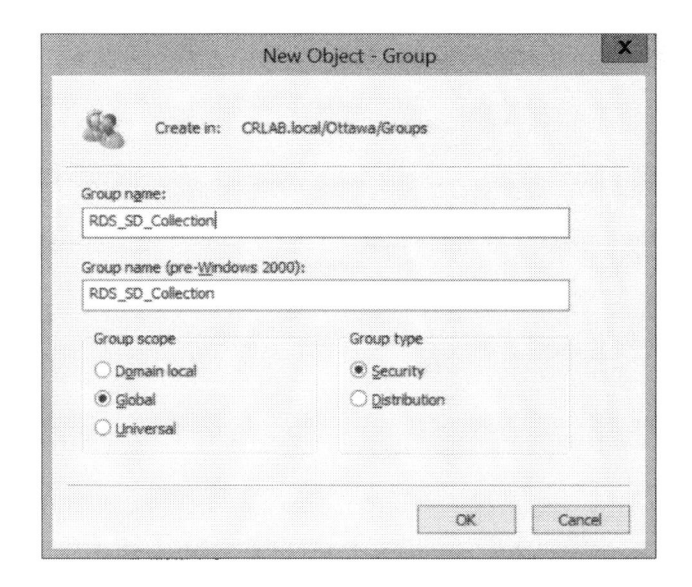

Then under 'Ottawa' | 'Users', create a new user named TestUser1.

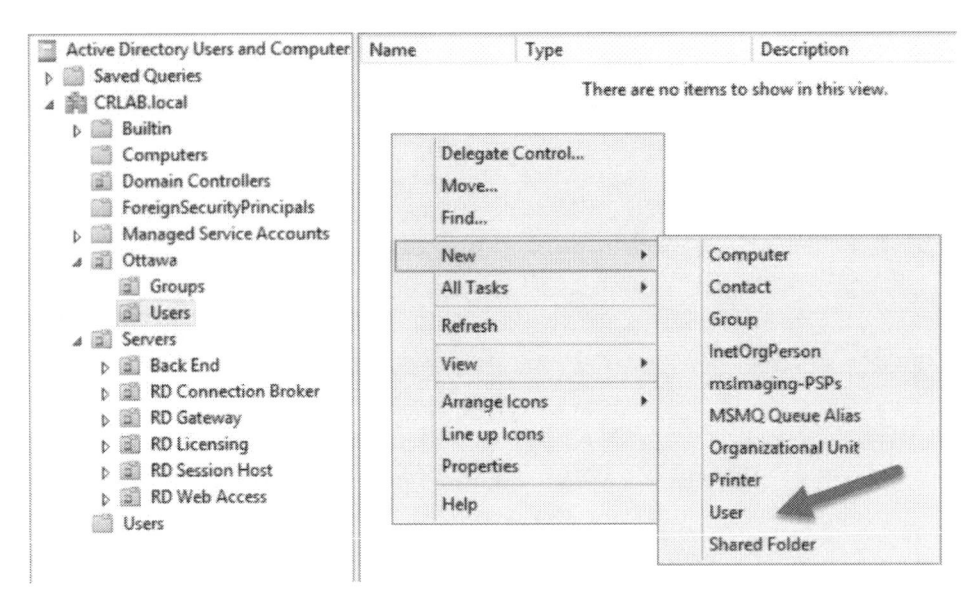

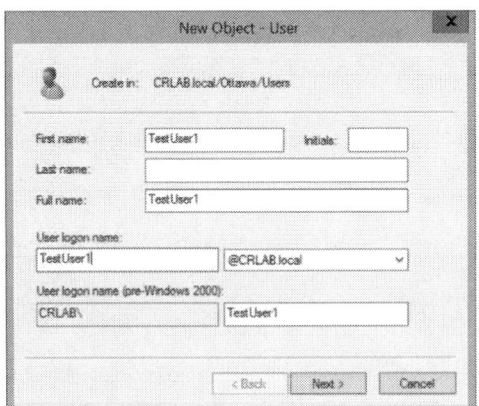

Double-click the user you just created and under the 'Member Of' tab make sure you add the 'RDS_SD_Collection' group.

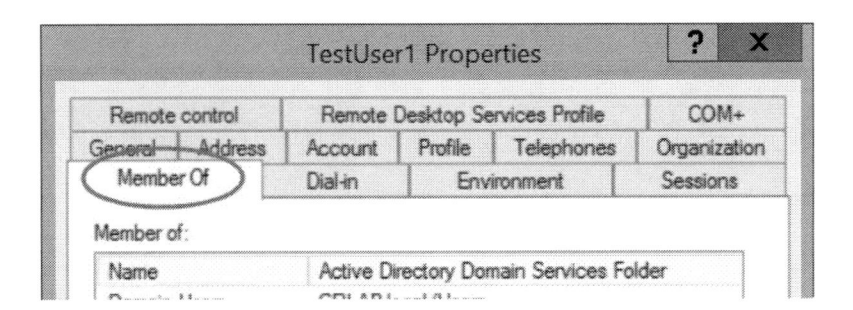

The next step is to create the actual session collection.

1. Launch 'Server Manager' on the server you used to perform the 'Standard deployment' (in our case CRLAB-DC01) and click on the 'Remote Desktop Services section.

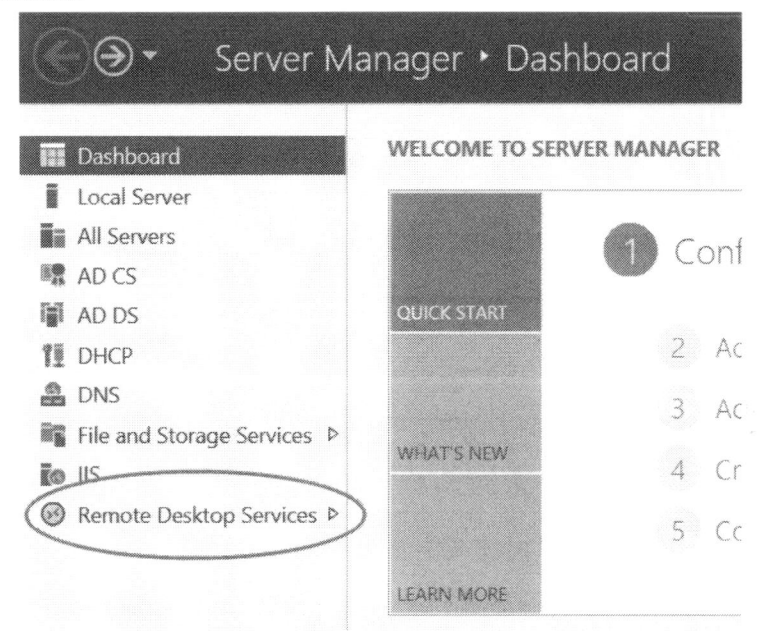

2. Under 'Collections', on the right pane, click on 'Tasks' and select 'Create Session Collection'.

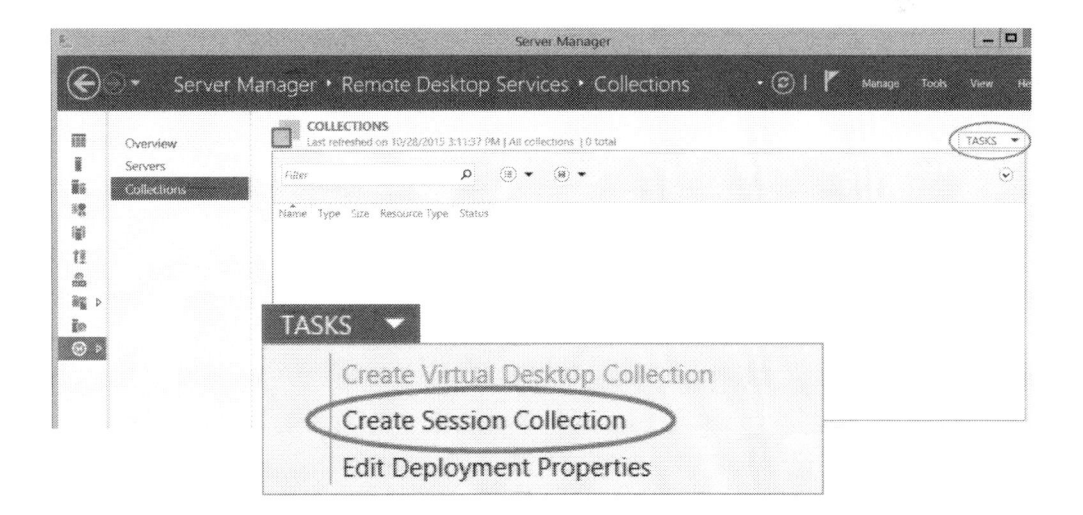

3. The wizard launches, showing the two pre-requisites to create a new session collection (user/group to assign it to and an RDSH available that is not part of any other collection – in our case, CRLAB-SH01). Click 'Next'.

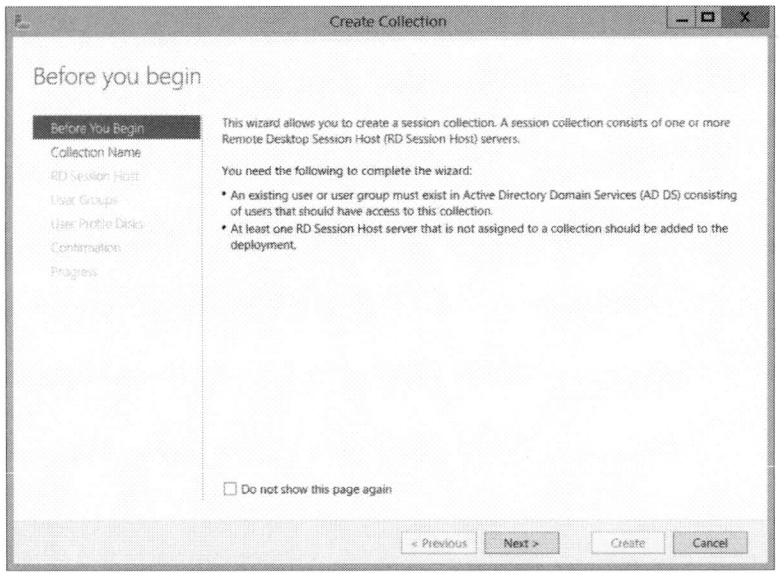

4. Now you need a name and description for your collection. In this example we will use "SD Basic Collection" but of course, on a real deployment you would choose a meaningful name that clearly describes the purpose of such collection. Enter the name and description and click 'Next'.

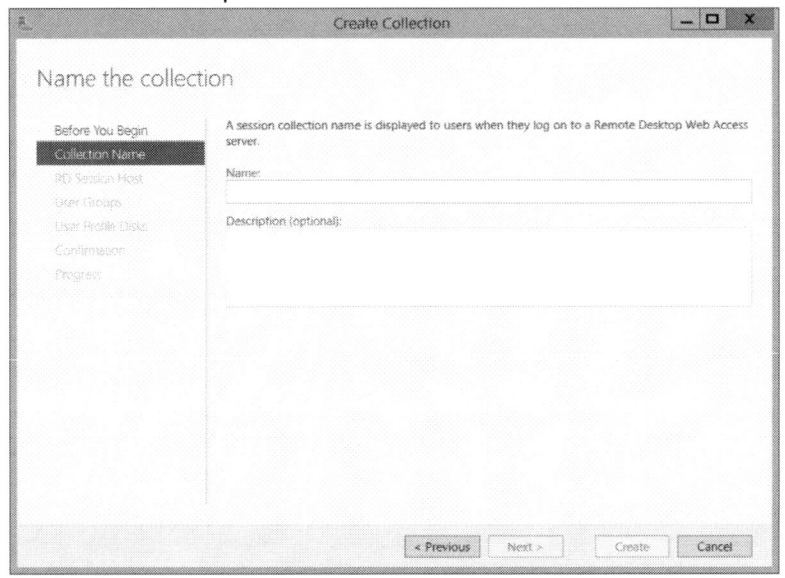

5. You will see the RDSHs that were added as part of the standard deployment (in this case, we only selected CRLAB-SH01). So click on it, click the arrow button and then click 'Next'. As mentioned before, an RDSH cannot belong to multiple collections. This may be confusing if you are coming from a Citrix background with its 'silos'.

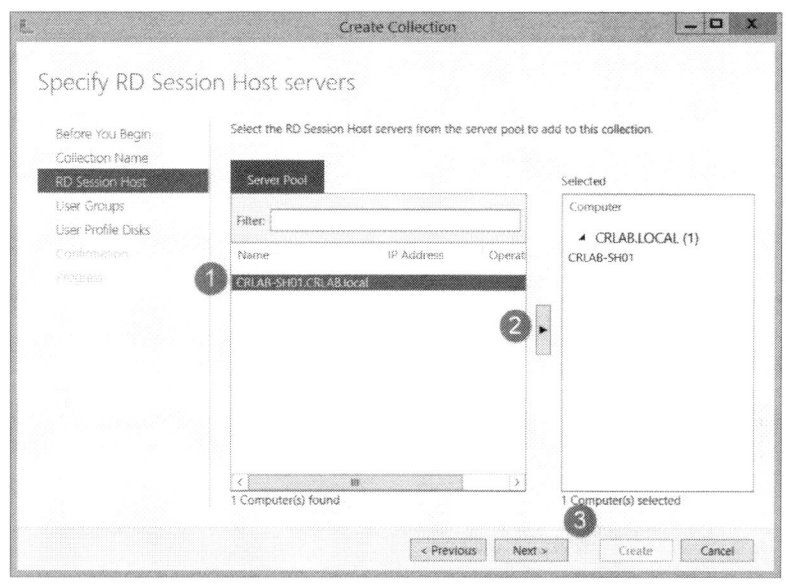

6. By default, the wizard adds the group 'Domain Users'. Select it and click 'Remove'. Then click 'Add' and search for the group we created previously, 'RDS_SD_Collection'. Click 'Next'.

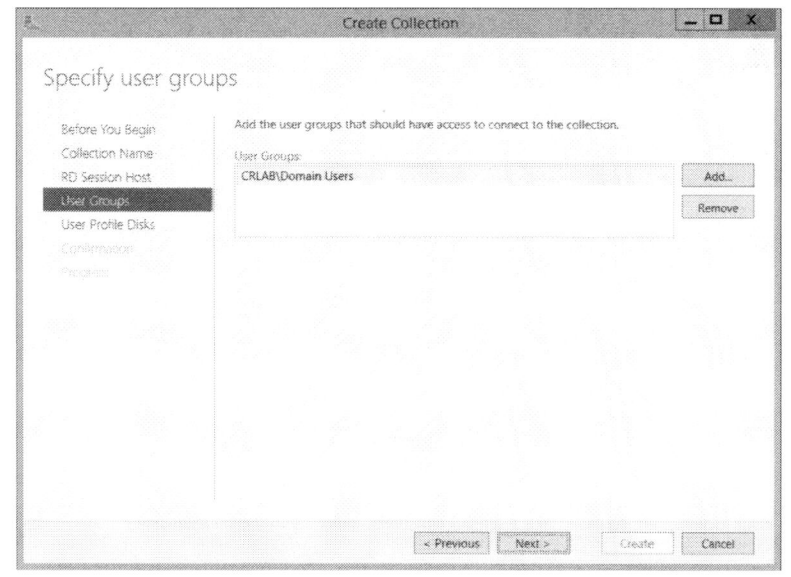

7. For now, uncheck 'Enable user profile disks' as we will discuss it later. Click 'Next'.

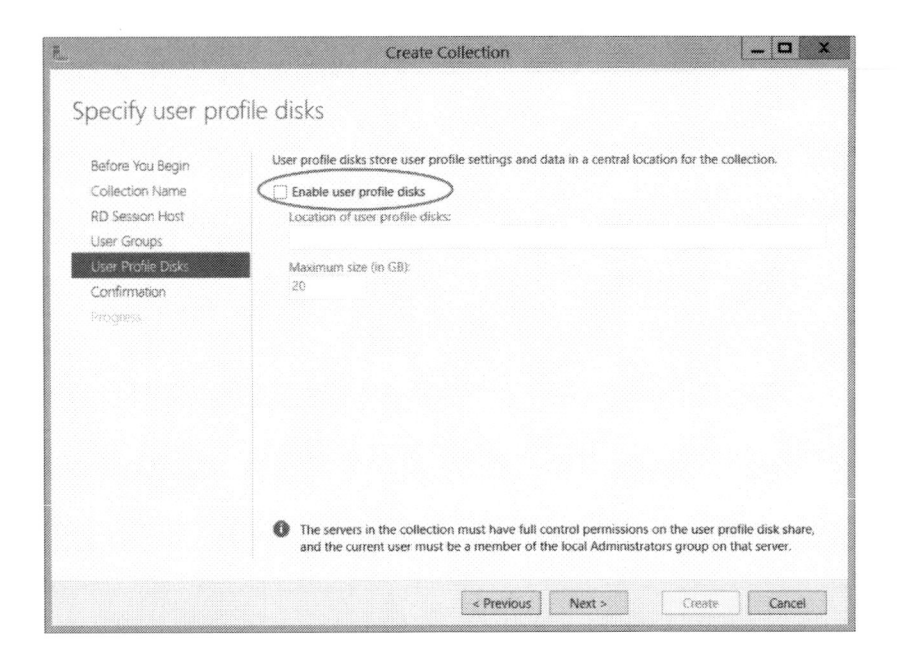

8. Review the settings for the collection you are about to create and click 'Create'.

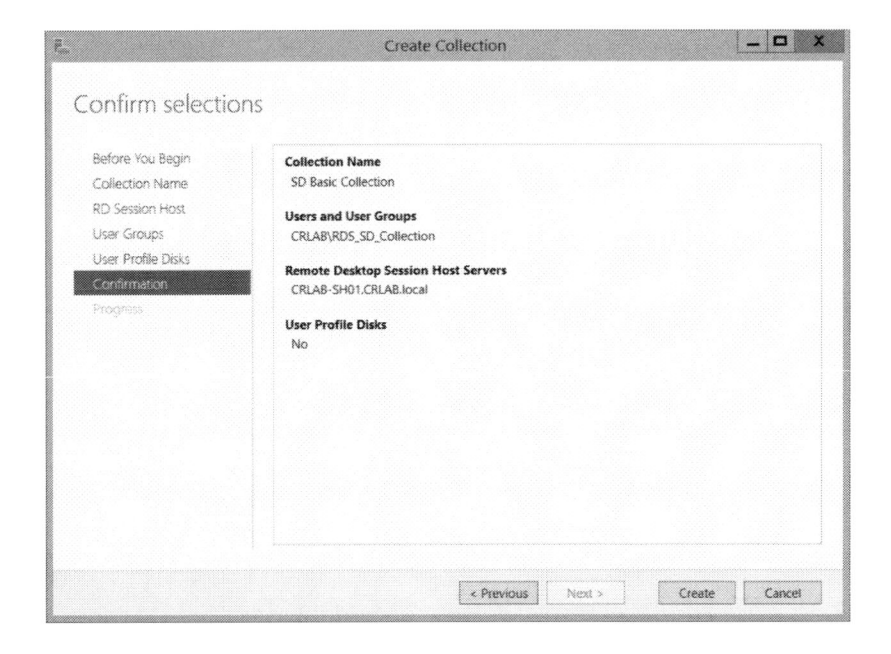

9. The wizard will show you a progress bar for each step.

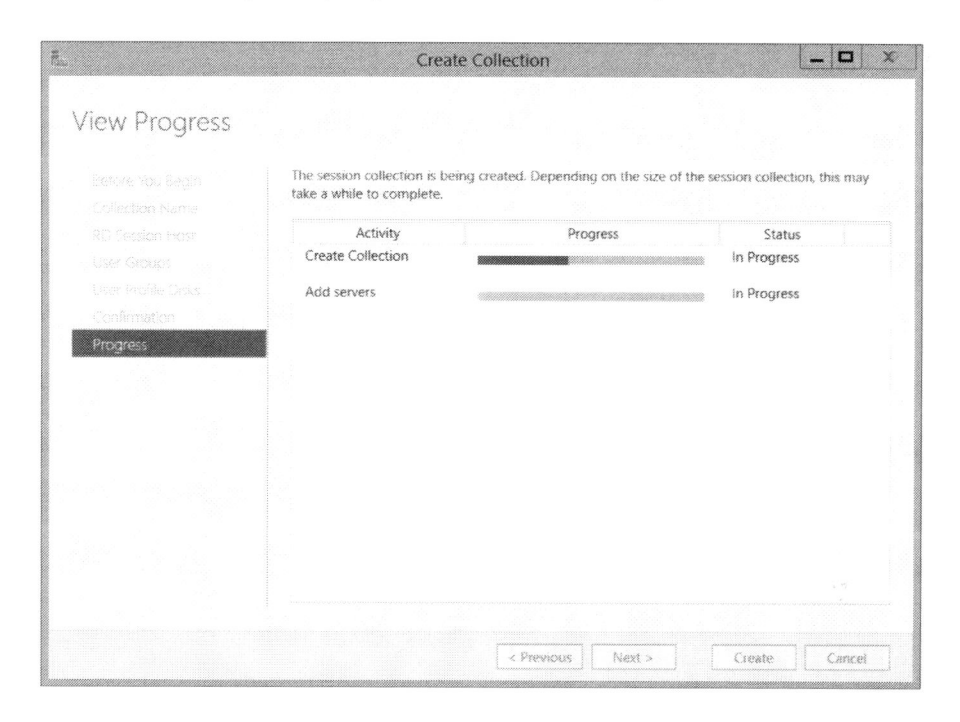

10. If everything works, you will get a 'Succeeded' status for both tasks and the wizard will show you which servers were added to the collection (in this case CRLAB-SH01). Click 'Close'.

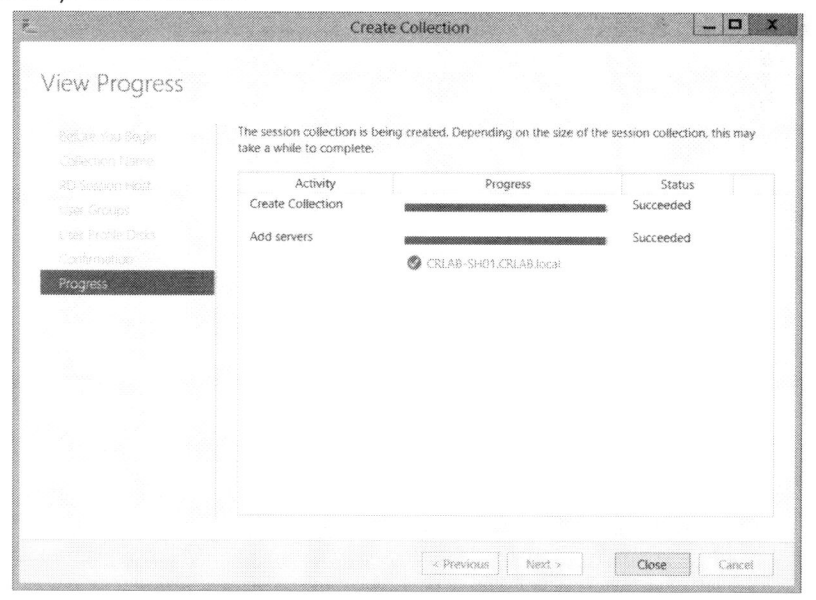

If you go back to RDMS, under 'Collections' now you should see your first session collection.

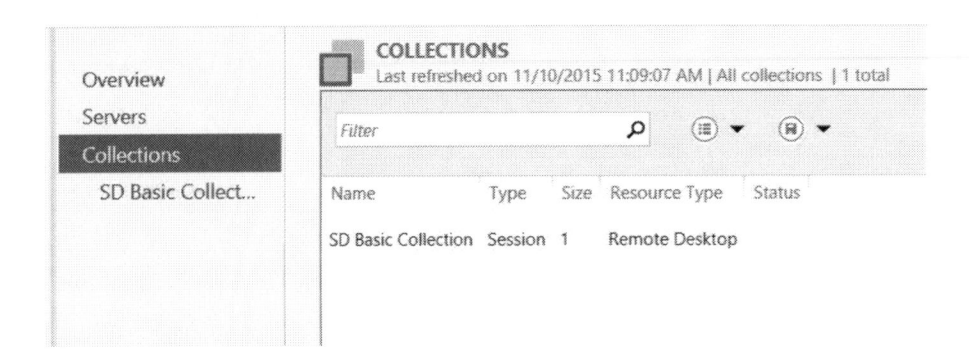

Congratulations. You just finished your first 'Standard deployment' with a brand-new collection. Users should be able to access this immediately through the RDWA portal (remember, always https://RDWA_NAME/rdweb). Of course, there is much more we can do with a collection so keep reading.

Session Collection overview

Previously you have configured a basic session collection using the built-in wizard. Next, we will review what the wizard created and which additional settings are available in a session collection.

ⓘ **Note:** You can associate a session collection to two different resource types: a 'Remote Desktop' or a 'RemoteApp'. For now, we will focus on RemoteApps but will certainly explain the differences between these as we move along.

Open 'Server Manager' again and click on the session collection you just created, 'SD Basic Collection'.

Before going through all the settings in a collection, let's take a look at everything you can find on the collections pane. As you can see, it has four main sections:

- **Properties:** shows the basic settings for a session collection. As we mentioned, there is more to it than what you see on the wizard (simply click Click 'Tasks' | 'Edit Properties' for a quick peek on what is available).

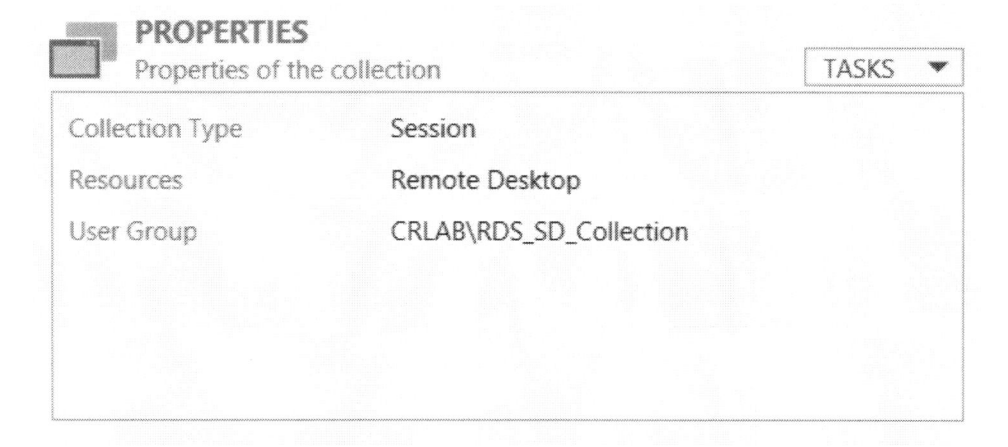

PROPERTIES
Properties of the collection   TASKS ▼

Collection Type	Session
Resources	Remote Desktop
User Group	CRLAB\RDS_SD_Collection

- **RemoteApp Programs:** here you have the RemoteApp programs currently published on this session collection. This is where you add, delete or modify RemoteApps. Therefore, without further delay, it is time to explain what a RemoteApp is then.

Back in the days when RDS was called 'Terminal Services', users would connect to the terminal servers and get what we called a 'full desktop'. As the name implies, this was what we know as a windows desktop. Start Menu, taskbar, systray, these were all there. Exactly like any other desktop. Citrix at one point introduced the concept of a published application, where only a particular application would be shown to the user (i.e. Microsoft Word), removing everything else (no start menu, no taskbar, etc). This application looked and behaved like a regular, locally installed application. Windows Server 2008 was Microsoft's first attempt to deliver 'published applications', named 'RemoteApps'. Resuming: RemoteApps are simply applications running on the RDSH, displayed on the endpoint, without any other visual element as seen on a Windows desktop (so no start menu, etc).

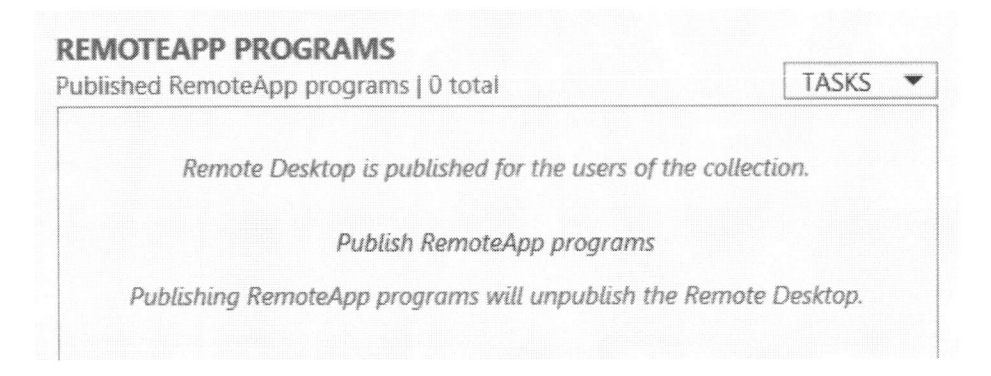

REMOTEAPP PROGRAMS
Published RemoteApp programs | 0 total   TASKS ▼

Remote Desktop is published for the users of the collection.

Publish RemoteApp programs

Publishing RemoteApp programs will unpublish the Remote Desktop.

- **Host Servers:** shows all the RDSHs tied to this session collection. That means when users connect to a desktop or RemoteApp part of this collection, they will run these in one of the RDSHs in the collection. Here you can also put a server in what we call 'drain mode' (more on that later).

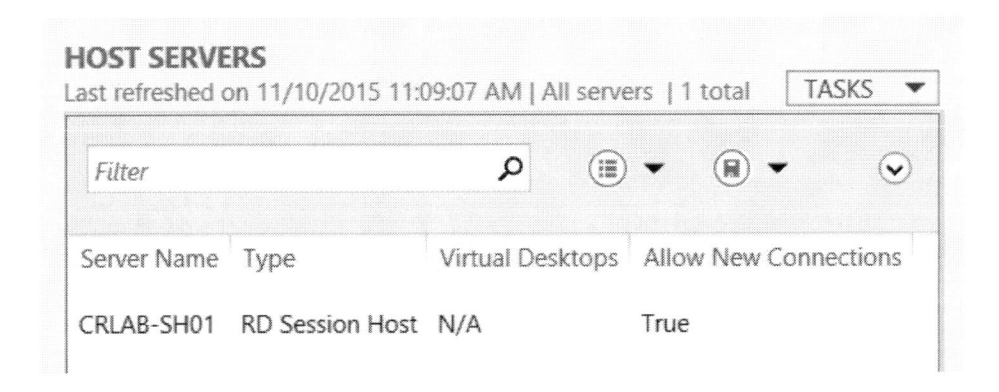

HOST SERVERS
Last refreshed on 11/10/2015 11:09:07 AM | All servers | 1 total   TASKS ▼

Server Name	Type	Virtual Desktops	Allow New Connections
CRLAB-SH01	RD Session Host	N/A	True

- **Connections:** lists all the connections currently established to any of the RDSHs part of the collection. From here, you can also perform some basic actions like disconnecting users, sending them messages or logging them off.

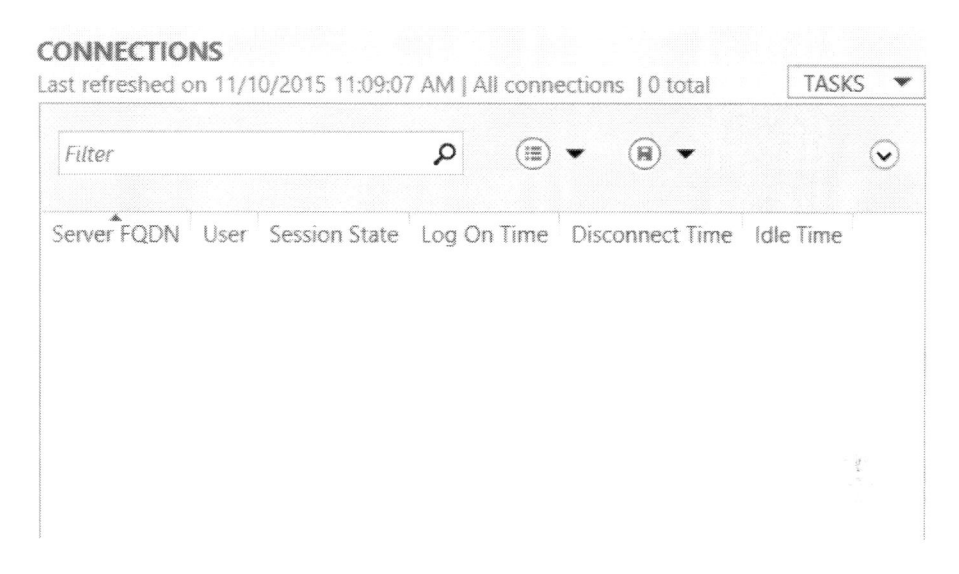

Now that we covered all the important aspects of a session collection, let's take a look at the advanced settings available in a collection.

Still under server manager, collections section, click on 'Tasks' | 'Edit Properties'.

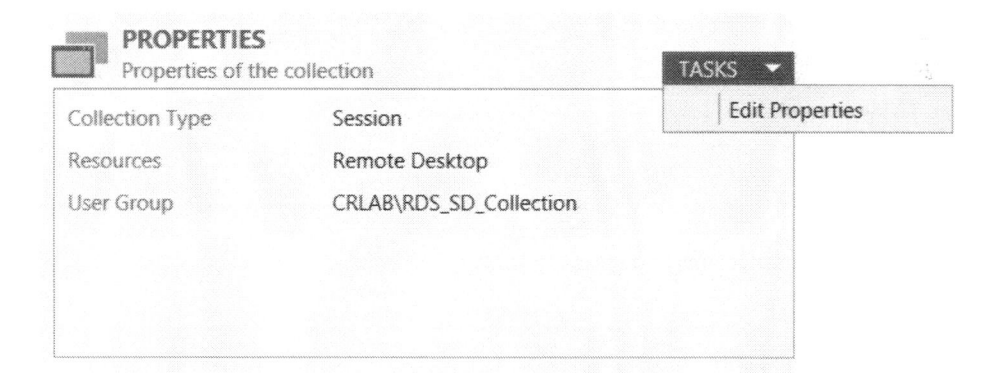

We can now explore a little bit more about a collection.

Collection Properties

Once you click on 'Edit Properties' RDMS will open the properties window for that particular collection.

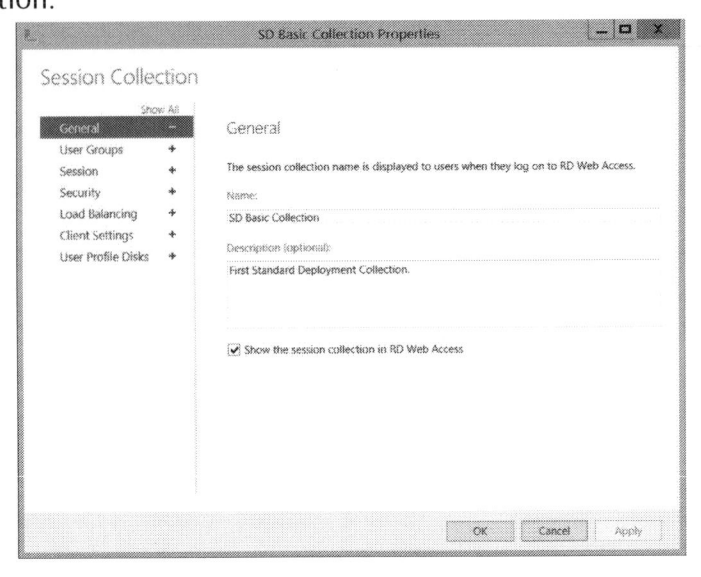

Let's take a look at each option available.

General

Shows the basic information (name and description) of the collection. It also allows you to set if it will be shown or not on the RDWA portal (remember, the website we used to launch an application when we performed a 'Quick Start' deployment).

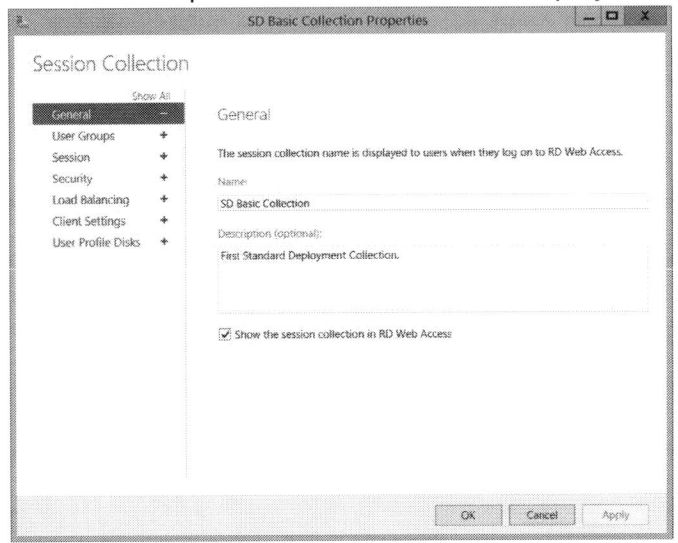

User Groups

Shows the groups that have access to the collection and allows you to add and remove groups as required. The wizard adds the group selected when setting up the collection as shown here.

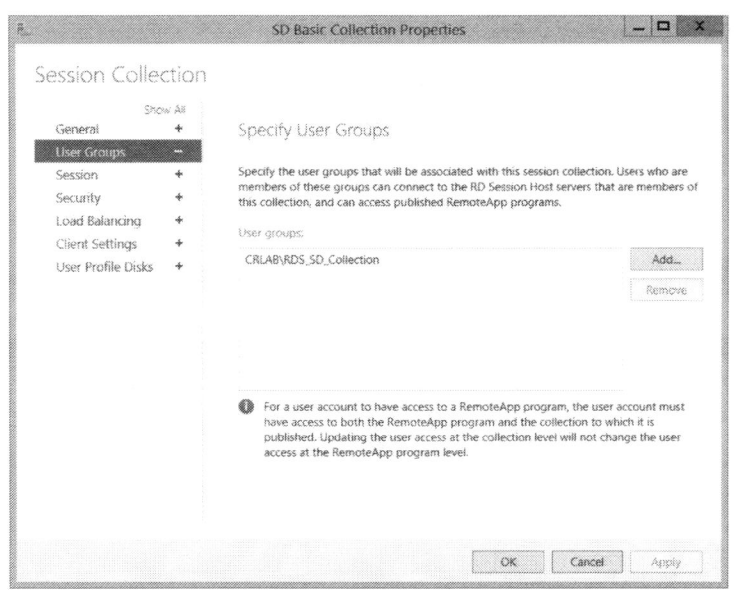

ⓘ **Note:** you can also control access at the RemoteApp level. This means users must have access to the collection and all RemoteApps in order to see and launch them. By default, when a RemoteApp is created, all users with rights to the collection are automatically added to the RemoteApp security.

Session

This tab allows you to change the timeouts related to the connections established to the RDSHs. By default, no matter what happens, sessions are never terminated from the server what is not a good thing (you want sessions to be terminated at one point in order to avoid performance issues due to things like memory leaks). Ideally you want to change the default values. Let's do a quick review on these timeouts, in case you are not familiar with them.

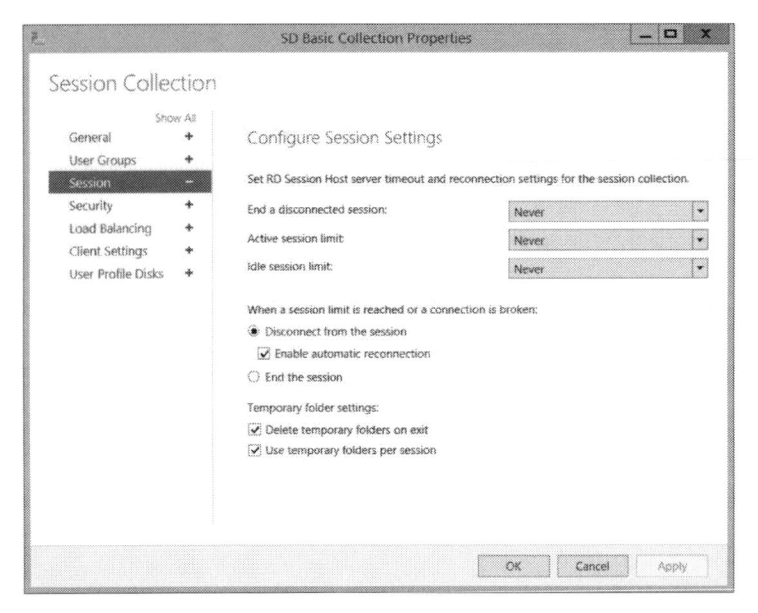

- **Disconnected session:** when a session is not logged off properly (for example, user clicks on the close button on the top right corner of the Remote Desktop Client or the network connection drops for whatever reason), it goes into a disconnected state. In this case the session is still running on the server but with no connection to an endpoint (the client machine). This setting prevents such sessions from remaining on the server indefinitely. As long as this timeout is not reached, the session will remain on the RDSH and users will be able to reconnect and start working exactly where they were before disconnecting.

- **Active session:** sets for how long a user session can be active before being disconnected or terminated (logged off). Usually this is not used but in certain regulated environments, users may not be allowed to work for more than a certain number of hours. This setting enforces that.

- **Idle session:** If the user connects and does not perform any work (no keyboard and mouse input), the idle timer starts and once it reaches the idle timeout set here, the connection is disconnected or terminated.

After setting the timeouts as per your needs, the next step is to decide what the server is supposed to do once sessions reach such timeouts. In most cases, we want to disconnect the sessions and then keep these running for a certain period. This will allow users to reconnect to their sessions if required and guarantee unused sessions do not remain on the RDSHs.

The final option controls how the RDSHs deal with temporary files and folders.

ⓘ **Note:** Group Policies can also enforce these timeout settings. That is why we mentioned the issue seen where the deployment wizards fail if any of these are being applied to your servers. For that reason, we advise you to use RDMS to configure timeouts, in order to prevent a potential conflict with a GPO.

Security

Here you control the 'Security Layer' and 'Encryption Level' of the RDP connection (meaning the connections established between the users' endpoint and the RDSHs). It also allows you to enforce that only computers capable of using 'Network Level Authentication' (NLA) connect.

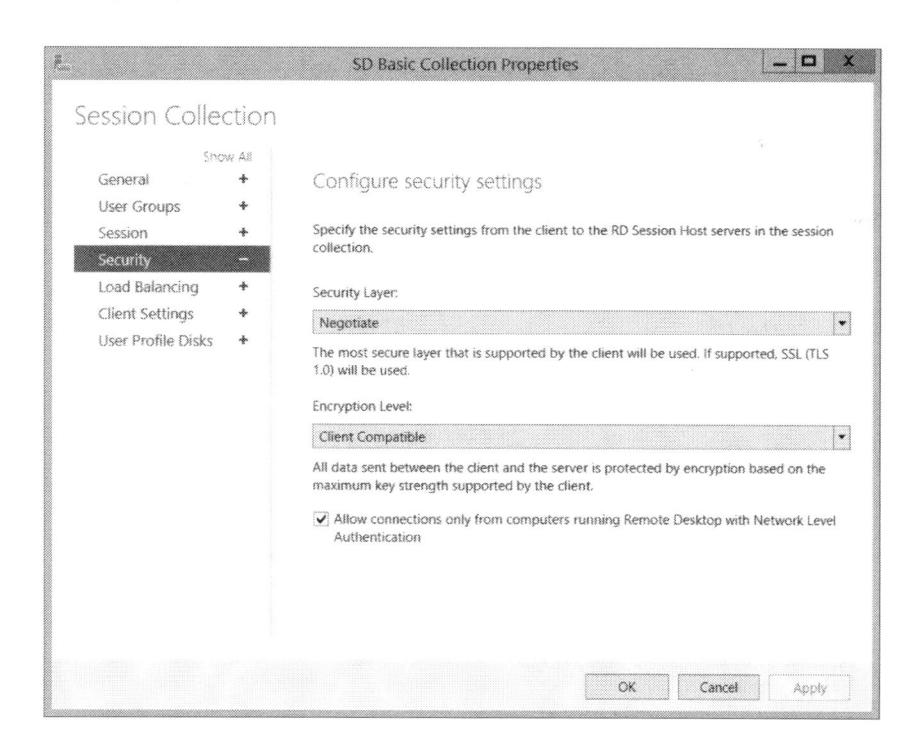

ⓘ **Note:** Network Level Authentication (NLA) is a technology that requires the connecting endpoint to authenticate before the session is established. If NLA is not used, the server logon screen is immediately accessible what not only may waste server resources but could also lead to Denial-of-Service (DoS) attacks.

Load Balancing

As previously discussed, one of the roles of the RDCB is to spread the user load equally across all your RDSHs. This tries to guarantee performance is virtually the same no matter which server a certain user logs in. Here you can adjust the maximum number of users you want per server (normally determined by performing what we call 'Load Testing' – more on that later) and also the relative weight for each RDSH (in case they are different – typical example is physical servers where CPUs and total memory are not the same).

ⓘ Certain conditions may override the RDCB load calculation. One typical example is when a user has a disconnected session. Ideally, you want the user to reconnect to his existing session so he can start working from where he left off. This is the behavior no matter what the load is on that particular RDSH at the time of the reconnection.

Client Settings

This tab controls how the RDSHs will handle the local resources on the endpoint, when it connects to a session. For example, you can disable access to the clipboard so users are not able to copy and paste between the local PC and the RemoteApp or Remote Desktop.

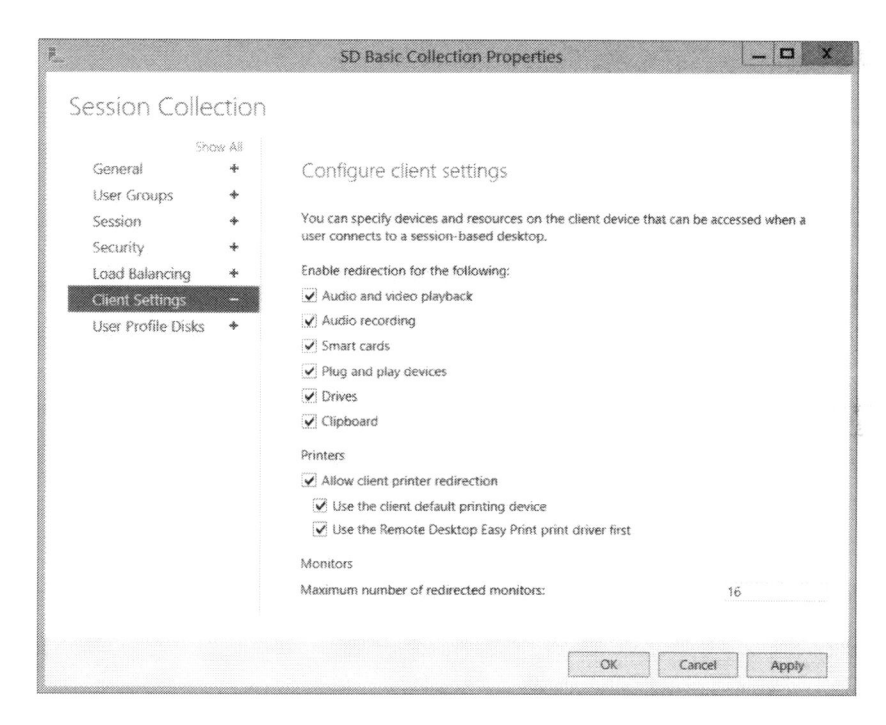

Printers are a little bit more complex due to the way the RDSH creates the printer within the user session. We will get to that in a bit. For now, simply use the default settings. For all other options, disable the features you do not need (important to mention logon times may be affected by how many local devices you are trying to map within your remote session. Reason why we do recommend disabling anything that is not needed).

ⓘ As with the timeout settings, Group Policies can control many of the redirection options, so be aware of potential conflicts between these and what is set using RDMS.

User Profile Disks

User profile disks (UPD) were introduced with Windows Server 2012. In short, UPD redirects the whole user profile (what you see under C:\Users\%username%) to a central location but unlike roaming profiles, it uses a single VHD file for each user at the remote share. As UPD offers several customization options, we will cover it in more details in a separate section.

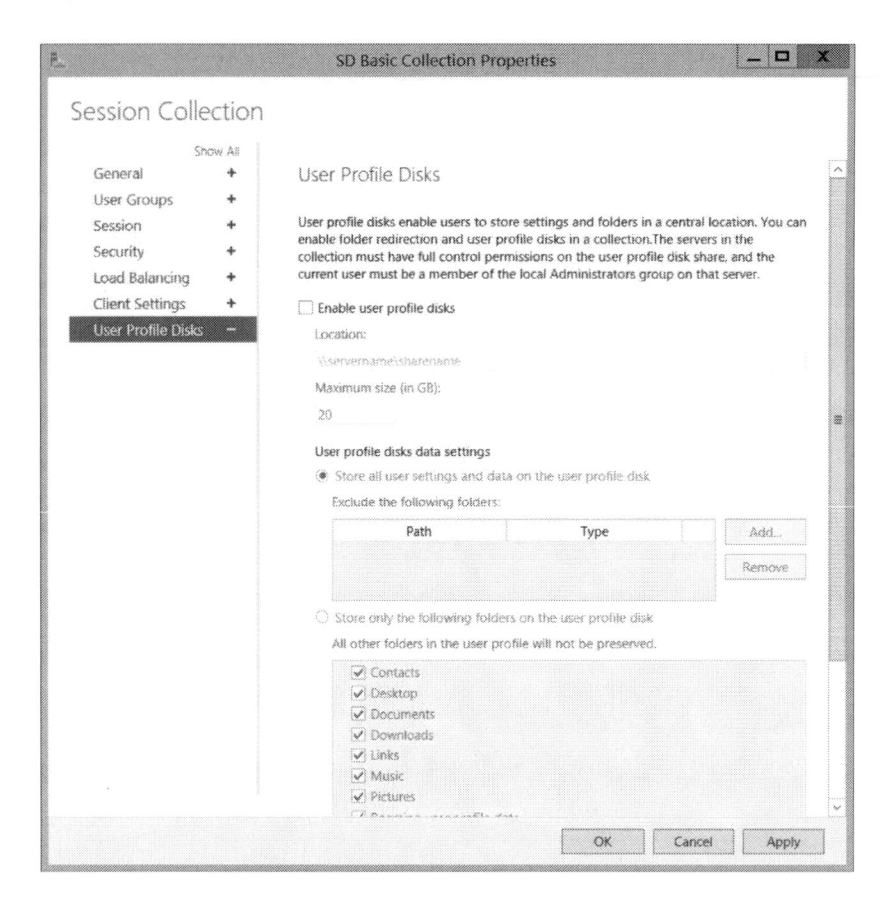

[User Profile Disks configuration screenshot showing SD Basic Collection Properties dialog]

That covers all you have for a session collection. If you worked with previous versions of RDS you certainly noticed some of these are not new. The key thing is you can manage these in a centralized way, instead of being scattered all over the place like in Windows Server 2008 R2 RDS.

Publishing RemoteApps

Up to Windows Server 2003 Terminal Services (remember, RDS was called Terminal Services or TS for short), users could only connect to what we call a 'full desktop'. That means once connected, they would see a Windows desktop, virtually identical to what they had on their local PCs. Start Menu, taskbar, systray and so on were all there.

At the time the main issue with that approach was when users still needed access to something on their local PCs. Switching back and forth between their RDS full desktop and the local PC was not really friendly and often led to confusion.

Windows Server 2008 introduced what in Citrix jargon is called a 'published application', and named it 'RemoteApp'. The idea is very simple. Instead of showing the user a full desktop with all its elements, RemoteApps allow administrators to provide single applications to the users, that look and behave almost like a locally installed one. Most users might not even see the difference between a local application and a RemoteApp. Of course, by not having to launch a full desktop and all the resources that come along with it, RemoteApps tend to use fewer resources and in case multiple apps are launched by the same user, the same session is used (meaning all RemoteApps run within the same session, within the same server).

ⓘ It is important to understand a key difference between a RemoteApp and a full desktop: full desktop sessions rely on explorer.exe/userinit.exe for the shell; RemoteApp sessions do not, relying on rpdshell.exe/rdpinit.exe instead. This may cause issues with applications (i.e. incorrect window sizing, windows not showing, etc.). Therefore, it is important to test your applications before a rollout in order to avoid unexpected surprises. This is also how we troubleshoot applications within RDS. Test them on an RDS full desktop in case you see odd issues with your application when doing RemoteApp. If the issue is not there, the shell is the culprit.

In addition, RemoteApps can be published in different ways. You can make them available directly on the RDWA page but also completely integrated to the local PC (running Windows of course) start menu or start screen (depends on the version of Windows).

Enough talking. Let's get our hands dirty and start deploying some RemoteApps on the session collection we just created.

1. On CRLAB-DC01 launch 'Server Manager' and under 'Remote Desktop Services' you should see 'SD Basic Collection' under 'Collections'. Click on it.

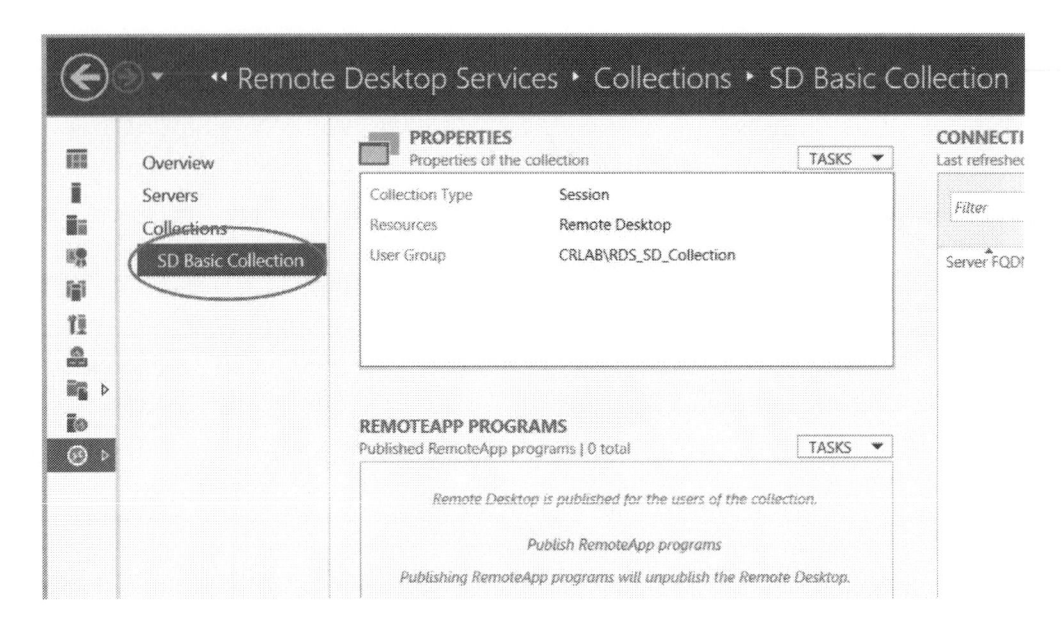

2. Under the 'RemoteApp Programs' section, click on 'Tasks' and select 'Publish RemoteApp Programs'.

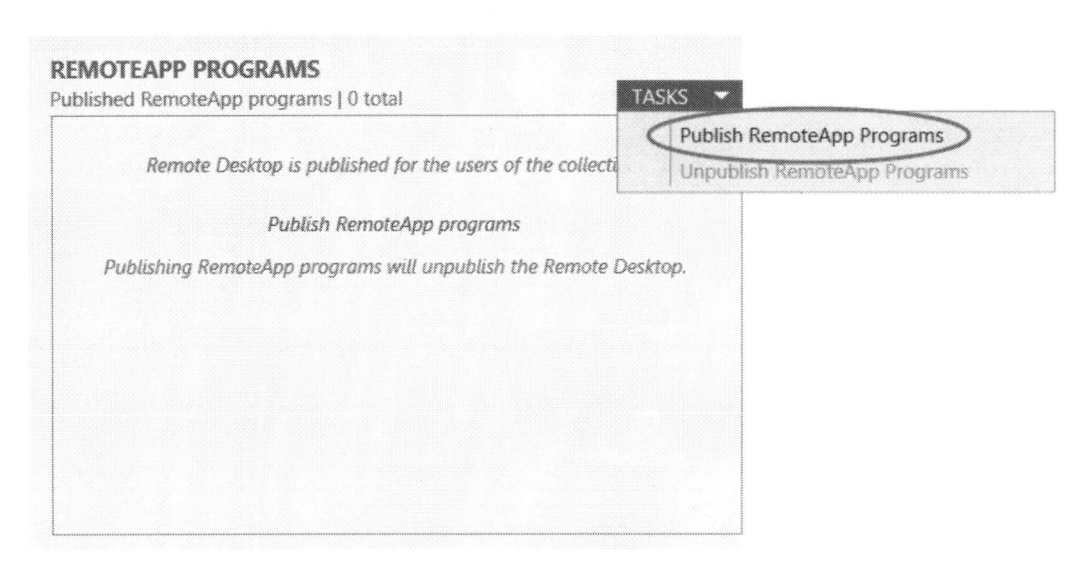

3. The wizard will launch and show a list of common applications retrieved from the session host you selected as part of the 'Standard deployment'.

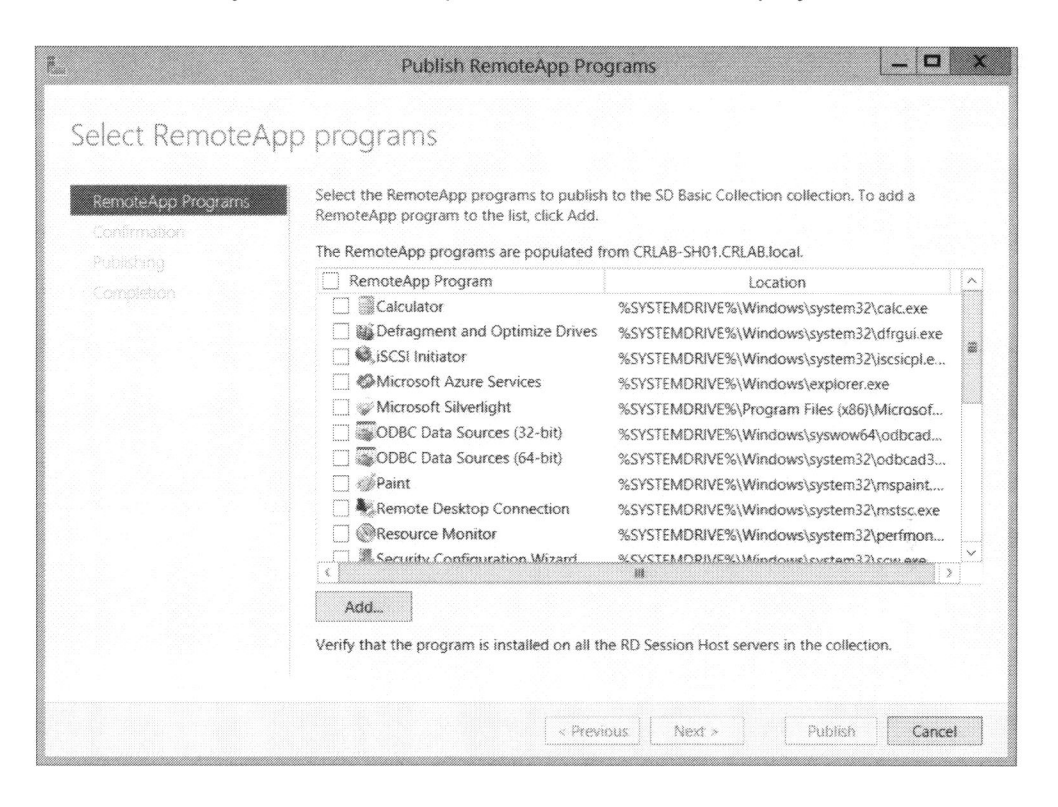

The wizard will show you the most common apps, including applications you had previously installed (i.e. Microsoft Office). In case you do not see a certain application, you can always click 'Add...' and browse to the required executable in order to publish it to your users. As this is a test environment, let's go ahead and publish 'Paint'.

ⓘ In this particular example, we only used a single RDSH server. In a production environment with multiple RDSHs in your collection, make sure these are all identical (with the exact same applications - installed and configured identically). Otherwise, you will end up with RemoteApps launching only on some RDSHs or even worse, different user experience depending on which RDSH the user connects. Also understand that the RemoteApps shown on this dialog come from the first RDSH in your collection and not from all RDSHs (so, no, there is no 'merge' here). One more reason to make sure all RDSHs are identical.

4. Select the application we want to publish, in our case 'Paint', and click 'Next' (you can select multiple applications at once if needed). The wizard will show you the confirmation screen so you can check if the RemoteApps you want to publish are correct. Click 'Publish'.

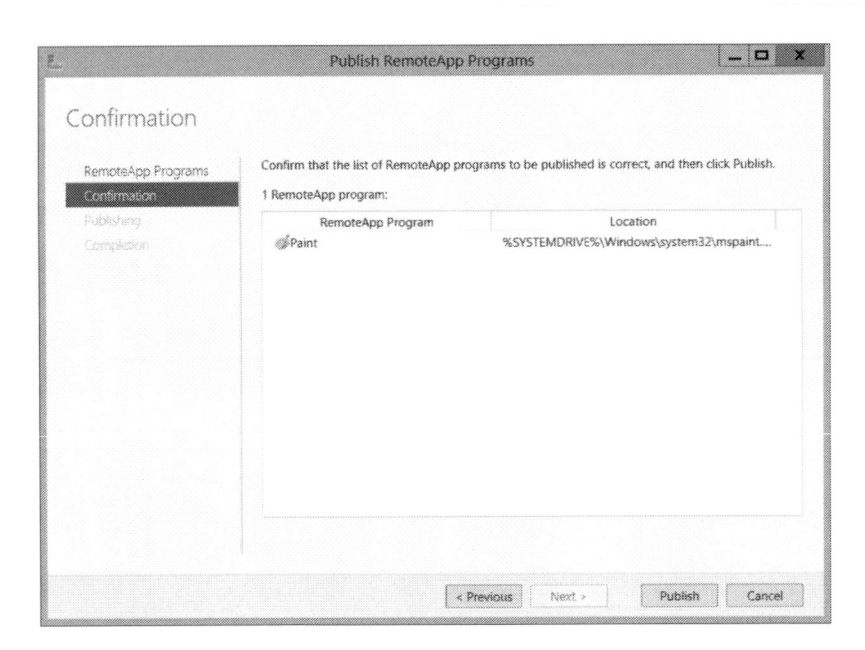

5. After a couple seconds, the wizard will finish. Click 'Close'.

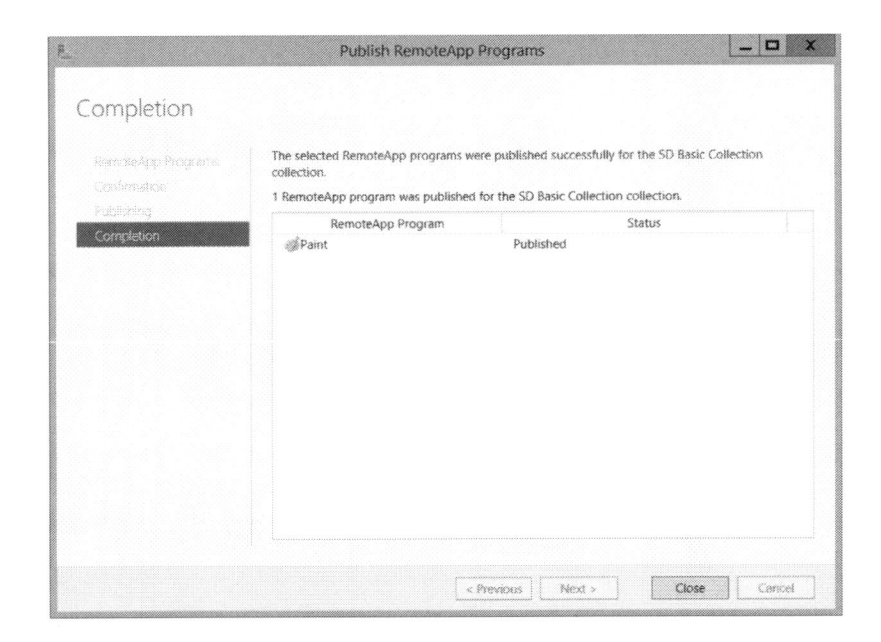

Page 66 | RDS - The Complete Guide

6. Back to the 'Server Manager' console, we can now see our first RemoteApp under 'Remote Programs'.

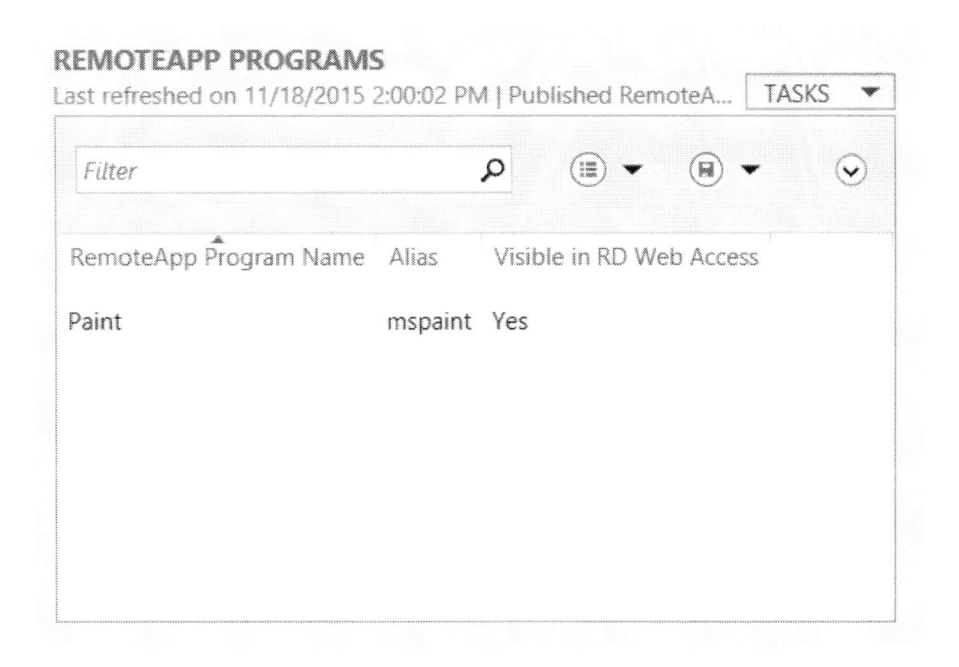

REMOTEAPP PROGRAMS
Last refreshed on 11/18/2015 2:00:02 PM | Published RemoteA... | TASKS ▼

RemoteApp Program Name	Alias	Visible in RD Web Access
Paint	mspaint	Yes

Before we dig into the more advanced properties of a RemoteApp, let's take a look at how this is all presented inside RDWA. After all, this may be the entry point for most users when accessing their applications. As we selected CRLAB-WA01 for the RDWA role, open https://crlab-wa01.crlab.local/rdweb using Internet Explorer and logon as TestUser1 (remember, we created this user account on AD earlier). You should see this:

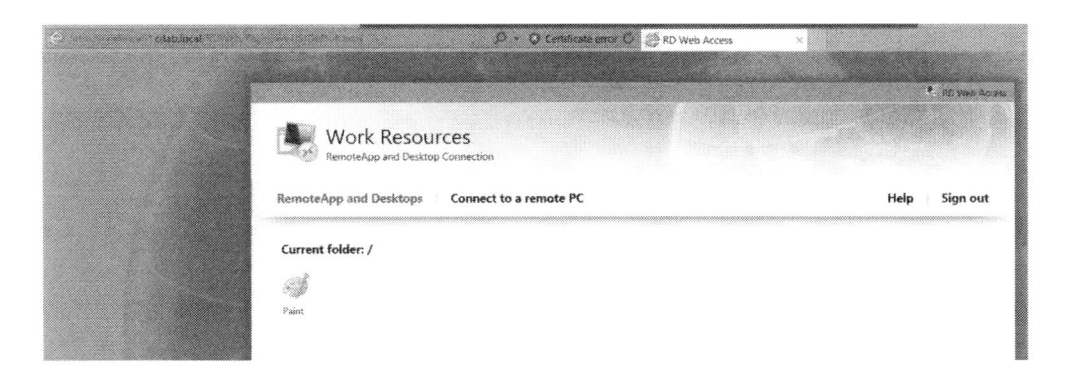

ⓘ Note: you will get a warning regarding a certificate mismatch when accessing the RDWA site. This is expected as the RDWA server is using a self-signed certificate that is not trusted by your endpoint. This is fixed when we deploy a proper certificate on the RDWA server. You may also get an add-on popup for the 'Microsoft Remote Desktop Web Access Connector' add-on. You can safely enable it.

That is all you need to publish RemoteApps. Fairly simple and straightforward.

Now, back to our RemoteApp, let's take a look at some of its configuration options that cannot be set initially. Under 'RemoteApp Programs', right click 'Paint' and select 'Edit Properties'.

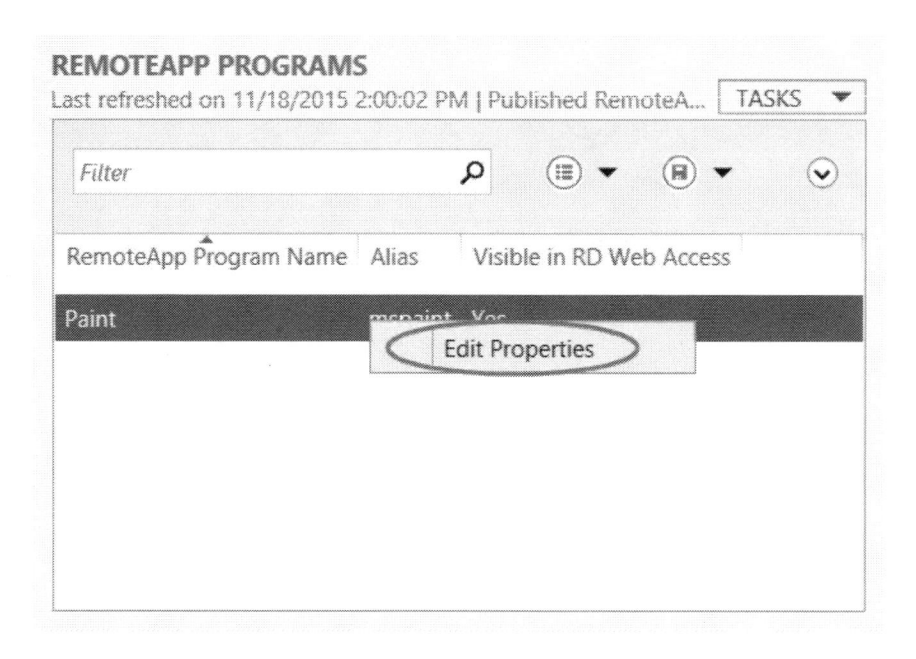

REMOTEAPP PROGRAMS
Last refreshed on 11/18/2015 2:00:02 PM | Published RemoteA... | TASKS ▼

Filter

RemoteApp Program Name | Alias | Visible in RD Web Access

Paint

Edit Properties

These are all the options for a RemoteApp:

General
Here we can change the program name for the RemoteApp (the name users will see), view its alias, icon and path for it on the RDSH server. You can also set if it will be available on the RDWA site and if you want it to be under a particular folder. This greatly helps organizing applications for the users as you can group similar ones in a single folder (if you worked with RDS under Windows Server 2008 R2, this was not

there and it was a major grief for users when you had hundreds of apps). Another thing to keep in mind is the fact you cannot select a particular icon for your application using this GUI. This is possible when using PowerShell, what we will cover later on.

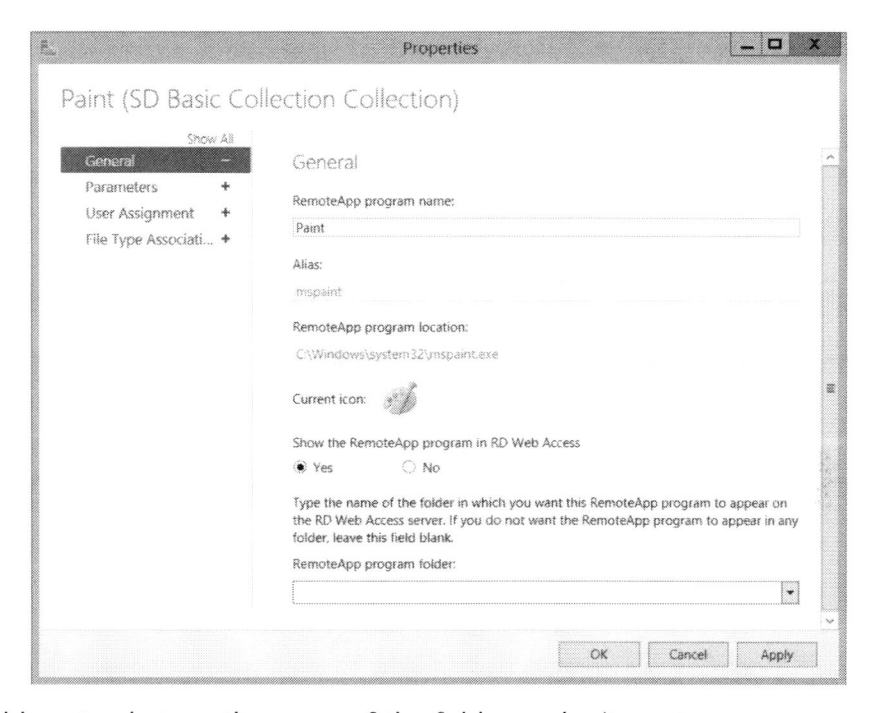

To create a folder, simply type the name of the folder under 'RemoteApp program folder' and click 'Apply'. Try it with a folder named 'Enterprise Apps'. If you log back into RDWA as TestUser1 you should now see this:

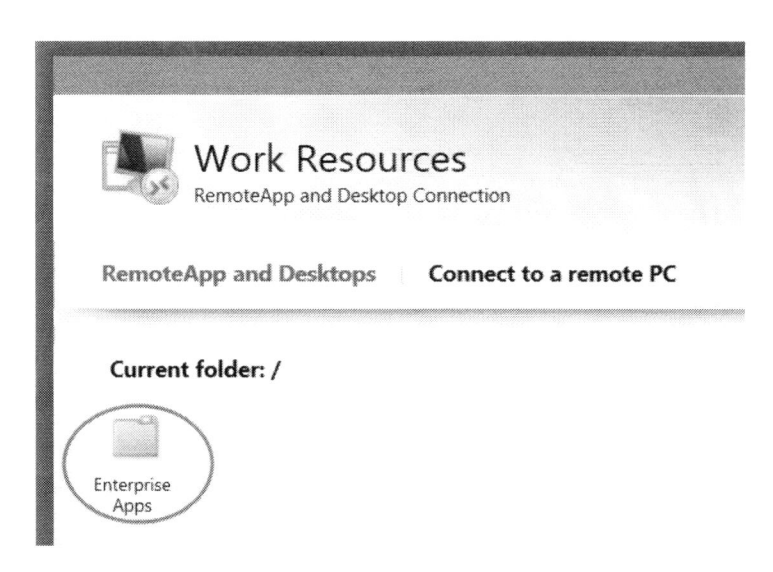

When publishing an additional RemoteApp you can now select the folder you just created or enter a name for a new folder.

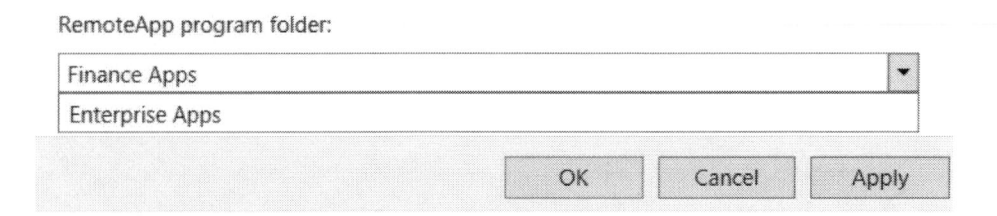

RemoteApp program folder:
- Finance Apps
- Enterprise Apps

Keep in mind that when you remove the last RemoteApp in a folder, that folder will be automatically removed. This prevents an empty folder being available to your users under RDWA.

Note: you cannot have subfolders. This means it is a single level hierarchy for your RemoteApps (what is already very useful).

Parameters

Here you can add any command line parameters your application may need. This allows for example, two configurations for the same executable (i.e. one points to a production database, another to a test one). Simply add the required parameters under 'Always use the following command-line parameters'.

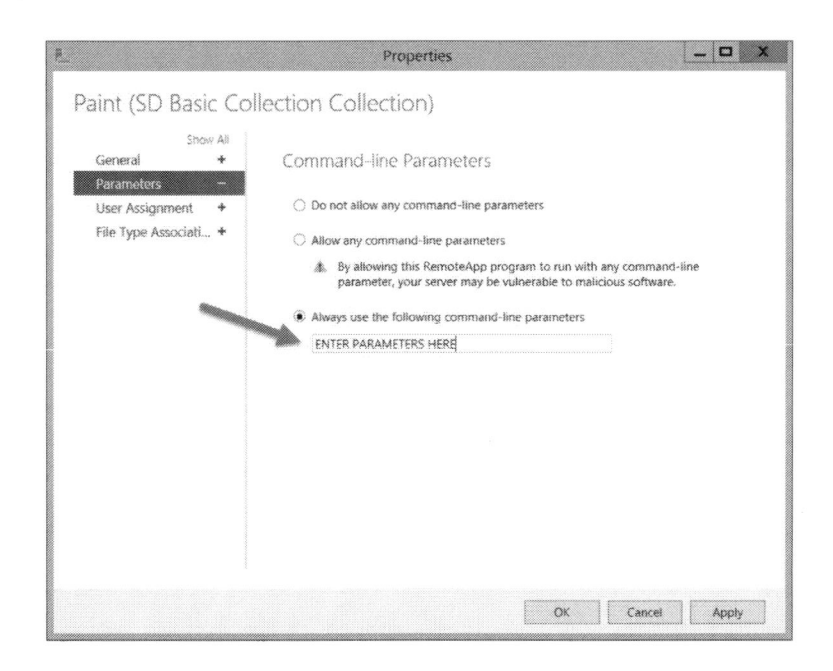

User Assignment

Here you can further tweak access rights to the RemoteApp. As previously mentioned, by default all users with rights to the session collection will inherit rights to each RemoteApp under that collection. By selecting 'Only specified users and groups', you can change the default behavior.

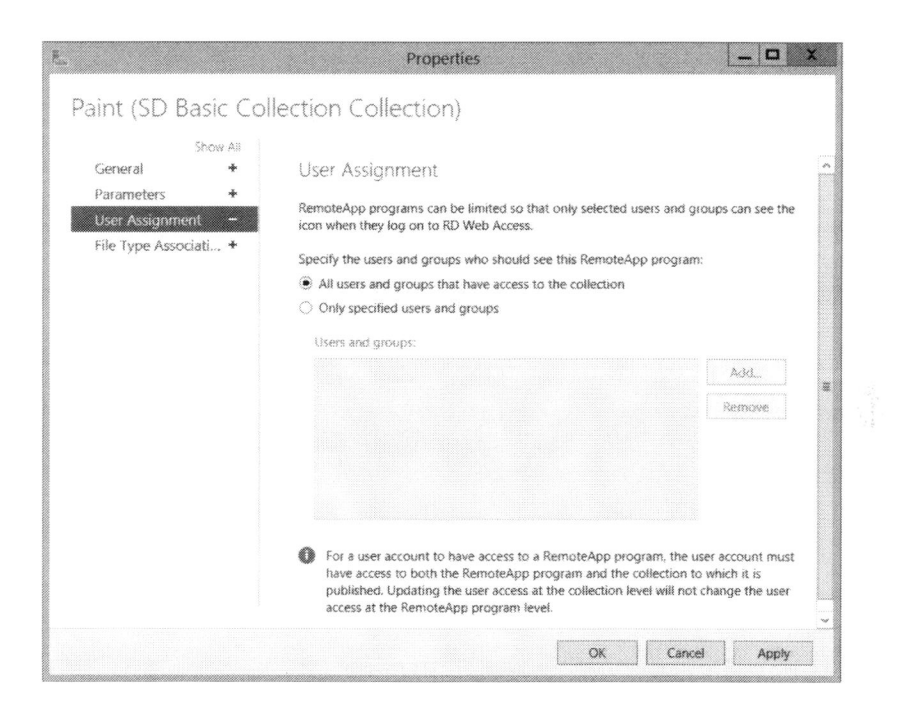

ⓘ **Note:** we highly recommend you to use application-specific groups (i.e. Microsoft Office Standard Users, Microsoft Project Users, etc) and to edit the RemoteApp to use them. This will greatly simplify managing application access. For that reason, we also avoid adding individual users to applications, except when troubleshooting issues. Another very important thing here is to keep in mind that user assignment is not to be used as a security measure to prevent users from running particular applications. It does hide these apps from them (i.e. on RDWA) though. If you do have a need to completely remove access to an application from a user, you will need to look into NTFS permissions or Microsoft's own AppLocker.

File Type Association

As the name implies, you are able to configure the file type associations (FTAs) you want to tie to this particular RemoteApp. This means when a user tries to open a local file on his PC, the RemoteApp that handles that particular FTA will start and open the file, as if it were a local application.

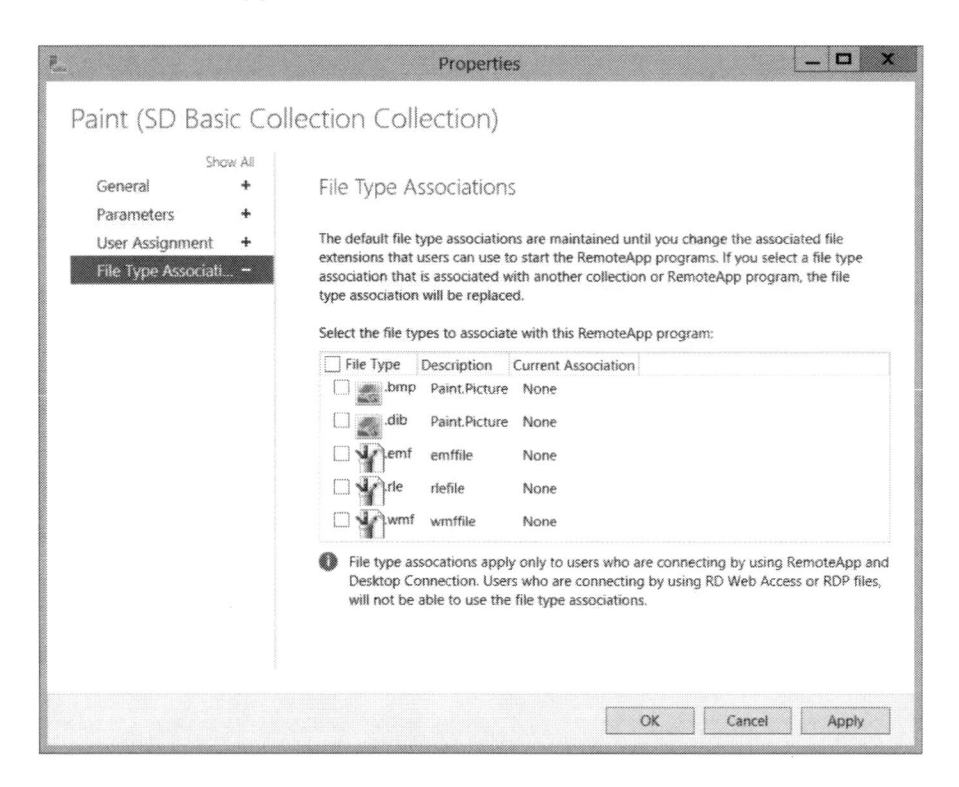

ⓘ It is important to mention this does not work for RemoteApps launched through RDWA. You will need to configure the PC to use the RDWA feed for that. More on that later.

Adding RDSH Servers

Now that you have a working 'Standard Deployment', it is time to expand it. So far, we have three servers on the deployment: RDCB, RDWA and one RDSH. First step to a highly available RDS environment is to make sure we do have multiple RDSHs available. This will also allow us to host more users at any given time, spreading their sessions over all the RDSHs.

Let's get to work and add one more server. In this case, we will add CRLAB-SH02 (as it is indeed supposed to be an RDSH).

1. As we did our 'Standard Deployment' from CRLAB-DC01, launch 'Server Manager' on it and select '3. Add other servers to manage'.

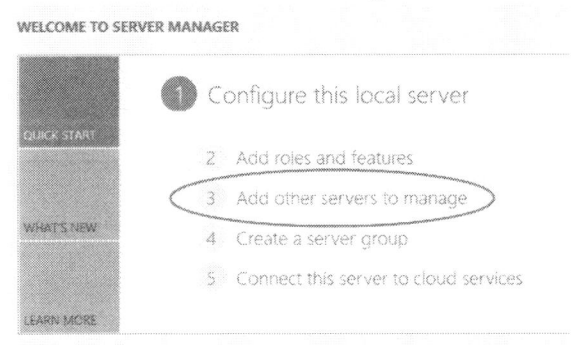

2. Type crlab-sh under 'Name(CN)' and click 'Find Now'. This will return all servers with names starting with CRLAB-SH. Select 'CRLAB-SH02' and click the arrow button to add it to the right pane. Click 'Ok'.

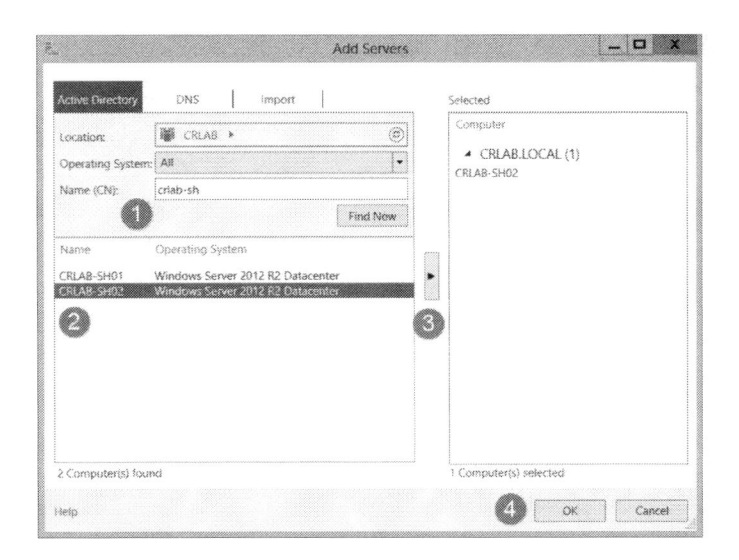

3. Now click on 'Remote Desktop Services' on the left. This will open the 'Overview' page we discussed earlier. Under 'Deployment Overview' right-click the 'RD Session Host' icon and select 'Add RD Session Host Servers'.

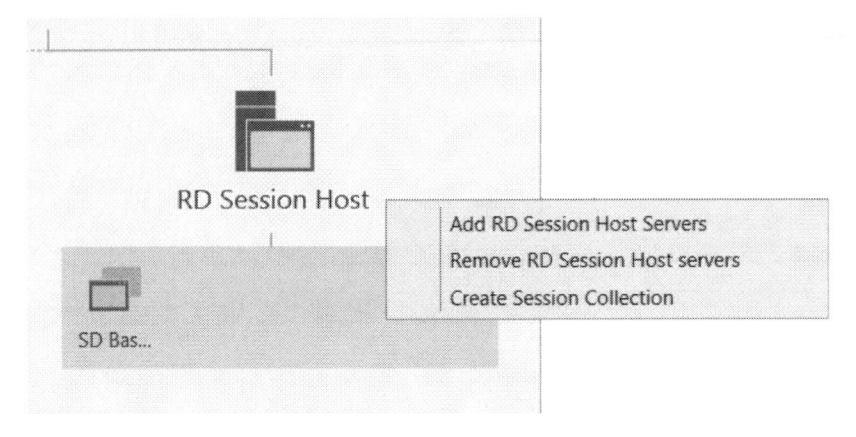

ⓘ **Note:** there are several ways to add a new RDSH server to an existing deployment. Just on the 'Overview' page, there are three different ways to do it (try finding them)! Later in this book, you will learn how to use PowerShell to do it.

4. Select 'CRLAB-SH02' and click the arrow button to add it to the 'Selected' list. Click 'Next'.

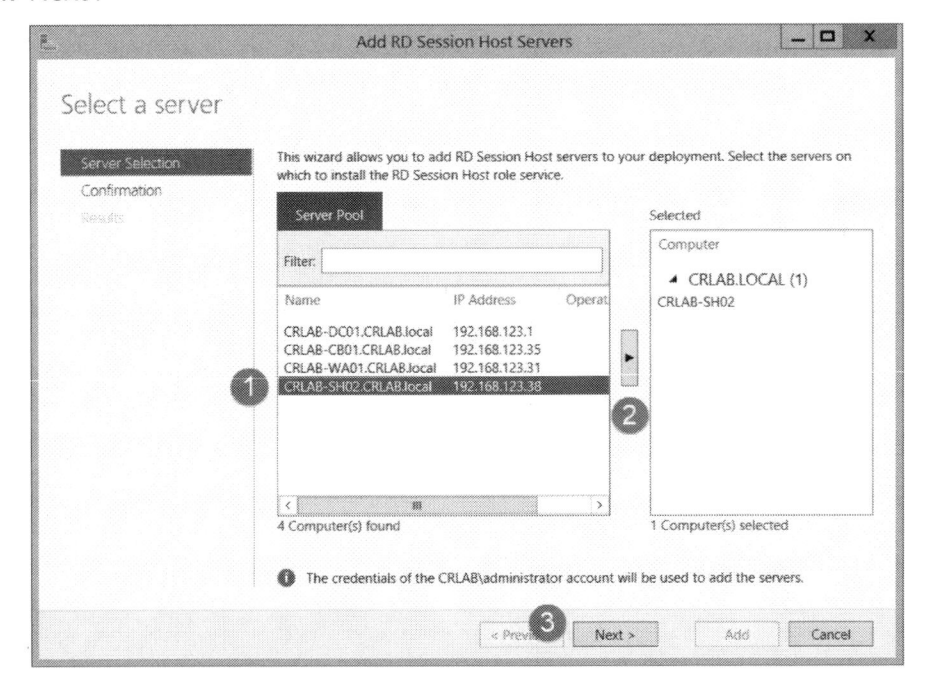

Page 74 | RDS - The Complete Guide

5. The wizard will show you the server you selected on the 'Confirmation' page. Click 'Restart remote computers as needed' and then click 'Add'.

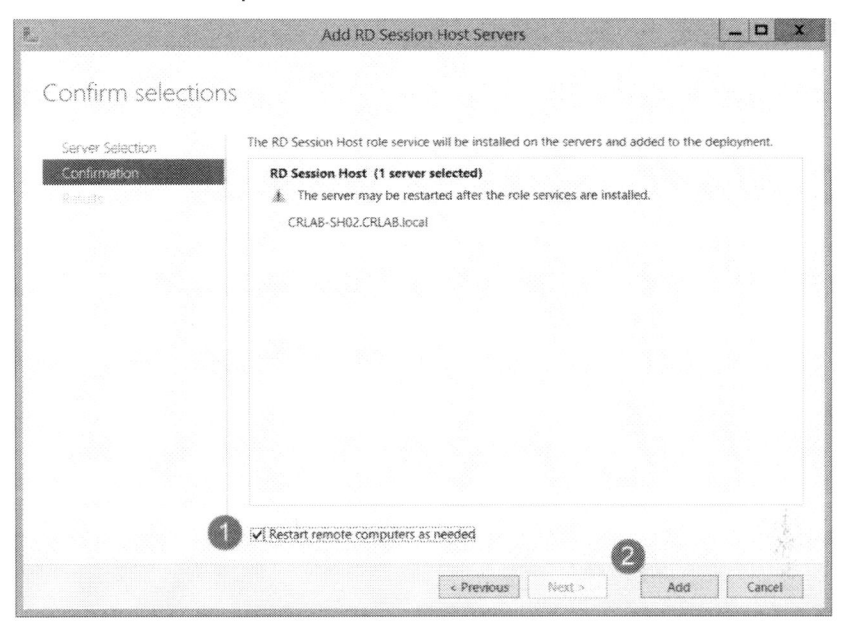

6. The wizard will display the installation status and at one point, it will show you the server is restarting. If everything works as expected, you should see 'Succeeded' under 'Status. Click 'Close'.

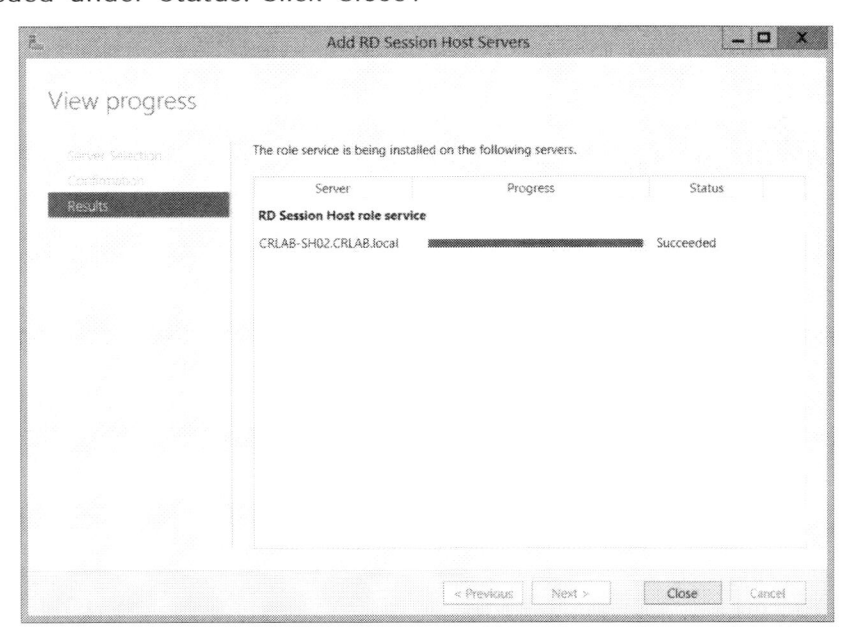

7. Back to the 'Overview' page, you will notice under 'Deployment Servers' on the left, the server we just added, 'CRLAB-SH02'.

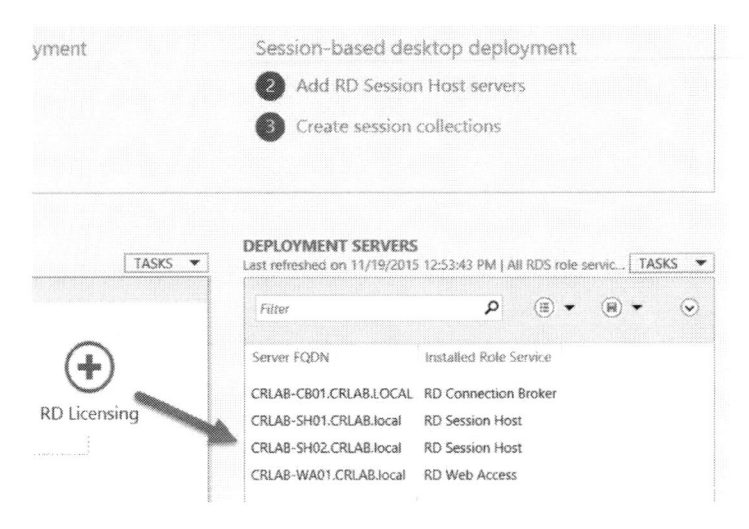

However, we are not finished yet. As you remember, a deployment may have multiple session collections. When we add a server to the deployment, it just sits there, not part of any collection. Therefore, we must add it to a collection in order for users to use it.

8. Under 'Collections', select 'SD Basic Collection' (the one we created previously) and under 'Host Servers' click 'Tasks' and then select 'Add RD Session Host Servers'.

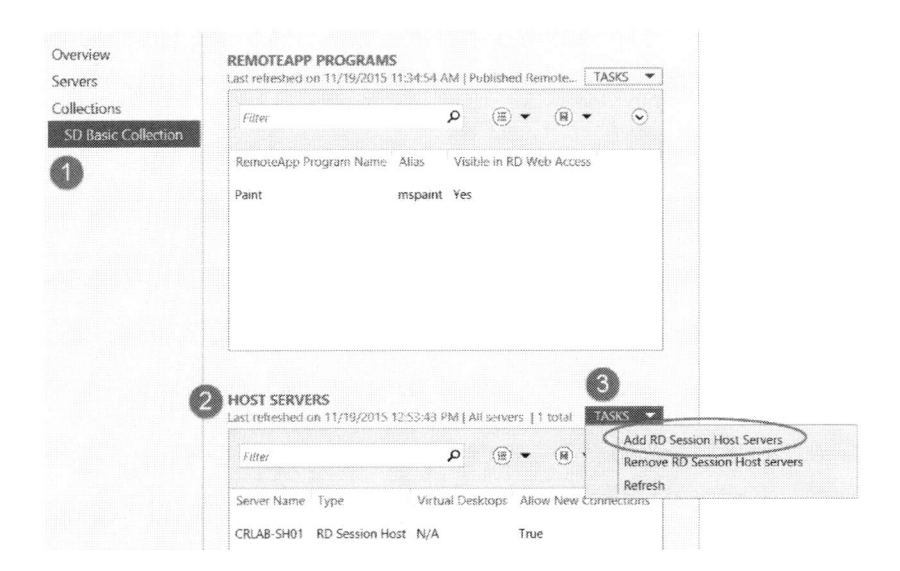

Page 76 | RDS - The Complete Guide

9. Select 'CRLAB-SH02' and click the arrow button. Then click 'Next'.

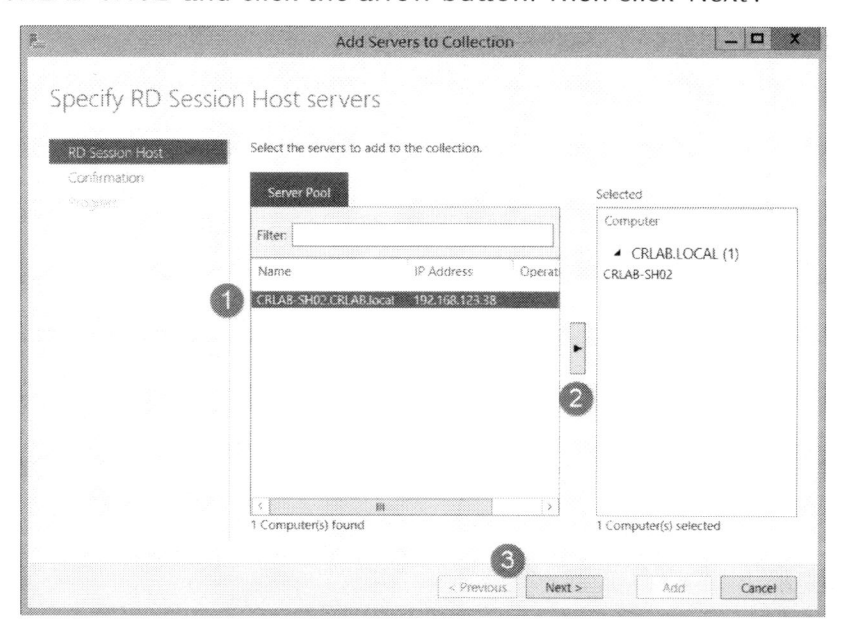

10. Under 'Confirmation', we can see the name of the server we are adding. Click 'Add'.

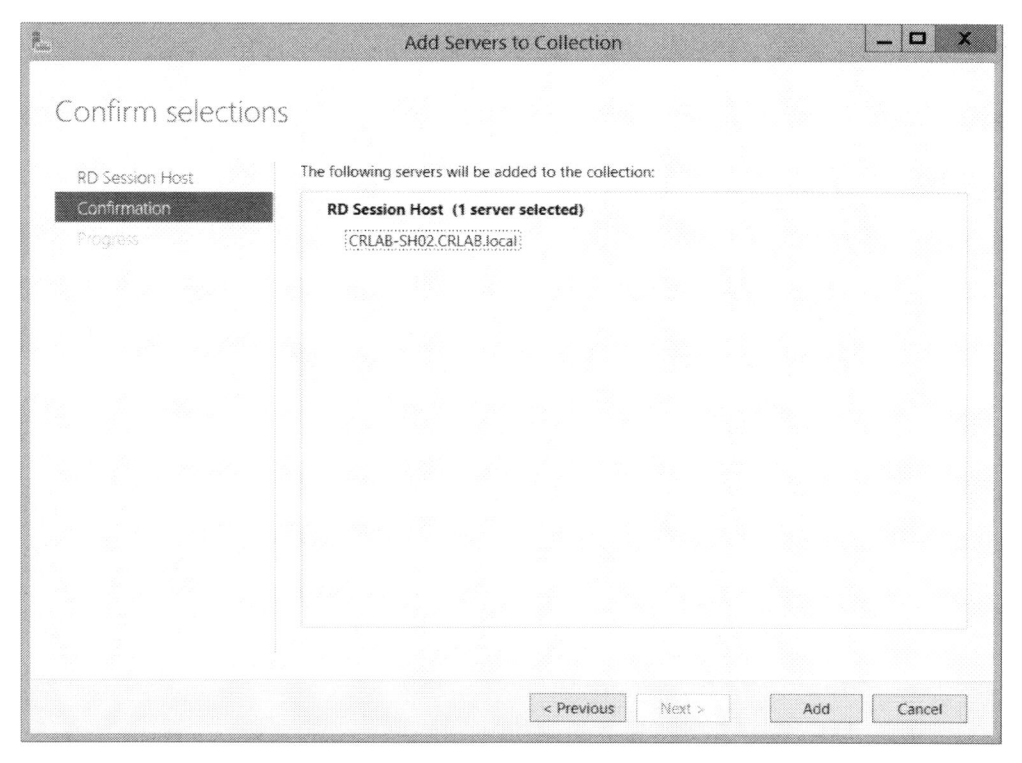

11. If everything works as expected, you should see 'Succeeded' under 'Status. Click 'Close'.

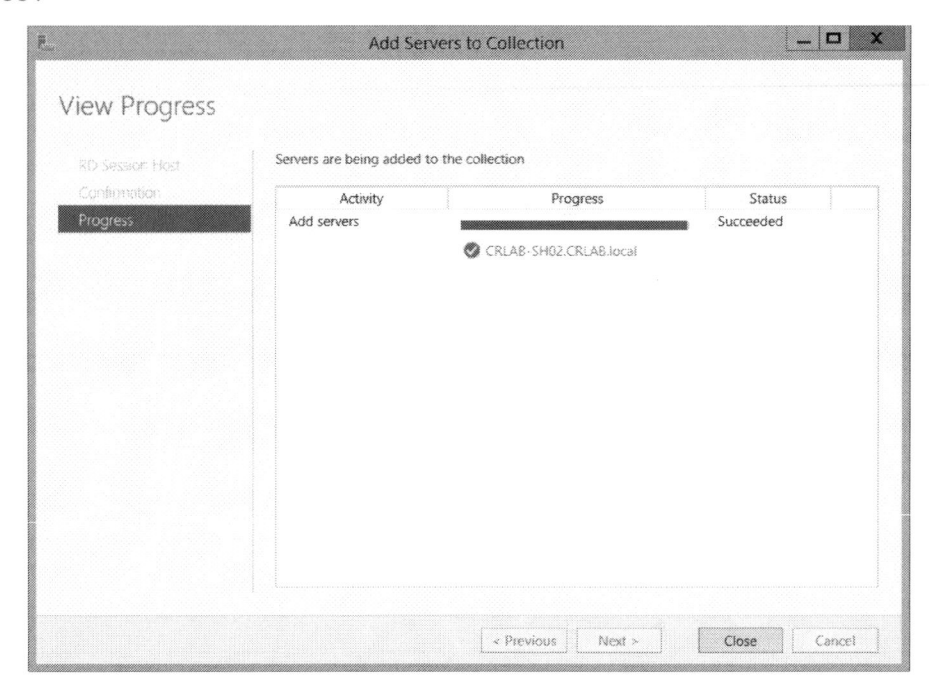

12. We can now see both RDSHs under 'Host Servers'.

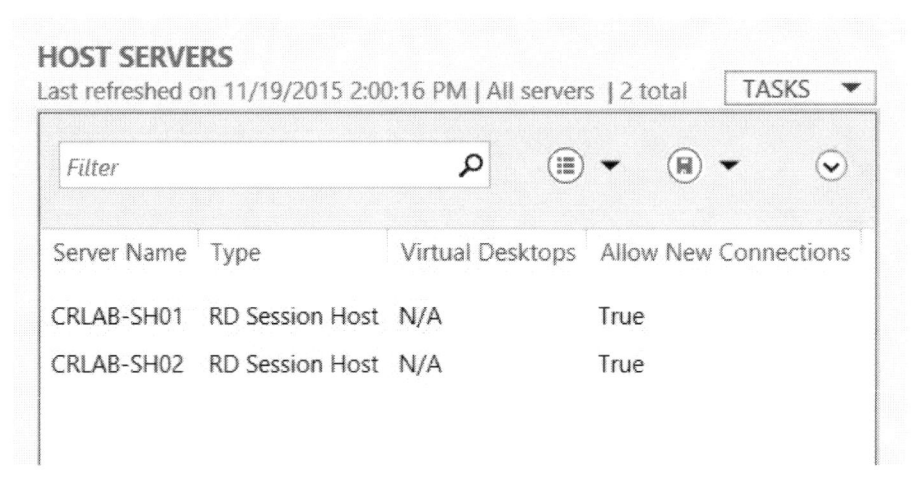

This completes the process of adding a new RDSH to a collection. Simple eh? Yes and no. The wizards did a lot for us under the hood. If you remember the process under Windows Server 2008 R2, we can bet you find RDS 2012 R2 much easier. So let's take a look at what was actually done for us and how much time that saved.

1. As the first step, it adds the selected RDSH to the RDCB farm (that is how we call a group of RDSHs managed by the RDCB). This allows the server to start accepting connections, dispatched by the RDCB. If you ever used RDS 2008 R2, we used to refer to this process as 'Adding an RD Session Host server to an existing RD Connection Broker farm'. This was either a manual process or something done by GPO. Yes, it was sort of messy and with room for error. RDS 2012 R2 greatly simplifies all that.
2. Next, this RDSH inherits the properties of our session collection. Remember that we showed you all the properties you can set for a collection (i.e. session timeouts, UPD settings, etc.).
3. Finally, this RDSH gets all the RemoteApps part of that collection. As you remember, we published 'Paint' to the collection that had CRLAB-SH01 as the only RDSH. By adding CRLAB-SH02 to this collection, it gets all the RemoteApps automatically. Again, back in the RDS 2008 R2 days this would require a manual process in the RemoteApp manager on the RDSH (this tool no longer exists on Windows Server 2012 R2) by either adding all RemoteApps manually or by using one of the two import/export procedures. Far from enterprise ready if you ask us.

(i) If you are the type of person that likes to see what happens under-the-hood, open the registry on CRLAB-SH02 and browse to *HKLM\Software\Microsoft\Windows NT\CurrentVersion\Terminal Server\TSAppAllowList\Applications*. You should see our amazing 'Paint' corporate app there.

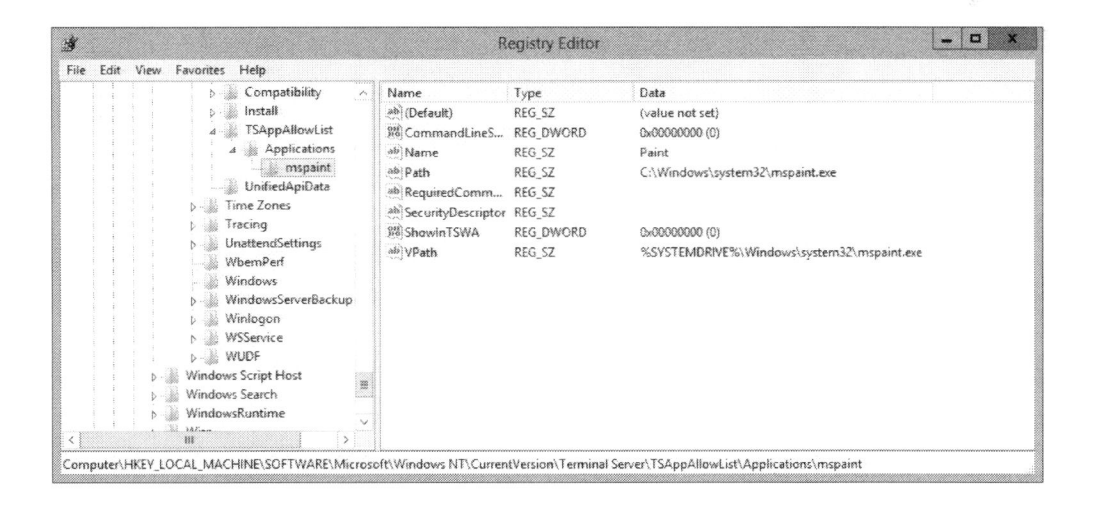

Before moving ahead and further enhancing our deployment, let's quickly explain a common mistake seen when managing RDSHs part of a collection (or farm for that matter). On an endpoint (desktop or even our CRLAB-DC01), if you launch MSTSC.EXE and try to connect to one of the RDSHs, in this example, CRLAB-SH02, you will get with the following error:

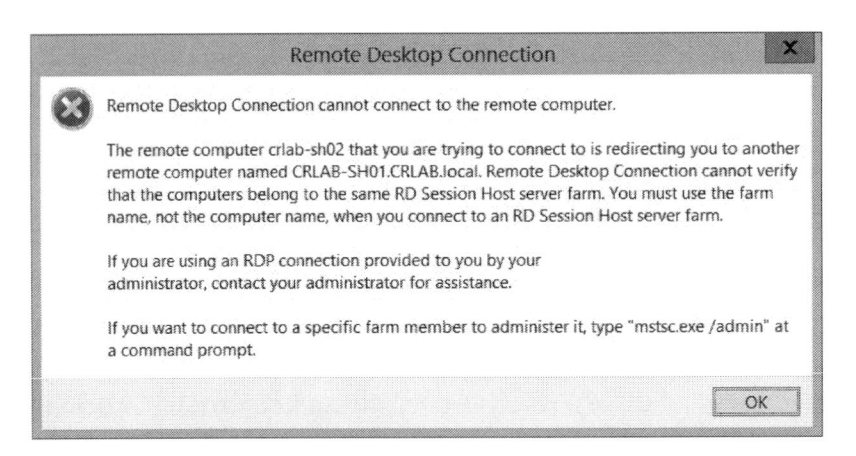

> **Remote Desktop Connection**
>
> Remote Desktop Connection cannot connect to the remote computer.
>
> The remote computer crlab-sh02 that you are trying to connect to is redirecting you to another remote computer named CRLAB-SH01.CRLAB.local. Remote Desktop Connection cannot verify that the computers belong to the same RD Session Host server farm. You must use the farm name, not the computer name, when you connect to an RD Session Host server farm.
>
> If you are using an RDP connection provided to you by your administrator, contact your administrator for assistance.
>
> If you want to connect to a specific farm member to administer it, type "mstsc.exe /admin" at a command prompt.

This happens because CRLAB-SH02 is aware it is part of a collection and therefore, it contacts the RDCB responsible for this deployment, in our case, CRLAB-CB01. The RDCB then redirects you to any server part of the collection. That is why we see a reference to CRLAB-SH01 in the error message. How can you avoid this? Simply use the /ADMIN switch when invoking MSTSC.EXE. This will prevent the connection going through the RDCB.

> ⓘ **Note:** the following conditions are true when using the /admin switch:
> - When remotely administering a server, no RDS CAL is used.
> - Time zone redirection is disabled.
> - The RDS Session Broker redirection is disabled.
> - Plug and Play device redirection is disabled.
> - The remote session theme changes to 'Windows Classic'.
> - RDS Easy Print is disabled.
>
> Another thing to keep in mind is, if using UPD, it does apply to administrators as well, even if using the /ADMIN switch. Be aware of that when managing RDSHs.

We will cover this in more detail in the RDCB HA chapter later on, where we will also show you how end users could manually connect to the RDCB farm by using MSTSC.EXE (not that you want that).

Setting up RDCB HA

On our quest towards a highly available RDS environment with no Single Point of Failure (SPOF), we fixed the RDSH layer by adding a second RDSH (so if one goes down, you still have one server to host user sessions). The next step is to address the RDCB HA. As explained earlier, the RDCB plays a crucial and central role. So let's take a deeper look at the RDCB.

Basic understanding of the RD Connection Broker

In a nutshell, the RDCB server is responsible for three main tasks:

- **Session Load balancing**
    In most production environments, you do have multiple RDSHs available in order to avoid an SPOF. This guarantees an RDSH server is always available to host a user session. With multiple RDSHs now ready for your users, who is responsible for deciding where a user should go? This is one of the purposes of the RDCB. It uses a database that holds information about the user sessions (mainly to which RDSH the user is connected). By using this database, the RDCB determines which server has the least load (the least amount of concurrent connections) and sends a new incoming connection to that particular RDSH. As you remember, when we configured our first session collection, we had the option to set a relative weight for each RDSH.

    Configure load balancing settings

    If you are using more than one RD Session Host server, you can specify how many sessions to create on each RD Session Host server by using the Session Limit column. To prioritize how sessions are created on servers, use the Relative Weight column.

RD Session Host Server	Memory	Relative Weight	Session Limit
CRLAB-SH01.CRLAB.local	2.00 GB	100	999999
CRLAB-SH02.CRLAB.local	2.00 GB	100	999999

    The RDCB uses these to decide where to guide a new incoming session. You should only change the relative weight in case your servers are different resources wise. For example, a server with more CPUs and RAM would get a higher relative weight. Regarding the session limit number, ideally you would load test your RDSH to determine the maximum number of users that can still work with acceptable performance and then set the session limit to that.

ⓘ **Note:** as you realize by now, the RDCB does not account for CPU, memory and several other parameters when deciding which server has the least load. Unfortunately, it uses only the total number of sessions. That is where third party products come to the picture, with much more robust and fine-tuned load balancing mechanisms.

- **Reconnecting disconnected sessions**
  The RDCB database also holds information about disconnected sessions (user sessions that have been closed but not logged off). When retrieving the best RDSH to start a new user session, the RDCB will check if the user has a disconnected session and if that is the case, it will redirect the user to that particular RDSH where he was working when the disconnection happened. This guarantees the user will be able to return to his session in case he accidentally closes it or the network misbehaves and drops the connection.

- **Serve initial connections**
  The final task of the RDCB is to handle the initial connections the endpoints will perform when accessing the farm. This means the endpoints, running the RDP client (Remote Desktop Client is another name), first reach the RDCB and then connect to a different RDSH, as instructed by the RDCB. In case you are familiar with RDS on Windows Server 2008 R2, you probably heard the term 'RD Dedicated Farm Redirection'. This used to be a setting on the RDSH. You would have a separate server (or the RDCB itself) as an RDSH and set to be a dedicated redirector. The endpoints would reach that server and after contacting the RDCB, it would redirect you to the correct server (as instructed by the RDCB). Technically this RD dedicated redirector was an RDSH running in 'drain' mode.

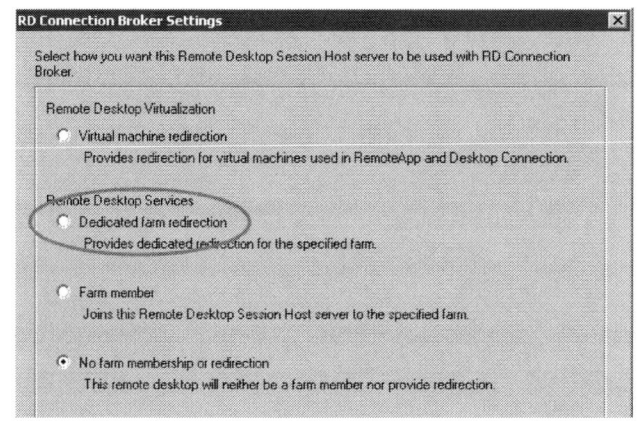

ⓘ Running an RDSH in 'drain' mode simply means that server will not accept any new sessions but will keep existing ones running (in case there are any). Normally we drain a server when we need to perform maintenance tasks on it, until there are no more users on that server. The dedicated redirector was an RDSH always in drain mode.

As you can see, in RDS 2012 R2, the RDCB is the dedicated redirector, even though this term is nowhere to be seen. What happens when we have multiple RDCBs, for HA purposes is another story. Keep reading.

Setting up RDCB High Availability

Now that you know everything about the RDCB and still on our quest for full HA, it is time to get our hands dirty. We will create an additional RDCB and setup HA between the two RDCBs in our deployment. In order to do it, there are a couple pre-requisites we must meet:

1. We need a SQL Server. All RDCBs must have write access to it.
2. All RDCBs need the Microsoft SQL Server Native Client installed.
3. All RDCBs must have static IPs.
4. We need a DNS entry that points to all RDCBs.

Let's get these four requirements done and take a look at why we need them and how they work.

First, why do we need a SQL Server? If you ever used RDS on Windows Server 2008 R2, you probably remember what it took to make the RDCB highly available. You had to install and configure Windows Clustering. Yep. This does not mean it is cleaner with RDS 2012 R2. It is still ugly and you will understand why. But hey, better than dealing with clustering.

On RDS 2012 R2, the clustering requirement is long gone and HA works in an active-active mode, instead of the active-passive one on RDS 2008 R2. One of the reasons it can be active-active is that it uses a central place to store the connection information. This is where SQL Server comes to the picture. The RDCBs in HA read and write information about user sessions to this centralized SQL Server database, what means all RDCBs know what is going on sessions-wise.

As we already have an RDCB up and running, where does it save that information when there is no HA? Locally of course. Right inside the folder %systemdrive%\windows\rdcbDb.

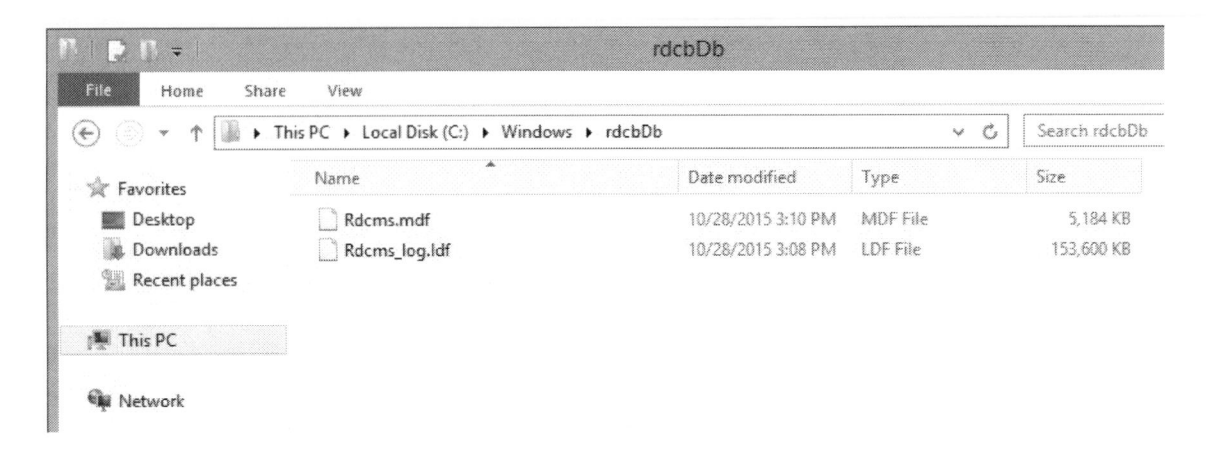

In this case, the data is stored in a Windows Internal Database (WID). For most environments, this is fine but there is indeed a performance penalty on large environments, when using it. In that case, SQL is the way to go. Microsoft even published a whitepaper, "RD Connection Broker Performance and Scalability" that shows the impact of WID on the RDCB performance.

As we are trying to get rid of all SPOFs, SQL is needed. Let's take a quick look on how to get SQL Server up and running. In our case, we installed SQL Server 2012 Enterprise Edition. However, any version from SQL Server 2008 R2 and above is supported. Please note this quick 'SQL Install Guide' does not cover the actual SQL HA or even best practices. Be warned.

Installing SQL Server

For this lab environment, we got SQL Server 2012 with Service Pack 2 and installed it on CRLAB-SQ01 (as expected). The steps you need to follow are:

1. Launch the setup program and under 'Installation', click 'New SQL Server stand-alone installation or add features to an existing installation'.

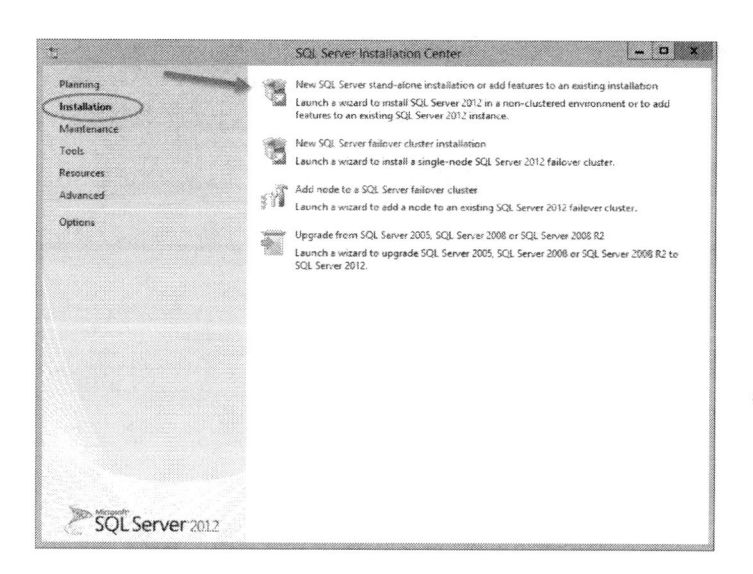

2. The wizard will perform some pre-checks to make sure no potential issues may occur during the install (i.e. proper administrator rights). Click 'Ok'.

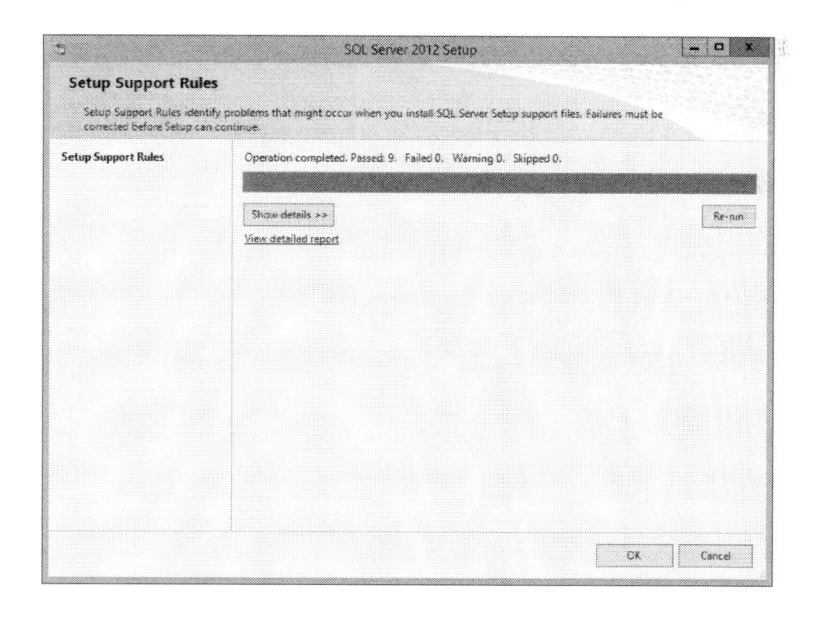

3. Enter or accept the product key (in case one is shown) and click 'Next'.

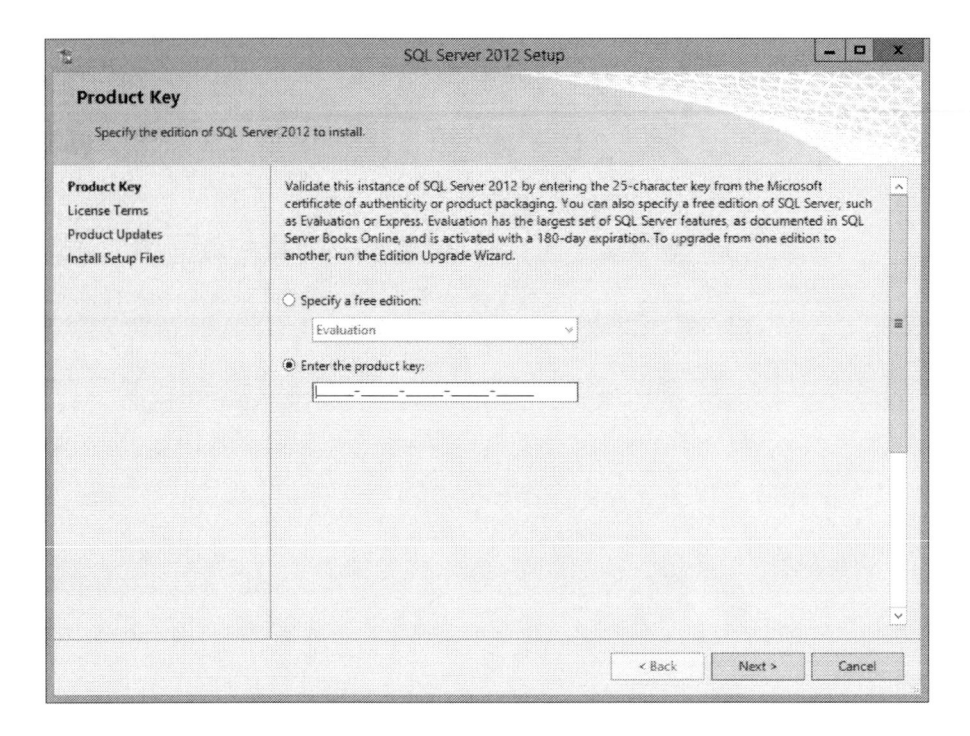

4. Accept the license terms and click 'Next'.

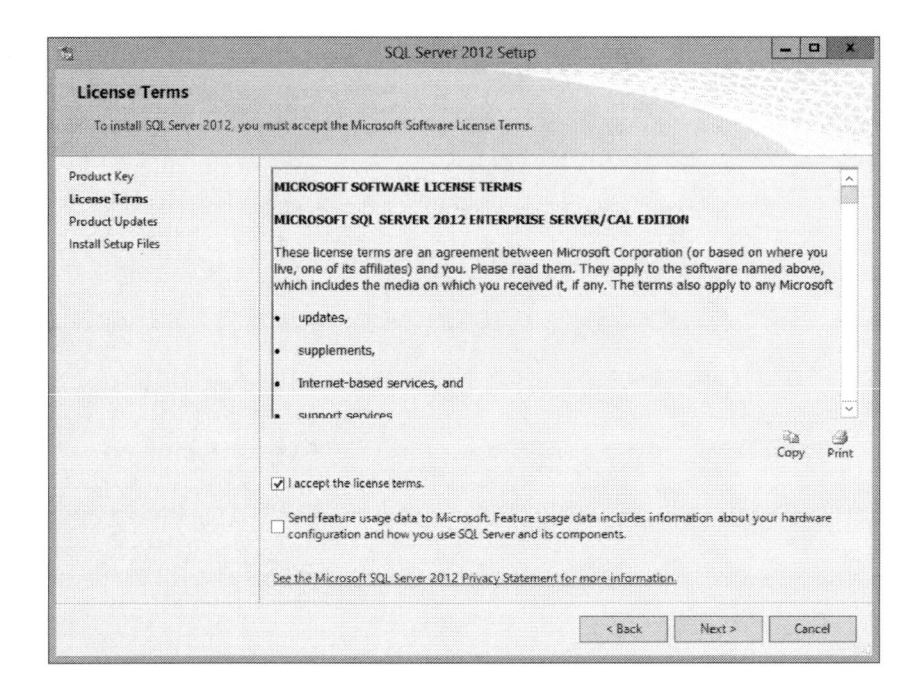

5. The wizard will do some more pre-checks and show whatever it finds. Click 'Next'.

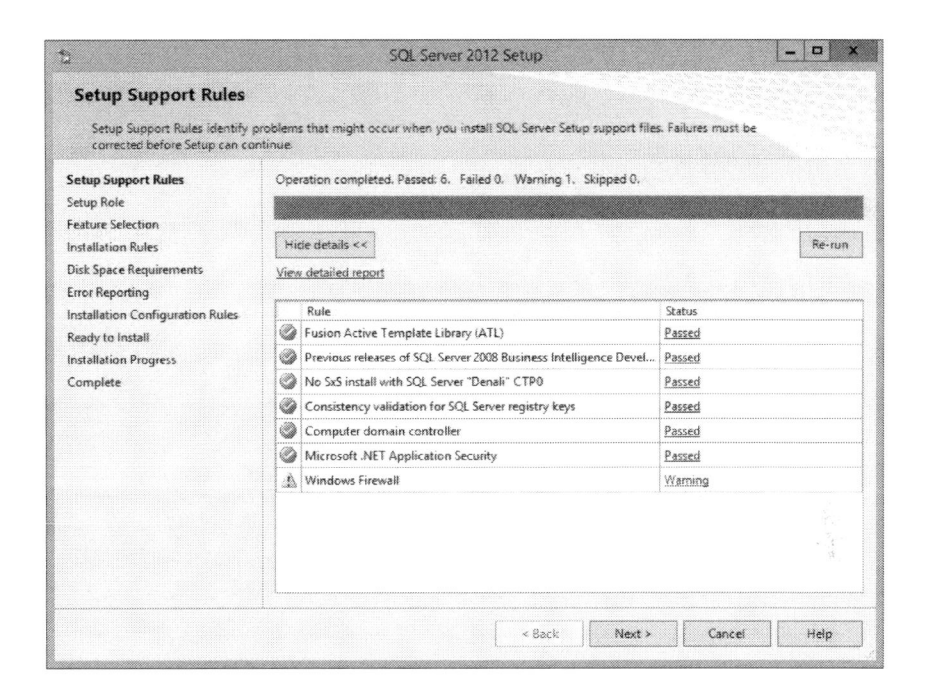

6. Select 'SQL Server Feature Installation' and click 'Next'.

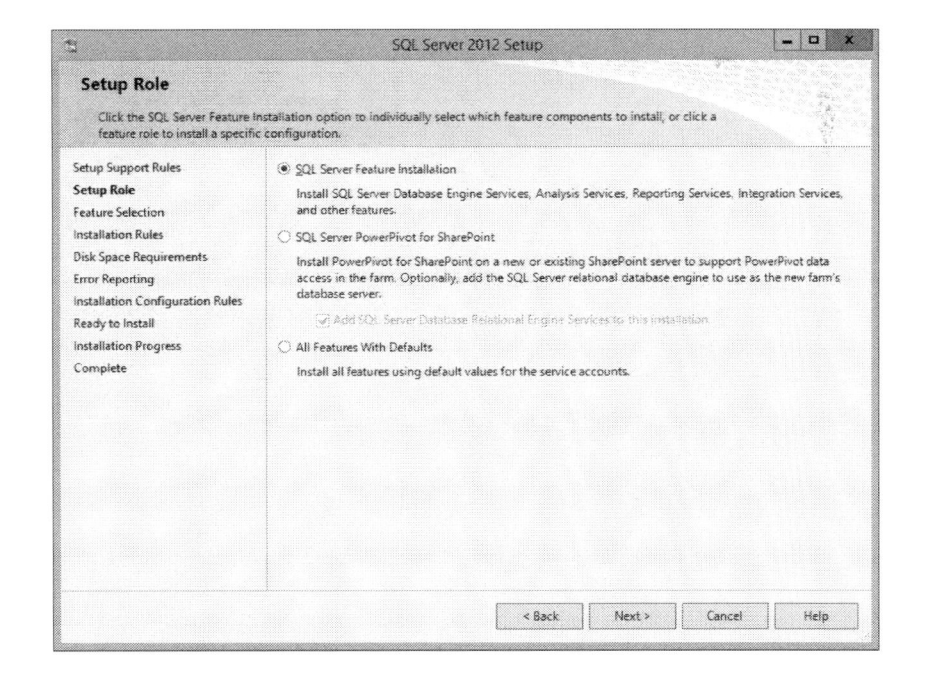

7. Check 'Database Engine Services' and 'Management Tools – Basic' and 'Management Tools – Complete' and click 'Next'.

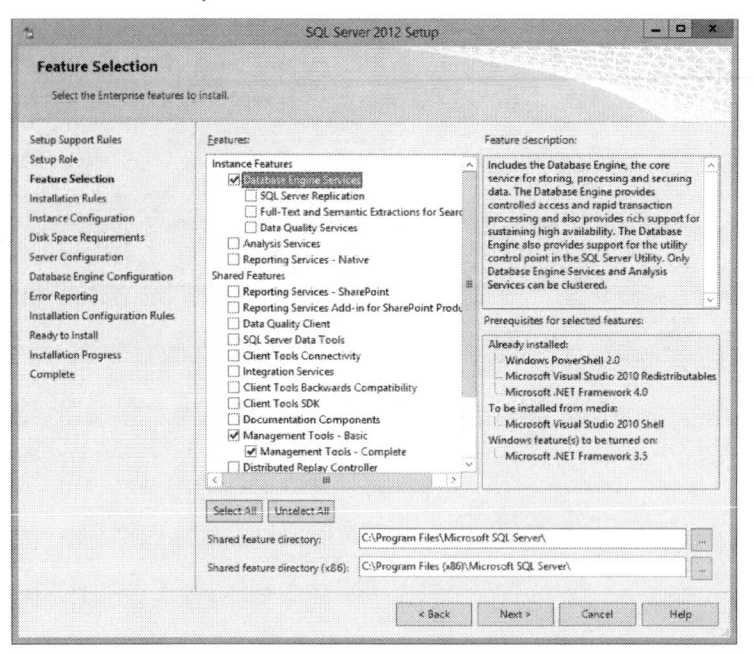

8. Yes, another installation check. Not sure why the installer has to check so many things but hey, I am no SQL MVP. So, click 'Next'.

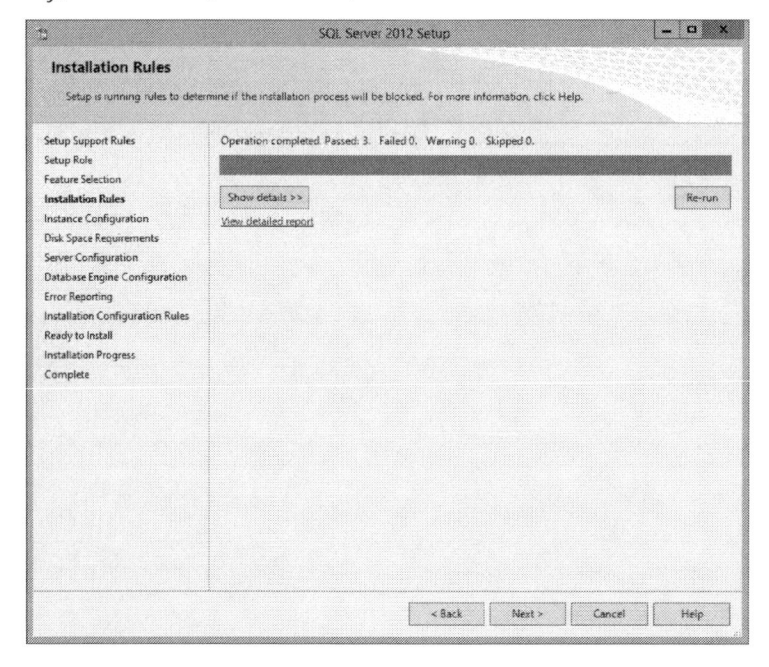

9. As this is a test environment, accept the defaults and click 'Next'.

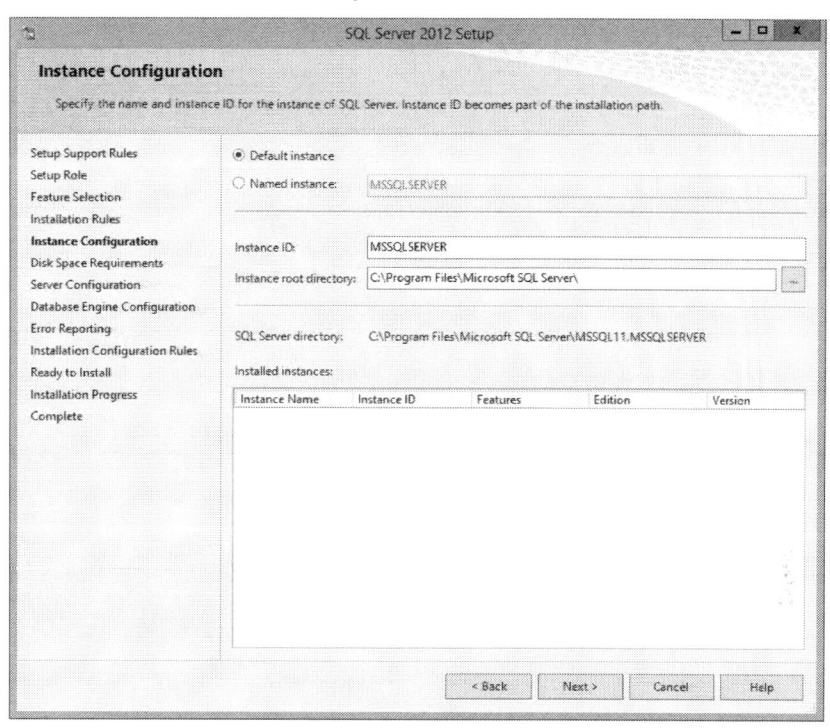

10. Now it is checking for disk space. Not sure why it did not check for that on one of the previous thirty-five checks. Click 'Next'.

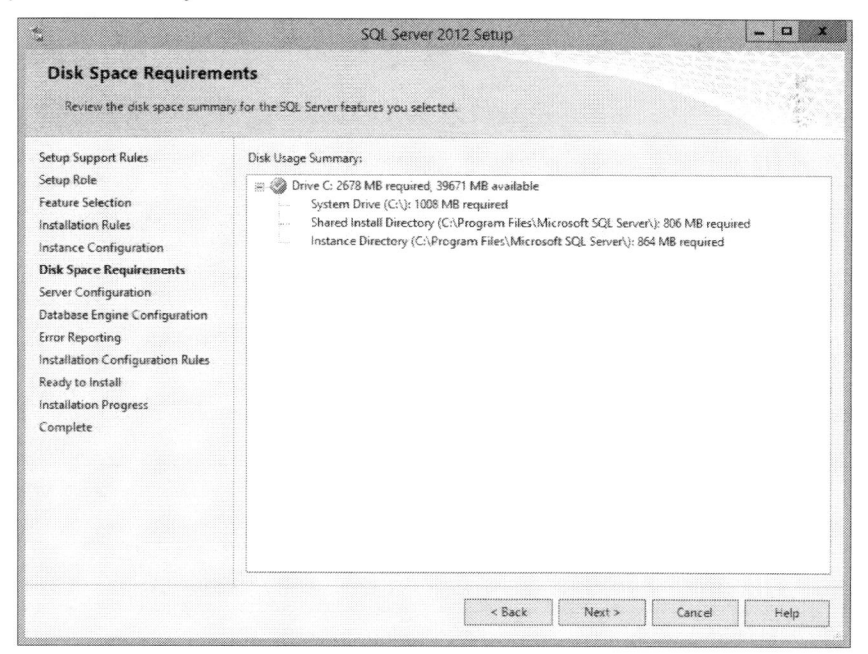

11. Accept the defaults and click 'Next' (just want to make sure you understand this is a lab environment and as such, we may not be following best practices when setting up this SQL Server).

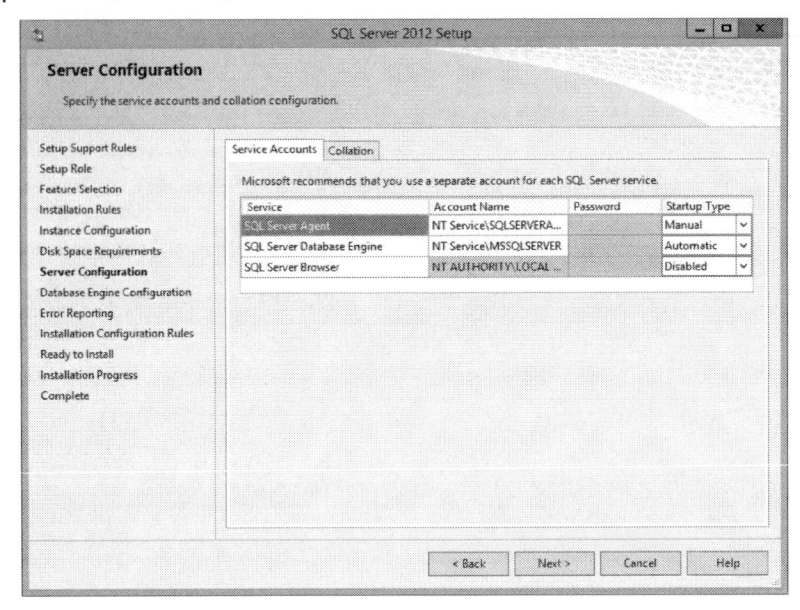

12. Select 'Mixed Mode (SQL Server authentication and Windows authentication' and enter a password for the SA account. Click 'Add Current User' (so it becomes a SQL Server administrator) and click 'Next'.

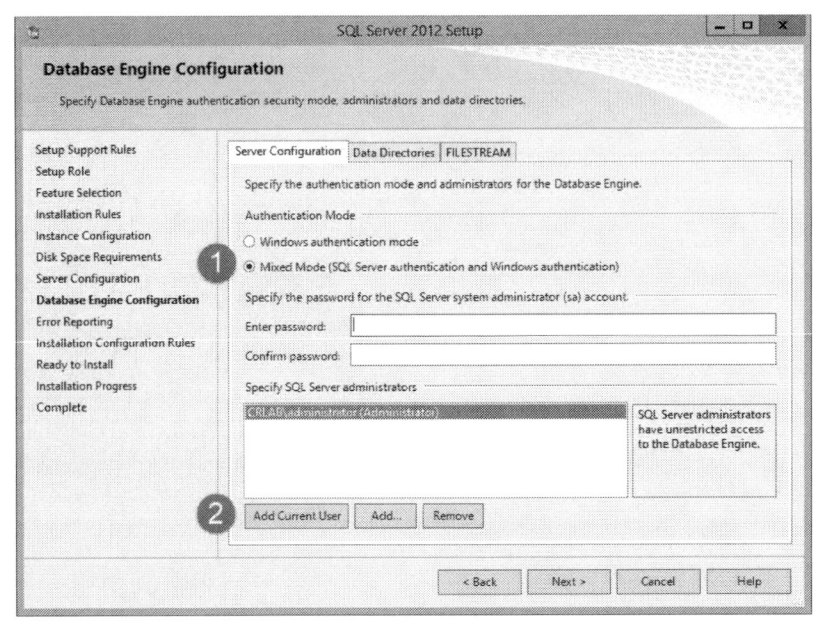

13. Accept the defaults for 'Error Reporting' and click 'Next'.

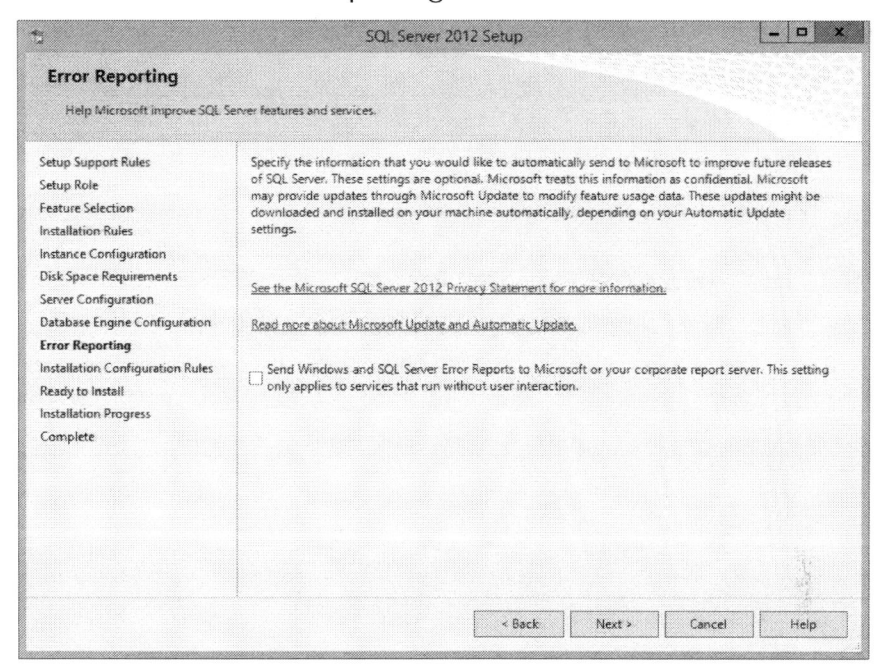

14. Yes, another installation check for whatever reason. Click 'Next'.

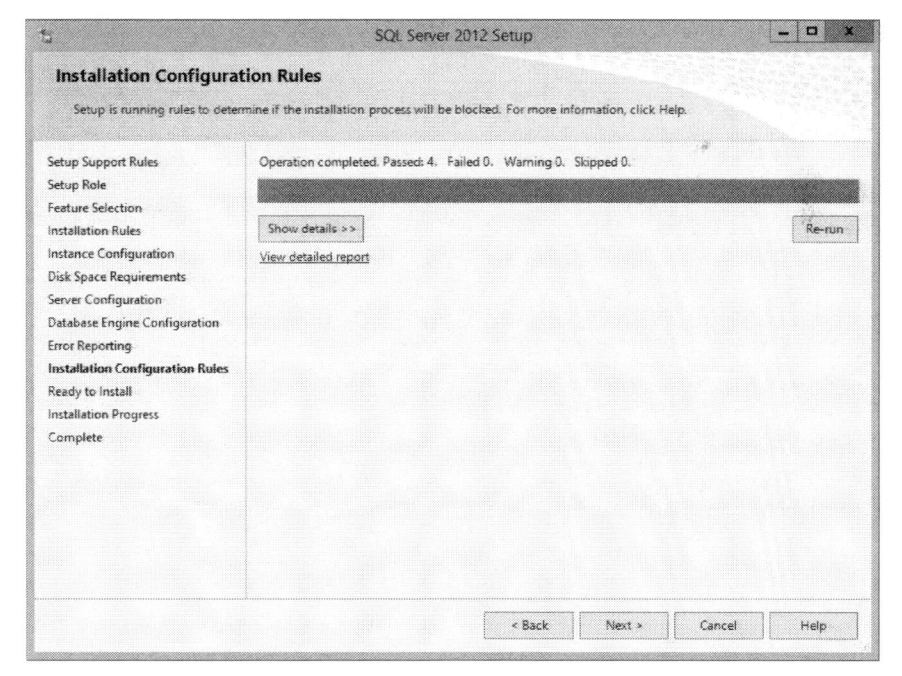

15. Finally the installation will proceed. Click 'Please Lord, Install'. Ok it is just 'Install'. Just click it before the setup program decides to run another check.

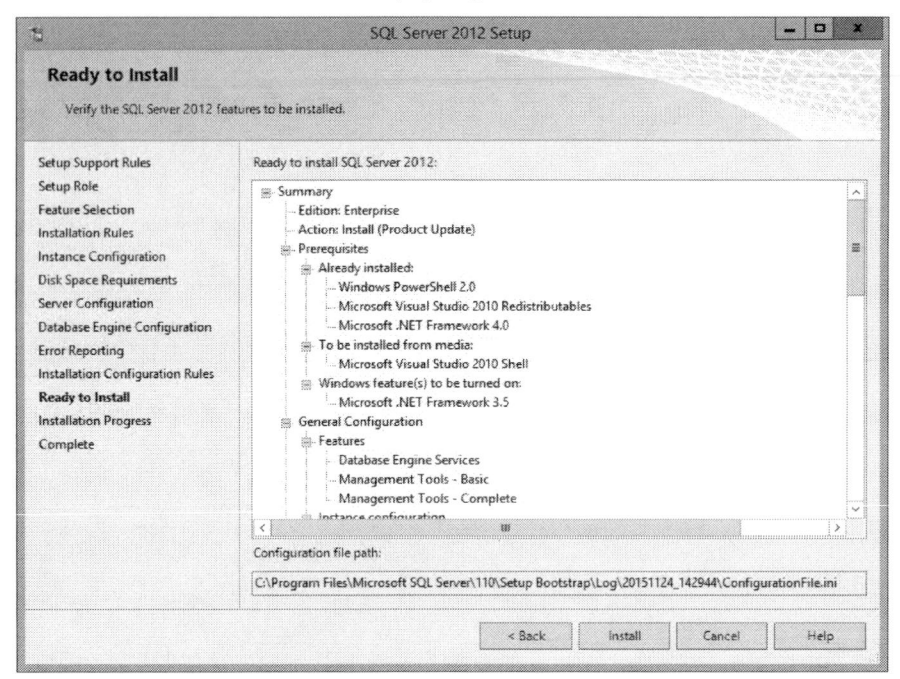

16. The installer will show its progress.

17. All done. Click 'Close'.

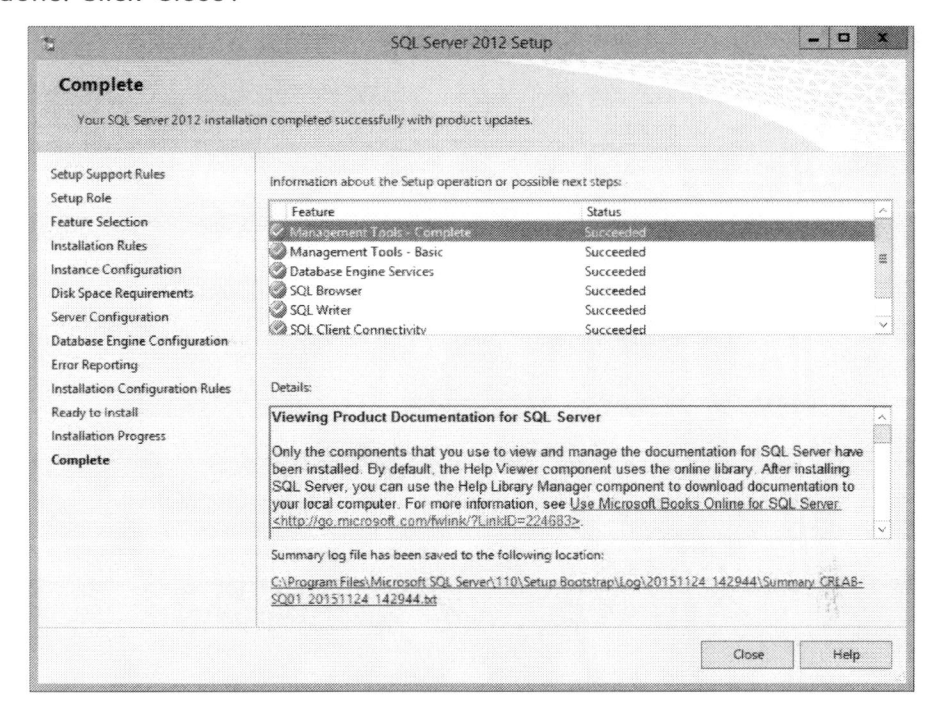

Great. We now have a working SQL Server. The next step is to give appropriate permissions to the RDCBs on the SQL server. On Active Directory, create a new group and name it 'RDCB_Servers'.

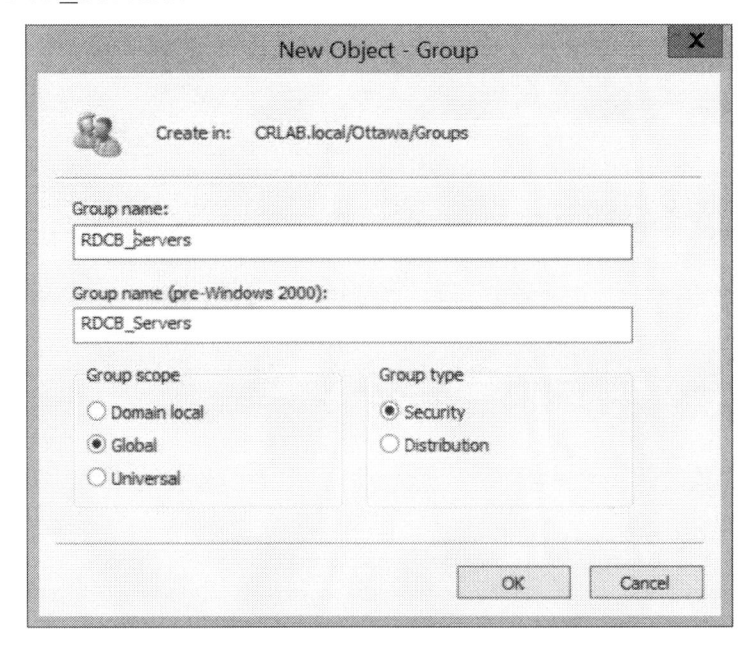

Add both RDCBs to that group.

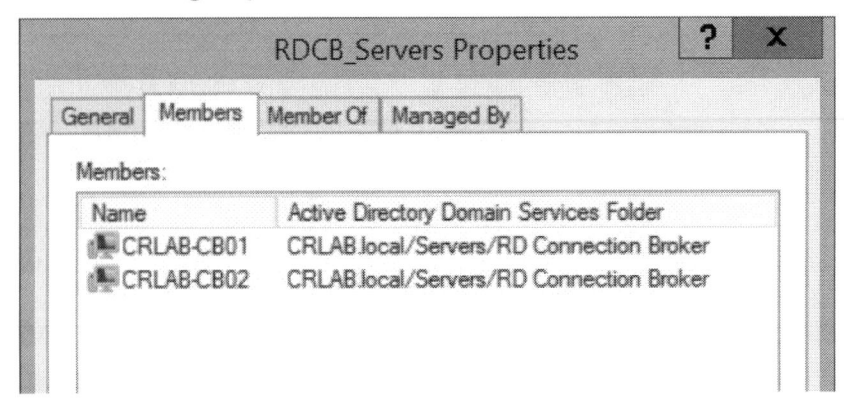

Back to the SQL Server, launch 'SQL Server Management Studio' and logon using the administrator or SA credentials.

Under 'Security' | 'Logins', right-click it and select 'New Login...'.

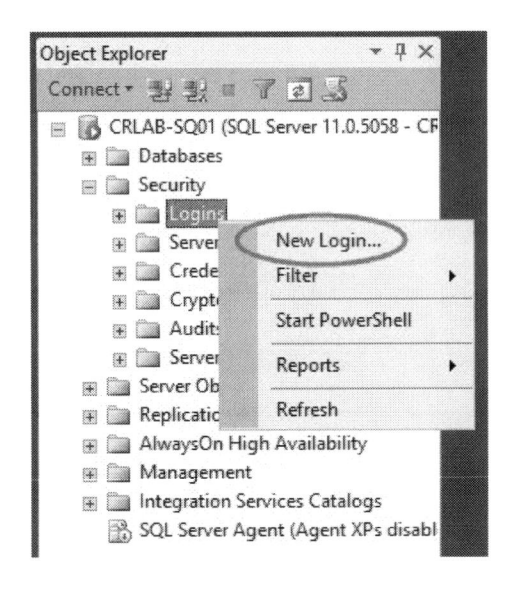

Under 'General', click 'Search' and make sure 'Groups' is checked under 'Object Types' and you select 'Entire Directory' under 'Locations'. Enter the name of the group we just created (RDCB_Servers) and click 'OK'.

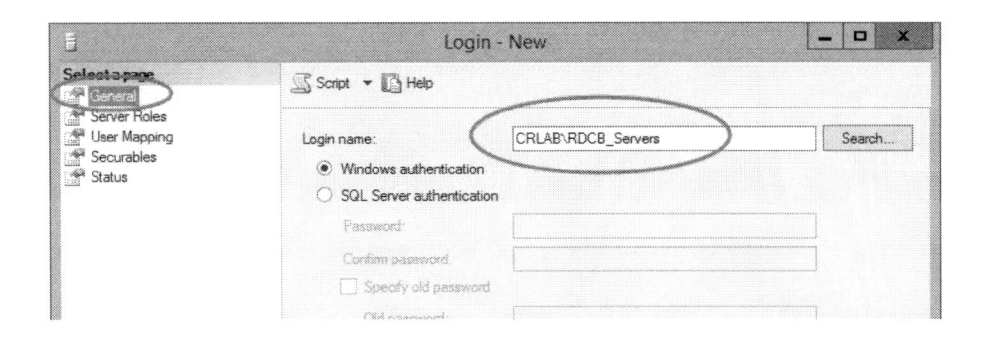

Under 'Server Roles', select 'dbcreator'. This is required as when we configure the RDCB HA, CRLAB-CB01 will be the one creating the actual database. Once this is done, you can certainly remove 'dbcreator' rights from this new login. Click 'OK'.

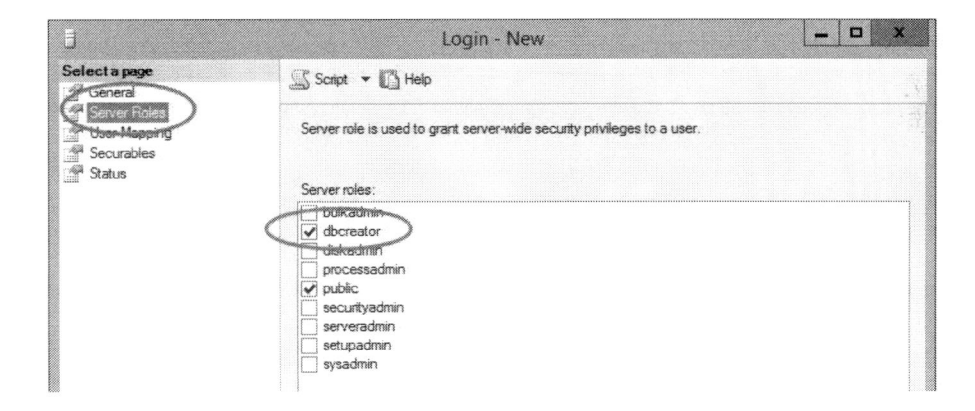

You should see the new login created under 'Logins'.

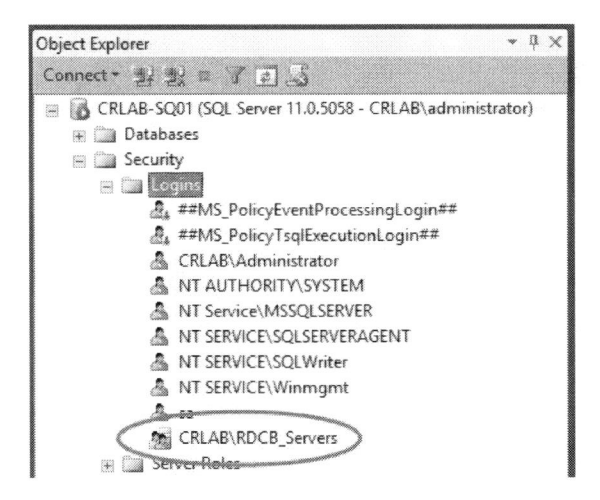

Now we need to get the 'SQL Server Native Client' on all RDCBs, in our case CRLAB-CB01 and CRLAB-CB02. You can download it here: http://www.microsoft.com/en-us/download/details.aspx?id=29065
(make sure the version of the native client matches the SQL version you are using)
You will find it under 'Install Instructions' | 'Microsoft SQL Server Connectivity Feature Pack Components'. Get the x64 one.

1. Go to the folder where you downloaded 'sqlncli.msi' and launch it. Click 'Next'.

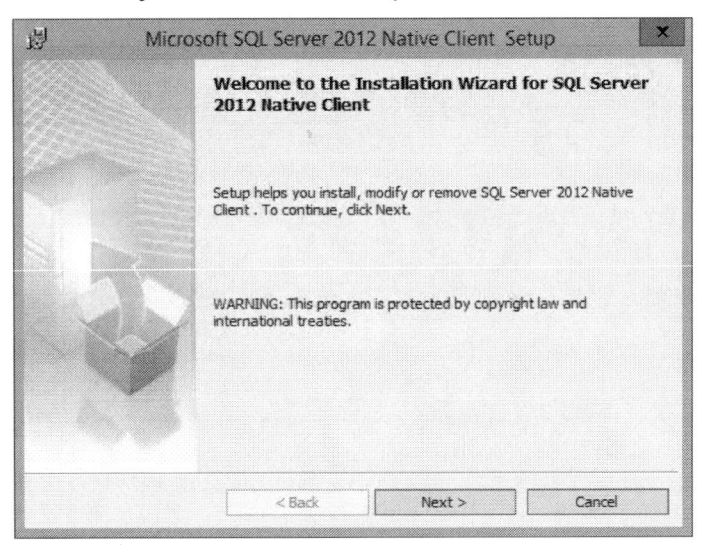

2. Accept the license agreement and click 'Next'.

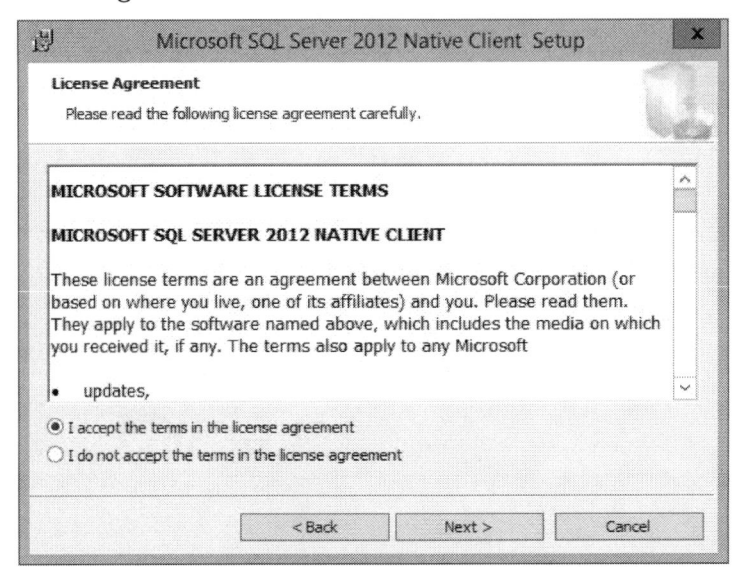

3. Make sure 'Client Components' is selected and click 'Next'.

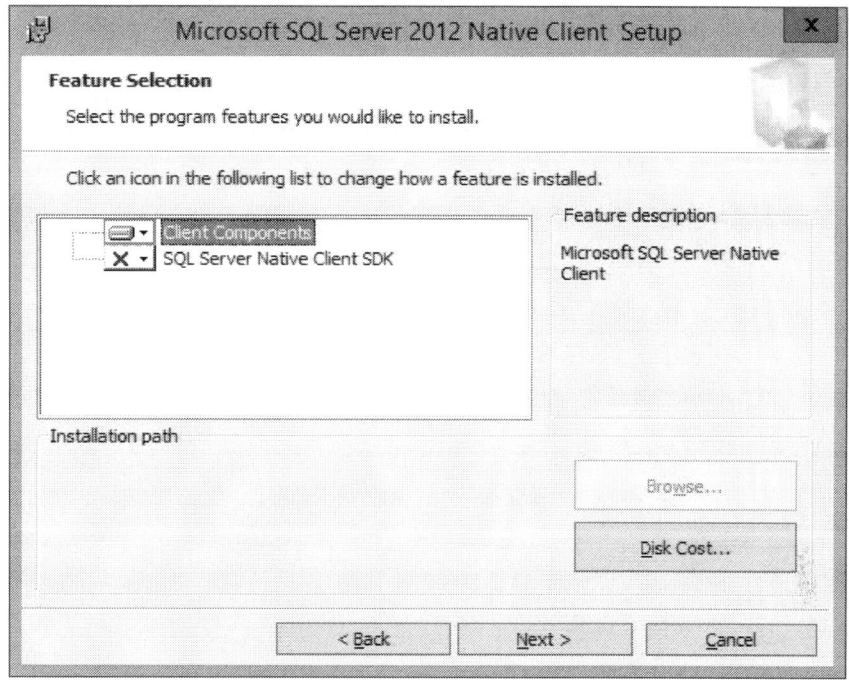

4. Click 'Install'.

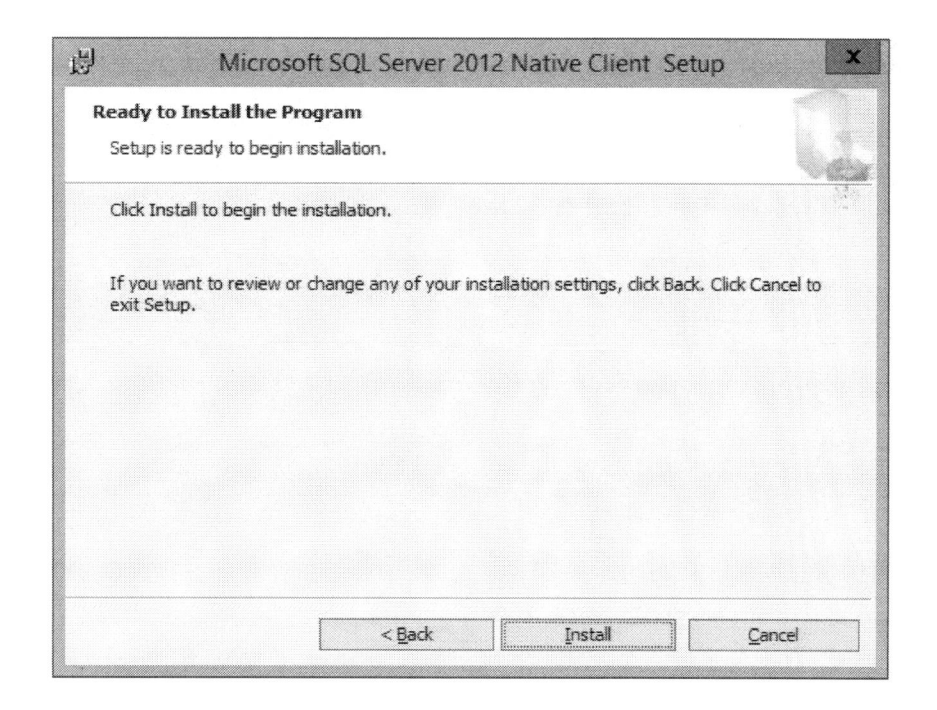

5. Click 'Finish'.

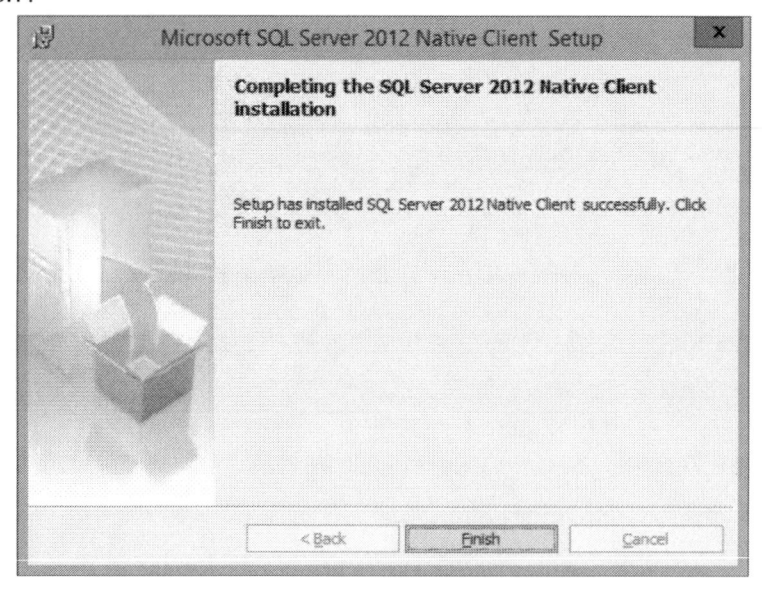

Next on the list is to make sure all RDCBs have static IP addresses. That is the case in our lab environment. Make sure that is your case.

Finally, we need a DNS record for the RDCB farm, pointing to all RDCBs (in our case, only two servers – you can indeed have HA with more than two RDCBs). You will need to use the DNS management console to do that. In our lab, we launched it on CRLAB-DC01.

Under 'Forward Lookup Zones' locate your domain name (in our case, CRLAB.local). Right-click it and select 'New Host (A or AAAA)...'.

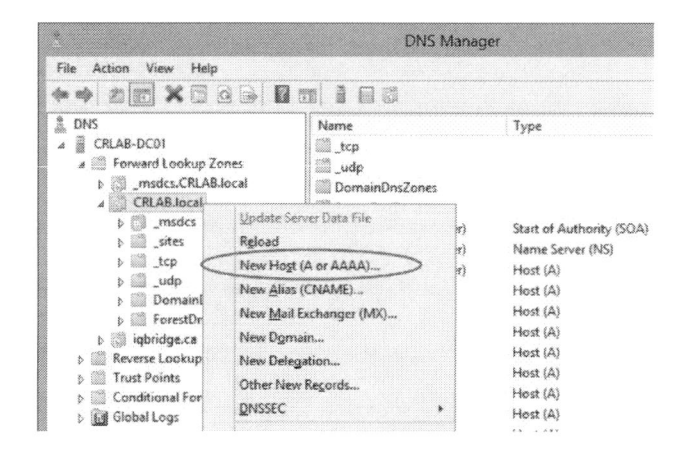

Create a record for each RDCB but with the name 'rdsfarm'. The IP address will be the one for each RDCB.

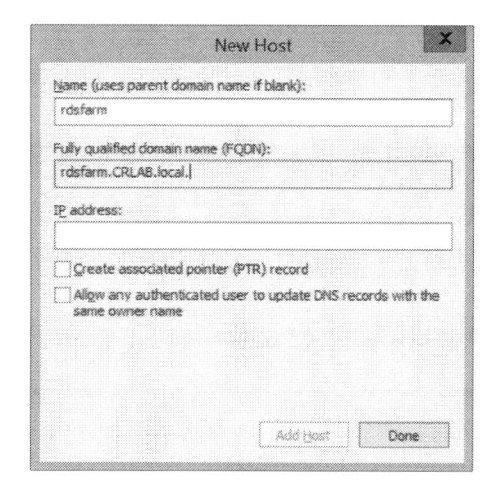

This is what you should have when done (your IPs will probably be different):

| rdsfarm | Host (A) | 192.168.123.35 |
| rdsfarm | Host (A) | 192.168.123.36 |

As you can see, we just used DNS Round Robin (DNS RR) to send requests to the farm to both RDCBs. In production, ideally, you would use a proper load balancer (i.e. Kemp LoadMasters, Citrix NetScalers, etc). Sure, you can even use Microsoft NLB but it is not the same. ☺

We are now ready to start setting up HA between the RDCBs. Setting up HA for the RDCBs involves two separate steps. First, we enable HA on the current RDCB, in our case, CRLAB-CB01. This will "move" the RDCB database (remember, a local WID) to the SQL Server. This step only prepares the RDCB to become highly available, as it is still using a single RDCB (itself).

Then, on the second and final step, we add extra RDCBs to the environment. Only after adding new RDCBs to the HA setup that our deployment will start using all RDCBs in an active-active highly available setup.

Time to do it.

1. Launch 'Server Manager' (in our case on CRLAB-DC01) and select '3. Add other servers to manage'.

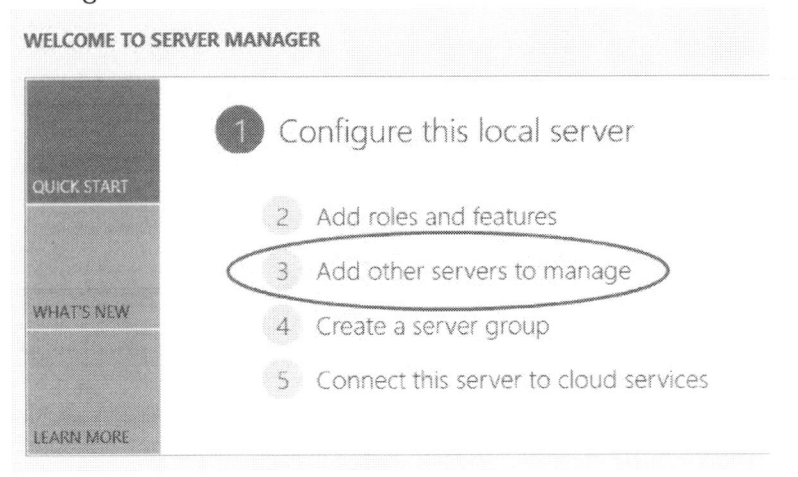

2. Type crlab-cb under 'Name(CN)' and click 'Find Now'. This will return all servers with names starting with CRLAB-CB. Select 'CRLAB-CB02' and click the arrow button to add it to the right pane. Click 'Ok'.

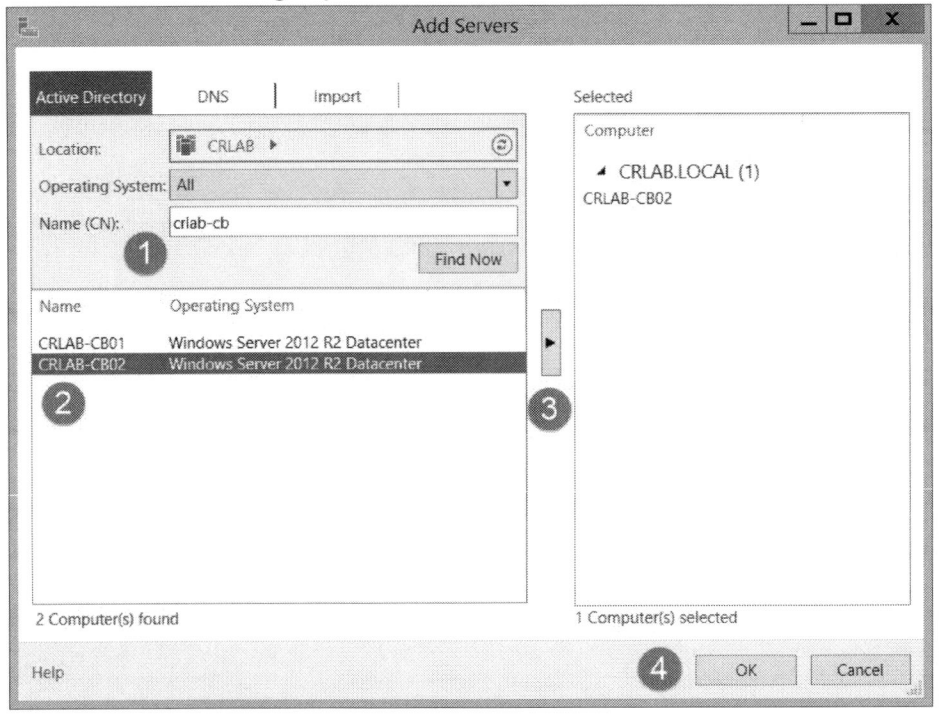

3. Now click on 'Remote Desktop Services' on the left. This will open the 'Overview' page we discussed earlier. Under 'Deployment Overview' right-click the 'RD Connection Broker' icon and select 'Configure High Availability'.

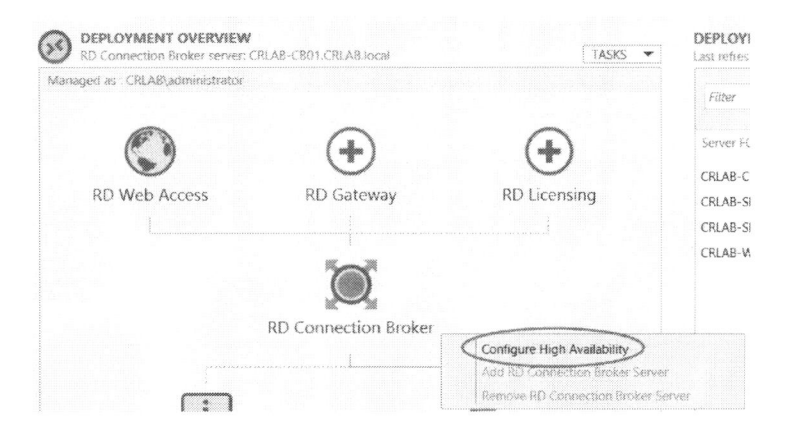

ⓘ Note: as you can see, the 'Add RD Connection Broker Server' option is unavailable. The reason for that is, as explained earlier, we first need to prepare the current RDCB for High Availability. Once that is done we can then add as many RDCBs as we want.

4. The HA wizard will launch, showing the four pre-requisites we discussed (and addressed) earlier. Click 'Next'.

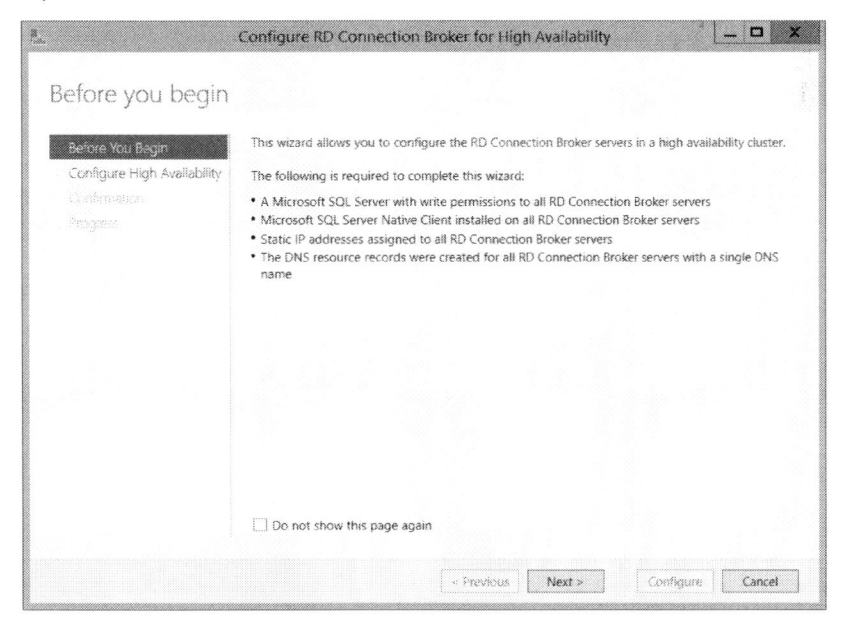

5. We now need to enter the specific connection string expected by the wizard (has to be exactly as expected otherwise it will fail), the folder name where the database will be stored (locally on the SQL Server) and the DNS Round Robin name we want to use (the one we created on the DNS server).

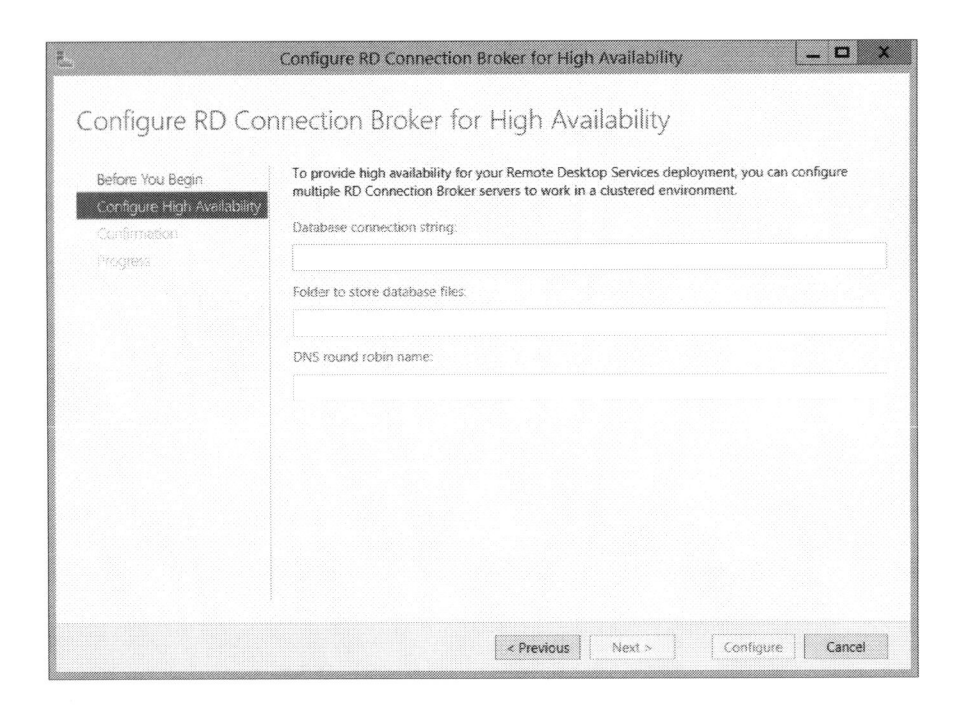

6. In our lab environment we used the following:
   a. **Database connection string:**
      DRIVER=SQL Server Native Client 11.0;SERVER=CRLAB-SQ01;Trusted_Connection=Yes;APP=Remote Desktop Services Connection Broker;DATABASE=RDCB
   b. **Folder to store database files:**
      C:\RDCB (in a production environment, your SQL administrator would probably tell you where that should go). Make sure this folder is created before launching the HA wizard.
   c. **DNS round robin name:**
      This is the name we entered when creating the two DNS records, rdsfarm.crlab.local.

      Enter all that and click 'Next' (make sure you use the correct version number, according to the 'SQL Server Native Client' you have on the

RDCBs. For example, SQL Server 2008 R2 uses version 10.0, while SQL Server 2012 and 2014 use 11.0).

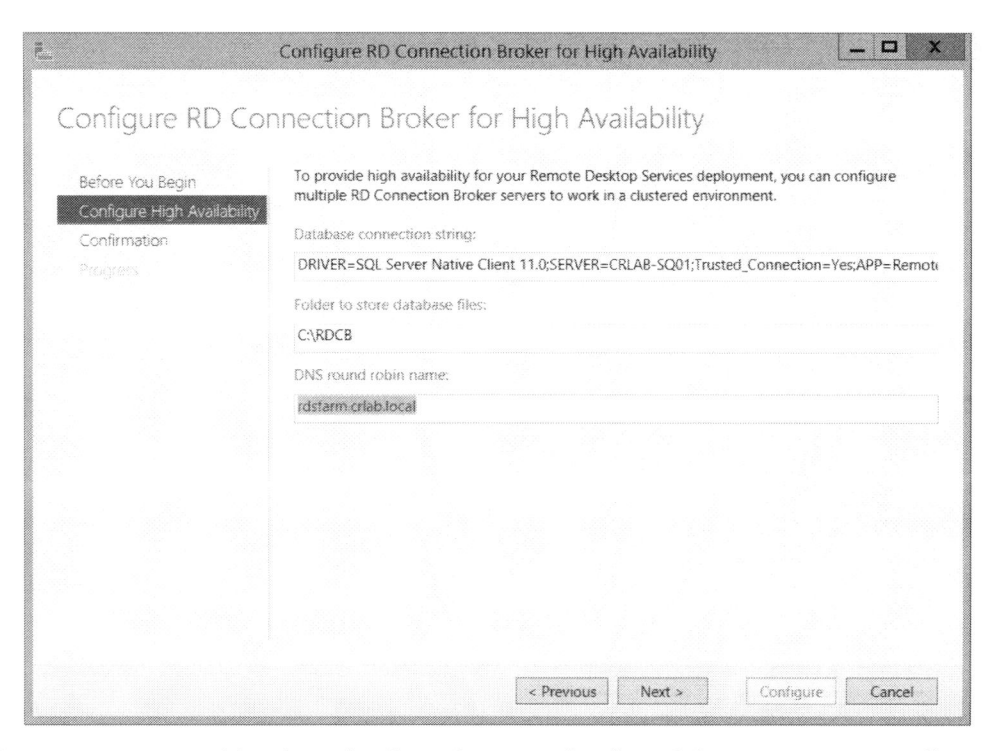

If you get an error like this, the first thing to check is if the SQL Server is allowing incoming connections (i.e. right port allowed on the Windows Firewall) and that you did add the AD group we created as a new login with proper rights on the SQL Server. In addition, if you installed the SQL Server using this guide, make sure you rebooted it.

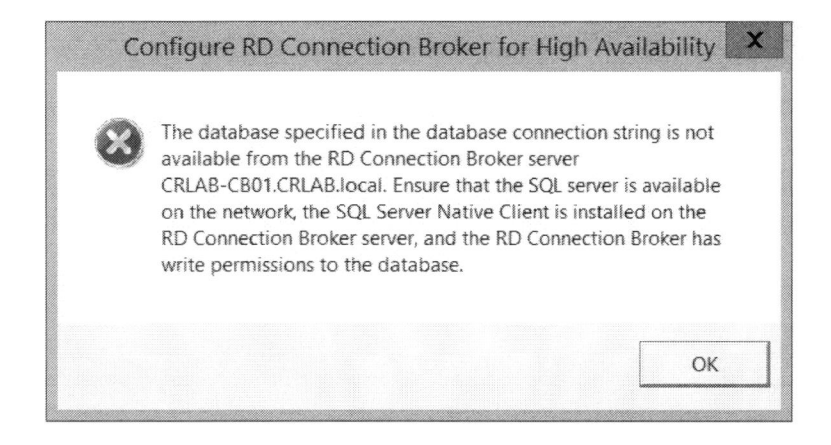

7. The wizard will show you a summary. Click 'Configure'.

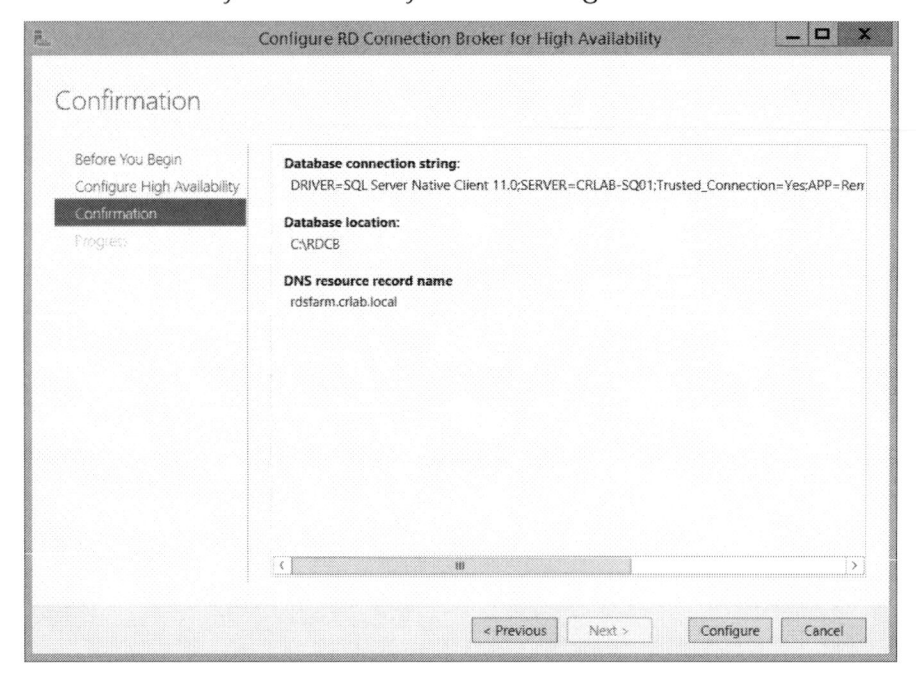

8. If you get this error, make sure the folder specified already exists on the SQL Server and the AD group we created for the RDCBs has full rights on it.

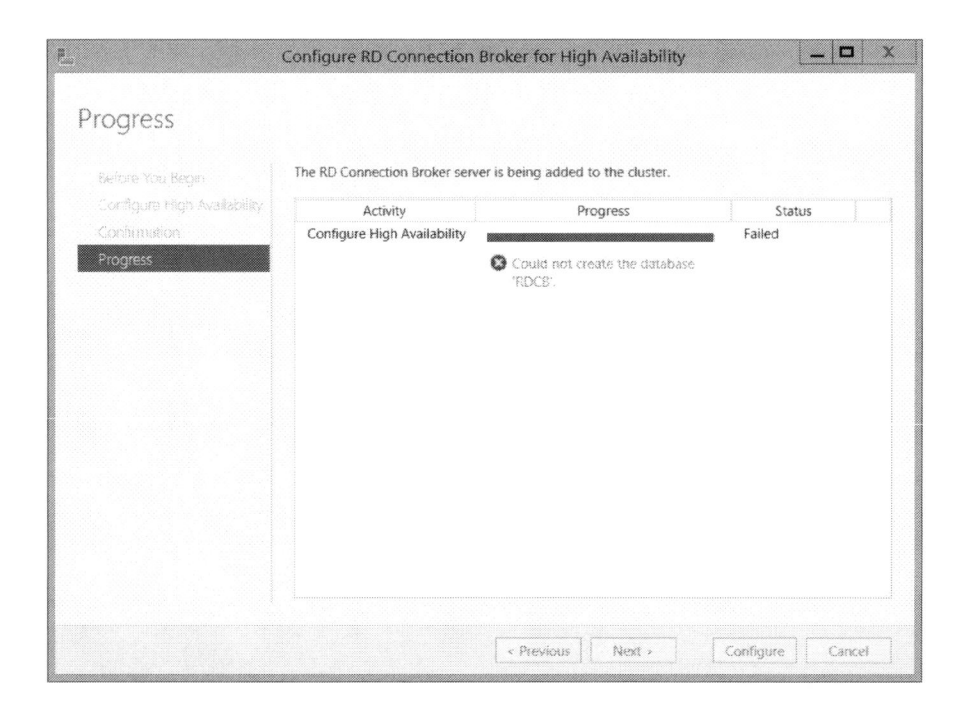

9. If everything works as expected you will see 'Succeeded' under 'Status'. Click 'Close'.

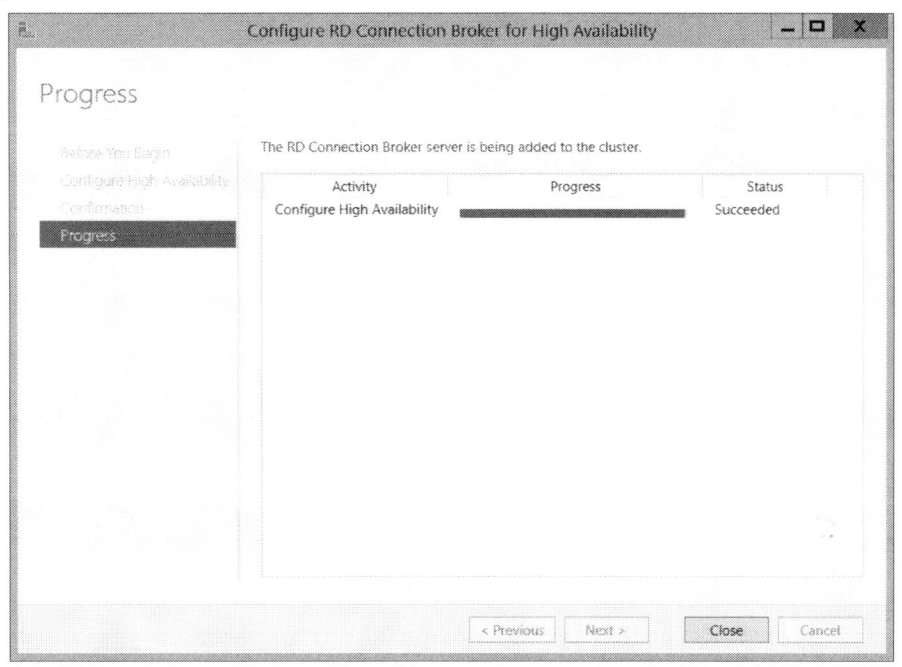

10. As the wizard finishes, we are now back to the server manage console and if you noticed, under 'Overview' we can now see '(High Availability Mode)' under the RD Connection Broker icon.

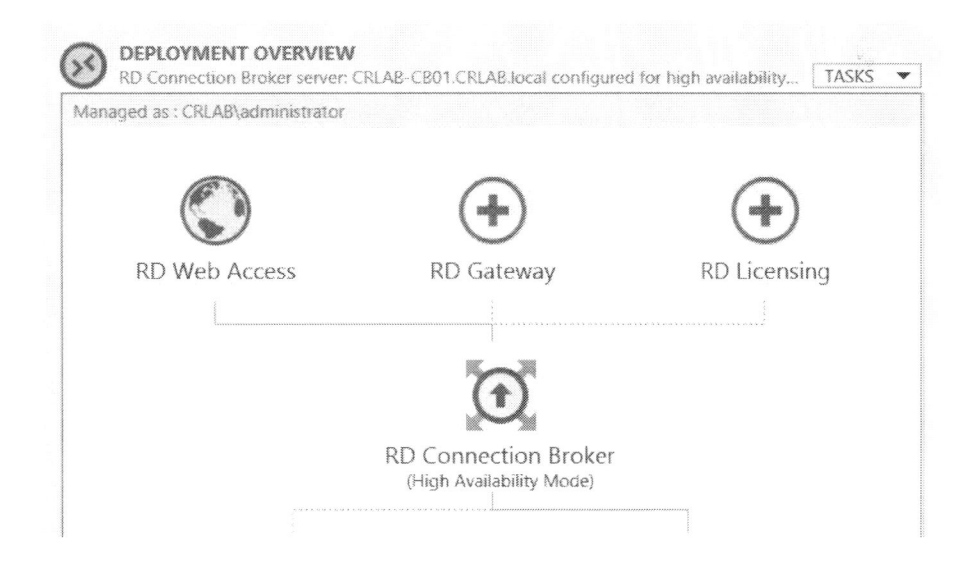

So what just happened? The wizard created a new database on the SQL Server we specified and then moved the configuration from the local database on the RDCB to the centralized one. You can easily confirm this by launching the 'Microsoft SQL Server Management Studio' on the SQL Server and checking it under 'Databases'.

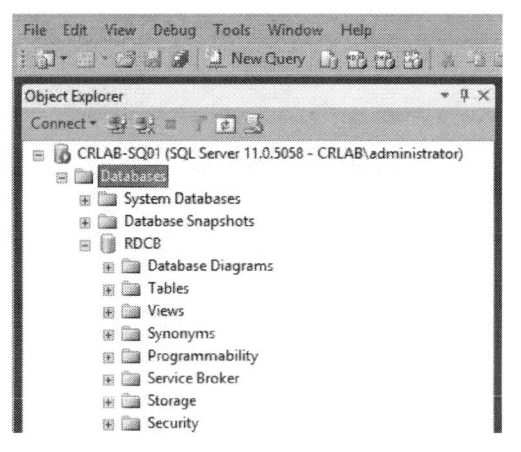

11. The final step is to give the RDCBs proper permissions to read and write to the database. On the 'Microsoft SQL Server Management Studio', under 'Logins', double-click the group we added previously. Under 'User Mapping' select the RDCB database and check 'db_owner' under 'Database role membership for: RDCB'. Click 'OK'.

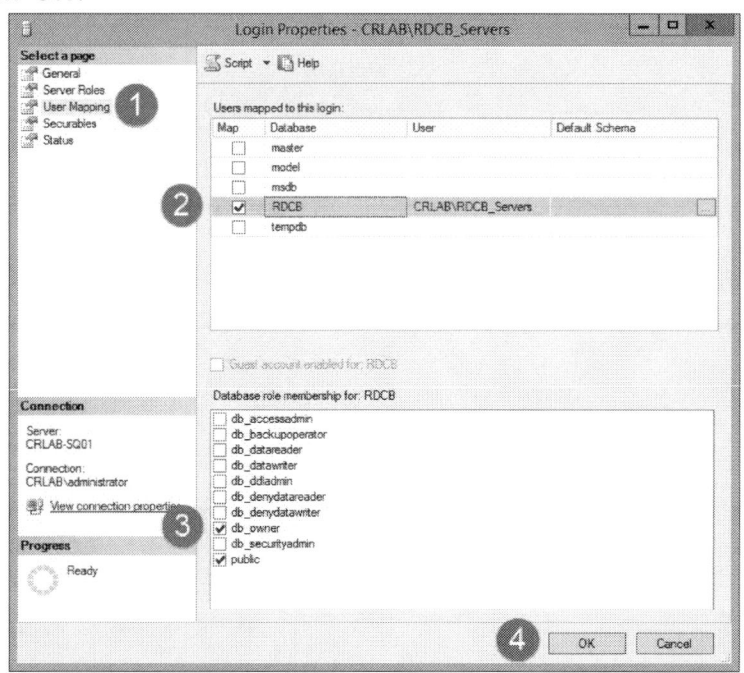

That is it for the first step. As you remember, step one was preparing the existing RDCB for HA. To wrap this up we now must add CRLAB-CB02 to the HA setup. Compared to the first step, this is a walk in the park.

1. Back to the server manager console on CRLAB-DC01, click on 'Remote Desktop Services' on the left. This will open the 'Overview' page we discussed earlier. Under 'Deployment Overview', right-click the 'RD Connection Broker' icon and select 'Add RD Connection Broker Server' which has now become available.

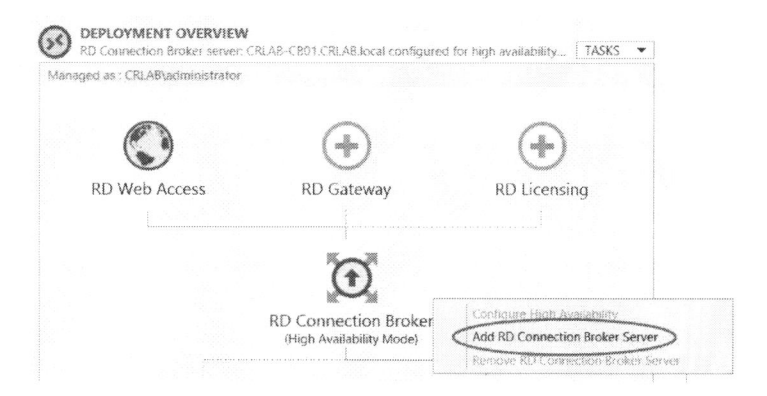

2. The wizard will launch one more time, showing the exact same pre-requisites as we saw earlier. Click 'Next'.

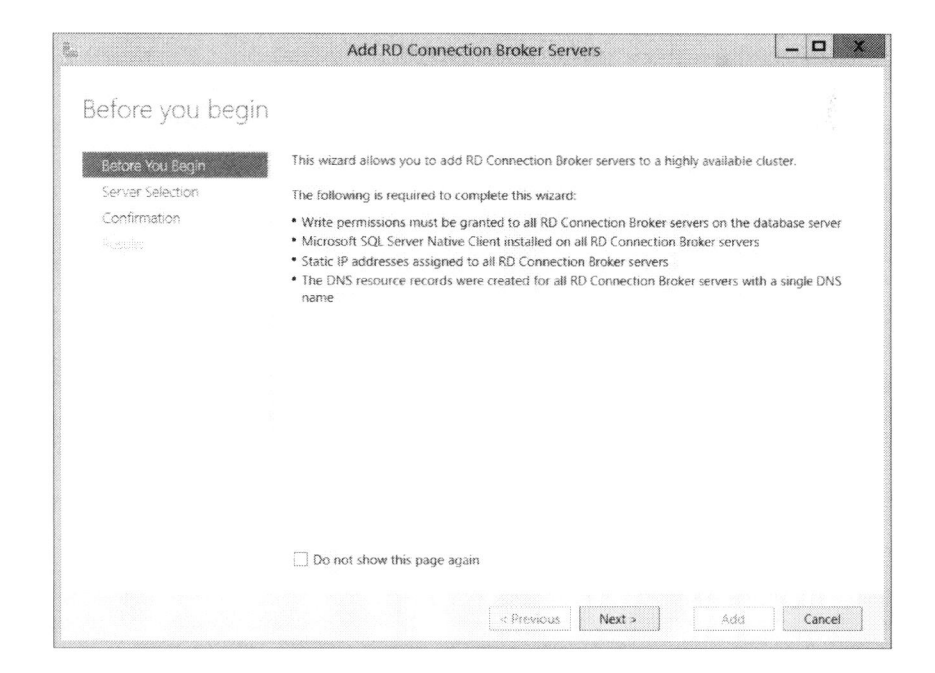

3. Select CRLAB-CB02 and click the arrow button. Click 'Next'. The wizard will take care of adding the RDCB role to the server for us.

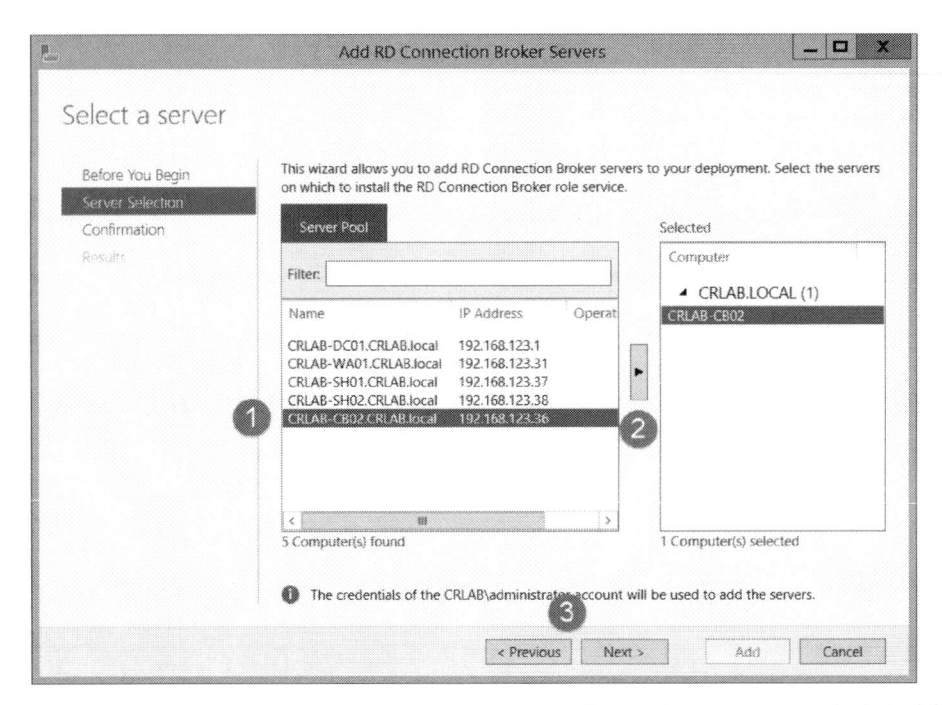

4. You can see what the wizard will do on the 'Confirmation' screen. Click 'Add'.

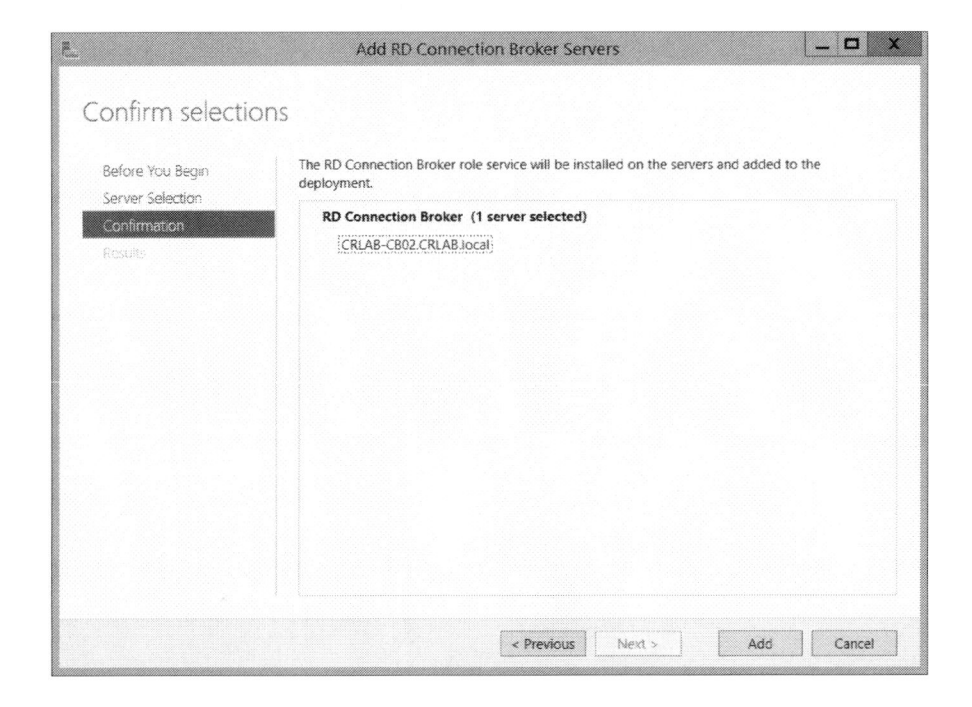

5. If everything worked as expected, you will receive a 'Succeeded' message under 'Status'. Click 'Close'.

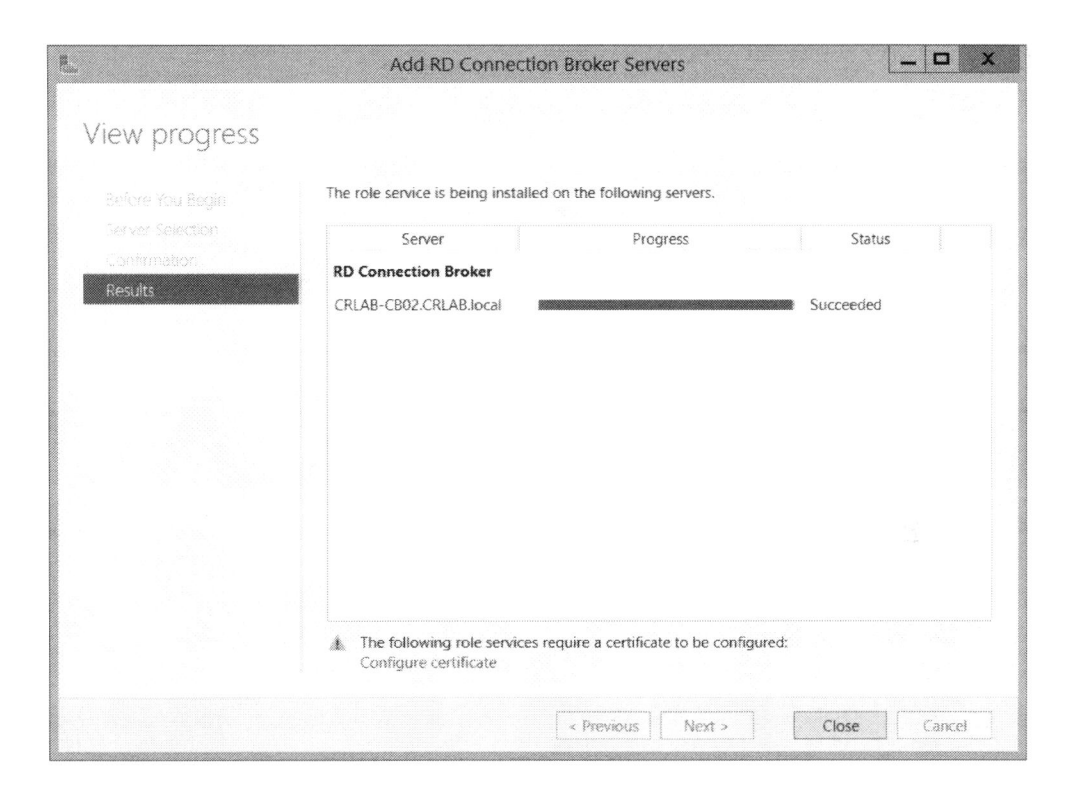

ⓘ **Note:** If you noticed, there is a little warning about certificates in the 'Progress' window. For now, do not worry about it too much. We have a whole section on certificates coming up soon. In addition, to prepare you for it, keep in mind certificates are one of the most annoying parts of RDS 2012 R2 and from what we can see, nothing will change for 2016 (even though setting up certificates is indeed easier with RDS 2012 R2 than in previous releases).

Now if you look at your deployment you should see something similar to ours, with five servers in total (two RDCBs in HA, two RDSHs and one RDWA). We are almost there on our goal towards a fully highly available environment.

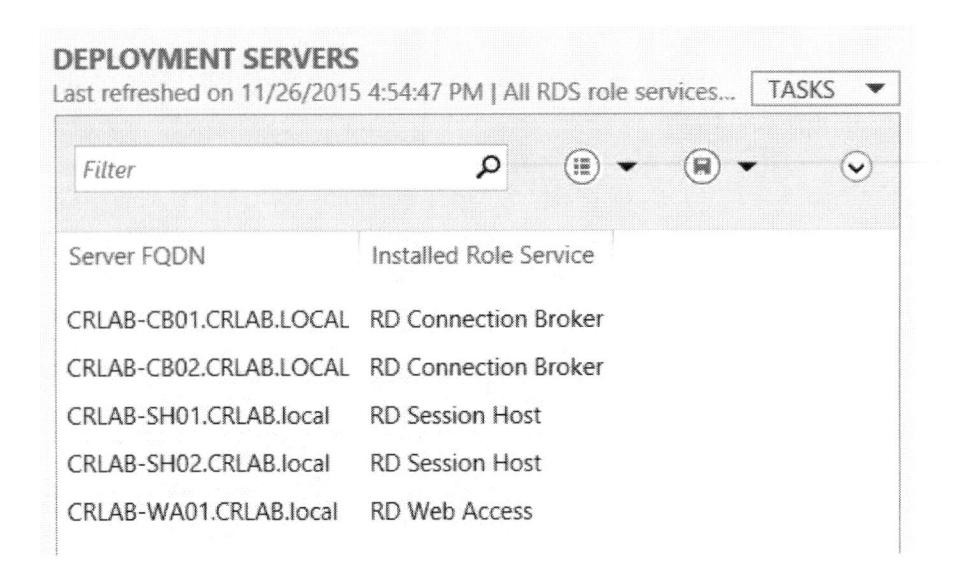

Server FQDN	Installed Role Service
CRLAB-CB01.CRLAB.LOCAL	RD Connection Broker
CRLAB-CB02.CRLAB.LOCAL	RD Connection Broker
CRLAB-SH01.CRLAB.local	RD Session Host
CRLAB-SH02.CRLAB.local	RD Session Host
CRLAB-WA01.CRLAB.local	RD Web Access

So what happened exactly once we enabled HA? With multiple RDCBs, all of these servers can handle the initial connection, redirect sessions to RDSHs (to keep the load spread) and reconnect sessions that were disconnected. The RDCBs exchange information about sessions using the SQL Server database. So how does an endpoint know to which RDCB it should connect? For published RemoteApps and desktops on the RDWA that we added to the deployment, this is configured automatically. When we start the RDCB HA wizard, it reconfigures the RemoteApps/Desktops to connect to the FQDN of the farm (in our case rdsfarm.crlab.local) instead of crlab-cb01.crlab.local (the first RDCB we had). As it changes what the RDWA delivers, this means it reconfigures the RSS feed used to integrate RemoteApps to the local start menu/start screen.

> ⓘ Digging a little deeper technically, on RDS 2012 R2 the RDCB also handles the initial connections. However, technically it is not an 'RD Dedicated farm redirector' like what we had on RDS 2008 R2. So if you create an RDP connection (.rdp file) to the RDCB on RDS 2012 R2, how does it know you want to connect to a certain collection and not to the RDCB itself? If you run mstsc.exe and point it to the RDCB and try to logon as a regular user, it will fail, as regular users do not have Remote Desktop permissions to logon remotely on the RDCB itself. The key here lies in the properties the RDP client holds, sent to the RDCB. If you open the .rdp file that is created on the client (when using the RSS feed) using Notepad you will notice the following:

full address:s:RDSFARM.CRLAB.LOCALworkspace id:s:RDSFARM.CRLAB.LOCAL

use redirection server name:i:1

loadbalanceinfo:s:tsv://MS Terminal Services Plugin.1.SD_Basic_Collect

alternate full address:s:RDSFARM.CRLAB.LOCAL

That is how the client is able to get to the RDCB for the initial connection.

We will cover all about connecting to the environment (not only to use apps but also to manage it) in a separate chapter. Time to deal with the certificates.

Adding Certificates

Now that we have a robust standard deployment, it is time to start adding certificates to the environment. Before we move ahead let us clarify a couple things. If you have been to any of Cláudio's presentations at BriForum (http://www.briforum.com) or E2EVC (http://www.e2evc.com) – by the way, great technical conferences – you probably know by now how much he hates certificates on RDS. As per Cláudio's comments, *"The main issue is simple: you need certificates and I am ok with that. The problem is Microsoft overused them, requiring a certificate on every single moving part you can think of, despite the fact companies in this space took a different approach and really only used them where needed. So resuming, it was a stupid decision by Microsoft if you ask me and the result is far from elegant, what I really do not appreciate"*.
With Cláudio's rant out-of-the-way, let's see how to get it up and running with the damn certificates.

As expected, certificates are key for having a working RDS environment. Most roles will not even work properly without them. That is the reason why we dedicated a whole section to certificates.

A quick note before we proceed: in production environments where you publish RemoteApps or desktops over the internet, it is highly recommended you use certificates issued by a well-known third-party authority (i.e. DigiCert, RapidSSL, etc). The reason for this is these certificates are trusted globally (what means any device, anywhere, will trust these). For this book, we chose to use self-signed or internally issued certificates (by setting up our own Certificate Authority – CA – on Windows Server 2012 R2).

It is important to understand certificates well, especially when dealing with access from both internal and external clients. First we will deal with an internal scenario and then show you how to change it to make it work internally and externally, using the exact same FQDN.

Internal Scenario

On the server you are using to manage the environment (CRLAB-DC01 in our case), open 'Server Manager' and under 'Remote Desktop Services' go to the 'Collections' section.

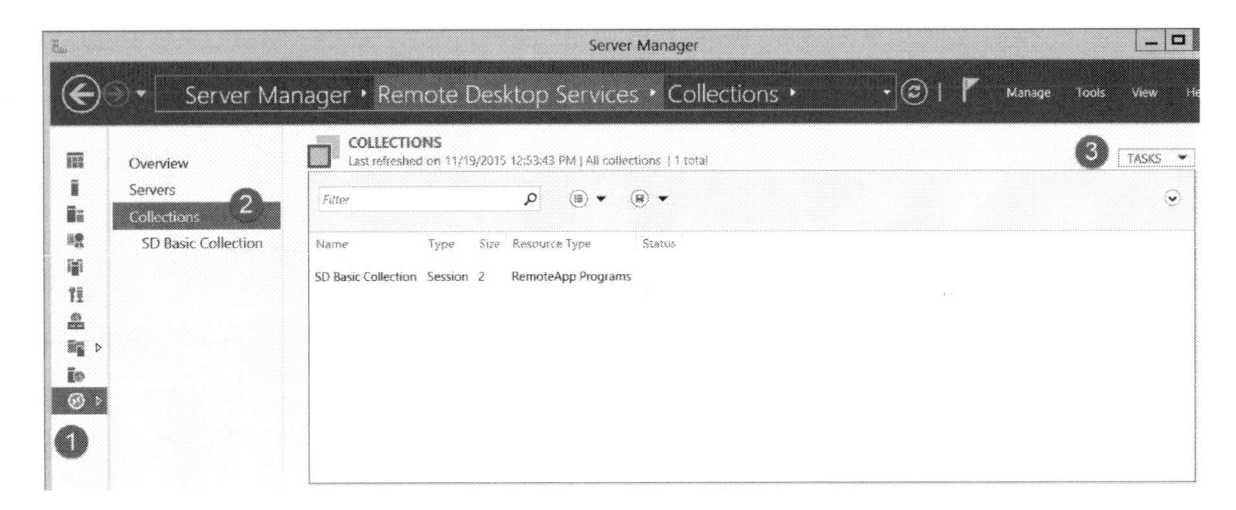

On the right side, click 'Tasks' and select 'Edit Deployment Properties'.

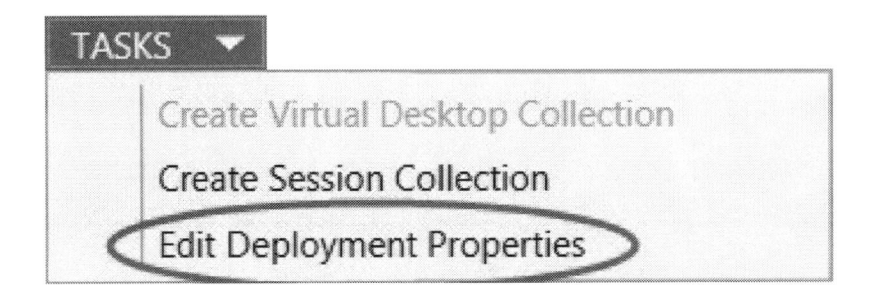

Click 'Certificates'. This will show you all the certificates in use with the RDS deployment (none at this stage).

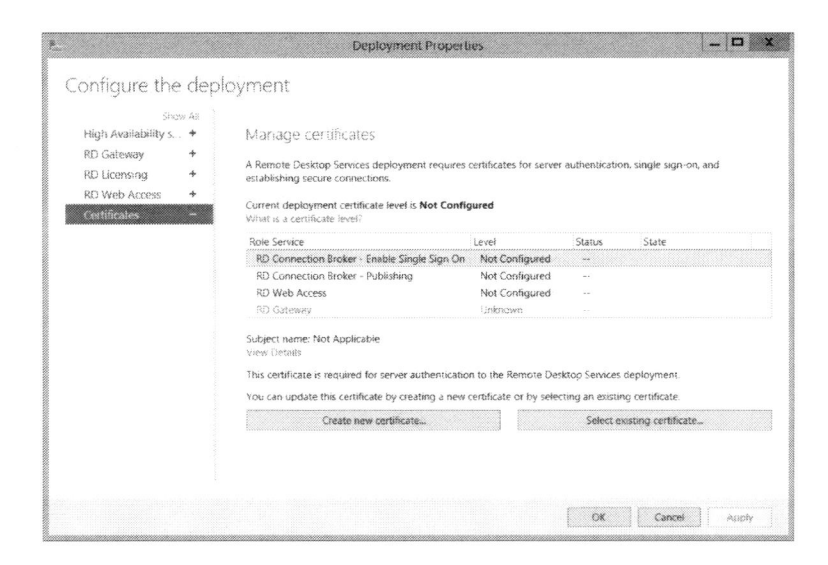

As mentioned before, Microsoft decided to use certificates for every single thing you can think of. The first step is to add a certificate for the RDCB single sign on role service. Select 'RD Connection Broker – Enable Single Sign On' and click 'Create new certificate...'.

For the name, use the same name chosen for the RDCB HA, in our case rdsfarm.crlab.local. Enter a password and make sure you select 'Store this certificate', so you can save it somewhere on the server. Select 'Allow the certificate to be added to the Trusted Root Certification Authorities certificate store on the destination computers' to allow this certificate to be loaded as a trusted one on the endpoints. Click 'OK'.

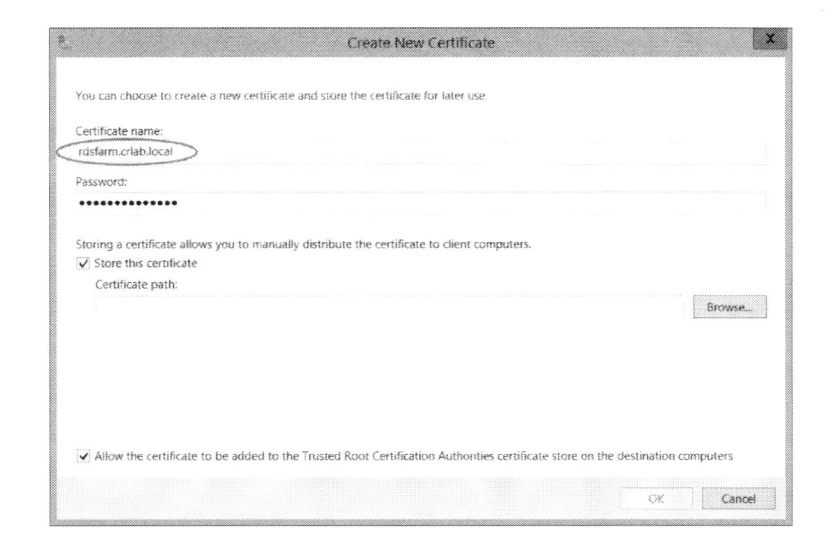

As you can see, now the state changed to 'Ready to apply'. This means it created the certificate and that we are ready to apply it to the RDCB by simply clicking 'Apply'.

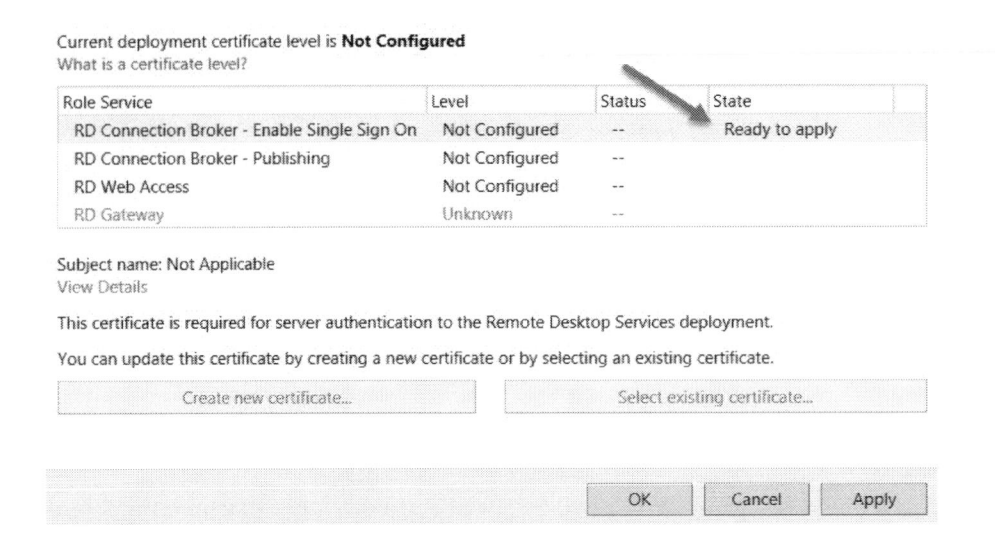

We cannot create any new certificates for the other role services until we apply this one. Once you click 'Apply', the state changes to 'Success'.

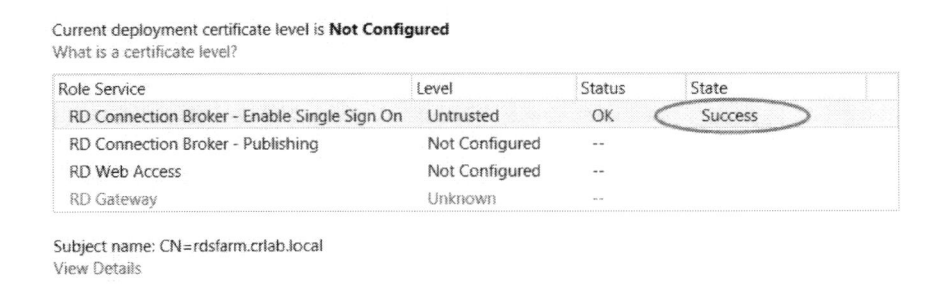

If you noticed, the certificate level changed to 'Untrusted' and the reason for that is quite simple: as this is a self-signed certificate, the endpoints will not trust it automatically, as they would if it was a publicly signed certificate (for example from Digicert, RapidSSL, etc). This is not a big issue in a lab environment but for production, it may pose additional challenges (i.e. making all endpoints trust the certificate).

Next, we need to set the certificate for the role service 'RD Connection Broker – Publishing'. You can simply use the certificate we just used. Click 'Select existing certificate...' and browse to the certificate file created on the previous step, entering the required password.

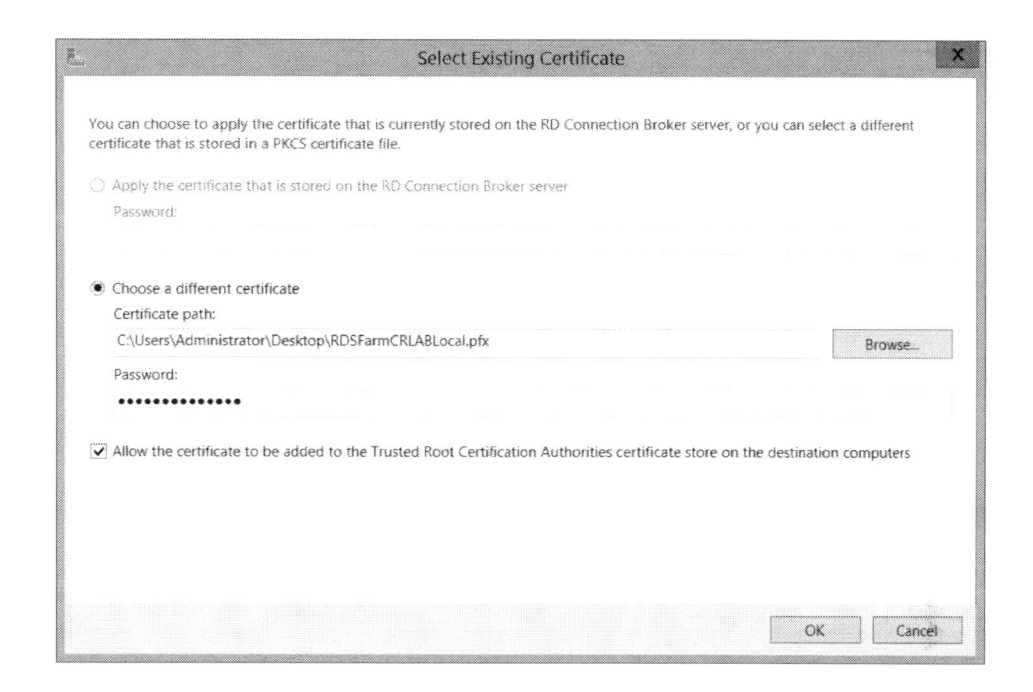

Click 'OK' and then 'Apply'. You should see 'Untrusted' and 'Success' exactly like before.

Now we need to set the certificate the RDWA will use. For this, we will create a new certificate, for the FQDN 'web.crlab.local', by following the exact same procedure we used when creating the certificate for 'rdsfarm.crlab.local'. Select 'RD Web Access', click 'Create new certificate...' and enter the required information.

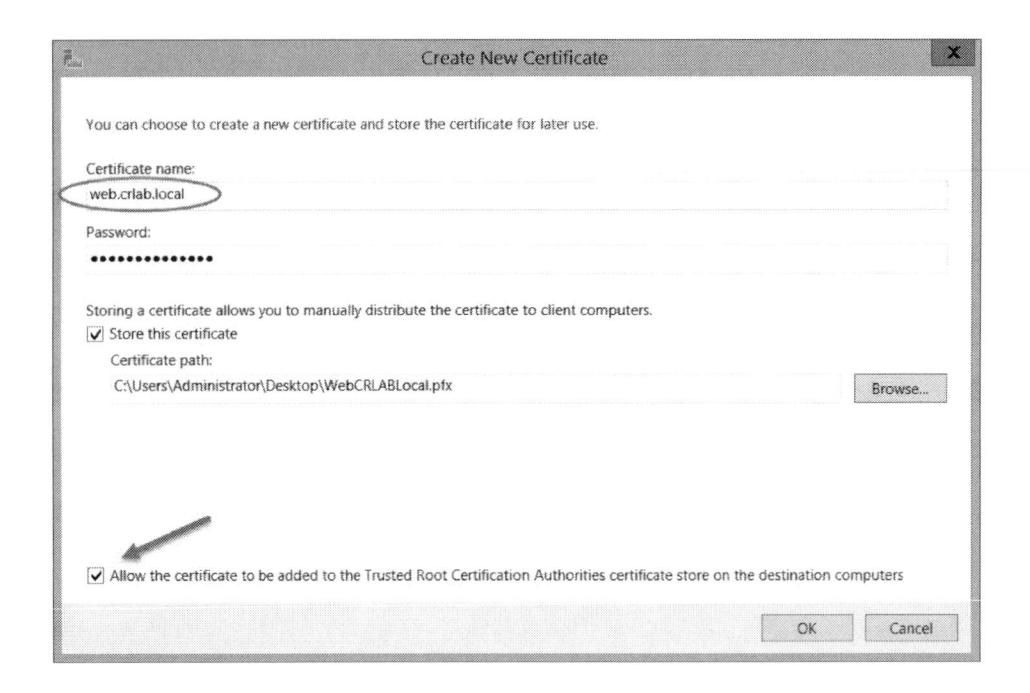

Click 'OK' and then 'Apply'. Now we have certificates for all the role services that are part of our deployment. We cannot add a certificate to the RD Gateway role service as we did not add such server (or role) to our deployment. We will take care of this later.

Setting up RDWA HA

Still in our quest for a perfect environment with no SPOF, the next step is to add another RDWA. As this is a critical component, (it is the web portal and the service responsible for the RSS feed – more on this later) we need to guarantee we always have an RDWA available. That is why we are adding a second one and finding a way to load balance these (as we did with the RDCB). Based on the server list for our environment, we will of course use 'CRLAB-WA02' for this. So let's do it.

1. Launch 'Server Manager' (in our case on CRLAB-DC01) and select '3. Add other servers to manage'.

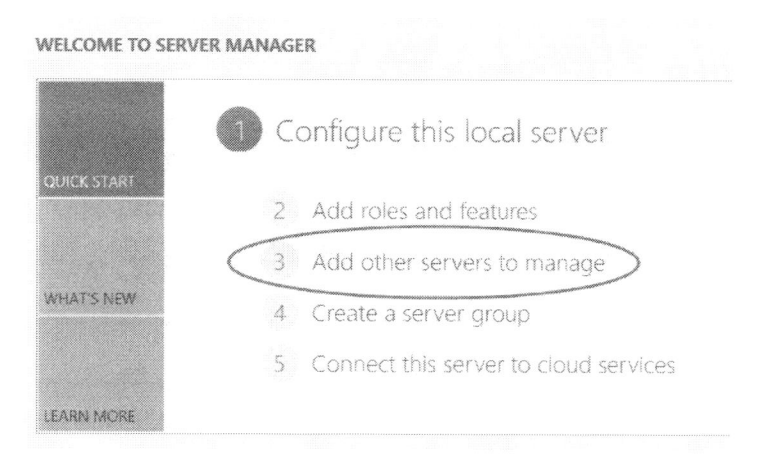

2. Type crlab-wa under 'Name(CN)' and click 'Find Now'. This will return all servers with names starting with CRLAB-WA. Select 'CRLAB-WA02' and click the arrow button to add it to the right pane. Click 'Ok'

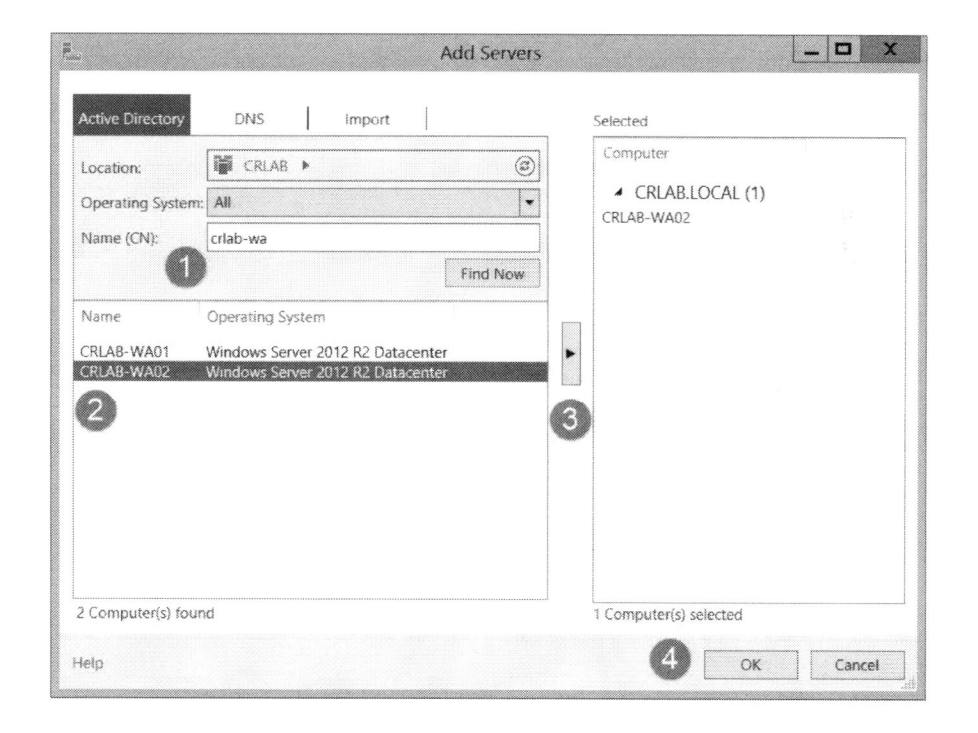

3. Now click on 'Remote Desktop Services' on the left. This will open the 'Overview' page we are now very familiar with. Under 'Deployment Overview' right-click the 'RD Web Access icon and select 'Add RD Web Access Servers'

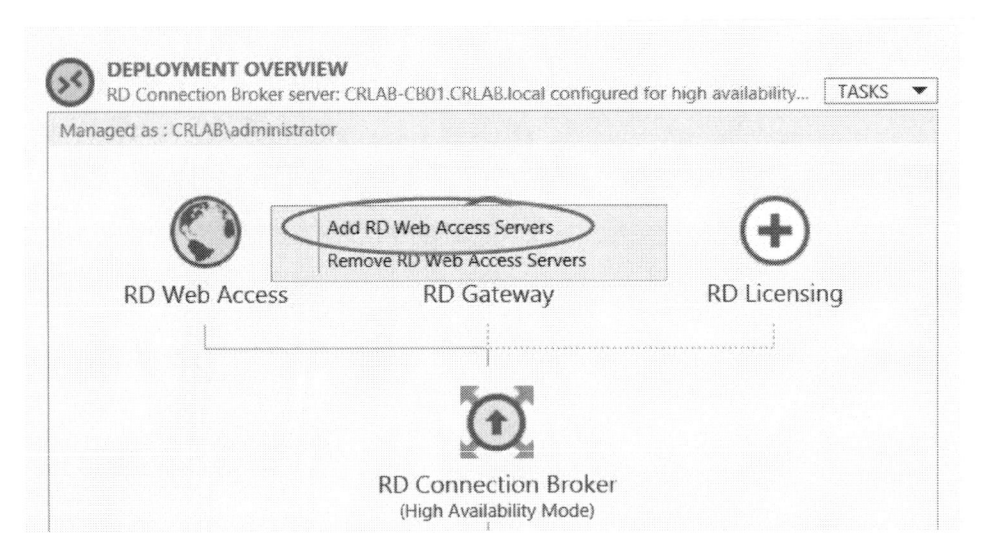

4. Select 'CRLAB-WA02', click the arrow button and click 'Next'.

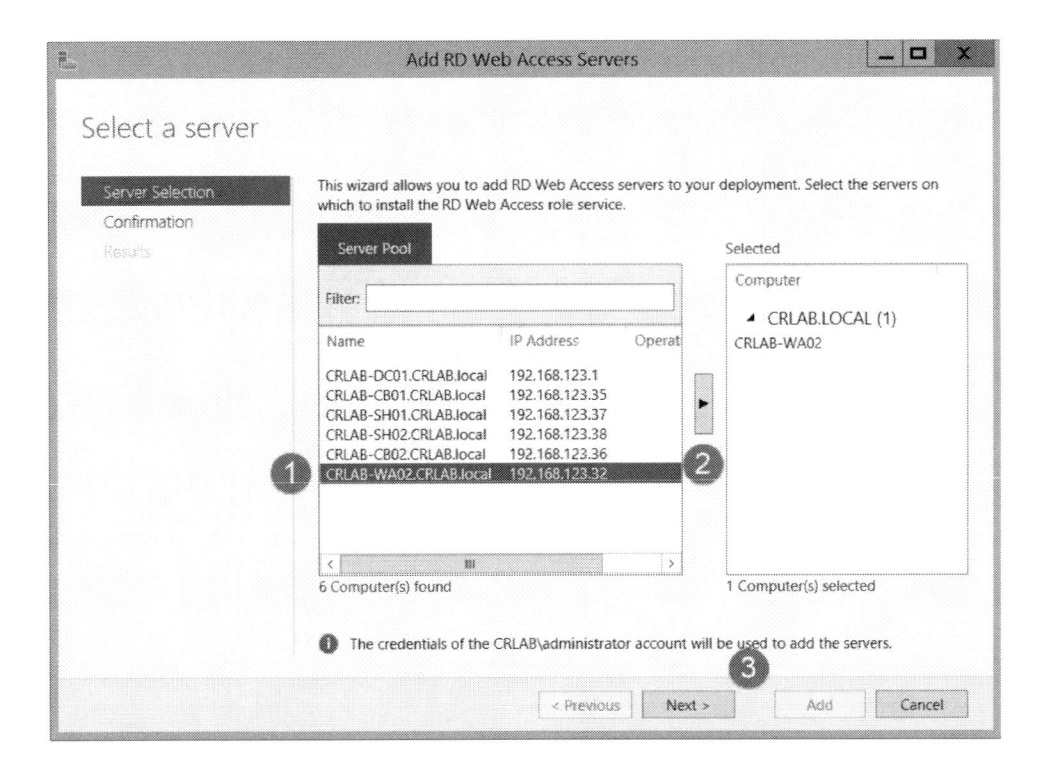

5. The wizard will show it is about to add 'CRLAB-WA02' to the deployment. Click 'Add'.

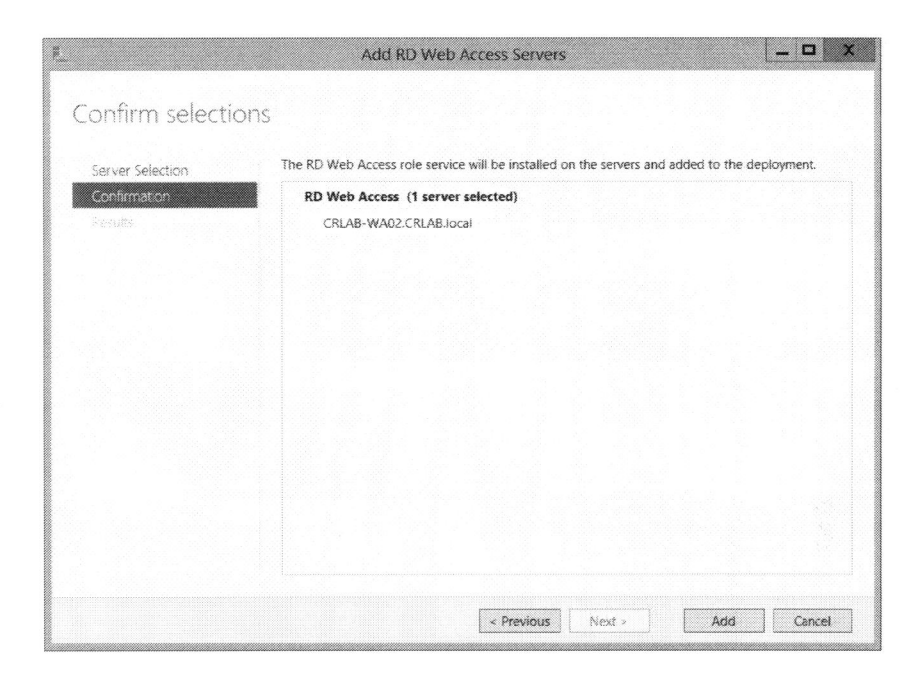

6. You will get confirmation the server was successfully added to the deployment. Click 'Close'.

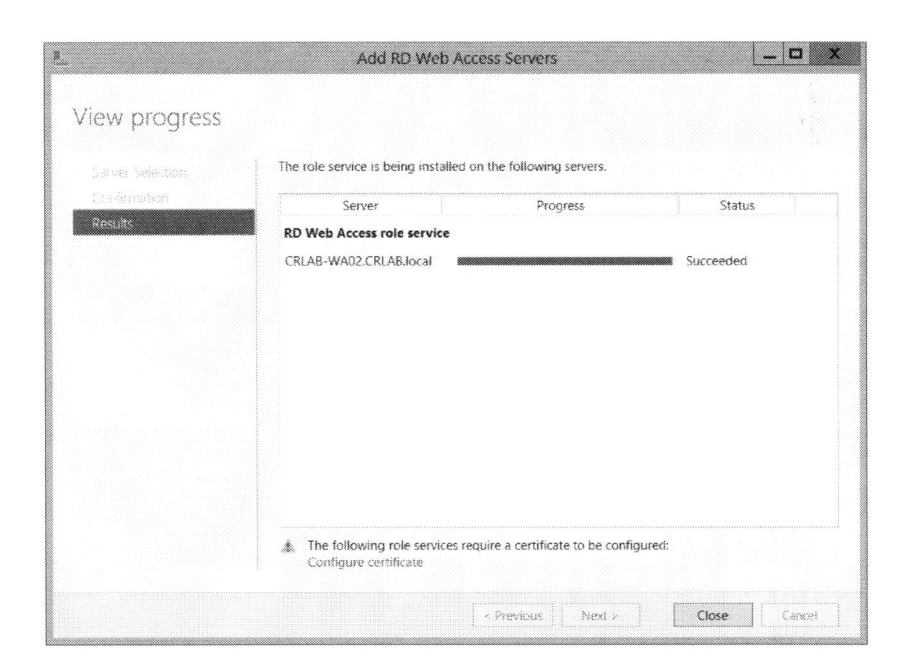

Now back to the 'Server Manager' screen you can see that 'CRLAB-WA02' was added to the deployment as a server running the RD Web Access role (as expected).

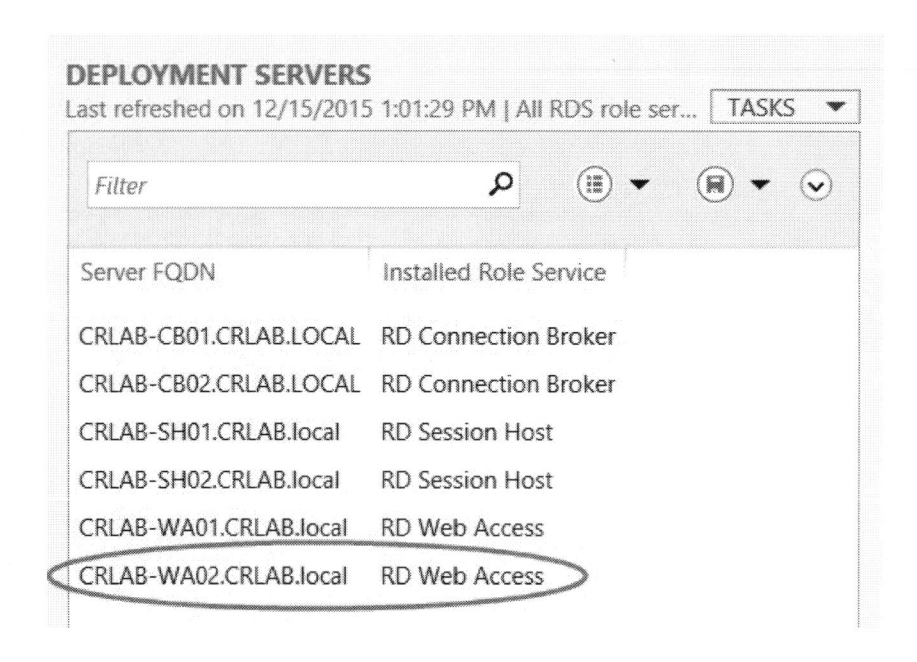

DEPLOYMENT SERVERS
Last refreshed on 12/15/2015 1:01:29 PM | All RDS role ser... | TASKS ▼

Server FQDN	Installed Role Service
CRLAB-CB01.CRLAB.LOCAL	RD Connection Broker
CRLAB-CB02.CRLAB.LOCAL	RD Connection Broker
CRLAB-SH01.CRLAB.local	RD Session Host
CRLAB-SH02.CRLAB.local	RD Session Host
CRLAB-WA01.CRLAB.local	RD Web Access
CRLAB-WA02.CRLAB.local	RD Web Access

The question now becomes, "With two RDWAs, how do I create a highly available pair and load balance them?" The answer here depends on several things, one being how critical the experience to the end users is to how much money you are willing to spend, since the RDWA role is simply a website like any other one. Let's check a couple of these options then.

DNS RR

This is the exact same thing we did when setting up HA for the RDCBs. If you remember, it relies on DNS. The idea is to create multiple DNS resource records and point these to the servers you want to load balance. For the RDWAs we used the FQDN web.crlab.local so we need to create two records for 'web' under the correct zone (CRLAB.local), pointing to the IPs of 'CRLAB-WA01' and 'CRLAB-WA02'.

As before, you will need to use the DNS management console to do that. In our lab, we launched it on CRLAB-DC01.

Under 'Forward Lookup Zones' locate your domain name (in our case, CRLAB.local). Right-click it and select 'New Host (A or AAAA)...'.

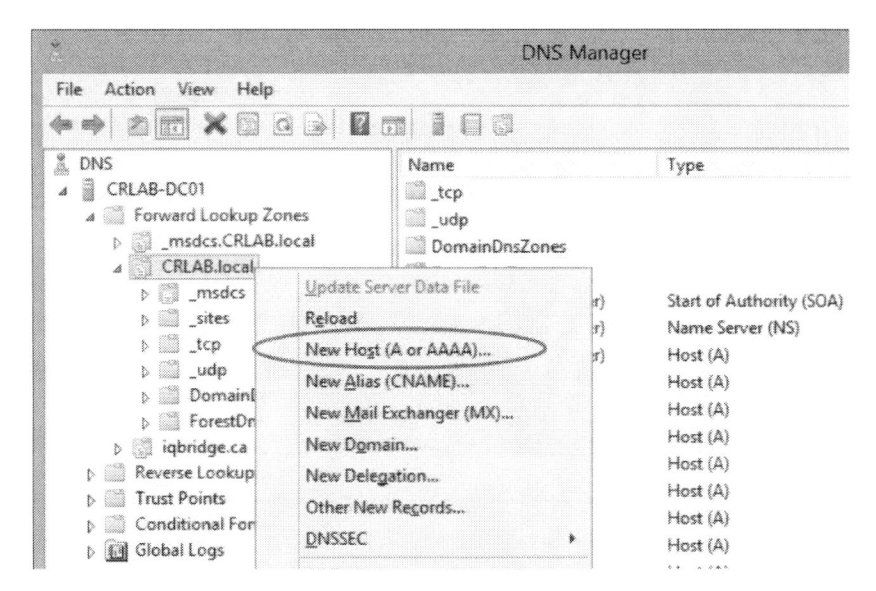

Create a record for each RDWA but with the name 'web'. The IP address will be the one for each RDWA.

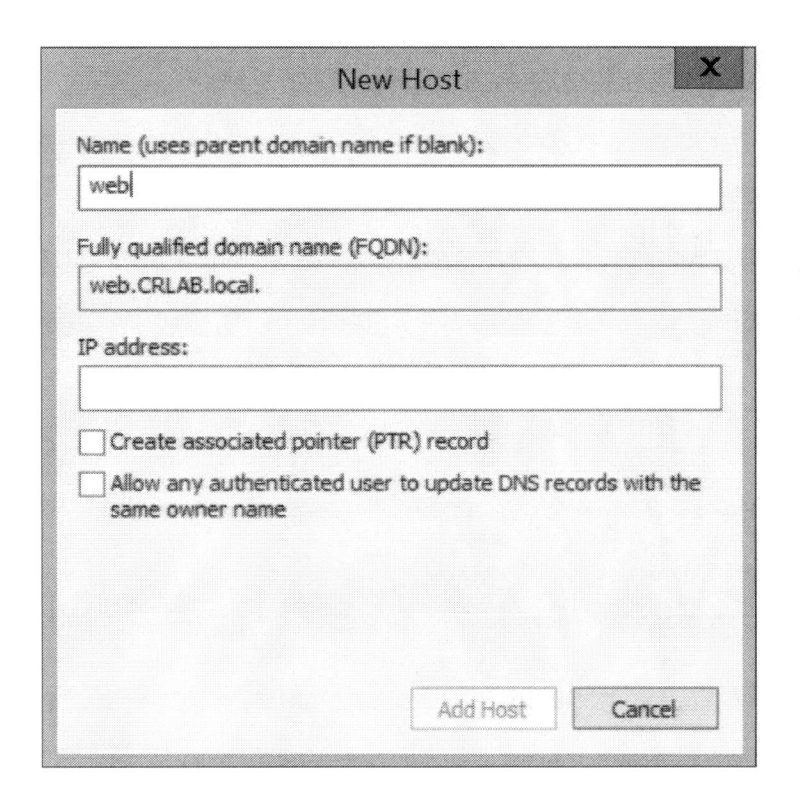

This is what you should have when done (your IPs will probably be different):

| web | Host (A) | 192.168.123.31 |
| web | Host (A) | 192.168.123.32 |

So now, if you browse to https://web.crlab.local/rdweb you should see the RDWA logon screen, ready to take on your users.

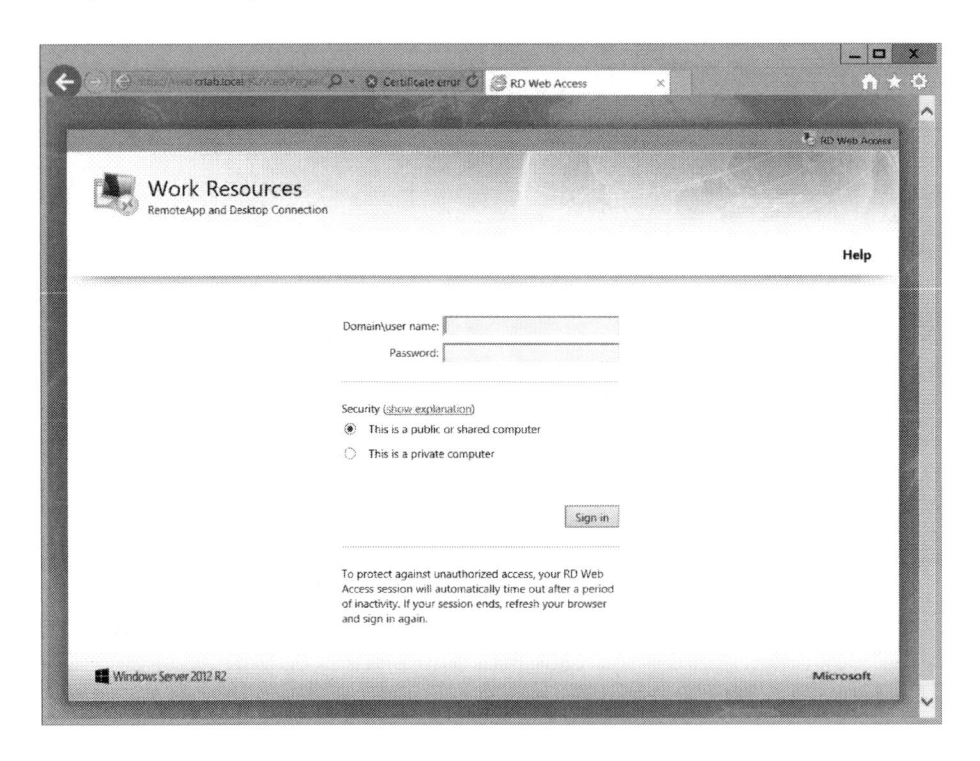

Keep in mind there are many downsides when using DNS RR. First, the DNS server is not aware if the backend servers (in this case, the RDWAs but this is valid for any service) are actually functional. The fact you can ping a server does not mean the services provided by such machine are actually working. The second issue is the IP address the client receives may be cached somewhere between the client and the servers. To make things even worse, DNS RR cannot even tell if the servers being load balanced are actually alive. That could result in a client not being able to access the RDWA because the DNS RR system returns an IP address of an RDWA that is down, even though another RDWA is up and running. So yes, DNS RR should be avoided but it is an easy and cheap way to achieve load balancing (and some sort of HA).

NLB

The second option is to use Network Load Balancing (NLB), a built-in feature on Windows Server. Unlike DNS RR, NLB is better at checking if the backend servers are available what certainly improves HA. Problem is NLB still works at the network level so it is not fully aware if the services in use are actually working. It assumes that if it can reach a server, all services provided must be working, what may not be true at all. Let's take a quick look at how to setup NLB.

Setting up NLB

1. On CRLAB-DC01 (or directly at the RDWAs) launch 'Server Manager' and click '2. Add Roles and Features'.

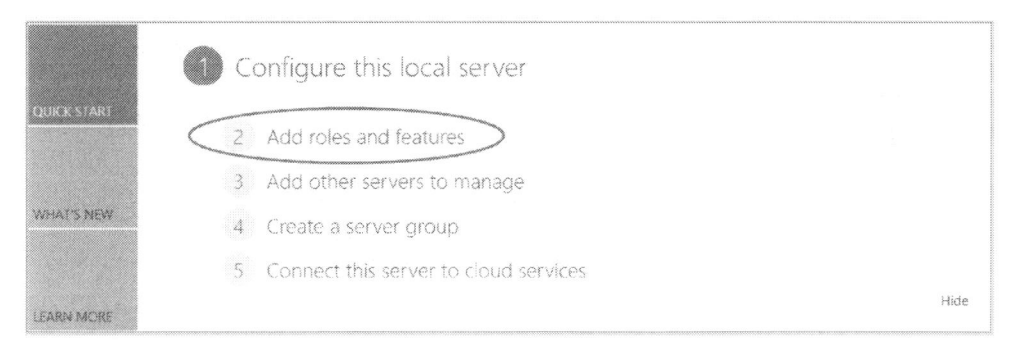

2. The wizard starts. Click 'Next'.

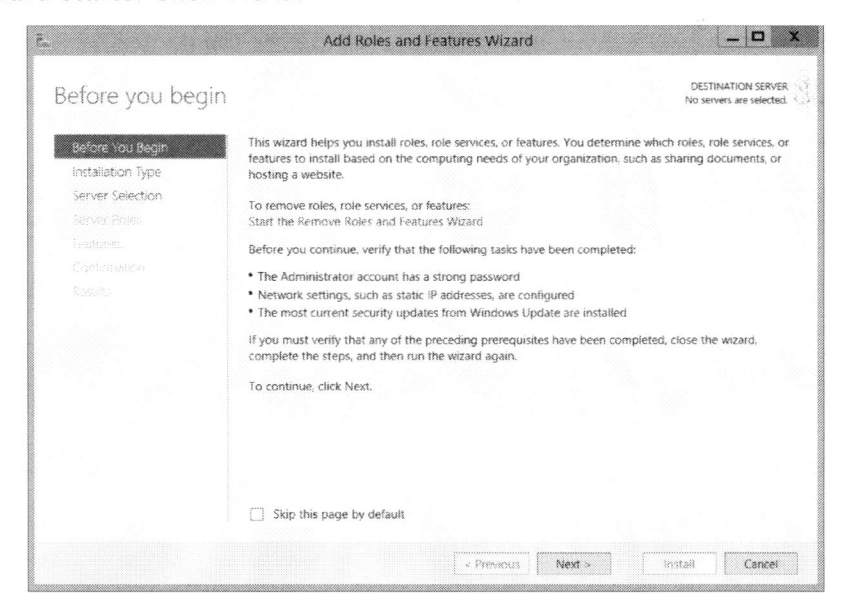

3. Select 'Role-based or feature-based installation' and click 'Next'.

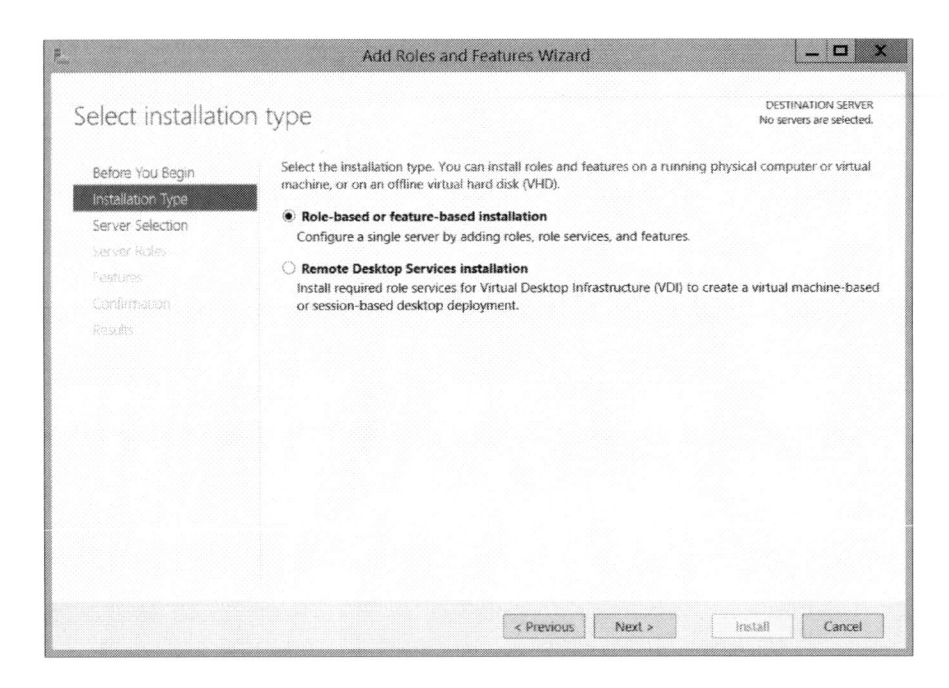

4. We have to do it one server at a time so select 'CRLAB-WA01' and click 'Next'.

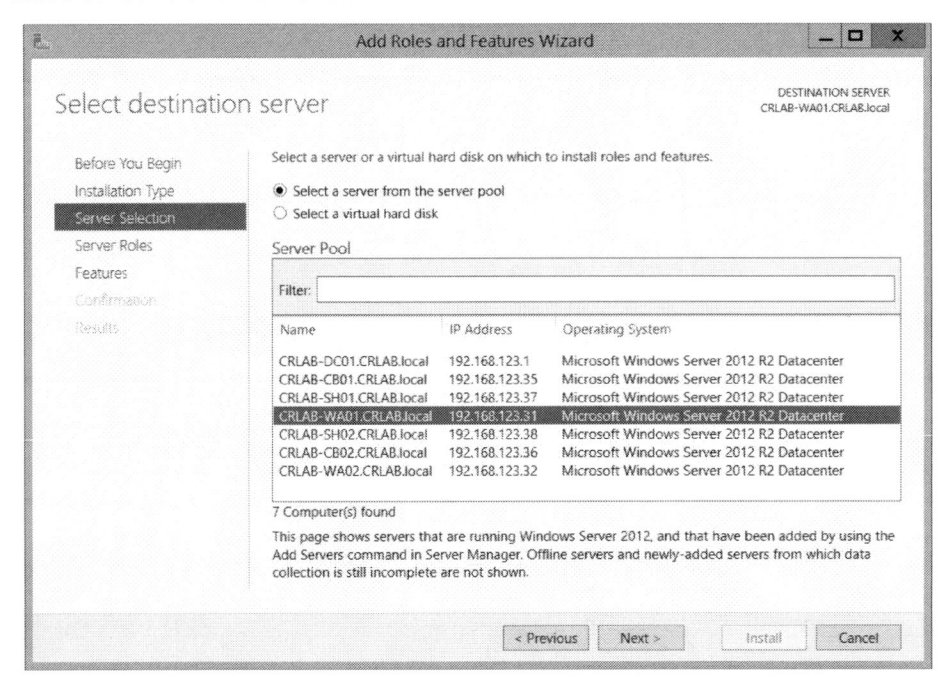

5. As NLB is just a feature (and not a role), simply click directly on 'Features' and select 'Network Load Balancing' (you may have to scroll down). Click 'Next'.

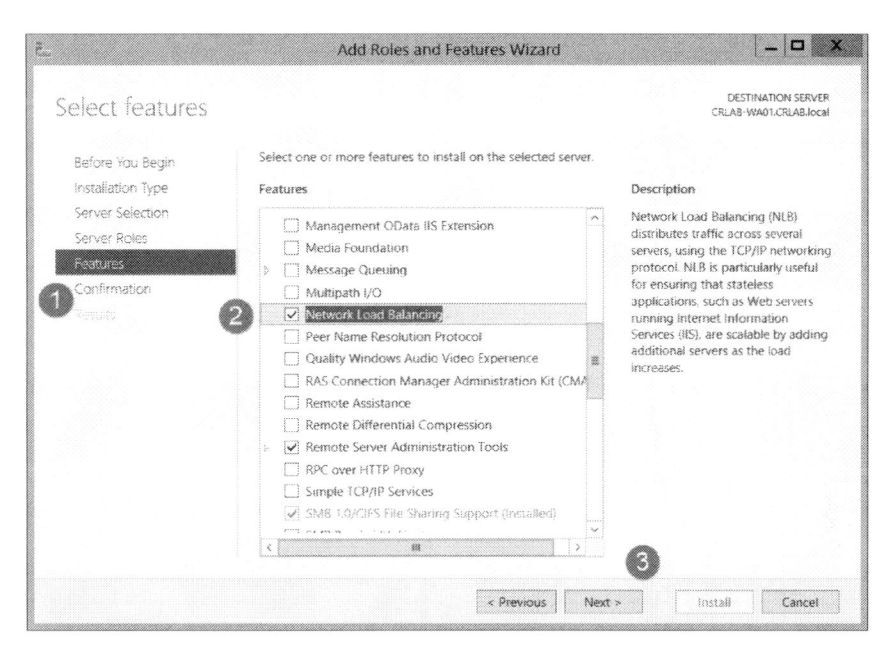

6. It will prompt you to install the 'Network Load Balancing Tools' for management purposes. Simply click 'Add Features'.

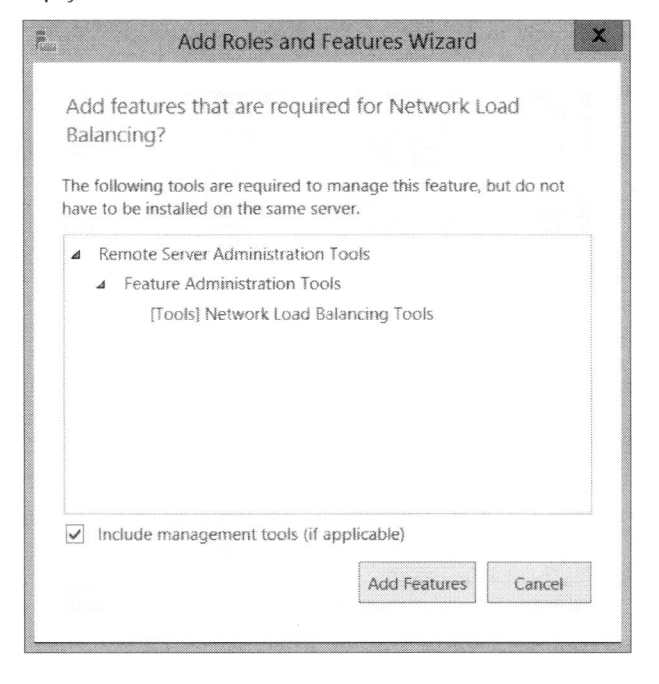

7. Check 'Restart the destination server automatically if required' just to make sure no restarts stay pending. Click 'Install'.

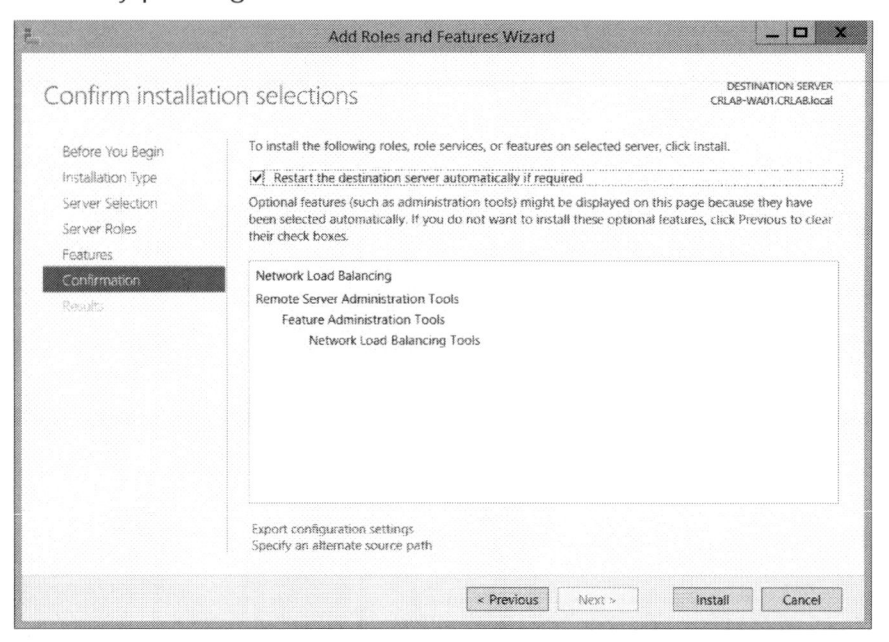

8. If everything works as expected you should get an 'Installation succeeded' message. Click 'Close'.

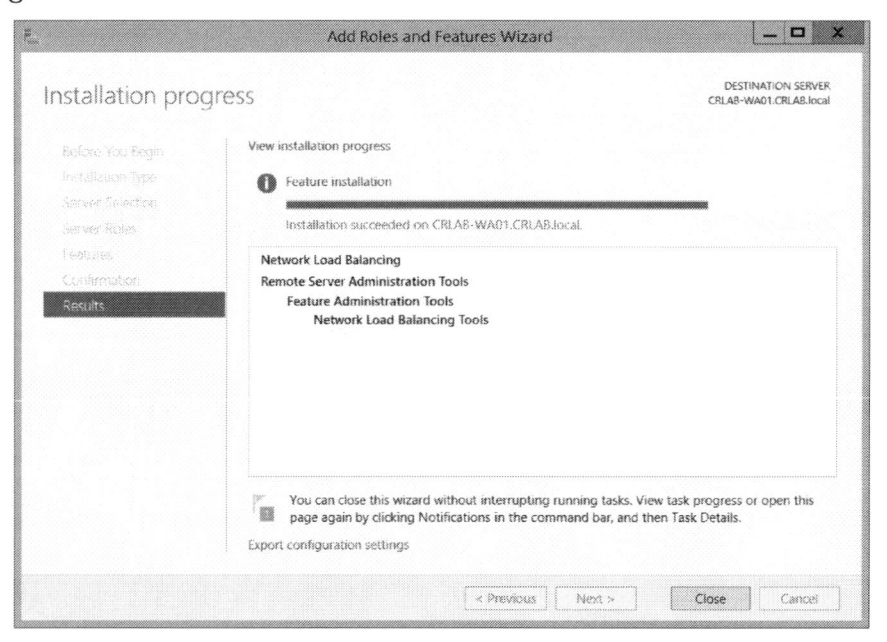

9. Simply repeat steps 4 to 8 but this time selecting 'CRLAB-WA02' as the target server where NLB will be added.
10. We are now ready to configure NLB for our RDWAs. Connect to 'CRLAB-WA01' and launch the 'Network Load Balancing manager' from the start screen.

11. The first step is to create a new cluster (basically the logical group containing all the servers we will be load balancing, the ports in use and so on). Right click 'Network Load Balancing Clusters' and select 'New Cluster'.

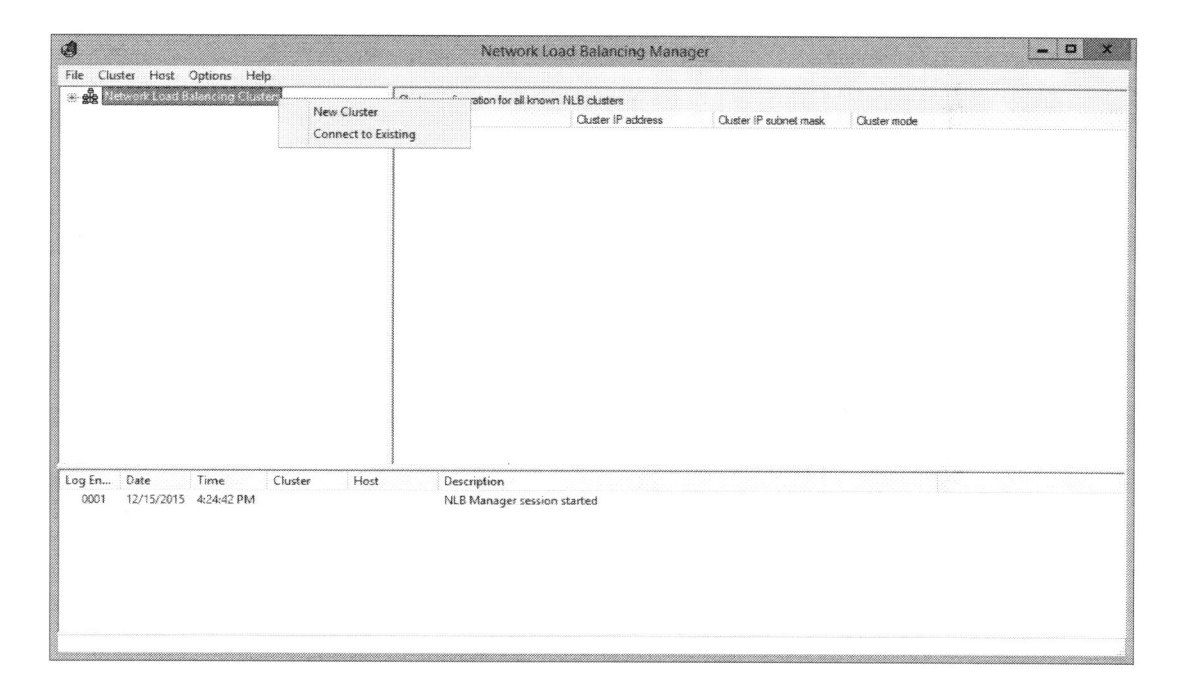

12. Now enter the name for the first server that we want as part of the cluster (in this case 'CRLAB-WA01') and click 'Connect'. This will show you the network interfaces on that server under 'Interfaces available for configuring a new cluster'. Select the right one (based on your network topology) and click 'Next'.

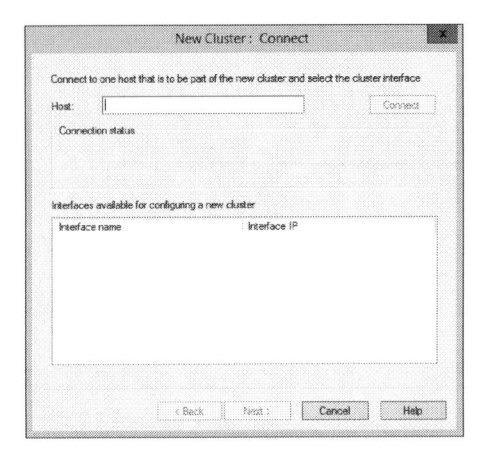

13. Simply accept the defaults and click 'Next'.

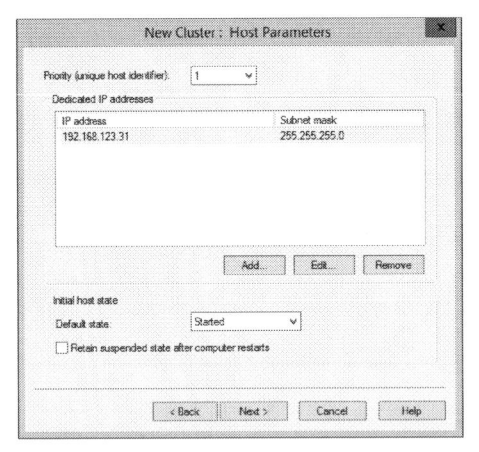

14. Now we have to specify the cluster IP address (this is referred in other load balancers like a Citrix NetScaler as a Virtual IP Address or VIP). It is the IP that will be used by clients to access the load balanced RDWA pair. Click 'Add'.

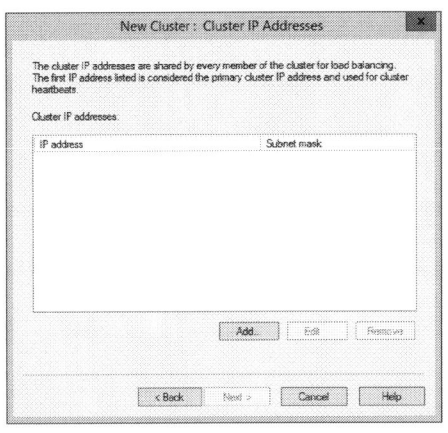

15. Enter an address not in use. Click 'OK' and then 'Next'.

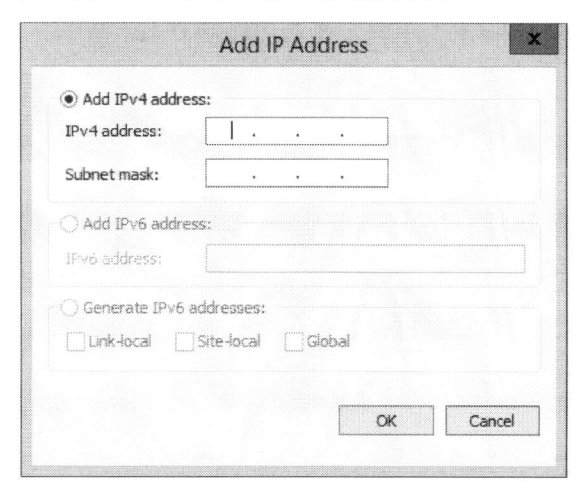

16. Under 'Full Internet name' enter the FQDN we chose when creating the certificate for the RDWA, 'web.crlab.local'. This is the name clients will use to connect to the RDWA pair. As you can see in this case we are using internal names (.crlab.local) so this will not work for external clients. We will get to that later. Just keep that in mind for now. Click 'Next'.

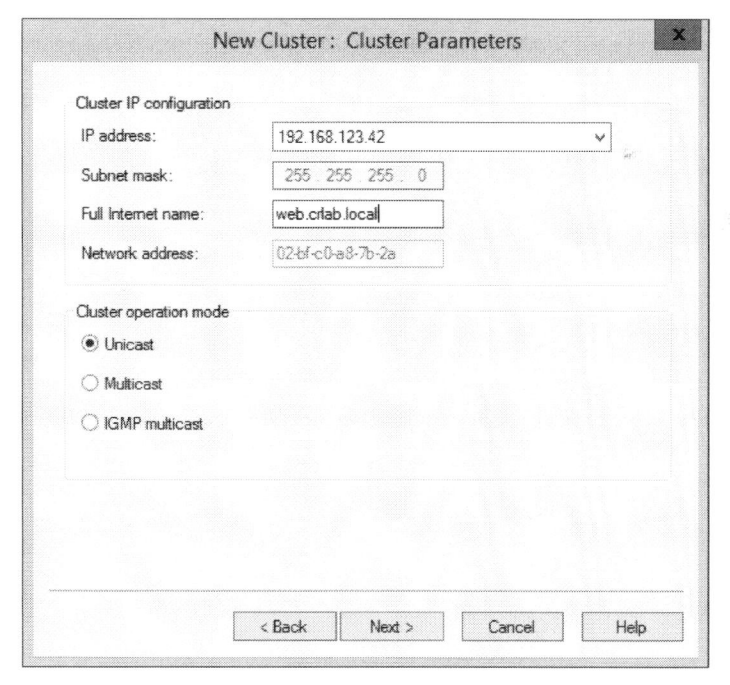

Note: If you only have a single network interface on the RDWAs (the case in our lab) make sure you use 'Multicast' for the cluster, if you do want to be able to RDP to any of the RDWAs later. Yes, we learned the hard way.

17. By default, NLB assumes you want to use all the ports for your VIP. In this case all we need is TCP 443 (HTTPS). The second thing is we want no affinity to make sure we do not get all clients from a certain location to be routed to a single RDWA all the time. Click 'Edit'.

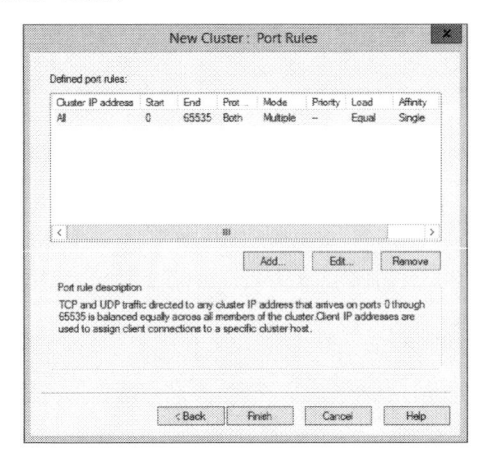

18. Change the ports used, the protocol and affinity. Click 'OK' then click 'Finish'.

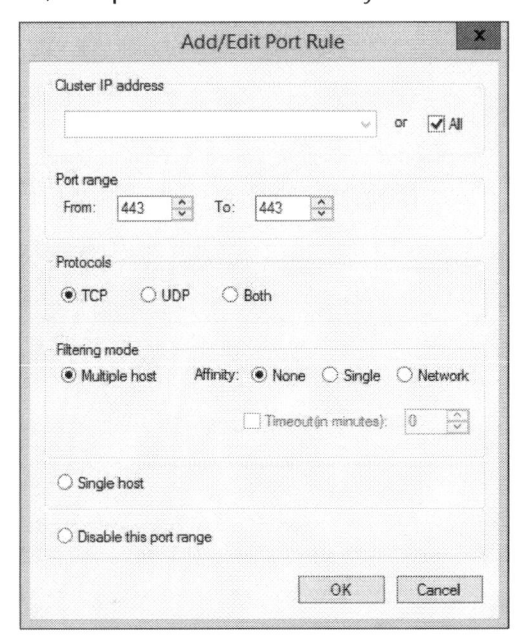

Page 130 | RDS - The Complete Guide

19. The configuration process may take a minute or so. Once it is done, you should see your NLB cluster up and running with one RDWA part of it.

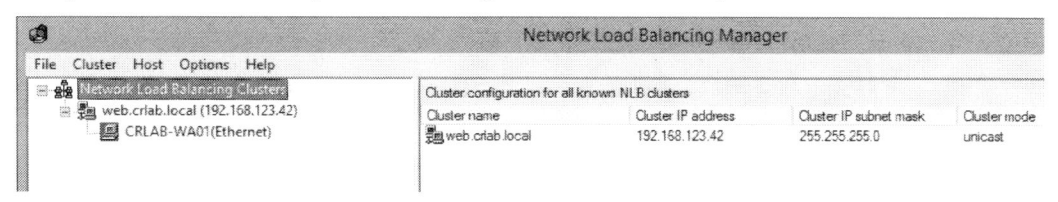

20. The final step is to add the remaining RDWA to it. Right click the cluster name (web.crlab.local) and select 'Add Host To Cluster'.

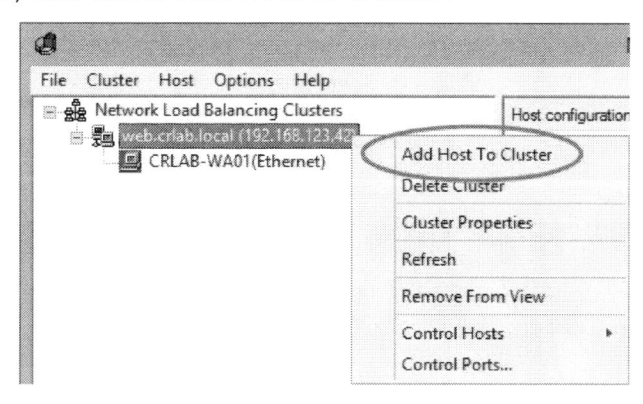

21. Enter 'CRLAB-WA02' under 'Host' and click 'Connect'. It should show you the network interface available. Select it and click 'Next'.

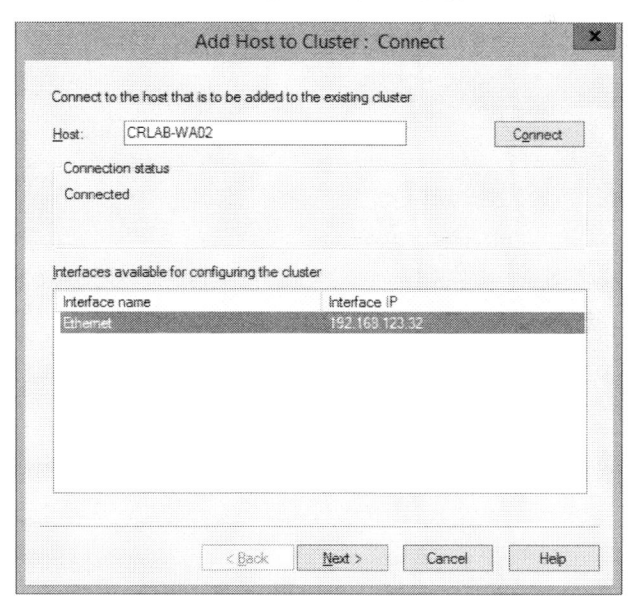

22. Accept the default settings and click 'Next'.

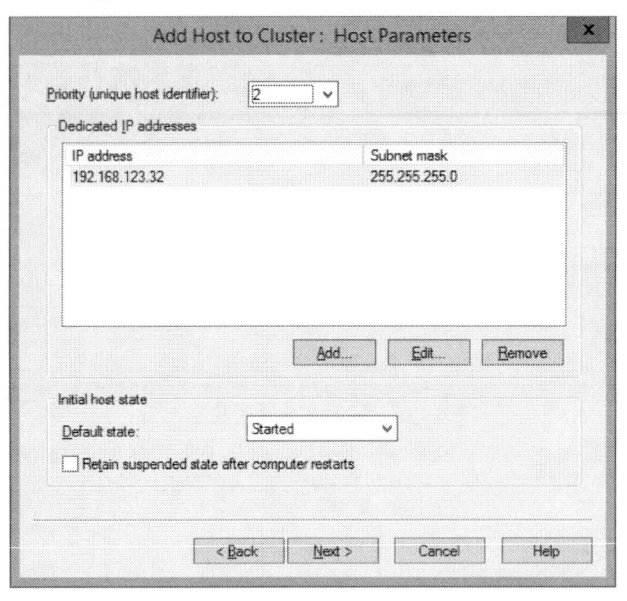

23. It will show you the correct port and settings currently in use in the cluster. Click 'Finish'.

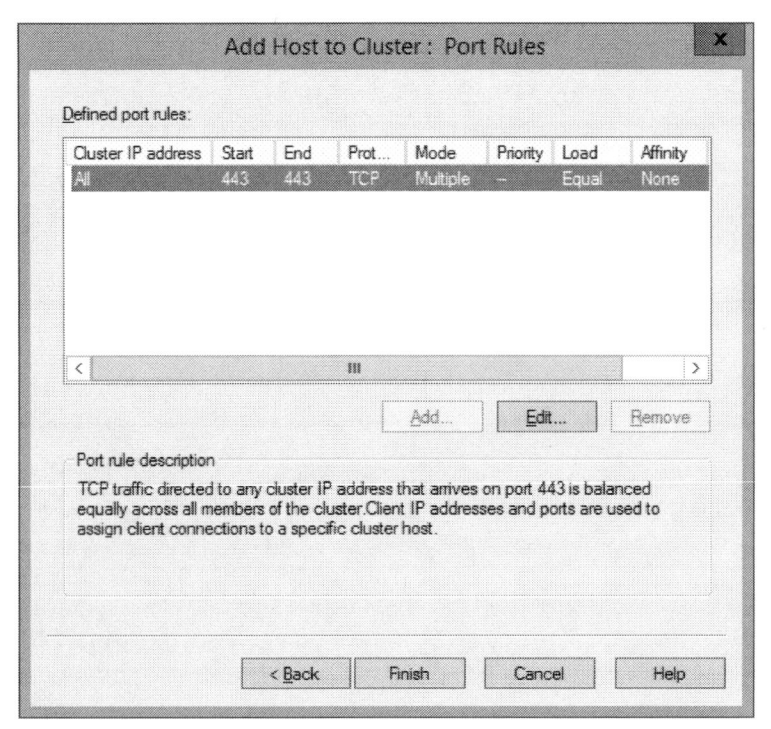

24. As before, it may take a while until everything is ready. The result is an NLB cluster with our two RDWAs on it, load balanced on port TCP 443 (HTTPS) and accessible on the FQDN 'web.crlab.local' (once we tweak the DNS record of course).

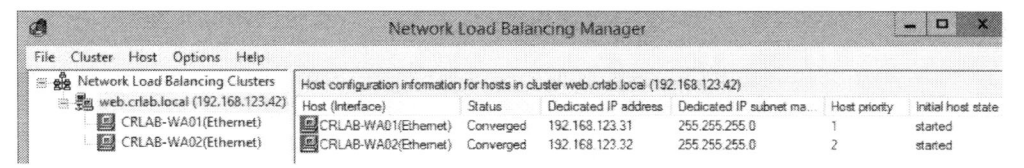

25. The last step is to remove the two DNS entries we created previously for the DNS RR and create a new one, this time pointing to the VIP of the cluster (in this case 192.168.123.42).

        web   Host (A)   192.168.123.42

26. You can test the configuration by launching Internet Explorer and opening https://web.crlab.local/rdweb. As the DNS record points to the NLB VIP, it will send the request to one if the RDWAs and you should see with the RDWA login screen (you will get a certificate warning before it – normal, as the certificates in use are not on the client trusted root CA store).

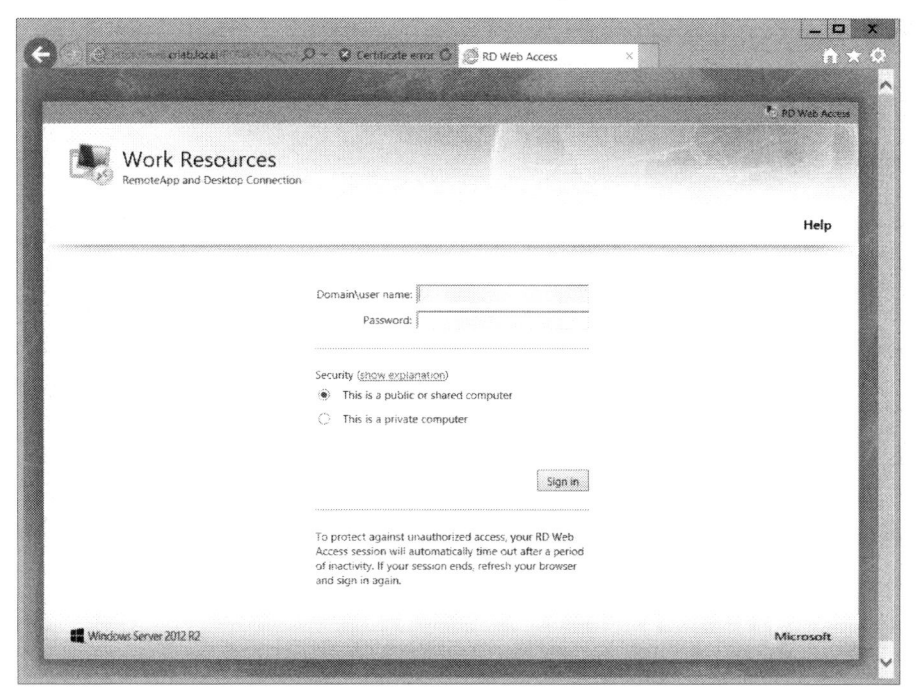

That is all for NLB. As you noticed, there is way more to it than what we covered here (i.e. Unicast vs Multicast). But as this is a book about RDS and not NLB, going through all that is beyond the scope of the book.

So now, let's take a quick look at the final (and probably best) option to load balance the RDWAs.

Hardware Load Balancing
As already mentioned, RDWA is a website like any other one, running on IIS. This means if you do have a hardware load balancer already in place (F5 BigIP, Citrix NetScaler, Kemp LoadMaster, etc) you can certainly leverage these to provide HA for the RDWA component.

We will not go through setting up a hardware load balancer as there are many options and the procedure to do it will greatly differ from device to device. It is just worth mentioning, some of these devices can be deployed as a virtual appliance (ready to be imported on Citrix XenServer, VMware ESXi or Microsoft Hyper-V) and free versions can be downloaded directly from the manufacturer website. Keep in mind they usually have bandwidth limitations on the free versions but considering the RDWA traffic is quite small, these could do the job easily even for environments with hundreds of users.

Some links for the free versions:

Kemp LoadMaster   **Citrix NetScaler VPX Free**

Based on our own experience, the Kemp LoadMaster seems to be the best product for this particular case. Higher bandwidth and much broader support for all hypervisors. In pure RDS implementations, we use this device, unless the customer already has something in place.

Note: No matter which load-balancing method you use (DNS RR, NLB or HW Load Balancer) keep in mind the certificate you used for your first RDWA must be present on all the RDWAs part of the load balancing (in our case, CRLAB-WA01 and CRLAB-WA02). Make sure the certificate is there on all servers. Also, if using a hardware load balancer, make sure you configure affinity, unless you do want to chase strange RDWA issues...

Adding RDGW

Still working on expanding our RDS deployment, this time we will add one of the most important role services to it, assuming you want to provide access to the RDS deployment over the internet. As explained before, the RDGW allows users to connect remotely over a secure, encrypted transport mechanism, using well-known protocols and ports. With RDS 2012 R2, Microsoft introduced an UDP based transport, to minimize the effects of latency and packet loss on RDP traffic. This means the RDGW now uses two ports, if you do want to leverage the new transport.

Without further delay, let's start adding our first RDGW to the deployment.

1. Launch 'Server Manager' (in our case on CRLAB-DC01) and select '3. Add other servers to manage'.

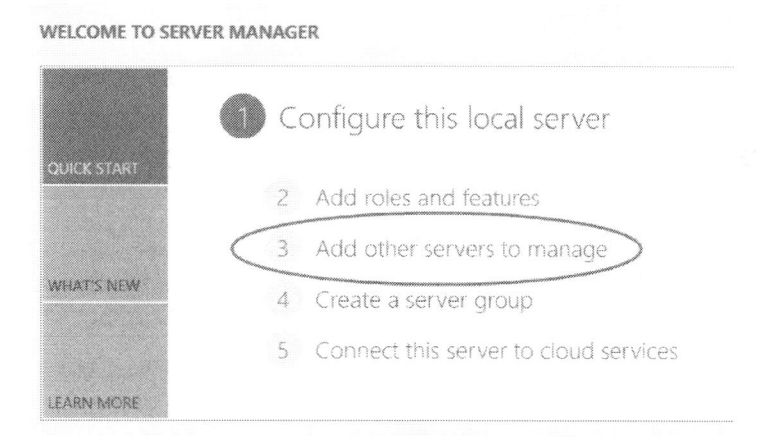

2. Type crlab-gw under 'Name(CN)' and click 'Find Now'. This will return all servers with names starting with CRLAB-GW. Select 'CRLAB-GW01' and click the arrow button to add it to the right pane. Click 'Ok'

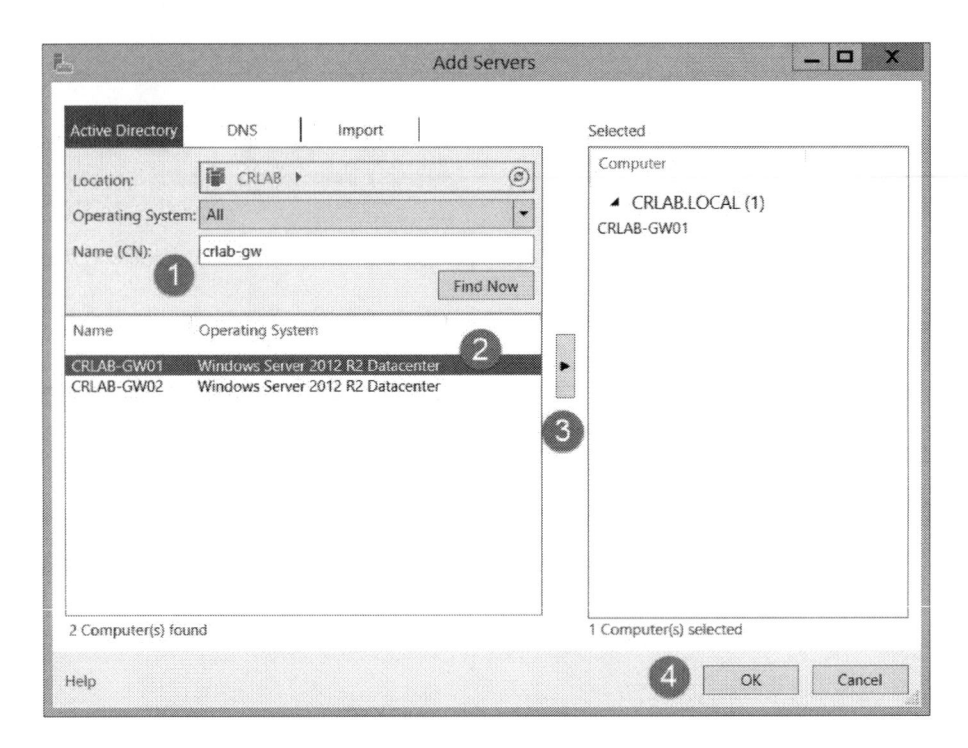

3. Now click on 'Remote Desktop Services' on the left. This will open the 'Overview' page we are now very familiar with. Under 'Deployment Overview' simply click the 'RD Gateway' icon.

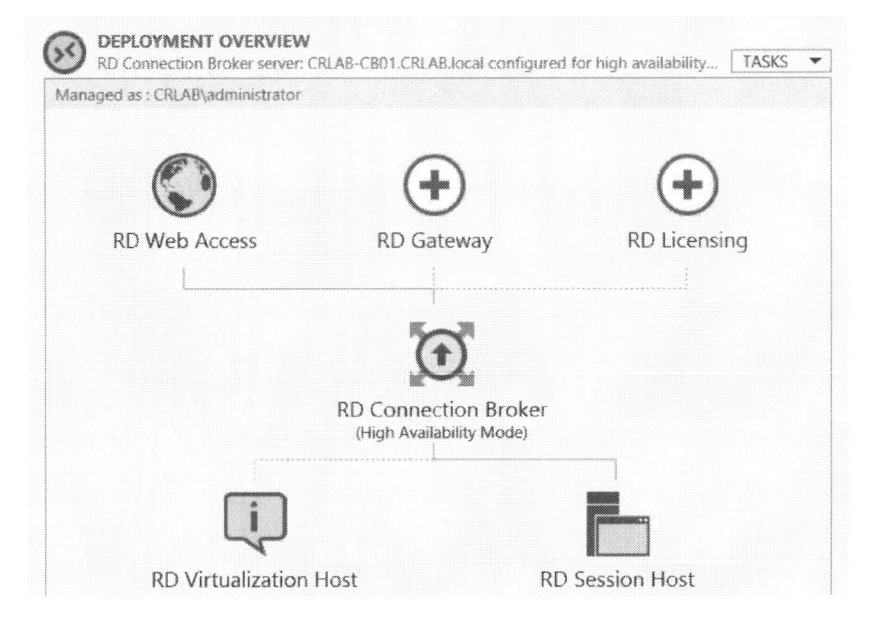

Page 136 | RDS - The Complete Guide

4. Select 'CRLAB-GW01', click the arrow button and click 'Next'.

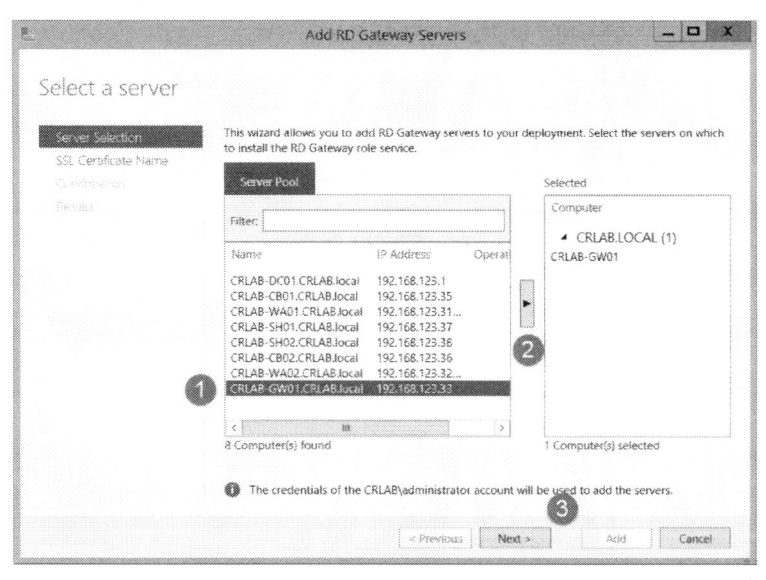

5. Enter the FQDN for the gateway. Normally users do not connect directly to it. Remember, this is why we have the RDWA. Of course, the RDWA somehow passes the information about the gateway to the client and therefore, the FQDN must be resolvable (hint: it is part of the .RDP file passed). As we are setting this up for internal use only at this stage, 'gateway.crlab.local' is good. When dealing with external access, you must use an FQDN that can be resolved from the outside, i.e. 'gateway.yourcompany.com'. Click 'Next'.

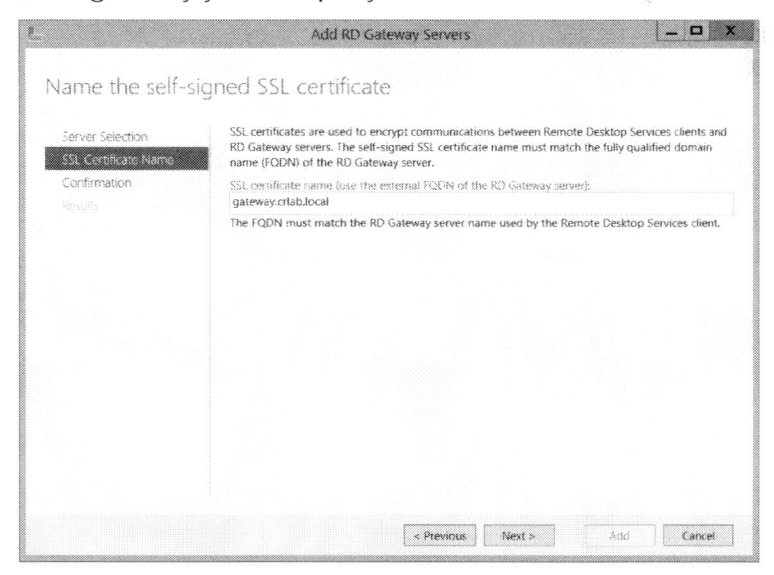

6. Review the information entered and click 'Add'.

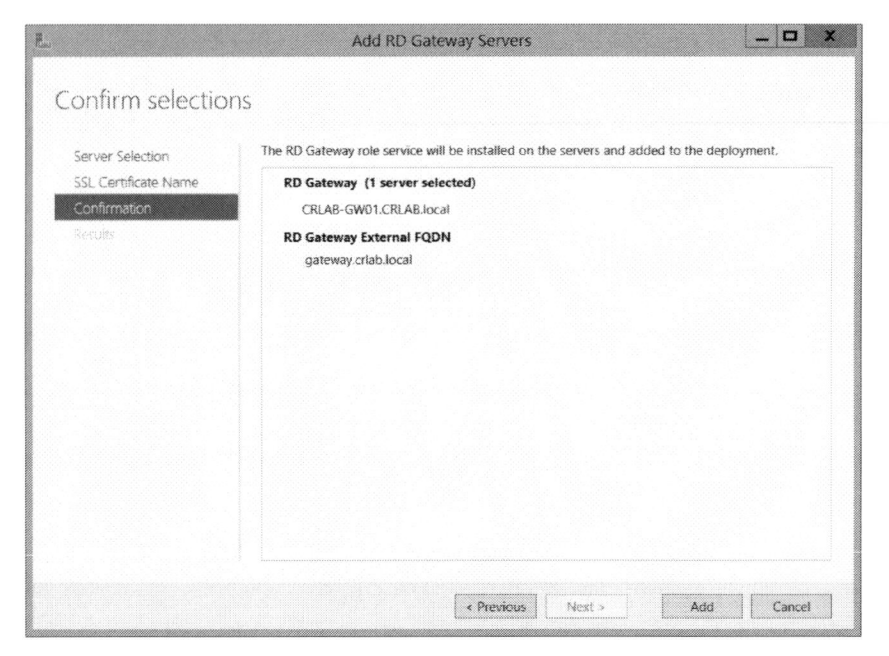

7. Once the wizard completes, you should see 'Succeeded' under 'Status'. Note the little warning about the certificates. This time we will go ahead and configure it. Click 'Configure certificate'.

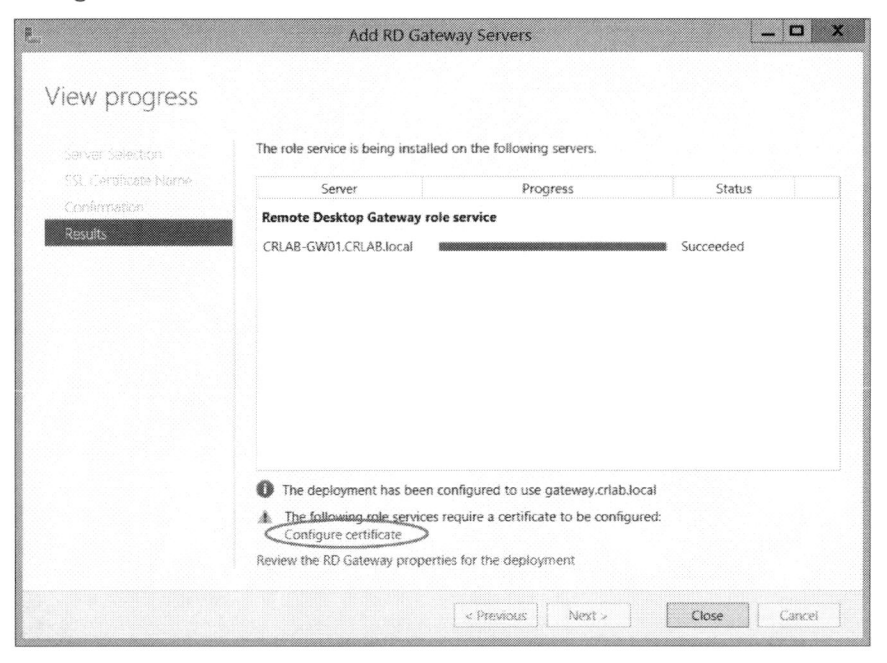

8. Now as the deployment does have an RDGW, you can now select 'RD Gateway' under 'Role Service'. Do it and click 'Create new certificate...'.

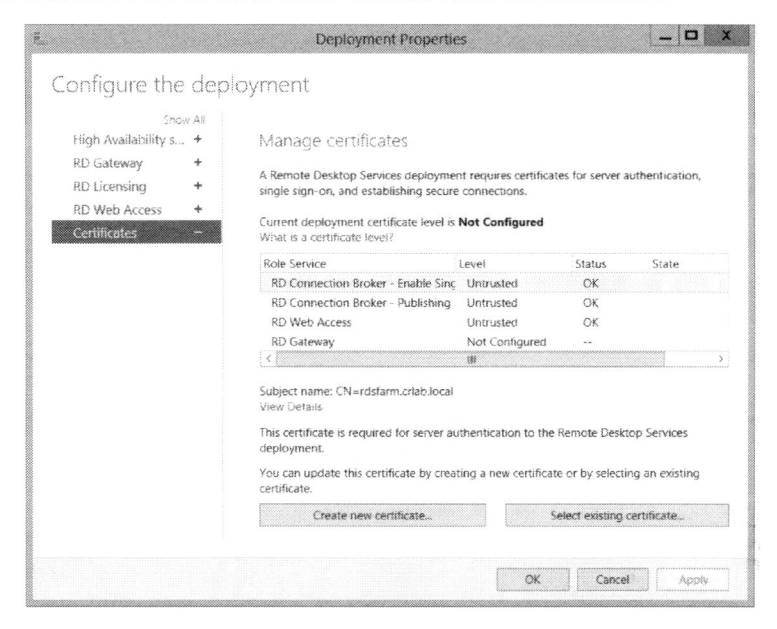

9. Enter the exact same FQDN used when adding the RDGW on step 5. In addition, one more time, we are using self-signed certificates since this is a lab environment. In production and especially when dealing with unmanaged clients, make sure you use SSL certificates signed by a well-known CA so the clients trust the certificate publisher automatically. Make sure you checked the checkboxes as shown and click 'OK'.

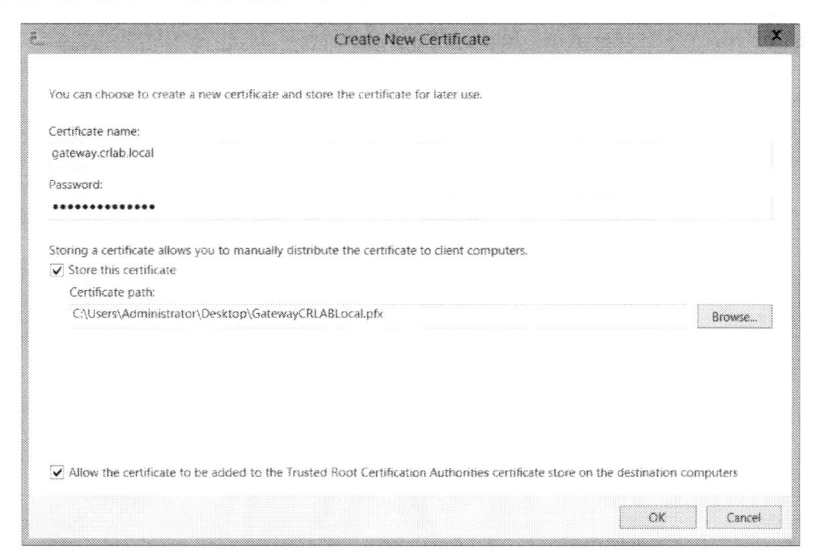

10. We are ready to deploy it. Click 'Apply'.

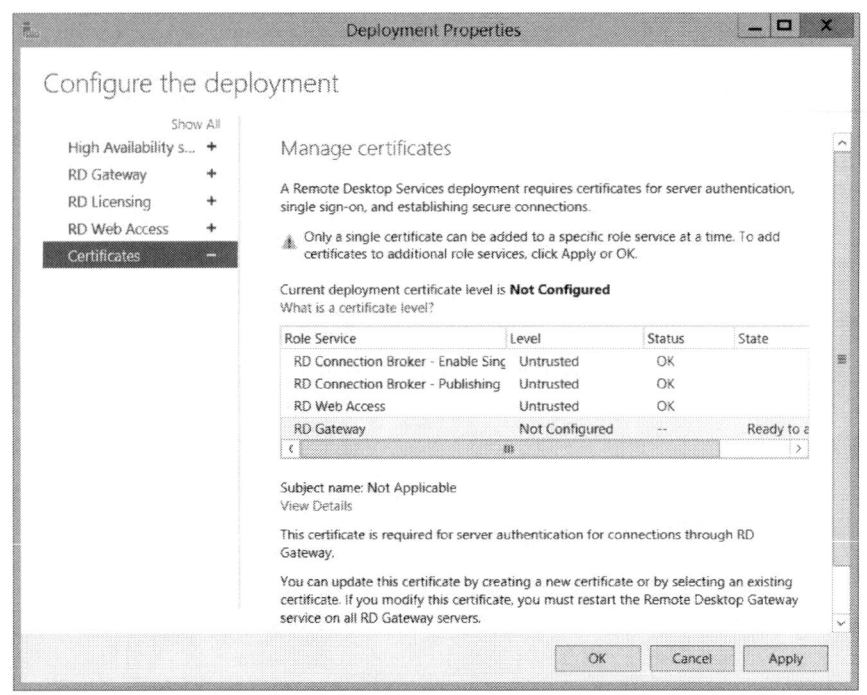

11. Success! We now have all the certificates in place. Click 'OK'.

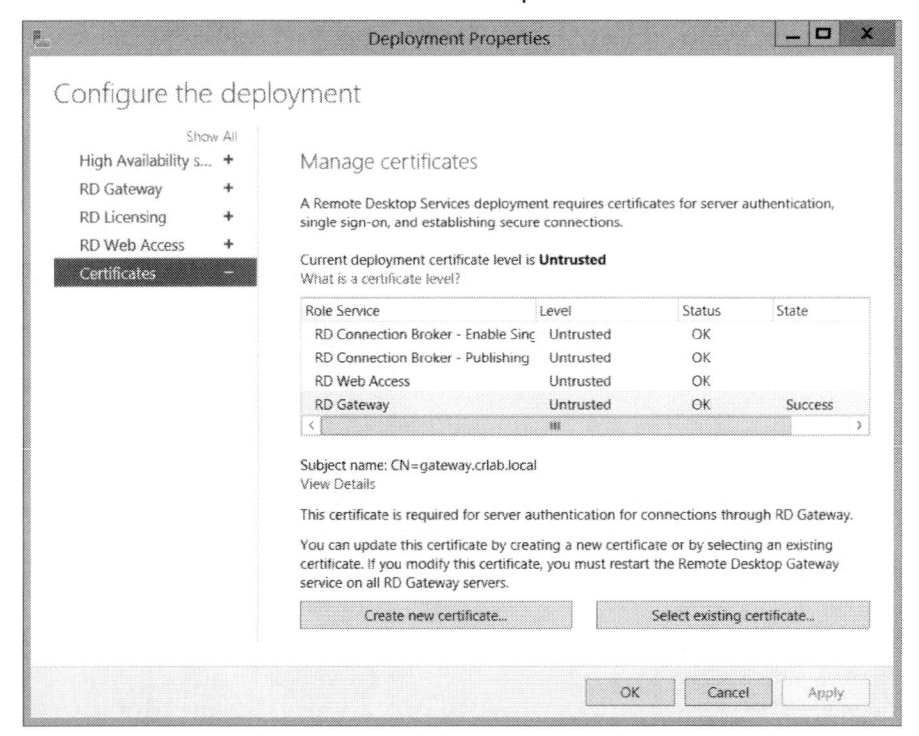

12. Simply click 'Close' and we are done with the wizard.
13. The final step is to make sure you do have a DNS entry for the FQDN created, in our case 'gateway.crlab.local'.

| gateway | Host (A) | 192.168.123.33 |

Looking at the 'Deployment Overview', we can now see the 'RD Gateway' icon has changed to indicate it is now setup and part of the deployment.

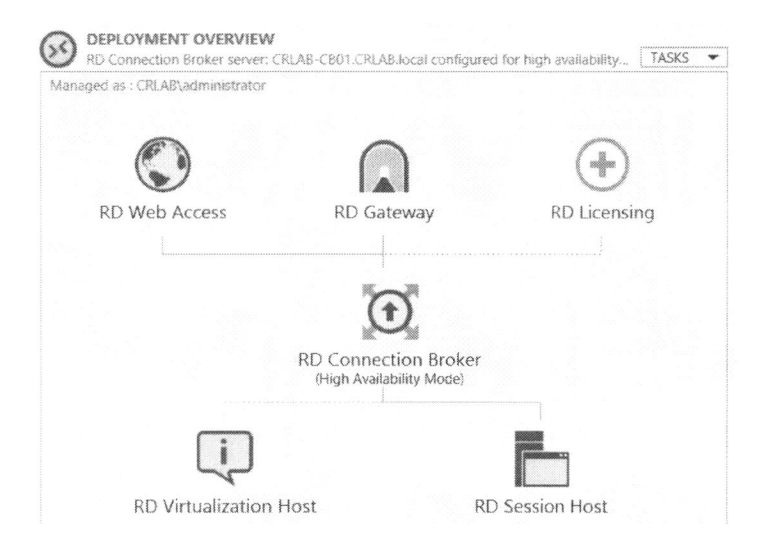

In addition, under 'Deployment Servers' we can see 'CRLAB-GW01' is now there.

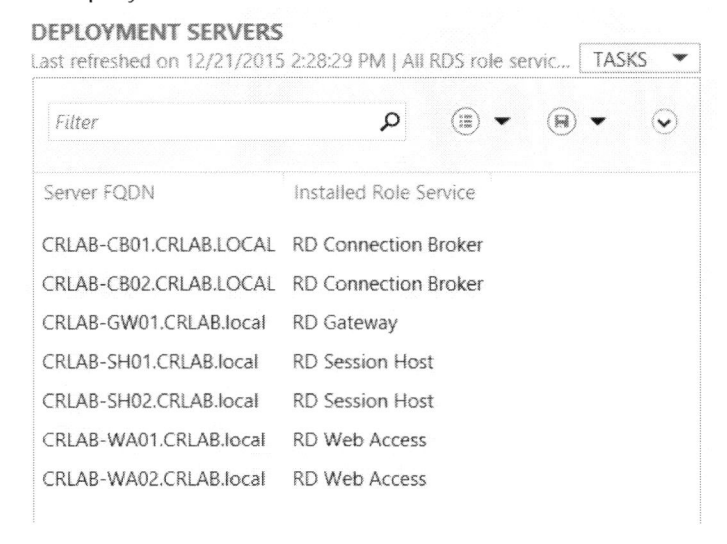

Server FQDN	Installed Role Service
CRLAB-CB01.CRLAB.LOCAL	RD Connection Broker
CRLAB-CB02.CRLAB.LOCAL	RD Connection Broker
CRLAB-GW01.CRLAB.local	RD Gateway
CRLAB-SH01.CRLAB.local	RD Session Host
CRLAB-SH02.CRLAB.local	RD Session Host
CRLAB-WA01.CRLAB.local	RD Web Access
CRLAB-WA02.CRLAB.local	RD Web Access

Now let's take a look at what was done at the 'Deployment' level. Under 'Deployment Servers' click on 'Tasks' and select 'Edit Deployment Properties'.

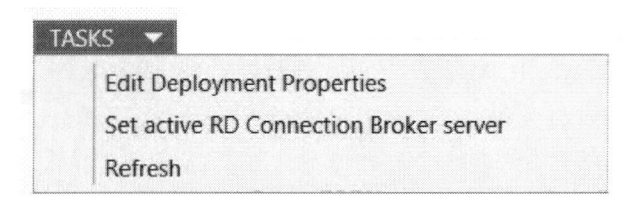

TASKS
- Edit Deployment Properties
- Set active RD Connection Broker server
- Refresh

As you can see under 'RD Gateway' once we used the wizard to add an RDGW to our deployment, it configured everything for us.

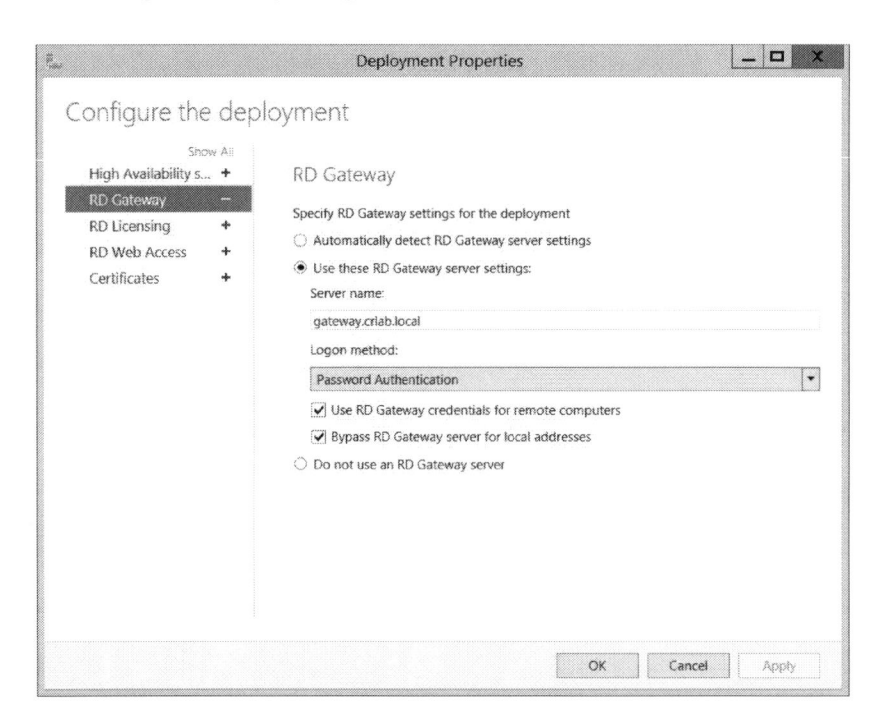

Some of the options we have exposed here are:

- 'Use RD Gateway credentials for remote computers': this setting is part of what allows for a single sign-on experience. This means an end user only enters his credentials once in order to access the environment. These are used on the RDGW and RDSHs. If users are prompted multiple times for their credentials, this is a good place to start your troubleshooting efforts.

- 'Bypass RD Gateway server for local addresses': as the description implies, this allows endpoints on the same network as the deployment to access the RDSHs without going through the gateway.

The RDGW configuration is much more than this though. When we mentioned the deployment wizards take care of all the 'gluing' when adding roles to the environment, we were not kidding. Of course, it takes care of the basics, to give you a working environment. Unfortunately, the 'Server Manager' console is not aware of all these RDGW settings. We still need to use a separate console for this, pretty much the same since the Windows Server 2008 days.

To check it out, logon to the RDGW ('CRLAB-GW01' in our case) and launch the 'Remote Desktop Gateway Manager' from the 'Start' screen.

This will open the 'RD Gateway Manager' console.

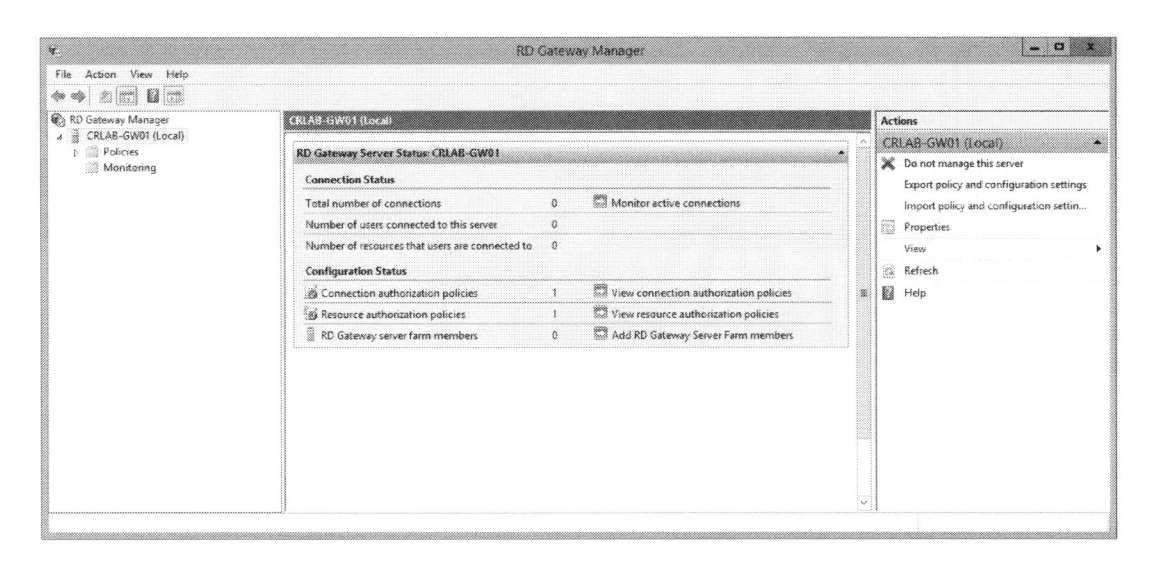

As you remember, the RDGW allows users to connect to the RDS environment over the internet in a secure way, working as an SSL proxy. Of course, for this to happen, the RDGW has to know which users get access to which resources. This is done by configuring two policy types inside the 'RD Gateway Manager'.

Connection Authorization Policy

A Connection Authorization Policy (CAP) defines which users or computers are allowed to access the RDS environment through the RDGW. It also handles device redirection settings (i.e. clipboard, printers, etc) and session timeouts (i.e. idle/active timeouts, etc).

Resource Authorization Policy

A Resource Authorization Policy (RAP) defines which resources (computers) are accessible through the RDGW. We can also configure the port that the RDGW will use when connecting to such resources. By default, this is port 3389/3391 (for RDP TCP/UDP traffic), but of course this varies depending on the resource.

So resuming what seems complicated, in order to connect to a resource that is behind the RDGW (an RDSH or a desktop OS in case of VDI) we need a CAP and a RAP in place (and properly configured). The RDP client passes that information to the RDGW and if a match is found, the connection is allowed. This means the user or the client connecting must be specified in the CAP and the target resource must be specified in the RAP.

Now that you know everything about the RDGW, let's take a deeper look at its configuration.

On the 'RD Gateway Manager' console, expand 'Policies' and select 'Connection Authorization Policies'. You will find a CAP already in place, created by the wizard once we added the RDGW to the deployment.

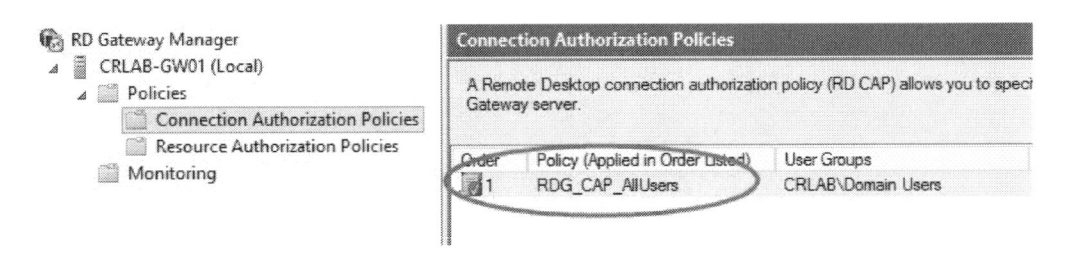

This allows the RDGW to work out of the box. Problem is, even though it works, this configuration is not ideal and you should change it as soon as possible and we will explain why: as you can see under 'User Groups', it lists 'CRLAB\Domain Users'. This means every single user on your domain now has access to the RDS deployment through the gateway. Even worse, the RAP created allows access to any computer on the domain. We can bet this is not what you want so let's change it.

Right-click the default policy created (RDG_CAP_AllUsers) and select 'Properties'.

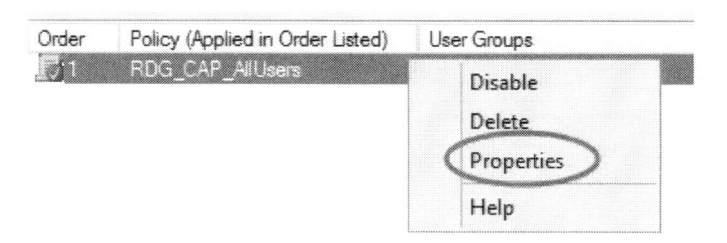

First step is under the 'General' tab, rename it to something more meaningful. A good example would be something like 'CAP_ SD_Basic_Collection'. This way you can easily identify it is a CAP policy that applies to the 'SD Basic Collection' collection that we deployed previously.

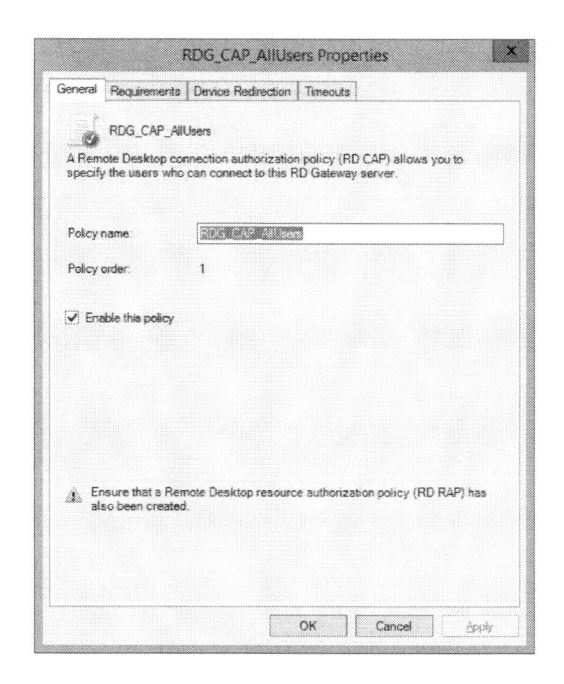

The next tab, 'Requirements', is probably the most important one on the RDGW. Here we define which resources (again, users or computers) can use the RDGW to connect. As mentioned, the wizard adds the 'Domain Users' by default what is really not a great idea.

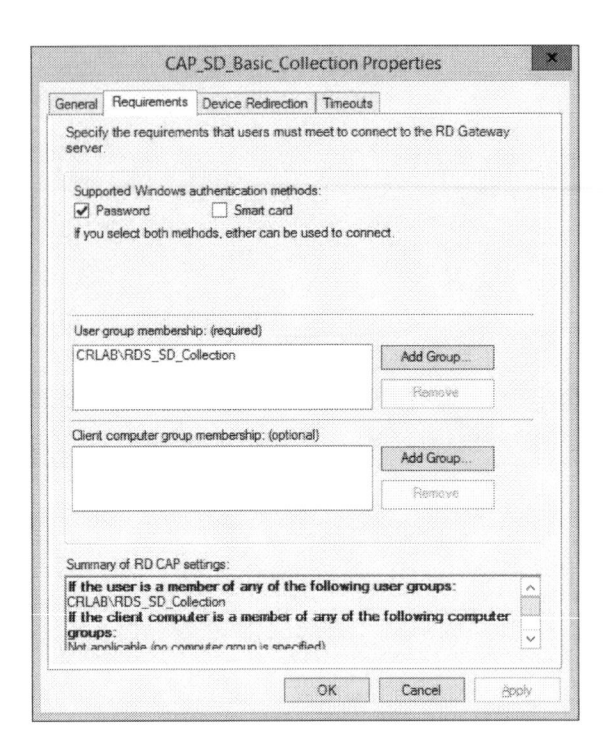

To fix this, select 'CRLAB\Domain Users' and click 'Remove'. Then click 'Add Group...' and add the group we created previously, 'RDS_SD_Collection'.

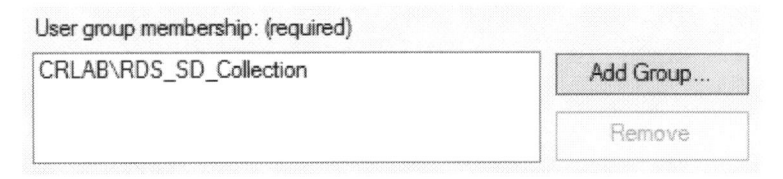

As you can see (and we mentioned that) you can also add client computers to the CAP. Problem is this requires these to be domain joined and in most cases when providing access to RDS over the internet, this is not something you want. Of course you can combine these two group memberships in one CAP. The end result is a CAP where the user trying to connect must be a member of the specified groups and the client computer must be member of the specified groups as well. Basically an 'AND' and not an 'OR'. Keep that in mind when troubleshooting connectivity issues through the RDGW.

The next tab, 'Device Redirection' can be used to enforce redirection settings. If you remember, we discussed these settings before as they are part of a session collection. By default, this CAP is configured to allow redirection of all client devices.

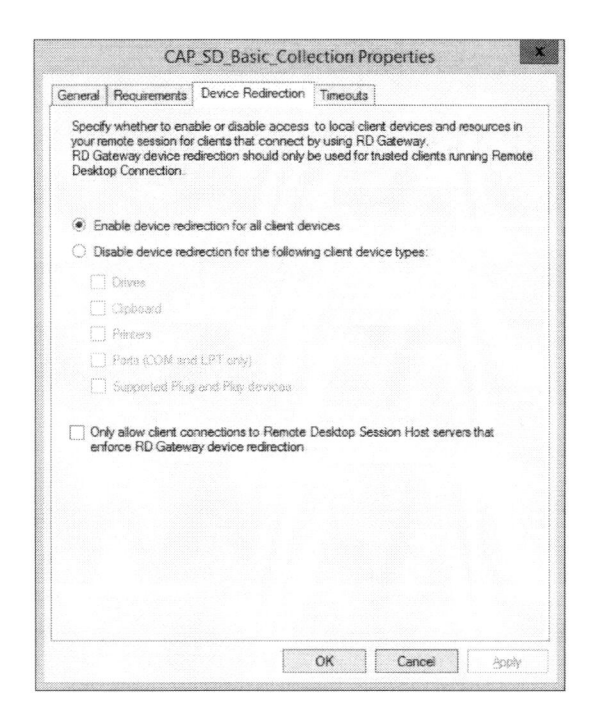

The final tab, 'Timeouts', as the name implies, controls timeout settings. This was also there, part of a session collection. Yes, these are the RDP timeouts for the sessions.

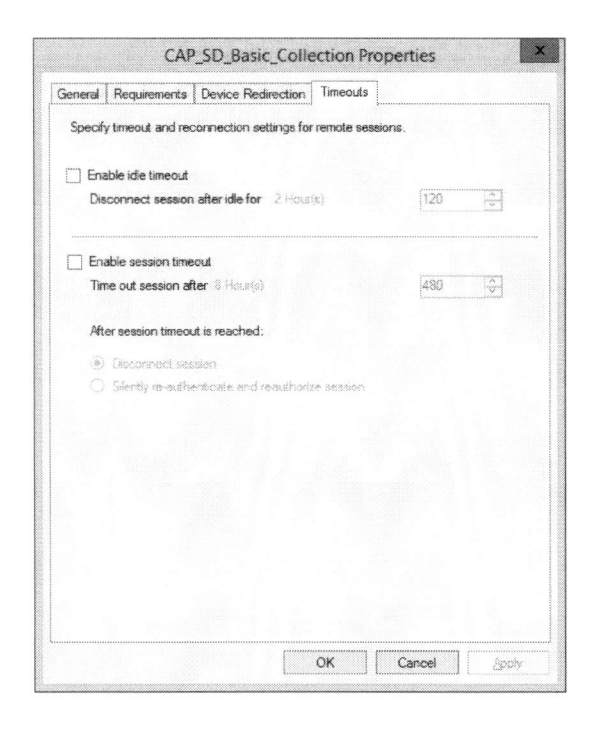

Now that we fixed the RAP, time to take a look at the RAP the wizard created. Right-click the RAP 'RDG_AllDomainComputers' and select 'Properties'.

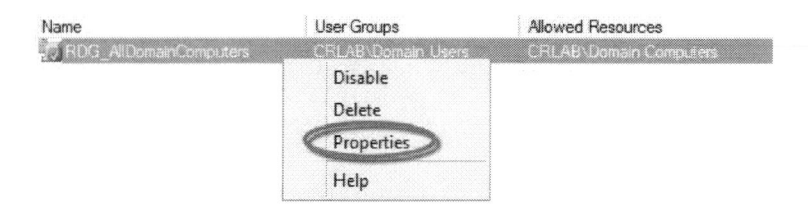

Under the 'General' tab we will rename the RAP to something more appropriate.

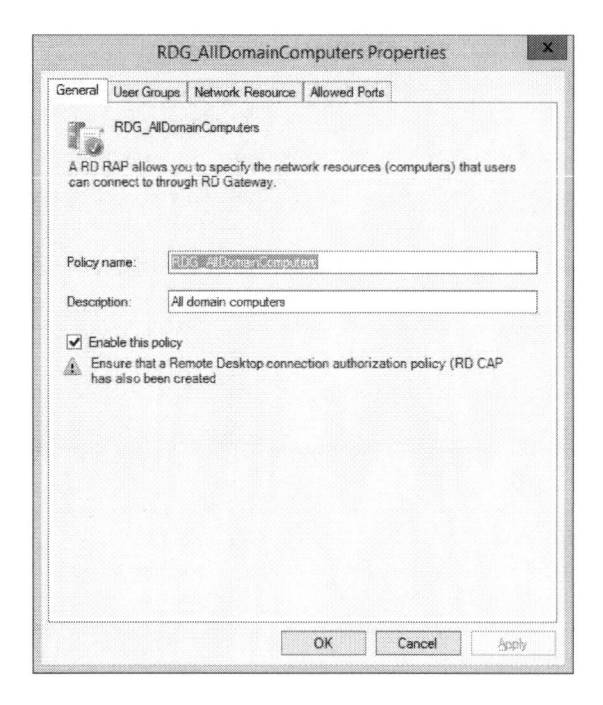

As before we suggest you change it to 'RAP_SD_Basic_Collection' so it follows the same standard as our CAP and matches our session collection.

On the 'User Groups' tab we can define the groups we would like to allow access to the resources on the RAP. You might be asking yourself why we have to specify groups in both places, CAP and RAP. The answer is simple but at the same time potentially confusing. This allows you to create a single CAP with a broader group of users on it and then create multiple RAPs containing smaller groups, each one accessing different resources. If you only have one group of users that will access the exact same resources, then it makes sense to use in the RAP the exact same group you used in the CAP. Got it?

So remove the 'CRLAB\Domain Users' group and add our 'RDS_SD_Collection' group for this RAP.

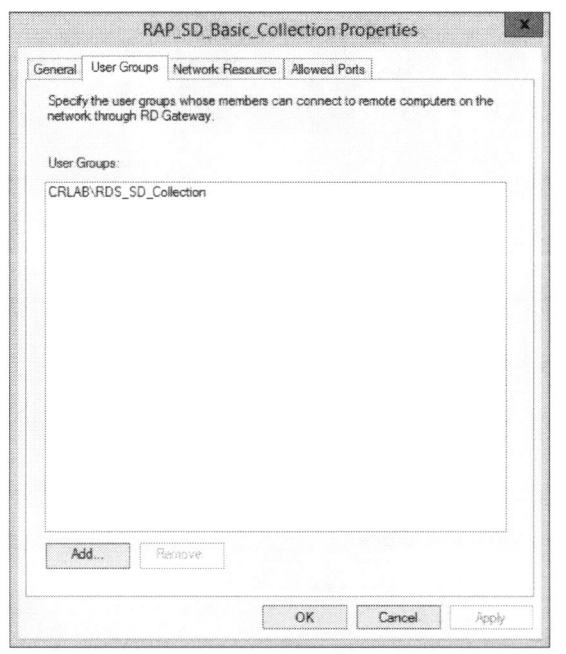

In the 'Network Resources' tab, we specify the resources that will be accessible to the users. As you can see the wizard basically gives all your users access to all computers within your domain. No good.

ⓘ **Note:** The fact the default RAP and CAP created during the installation of the 'RD Gateway' role allow access to all domain computers by all domain users might sound scary. And it is. However, that said, note that such users would still need remote access to the resource in question. This means the user also needs to be a member of the 'Remote Desktop Users' group on that resource. Regardless, we still advise you to change the default CAP and RAP according to your needs immediately after the installation of the 'RD Gateway' role. You have been warned.

So change the default setting to allow access only to our RDSHs. As we have not created such group yet, time to do it. Create a group called 'RDS_SD_Collection_Servers' and add both RDSHs to it ('CRLAB-SH01' and 'CRLAB-SH02').

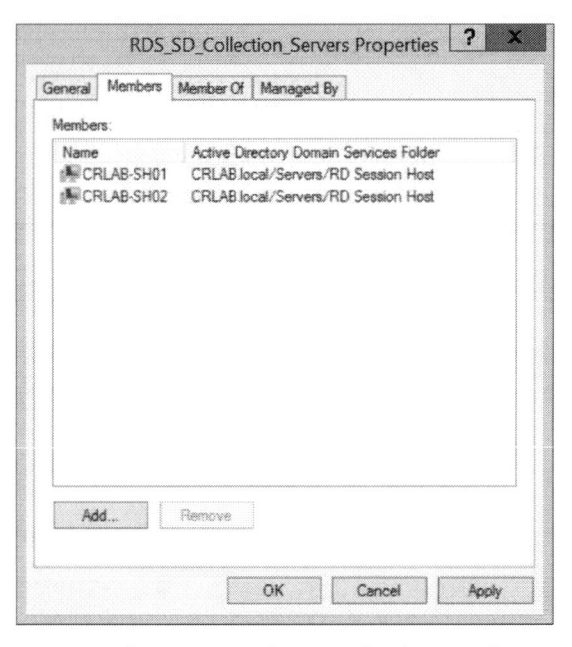

We can then add this group to the RAP, replacing the 'CRLAB\Domain Computers' group.

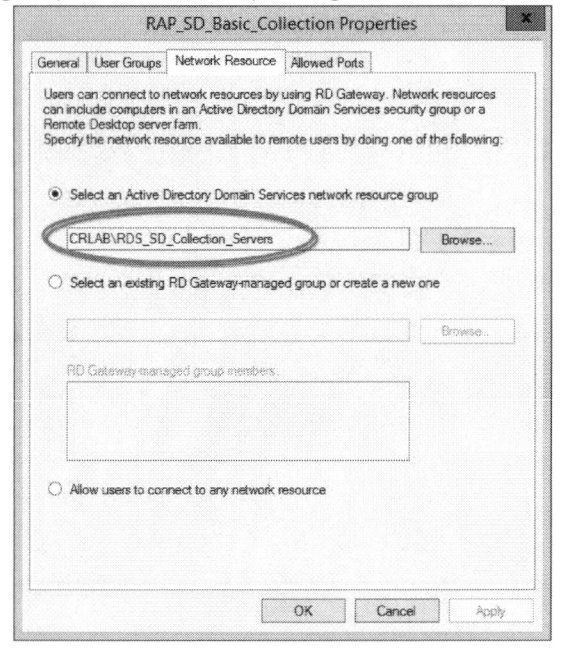

If you noticed, there is also an option called 'Select an existing RD Gateway-managed group or create a new one'. So what is this? It is actually a cool feature of the RDGW. Imagine you would like to use the RDGW to allow users to connect to a resource that is not part of your domain (or forest). An RDGW managed group allows you to define a group that exists only inside the RDGW itself. For example, you could create a group called 'My Resources' and add resources to it based on hostnames, FQDNs or even IP addresses. As long as the RDGW can resolve and reach such resources you are good to go. Interesting eh?

ⓘ **Note:** this is a very important one. When using RDCB HA, you must use RDGW managed groups as the RDCB HA FQDN (the DNS name) is not a computer object in AD. So, click 'Select an existing RD Gateway-managed group or create a new one' and create a new group. Add the RDCB HA FQDN and all the RDSHs (both FQDNs and IP addresses) to the group. Otherwise, you will get an error like this:

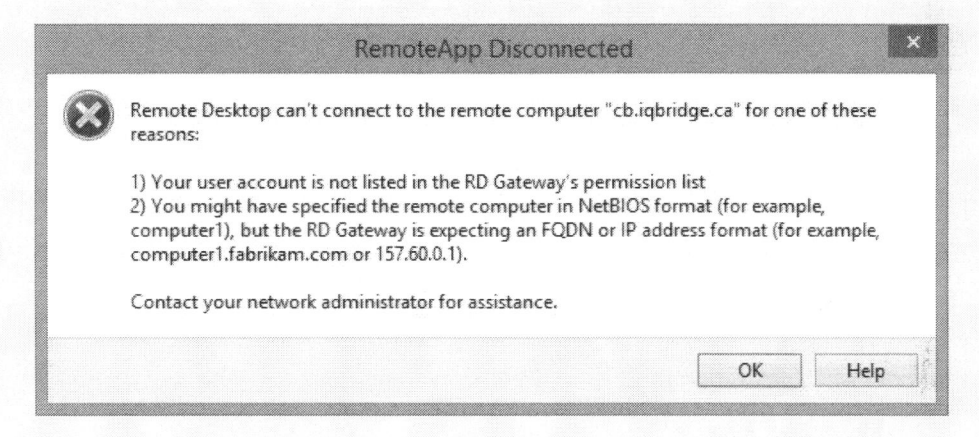

The group should be similar to this:

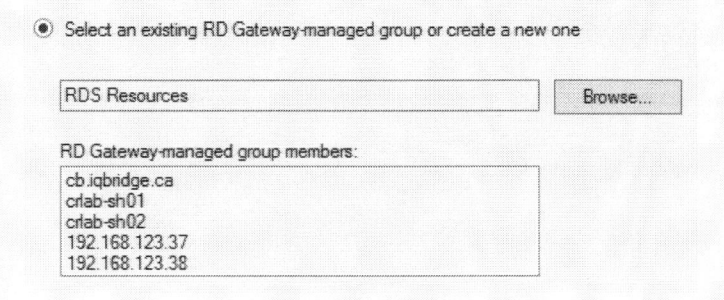

The final tab, 'Allowed Ports', does what it says. Here you define the ports that will be accessible. By default, port 3389 (RDP TCP) is there but you can define a different port, or even multiple ports if needed for a particular resource.

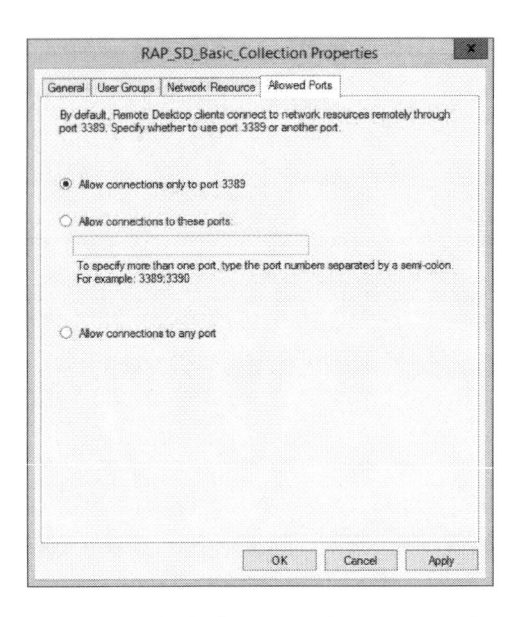

That is all for CAPs and RAPs. Hopefully by now the RDGW does not look like that crazy black box anymore.

> ⓘ **Note:** A good way of preserving the RDGW configuration is by exporting it on a regular basis, or before any changes are performed, to a secure location. This way you not only have a track record all changes but can easily revert these in case something happens. Exporting and importing can be done by right-clicking the server inside the 'RD Gateway Manager' console and selecting 'Export policy and configuration settings' or 'Import policy and configuration settings'. All the settings are stored in a .xml file. Pretty handy.

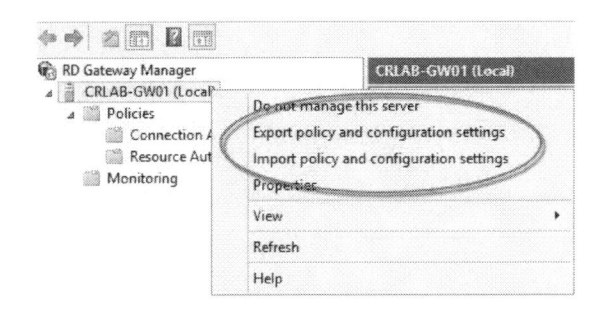

You can also use the 'RD Gateway Manager' console to monitor all sessions going through the RDGW. Simply click on 'Monitoring'. From there, on the right hand pane you will see all sessions (and if you feel like, disconnect them).

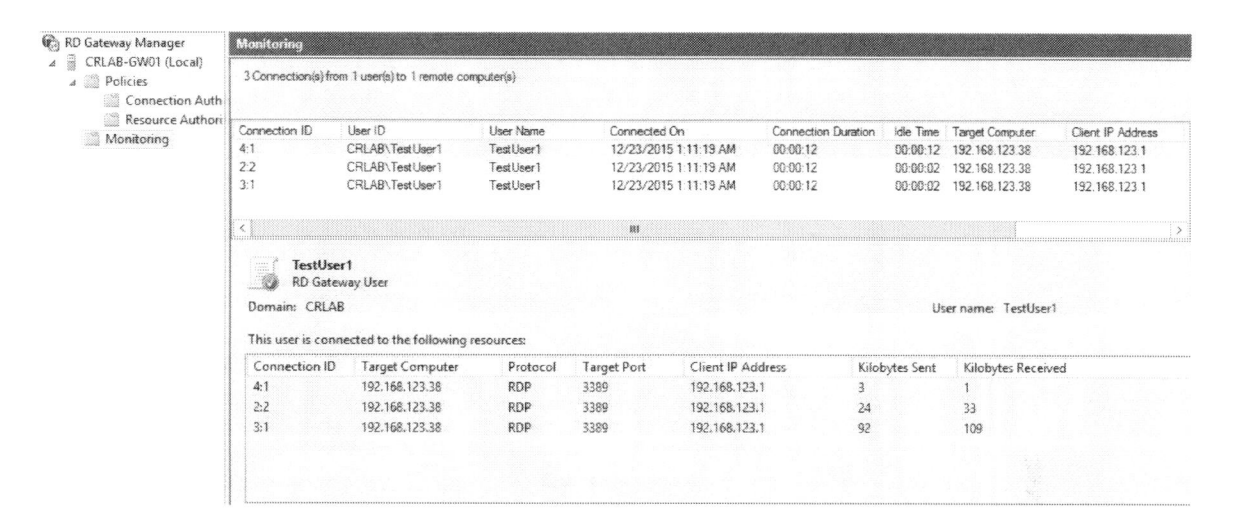

Connection ID	User ID	User Name	Connected On	Connection Duration	Idle Time	Target Computer	Client IP Address
4:1	CRLAB\TestUser1	TestUser1	12/23/2015 1:11:19 AM	00:00:12	00:00:12	192.168.123.38	192.168.123.1
2:2	CRLAB\TestUser1	TestUser1	12/23/2015 1:11:19 AM	00:00:12	00:00:02	192.168.123.38	192.168.123.1
3:1	CRLAB\TestUser1	TestUser1	12/23/2015 1:11:19 AM	00:00:12	00:00:02	192.168.123.38	192.168.123.1

TestUser1 — RD Gateway User
Domain: CRLAB   User name: TestUser1

This user is connected to the following resources:

Connection ID	Target Computer	Protocol	Target Port	Client IP Address	Kilobytes Sent	Kilobytes Received
4:1	192.168.123.38	RDP	3389	192.168.123.1	3	1
2:2	192.168.123.38	RDP	3389	192.168.123.1	24	33
3:1	192.168.123.38	RDP	3389	192.168.123.1	92	109

ⓘ **Note:** the 'Monitoring' section in the 'RD Gateway Manager' shows multiple connections per session. This is because Windows Server 2012 and up (using RDP protocol 8.X and up) is able to communicate with clients using both TCP and UDP transports. UDP provides a much better experience over challenging WAN conditions (i.e. 3G/LTE). Of course, UDP may not always work due to proxies, firewalls and so on. In such cases, the RDP 8.X protocol and up will automatically fall back to TCP only. We will discuss this in more details in the RemoteFX section.

Setting up RDGW HA

Now that we have multiple RDCBs, RDSHs and even RDWAs, the next step is to make sure your RDGWs are highly available. So how can we achieve that?

If you remember how we addressed the RDWAs HA, the process is the same with one exception: you cannot use DNS RR and we will explain why. As you noticed under 'Monitoring' on the 'RD Gateway Manager' a client ends up using multiple ports due to the UDP transport. However, there is more to the problem. With RDS 2012, Microsoft made a fundamental change on how the RDGW works, in order to maximize its performance.

When a client connects to the RDGW, two SSL tunnels are established from the client to the RDGW (for incoming/outcoming traffic). The RDGW then establishes a main channel over each tunnel for communications, relying on what is called a 'transport' to create such channels. Back in the RDS 2008 R2 days this was done using RPC over HTTP. Due to the way it works, performance quickly degraded when handling multiple clients. With RDS 2012 Microsoft added a pure HTTP transport, making it much more scalable. This is what clients using RDP 8.X and higher will attempt to use when connecting. For backwards compatibility, the RPC over HTTP transport is still there. That is why DNS RR cannot be used anymore. The traffic cannot be split over multiple gateways as it could be done using RPC over HTTP.

So, with DNS RR out of the picture, what are your options? The exact same two as before, NLB and hardware load balancers.

The NLB process is exactly the same as before but with a minor difference: you will need two ports (by default, TCP 443 and UDP 3391).

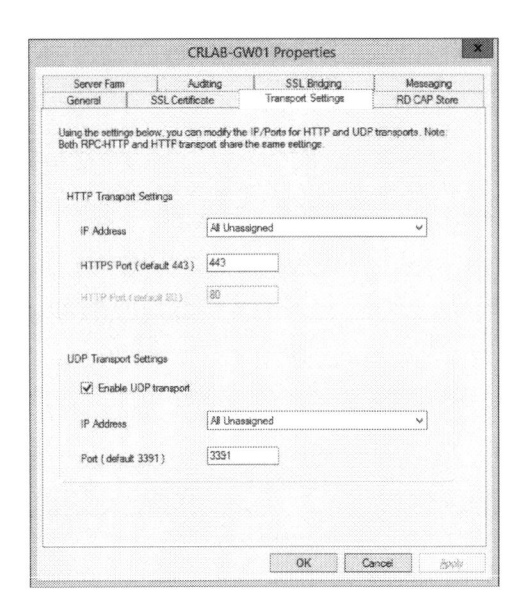

So resuming, this is how you make your RDGWs highly available:

1. Add a second RDGW to the deployment.
2. Use the exact same certificate on the RDGW you just added. To do this, simply reapply the gateway certificate using the 'Certificates' section under the deployment properties.

3. Export the RDGW configuration from the first RDGW and import it on the one you just added. This is required so all your RAPs and CAPs are the same on all RDGWs.
4. Use NLB or a hardware load balancer to create a VIP for the load balanced RDGW pair, load balancing ports TCP 443 and UDP 3391 (this time with affinity).
5. Modify or create a DNS record for the RDGW VIP.

I guess it is time to do it.

1. Launch 'Server Manager' (in our case on CRLAB-DC01) and select '3. Add other servers to manage'.

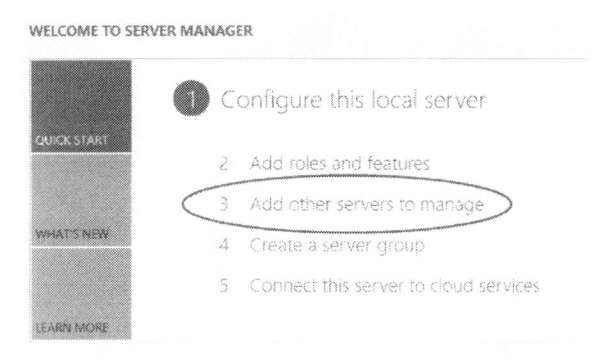

2. Type crlab-gw under 'Name(CN)' and click 'Find Now'. This will return all servers with names starting with CRLAB-GW. Select 'CRLAB-GW02' and click the arrow button to add it to the right pane. Click 'Ok'

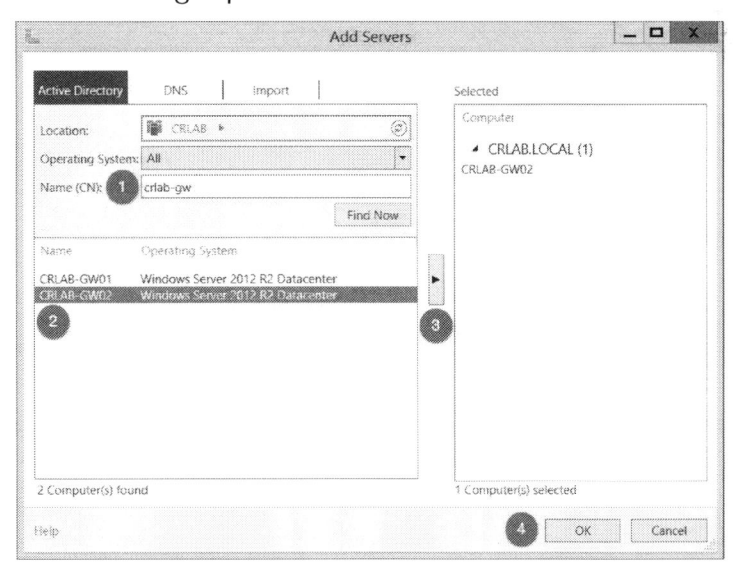

3. Now click on 'Remote Desktop Services' on the left. This will open the 'Overview' page we are now very familiar with. Under 'Deployment Overview' right-click the 'RD Gateway' icon and select 'Add RD Gateway Servers'.

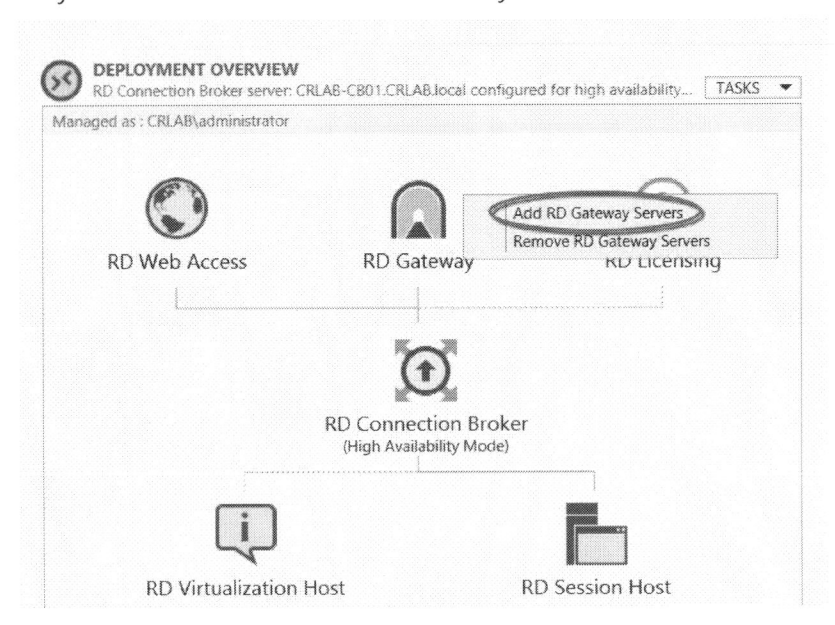

4. Select 'CRLAB-GW02', click the arrow button and click 'Next'.

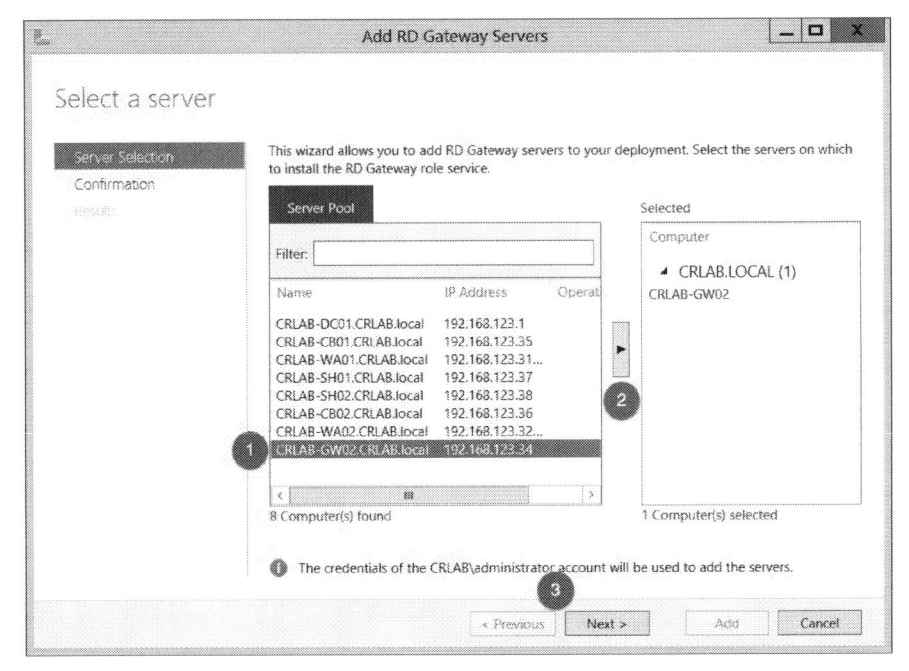

Page 156 | RDS - The Complete Guide

5. As we already have one RDGW in our deployment, the wizard shows us the FQDN in use. Just click 'Add'.

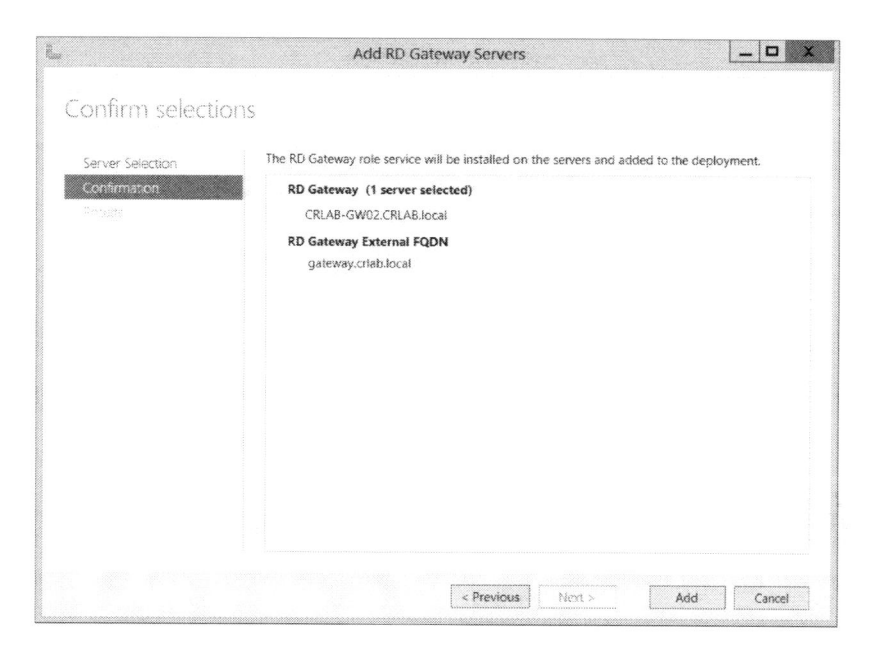

6. If everything worked as expected, you should see 'Succeeded' under 'Status'. Click 'Close'.

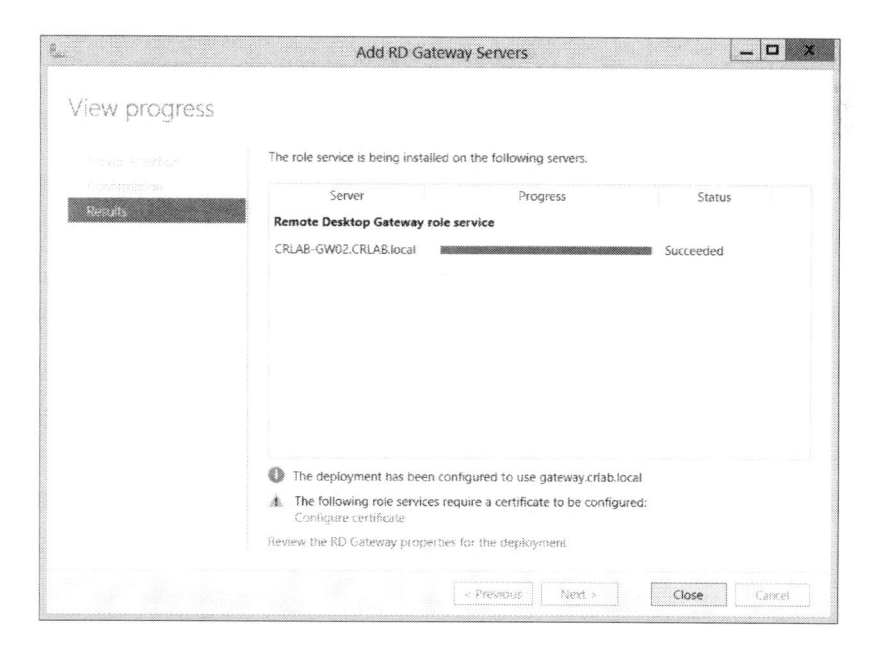

7. Now you must reapply the certificate to the RDGWs. Simply do that under the deployment properties.

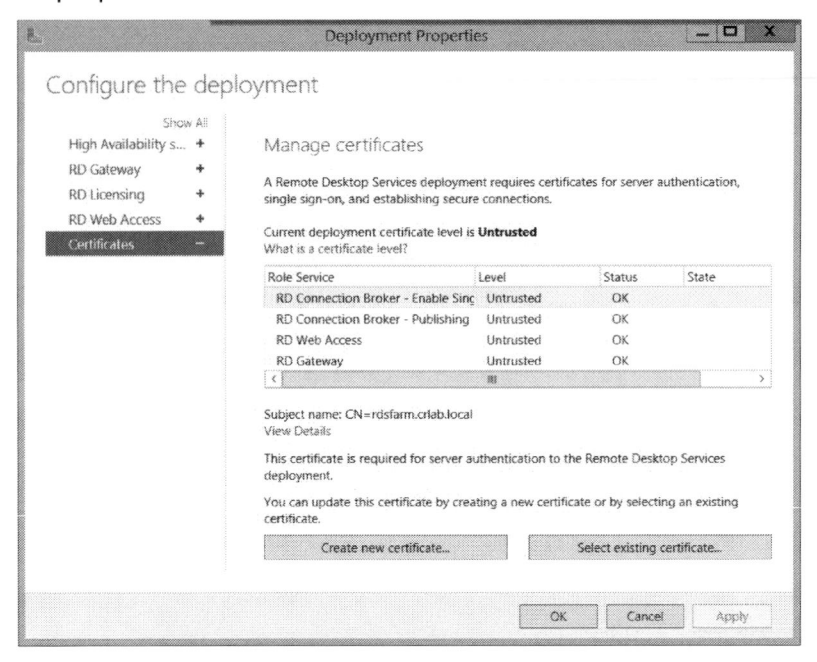

8. Finally, export the configuration on 'CRLAB-GW01' and import it to 'CRLAB-GW02' so the RAPs and CAPs are identical.

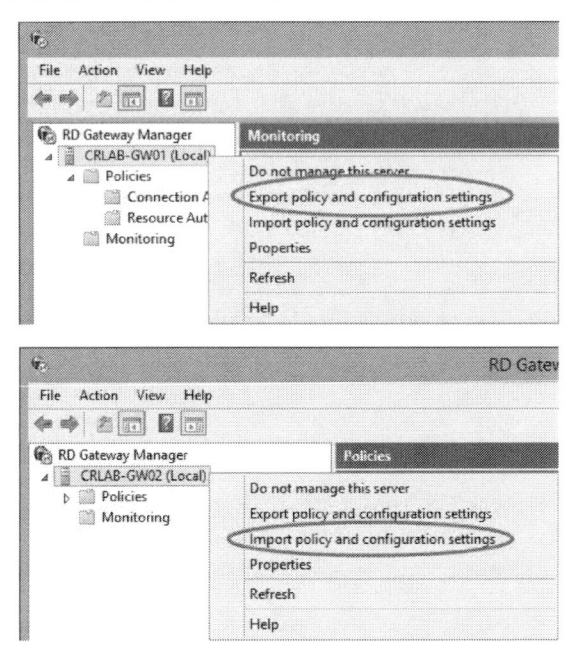

9. Once done, proceed with the NLB setup so we have a VIP for our RDGWs. On CRLAB-DC01 (or directly at the RDWAs) launch 'Server Manager' and click '2. Add Roles and Features'.

10. The wizard starts. Click 'Next'.

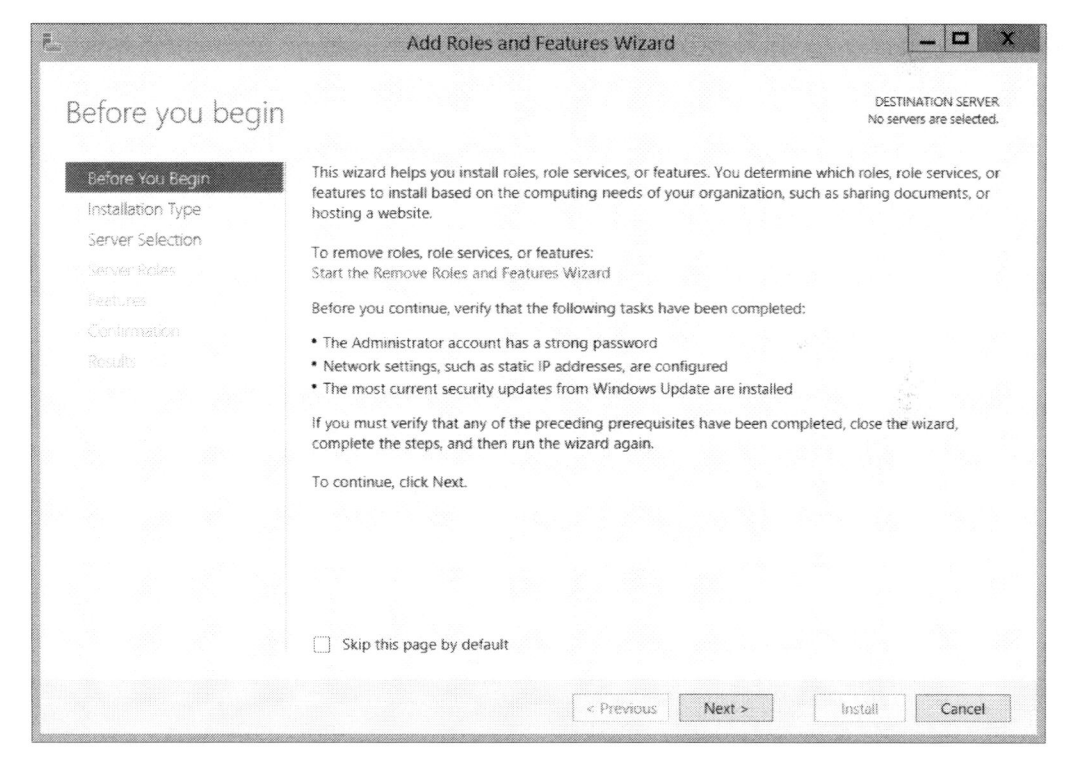

11. Select 'Role-based or feature-based installation' and click 'Next'.

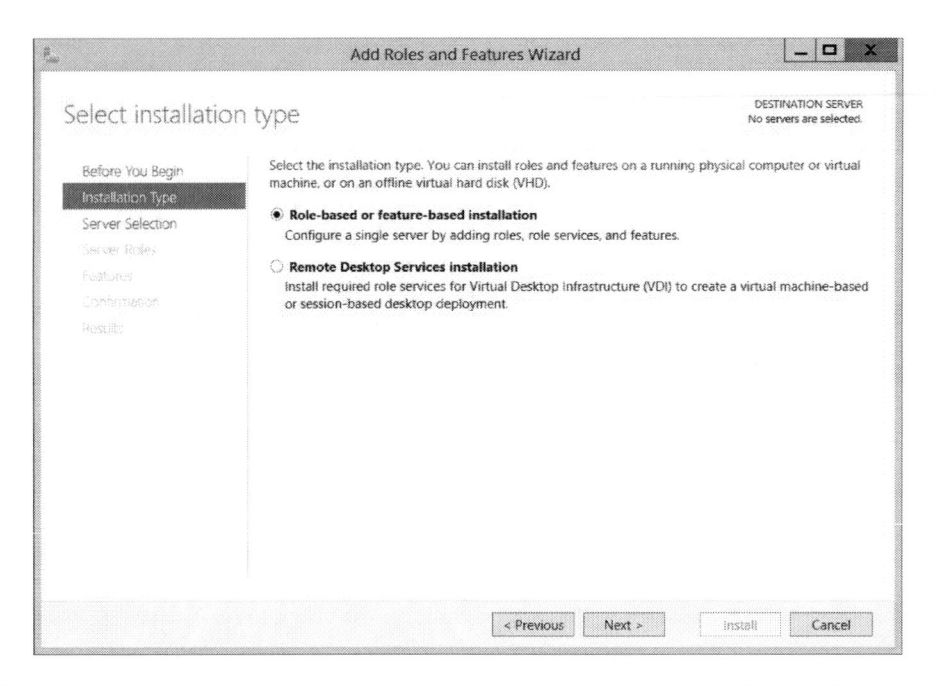

12. We have to do it one server at a time so select 'CRLAB-GW01' and click 'Next'.

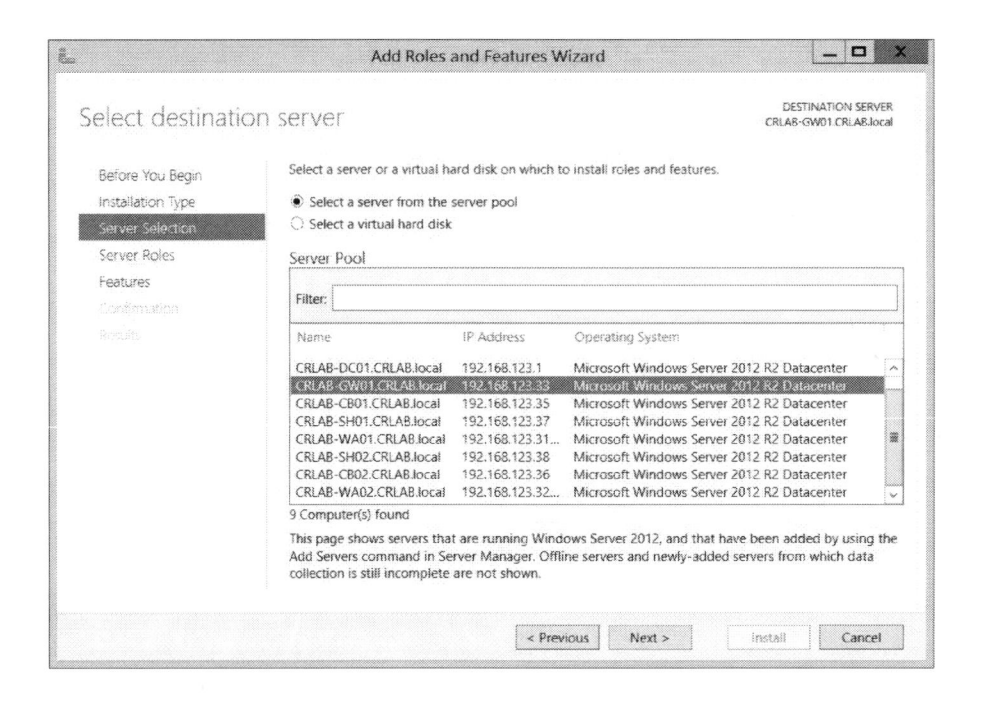

13. As NLB is just a feature (and not a role), simply click directly on 'Features' and select 'Network Load Balancing' (you may have to scroll down). Click 'Next'.

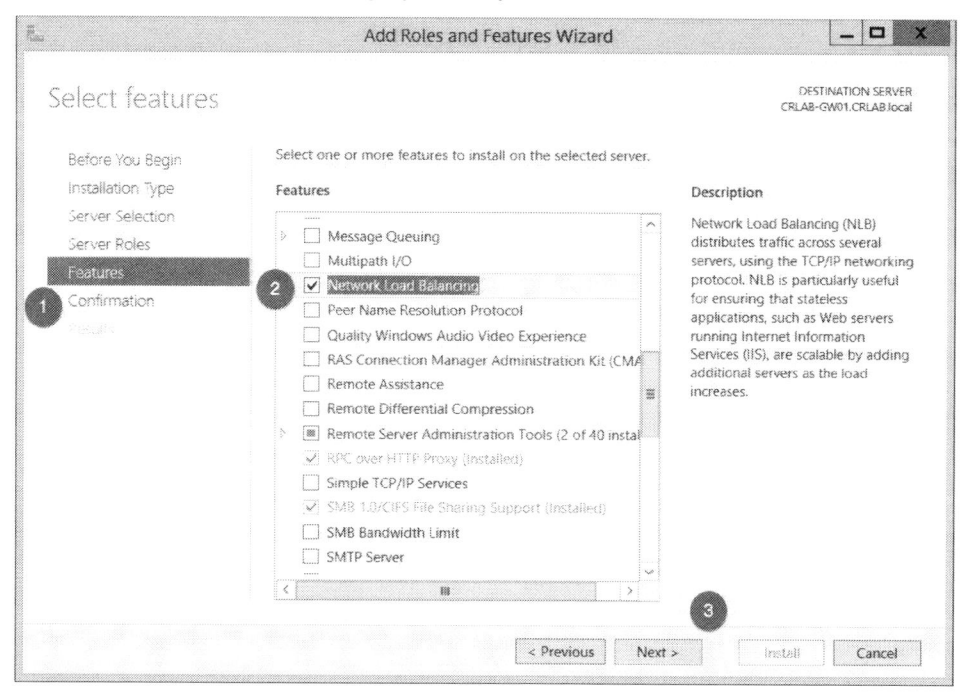

14. It will prompt you to install the 'Network Load Balancing Tools' for management purposes. Simply click 'Add Features'.

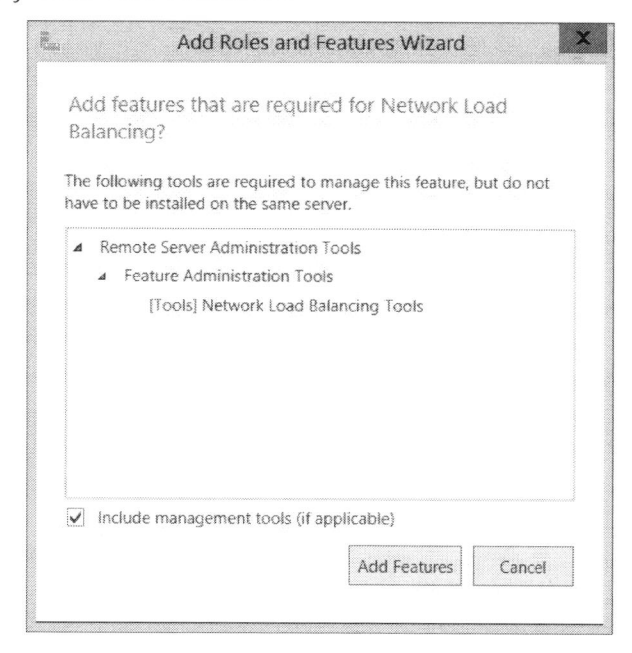

15. Check 'Restart the destination server automatically if required' just to make sure no restarts stay pending. Click 'Install'.

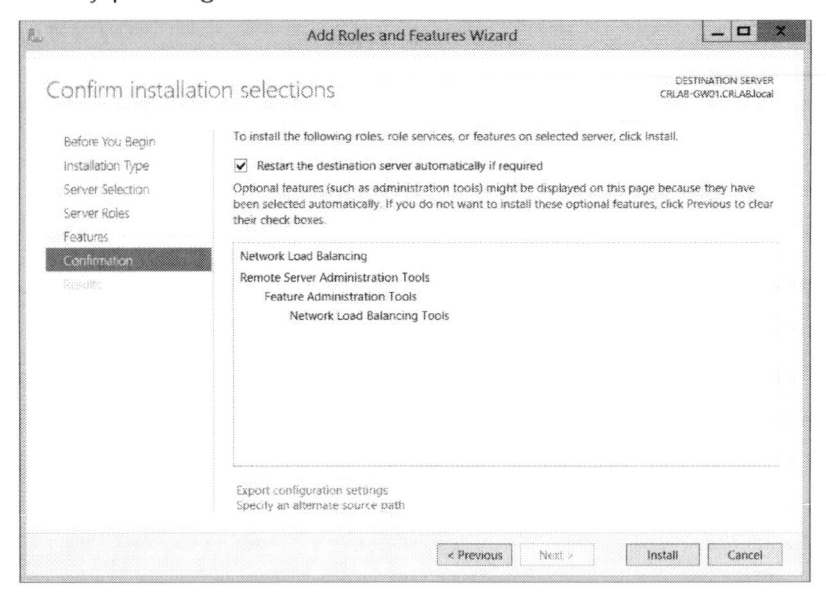

16. If everything works as expected, you should get an 'Installation succeeded' message. Click 'Close'.

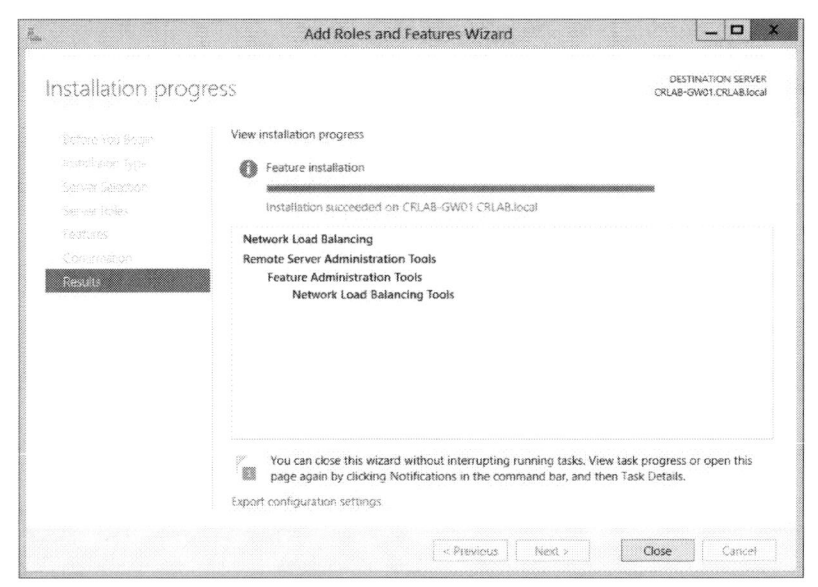

17. Simply repeat steps 7 to 13 but this time selecting 'CRLAB-GW02' as the target server where NLB will be added.

18. We are now ready to configure NLB for our RDGWs. Connect to 'CRLAB-GW01' and launch the 'Network Load Balancing manager' from the start screen.

19. The first step is to create a new cluster (the logical group containing all the servers we will be load balancing, the ports in use and so on). Right click 'Network Load Balancing Clusters' and select 'New Cluster'.

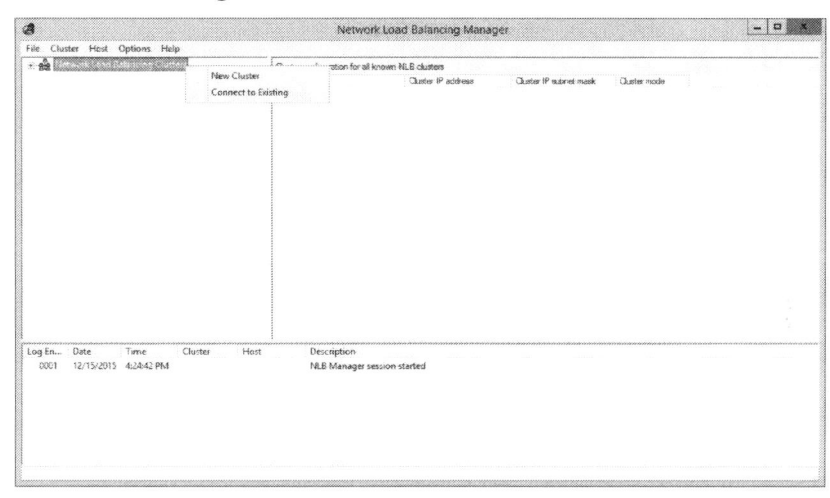

20. Now enter the name for the first server that we want as part of the cluster (in this case 'CRLAB-GW01') and click 'Connect'. This will show you the network interfaces on that server under 'Interfaces available for configuring a new cluster'. Select the right one (based on your network topology) and click 'Next'.

21. Simply accept the defaults and click 'Next'.

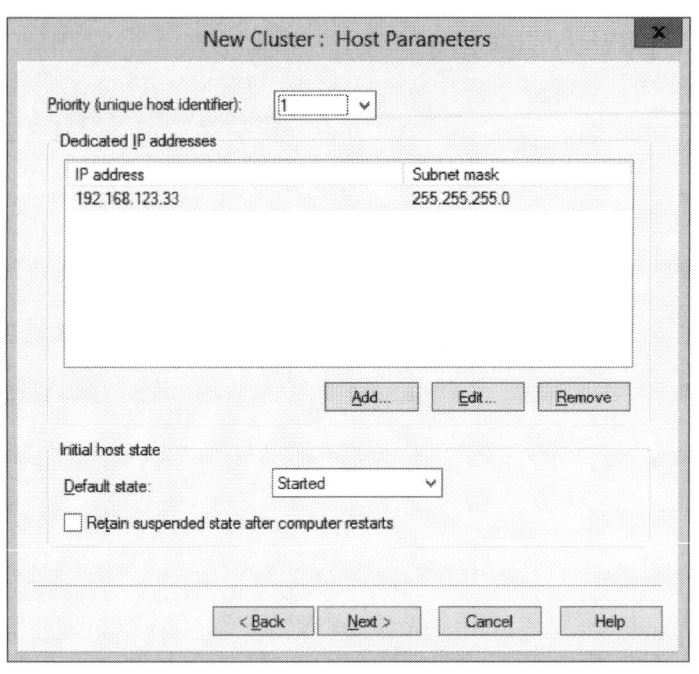

22. Now we have to specify the cluster IP address (this is referred in other load balancers like a Citrix NetScaler as a Virtual IP Address or VIP). It is the IP that will be used by clients to access the load balanced RDGW pair. Click 'Add'.

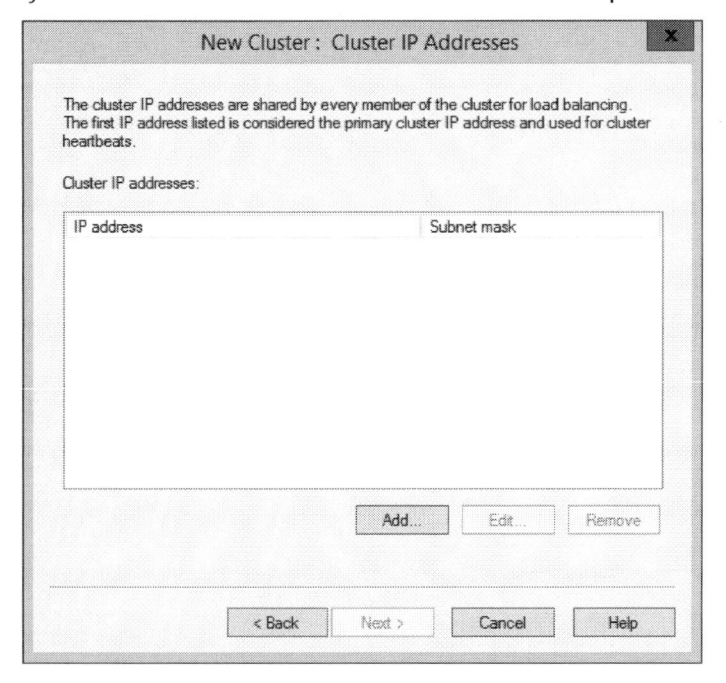

23. Enter an address not in use. Click 'OK' and then 'Next'.

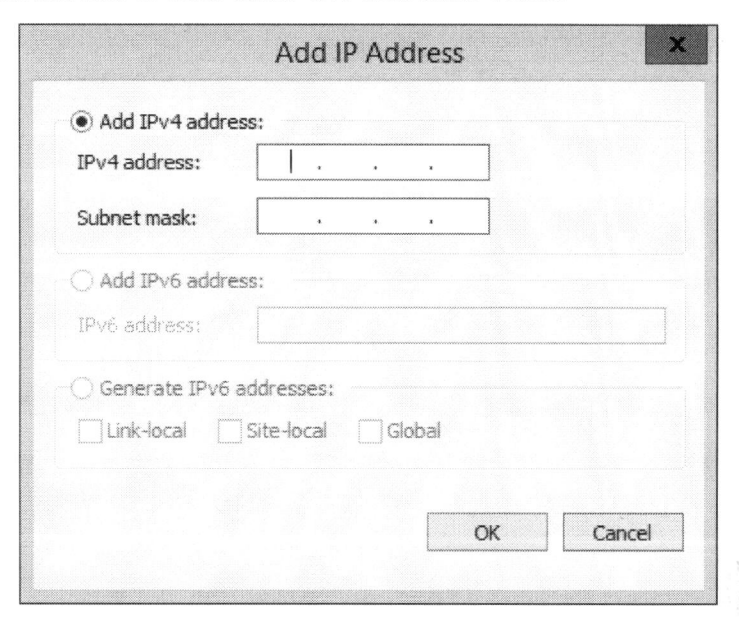

24. Under 'Full Internet name' enter the FQDN we chose when creating the certificate for the RDGW, 'gateway.crlab.local'. This is the name clients will use to connect to the RDGW pair. Again, as you can see in this case, we are using internal names (.crlab.local) so this will not work for external clients. We will get to that later. Just keep that in mind for now. Click 'Next'.

> ⓘ **Note:** If you only have a single network interface on the RDGWA=s (the case in our lab) make sure you use 'Multicast' for the cluster, if you do want to be able to RDP to any of the RDGWs later. Yes, we learned the hard way.

25. By default, NLB assumes you want to use all the ports for your VIP. In this case we need TCP 443 (HTTPS) and UDP 3391 (for the UDP transport). Unlike the RDWA VIP, for this we do want affinity. Click 'Edit'.

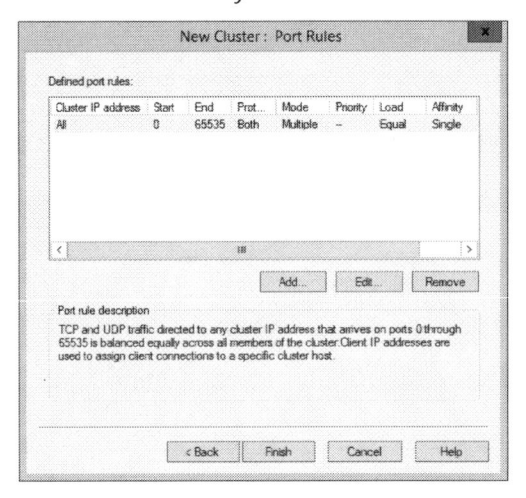

26. Change the ports used, the protocol and affinity (you need to do it twice, one for TCP 443, one for UDP 3391). Click 'OK' then click 'Finish'.

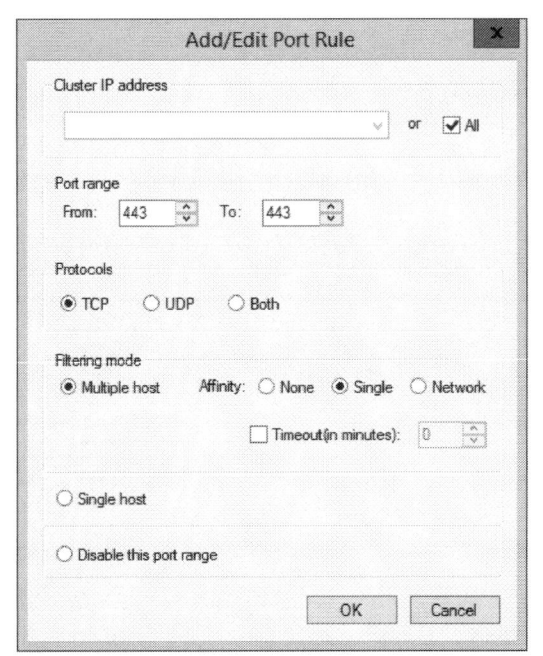

Page 166 | RDS - The Complete Guide

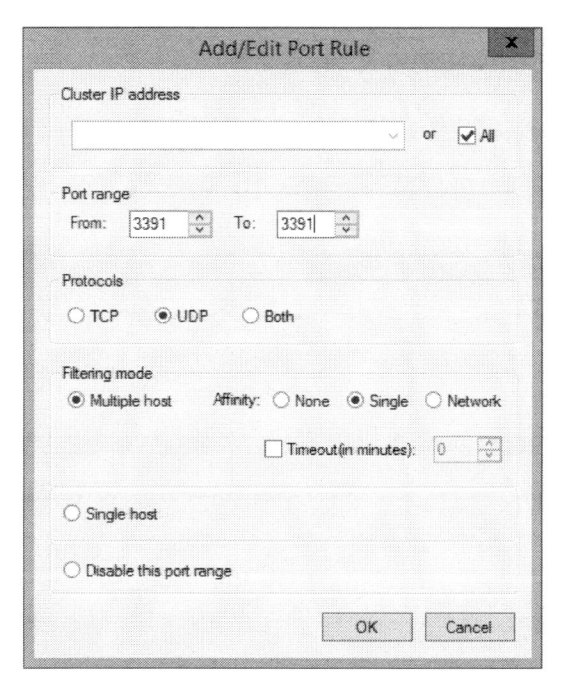

The configuration process may take a minute or so. Once it is done, you should see your NLB cluster up and running with one RDGW part of it.

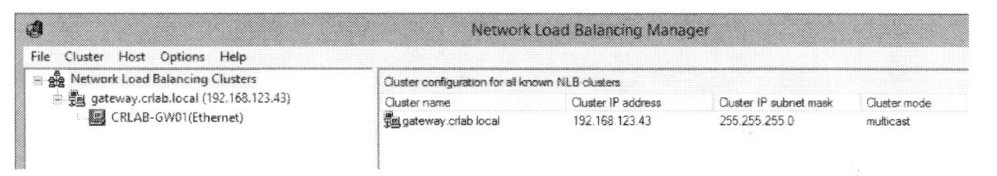

27. The final step is to add the remaining RDGW to it. Right click the cluster name (gateway.crlab.local) and select 'Add Host To Cluster'.

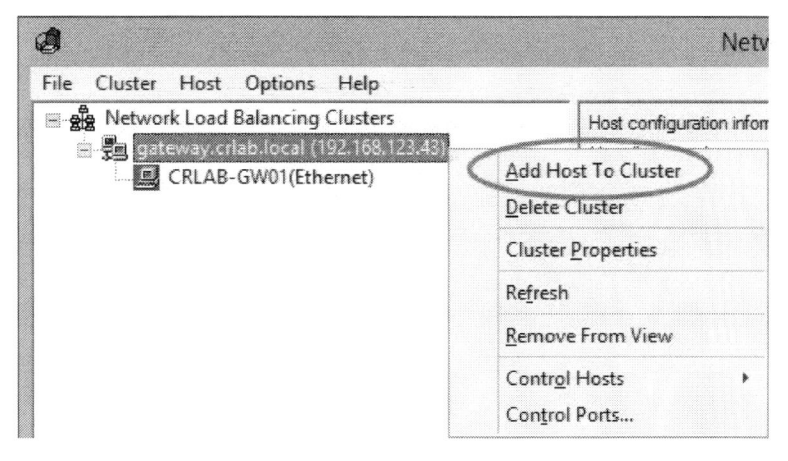

28. Enter 'CRLAB-GW02' under 'Host' and click 'Connect'. It should show you the network interface available. Select it and click 'Next'.

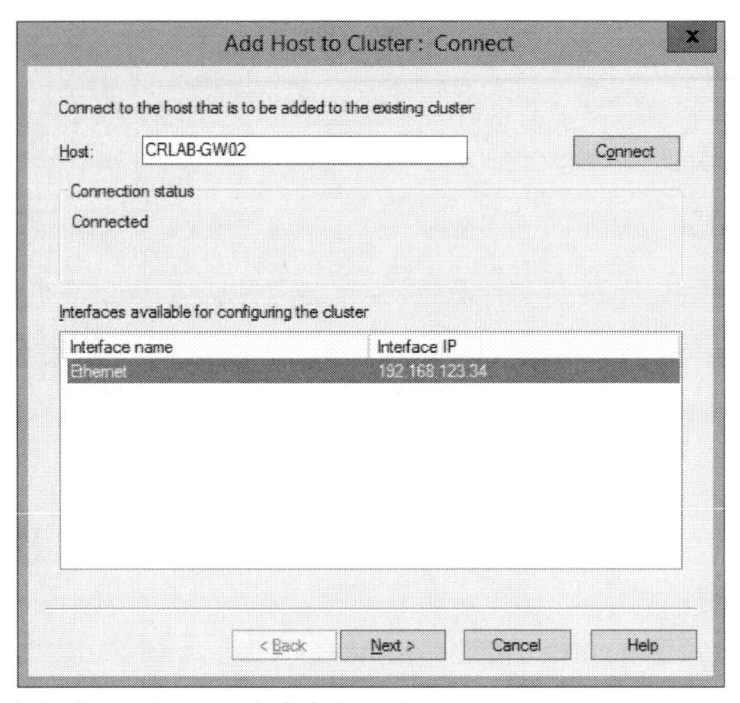

29. Accept the default settings and click 'Next'.

30. It will show you the correct port and settings currently in use in the cluster. Click 'Finish'.

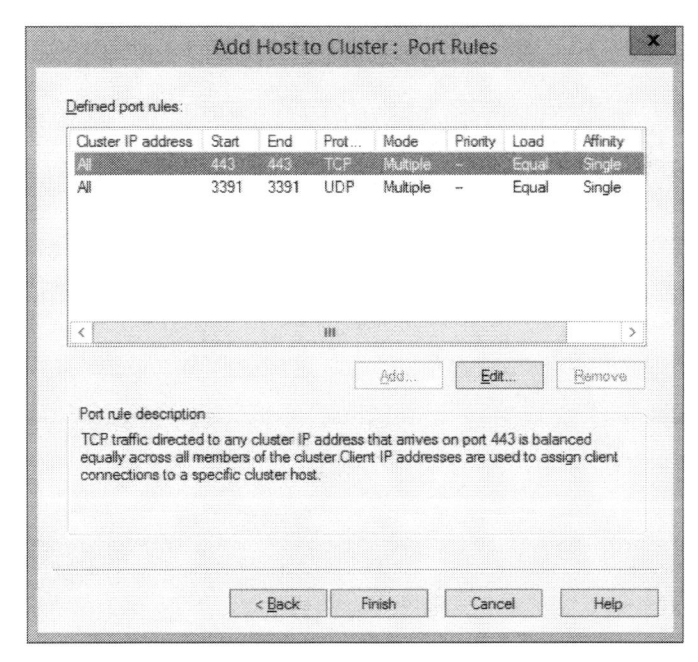

31. As before, it may take a while until everything is ready. The result is an NLB cluster with our two RDGWs on it, load balanced on port TCP 443 (HTTPS), UDP 3391 and accessible on the FQDN 'gateway.crlab.local' (once we tweak the DNS record of course).

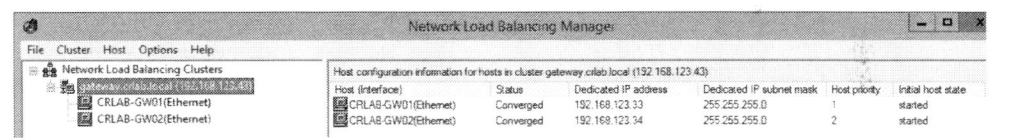

32. The last step is to update the DNS entry we created previously for the 'gateway.crlab.local' FQDN, pointing it to the VIP of the cluster (in this case 192.168.123.43).

    gateway   Host (A)   192.168.123.43

33. You can test the configuration by launching Internet Explorer and opening https://web.crlab.local/rdweb as multiple different users from different machines. This will connect the users using both RDGWs. Keep in mind you will need the certificate for the gateway (and ideally for RDWA and the RDCB),

loaded on all clients, under 'Trusted Root Certification Authorities' (if you are using self-signed or internally issued certificates on non-domain joined PCs).

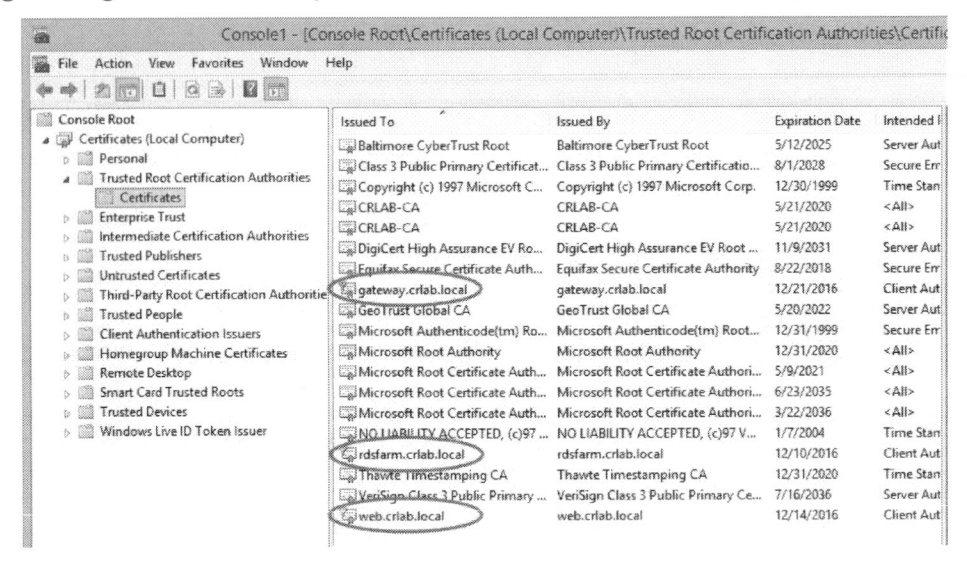

[Screenshot of Console1 showing Trusted Root Certification Authorities certificates, with gateway.crlab.local, rdsfarm.crlab.local, and web.crlab.local circled.]

That is all for RDGW NLB.

Adding RDLS

We are sure that one of the most discussed topics on the Microsoft forums regarding RDS is licensing (or printing, the two evils). We can definitely see the reasons for that. Since Windows NT 4.0 Server, Terminal Server Edition came out, people did not understand exactly how licensing worked. Fast forward it to 2018 and guess what? People still have no clue how licensing works, especially if you add VDI to the mix (let's not get into that – it would be a subject for a whole new book and sadly with no happy ending).

Even though it may seem confusing, if you read this section carefully we are sure you will understand how it works and will be able to figure out exactly what you need.

And before you ask us this question, RDS is not a license saving solution or miracle; although you are installing applications on the server itself (i.e. Microsoft Office) what could mean a single machine (if you have a single server RDS environment), this does not mean you will need only one single application license. Remember that multiple users will be able to access the application you just installed and therefore you must have as many licenses as needed to be legal. The savings you will have on an RDS environment do not come from software licensing.

Another key thing to keep in mind is what your application EULA says about running it under RDS. Certain applications may explicitly mention that running them under RDS violates its EULA. So, make sure you read the EULA for every single off-the-shelf application you intend to deploy under RDS and in case of doubt, contact the manufacturer.

Requirements

For each client connecting to a Windows Server 2012 R2 Session Host ('RDSH'), two licenses are required:

- Windows Server, Client Access License (CAL). A Windows Server 2012 R2 Client Access License (CAL) is required for each user or device (or combination of both) that accesses or uses the server software.

- Windows Server, Remote Desktop Services Client Access License (RDSCAL). RDSCALs are available in Per User/Per Device mode only. In Per User or Per Device mode, a separate RDSCAL is required for each user or device that accesses or uses the server software on any server. You may reassign an RDSCAL from one device to another device, or from one user to another user, provided the reassignment is made either (a) permanently away from the one device or user or (b) temporarily to accommodate the use of the RDSCAL either by a loaner device, while a permanent device is out of service, or by a temporary worker, while a regular employee is absent. RDSCALs are not available in Per Server mode as Windows sessions are not allowed in Per Server mode.

As you can see above, you must have two licenses in place for each user connecting to your RDSHs: a CAL and an RDSCAL. Usually the CAL is already in place in your company (as you need these to access any Windows Server you may have like a File Server, Print Server, etc) and are normally licensed per seat (although you can indeed license per server). Check with your network administrator (in case it is not yourself) what licenses you have in your company and if they are per seat or per server CALs.

The RDSCAL is needed by any device or user connecting to an RDSH, regardless of the OS they have on their machine (i.e. Windows 7, Windows 10, Mac OS X, Linux, etc). That is straightforward. It gets confusing when you add VDI to the picture as all the sudden it matters if you are connecting from a PC, if it is corporate owned or not and potentially even from where you are connecting. The bottom line is, if using VDI, be prepared for additional licensing on top of CALs/RDSCALs.

Licensing Modes

You have two options: 'Per User' or 'Per Device' RDSCALs. The difference between these, and figuring out which one to use, is easy to understand. As you know, everyone or everything connecting to an RDSH requires a license (RDSCAL). The question you need to ask is if you have more users than devices or the other way around.

For example, assuming you have fifty users in your company but they may access the RDSHs from multiple devices (i.e. office PCs and their iPads at home), it is easy to see the total number of devices at the end will be higher than the total number of users. If that is your case, 'Per User' licensing is the way to go (as you will need less RDSCALs).

On the other hand, if you have only twenty-five computers in the office that your fifty users share during two different shifts and you do not provide access to the RDSHs from anywhere else, it is clear you have less devices than users so it makes more sense (financially) to have 'Per Device' RDSCALs.

Another difference to consider is licensing enforcement. When the RDS environment is set to use 'Per Device' licensing, this is actually enforced. Once a user connects to an RDSH, a temporary RDSCAL is issued, valid for 90 days. After this license expires, the RDSH will try to get a permanent RDSCAL from the licensing server and if such license is not available, the connection to the RDSH will be denied. When set to 'Per User' licensing, such enforcement does not happen and users will still be able to work (meaning it is up to you to make sure you have enough licenses to be legal).

As you can see, the best way to handle licensing is to determine beforehand what you have (If more users or devices). Once you know this, simply set the RDS environment to use such licensing option (we will show you how to do it).

> ⓘ There is also a special license called 'External Connector License'. This is an unlimited license to be used for non-employee access (i.e. general public, suppliers, partners, etc.). If you are setting up your RDS environment for non-employee access, this may be the way to go.

So enough about RDS licensing theory. Let's get the last role service up and running so we can have a fully functional RDSH deployment.

1. Launch 'Server Manager' (in our case on CRLAB-DC01) and select '3. Add other servers to manage'.

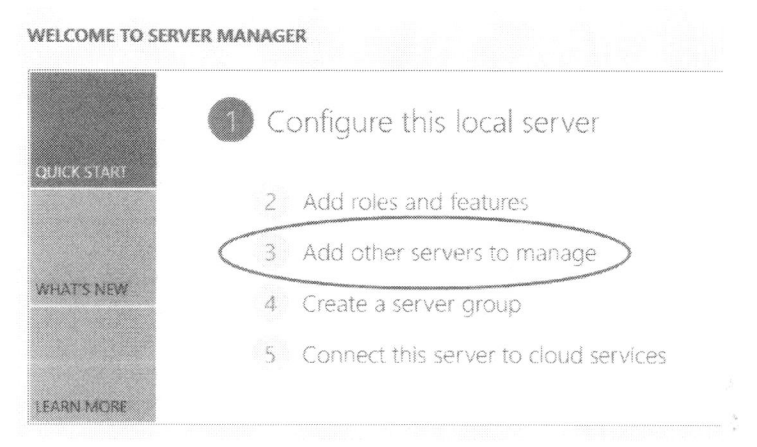

2. Type crlab-ls under 'Name(CN)' and click 'Find Now'. This will return all servers with names starting with CRLAB-LS. Select 'CRLAB-LS01' and click the arrow button to add it to the right pane. Click 'Ok'

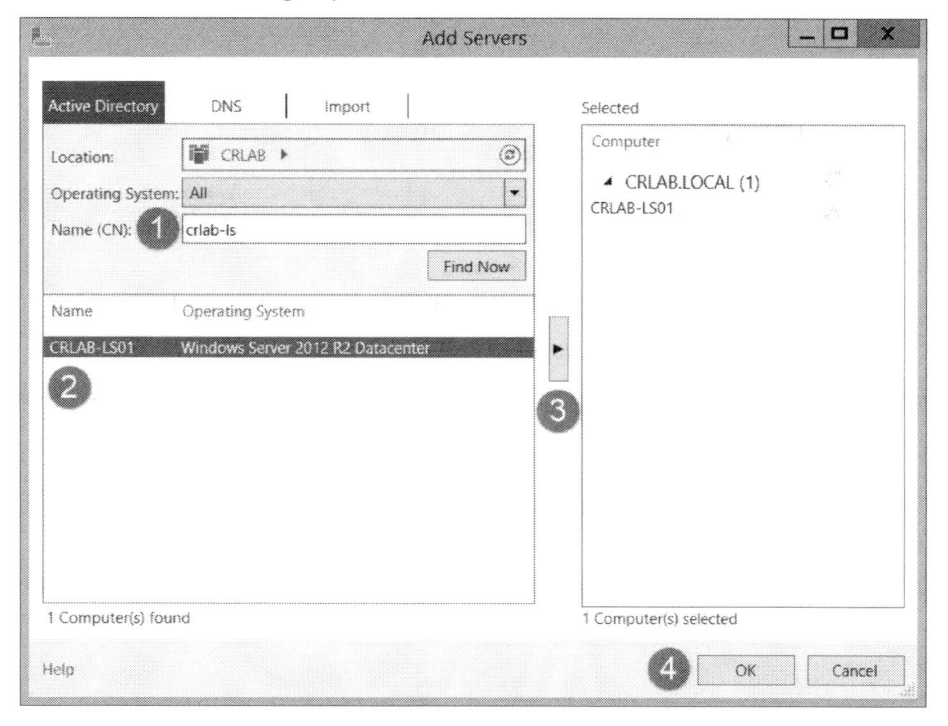

3. Now click on 'Remote Desktop Services' on the left. This will open the 'Overview' page. Under 'Deployment Overview' simply click the 'RD Licensing' icon.

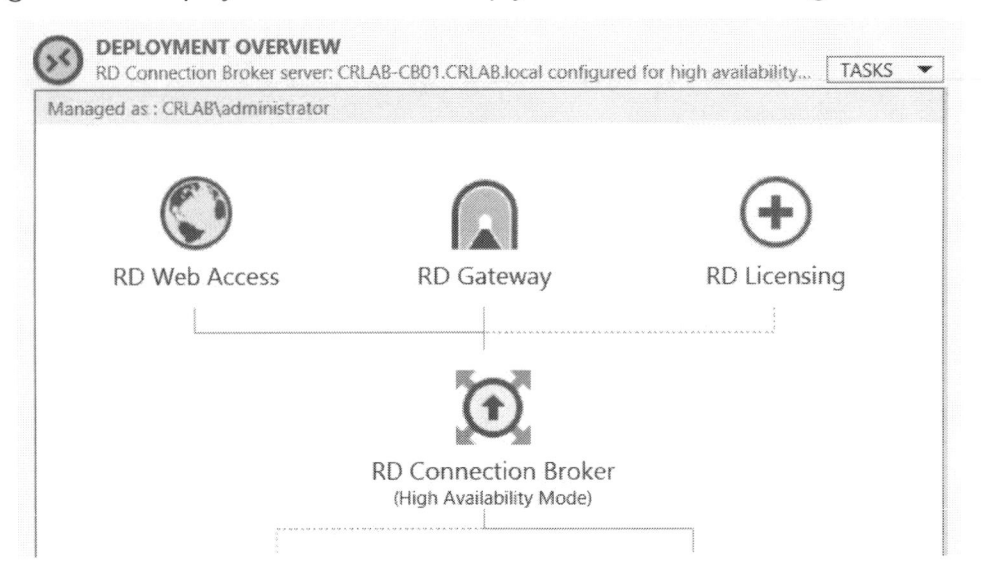

4. Select 'CRLAB-LS01', click the arrow button and click 'Next'.

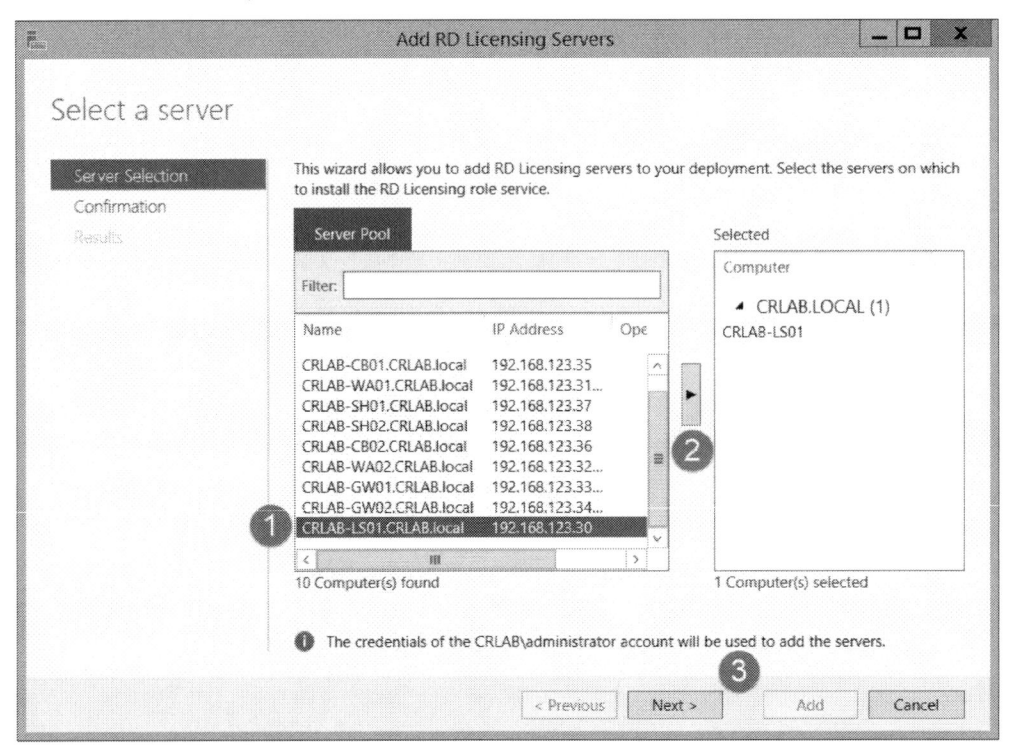

5. Confirm it is all as planned and click 'Add'.

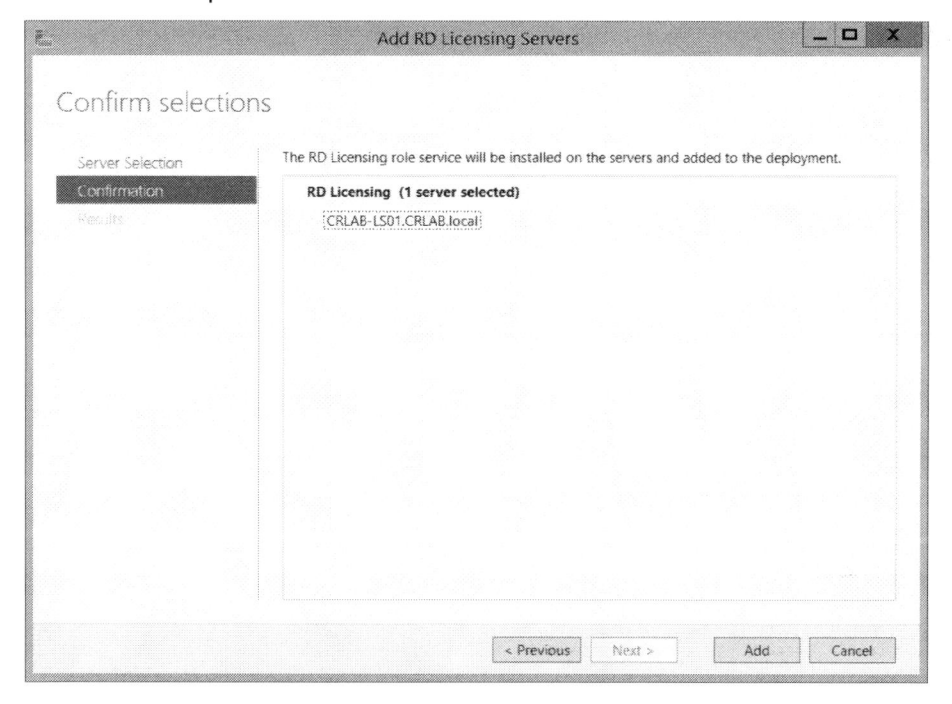

6. If everything went as planned, you got a 'Succeed' under 'Status'. Click 'Close'.

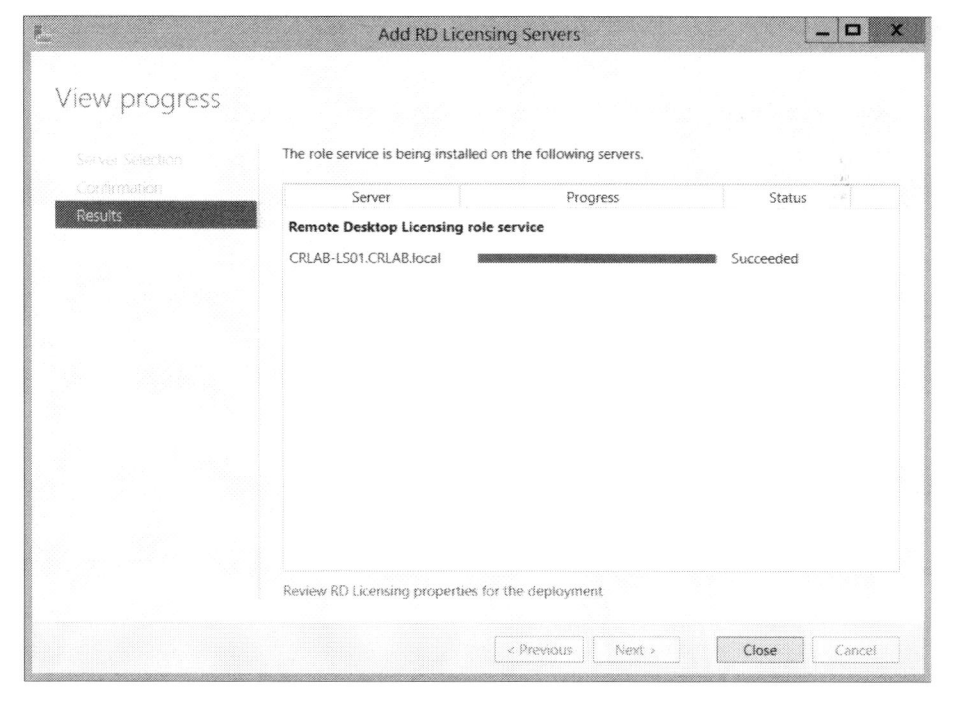

RDS - The Complete Guide | Page 175

The 'Deployment Overview' now shows that all roles have been provisioned. Congratulations, you now have a working RDS deployment, using every single role and almost fully redundant (we will get to that in one second).

Now that we have installed the 'RD Licensing' role, we must complete its configuration. If you remember from previous screenshots, select 'Edit Deployment Properties' under 'Tasks'.

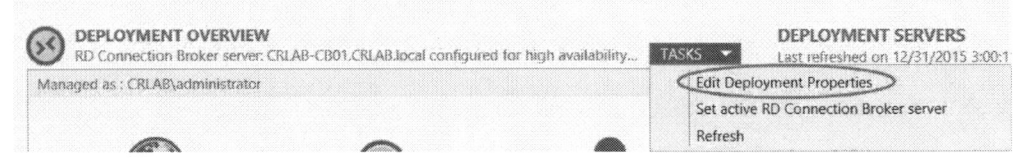

Under 'RD Licensing', you can see that by just adding an RDLS does not mean the configuration is done. We still need to select a licensing mode, as discussed previously. Select the one that makes more sense for your particular needs and click 'OK'.

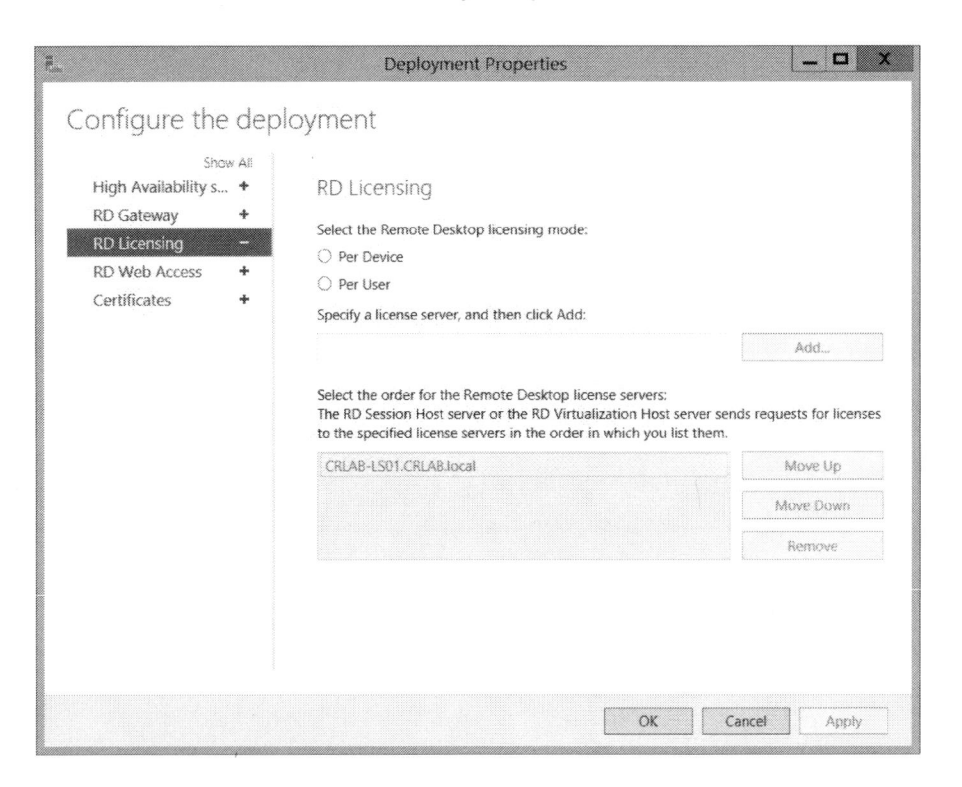

Next step is to activate the RDLS and add (if you have them ready) some RDSCALs. So, let's do it.

1. Logon to the RDLS ('CRLAB-LS01' in our case) and from the start screen, launch 'Remote Desktop Licensing Manager' (you can find it under 'Admistrative Tools' | 'Remote Desktop Services').

2. As you can see when launching it for the first time, the actual RDLS is not activated. If you have done it before with previous RDS versions, the procedure has not changed much at all. Just right-click the RDLS and select 'Activate Server'.

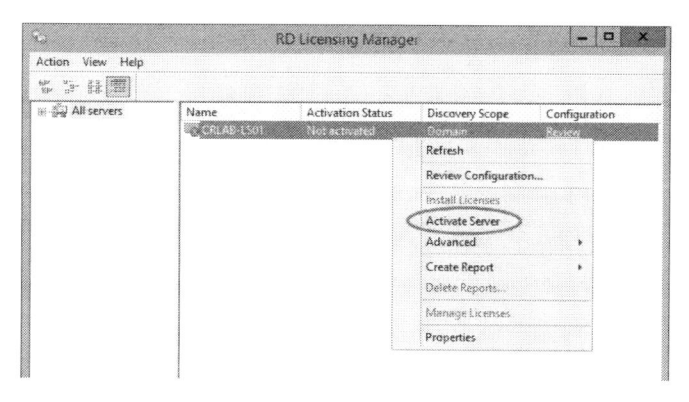

3. The wizard will launch. Click 'Next'.

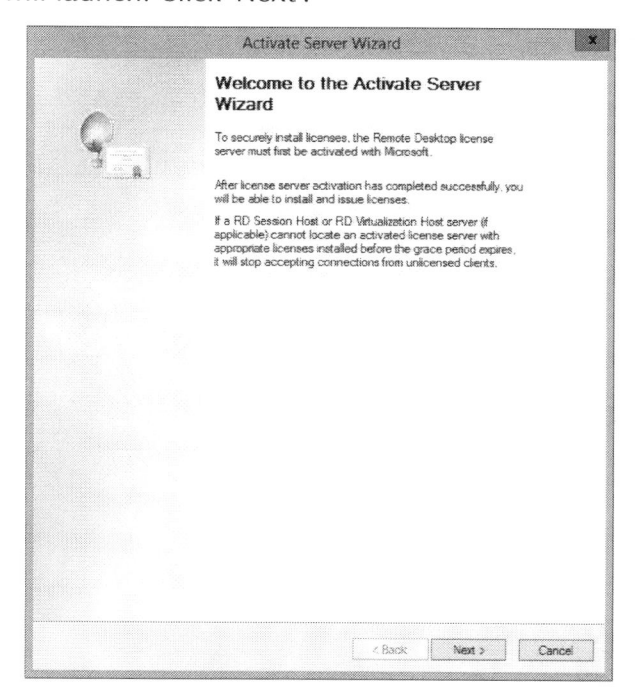

4. If the RDLS has access to the internet; select 'Automatic' and click 'Next'. This is the easiest. With no internet access, you will have to select 'Telephone' and call the number for your country as shown by the wizard. I assume you have internet access.

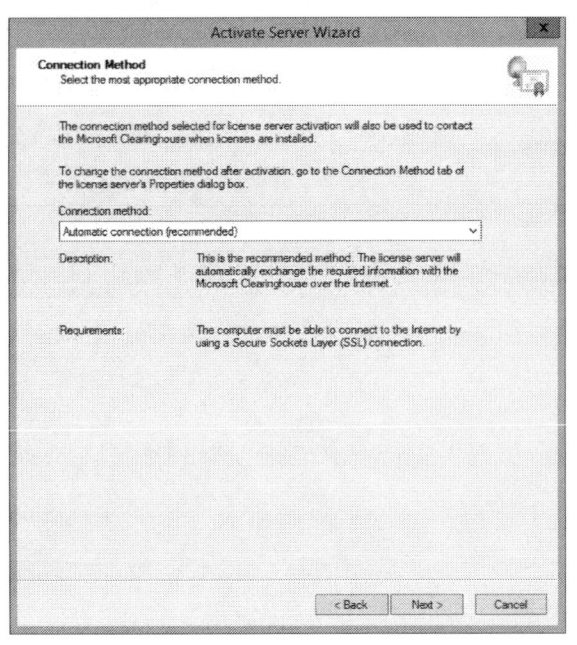

5. The wizard will contact the Microsoft Clearinghouse and if successful, will ask you for your information. Enter it accordingly and click 'Next'.

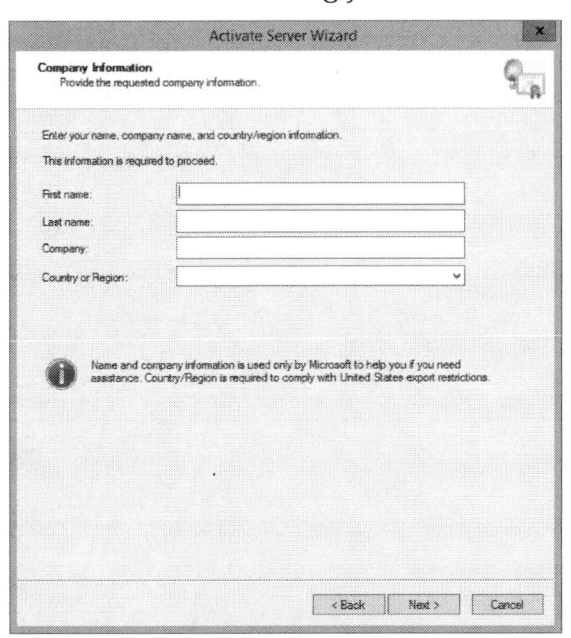

6. A bit more information can be entered here (although not mandatory). Enter it if you wish and click 'Next'.

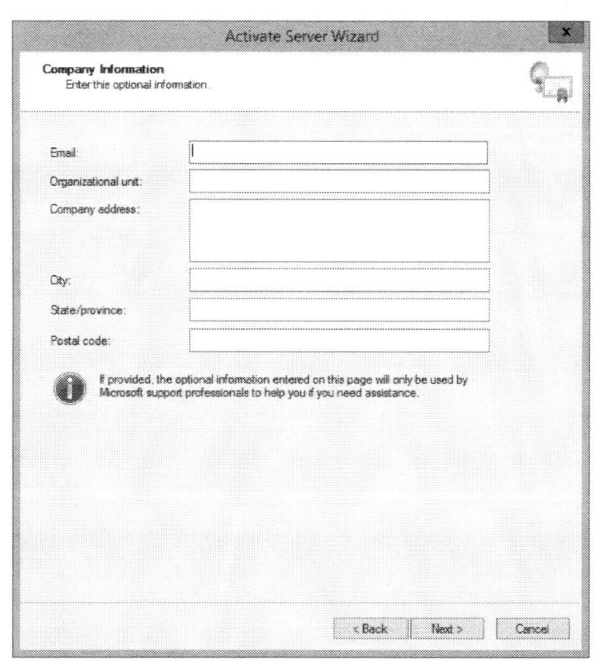

7. With that information, the wizard will contact the Microsoft Clearinghouse one more time. Uncheck 'Start Install Licenses Wizard now' and click 'Finish'.

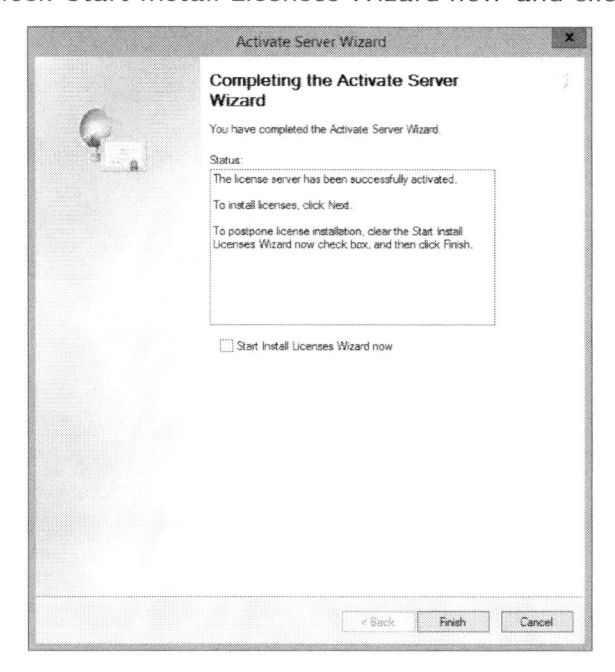

8. There is one more step. If you look at the 'Remote Desktop Licensing Manager' window, you will notice a warning icon on the 'CRLAB-LS01' server.

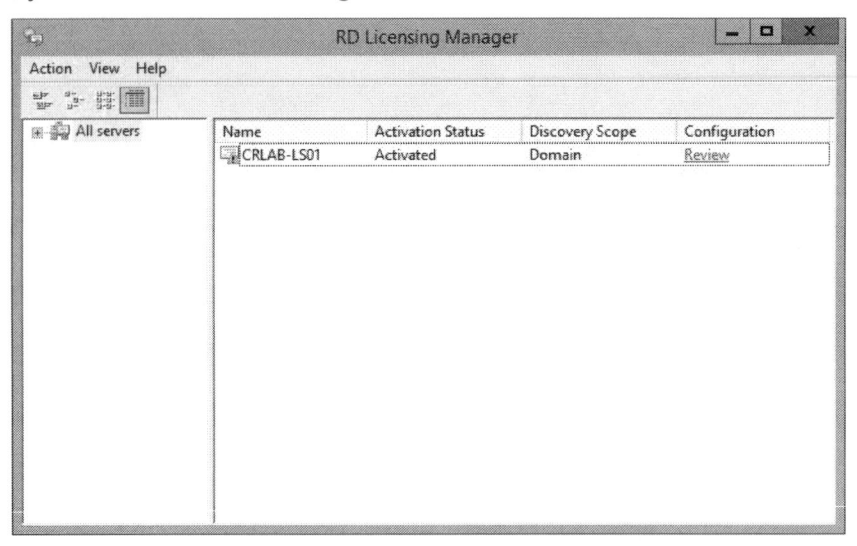

9. The issue is the RDLS has to be part of a particular group under 'Active Directory' so it can work properly. Simply click 'Review'. The RDLS configuration window will show up, clearly showing the issue. Click 'Add to Group'.

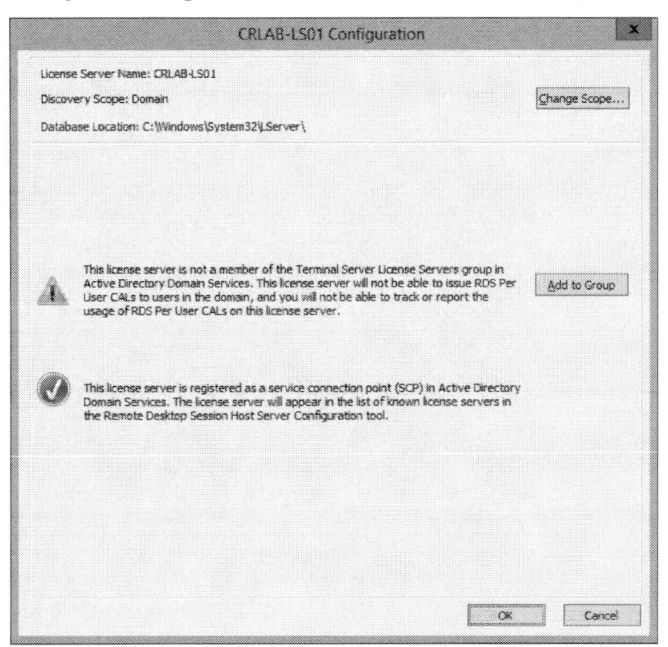

10. The wizard will mention you need 'Domain Admins' rights to perform that operation. If that is the case, simply click 'Continue' (if not, ask your AD guys to add the 'CRLAB-LS01' computer object to the 'Terminal Server License Servers' group on AD).

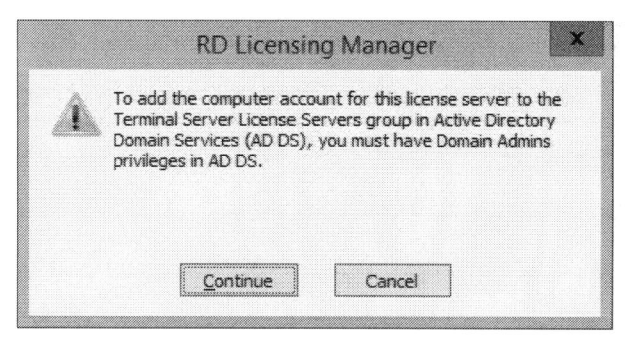

11. The wizard will show you it added the RDLS to the proper group. Click 'OK'.

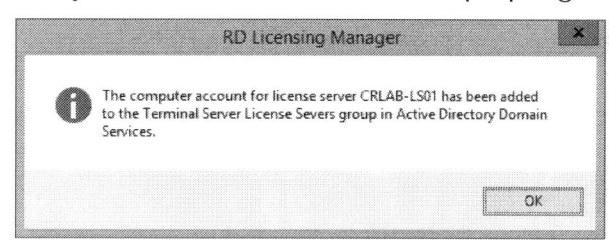

12. Everything is now happy in the RDLS land. Click 'OK'.

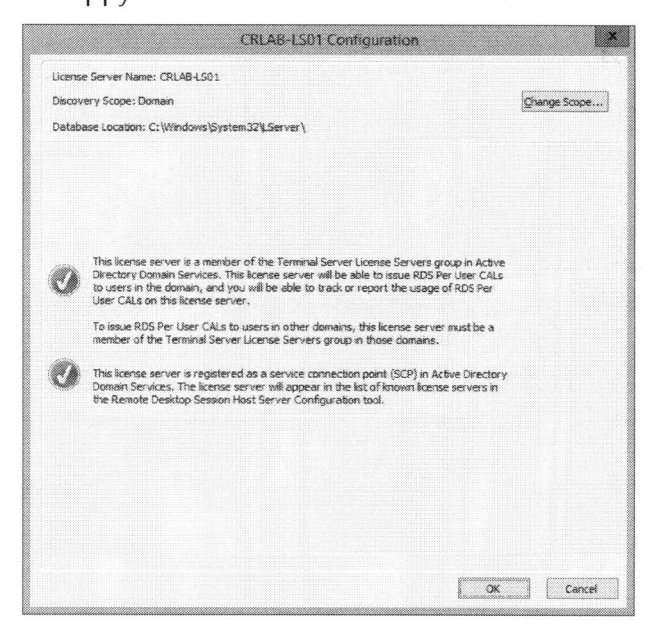

Now it would be the time to add your RDSCALs to the environment. Still under 'Remote Desktop Licensing Manager', simply right-click your RDLS and select 'Install Licenses' and follow the wizard accordingly (it will vary depending on the license agreement you have with Microsoft).

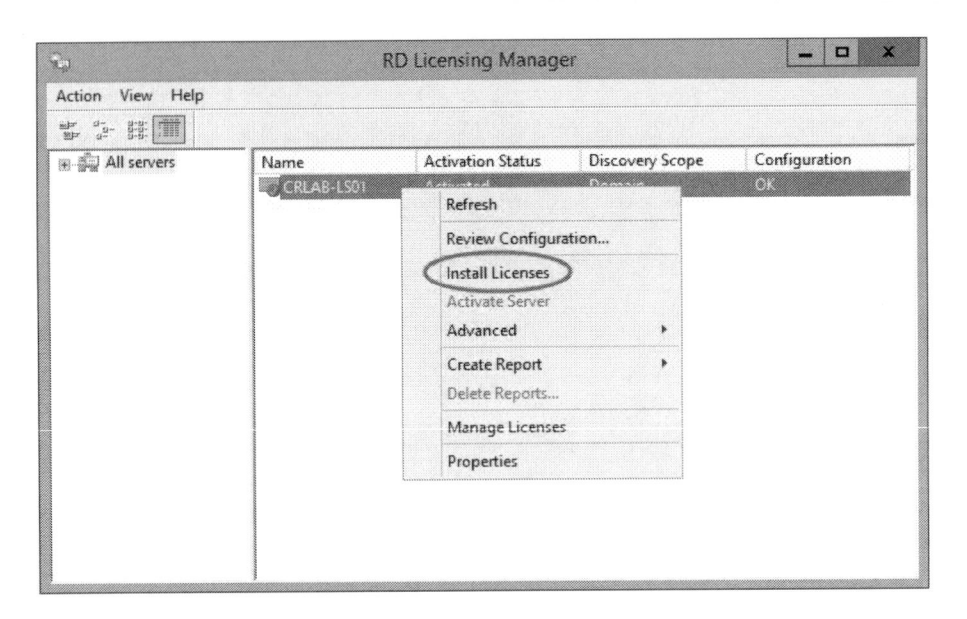

The final step would be to have a highly available RDLS. This is done by simply adding another RDLS to the deployment and activating it as per the steps above. You could them load half of your licenses on each RDLS. That said and legal considerations aside, what we recommend is to load the exact same amount of licenses on each RDLS (you do that by contacting the Microsoft Clearinghouse to get your RDSCALs reissued or reallocated). This guarantees a fully functional, fully redundant RDS environment with all your licenses available at any given time. Microsoft may not agree with that from a legal standpoint but hey, we are not lawyers.

Other than additional tweaks and settings to get the user experience a bit better, you now have a complete RDS 2012 R2 environment. Congratulations.

That said, there is only one thing missing. How to get this environment working over the internet? It is a bit of a tweak and dealing with certificates but that is what we will do next. Fix the environment so we can access it from anywhere, internally or externally, and all using a single FQDN. Stay tuned.

Fixing external access

Now we have a working environment that is fully redundant, at least from an RDS standpoint, and that works as expected internally. The question now is what if I want to access the environment from an external location (i.e. home or remote office)?

There are several things that need to be taken care of, all of them small. The first obvious one is you need to open ports on your firewall and point these to the VIP for the load balanced RDGWs (assuming you did everything as explained so far, you do have a pair of RDGWs with NLB). Which ports? You know them, TCP 443 and UDP 3391 (if you want to leverage all the goodies that came with RDP8.x). If you have (and you do) different servers for the RDGW and RDWA roles, you also need to open port TCP 443 pointing to the VIP for the load balanced RDWAs.

Now these external IP addresses (handled by the firewall), need FQDNs (i.e. gw.yourcompany.com, wa.yourcompany.com) so you must take care of that by creating proper DNS records for the external domain (yourcompany.com).

FQDN	External IP	Internal IP	Port
gw.yourcompany.com	X.X.X.X	RDGWs VIP	TCP 443
gw.yourcompany.com	X.X.X.X	RDGWs VIP	UDP 3391
wa.yourcompany.com	Y.Y.Y.Y	RDWAs VIP	TCP 443

If you do all that and try to connect, you will notice it will fail. Not just because of certificate errors (remember, we created certificates for local names, in our lab, 'web.crlab.local' and 'gateway.crlab.local') but name resolution. From the outside, no internal '.local' names can be resolved. This gives us a hint of what has to be done...

The fix is relatively simple. You will need to use proper external names for everything, no matter if accessing the environment internally or externally. If you remember, we used FQDNs for the RDCBs highly available pair, for the RDGWs and the RDWAs. Therefore, we must fix all these first.

The RDGWs and RDWAs we can do quite easily. Just a matter of creating proper certificates with the correct external FQDNs. The RDCBs is a bit more complicated. If you go back to the deployment, you can review what the FQDN in use is, but you cannot change it on the GUI.

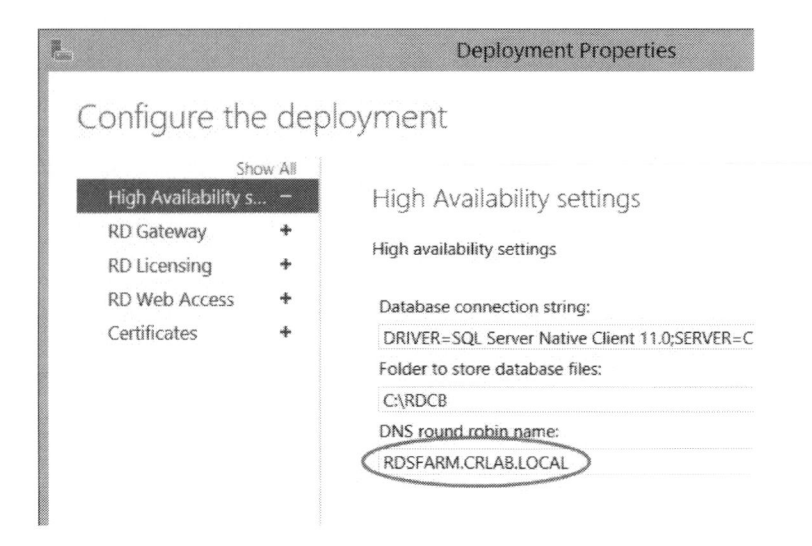

The solution? PowerShell. Before you ask, yes, we do have a full section on how to use PowerShell to do everything you did so far using the wizards. And more than that, we will also show you a tool we created, 'RDS-O-Matic' where you simply enter things like server names and IP addresses and the tool gives you the PowerShell script that creates the whole environment for you. Handy, eh?

So, let's first take care of the RDCB issue.

1. On the server you are using to manage the environment ('CRLAB-DC01' in our case), open a PowerShell prompt with elevated rights (right-click the PowerShell icon on the taskbar and select 'Run as Administrator').
2. Now use the following cmdlet to change it:

    Set-RDClientAccessName-ConnectionBroker "your_RDCB_FQDN"
    -ClientAccessName "fqdnYouWant"

3. In our case we used:

    Set-RDClientAccessName -ConnectionBroker "CRLAB-CB01.crlab.local"
    -ClientAccessName "cb.iqbridge.ca"

The active connection broker (the one doing whatever is needed on the RDS environment) is in our case, 'CRLAB-CB01'. Does not matter we have two in HA. The first one is normally the active one, unless you force a change (click 'TASKS' under the deployment properties and select 'Set active RD Connection Broker server'). That is why we used 'CRLAB-CB01'. Also, note you need the full name so make sure you use 'CRLAB-CB01.crlab.local'.

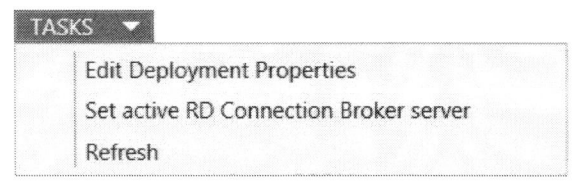

```
TASKS ▼
  Edit Deployment Properties
  Set active RD Connection Broker server
  Refresh
```

Now if you go back to the deployment properties you will see the new name in place (you may need to close 'Server Manager' and reopen it).

Deployment Properties

Configure the deployment

Show All
- High Availability s... −
- RD Gateway +
- RD Licensing +
- RD Web Access +
- Certificates +

High Availability settings

High availability settings

Database connection string:
DRIVER=SQL Server Native Client 11.0;SEF

Folder to store database files:
C:\RDCB

DNS round robin name:
(cb.iqbridge.ca)

Now before moving ahead, you must be asking yourself, "How internal clients will resolve such FQDNs?". The answer is, a new 'Forward Lookup Zone' on your internal DNS!

Once you do that, internal clients will get an internal IP address when trying to resolve the FQDNs we need. When they are connecting from the outside, the name resolution will be handled by external DNS, what means they will get the firewall IP addresses when outside and not the internal IPs when inside. That fixes our problem and more than that, gives users a single way to access the environment no matter if they are internal or external. Perfect.

Before we work on the DNS (you may need to ask someone else inside your company to do it, in case you have no rights), we need to think about the certificates. In our case, we need three, one for the RDGW VIP, one for the RDWA VIP and one for the RDCB HA FQDN. You can indeed get three certificates issued, one for each FQDN needed or simply go down the easiest route and get a wildcard certificate that will be good for all three (i.e. *.yourcompany.com). Some more paranoid security people may say it is better to have three certificates issued, one for each FQDN, instead of a single wildcard one. Our view here is simple: if one of these is compromised, chances are the CA has deeper issues to deal with and all three are potentially compromised already. Therefore, we always stick to wildcard certificates. However, as previously stated, we are no lawyers, not security specialists of any sort or paranoid. For us a wildcard always worked and so far, almost 20 years later since our first RDS deployment (Windows NT 4.0, Terminal Services Edition), we are still to see a compromised certificate on all the deployments we have worked with. It is then your call, if you want three separate certificates or a single wildcard one. For this book, we are using a single one.

Enough of certificates and FQDNs. Let's fix the internal DNS first.

1. On your DNS server, launch 'DNS Manager' (in our case, 'CRLAB-DC01'). You should see something like this:

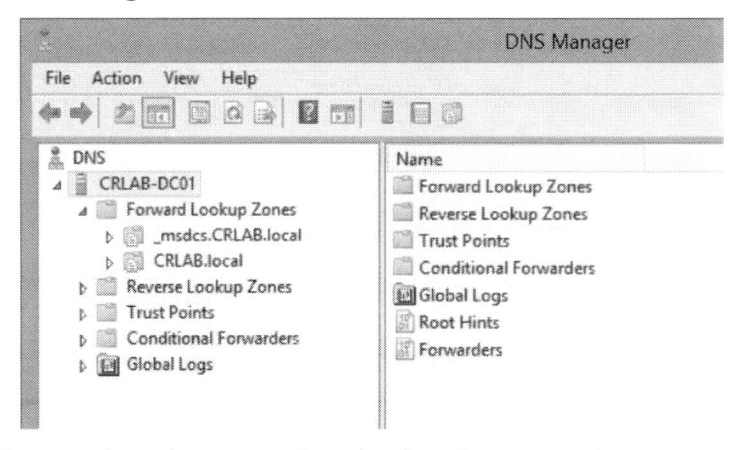

2. Right-click 'Forward Lookup Zones' and select 'New Zone'.

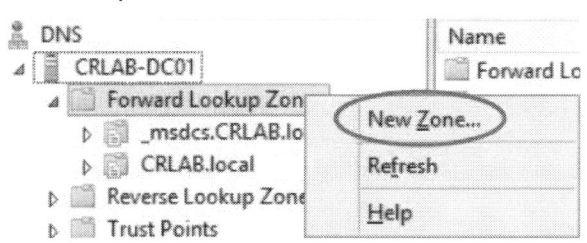

3. The wizard will launch. Click 'Next'.

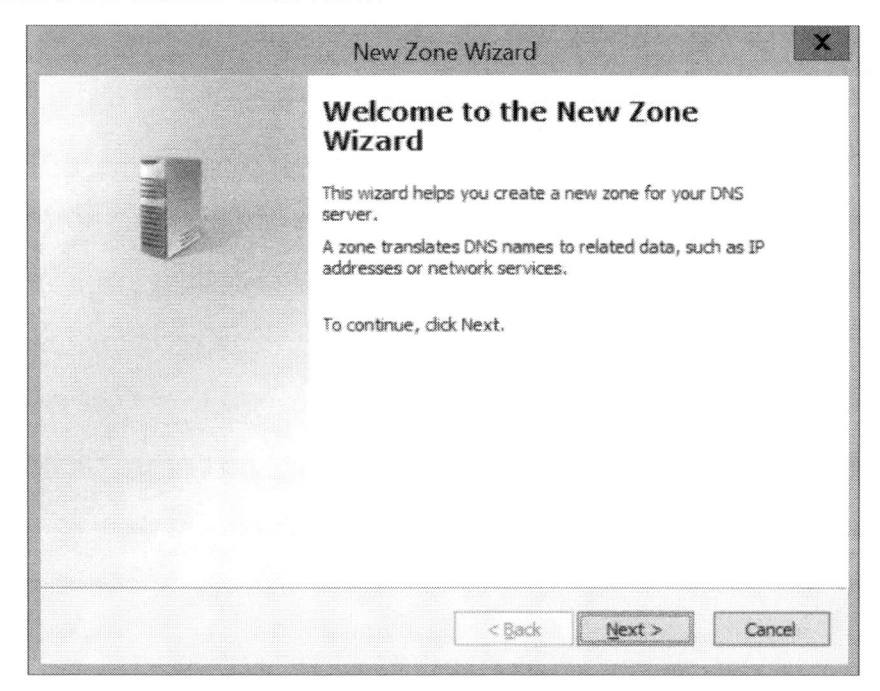

4. Select 'Primary zone' and click 'Next'.

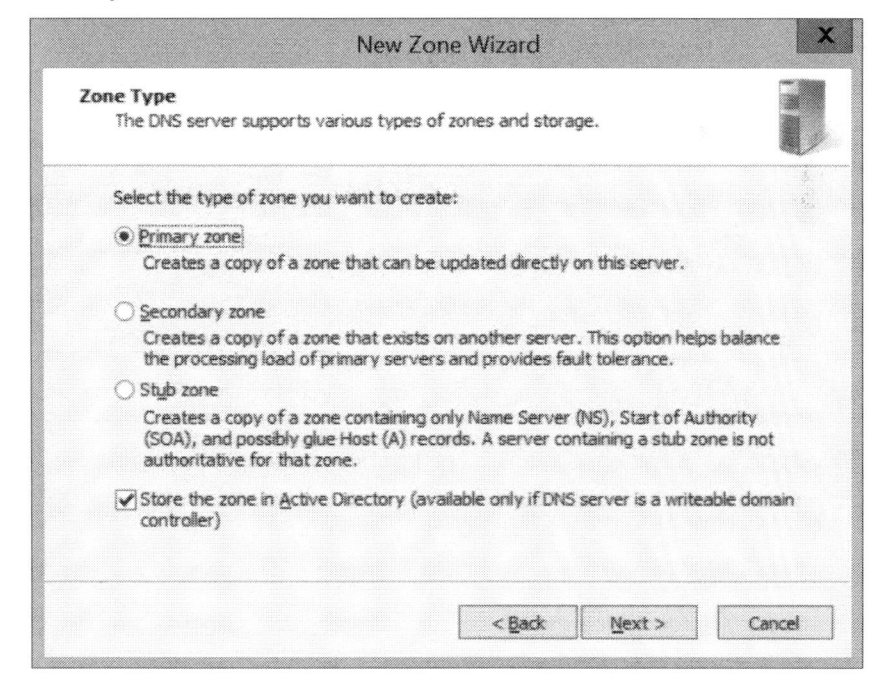

5. For our lab, the default option is fine (it may different for you). Click 'Next'.

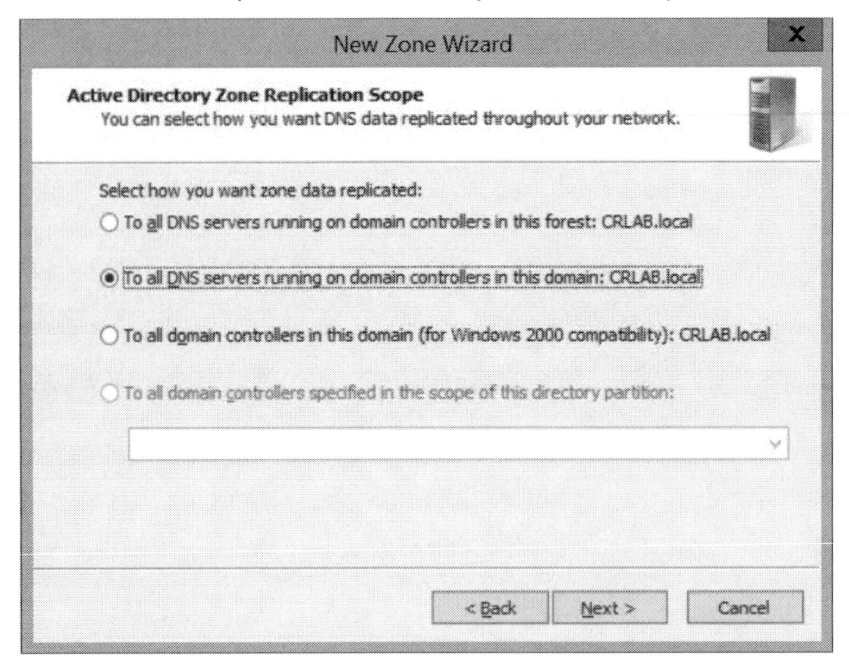

6. Enter the zone name. This is the external domain name that will be used on the certificates (in our case, this is 'iqbridge.ca', our company). Click 'Next'.

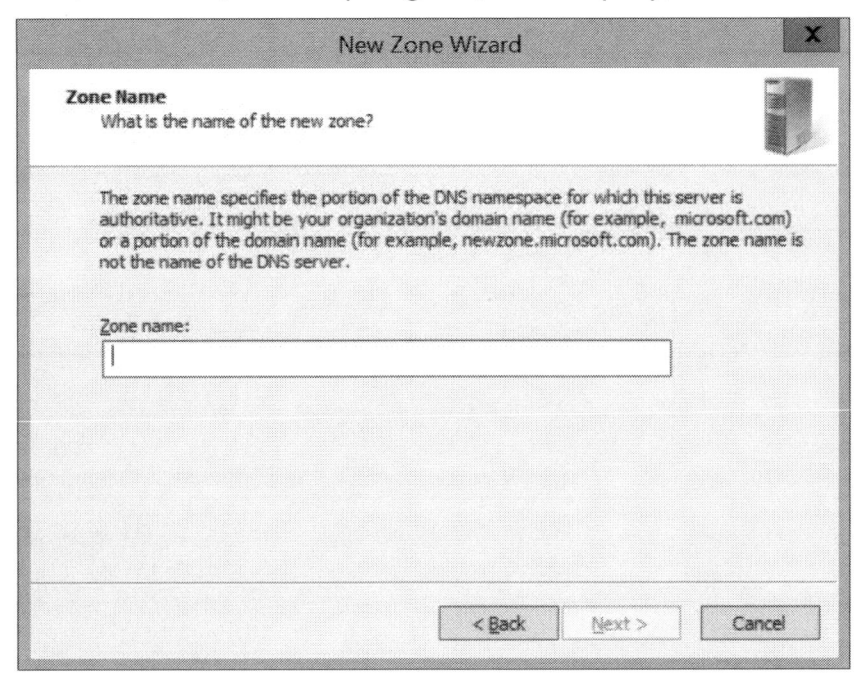

7. One more time we used the defaults but your case may be different. Click 'Next'.

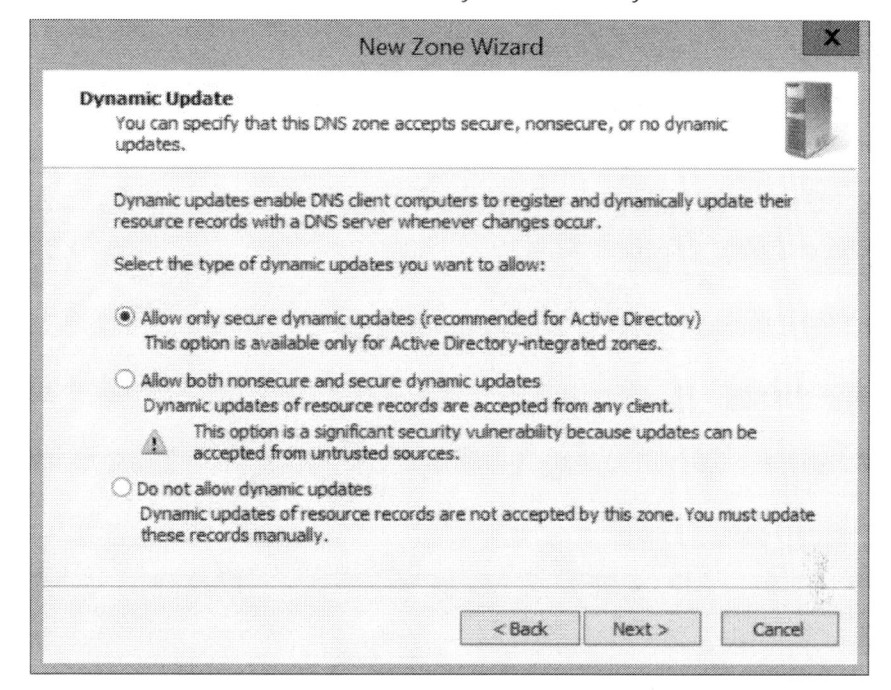

8. Click 'Finish'.

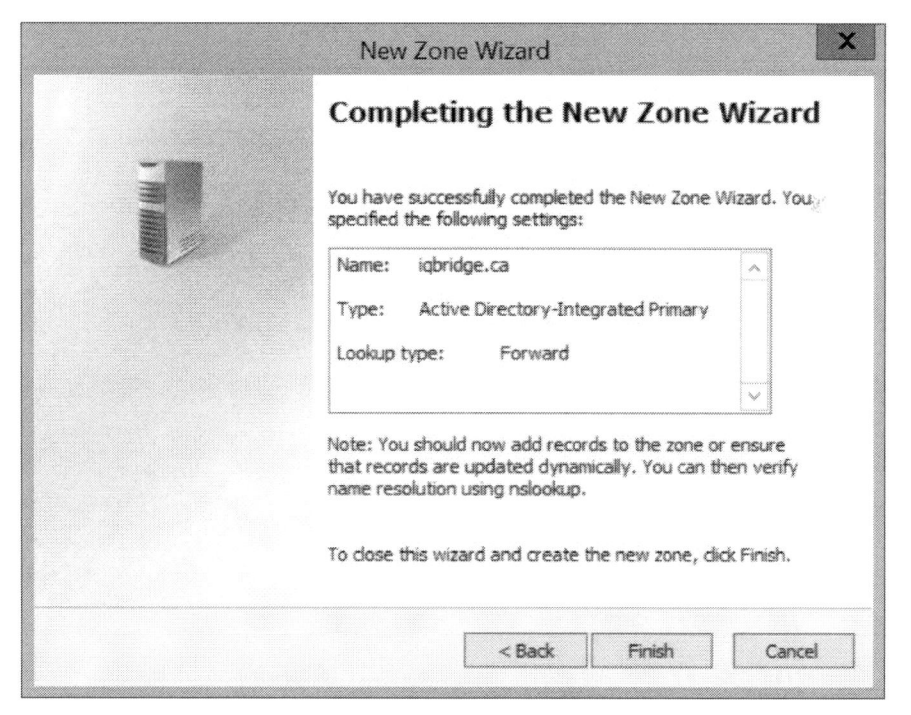

9. Now we can see the new zone created on the DNS.

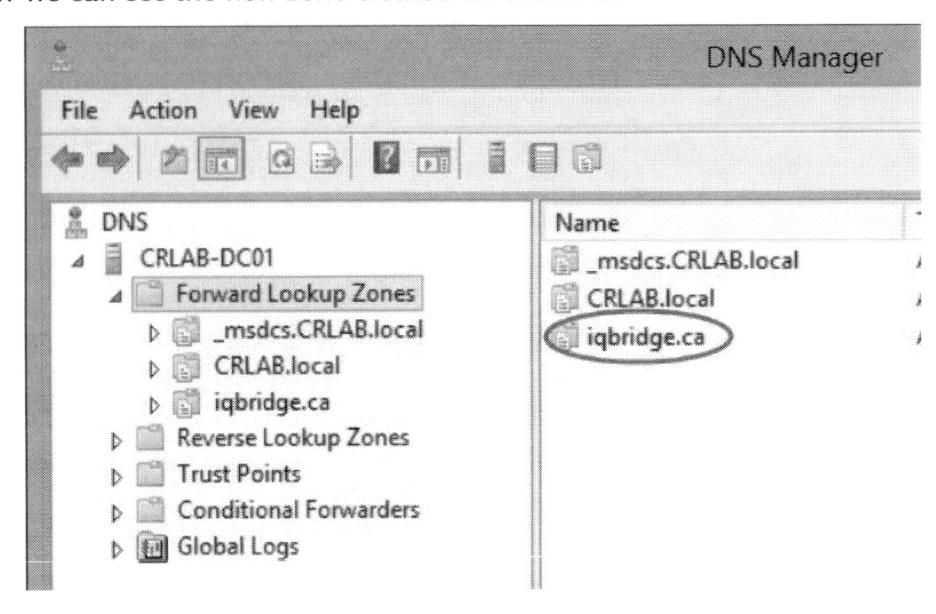

10. Next on the list is to create the proper records to handle the FQDNs we need. Right-click the new zone name and select 'New Host (A or AAAA)...'.

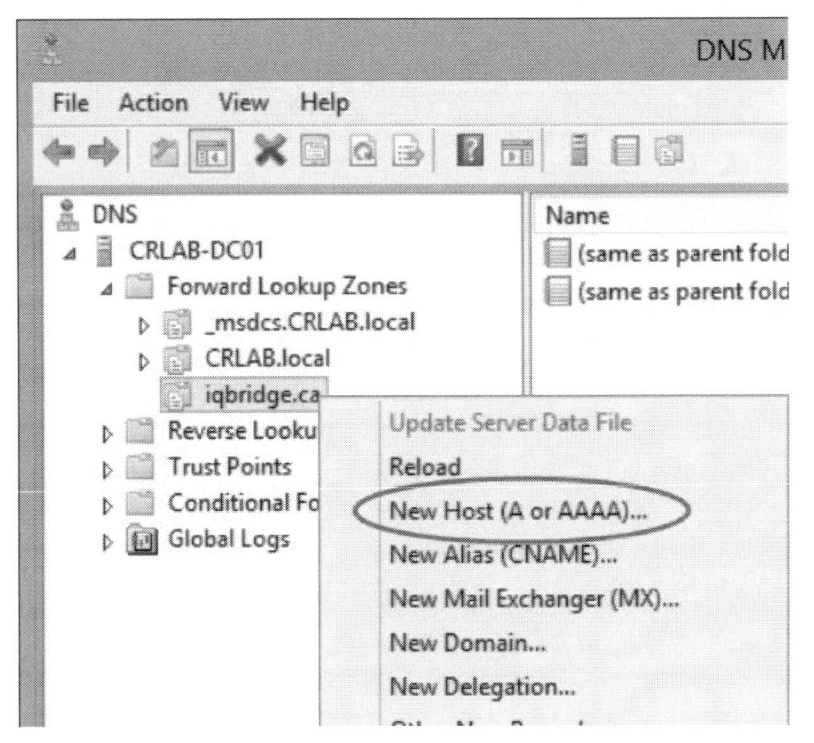

11. Enter the name we need under 'Name' and the correct IP address (the VIPs) and click 'Add Host'. You will have to do this four times (for the RDCBs, RDGWs and RDWAs). You may be asking "Why four times?". If you remember, when we setup the RDCBs HA, we created two DNS records as we used DNS RR for load balancing the RDCB traffic. That is why. If we had used NLB or a real load balancer then we would only need three records created.

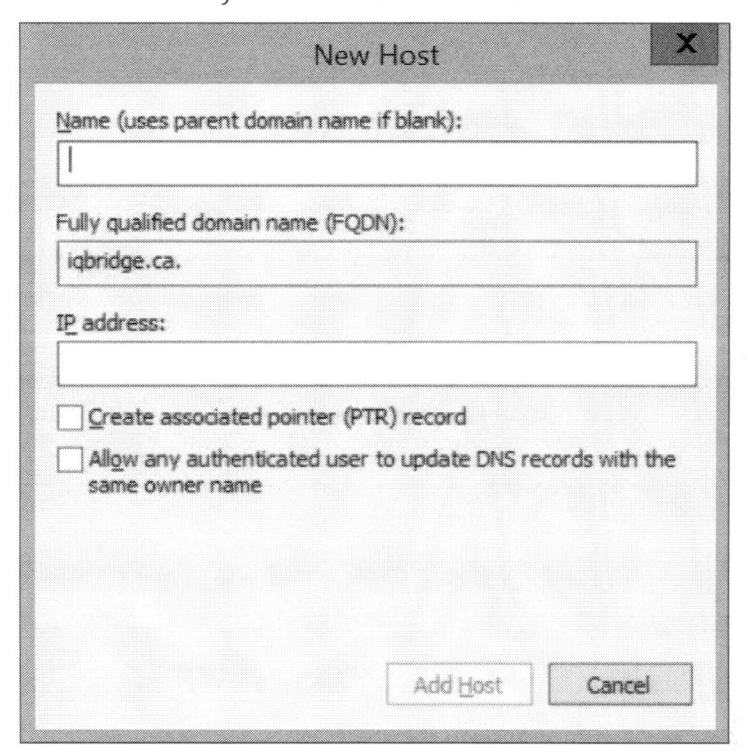

12. Once you are done you should have something similar to this:

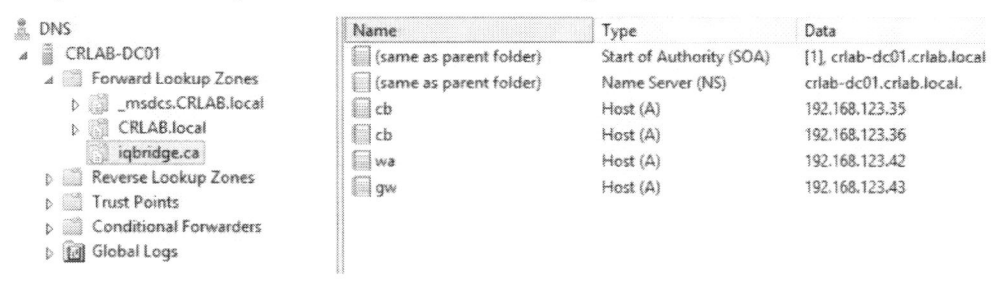

Name	Type	Data
(same as parent folder)	Start of Authority (SOA)	[1], crlab-dc01.crlab.local
(same as parent folder)	Name Server (NS)	crlab-dc01.crlab.local.
cb	Host (A)	192.168.123.35
cb	Host (A)	192.168.123.36
wa	Host (A)	192.168.123.42
gw	Host (A)	192.168.123.43

13. That is it for the DNS portion. If you go to a workstation that is part of the same domain and that uses the same DNS servers, you should be able to resolve all three FQDNs to the respective IP addresses.

The next step is to apply the certificates for each of the roles. In our case, as we are using a wildcard certificate, we simply use the exact same one for all role services.

1. Back to the deployment properties, go to the 'Certificates' section and select the 'RD Connection Broker – Enable Single Sign On' role service. Click 'Select existing certificate...'.

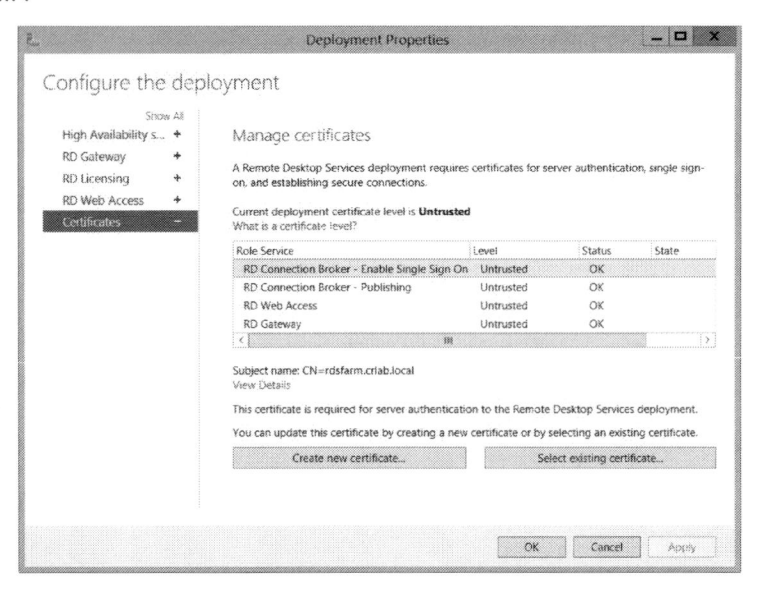

2. Browse to where you saved your certificate, enter the required password and make sure the check box to allow the certificate to be added to the 'Trusted Root Certification Authorities' is checked. Click 'OK'.

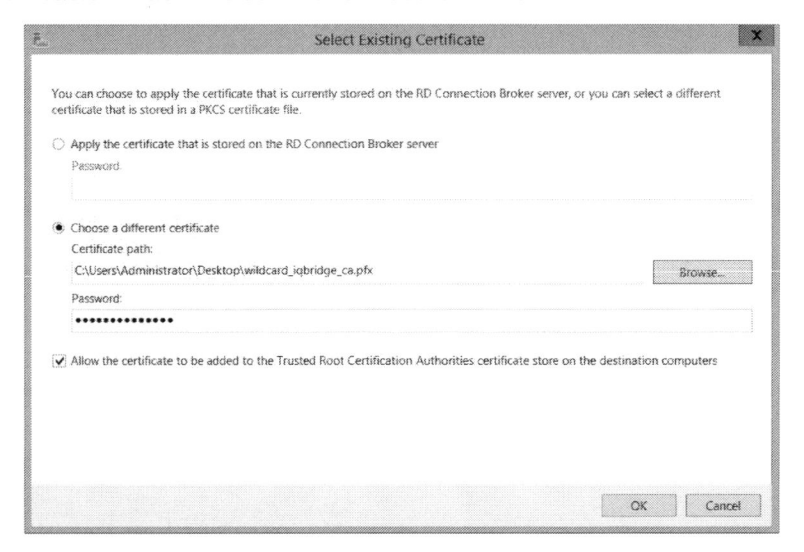

3. The state changes to 'Ready to apply'. Click 'Apply'.

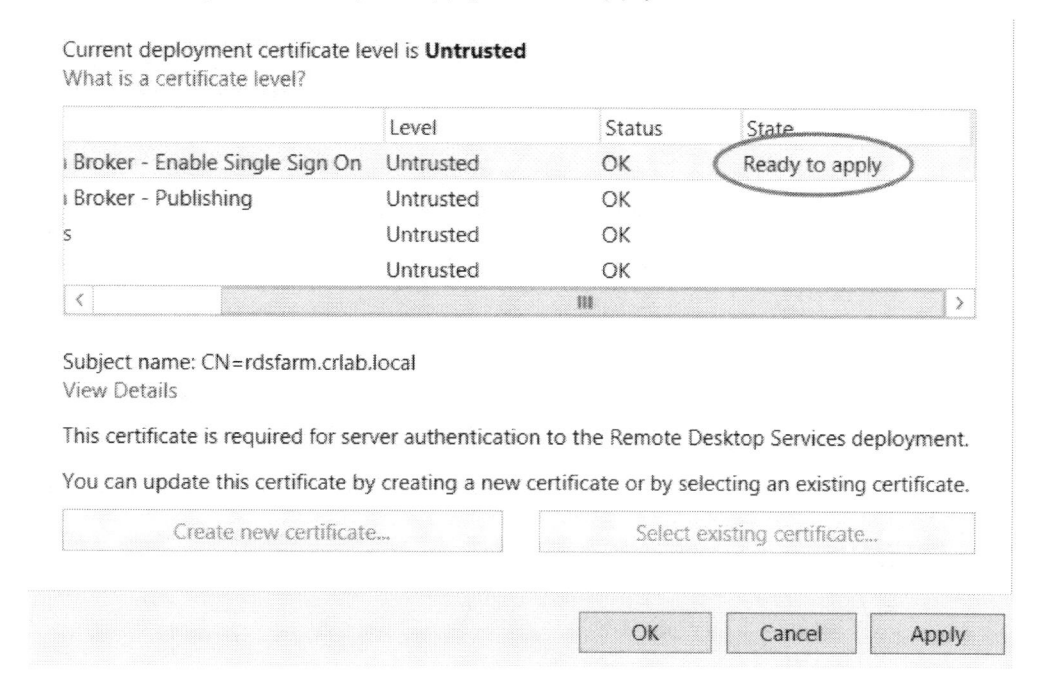

   Current deployment certificate level is **Untrusted**
   What is a certificate level?

	Level	Status	State
Broker - Enable Single Sign On	Untrusted	OK	Ready to apply
Broker - Publishing	Untrusted	OK	
s	Untrusted	OK	
	Untrusted	OK	

   Subject name: CN=rdsfarm.crlab.local
   View Details

   This certificate is required for server authentication to the Remote Desktop Services deployment.

   You can update this certificate by creating a new certificate or by selecting an existing certificate.

   [Create new certificate...]   [Select existing certificate...]

   [OK]   [Cancel]   [Apply]

4. As you can see, now the 'Level' changed from 'Unstrusted' to 'Trusted' as we are using a certificate issued by an external, trusted certificate authority and the 'State' now shows 'Success'.

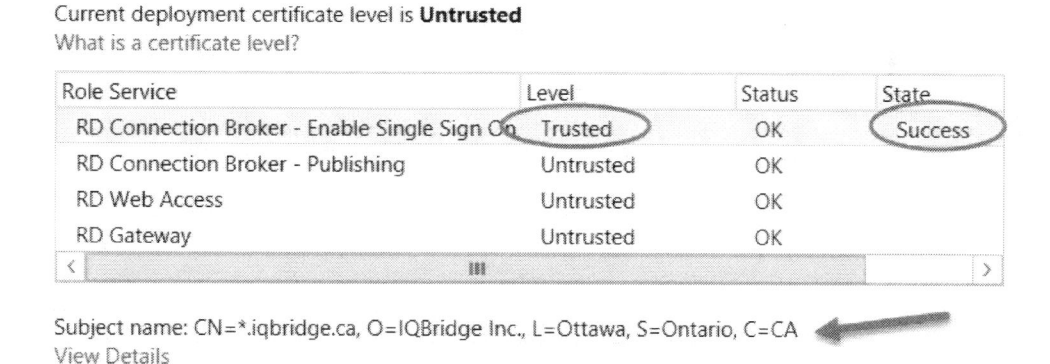

   Current deployment certificate level is **Untrusted**
   What is a certificate level?

Role Service	Level	Status	State
RD Connection Broker - Enable Single Sign On	Trusted	OK	Success
RD Connection Broker - Publishing	Untrusted	OK	
RD Web Access	Untrusted	OK	
RD Gateway	Untrusted	OK	

   Subject name: CN=*.iqbridge.ca, O=IQBridge Inc., L=Ottawa, S=Ontario, C=CA
   View Details

5. Repeat the exact same procedure for the three remaining role services, 'RD Connection Broker – Publishing', 'RD Web Access' and 'RD Gateway'. You should have something like this once the proper certificates are all in place:

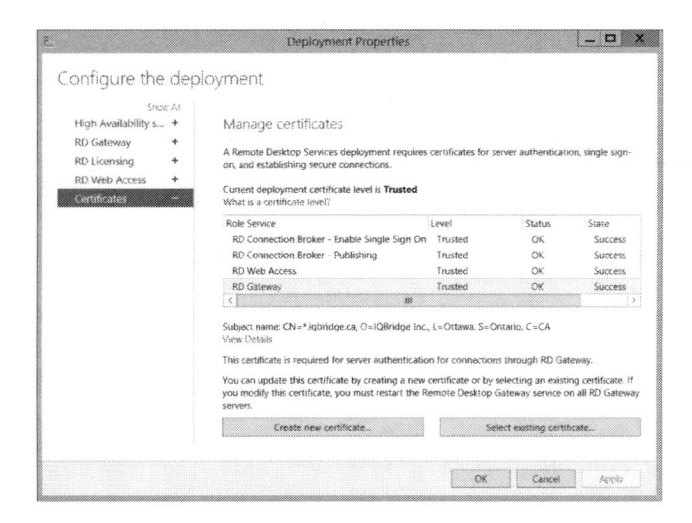

6. Final step is to change the name used for the gateway VIP. As we changed the certificate and created a DNS record for the RDGW VIP, the name here has to match it. In our case, 'gw.iqbridge.ca'. Enter the name you used and click 'Apply'.

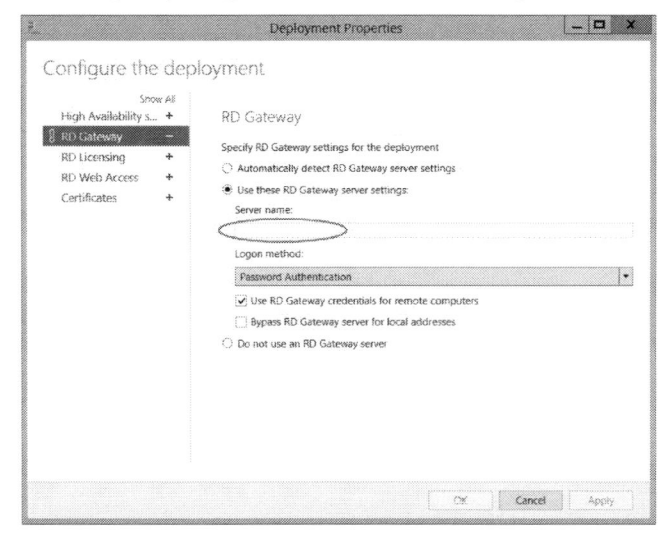

7. Now to be on the safe side, restart all the servers that are part of the deployment.
8. The final step of course is to change your firewall rules and redirect the appropriate traffic from the external IP addresses to the internal ones on the correct ports (remember the table we have at the beginning of this section). Once these are in place, you can test it internally and externally.

Congratulations. You now have a fully working RDS environment that is accessible from both internal and external clients and with redundancy for every single RDS component.

Enhancing your Standard Deployment

Now that you have a working RDS deployment, it is time to start enhancing it. The first issue we need to address is user roaming. If you are not familiar with the terminology, let's do a quick overview of the issue and how this was normally addressed and what Windows Server 2012 and higher changed.

When users launch a session (full desktop or RemoteApp, it does not matter), they are redirected to an RDSH and end up logged in to that server. This means a user profile is created on that server under C:\Users\%username%. Exactly like when you logon to your PC at home or work.

Anything the user does at that stage is then saved to his profile (again, the C:\Users\HisUsername folder). This includes little things like Microsoft Office preferences, Java preferences, his files and so on. If you look under your profile folder you will notice folders like Downloads, Documents, Music and so on.

The issue is when dealing with multiple RDSHs that are load balanced, you cannot predict on which RDSH the user will logon. If he is on 'CRLAB-SH01' today and configures everything the way he likes it, the user expects to see all that if tomorrow his session is on 'CRLAB-SH02'.

By default, out-of-the-box, this is not the case. His profile is not copied to any other server. Worse than that, the same user ends up with different profiles on each server he logs in. No good. The Microsoft way to address this is to use what is called a 'Roaming Profile'. If you look at the user properties on AD this is what you see:

If you noticed, there are two tabs named 'Profile' and 'Remote Desktop Services Profile'. This is where you control the user profile. Now, what is the difference?
Simple. If something is set under 'Profile', it will be used no matter where the user logs in. This includes workstations, laptops or RDSHs that are domain joined. Now if you set something under 'Remote Desktop Services Profile', it will only be used when the user logs in to an RDSH. This is a very important thing to keep in mind. In most cases you do not want to mix the profile that is in use on workstations or laptops and your RDSHs. Keep that in mind.

Now once you click on the 'Remote Desktop Services Profile' tab, this is what you see:

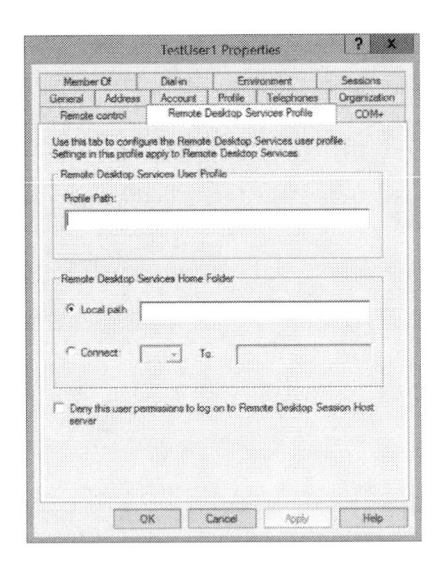

This tab controls the following settings:

- **Profile Path:** usually the UNC path to the user profile (i.e. \\fileserver\profileShare\%username%). This is a network location (remember, all RDSHs will be reading off a common location) where the profile is stored.
- **Remote Desktop Services Home Folder:** out-of-the-box this points to the same place as the profile. Normally we redirect it to another UNC path and set applications like Microsoft Office to use it as the default 'Documents' or 'My Documents' folder.
- There is also a small checkbox that if checked, will deny access to any RDSHs. The first place to check if a user complains he cannot access the environment.

If you do not redirect folders within the user profile, the actual profile folder can grow quite a lot what will make logons and logoffs potentially slow. The reason for that is the fact the system, once a profile is set, will compare what is locally saved on the machine the user is logging in and what is on the UNC share and copy what is needed. You may say this is not that bad. Problem is, if you do not do anything with the local copy stored on every single RDSH, after hundreds of users logged in to these machines, you may run out of disk space. That is why we normally set a policy that will delete the locally cached copies when the users logoff from the RDSHs.

Then we run into a catch 22. If you do that, it means every time a user logs in, his full roaming profile will have to be copied to that particular RDSH. Yes, that is correct. Therefore, if it is a huge profile with thousands of files, logon times will suffer quite a lot. This is the main reason you must redirect certain folders out of the profile and keep the profile and the home folder on different paths. This will make the profile as small as possible. Just be careful with which folders you redirect (looking at you, 'AppData') as this may actually hurt performance. Make sure you test all that with your particular environment and applications. If you are wondering where that is set, this is what you see under the 'Group Policy Management' console for a particular policy:

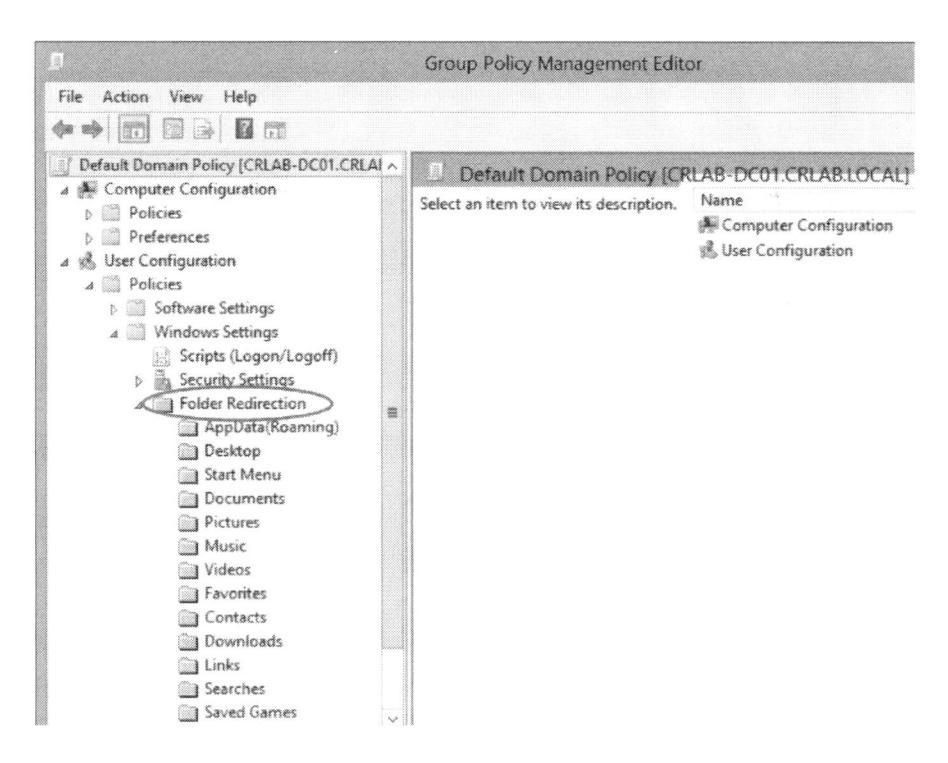

Note: one cool thing that you can do that most people do not realize is to use environment variables for the UNC path on the profile. Imagine an environment where you have RDSHs in San Francisco and Tokyo. If you enter an UNC path for a file server in San Francisco, when users logon to the RDSHs in San Francisco the logon process will be quick as the file server is on the same location as the RDSHs. Now if the user logs in to a server in Tokyo, that server will have to pull down the profile from the file server in San Francisco. Not good. That is where an environment variable is helpful. You can define something like 'HOMEFILESERVER' on the RDSHs in San Francisco to be 'FILESERVER-SF' and on the RDSHs in Tokyo to be 'FILESERVER-TK'. Then you set the profile path to something like \\%HOMEFILESERVER%\%USERNAME%. No matter to which RDSH the user connects to, he will always get a profile from a file server that is at the exact same location as the RDSHs and the logon speed will remain pretty much the same.

Now that you know what a roaming profile is, time to use it. Guess what? We will not be using roaming profiles. With Windows Server 2012, Microsoft introduced what is called a 'User Profile Disk' (UPD). The idea is the whole profile folder gets saved to a disk in VHDX format and once the user is logged in, this single VHDX file is mounted and linked to the profile path. From a system perspective, it shows up and behaves as if it was indeed a local folder under 'C:\Users\%username%'. However, the reality is that single file is stored on a file server and is never copied locally to the RDSHs. This makes the logon process much faster. This is the new way of dealing with user profiles and we will show you how to do it now.

Configuring User Profile Disks

Before we jump into the UPD setup, let's dig a little deeper into roaming profiles and how these work under Windows.

Regardless of how you logon to a machine (Desktop OS or Server OS, locally or remotely), your user settings will always be stored on your user profile. As mentioned before, by default the system stores it in the Users folder under the system drive (as this is normally the C: drive, the location will be C:\Users). Each user gets his own, unique and private folder under it. One important thing to remember is there will always be a C:\Users\%username% folder, no matter if the profile is local or roaming. A roaming profile simply gives you a starting copy the system will copy locally and keep it there until the user logs off. At that point whatever has changed will be copied over to the remote location and if you set the policy to deal with the locally cached copy, it will be deleted.

Now, what exactly are 'User Profile Disks'? Originally, UPDs were created to address a need seen when doing VDI. As you remember, RDS has two main flavors: the session-based deployment (what we have been doing so far in this book) and the virtual machine based one (yep, VDI). When using VDI, you publish a VM per user based on RD Virtualization Hosts instead of multiple sessions based on RDSHs.

When going down the VDI route you can deploy 'Personal VMs' and 'Pooled VMs'. The main difference is personal VMs assigns one VM to one user and that association never changes. It becomes, as the name implies, the user personal VM and anything he does or changes is saved locally on the VM itself (yes, like your PC). With pooled VMs, users share a pool of VMs that are always in a pristine state. That is why the user loses that personalization capability. To take advantage of pooled VMs (being able to always deliver a pristine VM) and still allow personalization, Microsoft created UPD, introduced with Windows Server 2012. So even though UPD was born to address a VDI need, as it addresses the personalization requirements and fixes many of the issues seen with roaming profiles, it made its way to the session based deployment.

Briefly, a UPD is a VHDX file, created on a per user basis and stored on a central network location. Inside this single VHDX file you will find the complete user profile, meaning everything you would normally see under C:\Users\%username%. When UPD is enabled and a user logs in, his VHDX file is mounted on the fly and C:\Users\%username% becomes a link to the mounted VHDX file. All the settings under C:\Users\%username% are then stored directly there. Given how it works, this is completely transparent to the applications what means full compatibility. Another advantage of this approach is that, in contrast to roaming profiles, settings that applications store under the Local and LocalLow folders (special folders under C:\Users\%username%) will also be saved. This helps a lot with poorly written applications (great example, Java). Out-of-the-box everything goes into the UPD but it is possible to define specific folders if you want to keep the UPD size under control.

Time to work. As you remember, we have a file server ready to go in our lab. That is 'CRLAB-FS01'. This is where we will have all the UPDs stored. Make sure you have space available, ideally on a second drive.

1. Logon to the file server ('CRLAB-FS01') and launch 'Server Manager'. Click on '2. Add roles and features'.

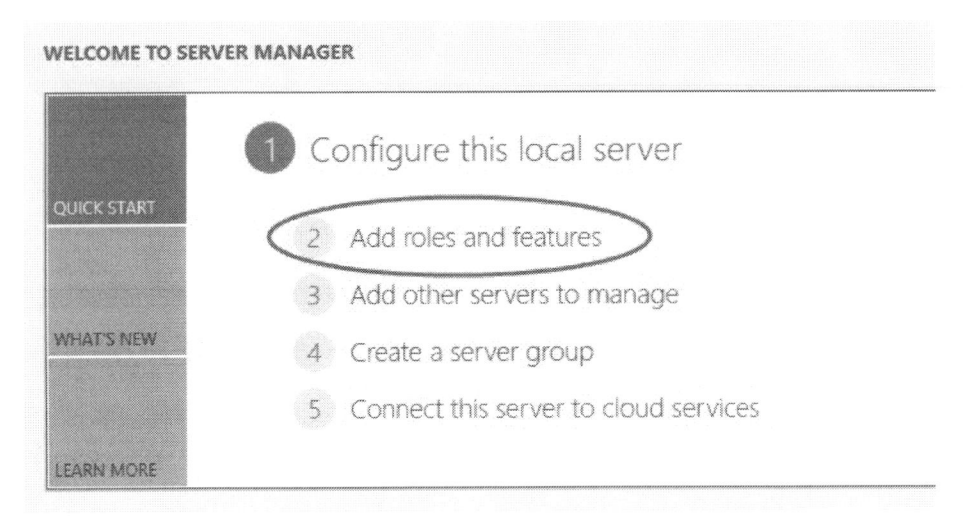

2. The wizard will launch. Click 'Next'.

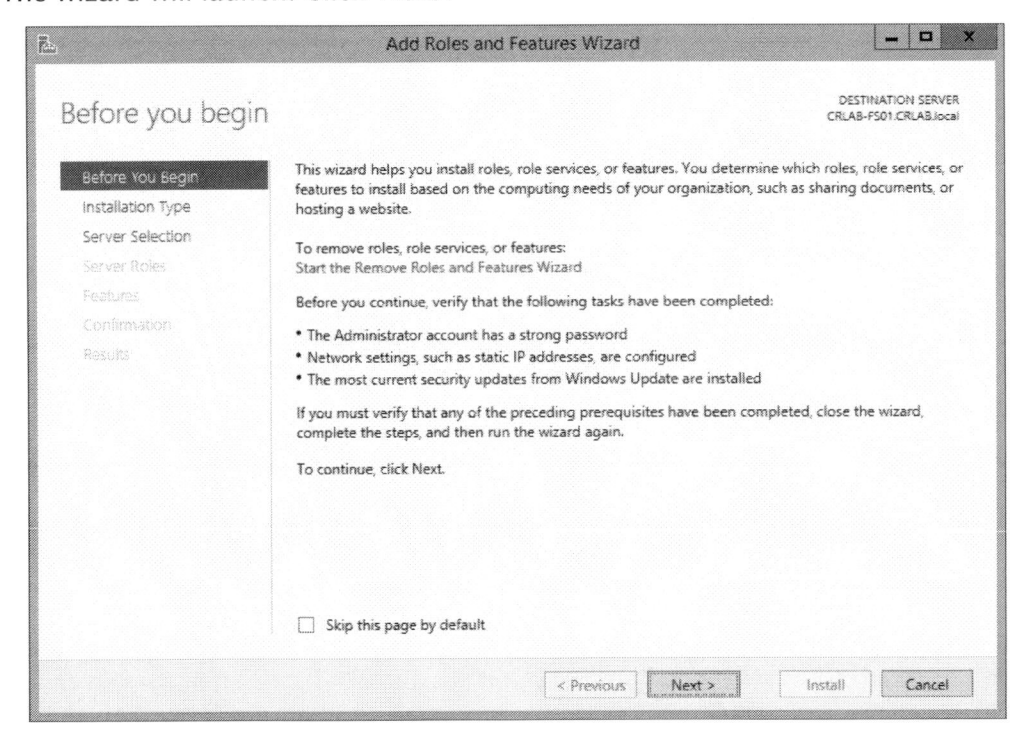

3. Select 'Role-based or feature-based installation' and click 'Next'.

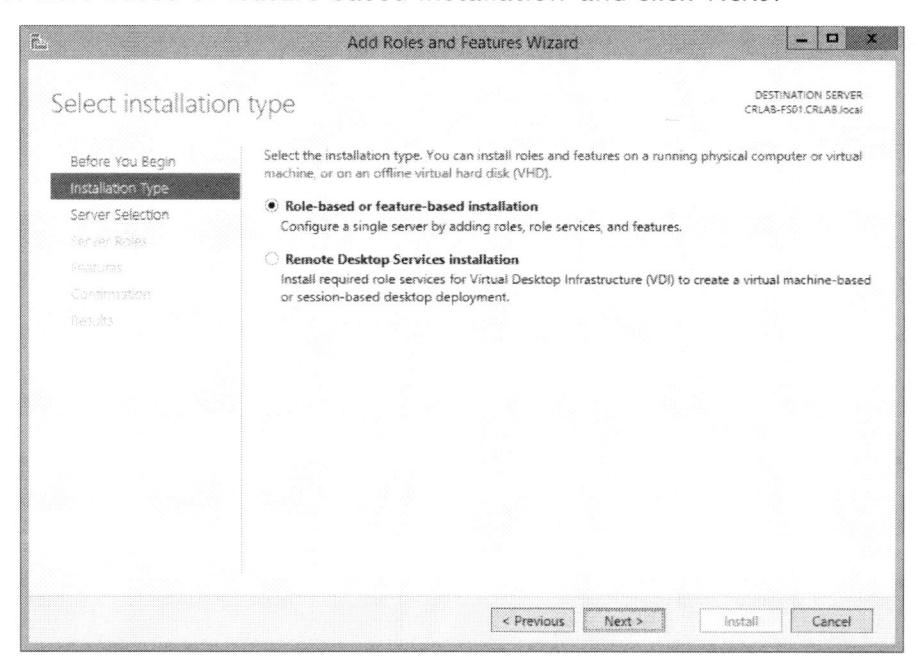

4. As we are performing this right on the file server, it should show itself on the server pool list. Click 'Next'.

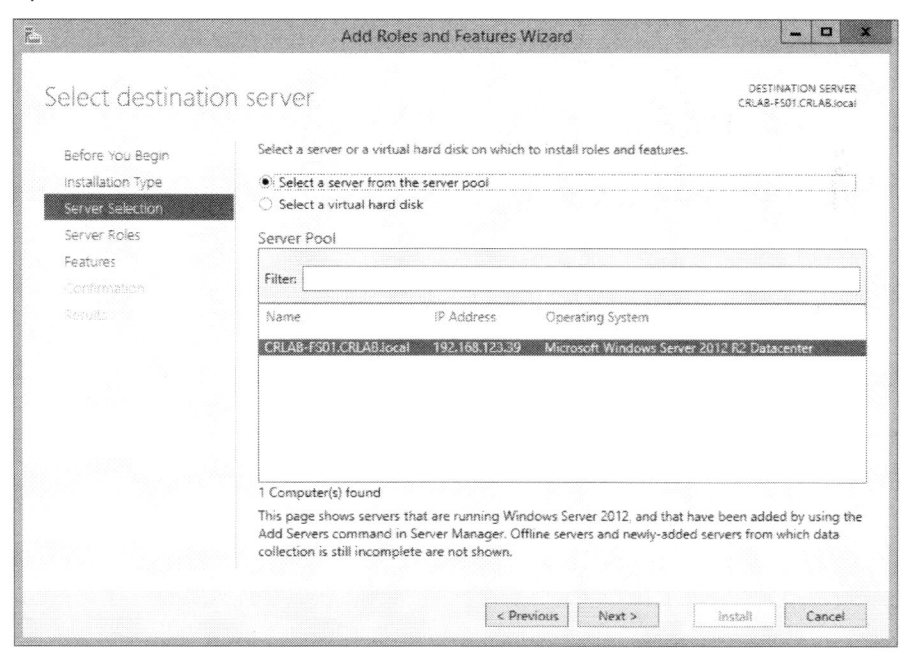

5. Make sure 'File Server' is checked (this is installed with Windows Server 2012 R2 by default).

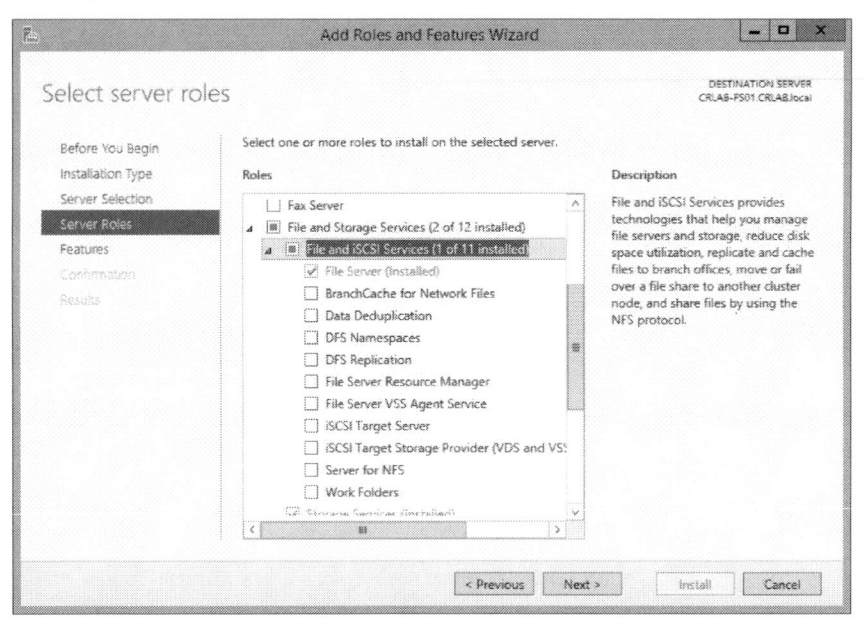

6. If the role is not there, simply install it and finish the wizard. The next step is to create a folder that will hold all the UPDs. For our lab, something under the C: drive will do the trick. When in production, make sure you use a separate drive to host your UPDs, and not the system drive. That said, we will use C:\UPD. Make sure the users on the collection do have access to it (in our case, 'RDS_SD_Collection').

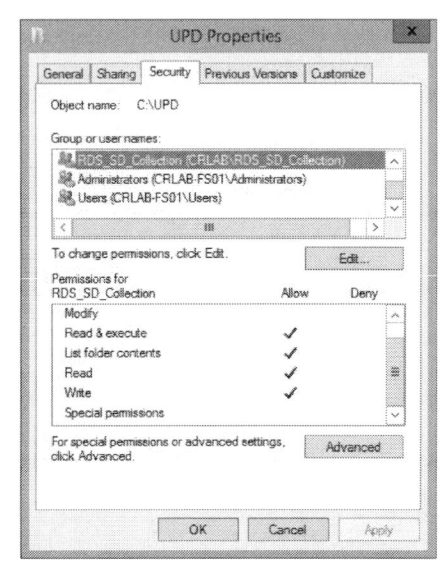

7. Next, we need to create a share to that folder with the correct permissions for the 'RDS_SD_Collection' group. Just launch the 'Server Manager' console on 'CRLAB-FS01' and on the left, select 'File and Storage Services' and click on 'Shares'. Under 'Tasks', select 'New Share'.

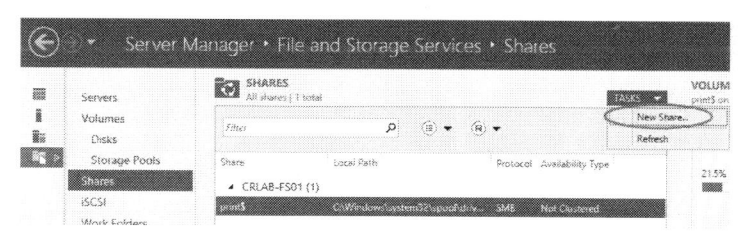

8. As this is a lab environment, select 'SMB Share – Quick' and click 'Next'.

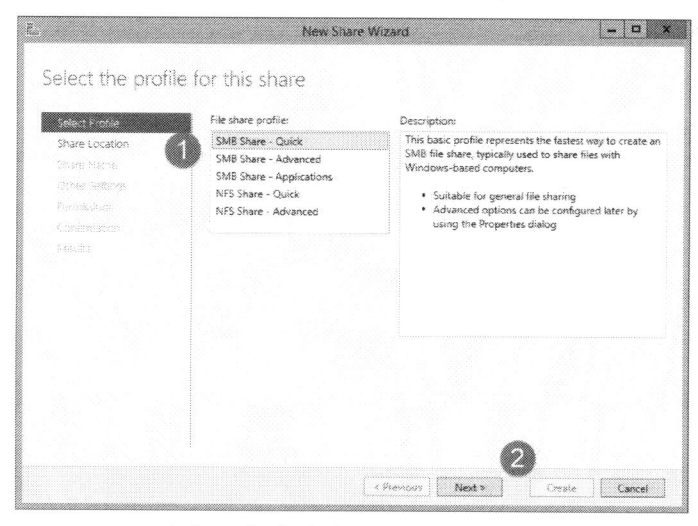

9. Select 'Type a custom path:' and click 'Browse'.

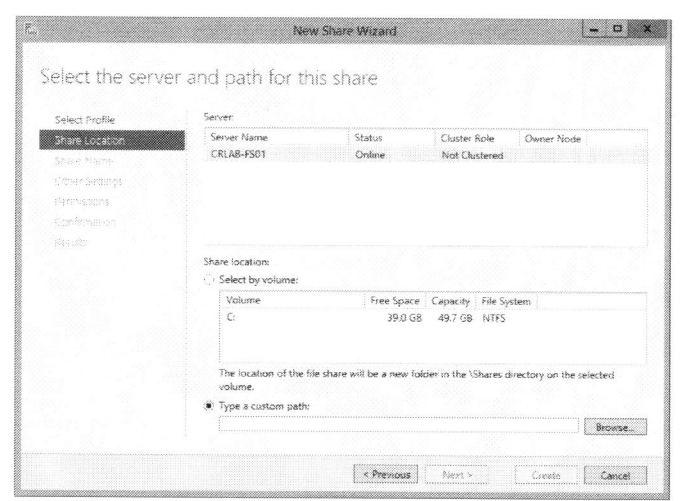

RDS - *The Complete Guide* | Page 203

10. Select the 'UPD' folder we just created and click 'Select Folder'. Then click 'Next'.

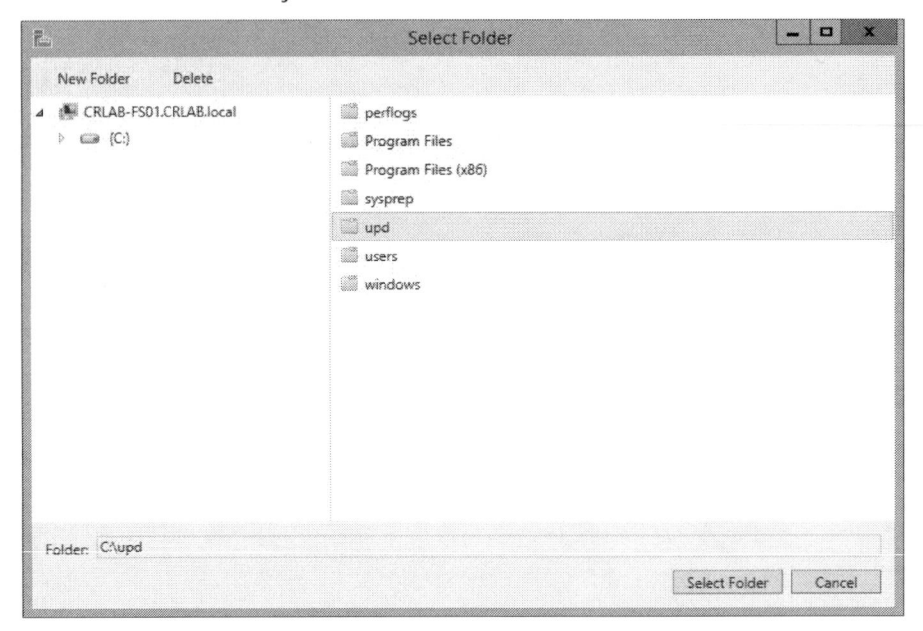

11. Enter the share name you want to use (we accepted the default – if you want, add '$' to the 'Remote path to share:' to make it hidden, i.e. '\\CRLAB-FS01\upd$). Click 'Next'.

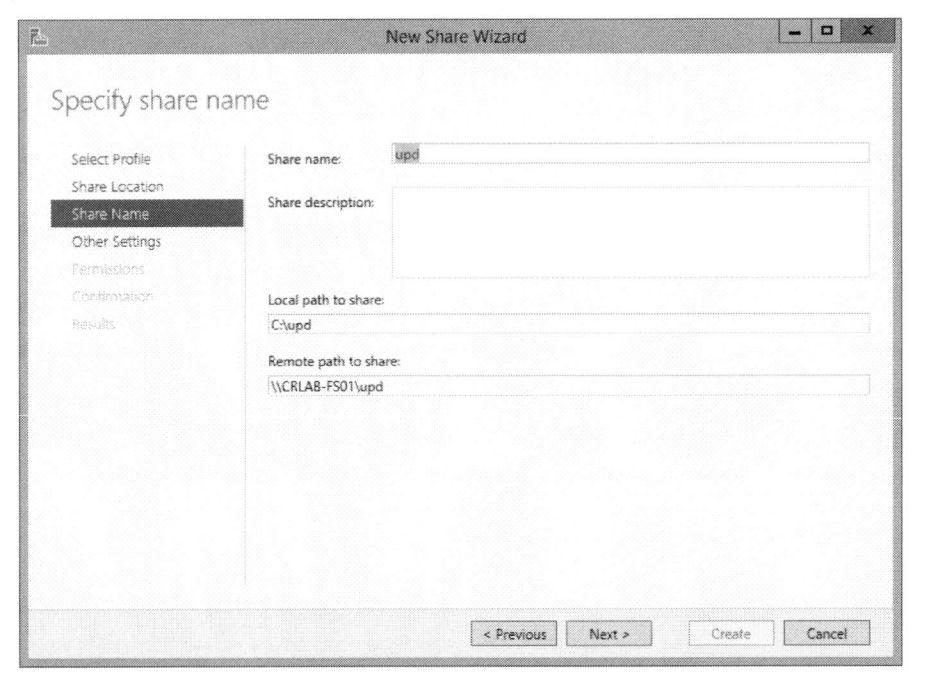

12. Uncheck everything and click 'Next'.

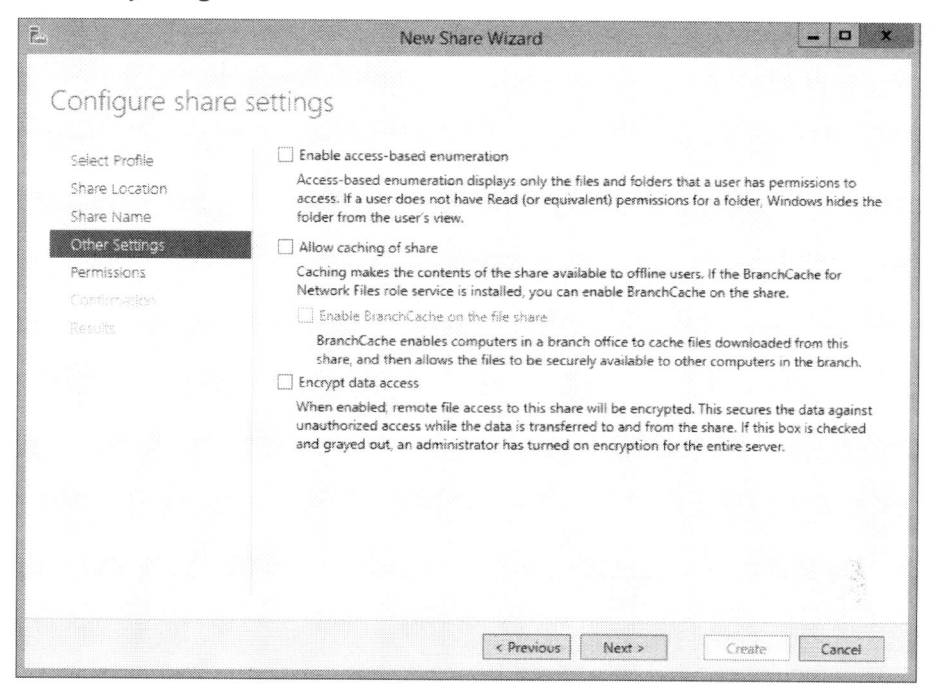

13. Accept the default permissions and click 'Next'.

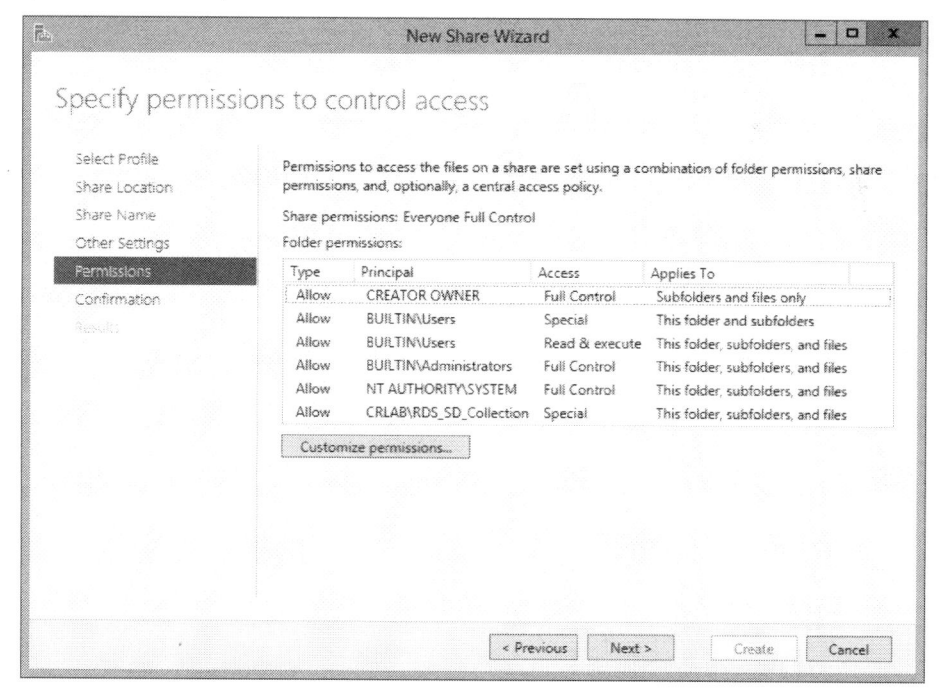

14. Confirm everything and click 'Create'.

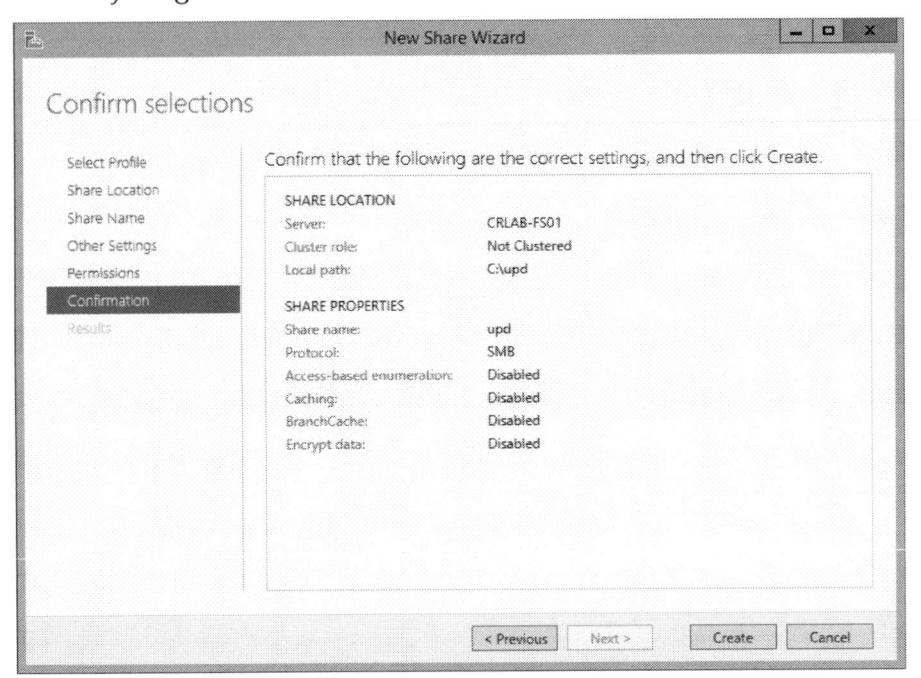

15. The wizard will finish and have everything ready to go. Click 'Close'.

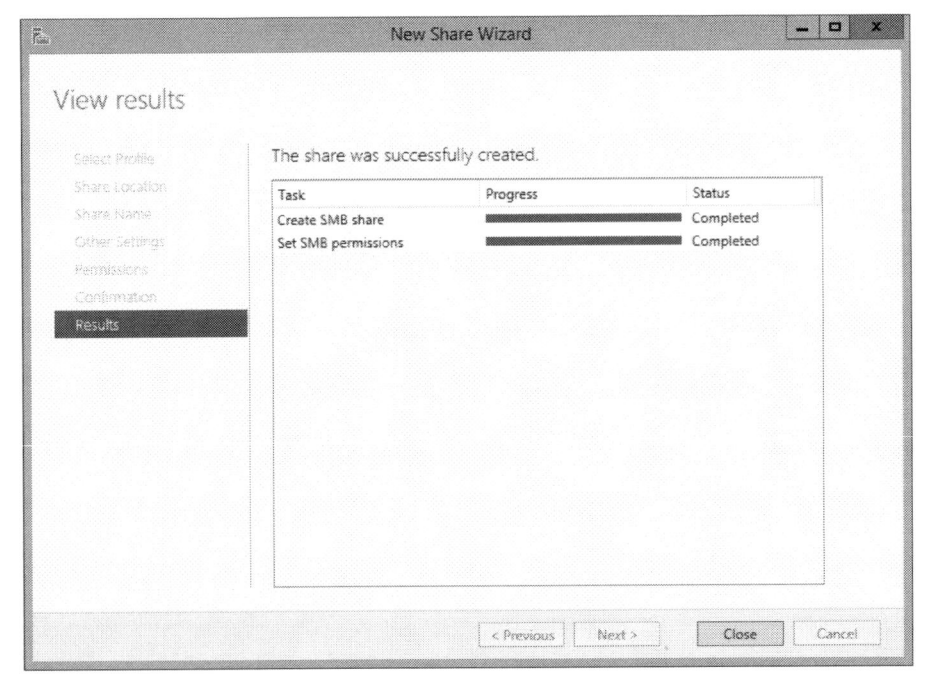

16. If you browse from any other machine to '\\CRLAB-FS01' you will see the share ready for us and of course with no content. We are ready for the UPD setup.

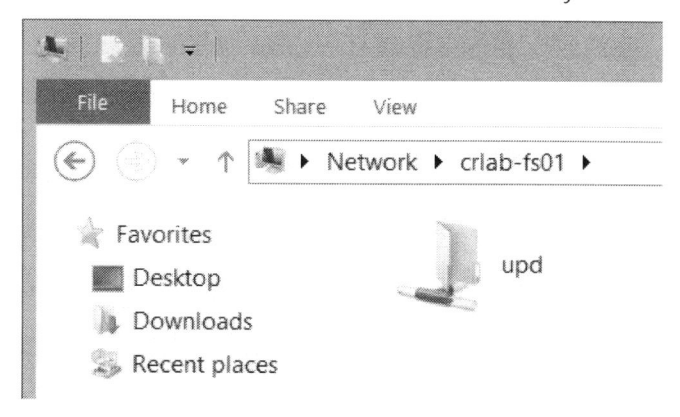

17. If you remember, the UPD setting is part of a session collection. So we need to launch 'Server Manager' on the server managing the whole deployment ('CRLAB-DC01' in our case) and under our session collection 'SD Basic Collection', edit its properties.

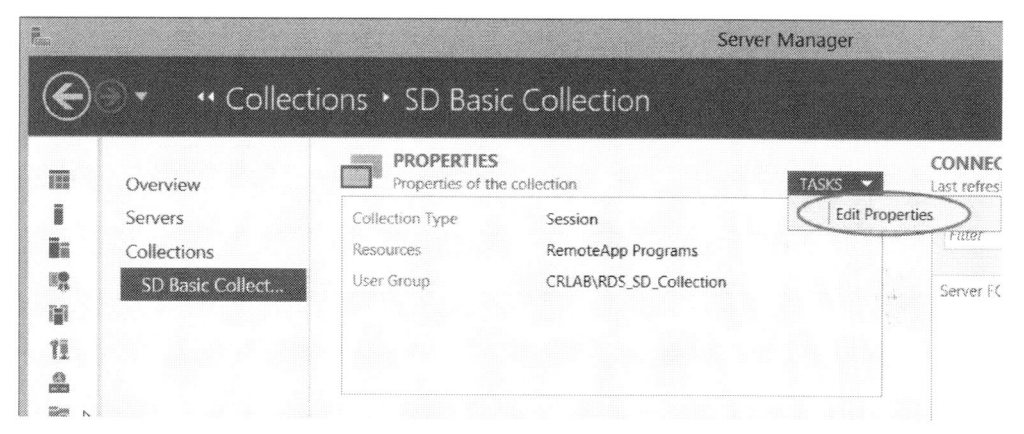

18. Under 'User Profile Disks' check 'Enable user profile disks' and enter the path to the share under 'Location'. For the size we chose 2GB as this is more than enough for our testing purposes. We will also use the default settings regarding which folders to store under the UPD (as we mentioned previously, you can customize it only to include particular folders). Click 'Apply'. The system will create a blank (template) UPD under the share. Simply click 'OK'.

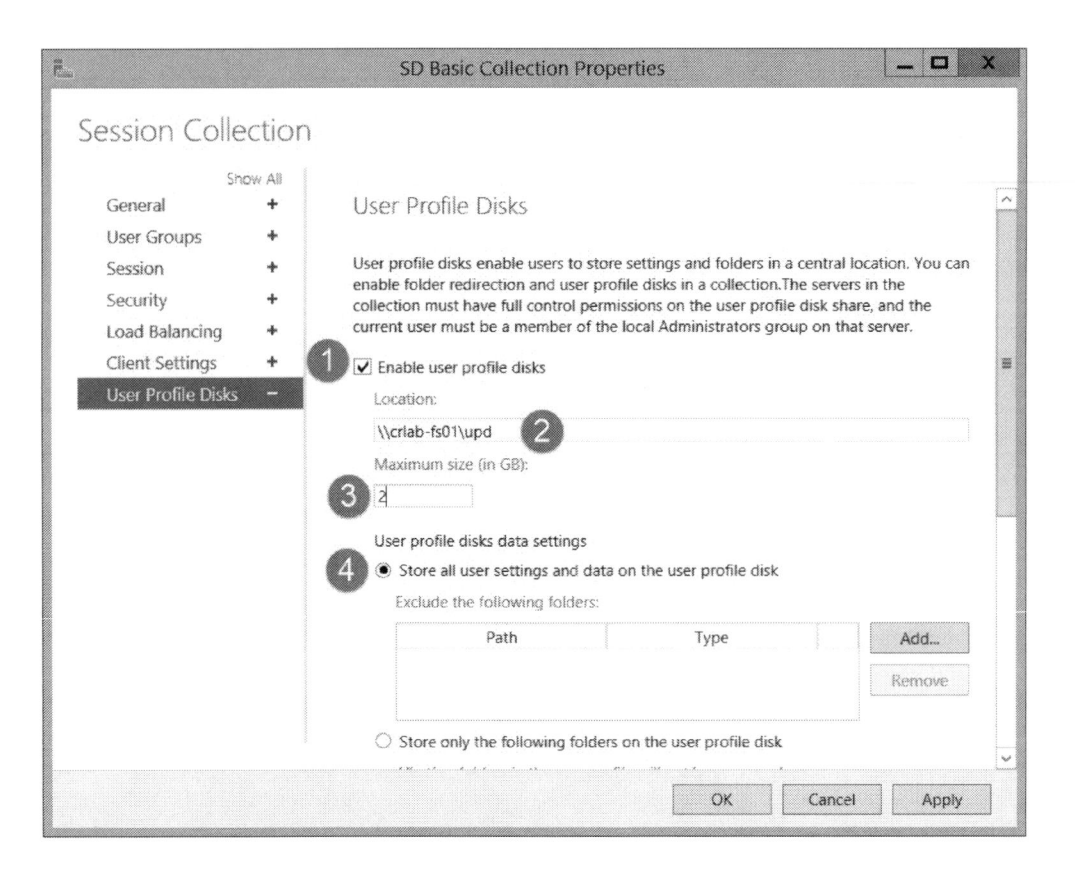

19. If you browse the share you just created, you will find a .VHDX file named UVHD-template.vhdx and as the name implies, every user will get his own .VHDX file based on this template. This also shows the UPD setup was successful.

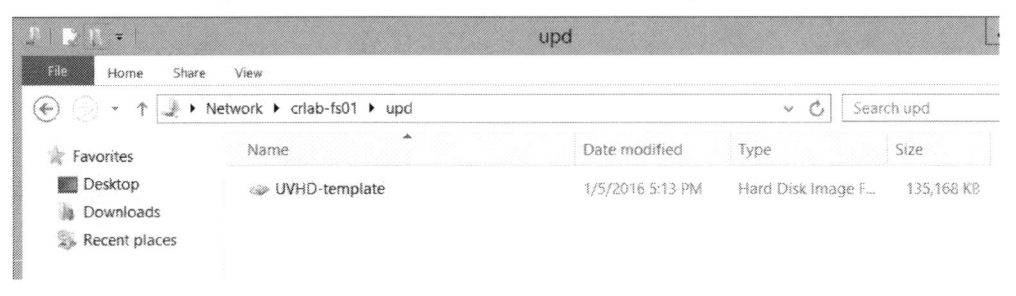

20. UPD is now ready to go.

To verify everything is working as expected, go to a workstation and logon to the environment through the RDWA using a test account (in our case, CRLAB\TestUser1). As soon as we are in, the system creates the .VHDX file for our user on the network share. To make our lives easier, Microsoft decided to use the SID of the user on AD instead of the user name. Keep that in mind.

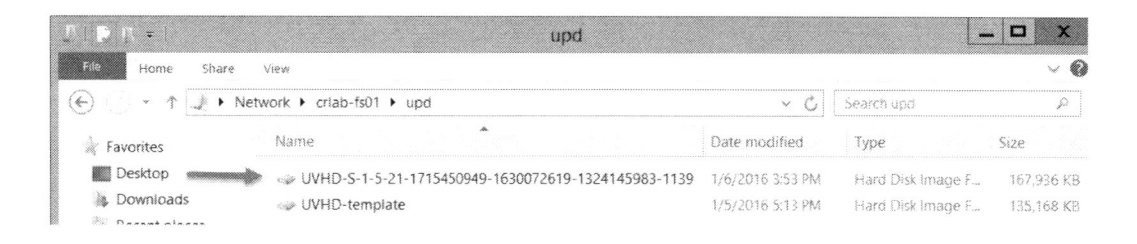

Note: you can download and use the 'ShowUPDFolderDetails.ps1' PowerShell script that Freek created directly from Technet.

https://gallery.technet.microsoft.com/Retrieve-usernames-for-a-94780a9e

It retrieves all the UPD names from the share where they are stored and shows (or exports to a text file) to which user each UPD file belongs to. Very handy.

Since it is just a regular .VHDX file, we can mount it to look inside it. Just go to the share, right-click the .VHDX file and select 'Mount'.

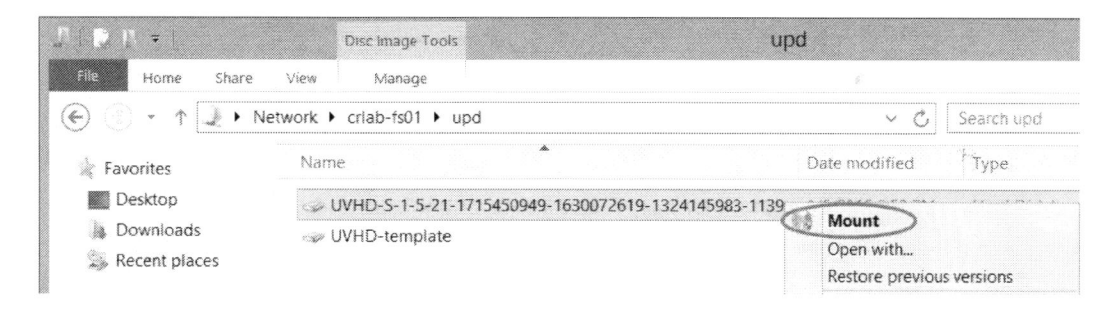

The machine you are on will mount it and assign a local drive letter as any other drive (in our case, E:). Inside it, as expected, we can see the whole user profile as you would normally see under C:\Users\%username%.

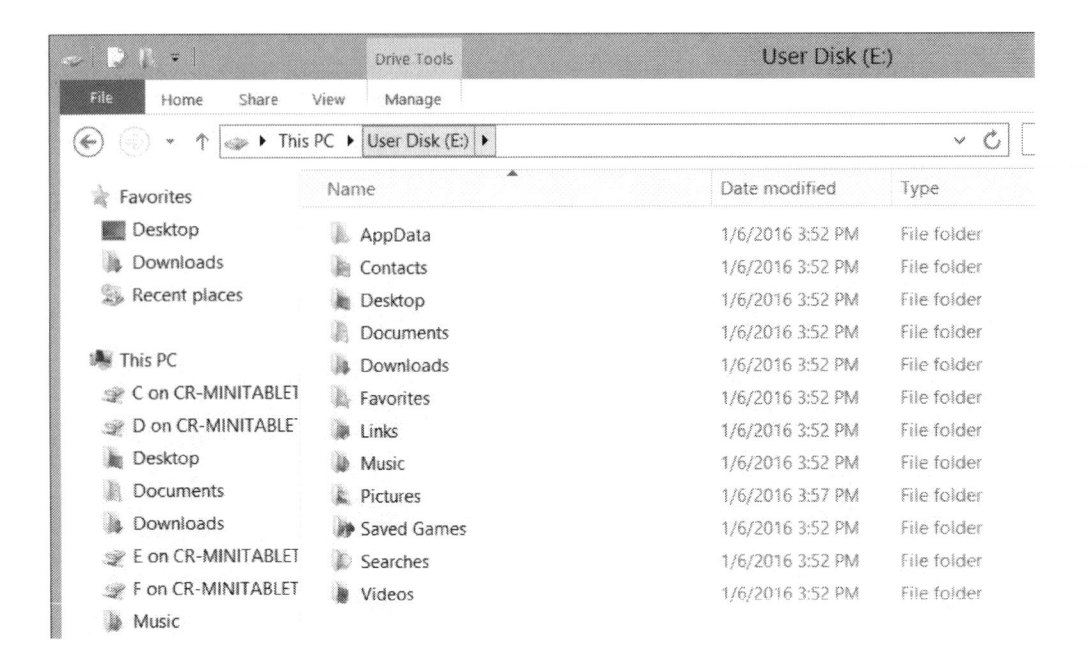

As mentioned before, Group Policies can be used to redirect certain folders out of the UPD file, what will reduce its size. Most folders can be redirected without any issues but special consideration should be given to AppData. Make sure you test all your applications (performance wise) with and without AppData redirection. If you have any questions about AppData, just email Shawn Bass. ☺

It is important to understand, and we cannot mention this enough, that UPD is configured on a per session collection basis. This means if you have multiple session collections providing different applications, user settings between these collections will not roam. Instead, a user with access to multiple collections will (if UPD is configured on both) get a different UPD per collection. The main reason behind this limitation is to prevent temporary profiles. As explained before, UPD is based on a VHDX file per user, and as such, can only be mounted once with write permissions. Therefore, if you had the same UPD file used across multiple collections, a user launching two RemoteApps from two different collections at the same time, would end up with a temporary profile in one of the servers as the VHDX would be already mounted.

Customizing RDWA

Going a bit further with our enhancements, it is time to look at what we can do with the RDWA landing page. As you remember, this is what the default RDWA site looks like:

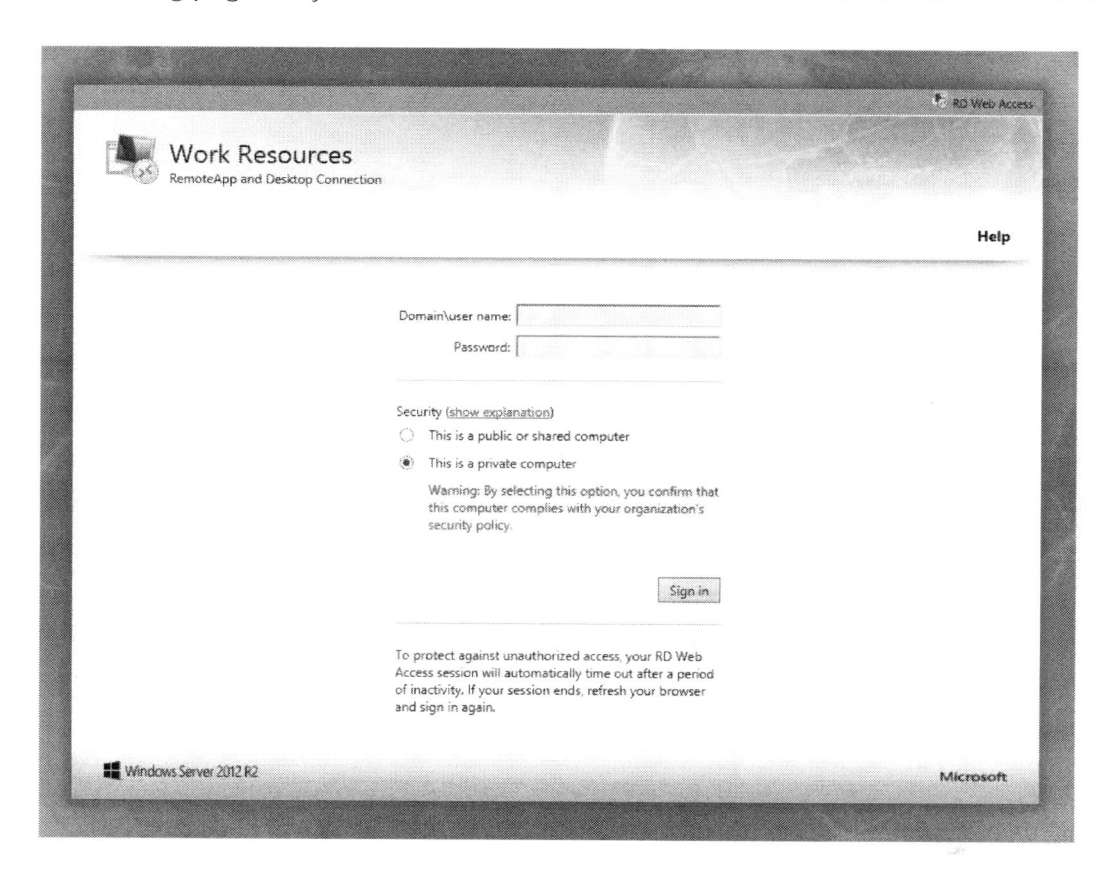

There are several ways to customize it to match your company website design. For example, you can easily change text messages, logos and so on. This is what this section is all about.

New to Windows Server 2012, you can find a file named RDWAStrings.xml under C:\Windows\Web\RDWeb\Pages\en-US on your RDWA. Keep in mind that as we are load balancing these servers, any modifications performed will have to be copied over to the other RDWA. This file contains some of the basic strings used on several RDWA pages. As this is a simple .XML file (text) you can edit it using notepad. By default, this is what this file looks like:

```xml
<?xml version="1.0"?>
<rdwastr:strings xmlns:rdwastr="urn:microsoft.com:rdwastrings">
  <string id="PageTitle">RD Web Access</string>
  <string id="NoScriptWarning">
      <p id="NoScript1">RD Web Access requires JScript. This Web browser either does not support JScript, or scripts are being blocked.</p>
    <br/>
    <br/>
    <p id="NoScript2">To find out whether your browser supports JScript, or to allow scripts, see the browser's online Help.</p>
  </string>
  <string id="HeadingRDWA">RD Web Access</string>
  <string id="HeadingApplicationName">RemoteApp and Desktop Connection</string>
  <string id="Help">Help</string>
  <string id="SignOut">Sign out</string>
  <string id="SearchingForApps">Searching for available RemoteApp programs... </string>
  <string id="CurrentFolder">Current folder: </string>
  <string id="ParentFolder">Up</string>
  <string id="OptimizeMyExperience">Optimize my experience for a LAN network when connecting to the computer or application.</string>
  <string id="PrivateComputer">I am using a private computer that complies with my organization's security policy.</string>
  <string id="MoreInformation">More information...</string>
  <string id="PrivateMore">By selecting this option you can save your credentials so that they can be used in the future when connecting to these programs. Before you select this option, please ensure that saving your credentials is in compliance with your organization's security policy.</string>
  <string id="HideMore">Hide additional information...</string>
</rdwastr:strings>
```

Under C:\Windows\Web\RDWeb\Pages we can also find another file, Web.config, which gives us some additional options. For example, you can configure whether or not you want to hide the 'Remote Desktop' tab users see when they logon to the RDWA, so they can only access your RemoteApps. To do that simply change the following under Web.config:

```
<add key="ShowDesktops" value="true" /> (change to "false")
```

You can also use this file to preset redirection options for Printers, clipboard and so on (these two examples you can set respectively under 'xPrinterRedirection' and 'xClipboard').

If you want to change any of the logos and other images, these are all stored under C:\Windows\Web\RDWeb\Pages\images.

If you checked all the files we mentioned so far you noticed there is no reference to the text shown right on the first page, "Work Resources". There is no way to change it on the files. However, we can do it using PowerShell. Simply use the following command on the server managing the environment (in our case, 'CRLAB-DC01'):

SYNTAX
    Set-RDWorkspace [-Name] <string> [-ConnectionBroker <string>] [<CommonParameters>]

So for our needs:

    set-RDWorkspace -Name "RDS 2012R2 Book" -ConnectionBroker "CRLAB-CB01.CRLAB.local"

This command will update both RDCBs as well both RDWAs. The result is this:

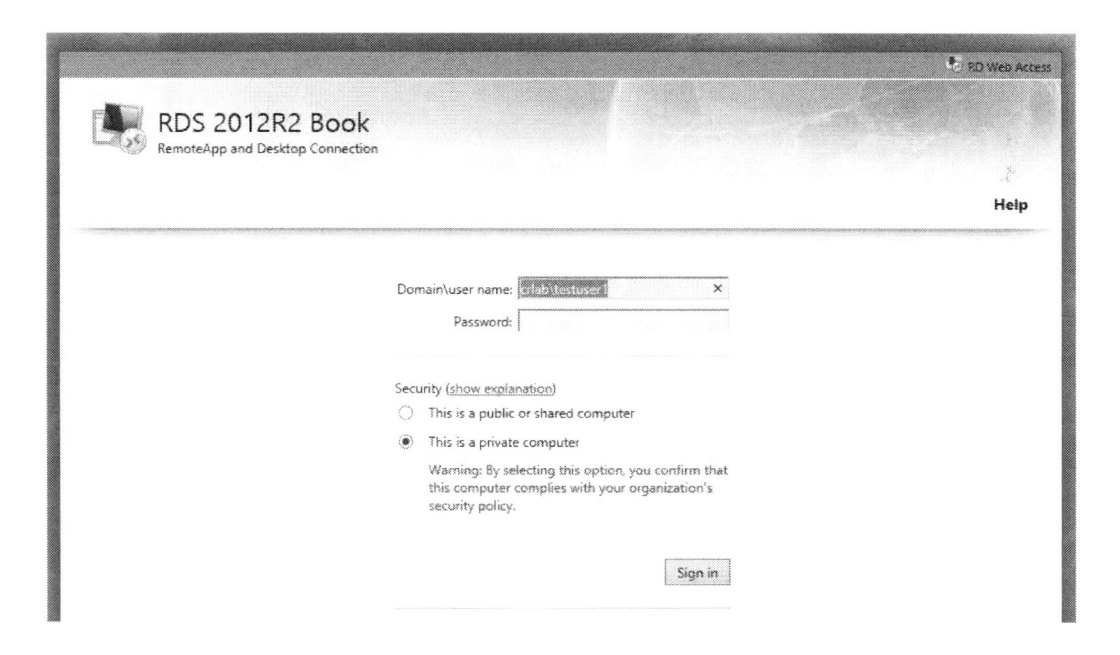

With Windows Server 2012, Microsoft introduced the ability to customize the RDWA pages using what is called a 'central style sheet' or 'CSS' for short. It is a file named 'Site.xlst' that you can find under 'C:\Windows\Web\RDWeb\Pages'.

If we want to review or change certain settings the RDWA uses, all we need to do is to launch 'Internet Information Services (IIS) Manager' on the RDWA.

Under the 'RDWeb' site, if we double-click 'Application Settings', we can find settings like the workspace name (the one we just changed using PowerShell), its ID and even the RDCBs we are using. As you may have guessed, all the wizards we ran previously, when creating the deployment, set these.

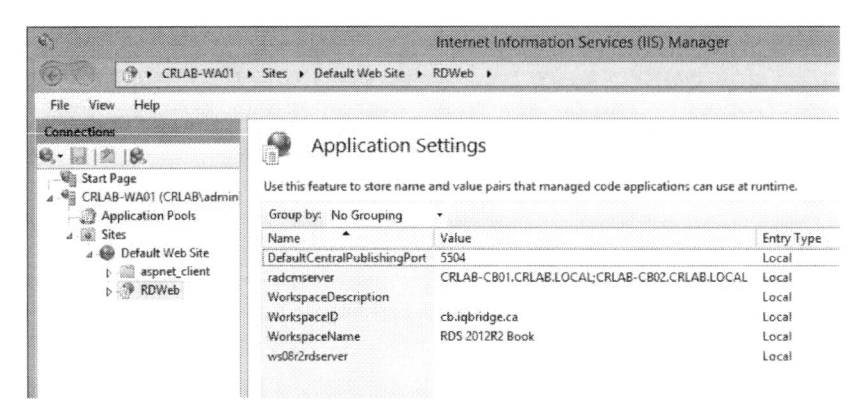

The 'Application Settings' at the 'Pages' level also contains some of the connection settings used on the 'Connect to a Remote PC' tab.

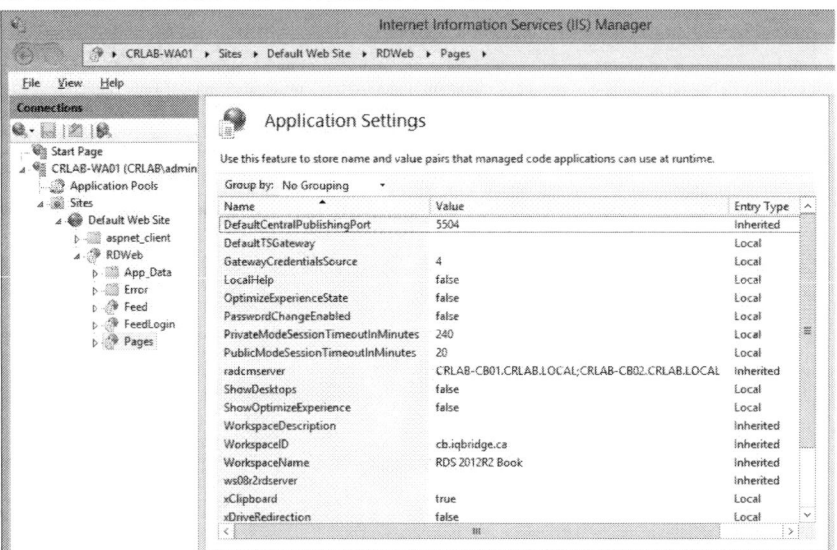

One of the settings we would like to highlight here is the PasswordChangeEnabled one. By default, it is disabled. Before Windows Server 2012, a user with an expired password was not able to logon at all, as the RDWA page would not provide a way to change an expired password. This is now possible (since Windows Server 2012 was released). All you need to do is to enable the PasswordChangeEnabled option here. After that, when a user tries to logon with an expired password he will be notified and will see a link to a page where he will be able to change it (the page is 'passwords.aspx'). Great, eh?

By clicking on the link provided, the user is presented with the page shown below, where he can then change his expired password.

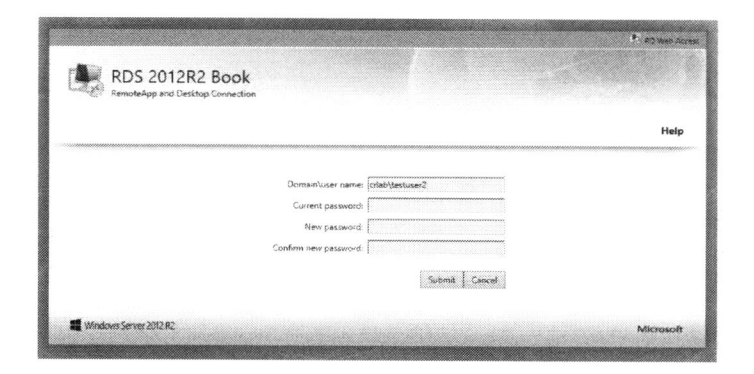

Note: we found a bug on RDWA and you will probably notice when looking at the password change page above. The text seen at the top left corner will not be the same as the one you set using the PowerShell cmdlet. To fix this, open the password.aspx file under 'C:\Windows\Web\RDWeb\Pages\en-us' and change line 14 to match the workspace name you chose. This is the line we are talking about:

string L_CompanyName_Text = "RDS 2012R2 Book";

For our final customization, we will show you how to redirect the default page to the RDWeb one. What we mean is if the user simply types http://wa.iqbridge.ca (this is our FQDN after fixing the environment for internal/external access) he is presented with the default IIS page:

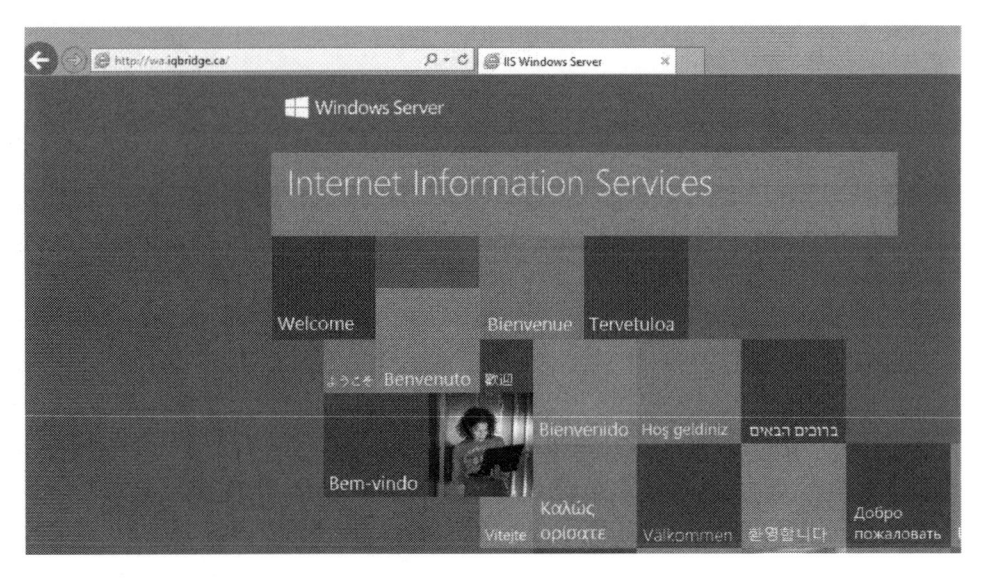

This is not good right? Ideally, we would like to redirect the user (no matter if he uses http or https) to the RDWeb page. So, let's do it:
1. Launch 'Internet Information Services (IIS) Manager' on the RDWA server (you must do this on both RDWAs, as we do have them in HA).
2. Select 'Default Web Site' on the left and then double click 'HTTP Redirect' on the middle pane.

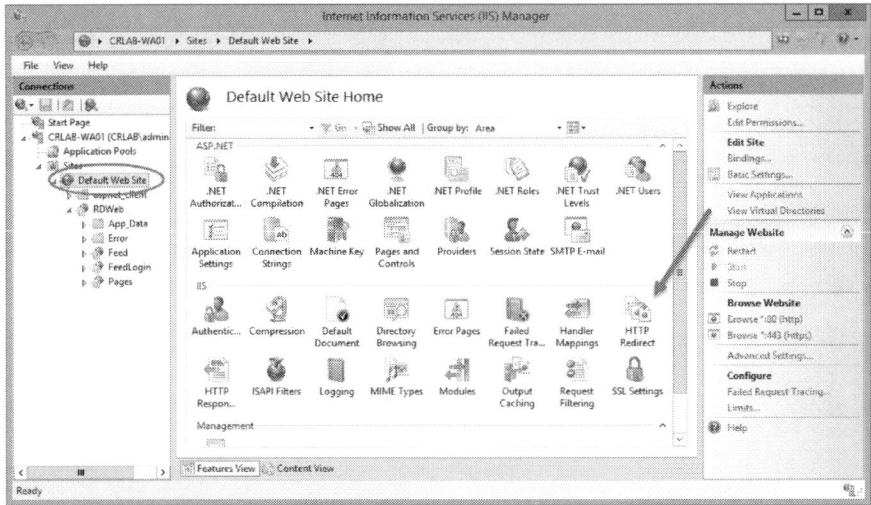

3. Select 'Redirect requests to this destination' and enter the path to the RDWeb site (in our case https://wa.iqbridge.ca/RDWeb). Make sure you also select 'Only redirect requests to content in this directory (not subdirectories)'. Click 'Apply'.

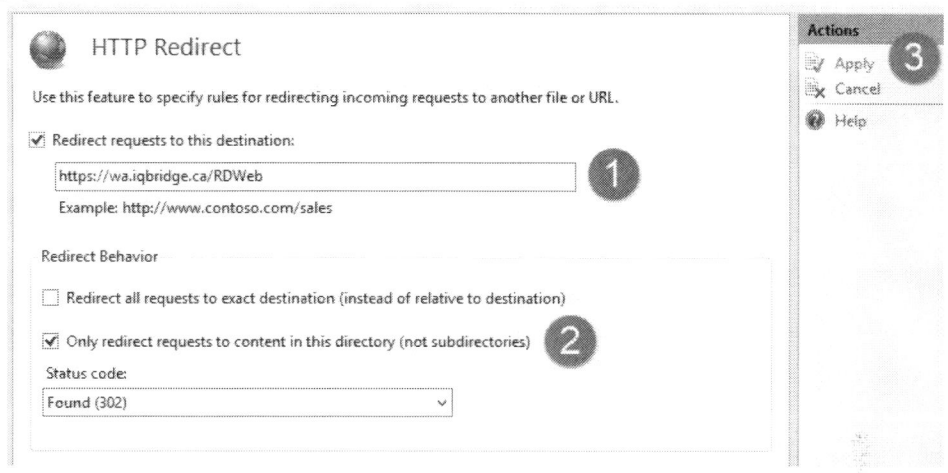

4. No need to restart anything. Now, no matter what the user uses (http or https) he will be redirected to the main RDWeb page. Perfect!

For additional customization options we recommend you take a look at the following articles by Arjan Mensh:

https://msfreaks.wordpress.com/2013/12/29/step-by-step-customizing-rd-web-access-2012-r2/
https://msfreaks.wordpress.com/2014/01/02/step-by-step-customizing-rd-web-access-2012-r2-part-2/
https://msfreaks.wordpress.com/2014/01/02/step-by-step-customizing-rd-web-access-2012-r2-part-3/
https://msfreaks.wordpress.com/2014/07/22/properly-removing-the-domain-prefix-requirement-from-rd-web-access-2012-r2/
https://msfreaks.wordpress.com/2015/01/14/rd-web-access-automate-bing-wallpaper-integration/ (one of our favorite modifications).

This is what it looks like after using the Bing wallpaper modification:

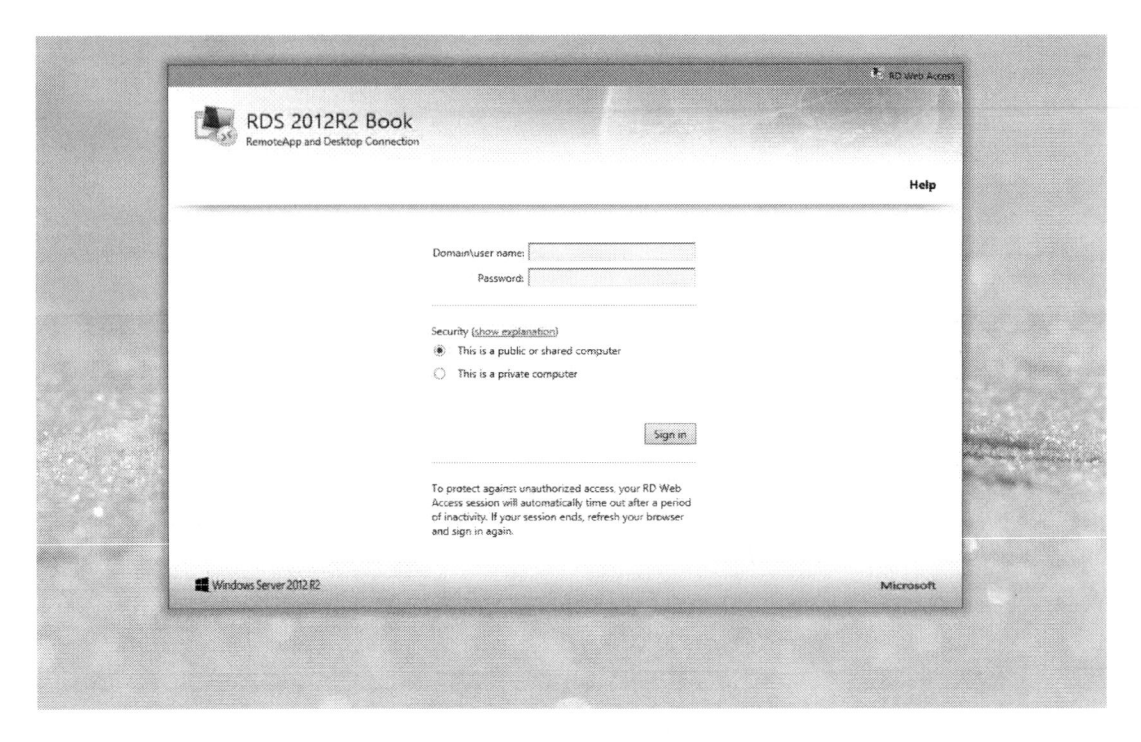

The PowerShell script to download the Bing wallpaper can be found here (amazing work by Michael Verbeek):

http://www.microsoftpro.nl/2015/01/19/using-the-daily-bing-wallpaper-as-desktop-background/

Just use a scheduled task and your RDWA page will change every single day for a great look and feel. ☺

That is all for RDWA customizations.

Performing a Role Based Deployment

The past section, "Performing a Standard deployment" has been a very big part, if not the biggest one, of this book so far. We have spent quite some time on the scenario-based deployments, as they were introduced for the first time with Windows Server 2012.

However, we still have the traditional role-based deployment available. Role-based deployment is not new, and has been around since Windows Server 2008 and could, theoretically, still be used as an alternative to the quick and standard deployments you just learned.

You can still use the role-based deployment to add additional roles besides the ones related to RDS. For RDS however, it makes more sense to use the scenario-based deployment. In addition, the reason for doing that, now that you went through deploying a fully functional RDS deployment, is simple. Why would you want to install the RDS roles all separately and then try to "glue" them together by using the new Server Manager console? It is just too much room for error. Something can go wrong and certainly will.

There are only two scenarios where we can see anyone doing a role-based RDS deployment instead of using the quick/standard ones. The first obvious one is simple to see, especially if you come from a Citrix background. Citrix Xenapp runs on top of RDS, as an add-on. Therefore, the RDS Session Host role must be there in order for XenApp to load. And as it is RDS based, licensing is a requirement. Therefore, at the end, even if using Citrix XenApp, you still need RDSHs and RDLS.

The second scenario is one that most people do not even realize it is possible: installing RDGWs to provide remote access to any sort of machine inside your network. Yes, you can do that and without any additional RDS role. No RDCB, RDWA, RDSH required. With a proper CAP/RAP you can have the RDGW (load balanced too as we showed you previously) as an entry point to any machine on your network, as long as RDP access is enabled on such machines. This means people would be able to connect to their desktops on their desks at the office, from their home machines if you allow them to. Great scenario if you ask me, and again, one that people are not even aware of.

We cannot think of any additional scenarios though. Actually, there may be another one but, in our opinion, it makes no sense and you will see why. Let's say you want to publish just a single RDSH for a small number of users, where you do not need RemoteApps or Connection Brokering. In that case, you could simply install the RDSH role on that one server, using the role-based deployment. Let's do it so you can understand what the problem with this approach is.

1. For this we created a temporary server, 'CRLAB-SH03' but this can be done on any server. Launch the 'Server Manager' console and select '2. Add roles and features'.

   1 Configure this local server

   2 Add roles and features

   3 Add other servers to manage

   4 Create a server group

   5 Connect this server to cloud services

2. The wizard will launch. Click 'Next'.

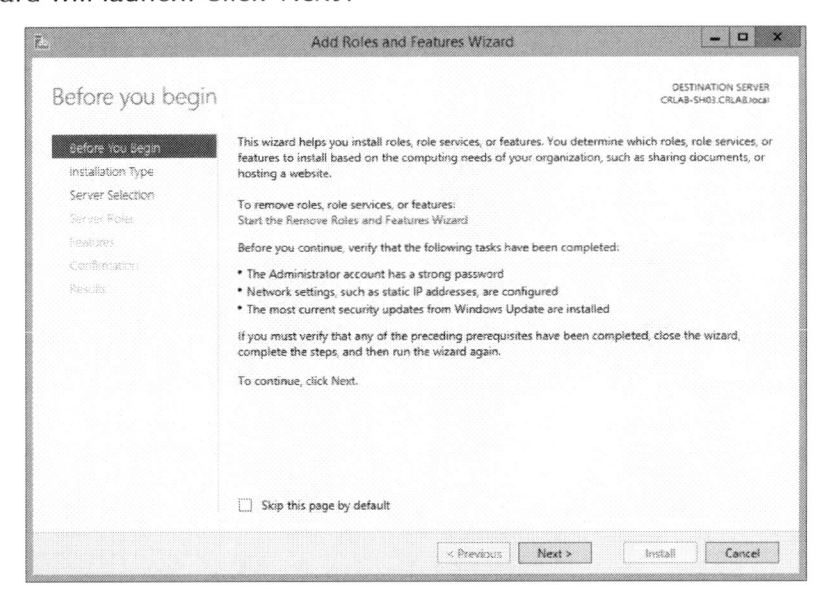

Page 220 | RDS - The Complete Guide

3. Select 'Role-based or feature-based installation' and click 'Next'.

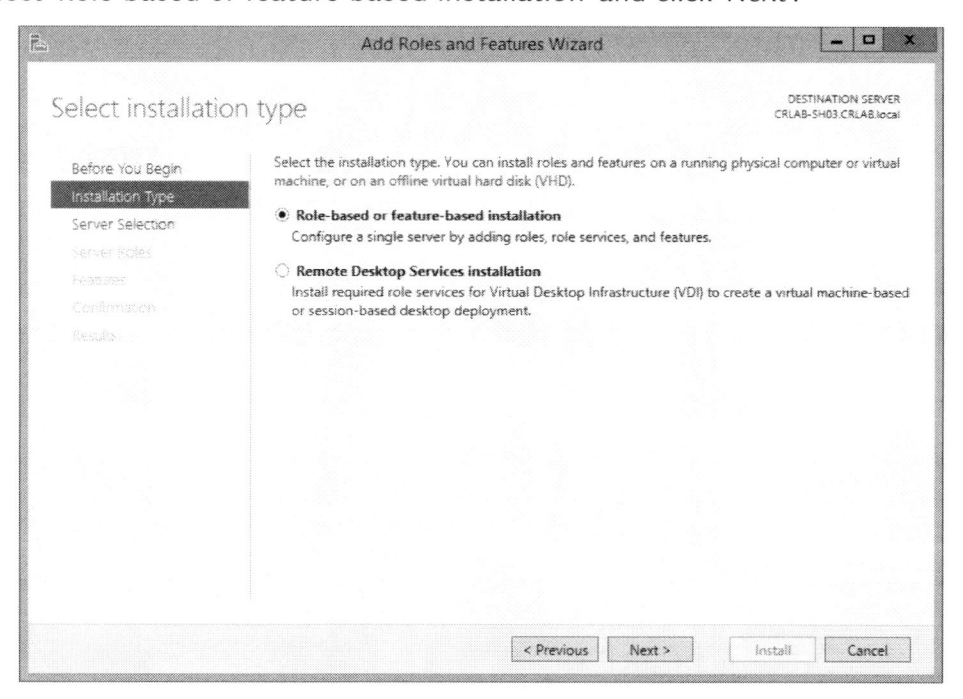

4. As we are doing this directly on the local server, simply click 'Next'.

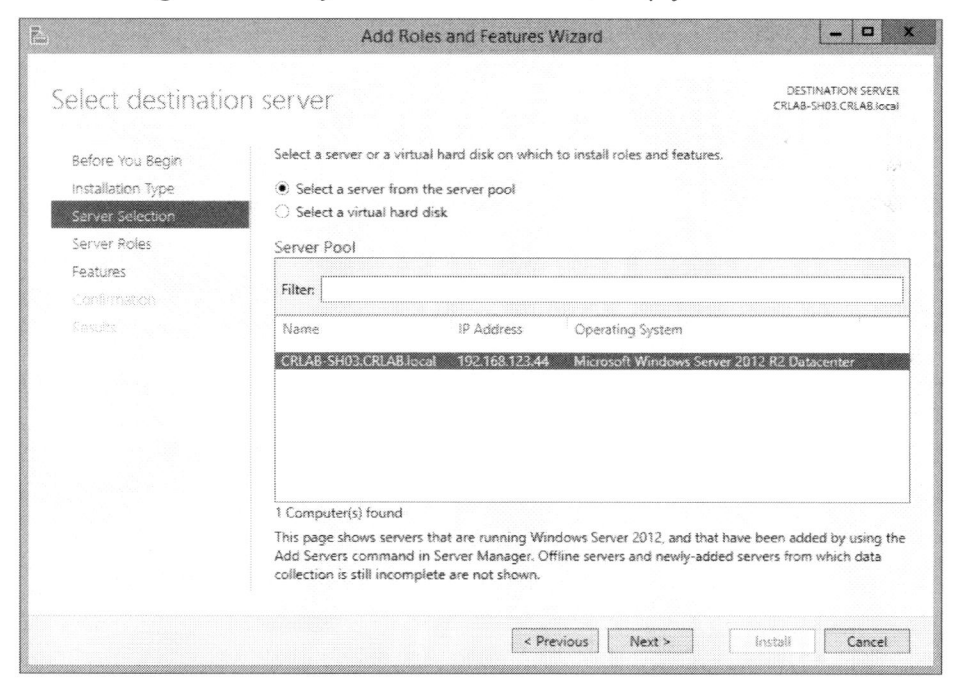

5. Select 'Remote Desktop Services' and click 'Next'.

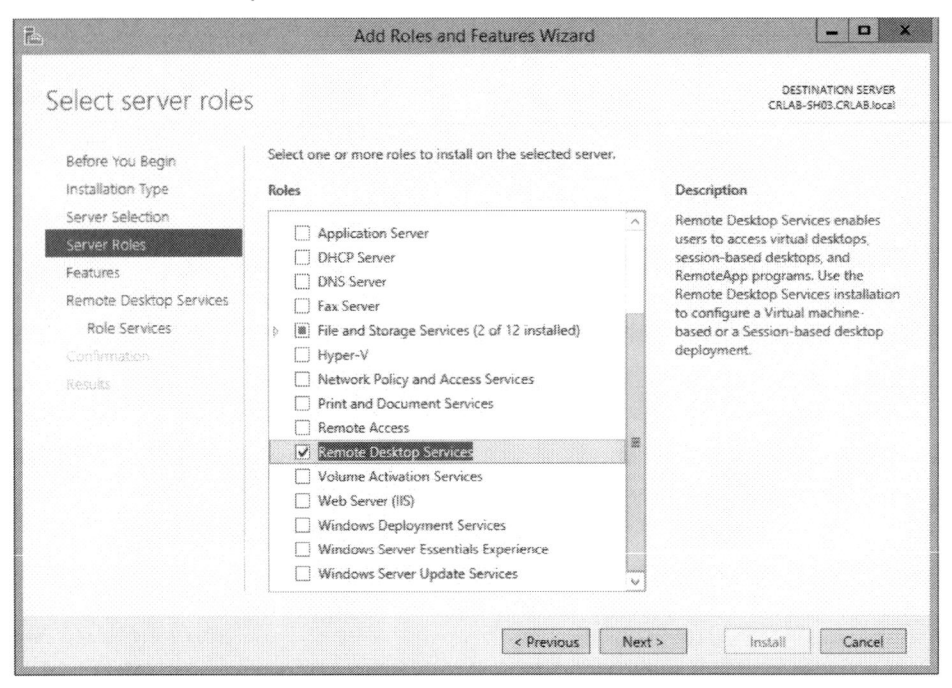

6. As this is just an RDSH, there is no need for any additional feature. Click 'Next'.

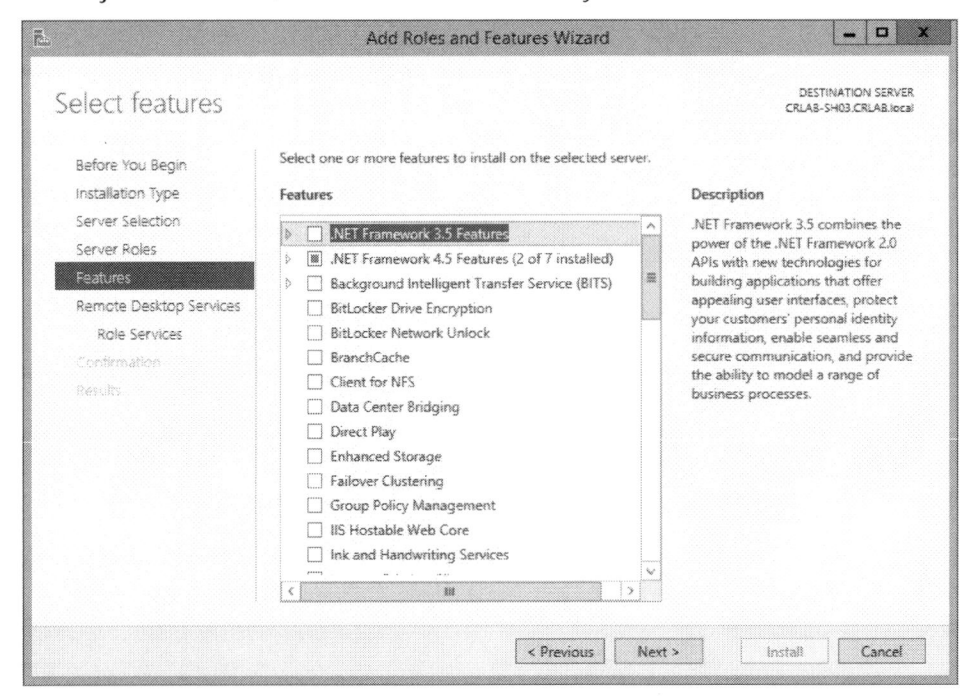

7. The wizard gives us a little background on what RDS is ☺. Click 'Next'.

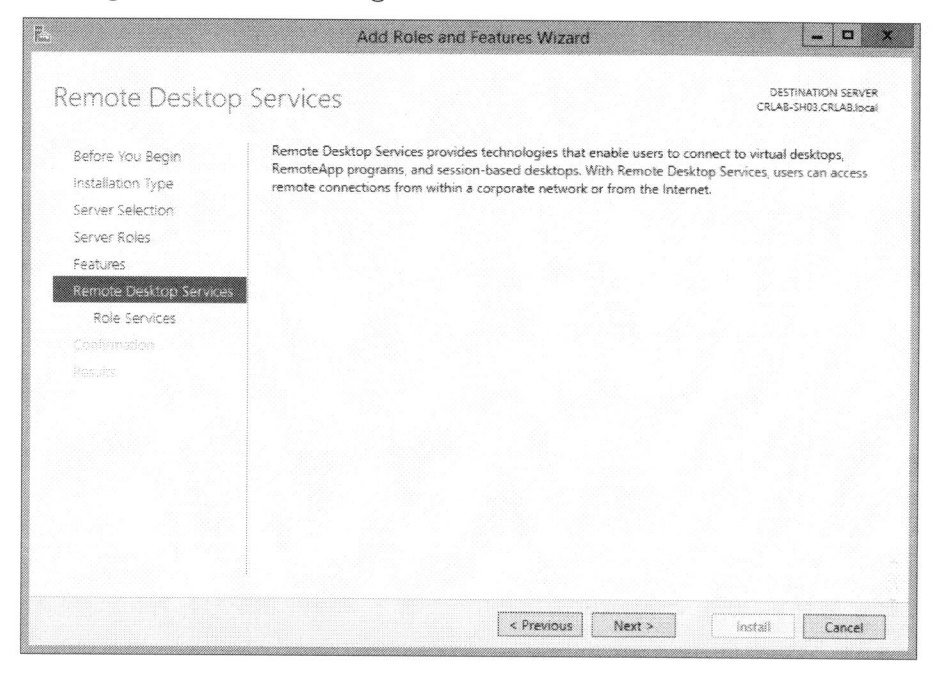

8. All we want is RDSH. Select 'Remote Desktop Session Host' and click 'Next'.

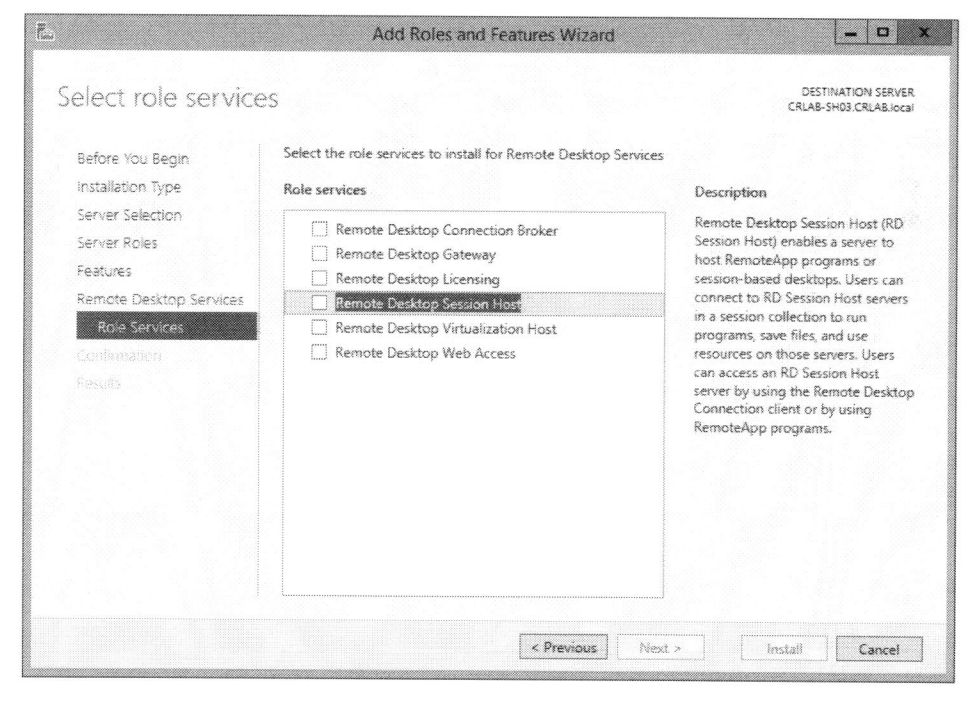

RDS - The Complete Guide | Page 223

9. The wizard will prompt you about additional features required. Just click 'Add Features' and then click 'Next'.

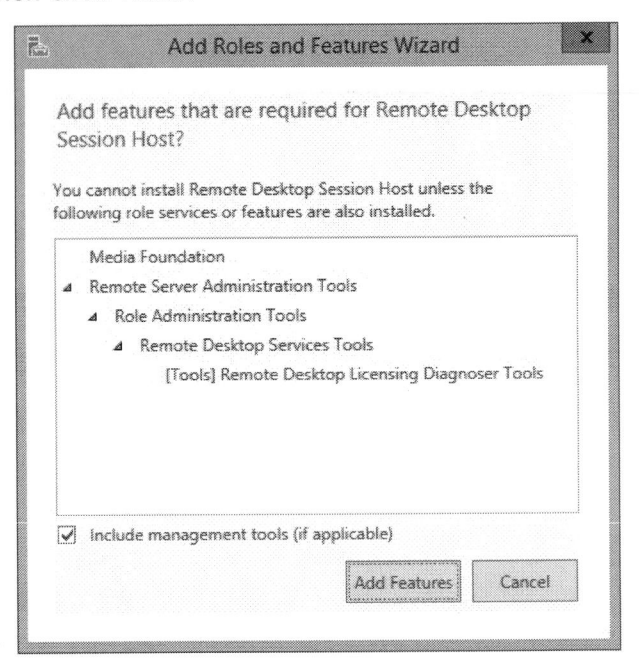

10. Review your selections and click 'Install'. Make sure you select 'Restart the destination server automatically if required'.

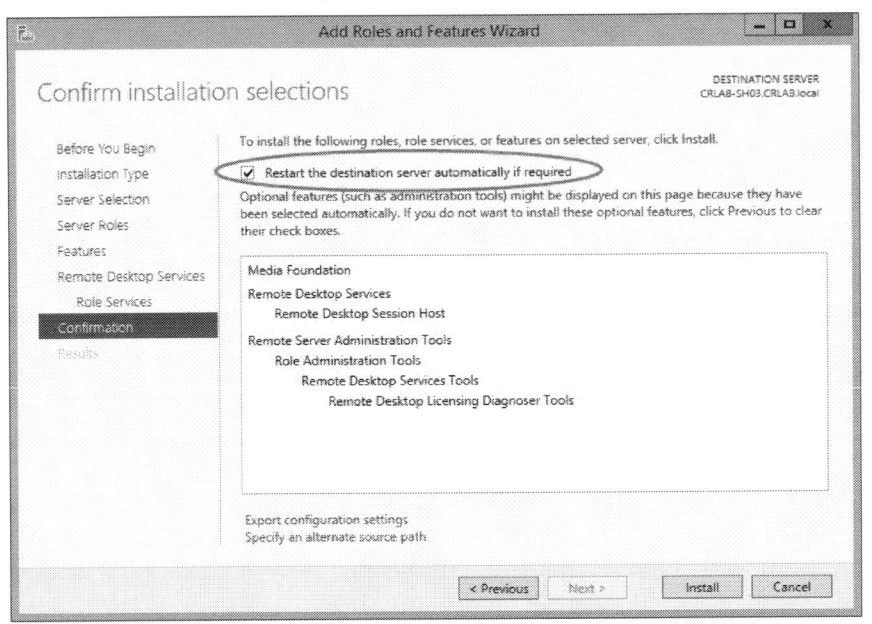

11. The server will reboot. Log back in and you will see the wizard just showing us it all went well. Click 'Close'.

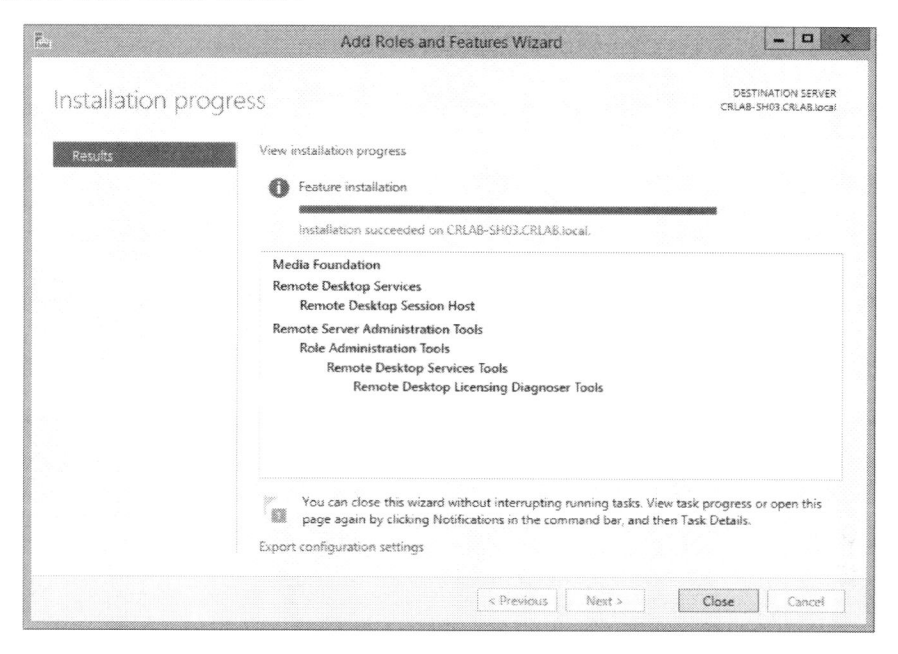

Everything seems great, right? If you launch the 'Server Manager' console and click on the 'Remote Desktop Services' section on the left, you will notice the following:

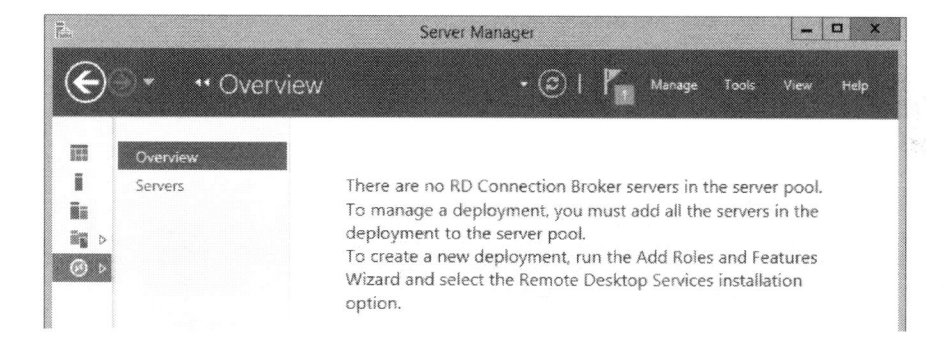

As explained earlier, RDS on Windows Server 2012 and up, relies on having an RDCB available as part of the deployment. As in this example we do not have one, even though you would be able start sessions to this RDSH, there would be no way to configure or manage it using the 'Server Manager' console.

By now, given all you learned about RDS so far, I can bet you are thinking "Well, let's just add the RDCB role here!". Ok, I will follow your thoughts then. Let's add it.

We just repeat the steps above but this time instead of selecting 'Remote Desktop Session Host' we select 'Remote Desktop Connection Broker'.

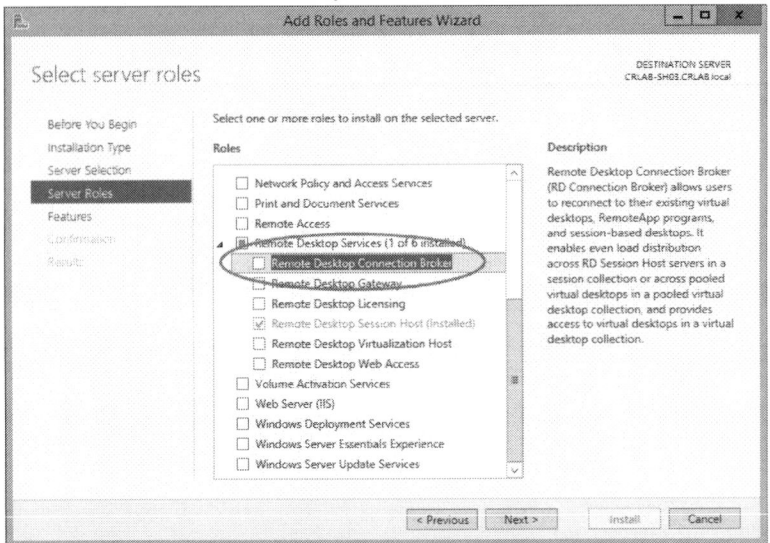

So now, if you launch the 'Server Manager' console one more time, that warning must be gone. Nope.

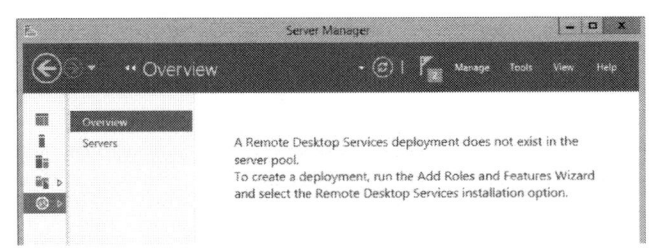

As you can see, even with an RDCB as part of our environment, running on the same server, it tells us to run the scenario-based deployment. At the end, does it make sense to use the role-based deployment to deploy RDS? Not at all.

If you try to fix this by using the 'Remote Desktop Services installation' option, it will detect the RDCB and will wrap it up for you. What leads us to the exact same thing if we had used it in the first place!

Something similar happens when you try to deploy RDS without a domain. You will see it does not allow you to do it, as it is one of the pre-requisites for the deployment. You can certainly deploy a full RDS environment in a domain controller (unbelievably, it is now a supported scenario) but this is not something we would recommend, regardless of what the support policy is. ☺

Using the RemoteDesktop PowerShell Module

So far, we have been deploying and configuring RDS using the 'Server Manager' console that comes with Windows Server 2012 R2. That is great, but one of the best things introduced with Windows Server 2012, and refined with 2012 R2 and later releases, is the fact you can do about anything with PowerShell. To give you an idea, over 70 cmdlets are available for RDS.

In this chapter, we will walk you through some of the PowerShell commands that come with Windows Server 2012 R2. Stay tuned.

Importing the RemoteDesktop module

The first step when using PowerShell for any of the services available within Windows Server 2012 R2 is to import the corresponding PowerShell module. This is done by using the 'Import-Module' command, passing the proper name as a parameter. In our case, as you guessed it, it is called RemoteDesktop.

Installing a Session Based Desktop Deployment

Now that we have the proper module loaded, let's start by creating a 'Session –Based' desktop deployment. The syntax for this command is

SYNTAX
   New-SessionDeployment [-ConnectionBroker] <String> [-SessionHost] <String[]>
   [[-WebAccessServer] <String>][<CommonParameters>]

Exactly like when using the 'Quick' or 'Standard' scenario-based deployment via the GUI, we need to specify the hostname of the server that we want to install the RD Connection Broker, RD Web Access and RD Session Host roles on.

To achieve the same result as when we used the GUI, we use the following command:

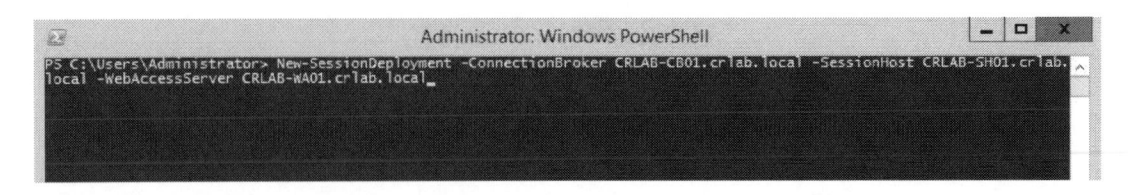

```
PS C:\Users\Administrator> New-SessionDeployment -ConnectionBroker CRLAB-CB01.crlab.local -SessionHost CRLAB-SH01.crlab.
local -WebAccessServer CRLAB-WA01.crlab.local_
```

Note that this installs the RDCB, RDWA and RDSH roles on the servers specified. But, as you may have guessed, it does not create an initial collection and therefore we have no session collections yet. The reason for this is the 'New-SessionDeployment' command is in fact a standard deployment. If we specify a single server for all three roles, you would end up with the same as a quick deployment via the GUI but without a session collection.

Creating a Session Collection

The next step is to get a session collection going. As expected there is a command for that, 'New-RDSessionCollection'.

SYNTAX

New-RDSessionCollection [-CollectionName] <string> -SessionHost <string[]>

[-CollectionDescription <string>] [-ConnectionBroker <string>] [<CommonParameters>]

To create a new session collection, we need to specify the name we want for it, a session host, a description and a connection broker. After the command finishes we receive confirmation and a summary of what has been configured for us.

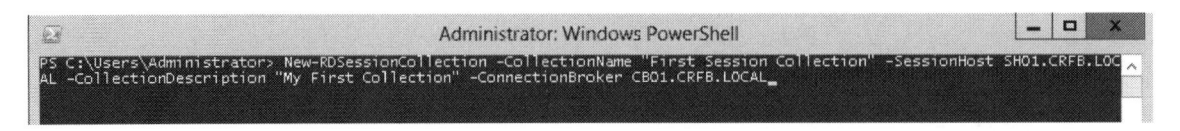

```
PS C:\Users\Administrator> New-RDSessionCollection -CollectionName "First Session Collection" -SessionHost SH01.CRFB.LOC
AL -CollectionDescription "My First Collection" -ConnectionBroker CB01.CRFB.LOCAL_
```

Note that, just like when performing a 'Quick Deployment' using the GUI, by default the group <domain>\domain users will be assigned to the collection that was just created. We assume you do not want to give access to every single user and if that is indeed the case, you will want to change that. This is done by using the command Set-RDSessionCollectionConfiguration which allows you to change any configuration setting for a particular session collection.

Creating Remote Apps

The RemoteDesktop PowerShell module can also be used to create and maintain RemoteApps. To do this, we use the command 'New-RDRemoteApp'.

SYNTAX

    New-RDRemoteApp [-CollectionName] <string> -DisplayName <string> -FilePath <string>
    [-Alias <string>] [-FileVirtualPath <string>] [-ShowInWebAccess <bool>] [-FolderName
    <string>] [-CommandLineSetting <CommandLineSettingValue> {DoNotAllow | Allow | Require}]
    [-RequiredCommandLine <string>] [-UserGroups <string[]>] [-IconPath <string>] [-IconIndex
    <string>] [-ConnectionBroker string>] [<CommonParameters>]

We need to specify an unique alias, a display name, the location for the application, the session collection name we want to assign it to and the name of the RD Connection Broker server. As an example, to create a RemoteApp for mspaint.exe we use the following command:

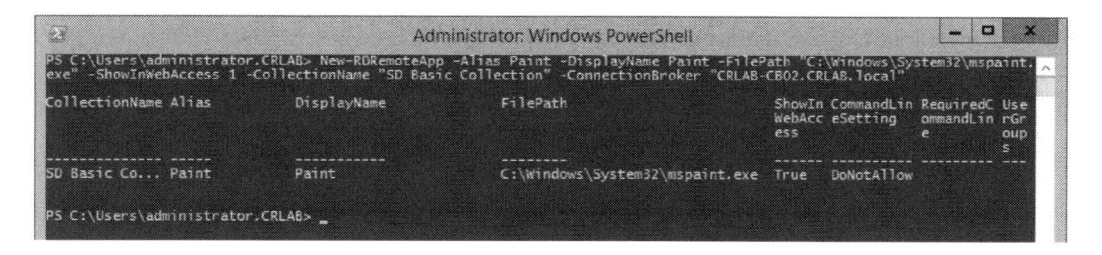

If we refresh the 'RemoteApp Programs' section in the 'Server Manager', the RemoteApp is now there:

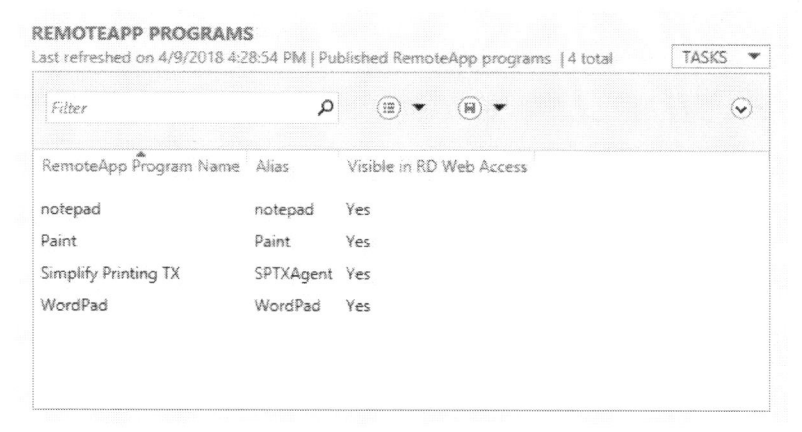

And since we forced a 'True (1)' value for the parameter -ShowInWebAccess (which is optional) the RemoteApp is available in RD Web Access too.

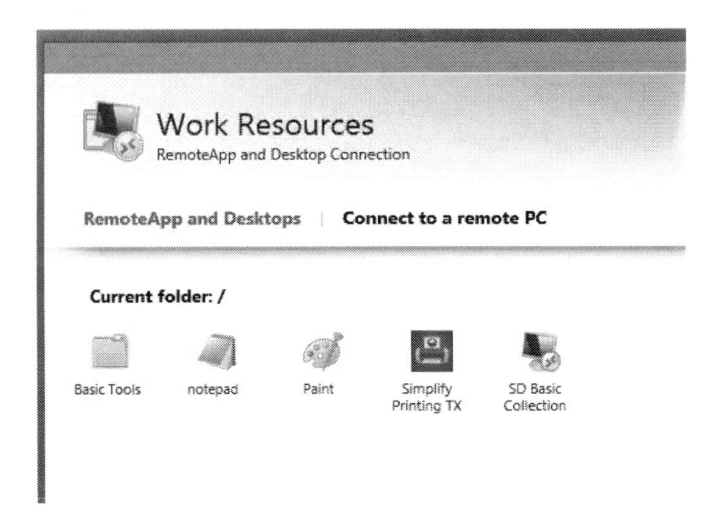

If we did not want that to happen we would use '-ShowInWebAccess 0' as a parameter. After a RemoteApp is created you can change all its properties using the command 'Set-RDRemoteApp'.

Configuring RD Gateway settings

Now that we learned how to create a deployment and some RemoteApps, time to dig deeper into the RDS environment. Let's take a look at how to use PowerShell to configure the RD Gateway for our deployment.

The syntax for this command is

SYNTAX
    Set-RDDeploymentGatewayConfiguration [-GatewayMode] <GatewayUsage>
    [[-GatewayExternalFqdn] <String>]
    [[-LogonMethod] <GatewayAuthMode>] [[-UseCachedCredentials] <Boolean>] [[-BypassLocal]
    <Boolean>]
    [[-ConnectionBroker] <String>] [-Force] [<CommonParameters>]

In this example we are going to specify a specific RD Gateway Server address, set the logon method to password authentication, let our users be able to use RD Gateway credentials for remote computers (to create a 'Single Sign-On' experience) and also bypass the RD Gateway Server for local addresses. All this can be done with a one-liner:

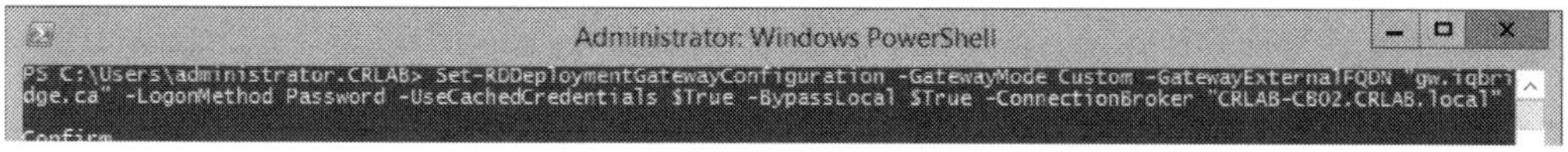

```
PS C:\Users\administrator.CRLAB> Set-RDDeploymentGatewayConfiguration -GatewayMode Custom -GatewayExternalFQDN "gw.iqbri
dge.ca" -LogonMethod Password -UseCachedCredentials $True -BypassLocal $True -ConnectionBroker "CRLAB-CB02.CRLAB.local"
```

After running this command, you are prompted with the following message:

```
Confirm
Changing RD Gateway settings of the Remote Desktop deployment. Do you want to continue?
[Y] Yes  [N] No  [S] Suspend  [?] Help (default is "Y"):
```

Just press enter (as 'Yes' is the default answer) and the above configuration will be set.

Configuring RD Licensing options

As the final item in this chapter, let's use PowerShell to configure the RD Licensing options for our environment. For this example, let's assume we want to start using the RD Licensing role on 'CRLAB-LS01' and configure a 'Per Device' licensing model. All we need to do is to use the following command:

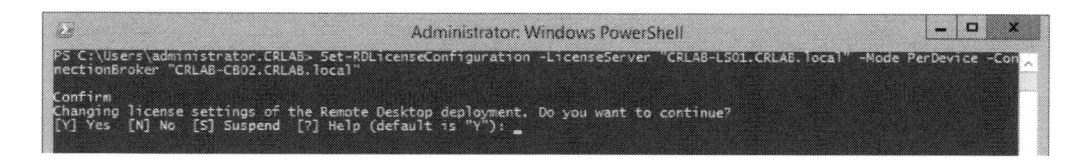

```
PS C:\Users\administrator.CRLAB> Set-RDLicenseConfiguration -LicenseServer "CRLAB-LS01.CRLAB.local" -Mode PerDevice -Con
nectionBroker "CRLAB-CB02.CRLAB.local"
Confirm
Changing license settings of the Remote Desktop deployment. Do you want to continue?
[Y] Yes  [N] No  [S] Suspend  [?] Help (default is "Y"):
```

When we open up the Server Manager Console and go to the Licensing tab of the Deployment Properties we can confirm that the specified settings have been changed.

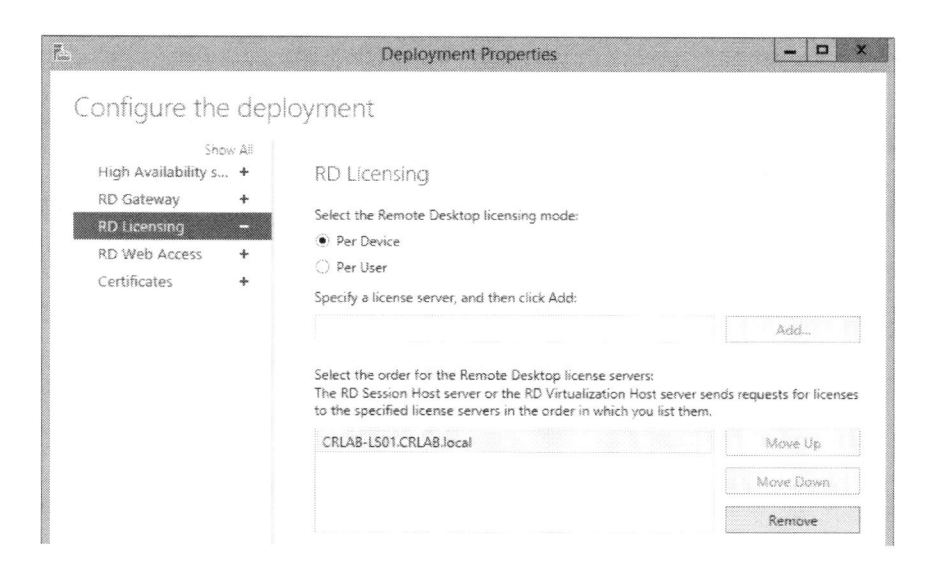

Finding your favorite RemoteDesktop cmdlet

All of the above commands are just some examples of what is possible with the RemoteDesktop PowerShell module. As we mentioned earlier, there are over 70 commands and to cover them all we would need to write a book on this one subject. The lesson here is to remember that everything (and more) that you can do using the GUI, you can do it using PowerShell and more than that, this should be the way for you moving forward as with PowerShell you can start automating your deployments what will certainly guarantee consistency.

To learn more about the other commands available, you can simply use the 'Get-Command -Module RemoteDesktop' command under PowerShell.

```
PS C:\Users\administrator.CRLAB> Get-Command -Module RemoteDesktop

CommandType     Name                                               ModuleName
-----------     ----                                               ----------
Function        Add-RDServer                                       remotedesktop
Function        Add-RDSessionHost                                  remotedesktop
Function        Add-RDVirtualDesktopToCollection                   remotedesktop
Function        Disable-RDVirtualDesktopADMachineAccountReuse      remotedesktop
Function        Disconnect-RDUser                                  remotedesktop
Function        Enable-RDVirtualDesktopADMachineAccountReuse       remotedesktop
Function        Export-RDPersonalVirtualDesktopAssignment          remotedesktop
Function        Get-RDAvailableApp                                 remotedesktop
Function        Get-RDCertificate                                  remotedesktop
Function        Get-RDConnectionBrokerHighAvailability             remotedesktop
Function        Get-RDDeploymentGatewayConfiguration               remotedesktop
Function        Get-RDFileTypeAssociation                          remotedesktop
Function        Get-RDLicenseConfiguration                         remotedesktop
Function        Get-RDPersonalVirtualDesktopAssignment             remotedesktop
Function        Get-RDPersonalVirtualDesktopPatchSchedule          remotedesktop
Function        Get-RDRemoteApp                                    remotedesktop
Function        Get-RDRemoteDesktop                                remotedesktop
Function        Get-RDServer                                       remotedesktop
Function        Get-RDSessionCollection                            remotedesktop
Function        Get-RDSessionCollectionConfiguration               remotedesktop
Function        Get-RDSessionHost                                  remotedesktop
Function        Get-RDUserSession                                  remotedesktop
Function        Get-RDVirtualDesktop                               remotedesktop
Function        Get-RDVirtualDesktopCollection                     remotedesktop
```

Troubleshooting the installation and configuration

So far, we have discussed the ways to deploy, configure and maintain your RDS deployment. The reality is, no matter how close you follow this awesome book, at one point or another you will certainly experience issues with RDS. That is where troubleshooting comes to the picture. In this chapter we will take a look at how to troubleshoot the RDS installation and configuration in case you run into errors or issues.

Windows Server 2012 R2 has several log files, trace logs, and event logs that can be very useful to troubleshoot your RDS environment. The following table gives you an overview of some of the logs available and where to find these (all of them can be seen with 'Event Viewer', under 'Applications and Services' | 'Logs' | 'Microsoft' | 'Windows' | 'TerminalServices-*').

Type	Name	Location
Event log	RDMS-UI Debug Log	Applications and Services Logs\Microsoft\Windows\RDMS-UI\Debug
Event log	Terminal Services Session Broker Admin, Analytic, Debug, and Operational Logs	Applications and Services Logs\Microsoft\Windows\TerminalServices-SessionBroker
Event log	Terminal Services Session Broker Client Admin, Analytic, Debug, and Operational Logs	Applications and Services Logs\Microsoft\Windows\TerminalServices-SessionBroker-Client

Enable tracing

If you need to troubleshoot an issue with the 'Scenario Based' Deployment or the creation of a session collection, you must first enable UI tracing. This can be done using the following steps:

1. Open command prompt with administrator rights and create a system environment variable named RDMSUI_TRACING, setting its value to 1.

```
C:\>set RDMSUI_TRACING = 1
C:\>
```
Administrator: Command Prompt

2. Launch 'Event Viewer' and click 'View' in the menu bar. Click 'Show Analytic and Debug Logs'.

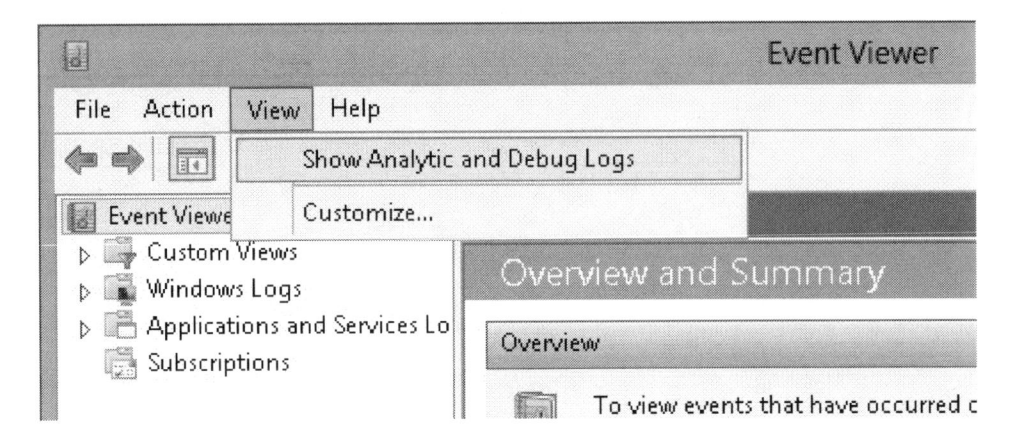

3. Still on 'Event Viewer', navigate to the following path: 'Applications and Services' | 'Logs' | 'Microsoft' | 'Windows' | 'RDMS-UI' | 'Debug'. Right click on 'Debug' and select 'Enable Log'.

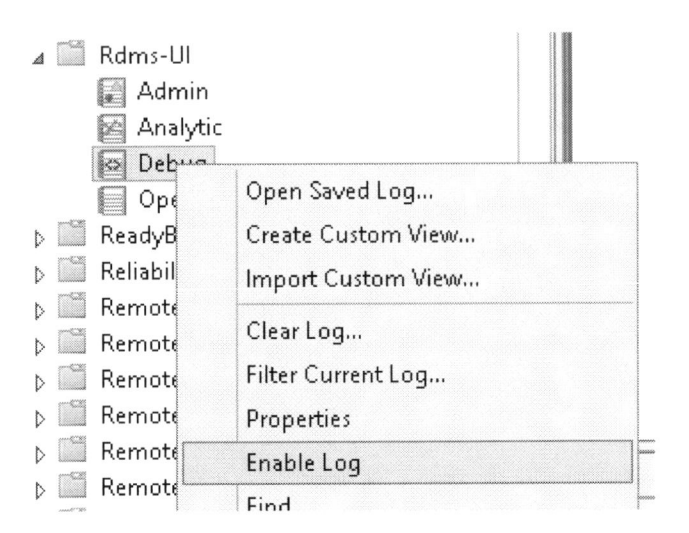

Page 234 | RDS - The Complete Guide

Troubleshooting using the debug log

The debug log shows very detailed information of all actions performed by the Server Manager GUI as well as direct PowerShell commands you may use within your RDS deployment. Aside from the debug log there is also the 'Operational' log inside the 'Rdms-UI' one.

```
▲ Rdms-UI
    Admin
    Analytic
    Debug
    Operational
```

This 'Operational' log shows global actions that have been performed.

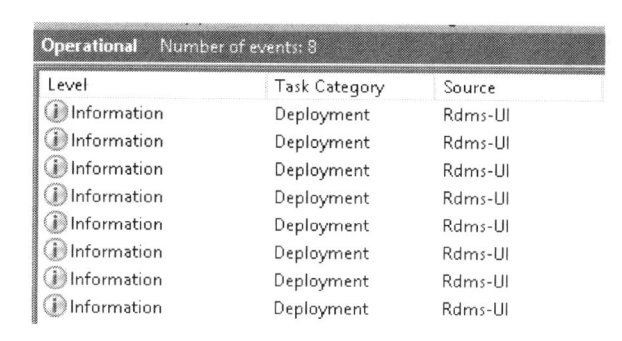

Level	Task Category	Source
Information	Deployment	Rdms-UI
Information	Deployment	Rdms-UI
Information	Deployment	Rdms-UI
Information	Deployment	Rdms-UI
Information	Deployment	Rdms-UI
Information	Deployment	Rdms-UI
Information	Deployment	Rdms-UI
Information	Deployment	Rdms-UI

Operational   Number of events: 8

For example, this log records events like:
- Scenario based deployment started
- RD Connection Broker Configuration Started on CRLAB-CB01.CRLAB.local
- RD Web Access Configuration Started on CRLAB-WA01.CRLAB.local

This is quite useful information if you want to get an overview of what is happening under the hood. If you do want to see the actions performed within your RDS deployment, the debug log is what you need.

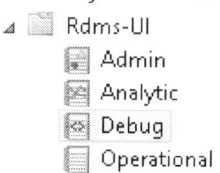

```
▲ Rdms-UI
    Admin
    Analytic
    Debug
    Operational
```

It will show you very detailed steps of what is happening with your RDS deployment. Some examples of what you can expect in this log are shown below:

Event 40961, Rdms-UI

General | Details

Component QuickDeployment: Job Progress Received for cmdlet: Unpublish remote desktop - -1% completed

Event 40961, Rdms-UI

General | Details

Component RdmsUI: ActiveServer: CRLAB-CB02.CRLAB.local

Event 40961, Rdms-UI

General | Details

Component RdmsMachinePool: MachinePoolServers: CRLAB-CB01.CRLAB.local,CRLAB-GW02.CRLAB.local,CRLAB-SH03.CRLAB.local,CRLAB-GW01.CRLAB.local,CRLAB-SH01.CRLAB.local,CRLAB-WA01.CRLAB.local,CRLAB-LS01.CRLAB.local,CRLAB-SH02.CRLAB.local,CRLAB-CB02.CRLAB.local,CRLAB-WA02.CRLAB.local

As you can see, the information collected and displayed is indeed very detailed. Therefore, in case of issues while performing an initial deployment or configuring additional settings for your deployment, the debug log might give you a very good idea on what is going on.

Troubleshooting sessions

On top of troubleshooting your RDS deployment during its deployment and configuration phases, from time to time you will certainly need to troubleshoot it once you have all in production. And as expected, there are various logs that contain information that could be valuable.

Once in production, a great place to start is the RDCB's event log (by now we are sure you know that 'RDCB' means 'RDS Connection Broker'). To show you some of what gets logged, as a test we launched 'WordPad' from the RDWA portal, using our client VM, 'CRLAB-CL01' and logged in as our 'testuser1' account.

As you remember from the table at the beginning of this chapter, the RDCB logs operational activities in the following event log:
'Applications and Services Logs' | 'Microsoft' | 'Windows' | 'TerminalServices-SessionBroker'
The actions we just described created four different log entries as seen below:

Level	Date and Time	Source	Event ID	Task Category
Verbose	4/10/2018 6:43:52 AM	TerminalServices-SessionBr...	818	RD Connection Broker proc...
Verbose	4/10/2018 6:43:52 AM	TerminalServices-SessionBr...	787	RD Connection Broker man...
Verbose	4/10/2018 6:43:50 AM	TerminalServices-SessionBr...	801	RD Connection Broker proc...
Verbose	4/10/2018 6:43:50 AM	TerminalServices-SessionBr...	800	RD Connection Broker proc...

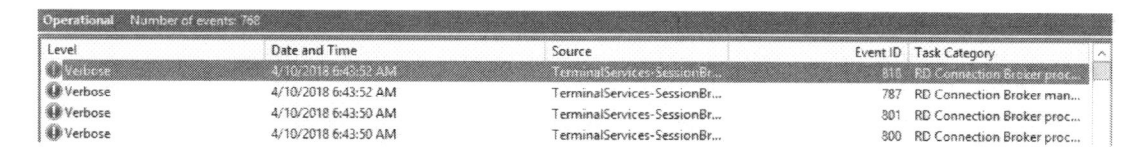

Let's take a deeper look on what exactly is being logged here. The first event (ID 800) shows the broker received a connection request. First, we see the user that performed the request, CRLAB\TestUser1. Then we can see the RDCB where the request originally came from, 'CRLAB-CB01.CRLAB.local'. Going deeper, we see something called the 'TSV URL'. This variable contains the path to the session collection. If you remember, this is also part of the properties seen in a .RDP file we discussed earlier. The initial application shows 'rdpinit.exe', meaning that the request is a RemoteApp and not a full desktop session.

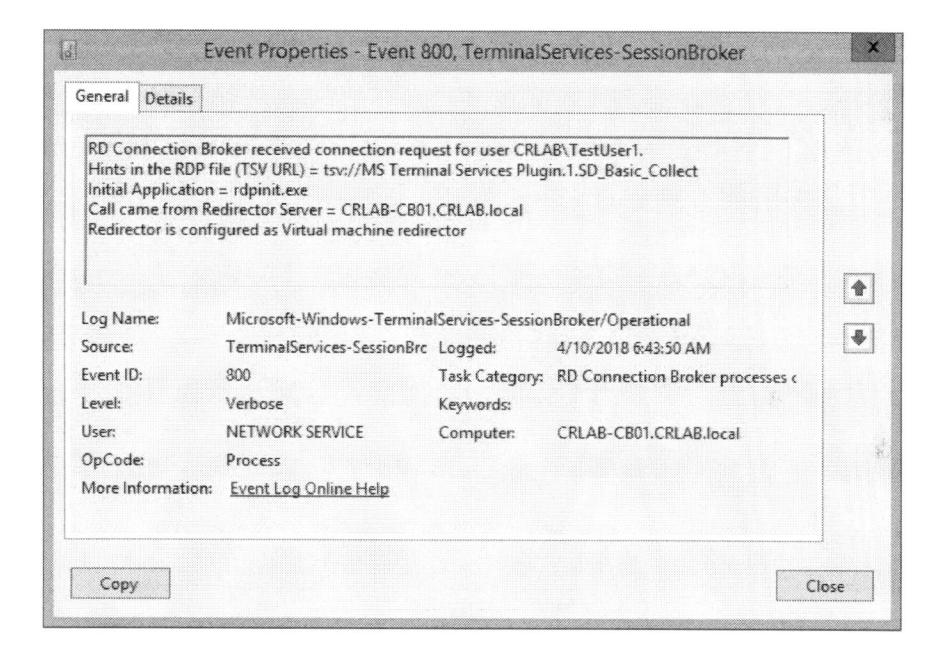

```
Event Properties - Event 800, TerminalServices-SessionBroker

General  Details

RD Connection Broker received connection request for user CRLAB\TestUser1.
Hints in the RDP file (TSV URL) = tsv://MS Terminal Services Plugin.1.SD_Basic_Collect
Initial Application = rdpinit.exe
Call came from Redirector Server = CRLAB-CB01.CRLAB.local
Redirector is configured as Virtual machine redirector

Log Name:     Microsoft-Windows-TerminalServices-SessionBroker/Operational
Source:       TerminalServices-SessionBrc   Logged:        4/10/2018 6:43:50 AM
Event ID:     800                            Task Category: RD Connection Broker processes c
Level:        Verbose                        Keywords:
User:         NETWORK SERVICE                Computer:      CRLAB-CB01.CRLAB.local
OpCode:       Process
More Information:  Event Log Online Help
```

The second event (ID 801) shows us the RDCB successfully processed the request by CRLAB\TestUser1. This log entry contains the target name of the RDSH, its target IP address, Netbios name and FQDN of the server that will handle that user session. It also shows 'Disconnected Session Found = 0x0'. As you know the RDCB holds a database of active, idle and disconnected sessions in order to be able to reconnect a user to a disconnected session. '0x0' means there was no disconnected session, and therefore a new session on 'CRLAB-SH01' will be created for the user CRLAB\TestUser1. Interesting, eh?

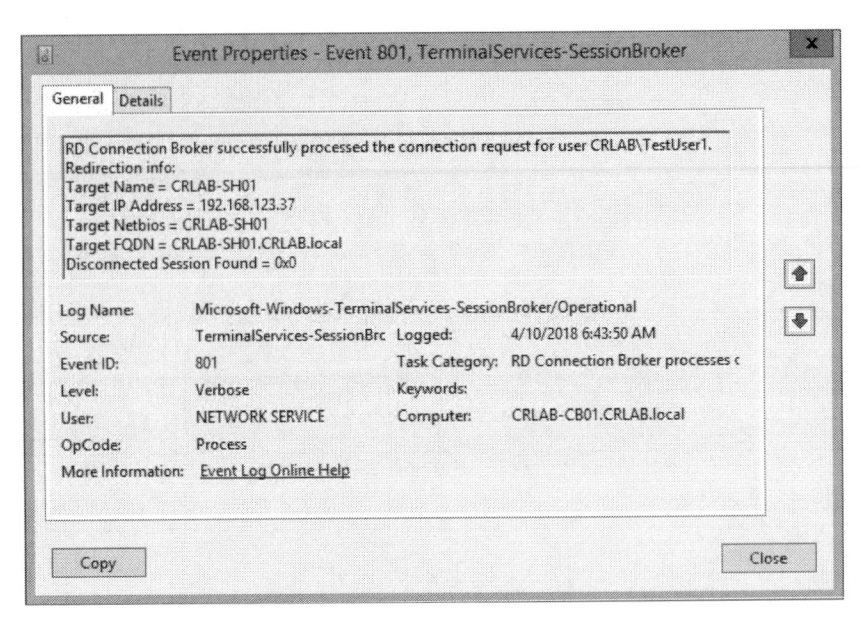

```
Event Properties - Event 801, TerminalServices-SessionBroker

General  Details

RD Connection Broker successfully processed the connection request for user CRLAB\TestUser1.
Redirection info:
Target Name = CRLAB-SH01
Target IP Address = 192.168.123.37
Target Netbios = CRLAB-SH01
Target FQDN = CRLAB-SH01.CRLAB.local
Disconnected Session Found = 0x0

Log Name:        Microsoft-Windows-TerminalServices-SessionBroker/Operational
Source:          TerminalServices-SessionBrc   Logged:         4/10/2018 6:43:50 AM
Event ID:        801                            Task Category:  RD Connection Broker processes c
Level:           Verbose                        Keywords:
User:            NETWORK SERVICE                Computer:       CRLAB-CB01.CRLAB.local
OpCode:          Process
More Information: Event Log Online Help
```

The next entry in the log (ID 787) shows us the session was successfully added to the RDCB database. We can also see the session ID for that session (which in this case is number 32).

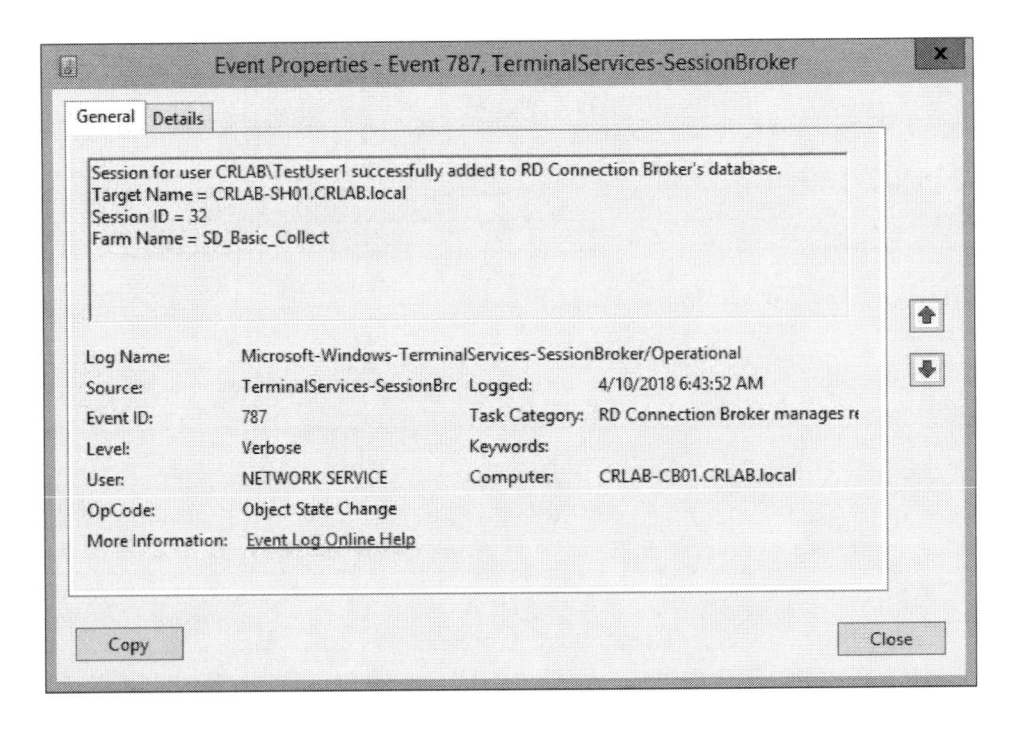

```
Event Properties - Event 787, TerminalServices-SessionBroker

General  Details

Session for user CRLAB\TestUser1 successfully added to RD Connection Broker's database.
Target Name = CRLAB-SH01.CRLAB.local
Session ID = 32
Farm Name = SD_Basic_Collect

Log Name:        Microsoft-Windows-TerminalServices-SessionBroker/Operational
Source:          TerminalServices-SessionBrc   Logged:         4/10/2018 6:43:52 AM
Event ID:        787                            Task Category:  RD Connection Broker manages re
Level:           Verbose                        Keywords:
User:            NETWORK SERVICE                Computer:       CRLAB-CB01.CRLAB.local
OpCode:          Object State Change
More Information: Event Log Online Help
```

The next event (ID 818) shows the user has successfully logged on to the session on the endpoint.

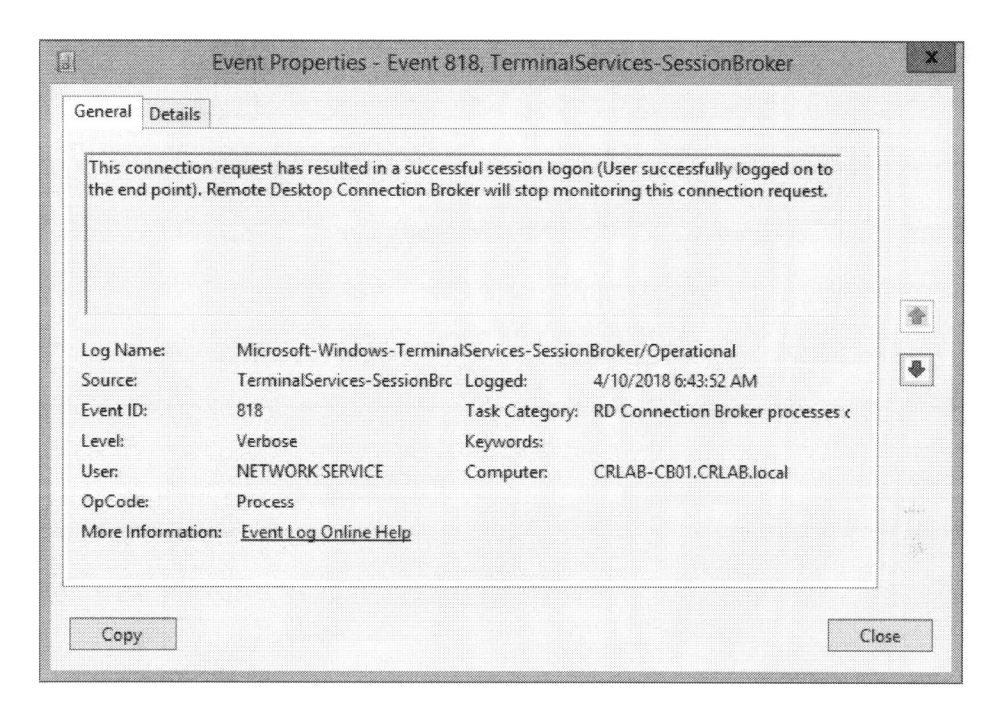

![Event Properties - Event 818, TerminalServices-SessionBroker dialog showing: This connection request has resulted in a successful session logon (User successfully logged on to the end point). Remote Desktop Connection Broker will stop monitoring this connection request. Log Name: Microsoft-Windows-TerminalServices-SessionBroker/Operational; Source: TerminalServices-SessionBro; Logged: 4/10/2018 6:43:52 AM; Event ID: 818; Task Category: RD Connection Broker processes; Level: Verbose; User: NETWORK SERVICE; Computer: CRLAB-CB01.CRLAB.local; OpCode: Process]

If you are curious about what the RDCB database looks like internally, let's take a quick look at it.

Launch the 'SQL Server Management Studio' on of SQL Server instance where the RDCB database is hosted and create a new query, providing the following expression (you may need to adjust the database name based on your deployment details):

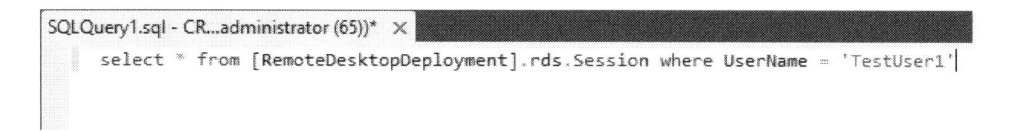

```sql
select * from [RemoteDesktopDeployment].rds.Session where UserName = 'TestUser1'
```

Once you execute the query, it returns the following information:

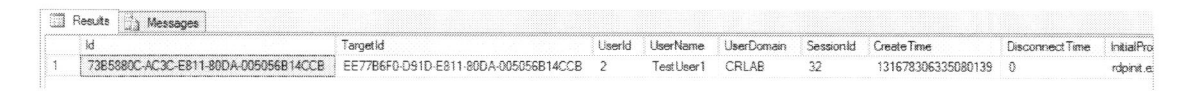

Id	TargetId	UserId	UserName	UserDomain	SessionId	CreateTime	DisconnectTime	InitialPro
73B5880C-AC3C-E811-80DA-005056B14CCB	EE77B6F0-D91D-E811-80DA-005056B14CCB	2	TestUser1	CRLAB	32	131678306335080139	0	rdpinit.e

RDS - The Complete Guide | Page 239

We can see details like the SessionId, Createtime and even properties like the resolution and color depth (just scroll to the side on the query return window).

Going back to our client VM, let's close the RemoteApp launched (remember, 'WordPad'). Launching the 'Server Manager' console on the RDCB, we can also view all the sessions on a deployment and even at the session collection level. If we look at the connections at the session collection level, we can see the user 'TestUser1' now has a disconnected session:

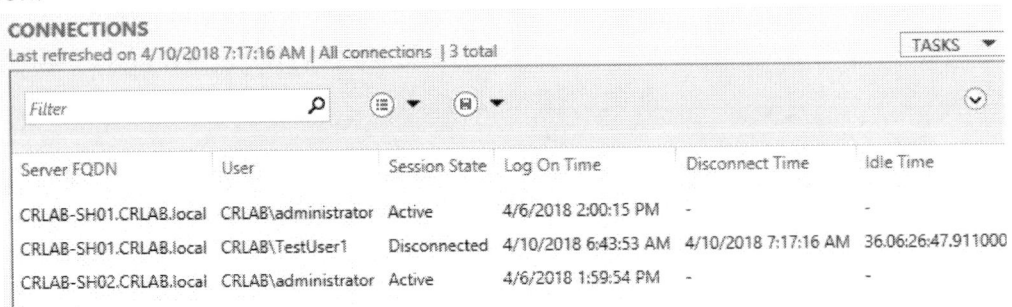

CONNECTIONS
Last refreshed on 4/10/2018 7:17:16 AM | All connections | 3 total

Server FQDN	User	Session State	Log On Time	Disconnect Time	Idle Time
CRLAB-SH01.CRLAB.local	CRLAB\administrator	Active	4/6/2018 2:00:15 PM	-	-
CRLAB-SH01.CRLAB.local	CRLAB\TestUser1	Disconnected	4/10/2018 6:43:53 AM	4/10/2018 7:17:16 AM	36.06:26:47.911000
CRLAB-SH02.CRLAB.local	CRLAB\administrator	Active	4/6/2018 1:59:54 PM	-	-

Refreshing the query we performed earlier shows this change. The record now shows a state of '4' and the 'DisconnectTime' gets updated:

	UserId	UserName	UserDomain	SessionId	CreateTime	DisconnectTime	InitialProgram	ProtocolType	State	ResolutionWidth	ResolutionHeight	ColorDepth
1	3	2	TestUser1	CRLAB	32	131678306335080139	131678326368078246	rdpinit.exe	2	4	0	0	0

Now let's go back to our client and relaunch the exact same RemoteApp as 'TestUser1'. Since this user has a disconnected session, he should be reconnected to that session by the RDCB.

Refreshing the event log on the RDCB, we see that three new events were added:

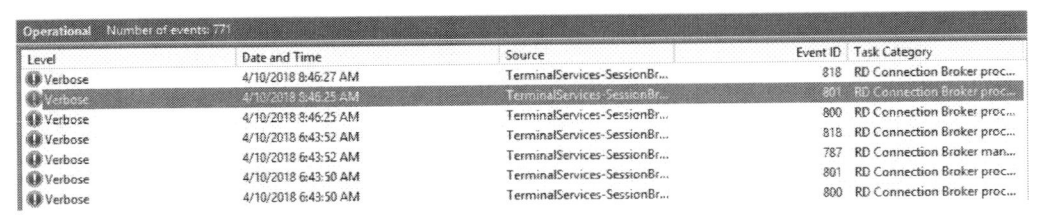

Level	Date and Time	Source	Event ID	Task Category
Verbose	4/10/2018 8:46:27 AM	TerminalServices-SessionBr...	818	RD Connection Broker proc...
Verbose	4/10/2018 8:46:25 AM	TerminalServices-SessionBr...	801	RD Connection Broker proc...
Verbose	4/10/2018 8:46:25 AM	TerminalServices-SessionBr...	800	RD Connection Broker proc...
Verbose	4/10/2018 6:43:52 AM	TerminalServices-SessionBr...	818	RD Connection Broker proc...
Verbose	4/10/2018 6:43:52 AM	TerminalServices-SessionBr...	787	RD Connection Broker man...
Verbose	4/10/2018 6:43:50 AM	TerminalServices-SessionBr...	801	RD Connection Broker proc...
Verbose	4/10/2018 6:43:50 AM	TerminalServices-SessionBr...	800	RD Connection Broker proc...

Again the 800 event ID which contains the same information as before. We also see ID 801, which now contains different information. The RDCB kept track of the disconnected session by TestUser1 as we can see since 'Disconnected Session Found' now contains '0x1' instead of '0x0'.

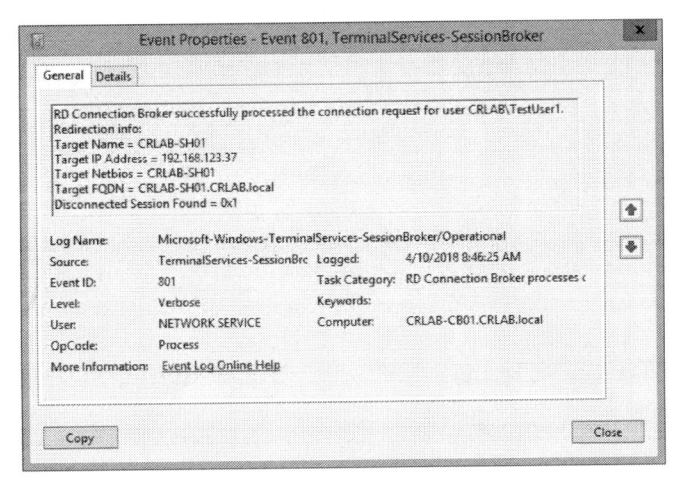

```
Event Properties - Event 801, TerminalServices-SessionBroker

General | Details

RD Connection Broker successfully processed the connection request for user CRLAB\TestUser1.
Redirection info:
Target Name = CRLAB-SH01
Target IP Address = 192.168.123.37
Target Netbios = CRLAB-SH01
Target FQDN = CRLAB-SH01.CRLAB.local
Disconnected Session Found = 0x1

Log Name:      Microsoft-Windows-TerminalServices-SessionBroker/Operational
Source:        TerminalServices-SessionBrc    Logged:          4/10/2018 8:46:25 AM
Event ID:      801                             Task Category:   RD Connection Broker processes c
Level:         Verbose                         Keywords:
User:          NETWORK SERVICE                 Computer:        CRLAB-CB01.CRLAB.local
OpCode:        Process
More Information:  Event Log Online Help
```

One more time, the last event we see is ID 818, which means the user has successfully logged on. Also note, that event ID 787 was not logged as an entry in the RDCB database already existed.

The RDSH that served the session for the user 'TestUser1' also records the logon, disconnect and reconnect events. It logs these events under
'Applications and Services Logs' | 'Microsoft' | 'Windows' | 'TerminalServices-LocalSessionmanager'.

The logon event (ID 21):

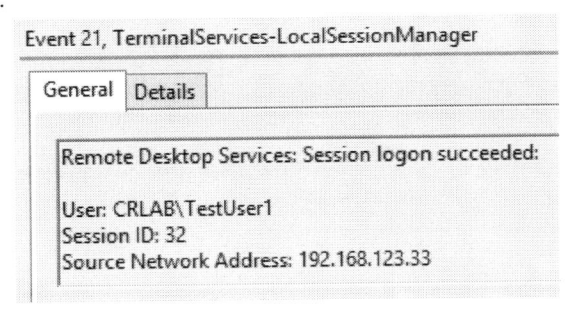

```
Event 21, TerminalServices-LocalSessionManager

General | Details

Remote Desktop Services: Session logon succeeded:

User: CRLAB\TestUser1
Session ID: 32
Source Network Address: 192.168.123.33
```

The disconnect (ID 24):

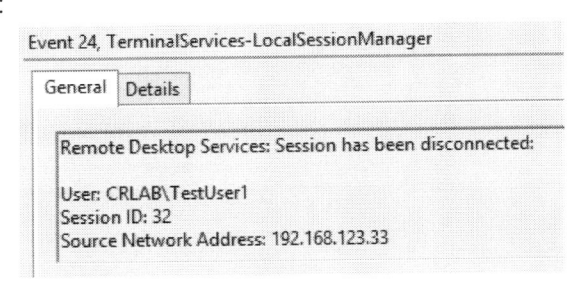

```
Event 24, TerminalServices-LocalSessionManager

General | Details

Remote Desktop Services: Session has been disconnected:

User: CRLAB\TestUser1
Session ID: 32
Source Network Address: 192.168.123.33
```

And the reconnect (ID 25):

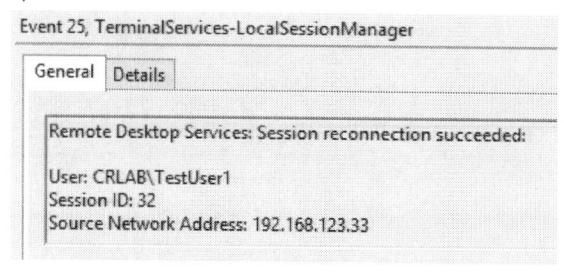

```
Event 25, TerminalServices-LocalSessionManager
General | Details

Remote Desktop Services: Session reconnection succeeded:

User: CRLAB\TestUser1
Session ID: 32
Source Network Address: 192.168.123.33
```

Troubleshooting RD Web Access

The RDWA server also has the ability to do trace logging. This can be useful in case you want to troubleshoot things like collections that are not being displayed on the web page, some collections appearing while others do not, or any other error messages that users might run into.

This trace is not enabled by default. To enable RDWA trace logging, you must perform the following steps (remember this has to be done on all RDWA servers in case you have multiple ones load balanced):

1. Launch notepad with administrative privileges on the RDWA server.
2. Open the file %SYSTEMROOT%\Web\RDweb\Web.config
3. Look for the section labeled 'system.diagnostics' and under it, modify the following (in **bold**): <add name="TraceTSWA" value="**4**" />
4. Remove the '<!--' and '-->' characters to uncomment the section seen below:
   <add name="FileLog"
        type="Microsoft.VisualBasic.Logging.FileLogTraceListener,
        Microsoft.VisualBasic, Version=8.0.0.0,
        Culture=neutral, PublicKeyToken=b03f5f7f11d50a3a,
        processorArchitecture=MSIL"
        initializeData="FileLogWriter" BaseFileName="RDWeb"
        Location="Custom"
        LogFileCreationSchedule="Daily"
        MaxFileSize="50000000"
        CustomLocation="\Windows\Web\RDWeb\App_Data" />
5. An RDWA log file will now be created in the following folder: %SYSTEMROOT%\Web\RDWeb\App_Data
6. In a command prompt with administrative rights, type 'iisreset' and press enter.

This log file contains very detailed information. For example, when we logon as 'TestUser1' on the RDWA page (without launching anything yet) the following is logged:

> 2018/04/10 09:11:55 [Info] 8 DomainUserName : crlab\testuser1.
> 2018/04/10 09:11:55 [Info] 8 UserIdentity : S-1-5-21-1715450949-1630072619-1324145983-1139.
> 2018/04/10 09:11:55 [Info] 8 ExtractInfoFromCookies returning : True.
> 2018/04/10 09:11:55 [Info] 8 Info from Form or Auth Cookie extracted : True.
> 2018/04/10 09:11:55 [Info] 8 SetupHttpContextUser returning : True.
> 2018/04/10 09:11:55 [Info] 8 Generating XML Feed compatible with schema version: Win8
> 2018/04/10 09:11:55 [Verbose] 8 Cloud Mode: False.
> 2018/04/10 09:11:55 [Verbose] 8 Radcm Server Name : CRLAB-CB01.CRLAB.LOCAL;CRLAB-CB02.CRLAB.LOCAL.
> 2018/04/10 09:11:55 [Verbose] 8 RDSH Server Names : .
> 2018/04/10 09:11:55 [Info] 8 Connecting to Centralized Publishing Server: CRLAB-CB01.CRLAB.LOCAL;CRLAB-CB02.CRLAB.LOCAL

Further down is where the RemoteApps are retrieved based on the security settings which can be set per RemoteApp and per session collection. This logging is very useful when trying to debug why certain RemoteApps are not shown.

> 2018/04/10 09:11:55 [Verbose] 8 Filtering apps for SID: S-1-5-21-1715450949-1630072619-1324145983-1139
> 2018/04/10 09:11:55 [Verbose] 8 >>>>> WordPad Checking Access
> 2018/04/10 09:11:55 [Verbose] 8 TSCheckAccess returned allow=1, SD=O:WDG:WDD:ARP(A;CIOI;CCLCSWLORCGR;;;S-1-5-21-1715450949-1630072619-1324145983-513)
> 2018/04/10 09:11:55 [Verbose] 8 ALLOWED access to app WordPad
> 2018/04/10 09:11:55 [Verbose] 8 >>>>> Simplify Printing TX Checking Access
> 2018/04/10 09:11:55 [Verbose] 8 Lookup returned allow=1, SD=O:WDG:WDD:ARP(A;CIOI;CCLCSWLORCGR;;;S-1-5-21-1715450949-1630072619-1324145983-513)
> 2018/04/10 09:11:55 [Verbose] 8 ALLOWED access to app Simplify Printing TX
> 2018/04/10 09:11:55 [Verbose] 8 >>>>> Paint Checking Access
> 2018/04/10 09:11:55 [Verbose] 8 Lookup returned allow=1, SD=O:WDG:WDD:ARP(A;CIOI;CCLCSWLORCGR;;;S-1-5-21-1715450949-1630072619-1324145983-513)
> 2018/04/10 09:11:55 [Verbose] 8 ALLOWED access to app Paint
> 2018/04/10 09:11:55 [Verbose] 8 >>>>> notepad Checking Access
> 2018/04/10 09:11:55 [Verbose] 8 Lookup returned allow=1, SD=O:WDG:WDD:ARP(A;CIOI;CCLCSWLORCGR;;;S-1-5-21-1715450949-1630072619-1324145983-513)
> 2018/04/10 09:11:55 [Verbose] 8 ALLOWED access to app notepad

> 2018/04/10 09:11:55 [Verbose] 8 >>>>> SD Basic Collection Checking Access
> 2018/04/10 09:11:55 [Verbose] 8 Lookup returned allow=1,
> SD=O:WDG:WDD:ARP(A;CIOI;CCLCSWLORCGR;;;S-1-5-21-1715450949-1630072619-1324145983-513)
> 2018/04/10 09:11:55 [Verbose] 8 ALLOWED access to desktop SD Basic Collection
> 2018/04/10 09:11:55 [Verbose] 8 Filtered apps stored in the cache for S-1-5-21-1715450949-1630072619-1324145983-1139

If the user enters an incorrect password, the following is logged:

> 2018/04/10 09:20:42 [Info] 17 User Name : testuser1, DomainName : crlab, Password : Non-NullOrEmpty, Private logon : True, LogonUser returned : False.
> 2018/04/10 09:20:42 [Info] 17 LogonUser() failed with error code 1326.
> 2018/04/10 09:20:42 [Info] 17 SetupHttpContextUser returning : False.

That is all from a troubleshooting standpoint. As you can see there is a lot of information being logged in at all times (assuming you did enable everything as explained here). That said, in most scenarios this is only done for troubleshooting purposes. Keep that in mind.

Accessing the environment

So far, we have covered pretty much everything related to the RDS backend and all its components. It is time to shift our focus to the next piece of the puzzle, the client side. Let's take a look at it now and discuss the different ways available when connecting to your RDS environment.

Since Windows Server 2012 R2, there are two main ways to connect to the RDS environment. The most common one, as you guessed, is indeed using the RDWA portal; the second one is using the RDWA feed that will populate the start screen (Windows 8 and later) or the start menu (in case you are using Windows 7 for whatever reason). Let's take a look at both options.

RD Web Access

We have already seen the first method, using the RDWA portal, for a bit in the previous chapters. RDWA can be accessed by browsing to the URL that is configured over HTTPS. As we have seen before, we can check which URL to use for RDWA by opening the 'RD Web Access' section in the deployment properties. As you noticed these are the internal URLs for all the servers hosting the RDWA role. To access these over the internet, you would need to allow traffic from the outside to these servers, by opening port TCP 443 at the firewall.

At one point we did create two DNS entries for the same FQDN, creating a simple DNS Round Robin, so connections are balanced between the two RDWAs. Later, we implemented a better HA solution, based on the Windows NLB and assigned a Virtual IP to the load balanced pair (what is indeed a much better solution).

Name	Type	Data
wa	Host (A)	192.168.123.31

So, in our case, no matter if the user is internal or external, in order to connect, all he needs to do is to open a browser and point to https://wa.iqbridge.ca/rdweb.

Doing it on our client, 'CRLAB-CL01', brings us to the following screen:

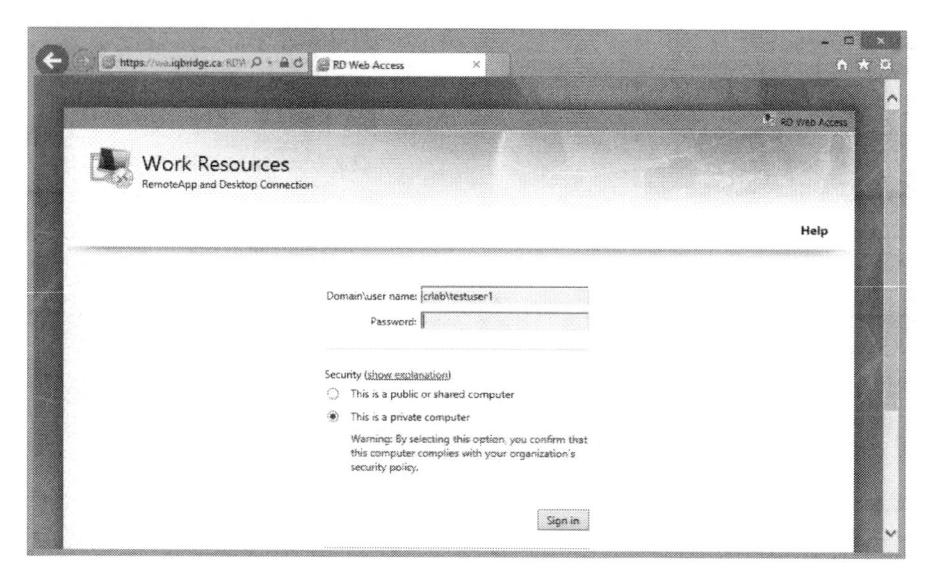

Once we provide valid credentials and click the 'Sign in' button, we are presented with the RemoteApps assigned to that particular user:

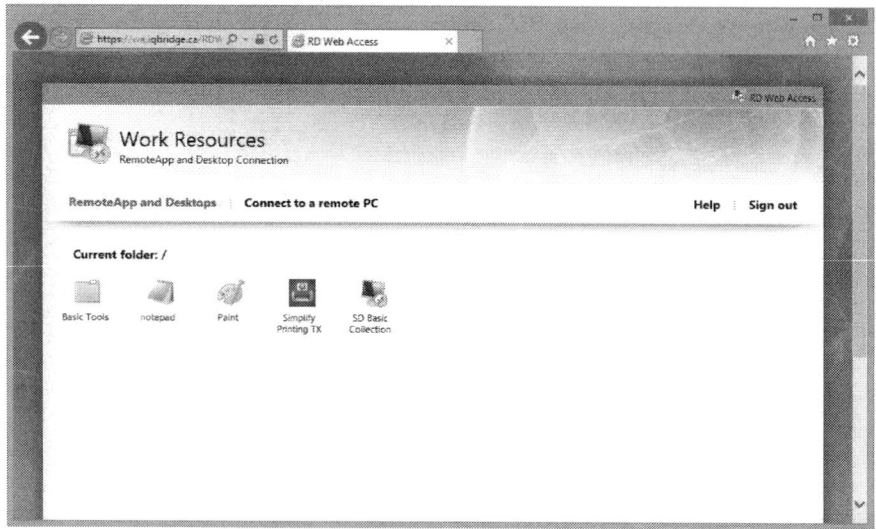

In order to launch any of the RemoteApps we simply click on it. Note that when launched, the RemoteApp runs seamlessly on your local desktop as if it was a local application. To differentiate between local and remote applications, when hovering over the application icon in the taskbar, it will show additional information.

If we were to launch a second RemoteApp (for example WordPad), the RDCB will make sure this application runs within the same session as the previous one. This means that all running RemoteApps for the same user run within the same session and RDSH (unless the user has access to multiple collections).

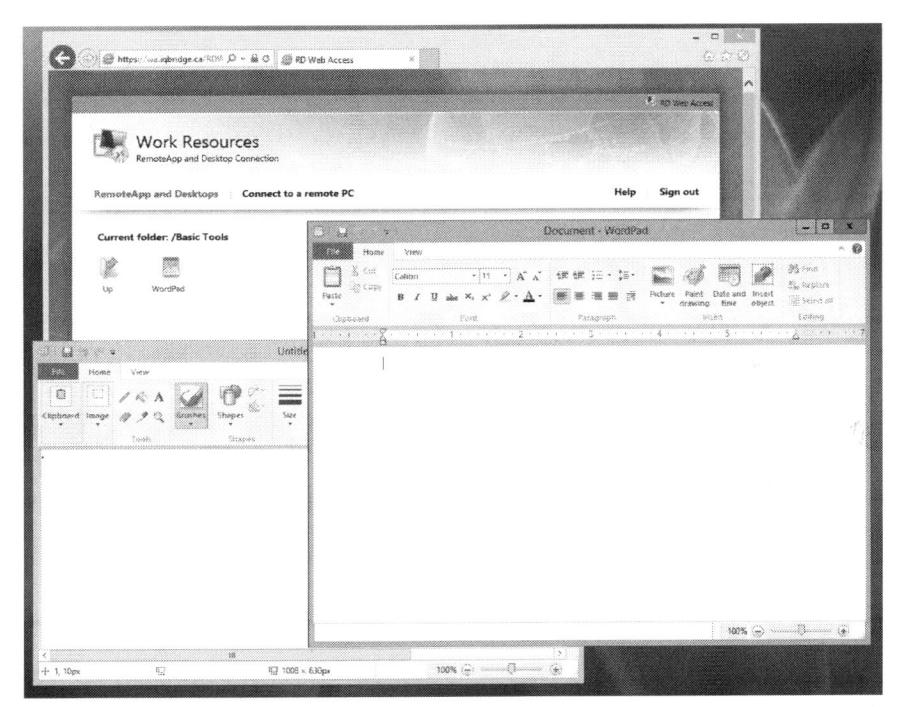

If you noticed, when logging in to the RDWA portal, you are presented with a balloon tip in the notification area:

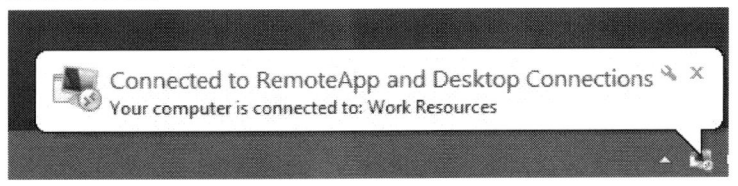

This confirms that you have successfully connected to the RDS environment. Using this systray icon, we can also disconnect and reconnect to it. For example, if you want to move your client machine to a different physical location (i.e. bring your laptop home) and continue to work from there you can click the icon in the notification area and select 'Disconnect from Work Resources".

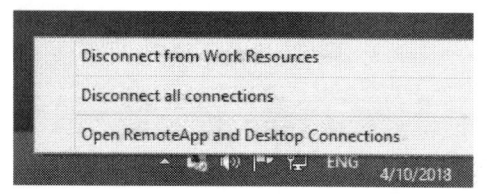

This closes the RemoteApps and leaves our user session in a disconnected state. We can confirm this by looking at the 'Connections' section for 'Remote Desktop Services' under 'Server Manager'.

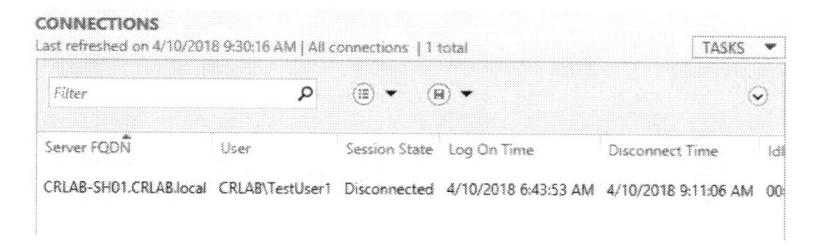

Once you log back in using the RDWA portal, simply launch any application you had open and the RDCB will reconnect you to that session (assuming a disconnect timeout was not reached).

Another feature available in the RDWA portal, in case you have not noticed, is the tab 'Connect to a remote PC'.

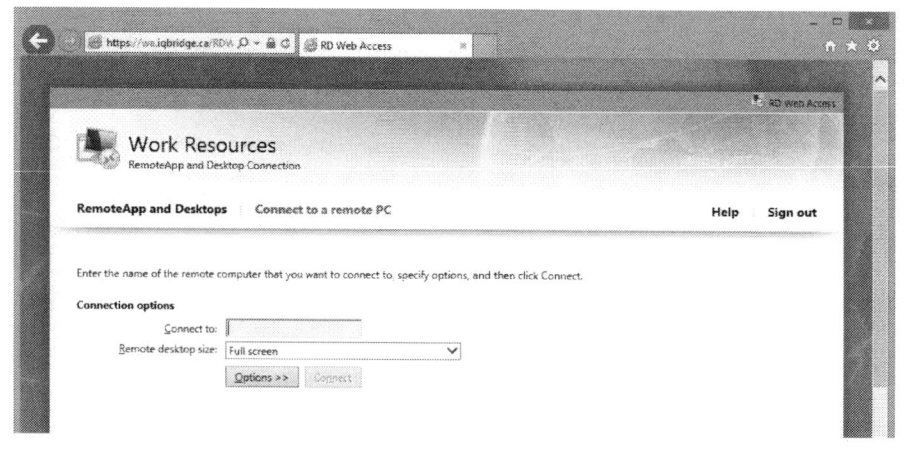

Through this option, it is possible to connect to an RDSH, a farm or a desktop (physical or virtual). Unlike RemoteApps, the connection in this case gives you a full desktop. If you click the 'Options >>' button, you are able to change some of the connection properties:

For example, if you provide the name of one of our RDSHs, you would get a full desktop session on that server. However, keep in mind the hostname you provide here must be resolvable and more than that, reachable on port TCP 3389, unless you use an RDGW. To configure an RDGW that will be used by this section of the RDWA portal, you must configure it in the 'Application Settings' section on IIS for all your RDWAs. Note that as we have seen earlier in the book, this is the same place where you can also change other session settings like redirection settings, time outs and so on.

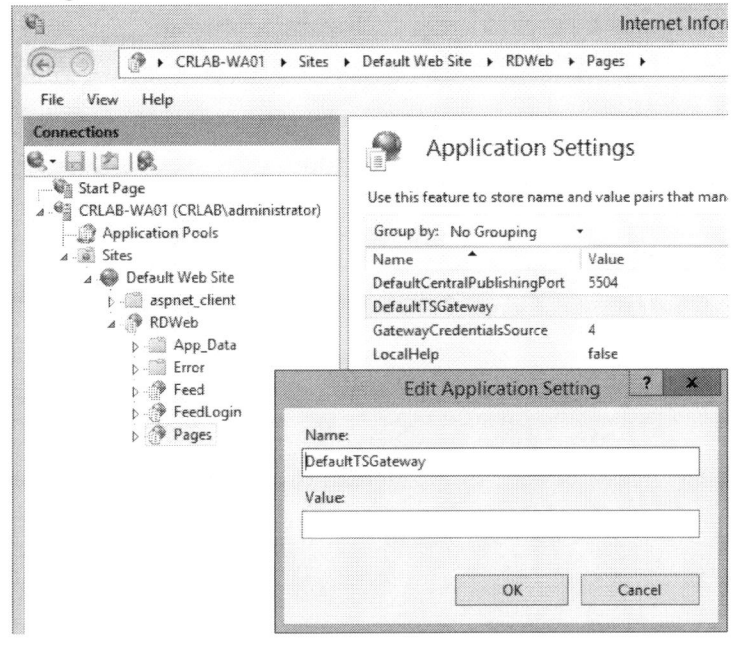

Remote App and Desktop Connections

As mentioned at the beginning of this chapter, there is a second way to connect to an RDS environment, that ends up creating shortcuts for your RemoteApps in the 'Start' screen or the 'Start' menu.

The first step required is to configure the client to connect to the RDWA web feed. For managed clients, all you need is to configure a GPO to set the 'Default connection URL'. This policy can be found under:

'User Configuration' | 'Policies' | 'Administrative Templates' | 'Windows Components' | 'Remote Desktop Services' | 'RemoteApp and Desktop Connections'

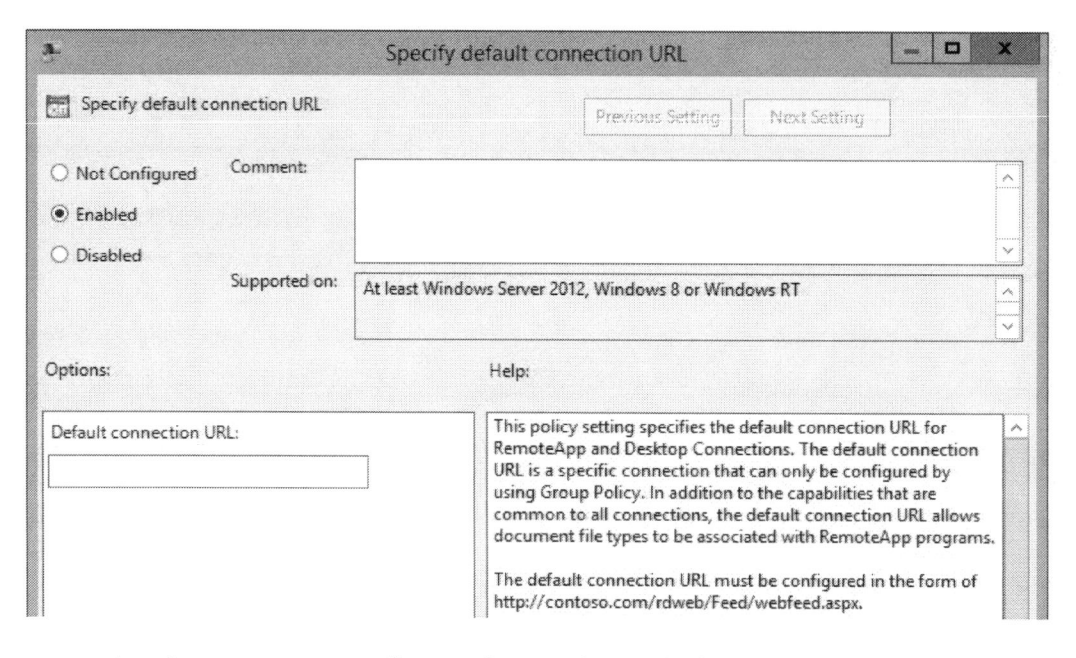

You can also let users manually configure the web feed URL either by using the control panel or the Remote Desktop Client universal app (in Windows 8 and higher). Unfortunately, we must say the current version of the Remote Desktop Client available on the Windows Store is not recommended, even if you are running Windows 10. We have experienced several issues with the app and unless you do have a reason to use it, just stick to the regular way available under 'Control Panel'.

Let's take a quick look at how this is configured (it is available on pretty much all versions of Windows, from Windows 7 and up).

1. Launch 'Control Panel' (the procedure is virtually identical for all versions of Windows starting with Windows 7). On the top right corner click 'Category' and select 'Large icons'.

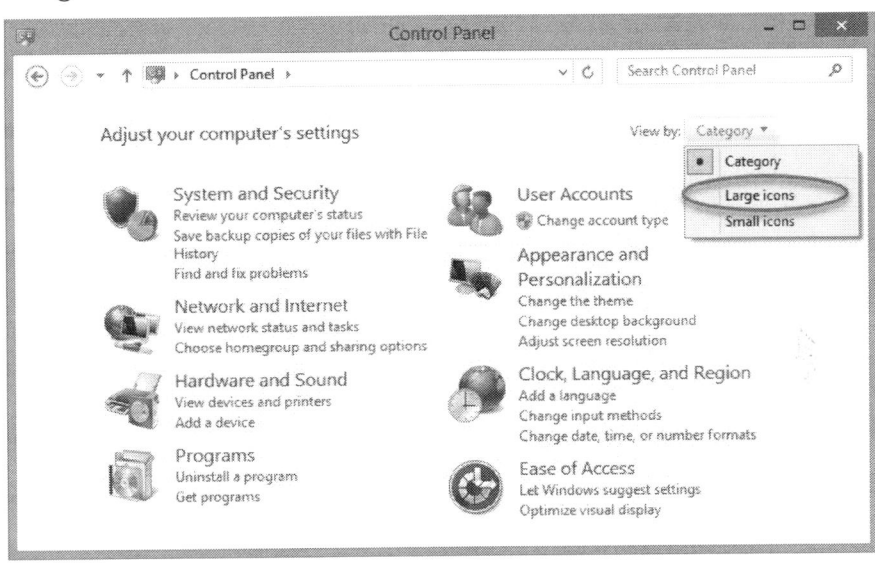

2. Click on 'RemoteApp and Desktop Connections' (you may need to scroll down to find it).

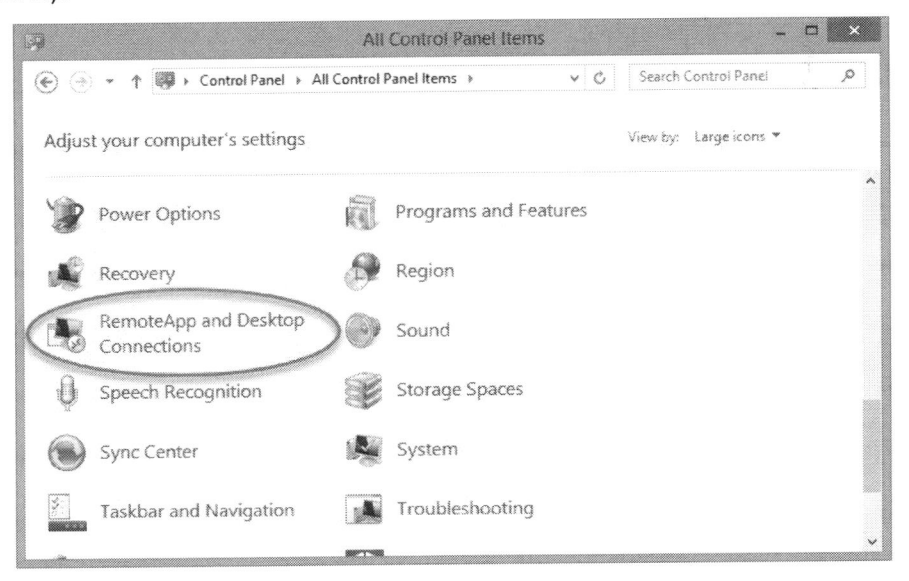

3. On the left, click on 'Access RemoteApp and desktops'.

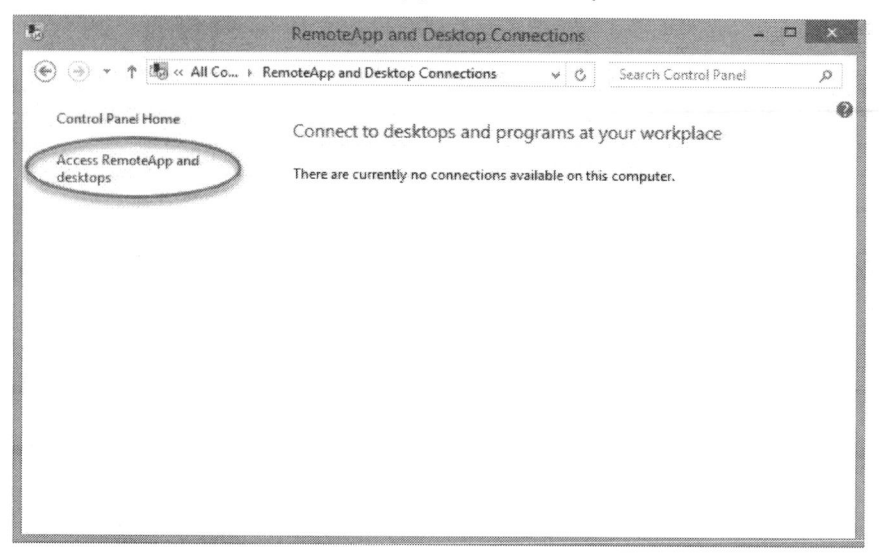

4. Enter the correct URL for the web feed. In our case, it is the single one, used for both internal and external users. By having a single URL, users will be able to roam between a corporate network and their home one for example, without losing access to their RemoteApps or desktops.

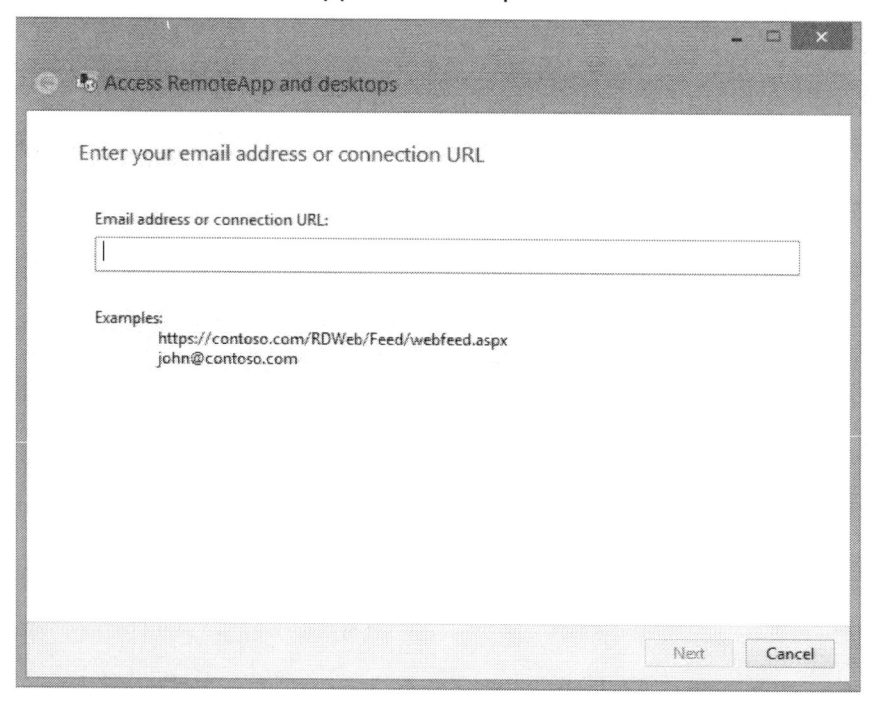

5. The URL entered will be displayed. Click 'Next'.

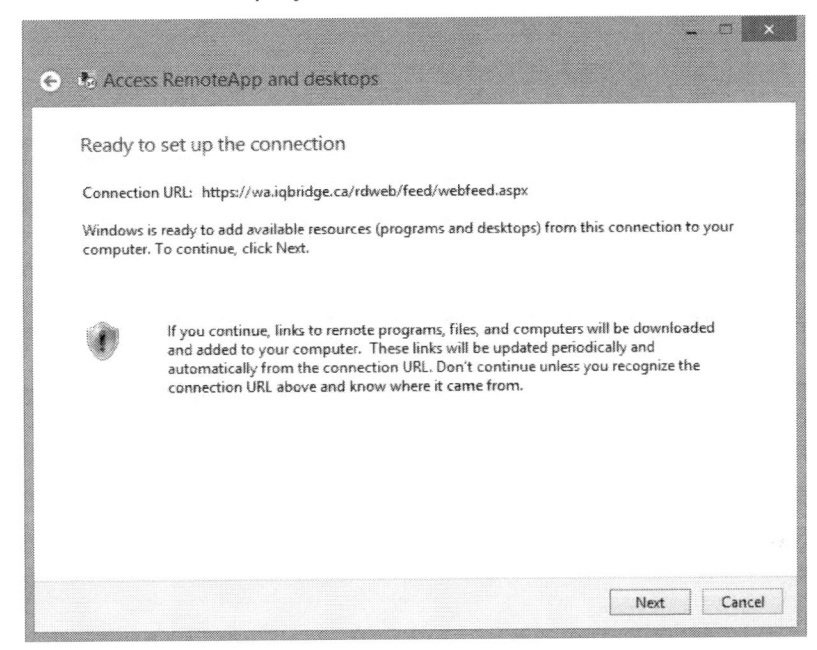

6. Enter your credentials (in our case we are using our 'TestUser1' account) and click 'OK'. You can select 'Remember my credentials' if you will always connect using the same account.

7. You should see the number of RemoteApps and desktops available for that particular user account. Click 'Finish'.

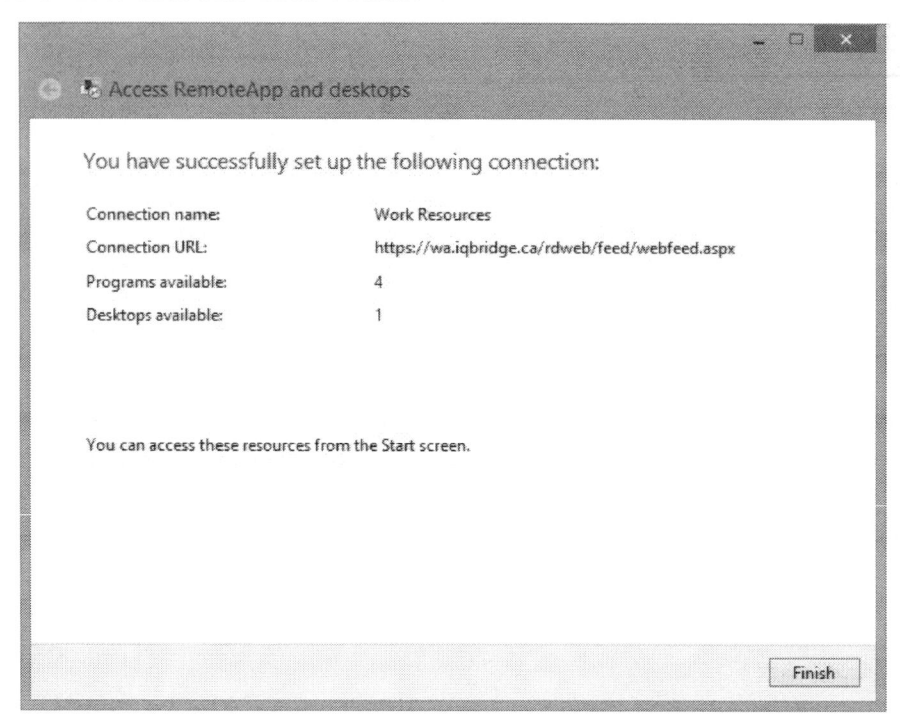

8. A summary of the resources available through the RDWA feed will be displayed.

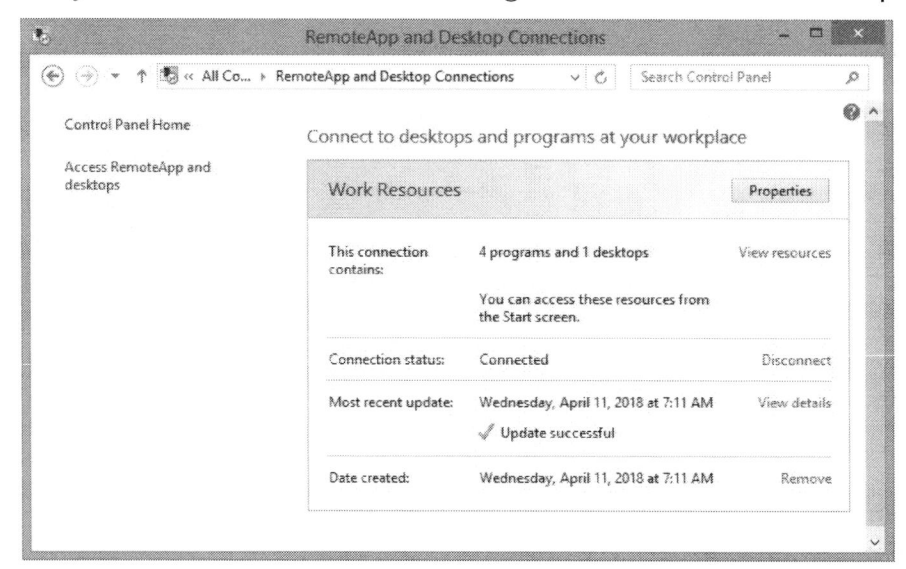

9. As mentioned before, the RemoteApps and desktops provided on the feed are now displayed under 'Apps' on the 'Start' screen or the 'Start' menu, depending on the version of Windows you are running on the client side.

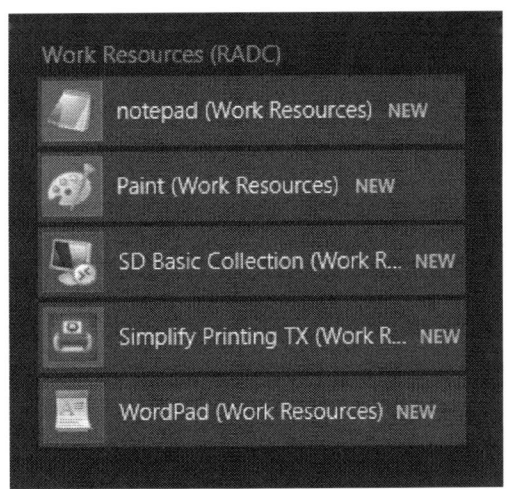

10. You can then pin these to the main 'Start' screen.

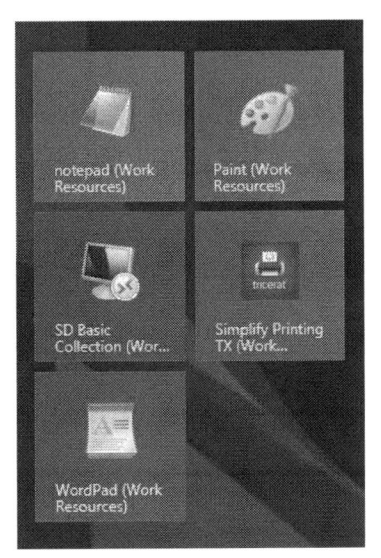

11. Clicking on any of them will launch the RemoteApp as if you were using the RDWA portal directly.

Session Collection resource types

It is important to realize that there is a significant difference in the way a session is launched using the 'Connecting to a Remote PC' tab and using the 'RemoteApps and Desktops' tab. In you launch a RemoteApp, an .RDP file is created on the RDSH based on the settings that we configured for that RemoteApp in the 'Server Manager' console. The .RDP file will be signed using the certificate we configured for the deployment, before being transferred to the client from where it is executed. Therefore, as a signed .RDP file is used, 'Single Sign-on' is possible.

When you connect using the 'Connecting to a Remote PC' tab, the .RDP file is actually created on the client itself based on parameters it gets from the RDWA (which reside in the web.config file and .aspx pages) plus the settings that might have been set using the options available within the same tab. As this .RDP file is not signed, once you launch it you will see a warning mentioning the publisher cannot be identified and due to this, 'Single Sign-on' will not work, prompting you for credentials as seen below.

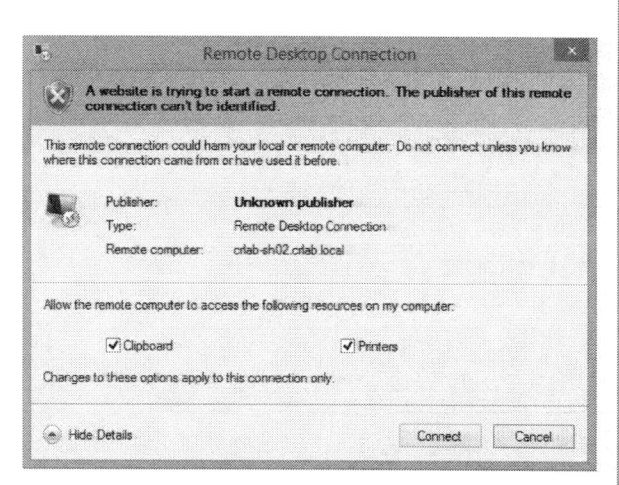

That said there is still ways to get you 'Single Sign-on' to an RDSH full desktop. The first way is a bit more complicated but given all you learned so far, we are certain you know exactly how to achieve this.

As you may have guessed, all you would need is to create a new session collection and assign different RDSHs than the ones used for your RemoteApps (as an RDSH host can only be part of a single session collection). Within that session collection you would not create any RemoteApps. With no RemoteApps available, the user receives a full desktop.

If no RemoteApps have been published inside a Session Collection, the Session Collection has "Remote Desktop" as the Resource Type. Meaning that a "RemoteApp" is available that launches a full desktop. If you unpublished all RemoteApps, the following is shown inside the Server Manager. Note that as soon as you publish a RemoteApp the Session Collection will change to the Resource Type "Remote Apps".

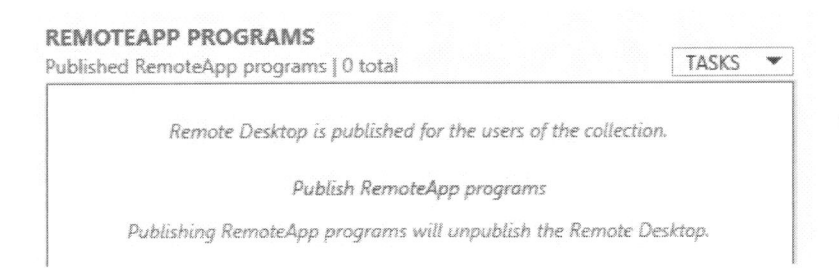

REMOTEAPP PROGRAMS
Published RemoteApp programs | 0 total   TASKS ▼

Remote Desktop is published for the users of the collection.

Publish RemoteApp programs

Publishing RemoteApp programs will unpublish the Remote Desktop.

If you have already published some RemoteApps and would like to revert to the 'Full Desktop' experience, you can use the PowerShell command 'Set-RDRemoteDesktop' or simply remove all RemoteApps using the 'Server Console' GUI.

SYNTAX
    Set-RDRemoteDesktop [-CollectionName] <string> [-ShowInWebAccess] <bool> [-ConnectionBroker <string>] [-Force]
    [-WhatIf] [-Confirm] [<CommonParameters>]

Once you run this command on the RDCB, you will receive a warning, clearly stating all RemoteApps will be removed (just confirm it):

```
PS C:\Users\administrator.CRLAB> Set-RDRemoteDesktop -CollectionName "SD Basic Collection" -ShowInWebAccess 1 -ConnectionBroker CRLAB-CB02.CRLAB.local
Warning: Removing published RemoteApp programs...
Allowing virtual or physical desktops to show in RD Web Access will remove all your published RemoteApp programs. Do you wish to continue?
[Y] Yes  [N] No  [S] Suspend  [?] Help (default is "Y"):
```

Looking at the 'Server Manager' console, under the RDS section you can see the collection now reflects this change, showing 'Remote Desktop' as the resource type:

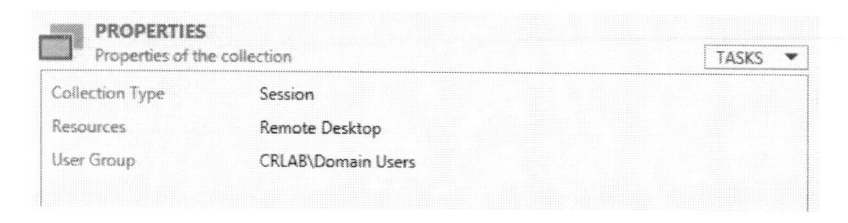

PROPERTIES
Properties of the collection | TASKS

Collection Type	Session
Resources	Remote Desktop
User Group	CRLAB\Domain Users

On the client, if you logon again to the RDWA portal we now see the following:

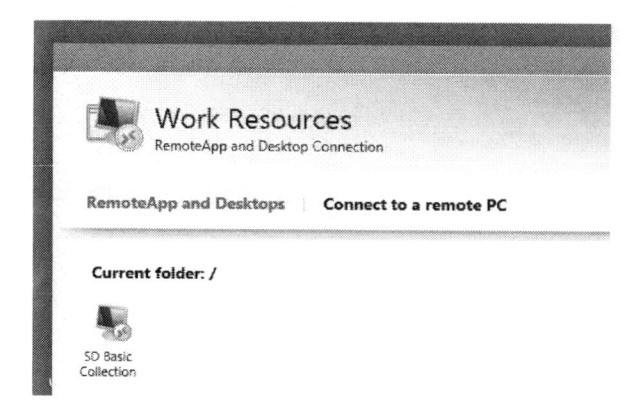

Work Resources
RemoteApp and Desktop Connection

RemoteApp and Desktops | **Connect to a remote PC**

Current folder: /

SD Basic Collection

We now have a full desktop available in the 'RemoteApp and Desktops' tab that will launch with 'Single Sign-on' as it is properly signed.

So far, the only downside with such approach is the fact you cannot mix and match RemoteApps and full desktops within the same session collection. Well, that is where the dirty tricks come handy. ☺

If you have RemoteApps published and you do want access to the full desktop at the same time, all you need to do is to set the following registry key (it is tied to the collection) on all your RDCBs:

Windows Registry Editor Version 5.00
    [HKEY_LOCAL_MACHINE\SOFTWARE\Microsoft\Windows NT\CurrentVersion\Terminal Server\CentralPublishedResources\PublishedFarms**YOUR_COLLECTION**\RemoteDesktops\SD_Basic_Collect]
    "ShowInPortal"=dword:00000001

The text highlighted above will have your collection name in the registry, truncated to sixteen (16) characters. You should be able to see the value 'ShowInPortal' there but set to '0'. Simply change it to '1' and once you refresh the RDWA page you should now see this:

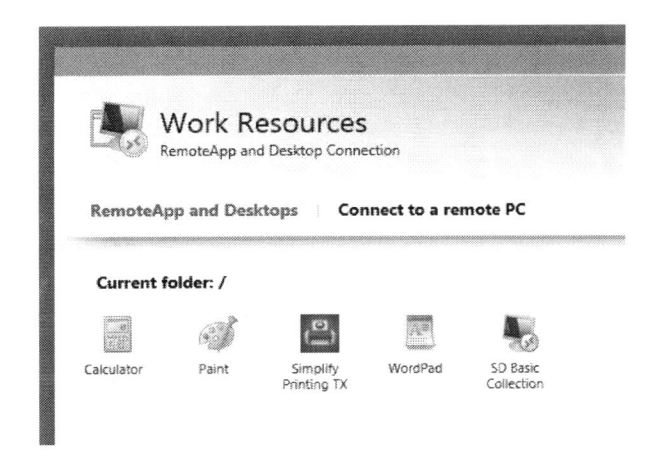

As you can see, RemoteApps and full desktop coming from the exact same session collection. Sweet.

Distributing RDP files

As many probably remember, with Windows Server 2008 and 2008 R2, you could distribute RemoteApps as .RDP and .MSI files (that you could use something like 'Systems Center Configuration Manager' to distribute to your endpoints). This was done using the 'RemoteApps Manager' tool.

As you realize by now, this is gone with Windows Server 2012 and up. Even though 'Server Manager' does its job centralizing the management for your RDS deployment, in case you need this capability, officially you just lost it.

That said, you do know about the RDWA web feed, that we configured previously. It even creates shortcuts on the 'Apps' section in the 'Start' screen and in the 'Start' menu. Well if that is the case, where these go?

These .RDP files end up here:

C:\Users\%username%\AppData\Roaming\Microsoft\Workspaces\{WorkspaceID}\Resource

Where {WorkspaceID} is a unique identifier for the workspace. On our client VM, 'CRLAB-CL01' we can see it there for our 'TestUser1' account:

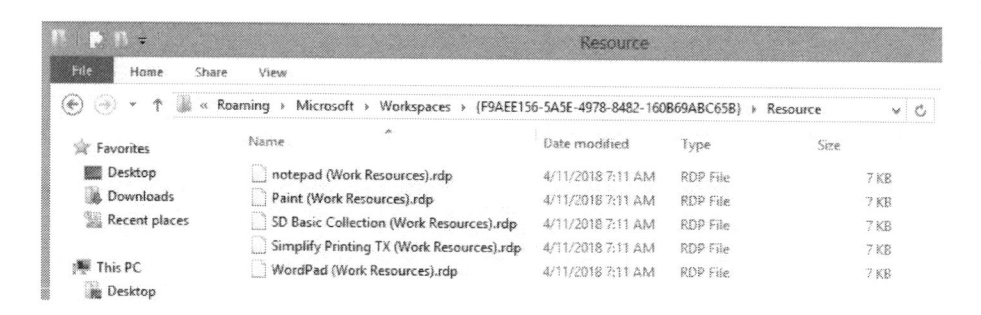

If you go up one level you will see another folder, named 'Icons' and as you have guessed, it has all the icons associated to these .RDP files.

So, what would stop you from distributing these .RDP files the way you used to do this with Windows Server 2008 R2? Technically nothing. However, since Microsoft removed this functionality with the Windows Server 2012 release, it probably means they do not want you to do that and almost certainly will not support you if you do it.

Looking at what is inside these .RDP files, you will probably recognize most of the options:

> redirectclipboard:i:1
> redirectprinters:i:1
> redirectcomports:i:0
> redirectsmartcards:i:1
> devicestoredirect:s:*
> drivestoredirect:s:*
> redirectdrives:i:1
> session bpp:i:32
> prompt for credentials on client:i:1
> span monitors:i:1

use multimon:i:1
remoteapplicationmode:i:1
server port:i:3389
allow font smoothing:i:1
promptcredentialonce:i:1
videoplaybackmode:i:1
audiocapturemode:i:1
gatewayusagemethod:i:1
gatewayprofileusagemethod:i:1
gatewaycredentialssource:i:0
full address:s:cb.iqbridge.ca
alternate shell:s:||WordPad
remoteapplicationprogram:s:||WordPad
remoteapplicationfileextensions:s:.rtf
gatewayhostname:s:gw.iqbridge.ca
remoteapplicationname:s:WordPad
remoteapplicationcmdline:s:
workspace id:s:cb.iqbridge.ca
use redirection server name:i:1
loadbalanceinfo:s:tsv://MS Terminal Services Plugin.1.SD_Basic_Collect
alternate full address:s:cb.iqbridge.ca
signscope:s:Full Address,Alternate Full Address,Use Redirection Server Name,Server Port,GatewayHostname,GatewayUsageMethod,GatewayProfileUsageMethod,GatewayCredentialsSource,PromptCredentialOnce,Alternate Shell,RemoteApplicationProgram,RemoteApplicationMode,RemoteApplicationName,RemoteApplicationFileExtensions,RemoteApplicationCmdLine,RedirectDrives,RedirectPrinters,RedirectCOMPorts,RedirectSmartCards,RedirectClipboard,DevicesToRedirect,DrivesToRedirect,LoadBalanceInfo
signature:s:AQABAAEAAAAtDwAAMIIPKQYJKoZIhvcNAQcCoIIPGjCCDxYCAQExCzAJBgUrDgMCGgUAMAsGCSqGSIb3DQEHAaCCDWkwggOvMIICl6ADAgECAhAIO+BWkEJGsa

We have highlighted some of the important properties. Note that the destination of the .RDP session is **cb.iqbridge.ca** which points to one of our RD Connection Broker servers (using Microsoft NLB). The other highlighted items will tell the RDCB that **cb.iqbridge.ca** is not our final destination server but that we are trying to connect to an RDSH which is part of a session collection.

RemoteFX

If you have been using RDS based on Windows Server 2008 R2, the term RemoteFX will probably sound familiar to you. RemoteFX was first introduced in Windows Server 2008 R2 Service Pack 1. Back then, RemoteFX was about being able to virtualize the Graphical Processing Unit (GPU) and having USB peripheral access in a VDI session.

With Windows Server 2012 R2 and up, RemoteFX has a much broader meaning. It is now considered to be the overall term for everything related to providing a high-end user experience. In addition, RemoteFX and all its new features are now applicable to both virtual machine-based desktop deployments and session-based ones.

With that in mind, let's take a quick look at some of the most important features of RemoteFX.

Single Sign-On, Email and web discovery of RemoteApps and Desktops

In the previous chapter ('Accessing the Environment'), we have already discussed the RemoteApp discovery. With Windows Server 2008 R2 you had the option to enter a web feed URL in order to retrieve the RemoteApps that were assigned to you. All you had to do was configuring a specific URL using the "RemoteApp and Desktop Connections" section available in the control panel.

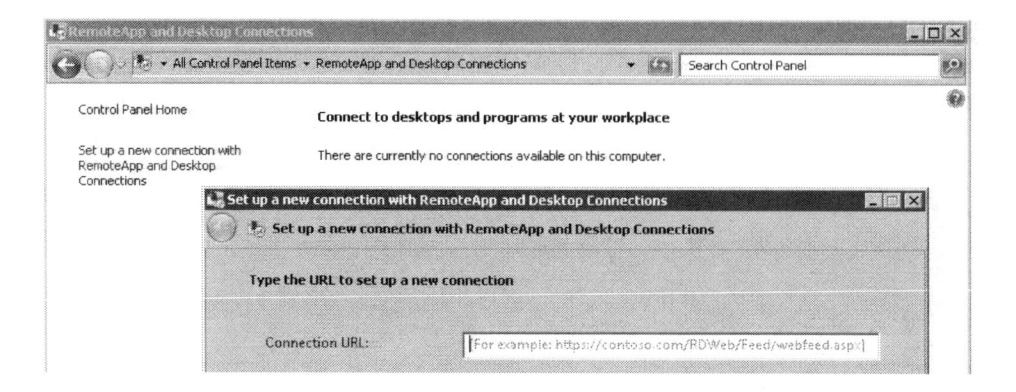

Part of what is underneath the RemoteFX umbrella is the ability to provide a corporate e-mail address instead of a URL. This is of course much more user friendly. The control panel interface introduced with Windows Server 2012 R2/Windows 8 is shown below (you can still see it is the same on Windows 10 Fall Creators Update):

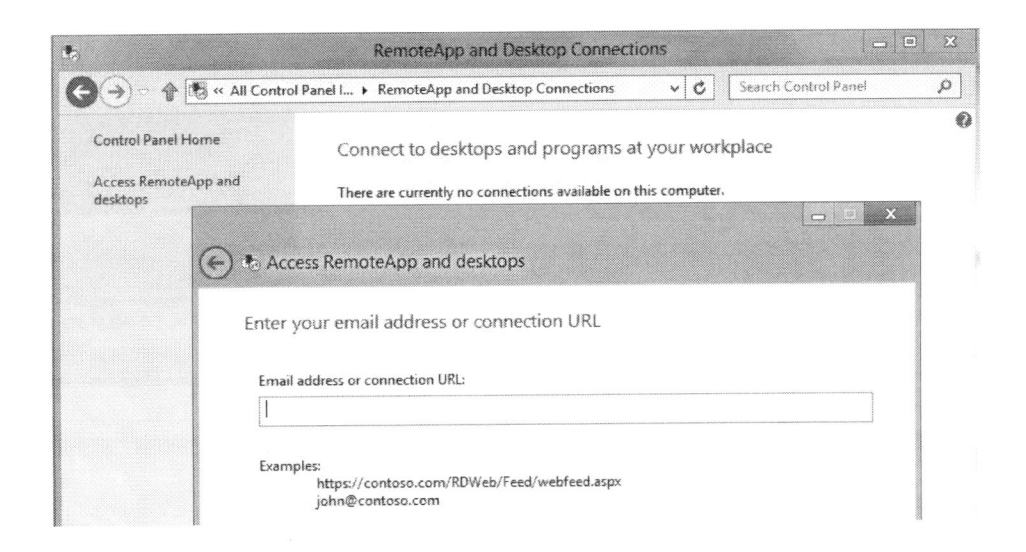

And as we have also seen in the previous chapter, this same option is also available in the Universal Windows Platform (UWP) RDP client.

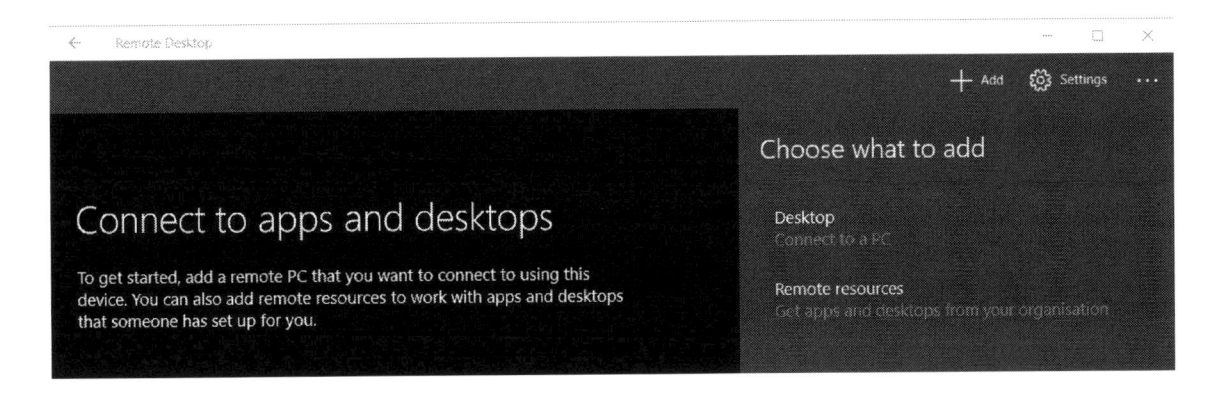

Windows Server 2012 introduced the ability to set the web feed URL using a Group Policy setting to deploy it to your managed clients. This GPO setting is called "Specify default connection URL" and can be found under:

'User Configuration' | 'Policies' | 'Administrative Templates' | 'Windows Components' | 'Remote Desktop Services' | 'Remote App and Desktop Connections'

You need to specify the URL in the following format:
http://RDWebFQDN/rdweb/Feed/webfeed.aspx

Adaptive Graphics

When establishing a remote desktop connection using previous versions of Windows with RDP 7.X (i.e. Windows 7 – Windows 10 Fall Creators Update ships with RDP 10.4), a single codec was being used to encode everything graphics related. This changed with the introduction of Windows Server 2012 and Windows 8, where different codecs are used for depending on the content being delivered. For example, a different codec is used for text, and another one for images and video. Each of these are optimized for that particular type of content.

With RDP 8.0, RemoteFX introduced a new codec that can encode a bitmap progressively, the reason why it is called 'Progressive Rendering'. In previous releases of the RDP protocol a user's session could freeze due to large bitmap transfers over the wire. With 'Progressive Rendering', a bitmap is transferred in stages, looking blurry at first and then getting shaper. Since text is handled by a different codec, you will notice that text content is always sharp.

Even though RemoteFX adapts to the current conditions, it allows you to enforce a particular setting based on your own environment. As usual, this can be done using a GPO under the following setting:

> 'Computer Configuration' | 'Policies' | 'Administrative Templates' | 'Windows Components' | 'Remote Desktop Services' | 'Remote Desktop Session Host' | 'Remote Session Environment'

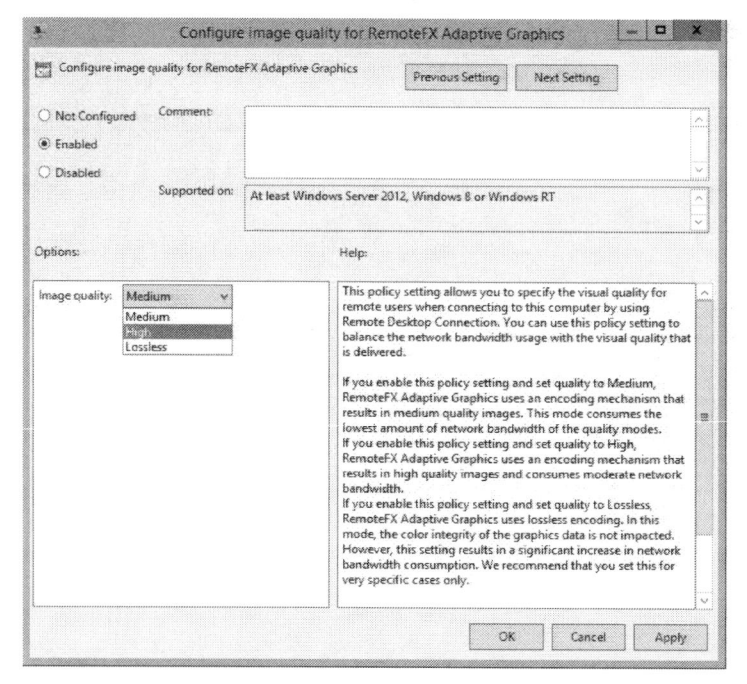

In that same location, you can also configure the way to use 'Adaptive Graphics'. The options are:

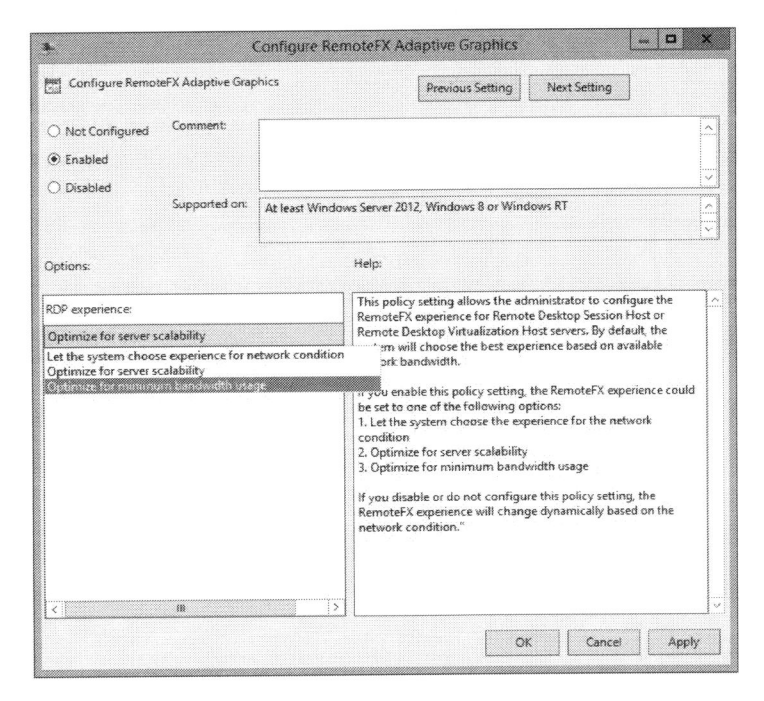

In case you are dealing with older clients (i.e. non-Windows based thin clients), in the same location, you can revert back to the codec that was used in Windows Server 2008 R2 SP1. Just enable the policy "Enable RemoteFX Encoding for RemoteFX clients designed for Windows Server 2008 R2 SP1."

Intelligent Transports

With previous versions of the RDP protocol, everything was TCP based. RDP 8.0 introduced UDP as a transport mechanism. Compared to TCP, UDP is a stateless protocol, providing a better experience over challenging WAN conditions. That said, the main challenge with UDP is making sure it is allowed and supported along the way between client and the server. Sometimes an UDP based connection may not be allowed or even possible. To overcome this, RDP version 8.0 and higher will automatically fallback to TCP if an UDP connection cannot be established. As expected, you can control such behavior with a GPO, under the following location:

'Computer Configuration' | 'Policies' | 'Administrative Templates' | 'Windows Components' | 'Remote Desktop Services' | 'Remote Desktop Session Host' | 'Connections'

The setting is 'Select RDP transport protocols' as seen below:

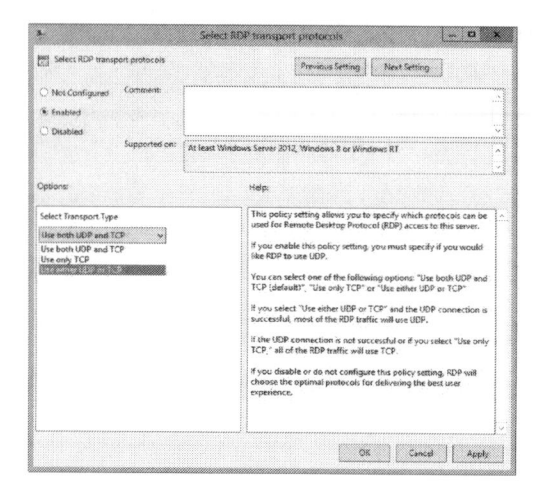

Multi touch

If you are using a touch device such as a tablet and you connect to an RDS environment, multi touch within that session is fully supported. You can use multi touch within the RDS session for both session-based or virtual machine-based deployments.

USB Redirection

With RemoteFX in Windows 7 SP1 USB redirection was introduced for usage within a single session. Windows Server 2012 and up support full USB redirection for both session-based and virtual machine-based deployments, providing session isolation for redirected devices so users on a RDSH will only see redirected USB devices for their own sessions. Dynamic in-session USB redirection is also fully supported. This means that you can mount and unmount USB devices at session runtime.

With Windows Server 2012, Microsoft introduced the ability to explicitly allow certain types of USB devices while disallowing others. This can be done on a particular session collection using the PowerShell command 'Set-RDSessionCollectionConfiguration'.

For example, you can use the following command to allow bluetooth USB devices:

> Set-RDSessionCollectionConfiguration –CollectionName "First Session Collection" – CustomRdpProperty "usbdevicestoredirect:s:{e0cbf06c-cd8b-4647-bb8a-263b43f0f974}" -ConnectionBroker crlab-cb01.crlab.local

To find the correct GUID for the device type you would like to allow please refer to following link:

http://msdn.microsoft.com/en-us/library/ff553426(v=vs.85).

Completing your RDS environment

We know you are eager to have your users connecting to the environment. After all you built it by the book. Literally. ☺

But before you do it, we highly recommend you do a bit of lockdown on the RDSHs not only to streamline the user experience but also to prevent some undesired results.

As users are sharing the RDSHs, it is very important to limit what the users can and cannot do on the servers. This is where Group Policy Objects (GPOs) and Group Policy Preferences (GPPs) come to the picture. Let's take a look at these, focusing on some basic configuration that will give you a great starting point for any RDS environment.

Basic GPO and GPP

The fact you now have a fully functional RDS environment does not mean it is ready for production though. Out-of-the-box, users may be able to see and do things we may not want (i.e. browsing and saving to the local C: drive and some of its folders).

GPOs and GPPs can and should be applied to tweak the RDSHs, locking them down and more than that, presenting a pre-configured environment to our users. There are so many GPO settings that apply to RDS that we could easily devote an entire book to this. Instead, we will show you some of the most common GPO/GPPs that are usually applied to RDSHs in production environments.

Regarding locking it down, there is one thing we must mention and explain, considering how many times we have heard it. You probably have heard it too: "As we are publishing RemoteApps instead of giving our users access to a full desktop, there is no need to any sort of lockdown". To make things worse, we have heard this from Citrix customers as well. As they are only using 'Published Applications' (the Citrix equivalent to RemoteApps), some truly believe no lockdown is required.

Of course, this is not only inaccurate but will certainly leave the server exposed in ways we do not want. The fact you are publishing RemoteApps and essentially hiding the desktop does not mean it is not there. If you think hiding is good enough, well you are now doing what we call 'security by obscurity' and trust us, this is not a good thing ☺. We do agree there are certain settings that simply do not apply when running RemoteApps like hiding certain parts of the taskbar. These aside, no matter if running

RemoteApps or full desktops, locking the environment down is indeed a very important task and one that you should not skip.

Before getting any deeper, let's chat a bit about the differences between computer and user settings and how to use them properly.

When dealing with GPOs for RDSHs, there are two types of settings. Settings that apply to the computer (the actual RDSH) and settings that apply to the user (the user logging in to the RDSH). In most cases, you will need both. To make your life easier, we recommend you create separate GPOs for these so you can easily identity and possibly reuse these GPOs.

These GPOs are most commonly applied to the OU holding your RDSHs (I am sure you do remember our OU structure as described at the beginning of the book). For a computer GPO simply link the GPO to the OU. User GPOs are a bit different. For them to work, you need to go through an additional step after linking that GPO to the OU. For this to happen, we need to use what is called the 'Loopback Processing Mode'. You will find it under:
'Computer Configuration' | 'Policies' | 'Administrative Templates' | 'System' | 'Group Policy' | 'Configure user Group Policy loopback processing mode'.

Just select if you want this to merge user settings with other policies or to replace these completely.

With all that in mind, let's take a look at some common GPO settings related to the RDSHs that you should use.

- **Logon Scripts.** Yes, some people will definitely say this is ancient and more than that, these are the culprit for all slow logons out there. The reality is, poorly written logon scripts can and will slow down the logon process. We agree on that. But that said, in many cases logon scripts can be faster than using GPOs and GPPs (i.e. importing a registry file with all the settings we want to control instead of setting each one individually through GPOs/GPPs). The lesson here is to use logon scripts where it makes sense, making sure you maintain and optimize them (yes, logon scripts with 10,000 lines will probably slow things down). You can set them under the following location:
'User Configuration' | 'Policies' | 'Windows Settings' | 'Scripts (Logon/Logoff)' | 'Logon'

- **Control Panel.** What we mean here is, what users should see (if anything) when they open the control panel. Usually we strip it down as much as possible but do not remove it completely (as there may be some items that are useful when dealing with the user experience). This is controlled under:
  'User Configuration' | 'Policies' | 'Administrative Templates' | 'Control Panel'

  The recommended ones are:
    - *'Always open All Control Panel Items when opening Control Panel'*. Set it to enabled. This forces the control panel to the 'icon' view (cleaner and easier to browse than the 'categories' one).
    - *'Show only specified Control Panel items'*. Here you are able to specify the control panel items you always want to show to the end users. This removes any other item that is not explicitly listed here. Be aware that you need to provide the control panel canonical names here. The most common items to show are: 'Devices and Printers', 'Language', 'Mouse', 'Personalization', 'Region' and 'Sound'. You can get the canonical names directly from MSDN:
    https://msdn.microsoft.com/en-us/library/windows/desktop/ee330741(v=vs.85).aspx#canonical_names

- **Add or Remove Programs.** Well this one we do think it is a no-brainer. Even though users typically lack local administrative rights (if they do, well, there is something wrong at your place) it does not hurt locking this down. We follow the motto 'Users see, Users touch' so we hide all we can ☺. This is controlled under:
  'User Configuration | 'Policies' | 'Administrative Templates' | 'Control Panel' | 'Add or Remove Programs'

  Here feel free to enable pretty much everything.

- **Personalization.** Yes, before you say anything, we know this is a heated topic in certain businesses. That said, we kind of do not care about what you think and according to our superior knowledge, users should not be allowed to personalize anything ☺. That is the main reason why we prevent access to most of these settings, controlled under:
  'User Configuration' | 'Policies' | 'Administrative Templates' | 'Control Panel' | 'Personalization'

- **Printers.** Usually we configure 'Point & Print' approved servers to control which print servers users can retrieve printers from (make sure you read the chapter about printing to understand the importance of restricting this) and of course set the appropriate policy to enforce users to only use this particular mechanism. This is controlled under:
'User Configuration' | 'Policies' | 'Administrative Templates' | 'Control Panel' | 'Printers'

    The recommended ones are:
    - 'Only use Package Point and print'. Set it to enabled.
    - 'Package Point and print – Approved servers'. Set it to enabled (enter your print servers FQDNs there).

- **Regional and Language Options.** This is a key one if you are dealing with Multilingual User Interfaces (MUI). The idea behind it is to have an English language OS and for each language you have to support, an MUI pack is installed. This allows you to serve users with different language requirements, all from the same base RDSH. Once the packs are installed you can enforce which language a particular group will see as the default by setting this GPO. This is controlled under:
'User Configuration' | 'Policies' | 'Administrative Templates' | 'Control Panel' | 'Regional and Language Options'

    The recommended ones are:
    - Restrict selection of Windows menus and dialogs language
    - Restricts the UI languages Windows should use for the selected user

- **Desktop.** This one controls several things the user will see or have access to on the desktop. Even though you may think these are not needed if using RemoteApps only, we highly recommend you to enforce these so no matter what delivery method you use (full desktop or RemoteApp) the environment will be properly locked down. These are controlled under:
'User Configuration' | 'Policies' | 'Administrative Templates' | 'Desktop'

    Many of these will apply depending on your environment but the most common we usually set are:
    - Remove the Desktop Cleanup Wizard
    - Hide Network Locations icon on the desktop

- Remove Properties from the Computer icon context menu
- Remove Properties from the Documents icon context menu
- Remove Properties from the Recycle Bin context menu
- Under 'Desktop' you can enforce a wallpaper (i.e. with your company logo). Just set it under 'Desktop Wallpaper' (make sure the file exists on all your RDSHs).

- **Network Connections.** Pretty much all users can see regarding network cards and their settings are controlled here. Even though some will certainly require elevated rights to work, the best approach is to indeed get rid of anything users can see. If they see something, they will touch it. I can assure you. The main reason why in most cases we enable all these settings (meaning in a restrictive way). This is all controlled under:
  'User Configuration' | 'Policies' | 'Administrative Templates' | 'Network' | 'Network Connections'

- **Registry and Command Prompt.** In our opinion, users should have no access to the registry and to the command prompt, unless you want to open a can of worms. This is controlled under:
  'User Configuration' | 'Policies' | 'Administrative Templates' | 'System'

  The two settings mentioned above are:
  - Prevent access to the command prompt (make sure you set 'Disable the command prompt script processing also' to 'No', unless you are sure no scripts of any sort that will be importing registry keys need to run).
  - Prevent access to registry editing tools (here 'Disable regedit from running silently' should be set to 'No' only if you fall into the case described above).

- **Task Manager.** More advanced users know they can press CTRL+ALT+END to access the task manager. Unless you control which executables users can launch, this is normally not something you want to allow users to do as they would be able to launch almost any process within the system. The good thing is, you can indeed prevent that. It is under:
  'User Configuration' | 'Policies' | 'Administrative Templates' | 'System' | 'Control + Alt + Del Options'
  The setting in question is:
  - Remove Task Manager

- **Windows Explorer.** Here you control many little things that usually most administrators do not even think about restricting. For example, if your users right-click the 'My Computer' icon, do they see 'Manage' on the menu that pops up? If they double-click 'My Computer' do they see the server drives (C:, D: and so on)? Yes, these are all controlled here and, in our opinion, should be carefully reviewed and of course implemented. These, with many others, are located under:
  'User Configuration' | 'Policies' | 'Administrative Templates' | 'Windows Components' | 'File Explorer'
  The settings we mentioned are:
    - Hide these specified drives in My Computer (if you need to hide specific drives, search for hidedrive.xls on the Internet. It will show you which value you must use based on the drive letters you want to hide. You will need to modify the ADMX template)
    - Prevent access to drives from My Computer
    - Hides the Manage item on the File Explorer context menu
  These are also enabled in most cases:
    - Remove Hardware tab
    - Remove Security tab
    - No Entire Network in Network Locations
    - No Computers Near Me in Network Locations

- **Internet Explorer.** In almost every RDS environment Internet Explorer is the browser used to access many web applications due to compatibility reasons. No matter if the application is hosted on your intranet or on an external site, it is always a good idea to lock down Internet Explorer due to security reasons. Its settings can be configured under:
  'User Configuration' | 'Policies' | 'Administrative Templates' | 'Windows Components' | 'Internet Explorer'

  We usually use the settings here to configure the homepage, 3rd party extensions and for hiding specific menus from Internet Explorer (so users do not go crazy, trying everything).

  Another important one is under 'Internet Control Panel' | 'Security', under 'Site to Zone Assignment List'. This is where you can add particular sites to certain zones, so these work as expected and with the most restrictive settings for that particular zone.

- **Remote Desktop Services.** Although there is an entire Group Policy section called 'Remote Desktop Services', it is important to mention that most of these settings can also be configured using PowerShell or even through the 'Server Manager' interface. In our opinion, there is no right or wrong way here. What is key, is to decide what to use and stick to it otherwise you will run into issues like not knowing for sure how a particular setting is enforced. The RDS relevant settings are located under:

  'User Configuration' | 'Policies' | 'Administrative Templates' | 'Windows Components' | 'Remote Desktop Services'

  A very important setting, that should be applied to all clients (not the RDS Servers) and that can also be imported as a registry key to non-managed PCs is under 'Remote Desktop Connection Client'. It is the 'Specify SHA1 thumbprints of certificates representing trusted .rdp publishers'. This controls the warning screen users will get when launching an RDP session, showing the message 'Do you trust the publisher of this remote connection?' or similar. All you need is to get the thumbprint from the certificate you used for the deployment (as in our case, the wildcard certificate) and set this policy.

- **Task Scheduler.** Settings related to the 'Task Scheduler' are usually configured, in order to prevent users from running, creating and deleting tasks. These settings can be configured under:
  'User Configuration' | 'Policies' | 'Administrative Templates' | 'Task Scheduler'

- **Windows Updates.** In an RDS environment, it is quite important to control how updates get pushed to the servers and which users may get notifications about these. Usually we control which updates are deployed using something like WSUS and only after extensive testing, simply because in the past, certain Windows updates did break RDS related components. Considering that in certain cases such updates cannot be uninstalled, you realize how important it is to make sure only updates known to work should be deployed. Regarding user notifications, well, if the user is not an administrator, he should never get any of these messages. These settings can be configured under:
  'Computer Configuration' | 'Policies' | 'Administrative Templates' | 'Windows Components' | 'Windows Update'

The settings we mentioned are:
- Allow non-administrators to receive update notifications
- Specify intranet Microsoft update service location

Now that we covered a bit regarding GPOs, time to take a quick look at GPPs. GPPs, part of a GPO, came from the DesktopStandard acquisition by Microsoft. Their PolicyMaker product allowed administrators to perform several tasks that were typically done using logon scripts (i.e. drive mappings). One of its key features was the filtering granularity allowed (i.e. only apply certain items if the user was running his session on a particular group of servers and only if that server was 64-bit and the moon was full – ok, I made up that last part) what is still a major problem when dealing with logon scripts.

As these are part of a GPO, GPPs can be controlled on a computer or user basis but again, with way more granularity. When you open an existing GPO, you can see the 'Preferences' folder, listed under both 'Computer Configuration' and 'User Configuration'.

As we can see above, GPPs allow you to control things like printers, drive mappings and even the shortcuts users may see on their desktops. Even though GPPs are easy to configure, it is worth mentioning that you pay a price for using them. In general, GPPs tend to slow down the logon process a bit, when compared to a basic GPO (remember, ControlUp Insights can show you that information, down to details where the slowness is during the logon process). In many cases, well-written logon scripts will probably be faster. But not everyone knows how to write well-written logon scripts. ☺

One of the most common tasks performed using a GPP is to modify registry keys under the user hive (HKCU), in order to configure specific applications or settings (i.e. a file type association can be controlled here, on a per-user basis).

For example, Adobe Acrobat Pro and Reader can indeed co-exist on the same machine. The trick is to install Reader first and then Pro and finally use a GPP to set the file type association for the users that are supposed to only use Adobe Reader, to Adobe Reader!

This is controlled by the following keys:

> [HKEY_CURRENT_USER\Software\Microsoft\Windows\CurrentVersion\Explorer\FileExts\.pdf\OpenWithList]
> "a"="AcroRd32.exe"
> "MRUList"="a"
>
> [HKEY_CURRENT_USER\Software\Microsoft\Windows\CurrentVersion\Explorer\FileExts\.pdf\UserChoice]
> "Progid"="AcroExch.Document.DC"

By creating a GPP to enforce these registry keys to the correct group, you can now have full control over the application that handles the PDF file type association. The main thing, as mentioned above, is how granular this can be.

Once the GPP registry item is created, open it and go to the 'Common' tab. Make sure the 'Item-level targeting' is checked. Click on 'Targeting...'

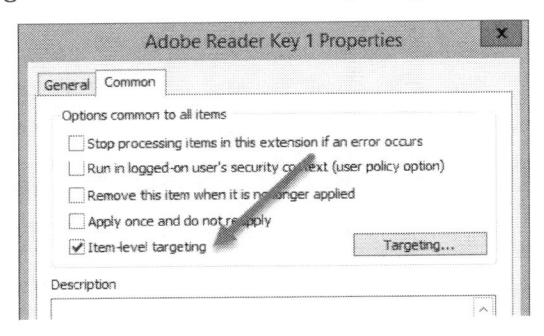

This shows you how granular it can be:

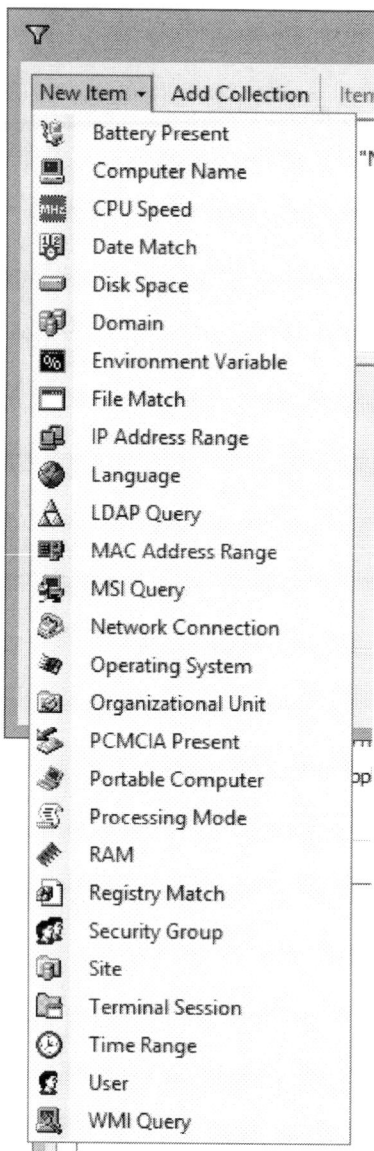

- Battery Present
- Computer Name
- CPU Speed
- Date Match
- Disk Space
- Domain
- Environment Variable
- File Match
- IP Address Range
- Language
- LDAP Query
- MAC Address Range
- MSI Query
- Network Connection
- Operating System
- Organizational Unit
- PCMCIA Present
- Portable Computer
- Processing Mode
- RAM
- Registry Match
- Security Group
- Site
- Terminal Session
- Time Range
- User
- WMI Query

It even allows you to detect if the user is inside a Terminal Session (see above, fourth item from the bottom!).

A huge difference if compared to regular logon scripts. To achieve the same level of granularity, a lot of work (and logic) has to go into your login script. It is clear that GPPs can achieve a lot in a much easier way. But as mentioned, make sure you understand the caveats when using these.

Customizing and locking down the 'Start' screen

On RDS 2012 R2, users are presented with a 'Start' screen, instead of a well-known 'Start' menu. This change, introduced with Windows 8/Windows Server 2012, further refined and modified with the Windows 10/Windows Server 2016 release created a huge headache for administrators, given there is still, in 2018, no easy way to implement a customized 'Start' screen/menu based on group membership.

With that in mind, there are still some ways to at least give users a customized, locked down experience. Using a GPO, we can set a pre-defined layout for the 'Start' screen, with all the required application icons for a particular group and locked down enough so no additional application icons can be added to it. Sure, that is indeed a drawback as users would not be able to change it but that said, it is indeed better than nothing.

To create a custom 'Start' screen and set it for your users, while hiding all the 'common' application seen under the 'Apps' section, follow these steps:

1. The first thing to be done is to create a custom 'Start' screen. We suggest you to use a test user account. Logon to one of your RDSHs as the user and customize the 'Start' screen as you wish, by pinning items under the 'Apps' section to it. You must click on the 'Start' button and then on the arrow at the bottom left corner:

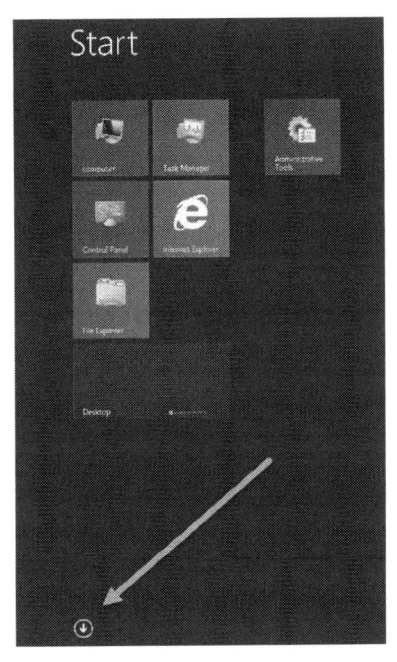

2. The 'Apps' section will appear. Right-click any application you want to see in the 'Start' screen and select 'Pin to Start'. Repeat this step for as many applications as you want.

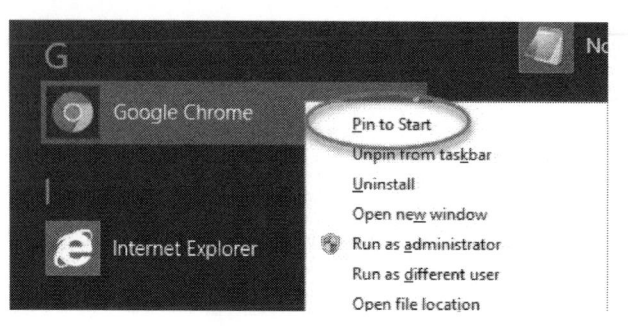

3. Back to the 'Start' screen, arrange the icons as you wish. Once this is done, open a PowerShell window and run the following command (make sure the path points to a folder that does exist):

    Export-StartLayout -Path C:\Temp\MyLayout.xml -As XML

4. Copy the file 'MyLayout.xml' to a shared location (in our case we copied to our fileserver, \\crlab-fs01\StartScreen\Common.xml). If you need different layouts for different groups, you must arrange the 'Start' screen and export it several times, so you end up with multiple XML files.

5. Now, create or modify an existing GPO and set the following 'Start Screen Layout' option under *'User Configuration' | 'Policies' | 'Administrative Templates' | 'Start Menu and Taskbar'*.

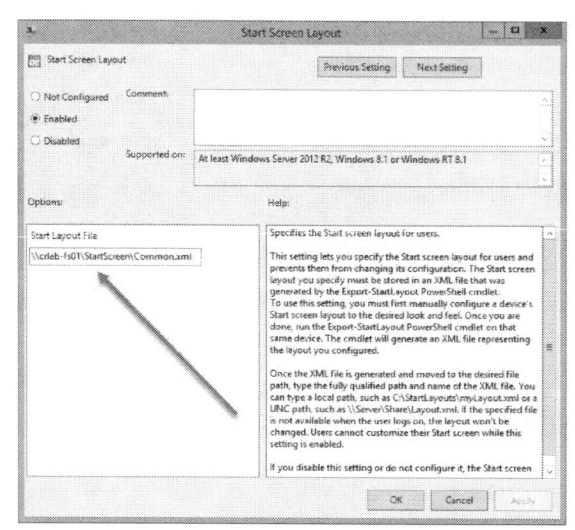

6. As you realize, if you need a custom layout per group, you will need multiple group policies. Also make sure these policies only apply to the required groups and not 'Authenticated Users' as in such case, administrators would get these restrictions in place.

7. The final step is to create a registry item that will remove all the extra applications from the 'Apps' section. Under *'User Configuration'* | *'Preferences'* | *'Windows Settings'* | *'Registry'* right-click it and select 'New' | 'Registry Item'.

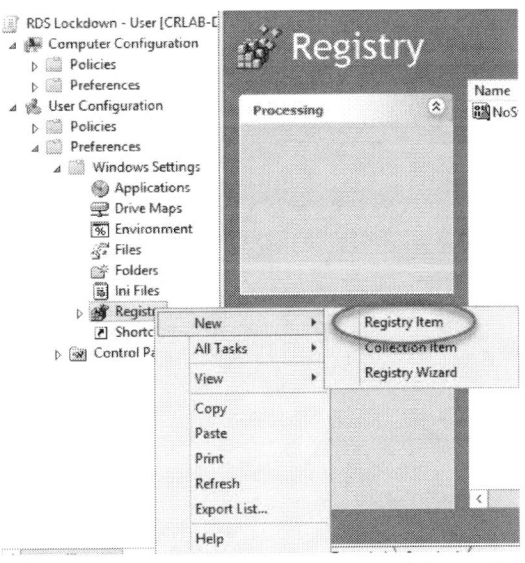

8. Set the value name 'NoStartMenuMorePrograms' to a REG_DWORD with a value of '1' (decimal or Hexadecimal). The key path must be set to 'Software\Microsoft\Windows\CurrentVersion\Policies\Explorer'. Click 'Apply'.

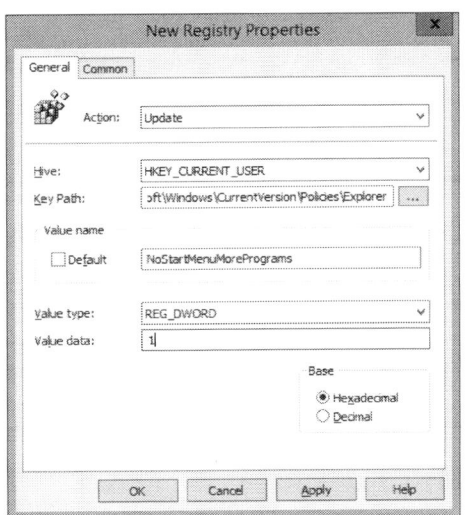

9. Assuming your policies are indeed correctly set (i.e. loopback processing mode is enabled, filtering is set to the correct groups, etc), once a user logs in, he should see something like this:

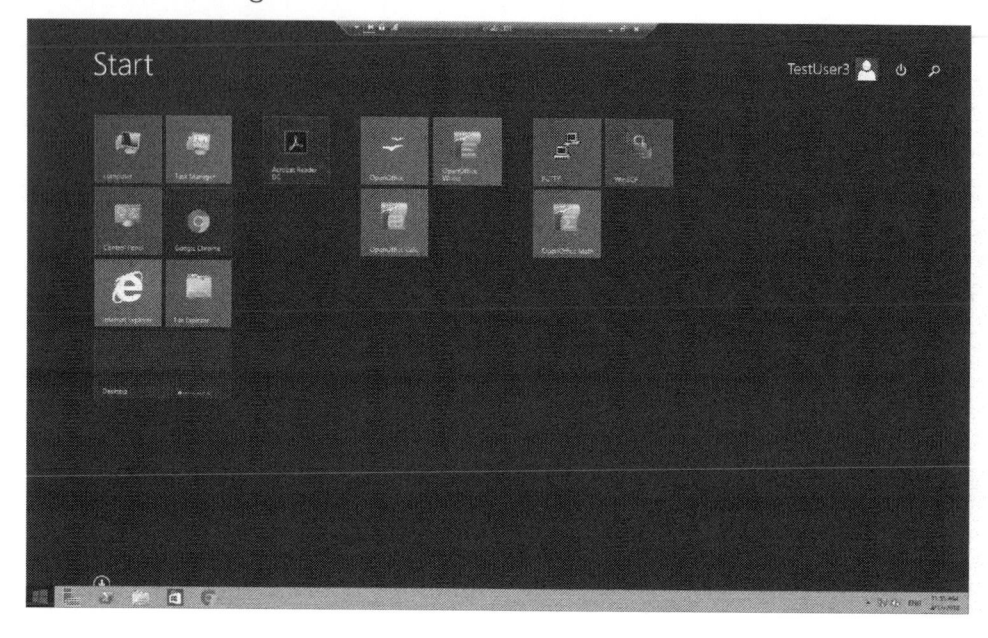

10. If the user clicks on the arrow at the left bottom corner, to access the 'Apps' section, he is presented with something similar to this:

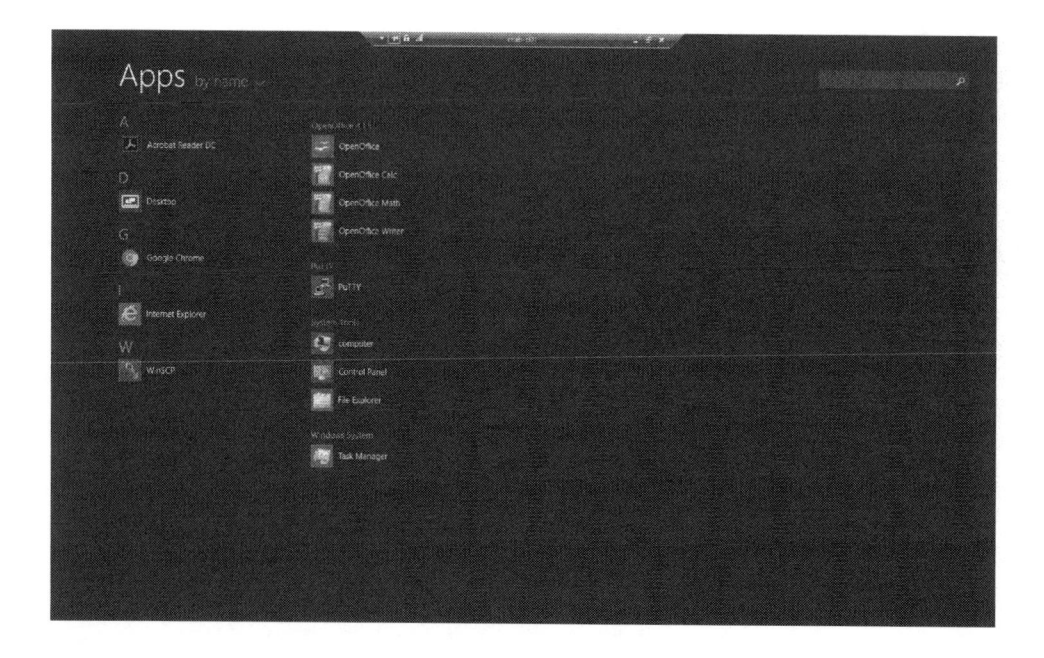

11. Success. Your users now have a customized 'Start' screen and with all the unnecessary applications removed from 'Apps'. The drawback here is just the fact this is indeed fully locked down. Users cannot right-click the apps to pin the to the 'Start' screen.

Now you may be wondering if it is possible to create a custom, initial 'Start' screen that all users would have initially and that could be customized by them. Yes, this is indeed possible but it is a very cumbersome process and more than that, without a centralized way of doing it, meaning you will have to do it for every single RDSH you may have.

The process is described on Jesse Boehm's website (a great resource – if you need a custom RDWA portal, or Citrix NetScaler one, he is the guy to do it). The article that shows it in details is this one:

https://biab.solutions/creating-default-roaming-profiles-for-microsoft-rds-and-citrix-xenapp-and-xendesktop-on-windows-2012-r2-for-end-users/

Does it work? Yes! Is it easy to maintain, especially with multiple RDSHs? Nope. Is there a better way to do it using what is available with RDS out-of-the-box? Unfortunately, no. ☹

Now, let's take a look at how applications behave under RDS and what to keep in mind, in terms of best practices, when dealing with them.

Installing applications

Now that you got a pretty good idea how to manage certain application needs (i.e. file type associations, creating customized 'Start' screens, etc), the next big question comes up: "Is there a special way to install applications on RDSH?". Unfortunately, there is no easy answer to this question and we will explain why.

First of all, there are developers and developers out there. Some do develop applications they should be proud of showing to their wives, moms and kids. Others, should be kidnapped and sent to a remote island where they would have to fight for food and water. Kind of a Kong, Skull Island type of place.

What that means is, there are great and terrible applications out there. Some will work just fine on RDSH, while others will require all sorts of tricks to get them going.

That is where the problem starts: installation. Since day one, RDS uses a mechanism that helps dealing with legacy, old or simply poorly written applications: the shadow keys.

The idea was simple: if something is written to HKCU (our Ol'Good HKEY_CURRENT_USER hive) during installation, these 'writes' were captured and automatically added to a user once he logs in for the first time. This 'mode' is triggered by opening a command prompt and typing 'CHANGE USER /INSTALL' and pressing enter (this has to be done on all RDSHs, when installing applications). Once the installation is done (and before a reboot), you go back to the command prompt and type 'CHANCE USER /EXECUTE' (press enter). Done.

These 'writes' will end up here:
HKEY_LOCAL_MACHINE\SOFTWARE\Microsoft\Windows NT\CurrentVersion\Terminal Server\Install\Software (64-bit processes)
HKEY_LOCAL_MACHINE\SOFTWARE\Wow6432Node\Microsoft\Windows NT\CurrentVersion\Terminal Server\Install\Software (32-bit processes)

Once a new user logs in, this mechanism will then add these keys for that user and the application should work as expected.

Now you may be thinking that as of today most applications, if not all, do handle this properly, eliminating the need for this mechanism. Well let me burst your bubble. While many may (and a BIG may here) work as expected, the reality is RDS to this day is used as a platform to deal with legacy apps. And as expected, the older the app, the higher the chances it was written with the always-for-a-single-user mindset. As we cannot predict which applications do work or not, we would say it is always a good thing to use the 'CHANGE USER /INSTALL' and 'CHANGE USER /EXECUTE' commands. If you are using something like SCCM to deploy packages to your RDSHs, it is a good thing to enforce such commands within the packages.

And before you ask if that mechanism is still present to this day, well, if that was not the case we would not be writing about it. ☺

Seriously, as of today, the mechanism is there. The thing is, when applications are compiled, you can set a flag (TSAWARE - https://msdn.microsoft.com/en-us/library/01cfys9z(v=vs.100).aspx) that will basically flag that application as 'RDS compliant' what means, there is no need for the shadow mechanism as the application does not write anything that is user specific during installation. As you probably guessed, many applications do have this flag set and still do not conform to the rules that dictate if that flag should or not be set. Yes, thank the developers we sent to Skull Island for that.

Of course, over the years things improved. Depending on the installer, RDSH can put itself into 'install' mode and take care of everything. But again, if you want to be on the safe side, always use the 'install' and 'execute' modes when installing applications.

"But what if I do not want to use this?". Well, your choice really. The reality is, if you do know your applications well, and what files/registry keys are needed to be there, you do not need to worry about anything. Use GPPs or another mechanism to inject registry keys and copy files during logon for example and you are all set.

The reality though is a bit different. We, the 'RDS guys', usually have no clue about what applications do or how they work. We expect developers or application owners to give us that information. With that in hand, sure, easy job to make sure the application works as expected.

Guess what? In many cases, more than I would like to deal with, developers and application owners have no idea whatsoever what their own application is doing. Seriously. The end result is, the 'RDS guys' end up having to use tools like 'Process

Monitor' (https://technet.microsoft.com/en-us/sysinternals/bb896645) to clearly see what an application is trying to do when something fails. Typical examples are writing registry values to keys the user has no rights to, attempting to write files to read-only locations or simply expecting files to be present in a hard-coded path for every single user. Now you understand why the population at Skull Island is growing at a very fast pace.

The lessons to be learned here are simple:
- Never trust any developer or assume they know what they are doing. Many do but way more do not.
- Try as much as you can to use the vendor provided MSI when installing applications. You can certainly leverage transform files, answer files, command line switches or anything else the vendor uses for pre-configuring application settings. That is all good. But avoid using repackaged installers, provided by the 'Application Team'. In most cases these were created assuming desktops as endpoints and not RDSHs. This is probably the most important point here. Keep this in mind, especially if the 'Application Team' is trying to push packages down to the RDSHs using SCCM or similar products. If that is the case, make sure you clearly understand what the package is doing. You have been warned.
- You can certainly avoid the shadow mechanism entirely by not using the commands mentioned above. Just understand that in certain cases you will have to push registry keys and/or files around to make sure the application works as expected the first time a user launches it. As of today, most applications should work out-of-the-box as they are flagged as TSAWARE but again, do not count on that at all times.
- Based on the above, use the 'install'/'execute' mechanism if you know you are dealing with an old application. But keep in mind that there is an issue regarding time stamps, assuming you do create new RDSHs way down the road, after the first ones were built. But considering that as of today most servers are built using some cloning/template mechanism, this should not be an issue. The issue arises when users logon to these newer servers and these keys have a newer timestamp than what is in the user hive. In such cases, the user hive gets overwritten (for that particular application). Therefore, the ideal solution is to use the shadow key mechanism when installing apps to determine if the application does require something to be pushed. If you see the new application keys under the registry locations we mentioned above, you know the application is not TSAWARE. In that case, take a note of the registry keys/values required

and use a GPP or similar solution to push the keys and delete what you see under the shadow keys. Yes, more management on your side but at least you know for sure the timestamps will not be an issue and you will have a much better understanding of your applications.

Tricerat's Simplify Profiles - Managing the user environment, the right way

So far, we learned how to manage the user environment using GPOs and GPPs. More than that, by now you understand how applications work under RDS and why you may need to manage certain registry keys and files for such applications.

Going back a little bit more, we covered User Profile Disks (UPD) and how to customize them so only certain folders are saved into it.

Looking at all that, what is the main lesson learned? The out-of-the-box solution does work but it is indeed cumbersome. And more than that, does not cover some very common scenarios in an elegant way. For example, users may be accessing applications from two different collections for whatever reason (i.e. due to incompatibility between the applications). If you remember, UPDs are assigned at the collection level what means if using multiple collections, multiple UPDs are required. While this may certainly work, it is not elegant and does complicate things from a management perspective.

That is where a solution designed to deal specifically with the user environment comes to the picture. Such solutions allow you to perform much more than simply roaming settings and data for your users. Application blocking, start menu and desktop customizations, registry/file roaming per process, it is all there.

The key thing about 'Simplify Profiles' is the fact it is, as its name implies, simple. As the product is part of the 'Simplify Suite' it also gives you a single console and simple architecture and can manage different platforms, what RDS on its own cannot do.

So, it is time to dig into 'Simplify Profiles' and see what it can do for you.

Before digging into the installation, it is worth taking the time to explain a bit about the components required and what each of them do.

'Simplify Profiles' is part of a suite, named as expected, 'Simplify Suite'. It includes several components, as explained below:

Component	Description
Simplify Console	As its name implies, this is the console where you manage everything. Here you create the assignments between users and objects (printers, applications, whitelists, etc).
Simplify Printing	Handles everything printing related, providing a true driverless printing environment on RDS. All the details about this and how to get it going are explained on the next chapter, 'Printing'.
Simplify Profiles	Allows you to have personalization for your user profiles but without relying on roaming profiles or similar technologies.
Simplify Lockdown	Controls what your users can and cannot run on your RDS servers, using for example blacklists/whitelists.
Simplify Desktop	Using Tricerat's own shell (TriShell), provides users with a controlled, customizable desktop experience. Wallpapers, start menu, taskbar, all configurable using the 'Simplify Console'.

With the basics out of the way, let's take a look at how to install and configure the components required to control our user environment.

Installing the 'Simplify Suite' console

This is the first step required as it will not only give us a console to manage the whole solution but also creates the required database.

1. Logon to the machine where you want the console installed (in our case, 'CRLAB-CL01') and launch the 'Simplify Suite' installer. Select the desired language and click 'Next'.

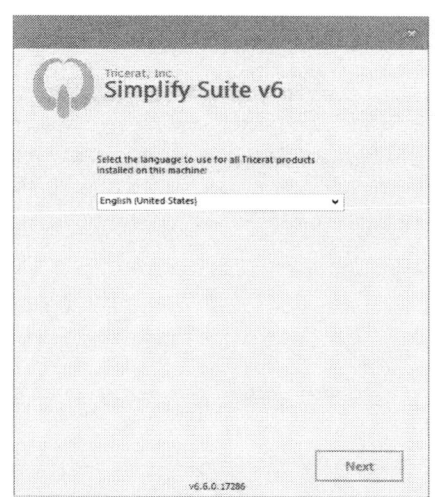

2. Agree to the licensing terms and click 'Next'.

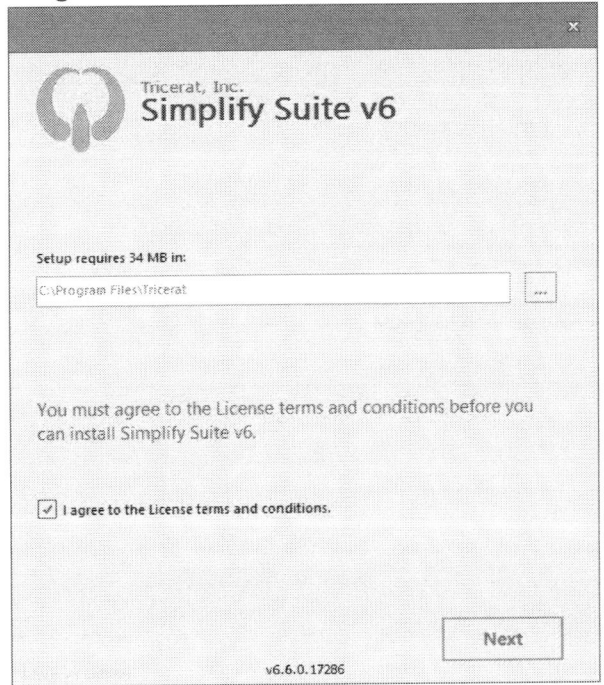

3. Select 'Simplify Console' and click 'Next'.

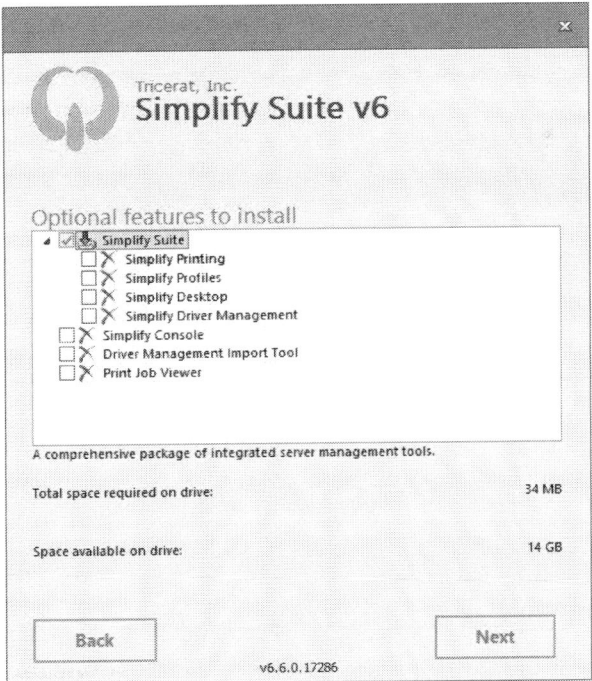

4. Enter the trial license you got from Tricerat (sent to the email you used to download the product) and click 'Next'.

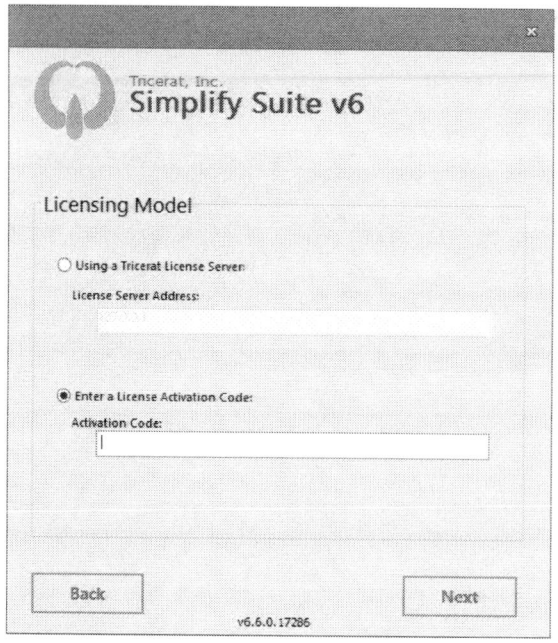

5. The installer will display some information about the SQL server setup procedure. Click 'Next'.

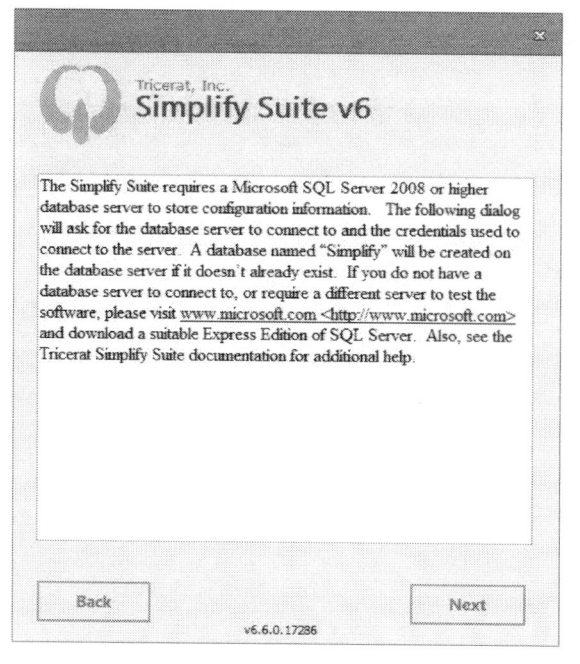

6. Select the SQL Server you will use (in our case, the same one we used for the RDCB HA, 'CRLAB-SQ01') and select the authentication method you want to use. The installer will show you the database name that will be created. Click 'Next'.

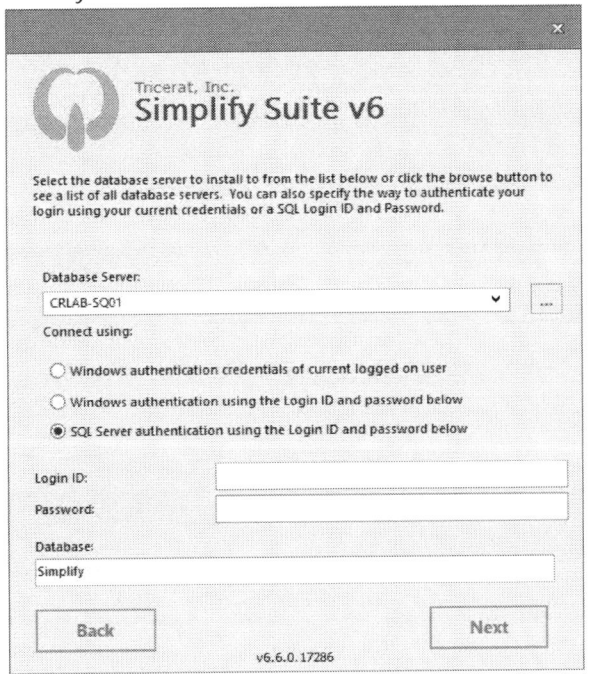

7. Click 'Install' to perform the installation.

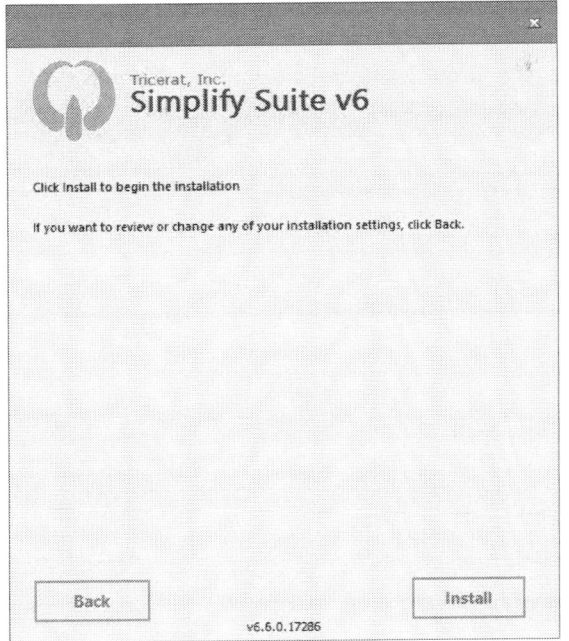

8. The setup procedure will start, showing you what is happening under the hood. Just wait...

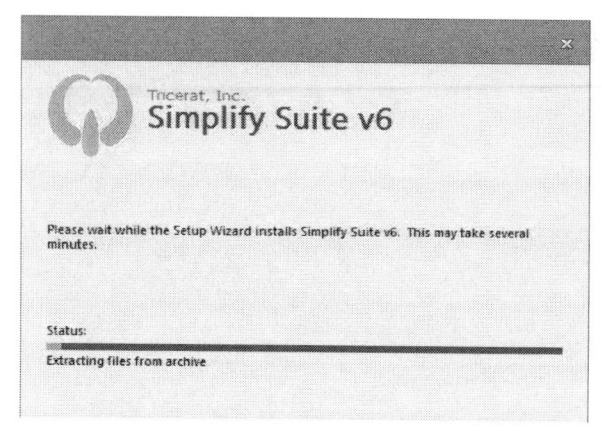

9. You are done. Click 'Finish'.

Installing the VDI/RDSH agent

Now that we have the console up and running, we need to install the required agents on our terminal servers. These will control the environment for our users, not relying on profiles, group policies or anything similar. Remember, it is all done within the 'Simplify Console'!

The installation is identical to the one we just did. The only differences are:
- You will perform it on your RDSHs.
- You will select different options.

Let's do it then.

1. Logon to every single RDSH and launch the installer. Select the desired language and click 'Next'.

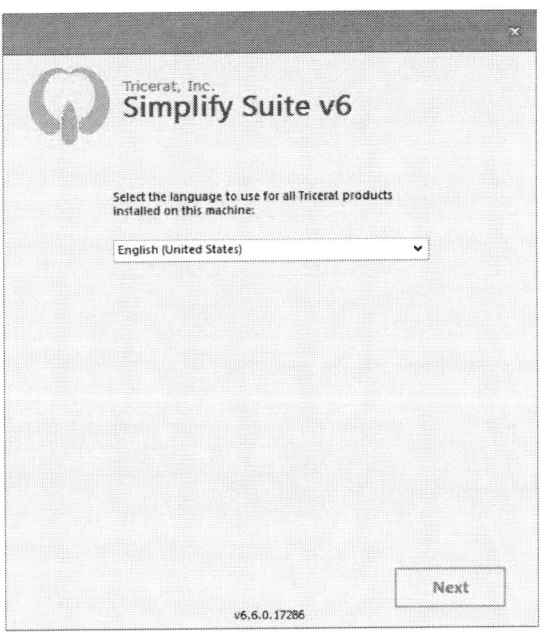

2. Agree to the licensing terms and click 'Next'.

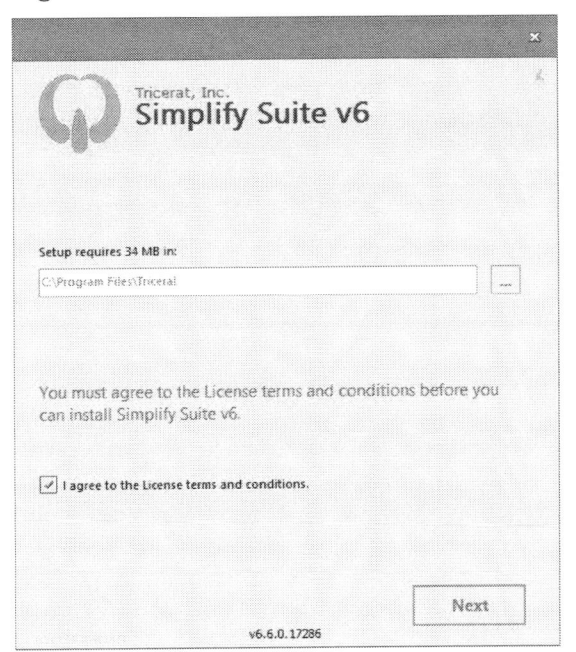

3. Select everything but 'Simplify Console' and click 'Next'.

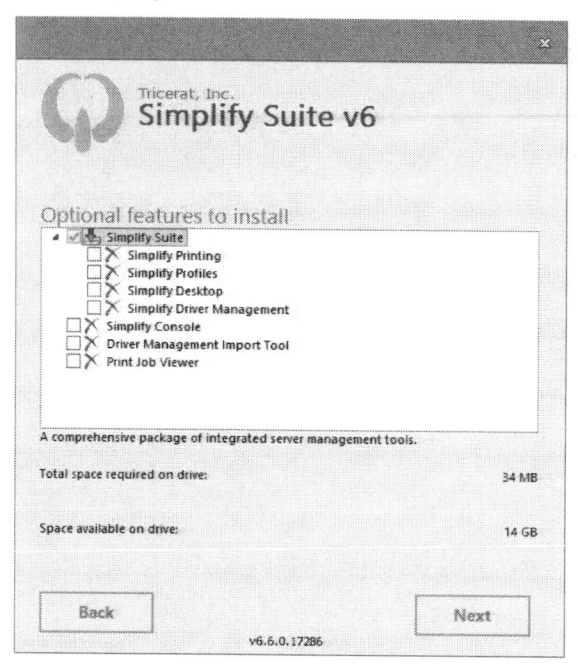

4. Enter the trial license you got from Tricerat (sent to the email you used to download the product) and click 'Next'.

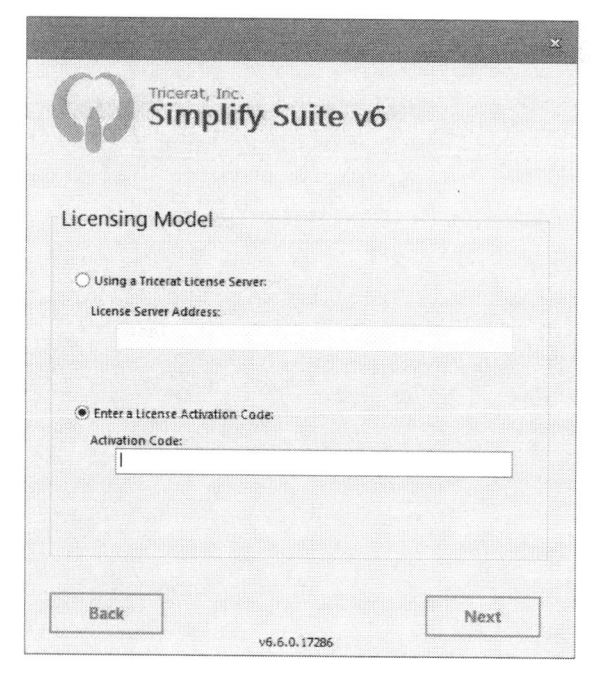

5. The installer will display some information about the SQL server setup procedure. Click 'Next'.

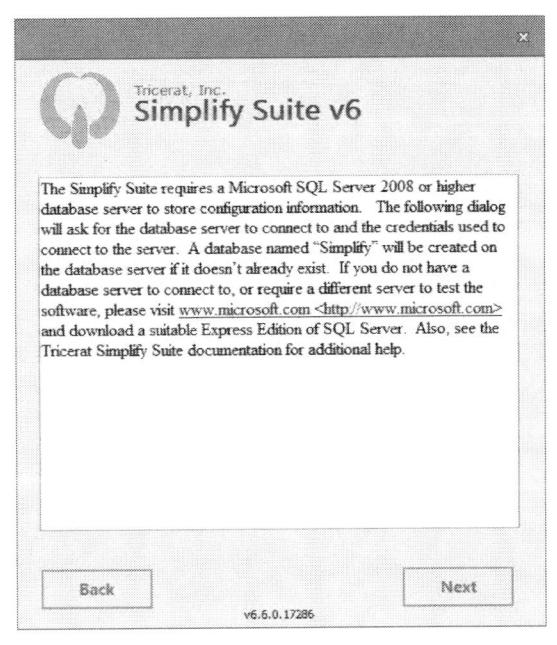

6. Select the same SQL Server and authentication method you used before. Click 'Next'.

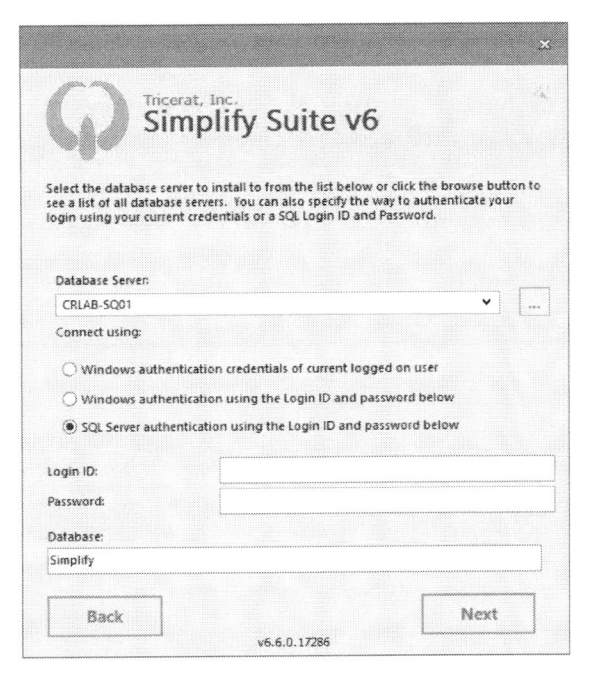

7. Click 'Install' to perform the installation.

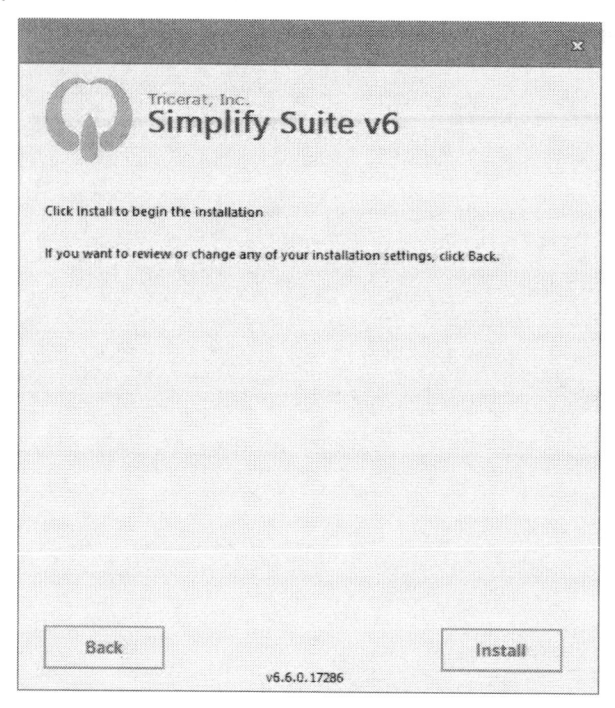

8. The setup procedure will start, showing you what is happening under the hood. Just wait...

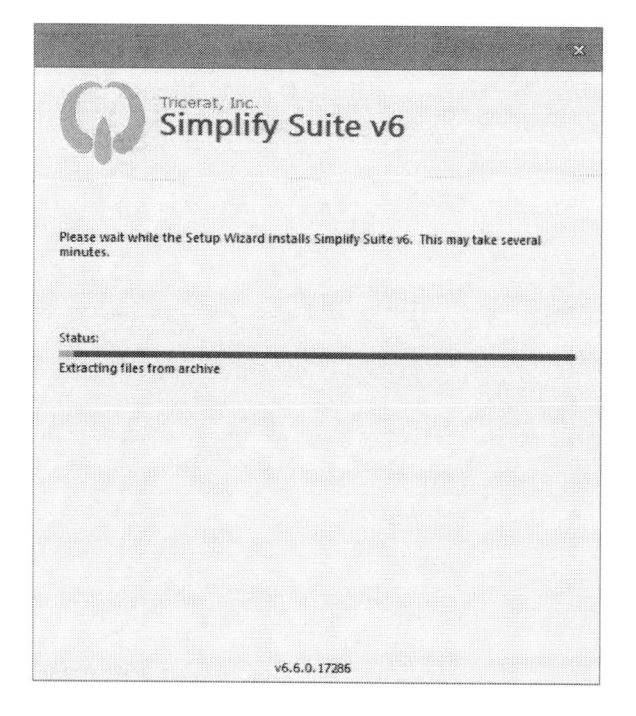

9. You are done. Click 'Finish'.

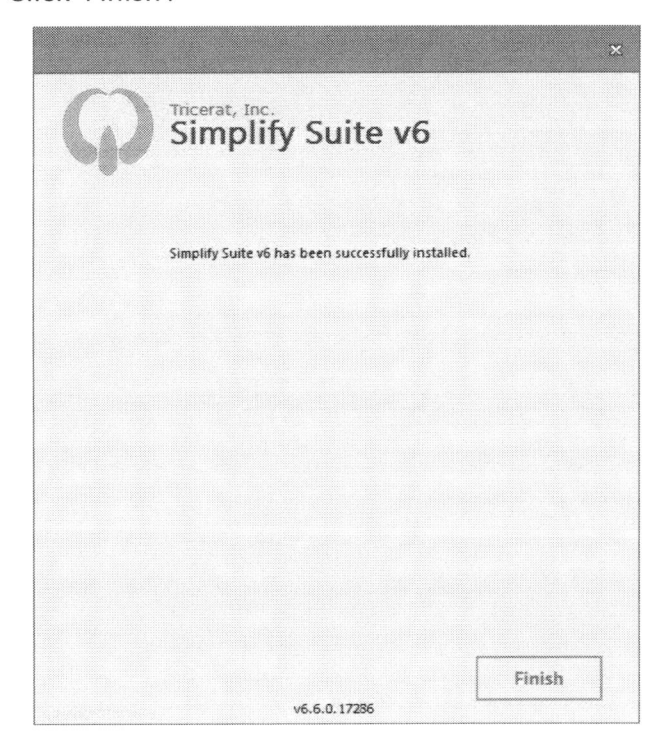

That is all you need on the RDSHs.

Note: as you selected 'Simplify Printing', on the next chapter the part that deals with installing 'Simplify Printing' on the RDSHs is therefore done. ☺

Creating the user environment

With all we need now in place, it is time for us to start creating a completely managed environment for our users. In order to highlight all the product capabilities, we will perform the following tasks:

- Create a custom desktop (enforce wallpaper, locked down taskbar, etc) based on a locked down shell (TriShell) with the shortcuts we want on it.
- Define applications that our users cannot use.
- Enforce certain registry settings.

Time to do it.

Creating a locked down desktop

First step, let's get a locked down desktop going, using the 'TriShell' from 'Simplify Desktop'.

1. On the machine where you installed the 'Simplify Printing' console, launch it. The console will load.

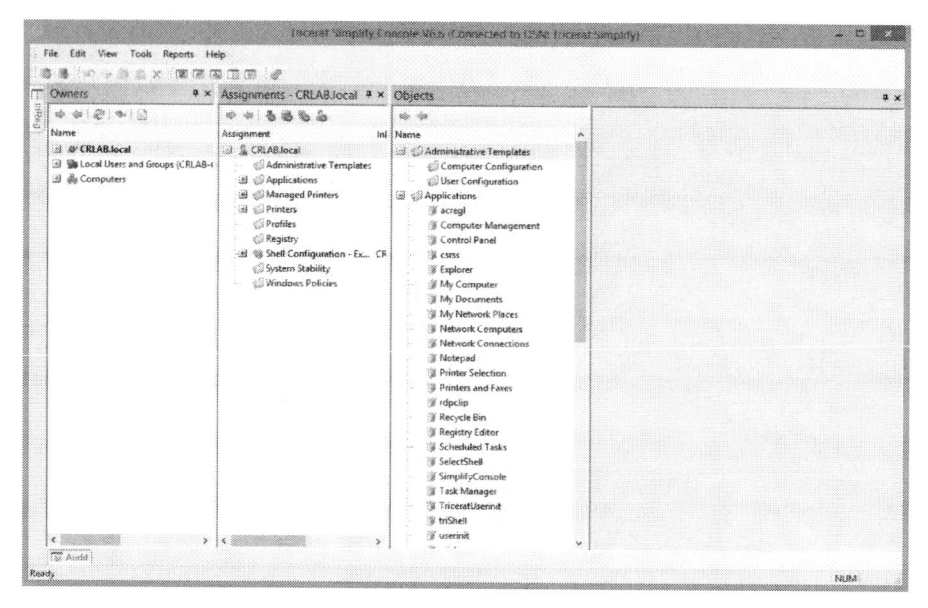

2. On the right-hand pane, under 'Shell Configuration', right-click triShell and select 'New Object'.

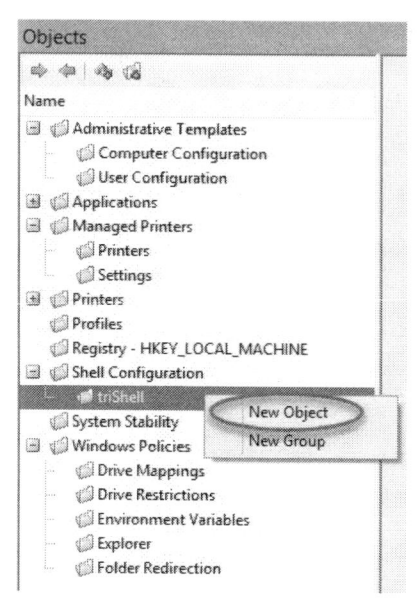

Page 296 | RDS - The Complete Guide

3. Rename it as desired.

```
□ 📁 Shell Configuration
   □ 📁 triShell
         📁 RDS Book
```

4. A new panel on the right-hand side will appear, showing you all the options for the locked down shell.

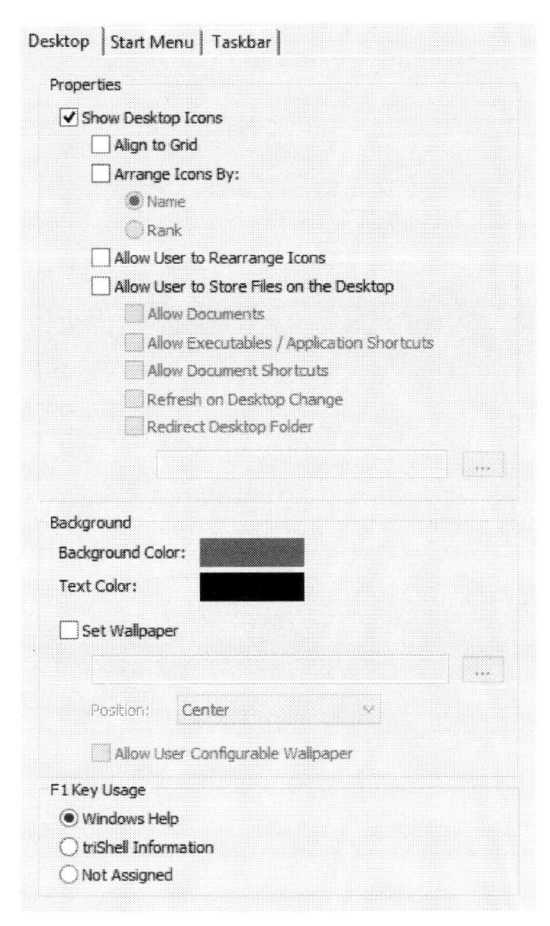

```
Desktop | Start Menu | Taskbar |
Properties
    ☑ Show Desktop Icons
        □ Align to Grid
        □ Arrange Icons By:
            ● Name
            ○ Rank
        □ Allow User to Rearrange Icons
        □ Allow User to Store Files on the Desktop
            □ Allow Documents
            □ Allow Executables / Application Shortcuts
            □ Allow Document Shortcuts
            □ Refresh on Desktop Change
            □ Redirect Desktop Folder
            [                              ] [...]

Background
    Background Color: [      ]
    Text Color:       [      ]
    □ Set Wallpaper
      [                              ] [...]
        Position: [Center      v]
      □ Allow User Configurable Wallpaper
F1 Key Usage
    ● Windows Help
    ○ triShell Information
    ○ Not Assigned
```

5. Let's set a particular wallpaper (it must be available in a folder on all your RDSHs) and make sure 'Allow User to Store Files on the Desktop' is unchecked (how many times have you had to redirect the desktop folder to avoid users saving stuff to it? Here it is a default setting, not to allow it).

6. For the 'Start Menu' we used the following settings (the text is indeed using some spaces at the beginning, to make it look good on the screen – you will understand what I mean by that):

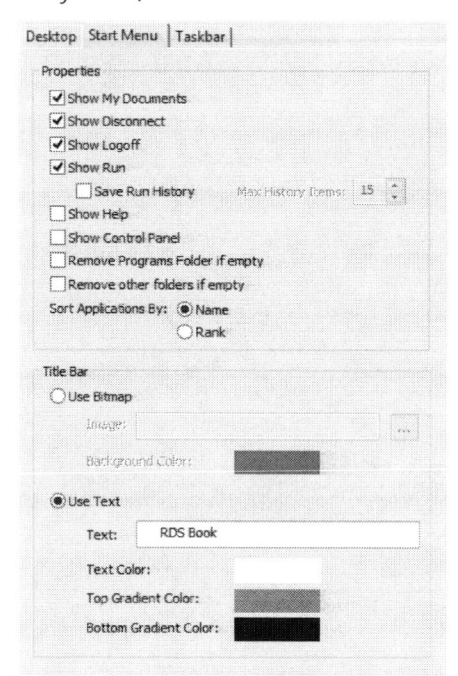

7. Finally, for the taskbar, we used the following:

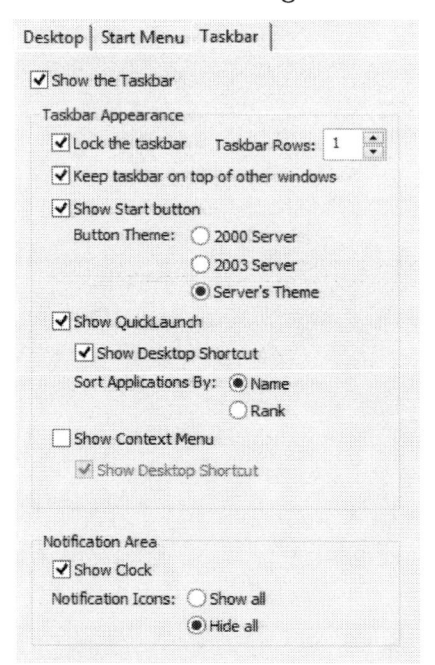

8. The next step is to drag-and-drop the newly created 'triShell' object, named 'RDS Book' to the user you selected in the first pane ('Owners'), shown in the middle one ('Assigments').

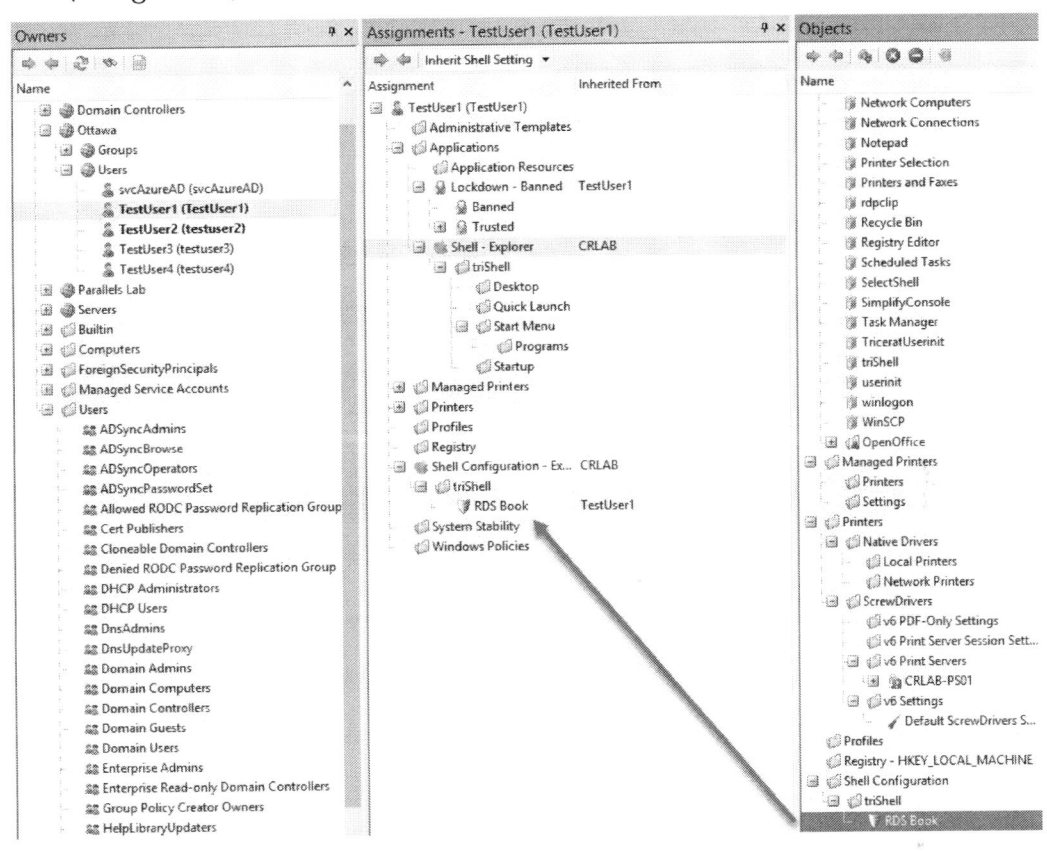

9. Now, right-click 'Shell – Explorer' in the middle pane for this user (in our case, 'TestUser1') and select 'triShell'.

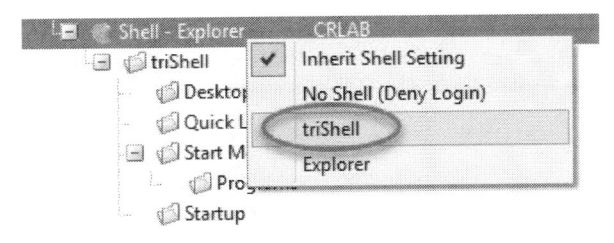

10. That is all. In a matter of minutes, you now have a locked down desktop for your user. If you go back to the RDWA, logon and launch a desktop as that user, this is what you see:

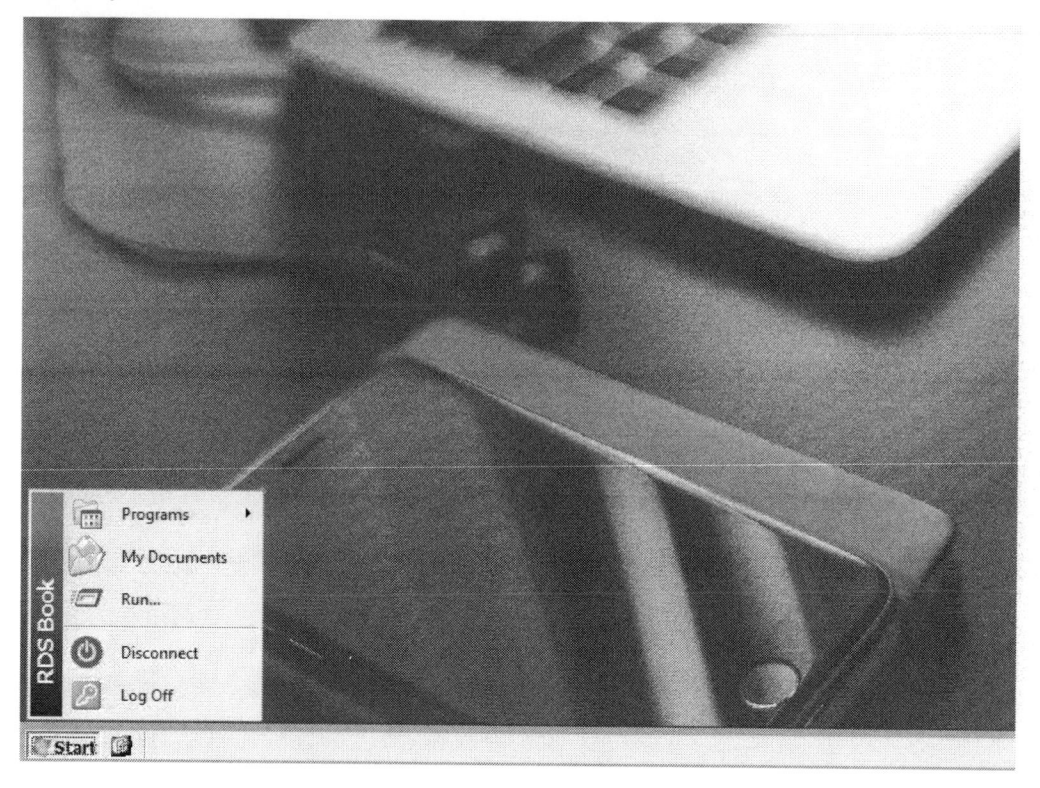

Success. It is worth mentioning the triShell does not have the same look-and-feel as seen on a Windows Server 2012 R2 or higher desktop (Tricerat is indeed considering creating a more modern, potentially similar to the Windows 10 interface). The reality is, this is an interface users are used to and that you can easily control, instead of dealing with the mess created by Microsoft with the Windows 8 and Windows 10 layouts. So, you get all the benefits of the underlying platform with the lockdown and customization capabilities you need.

Next on the list is to create some custom layouts for the 'Start' menu seen on the triShell. Let's create different ones for our two users, 'TestUser1' and 'TestUser2'. Before we can do that, we must create some application objects that we will then assign to the user 'Start' menu.

Let's do it.

1. As we have a couple applications installed on our RDSHs, still on the 'Simplify Suite' console, locate 'Applications' in the 'Objects' pane on the right.

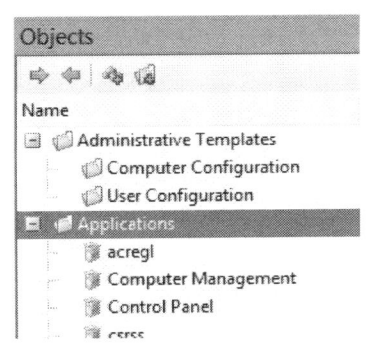

2. Right-click 'Applications' and select 'New Object'.

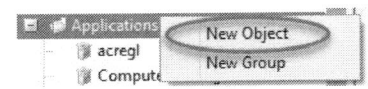

3. Enter a new name for the application object. In this example we will create an application object for 'Acrobat Reader DC' that we have installed on the RDSHs.

4. On the right pane, in the 'Properties' tab, enter the information for the application. As you can see, right there you can set how many instances of this application you want to allow in a session or even on the RDSH. This is extremely helpful when dealing with applications known to be resource hogs. This is something that RDS, out-of-the-box, does not offer.

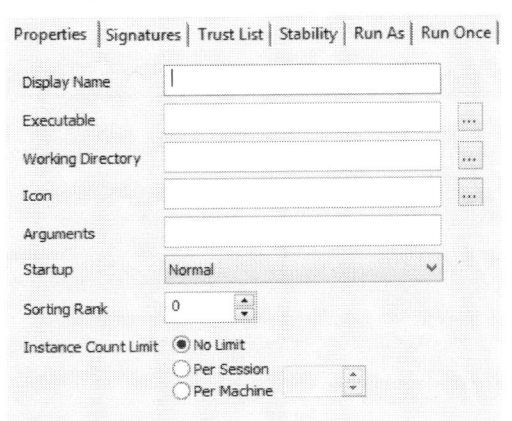

5. Once you fill in all the information, click the 'Apply changes' button. Make sure the paths you enter do not have any quotes and for the icon, use the same path as the main executable. Your screen should look similar to this:

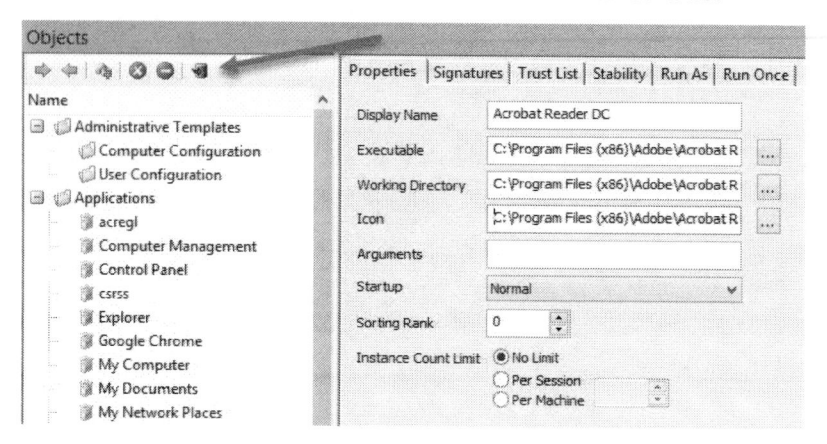

6. Repeat for as many applications as you want. In our case we created a bunch of them so we can build a nice 'Start' menu for our users. It is worth highlighting that the 'Simplify Suite' allows you to control how all these applications behave, guaranteeing they do not use all the resources available. This is done on a per-application basis and is controlled through the 'Stability' tab settings:

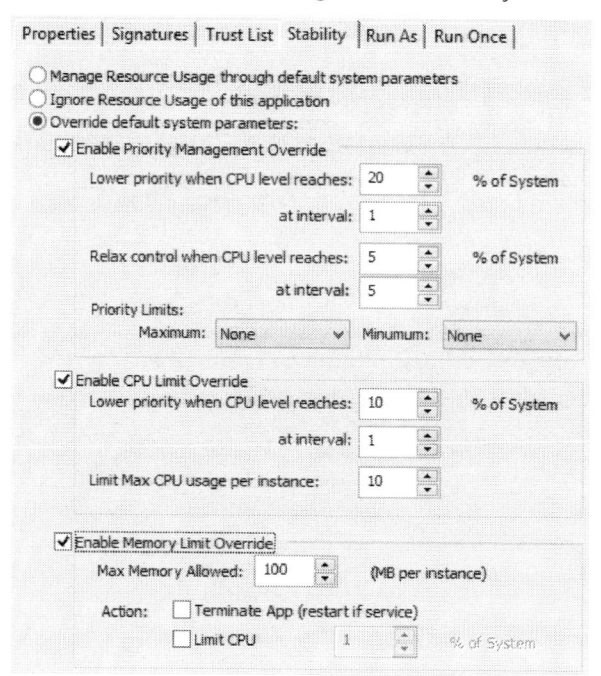

7. Now that we have several applications created, let's get a proper 'Start' menu going. You can do this at any level, OUs, groups and of course users. For this example, let's create two separate layouts, one for our 'TestUser1' and one for 'TestUser2'. On the left pane, 'Owners', select the user in question and in the middle pane, 'Assignments', under 'Applications' | 'Shell' | 'triShell' | 'Start Menu', create your folders. This is what we have done for our user 'TestUser1'.

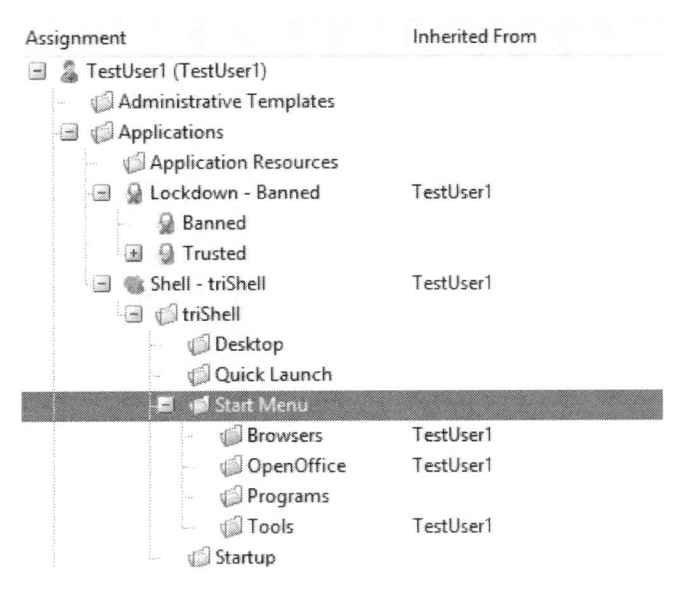

Assignment	Inherited From
TestUser1 (TestUser1)	
Administrative Templates	
Applications	
Application Resources	
Lockdown - Banned	TestUser1
Banned	
Trusted	
Shell - triShell	TestUser1
triShell	
Desktop	
Quick Launch	
Start Menu	
Browsers	TestUser1
OpenOffice	TestUser1
Programs	
Tools	TestUser1
Startup	

8. For our 'TestUser2' we built the following structure:

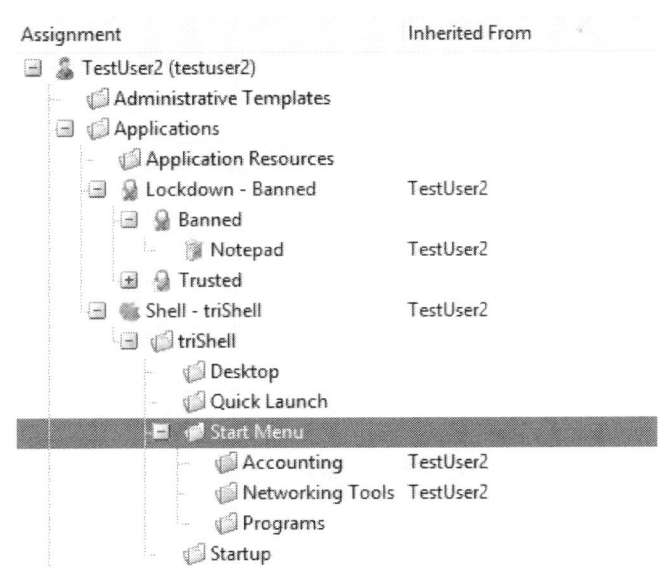

Assignment	Inherited From
TestUser2 (testuser2)	
Administrative Templates	
Applications	
Application Resources	
Lockdown - Banned	TestUser2
Banned	
Notepad	TestUser2
Trusted	
Shell - triShell	TestUser2
triShell	
Desktop	
Quick Launch	
Start Menu	
Accounting	TestUser2
Networking Tools	TestUser2
Programs	
Startup	

9. Now from the right pane, 'Objects', drag-and-drop the applications you just created to the folders under 'Start Menu' in the middle pane, for these users. The end result should be similar to this:

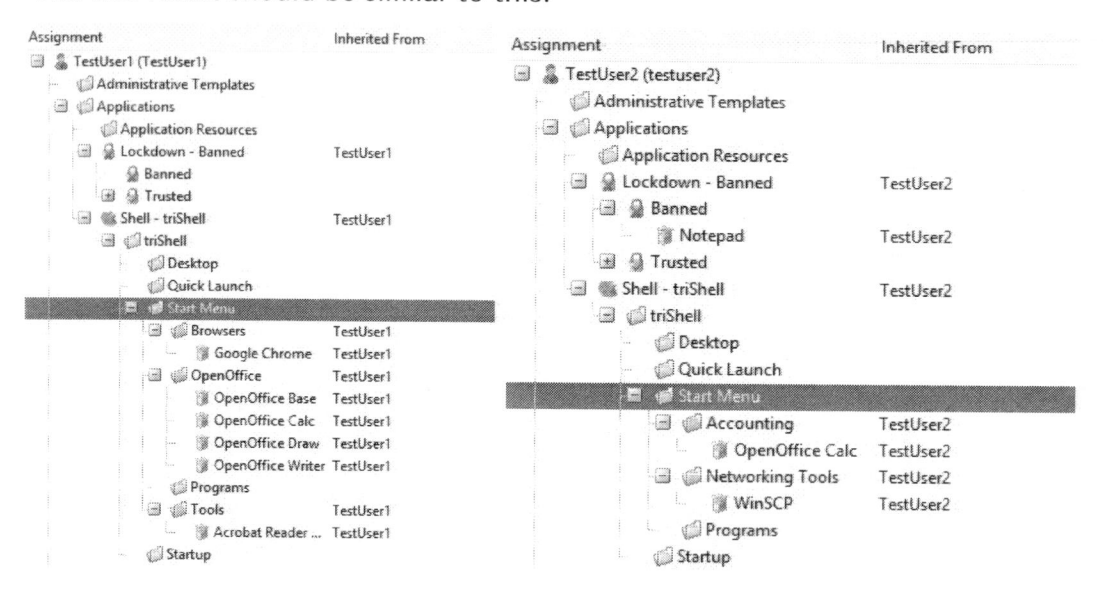

10. It is that simple. Now, just a matter of testing. Login to the RDWA portal and launch a full desktop. The 'Start Menu' will be exactly as we defined for these users.

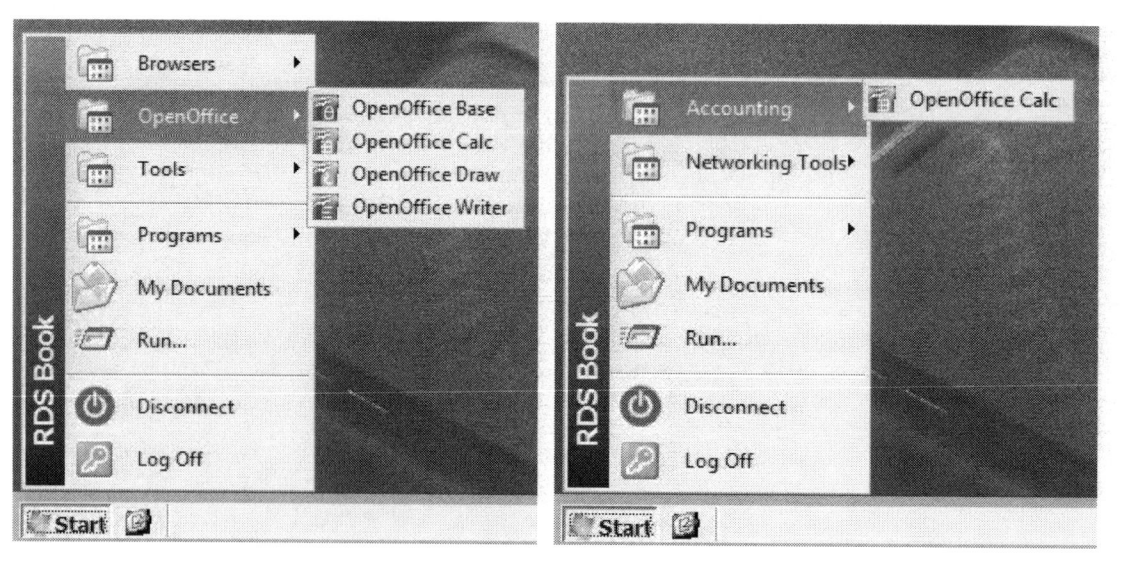

11. To finish this customization, let's drag-and-drop some applications to the 'Desktop', still under the 'triShell' section in the middle pane for these two users. In this example, we will add 'Google Chrome' and 'Acrobat Reader DC' to their desktops. The difference now is we will assign these at a higher level, in this case the OU where such users reside under AD. This assignment will look like this:

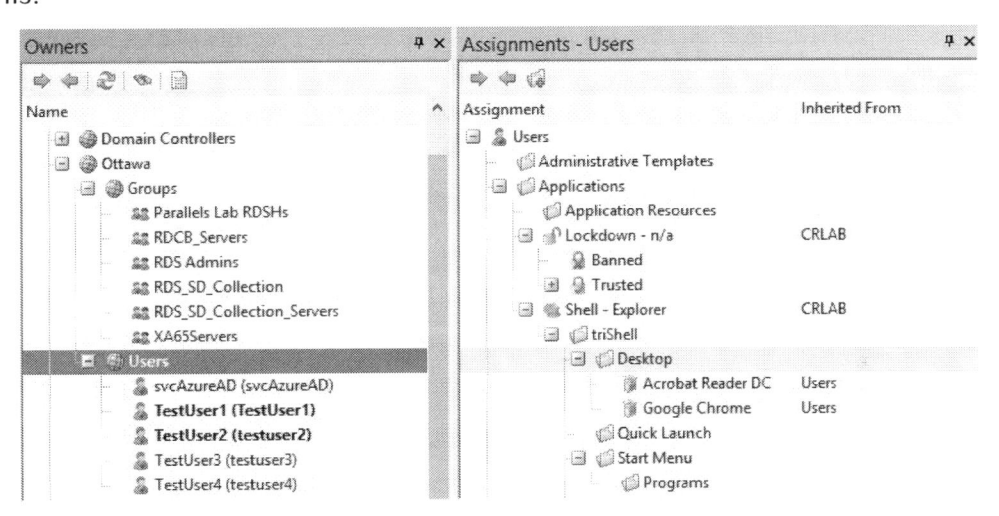

12. As you noticed, for the OU 'Users', we did not set the shell to triShell as you can see in the middle pane. But if you logon as any of these users, you will indeed get the two applications on the desktop. How is that possible? Well, simple. As the shell for these users is indeed triShell, it will inherit any triShell customizations from the OU and therefore the users will get the proper icons on their desktops as seen below:

We could keep going with these customizations, considering how easy it is when done with the 'Simplify Suite'. But we still have other things we want to enforce and set for our users, so let's keep moving.

Blocking access to applications

The next step in our lockdown/customization efforts is to define a couple applications the users cannot run. For this example, let's define 'Notepad' and 'WordPad' as evil apps and block these from running (I know you feel bad about 'Notepad', especially now that it has tabs on Windows Server 2019!). Let's do it.

1. The process is quite similar as before. First of all, we will create the two applications in the 'Objects' pane. The only thing we are doing differently now is in the 'Signatures' tab for each application we will select 'Use Name' and 'Only Name.Extension' as shown below.

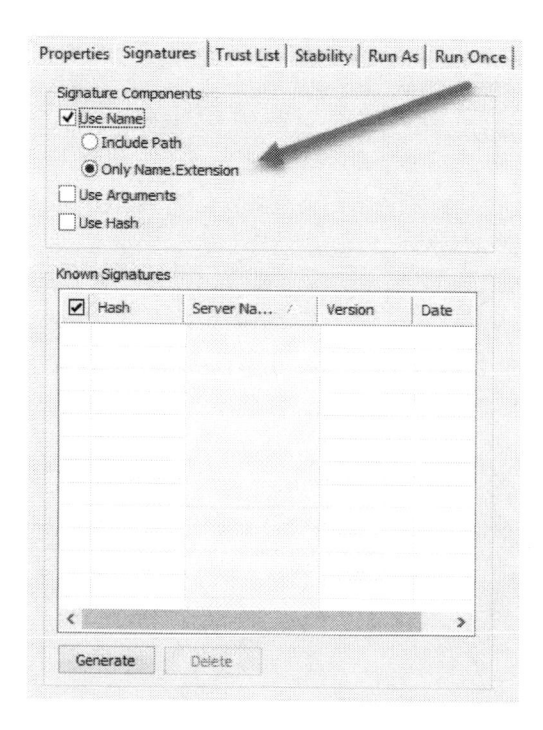

2. Now that we have the two applications created, let's define for the OU where these two users reside that such applications are not allowed. On the left pane select the OU (in our case 'Users') and in the middle pane, 'Assignments', right-click 'Lockdown – n/a' and select 'Use Banned List'.

Page 306 | RDS - The Complete Guide

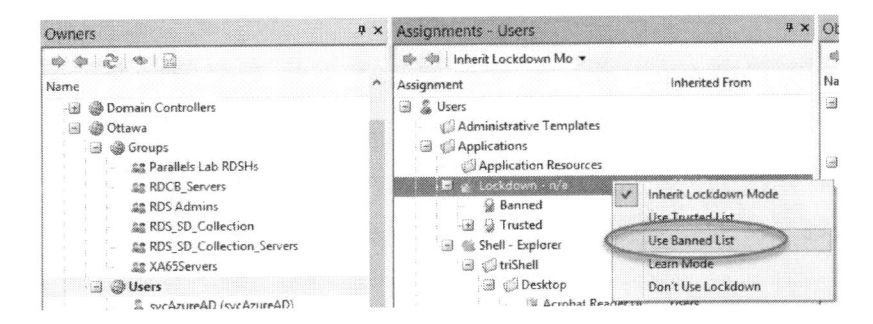

3. Right below it, you will see the icon saying 'Banned'. Simply drag-and-drop the two applications we will block from the right pane, 'Objects' to it. You should have something similar to this:

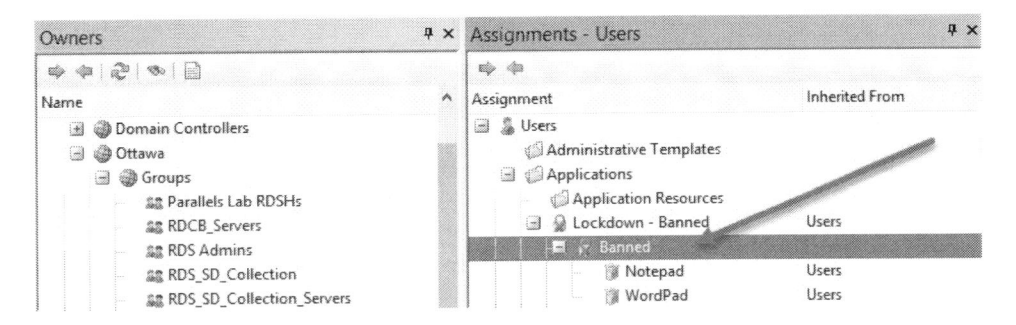

4. As the two users in question have the 'Banned' settings set to inherit, they will be blocked if trying to run these applications. Time to test it! Logon as any of these users and in the 'Start' menu, click on 'Run' and simply type 'notepad' or 'wordpad'. 'Simplify Suite' will kick in and you will get a message similar to this one:

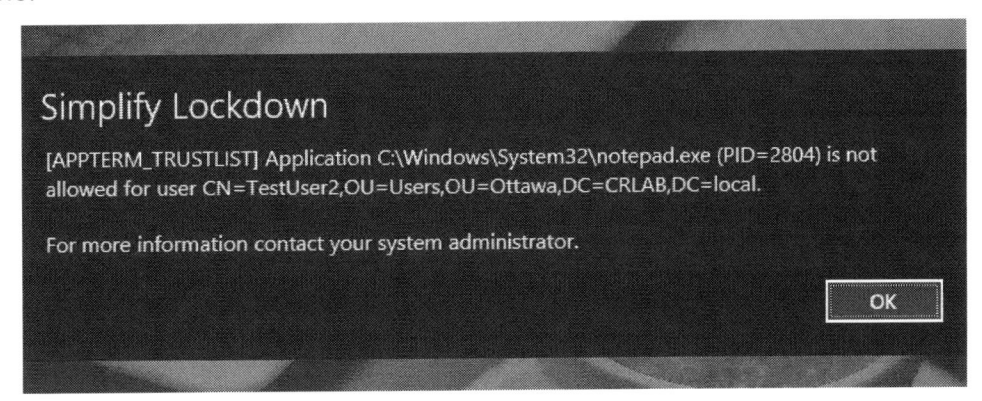

5. As we select 'Only Name.Extension' in the 'Signatures' tab for the application, no matter which 'notepad.exe' the user attempts to run, it will always be blocked. You may say, 'Ok, but what if I rename notepad.exe to myapp.exe? Will it run?'. Yes and no. ☺ It depends if you select 'Use Hash' under the exact same tab. If it is selected, even if the user manages to rename the file, the hash will be the same and execution will be blocked. In this case you must click the 'Generate' button and be pointing to the executable that is stored on the RDSHs of course. Pretty neat, eh?

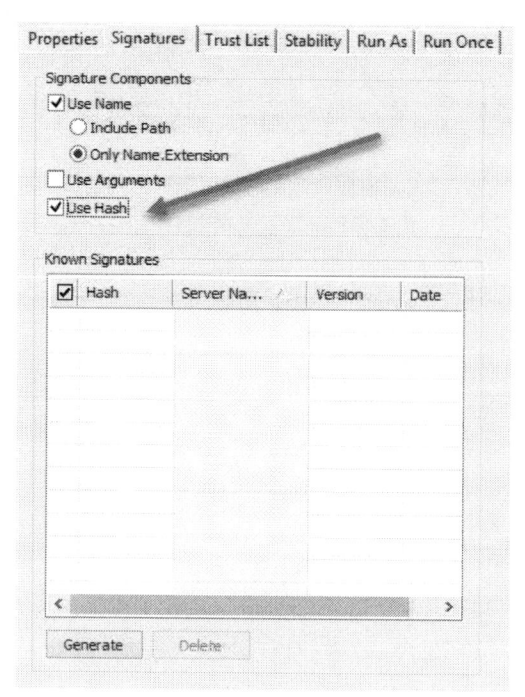

Dealing with the registry

The final step in our lockdown/customization efforts is to define a couple registry settings that we would like to enforce on our users. These may include little things like disabling first-time prompts (i.e. 'This application is not your default whatever, do you want to change it?' or the user having to accept an EULA) or even performance/stability settings for an application (you probably know about the 'bProtectedMode' for 'Acrobat Reader', don't you?). So, let's pick a couple ones we want to enforce and show how it is done.

1. The settings we want to enforce will disable the 'protected mode' for 'Acrobat Reader DC' and will prevent 'Google Chrome' from asking if it should be set as the default browser. The registry keys in question are:
   a. Adobe: [HKEY_LOCAL_MACHINE\SOFTWARE\Wow6432Node\Policies\Adobe\Acrobat Reader\DC\FeatureLockDown] "bProtectedMode"=dword:00000000
   b. Chrome: [HKEY_LOCAL_MACHINE\Software\Policies\Google\Chrome] "DefaultBrowserSettingEnabled"=dword:00000000
2. As these are machine settings (the hive is HKLM) we need to use a 'Registry – HKEY_LOCAL_MACHINE' object. Note these only apply at startup so once we create and assign it, the servers will need to be rebooted. We will create as a single item, named 'Optimizations'. So, in the right panel, right-click 'Registry – HKEY_LOCAL_MACHINE' and select 'New Object'.

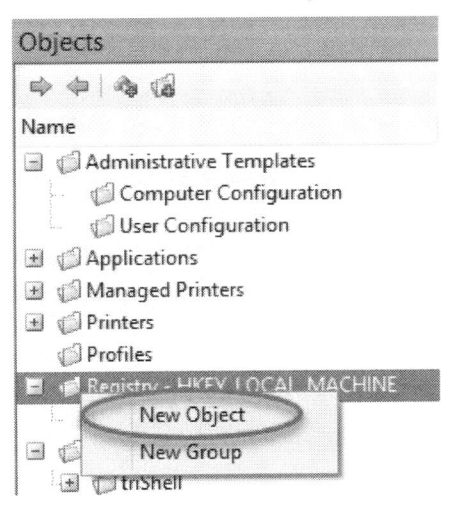

3. Name it 'Optimizations'.

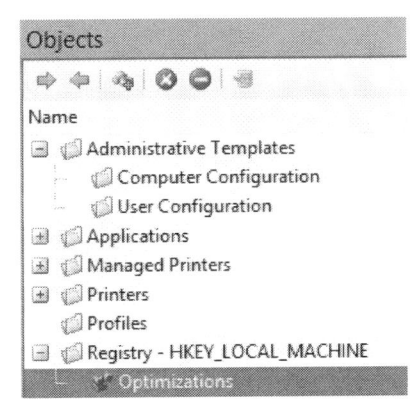

4. On the right side, browse to the hives where we need to create these keys. Depending where the console is running, these keys may not exist. Simply right-click a particular hive and select 'Create New Key'.

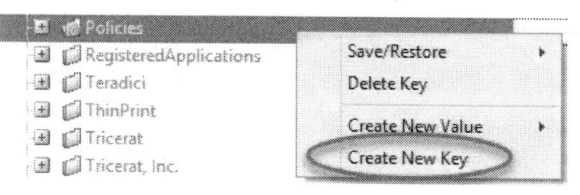

5. Once you have all the keys in place, right-click the one where the value must exist and select 'Create New Value' and choose the appropriate type required for it.

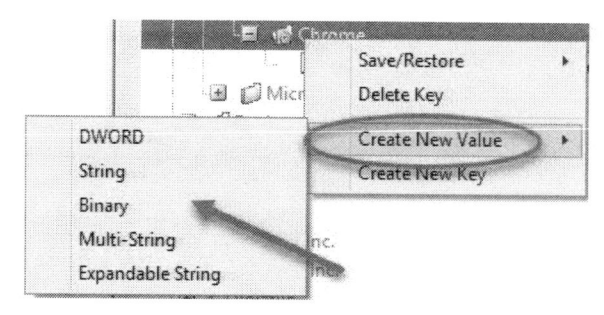

6. For the two keys we are setting in this example, your end result should look like this:

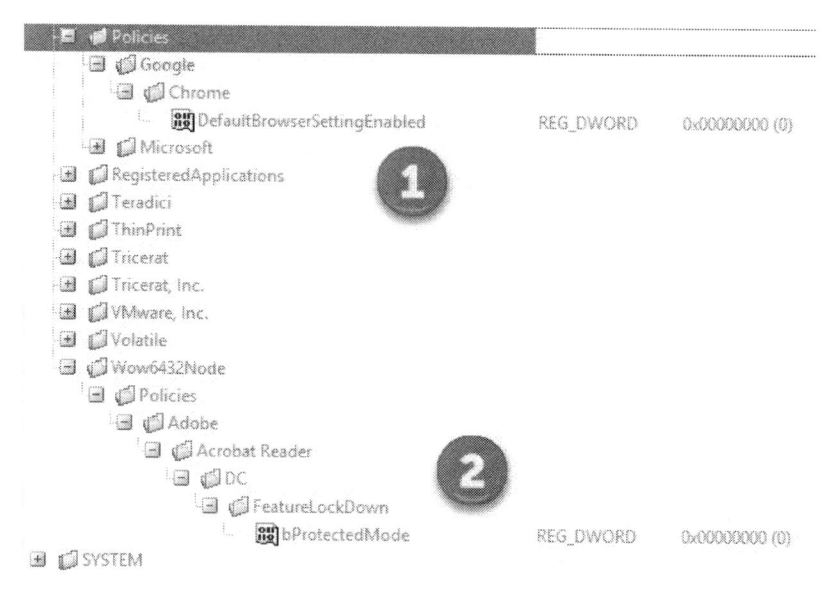

7. The next step is to enable which action we want for these keys. Simply right-click each of them and select 'Set This Value'. This will make sure the key is enforced every time the RDSHs reboot.

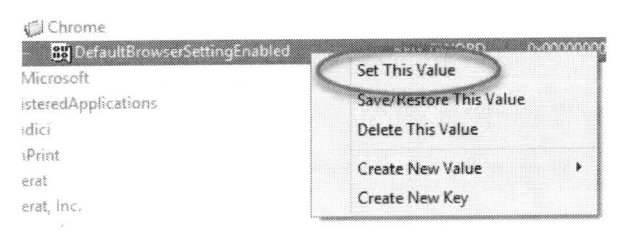

8. Once these are both set you should have something like this (make sure you click the 'Apply Changes' object at the top right corner):

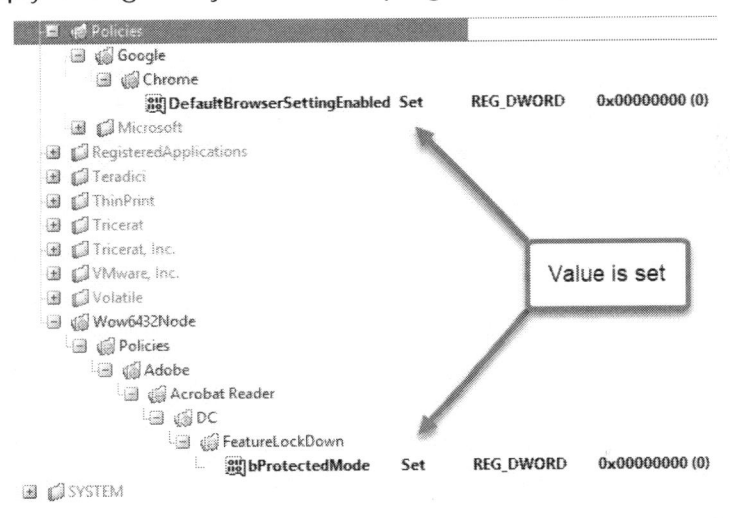

9. Now all we need is to drag-and-drop the newly created object, 'Optimizations' to the OU where our RDSHs reside on the 'Owners' panel, as seen below:

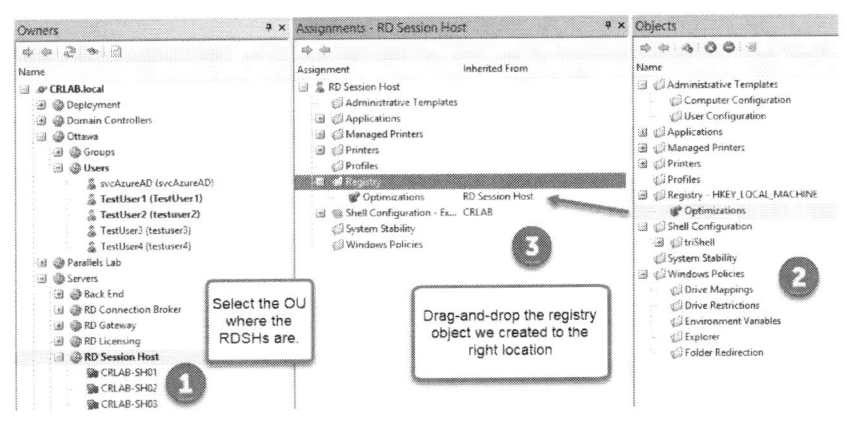

RDS - The Complete Guide | Page 311

10. That is all. If you now reboot the RDSHs, you will notice these keys are now in place, setting what we need for 'Adobe Reader' and 'Google Chrome'.

11. If you now try to logon as a regular user to the RDSHs, you will notice that 'Google Chrome' no longer bothers you about which browser is the default and that 'Acrobat Reader' is now set to work properly under RDSH. Neat, eh?

The main question you are probably asking at this stage we would bet, is relatively simple: "Can't I use a GPP to do this?". The answer is, "Yes". But that said, there are major differences with both approaches.

First of all, anything GPO or GPP related, requires you creating and maintaining GPO objects. In many cases, the RDS administrators do not have the required access to AD and may need to request that to a different department (many companies have people that deal with AD only). The 'Simplify Suite' covers it all. As seen below, you have everything in one place.

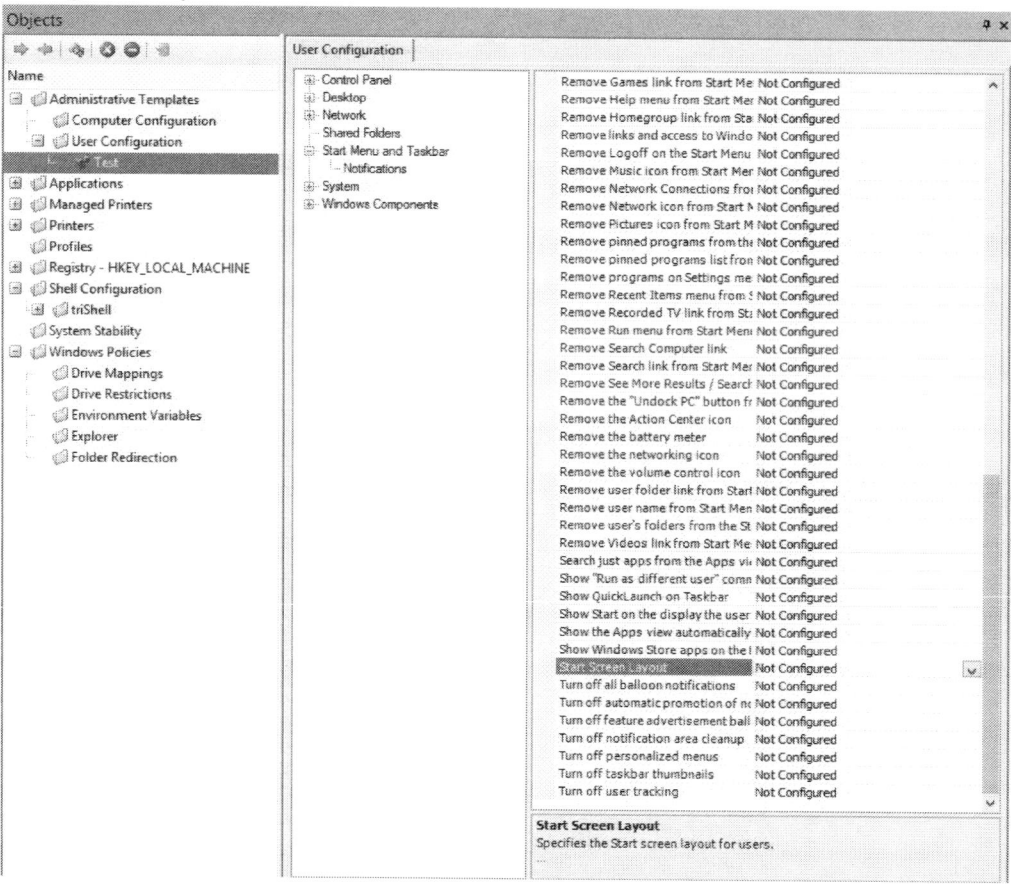

Your typical policies available from the administrative templates (see, we highlighted the one we used to create that customized 'Start' screen layout using a GPP) all the way to 'Drive Mappings' and 'Folder Redirection'.

Secondly, as you probably noticed, 'Simplify Profiles' is cross-platform. What does that mean specifically for RDS? Simple. It allows you to roam whatever settings on a per-application basis (if required) to any Windows platform. Users accessing a Windows 7 VDI environment may get the exact settings for a particular application if it is used as well on Windows 10 VDI or even on 2012 R2 and 2016 RDSHs. This is something that Windows itself cannot do it at all.

The beauty here is, you do not have to reconfigure a particular environment to handle the same application. It is just a matter of making sure all the endpoints in question do have the required 'Simplify Profiles' agent installed and all pointing to the same database.

That is the end of this chapter. We truly believe by now you clearly understand how to deal with the user environment and its applications; more than that, you know where the built-in solutions come short and how to go beyond that, using what we do consider to be the best product out there for the money: the 'Simplify Suite'.

Printing

Many of you guys (and girls I hope) reading this book probably have been using Citrix or even RDS, for years now. Printing has to be one of the topics, right there with profiles, that creates the most support calls and issues in any environment, and I am certain you would agree.

So, let me give you the good and bad news. As I am not a very optimistic person, let me start with the good news. Printing has certainly improved quite a lot since the early Windows NT 4.0 TSE product. I mean quite a lot. Even compared to printing in the RDS 2008 days. Much better now.

The bad news unfortunately, is the fact printing is still far from perfect and yes, still does not work as expected in many cases, especially when dealing with non-Windows endpoints, multi-functional printers (the ones that do everything, from printing to scanning and faxing. Some even heat up pizza) and network printers.

However, before we go ahead and dig into printing, we must understand how this mythical creature exists and behaves in an RDS deployment. For this to happen we need to take a look what goes under the hood when connecting to an RDS 2012 R2, from a printing standpoint, so you have a better understanding of the whole process. This will make you understand all its shortcomings and when looking for a way to solve a particular problem, it will help you deciding the best way to fix it.

Printer Types

There are only two printer types inside an RDS session (others may disagree but hey, it is our book, not theirs):

- **Local printer:** when the device is 'installed' on the RDSH and when you print something, the RDSH sends the job directly to the printer. As you can see there is really no distinction here if the printer is actually connected to the RDSH (i.e. a physical connection to a physical RDSH) or if it is a network printer (i.e. the RDSH has a TCP/IP port for RAW/LPD printing). The bottom line and important lesson here is the RDSH sends the job directly to the printer.

- **Redirected printer:** this is a special printer, created by the RDSH, once a user connects to it. A single user may have multiple redirected printers (one for each local printer he has on his local device, the endpoint connecting to the RDSH).

Drivers

This is a very important topic and if you understand it, you will probably save your hair and resolve at least half of all your printing problems. Seriously. Many still do not understand this.

When you connect to the RDSH server, what happens from a printing standpoint is quite simple:

1. If the Remote Desktop Client is configured to allow printing redirection (and if the gateway, policies, etc do NOT disable the redirection), the information about your local printers is passed to the RDSH. That means all your local printers and the drivers in use locally (depending on settings and policies, this can be changed so only the default printer is redirected).

2. The RDSH tries to find a suitable native driver. This means it will try to use a locally installed driver on the actual RDSH server. If the printer is supported out-of-the-box, meaning you did not have to download and install any driver on the RDSH, the server will create a local printer within your session, mapped back to your real printer, locally available on your endpoint. This printer will use the native, Windows driver.

3. If a driver is not found, a couple things may happen, depending on how everything is configured or locked down:
    a. The server will create the printer but using the Remote Desktop Easy Print driver. This is a universal driver, based on the XML Paper Specification (XPS for short). It works for most printers but it is Windows only. That means Macs or any other platform will not be able to print using Easy Print.
    b. The driver you have on the local endpoint may end up being copied to the server, and the printer will be mapped using this driver (native). This may happen if the user connecting has administrative rights (i.e. he is a local administrator on the server).

c. The first two scenarios listed failed (i.e. Easy Print is not allowed and copying drivers is not allowed) and the printer is not created. This will raise an event in the 'Event Log' under Microsoft | Windows | TerminalServices-Printers, Event ID 1111. It will say something like this: "Driver EPSON Artisan 730 Series required for printer IQB-EPSON1 (Artisan 730) is unknown. Contact the administrator to install the driver before you log in again."

Based on what we just explained, you may think the solution is quite simple: simply determine which printers you do not have the drivers for and install them on all your RDSHs. That is exactly what most people do.

Certainly, the number one reason why they have issues with printing on RDS. ☺

The issue is, the fact a certain printer driver is available for Windows Server 2012 R2 does not guarantee it is stable when used under Remote Desktop Services. Unfortunately, when such drivers are developed, very few vendors take the time to test them in a fully loaded RDSH, with several sessions printing at the same time. You will find the hard way that some drivers simply crash under load (but do work fine in a single user PC for example) and the first symptom reported by users is that all printers 'disappeared' from their sessions.

The only drivers known to work properly under RDS are the ones that came out-of-the-box with Windows Server 2012 R2. Resuming, anything that is there once you finished installing and updating the server. There are no guarantees that anything else you install will work properly.

That is why you should avoid as much as possible installing any printer drivers on an RDSH. Also, keep in mind there is no such thing as 'RDS certified' or 'TS certified' drivers. If it is not on the default server installation, you are on your own.

Flow

Before we dig into getting printing going the safest and most reliable way possible, using what is there out-of-the-box, it is quite important to understand how the print job travels when the user clicks 'Print' anywhere within his session.

There are two possibilities here:

1. **Redirected Printer.** In this case, the user has a printer defined on the endpoint he is using to connect to the RDS deployment (could be a physically attached printer – USB for example or a network printer – printing to a TCP/IP port, Windows print queue, etc). Once he connects, that printer is mapped within his session, using the Easy Printer or a native driver (Windows endpoint – non-windows, we will touch base on that later). Once he prints, the print job is sent over the RDP connection (using a virtual channel) back to his machine and from there the job is spooled.
2. **RDS local printer.** The printer in this case is defined at the RDSH level, as a network printer for example. The RDS prints directly to the printer, through a TCP/IP port or a Windows print queue for example. What the user has on his end is irrelevant and no printing traffic whatsoever is seen over the RDP connection.

The main difference here is simple: in the first case, the print job has to make its way back to the client and depending on the network conditions (bandwidth, latency, etc) the job may take quite a while and more than that, the bandwidth required may actually interfere with other things RDP uses within the session. However, more than that, it may actually affect other users within the same link.

Imagine a scenario where a couple users are working out of a remote, small branch office. All of them connected to the RDS deployment at HQ. The network link from the branch office to HQ is relatively small (i.e. a 10Mbit pipe used by ten users at the branch office).

When one user prints a large document, this has to travel all the way back to his local PC, over the RDP channel. Even though RDP does have a built-in mechanism to minimize performance degradation on his own session, the fact he may use a lot of bandwidth due to printing, may indeed affect all the other RDP sessions going through the same link.

Note: these two registry values control the bandwidth distribution between display and virtual channels:

HKLM\ SYSTEM\CurrentControlSet\Services\TermDD
- FlowControlDisplayBandwidth
- FlowControlChannelBandwidth

By default these are set at 70/30, what means 70% is reserved for display traffic (so his session does not 'lag') and 30% goes to the virtual channels (i.e. printing, file transfers, etc).

On the second case, the printing job never goes through the RDP channel. As the RDSH has the printers defined locally, it can print directly to them. Clearly the better alternative. The main issue is, not in all cases the RDSHs will have a direct connection to the printers (like in the branch office scenario illustrated above). However, if a direct connection is indeed possible, this should always be the way to go. Keep that in mind.

The only drawback with that approach is the fact (I can bet you guessed it already) you will always need the drivers for these 'direct' printers on the RDSHs. No Easy Print is available in that case. And if you do need drivers, that means all the potential issues with printer drivers and RDSH will be there, just waiting for you.

Resuming:

- **'Easy Print' Redirected Printers**
    - PROs
        - No need for drivers on the RDSHs.
        - No need to install and manage printers on the RDSH.
        - Works reasonably with many printers.
        - Bandwidth can be tweaked (see registry keys above).
        - Users can print anywhere, anytime.

    - CONs
        - Does not work with non-Windows clients
        - Job is always sent back to the client endpoint what could affect performance due to link saturation.
        - Even though this is a 'universal' printing solution, do not expect all printers in the universe will work with it. ☺
        - The same issue applies for the printer features. Some may not work.

- **'Native Driver' Redirected Printers**
    - PROs
        - Assuming the driver is stable (usually the case with the out-of-the-box ones), will give you almost all (if not all) features on a particular printer.
        - Bandwidth can be tweaked (see registry keys above).
        - Users can print anywhere, anytime.

    - CONs
        - You may need to use manufacturer drivers in case the out-of-the-box ones do not work. ☺
        - Job is always sent back to the client endpoint what could affect performance due to link saturation.
        - Could create a huge hassle depending on the manufacturer, as some drivers are indeed garbage.
        - As users change or upgrade their printers, getting the right driver and testing it, could potentially become a huge task.

- **Local RDSH Printers**
    - PROs
        - Printing job will never affect the actual RDP connections over a certain link as the job travels from the RDSHs to the printer or print server.
        - As it uses the native manufacturer driver, all printer features should work.
        - You have total control of the printing environment (permissions, drivers, etc).

    - CONs
        - You need to use native drivers. ☺
        - Could create a huge hassle depending on the manufacturer, as some drivers are indeed garbage.
        - Printing is limited to the location where the RDSH and the printers are (users will not be able to print at home if not using redirected printers for example).

Before you ask, and knowing you are probably wondering, what about non-Windows clients? The answer here is a bit more complicated as 'non-Windows' could mean a lot of extremely different things.

If you are thinking about anything mobile, the answer is simple. You cannot print. At all. Yes, no printing from iOS, Android and even Windows Phone. So that shiny tablet that you thought would make a great thin client, if you need to print from it, only workaround is print to PDF and then make that file somehow end up on the device so you can print it from there. Of course, you can print if the RDSH you are connected to has printers defined within your session. However, you cannot do fancy stuff like printing to 'Air Printers' or whatever Apple calls their stuff.

Linux and OSX are in better shape in that respect but still far from great. Linux, as there is no official Microsoft client for it, can be tweaked (I mean the third-party RDP clients, not the OS itself) so printing works and the RDSHs use the native driver for the redirected printers (assuming you have such drivers on the servers).

OSX on the other hand, will use the 'Microsoft Publisher Imagesetter' driver for the redirected printer. It is a PostScript based driver and seems to work fine. The main issue is it does lack things like compression so certain jobs simply grow huge when sent to the client, meaning they will use a lot of bandwidth and take time to print. Not ideal.

As a final note, if you want to minimize the hassle when deciding which printers to buy for an RDS deployment, simply do a quick search on google for 'HP printers + citrix' and look for the results that show a PDF from HP discussing all their printers within a Citrix environment. Pretty much everything listed there will apply to RDS. That said, yes, HP seems to be the most stable under RDS but other vendors have done a good job over the years on trying to make their solutions better (i.e. Canon, Xerox, etc).

Trying to fix the mess

Yes, you can see RDS printing is a mess and a big sore point on any RDS deployment. The good news is there are some ways, using out-of-the-box tricks, to minimize the problem. Keep in mind the word 'minimize'. It does not mean 'eliminating'.

Based on all you read so far about printing, it is really all about drivers. What to do and use when dealing with native drivers. The reason for that is simple: if you are not using native drivers, it means 'Easy Print' is in use and if it is working 100% for you, great. You are a very lucky IT person. The reality is most customers will have to deal with non-Windows clients, network printers, will need native driver features and so on and in that case, 'Easy Print' is not there.

With all this information in mind, the ideal workflow, in an attempt to minimize your printing issues, goes like this:

1. If the client supports 'Easy Print', try it. As mentioned, the RDSHs will create the printer using the 'Easy Print' driver. If that works as expected for you, you are all set.
2. Ok 'Easy Print' did not work as expected for you. The first thing you should try is to check if the printer you have works with an out-of-the-box driver. What I mean is simple. Many printer drivers ship with the OS. Simply add the printer to a VM for example and when prompted for the driver, pick one from the list you see. For example, if you have a new HP Color LaserJet something, try to print using a LaserJet 2600n driver. The idea is to pick the closest built-in driver that still works with your printer.

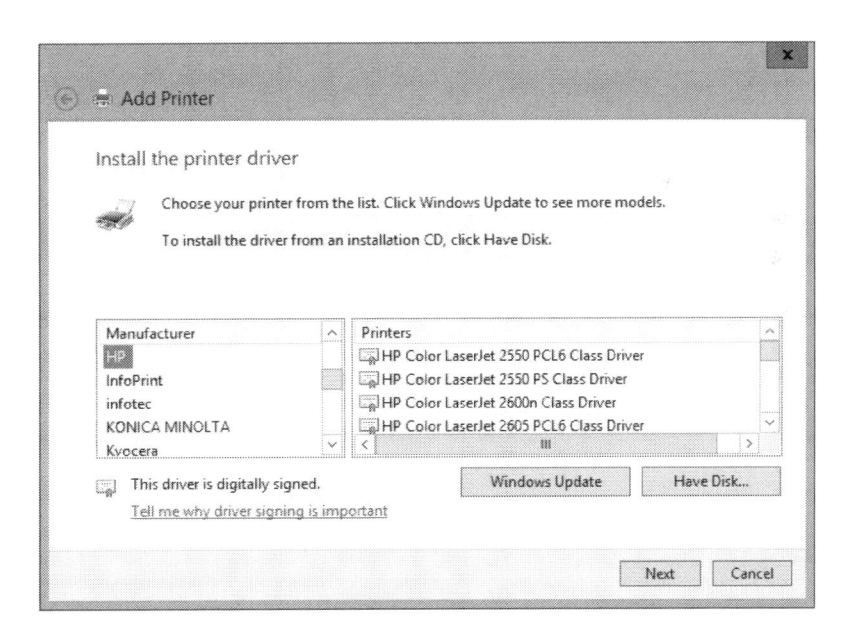

3. If that works, it is now a matter of telling the RDSHs if someone connects using printer 'X', the server should use driver 'Y'. This is done by creating what we call a mapping file (.INF) and setting a registry key pointing to it.
   a. Create a simple text file using notepad and paste this into it:
   ;PrintMapping.INF
   ;Printer mapping file for client-side to server-side drivers
   [Printers]
   "OEM Printer Driver Name" = "Windows Server 2012 R2 Driver Name"

   b. Replace 'OEM Printer Driver Name' with the exact driver name as seen on the client. Keep in mind this is case sensitive so you must type it EXACTLY as seen.
   c. Replace 'Windows Server 2012 R2 Driver Name' with the EXACT name seen on 2012 R2.
   d. For example, that line would look like this (in this example I took the driver name as shown on my Windows 10 PC and the one shown on the 2012 R2 print server I have, for the Epson Artisan 730):
   "EPSON Artisan 730 Series" = "Epson ESC/P-R V4 Class Driver"

   e. Save the file to a folder like C:\Windows\Inf on your RDSH, naming it "PrintMapping.inf". This has to be done to ALL RDSHs. Great, eh? You can make this simpler if you save the file to a share and use a startup script or Group Policy Preference (GPP) to copy it to all RDSHs.
   f. Change the registry key below on all RDSHs (again, another good candidate for a GPP so you do not have to touch the RDSHs directly):

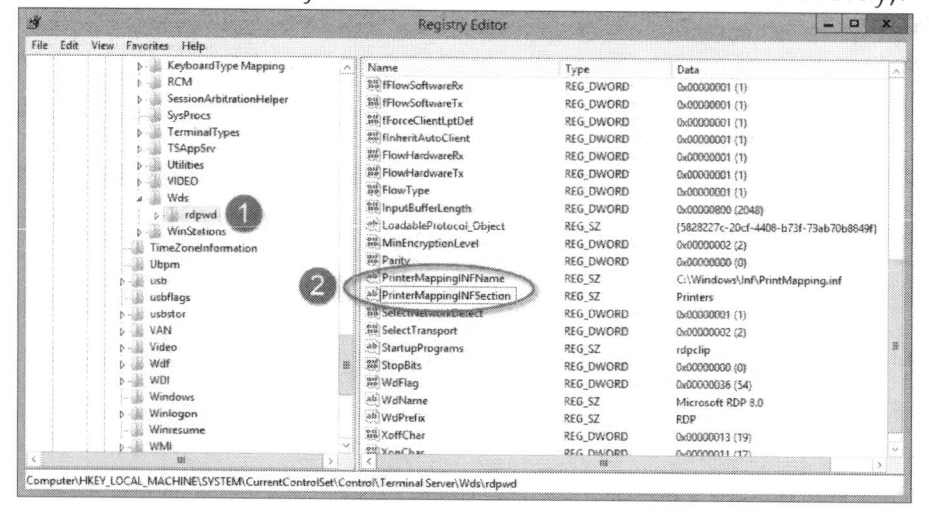

g. Done. Anyone connecting with that particular driver on the client, will get a printer auto created using the native 2012 R2 driver.

Note: in this case, you will also need to create a policy that will force the RDSHs to use the native driver first (if available) and then go for the 'Easy Print' one if a match is not found. This policy is located under Computer Configuration| Policies | Administrative Templates | Windows Components | Remote Desktop Services | Remote Desktop Session Host | Printer Redirection | 'Use Remote Desktop Easy Print printer driver first'. You must DISABLE it. This way the RDSHs will try to map the printer using the native drivers (or as specified on the INF file we just created) and if it does not find anything suitable, it will then use the 'Easy Print' driver.

4. If the mapping trick does not work, you can then try a native driver. Again, try it on a test server first and load it with users (not only a user or two – get real load on the test box). If everything works as expected you can then go ahead and deploy the driver in production, on all your RDSHs.

It is worth mentioning that some non-Windows clients will allow you to pass the driver name you are using on the client (i.e. certain Linux clients) and in this case the mapping idea still applies (so you can force a certain client printer on Linux to be redirected using a particular Windows Server 2012 R2 driver).

Tricerat's Simplify Printing - Fixing it for good

So far, you learned about printing and RDS. You probably realized it is a complicated matter due to poor drivers, ever changing client printers, mobile clients, road warriors and so on. In addition, to top it off, if you are dealing with a massive network-printing environment, with several network printers and print servers, you are in for a treat. By that, I mean you will lose all your hair and printing will still not work that great. If losing hair is your goal, you can just skip this whole section of this amazing, wonderful book (just reading your thoughts, our apologies).

The reality is, printing is indeed a very complex subject and for that reason, several companies started developing products to address that one single issue since RDS (or TS) was announced, back in 1998. These companies focus on printing and nothing else. If it were that simple, Microsoft would have fixed this for good a very long time ago.

Over the years, I had the chance to work with several of these products, in real production environments. From doing research and getting pricing on them, to deploying the whole thing for hundreds of customers. The bottom line for me, after using all of these products, is simple: 'Simplify Printing' scores high on all fronts. It is affordable, easy to deploy and manage and it does work. Again, we tested almost every single known printing solution for Citrix and RDS. You name it, we tested it.

So, let's take a quick look on how 'Simplify Printing' works and how to get it up and running, from start to end.

Setting up 'Simplify Printing'

Before going ahead and setting up 'Simplify Printing' we must explain a couple differences between the available editions, so you can decide which one you need it.

This simple table summarizes it, but a full detailed comparison is available here: http://www.tricerat.com/products/printing-solutions

Feature	ScrewDrivers® Universal Print Management Solution	Simplify Printing® Enterprise-Ready Solution	Simplify Printing TX® Mobile Printing Business Solution
Single driver for redirected printers	X	X	X
Single driver for networked printers (off print servers)	-	X	X
Printing from mobile devices (iOS, Android, etc)	-	-	X

As I mentioned, there is way more on each edition than what is stated above (hint: click on the link provided!) but the bottom line is this: if all you need is to deal with redirected printers and you do not want to deal with printer drivers ever again, all you need is the 'ScrewDrivers' product. If you need to handle network printers as well and want to take the same single driver approach, 'Simplify Printing' is the way to go. Finally, if you want to throw mobile devices to the mix and much more, go for 'Simplify Printing TX' (we will cover it – stay tuned).

Time to do it. For this first run, we will be setting up 'Simplify Printing' as the goal here is to have a driverless solution that can also handle network printers. To get to that point, we will perform the following:

1. Make sure we have a print server ready and with a network printer created on it (in our case we simply created a new VM, 'CRLAB-PS01' and installed an Epson Artisan 730 and an HP Color LaserJet 2600 on it - network connections to the actual printers) and tested them just to make sure we could print properly.

2. Install 'Simplify Printing' on a management computer (in our case, the Windows 8.X VM 'CRLAB-CL01'). This will install their management console and establish the connection to the SQL database (we are using the same SQL server used for the RDCB HA – make sure you use credentials that have the proper rights on the SQL Server then).

3. Install the 'Simplify Printing Print Server' on the print server 'CRLAB-PS01' and import the print server into the 'Simplify Printing' console.

4. Install the 'Simplify Printing' on the RDSHs.

5. Install the required client on the endpoints (required if printing to printers that are local to the endpoint, so you can have any sort of printer working).

6. Test it!

Installing the 'Simplify Printing' console

This is the first step required as it will not only give us a console to manage the whole solution but also create the required database. If you already installed the console in the previous chapter, you can skip directly to 'Installing the Simplify Printing server' section.

1. If you have not done this yet, logon to the machine where you want the console installed (in our case, 'CRLAB-CL01') and launch the installer. Select the desired language and click 'Next'.

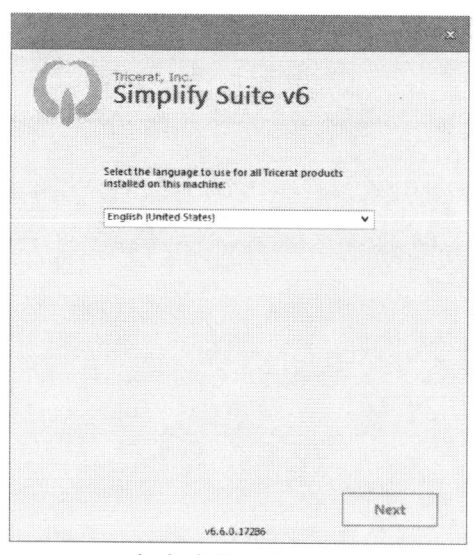

2. Agree to the licensing terms and click 'Next'.

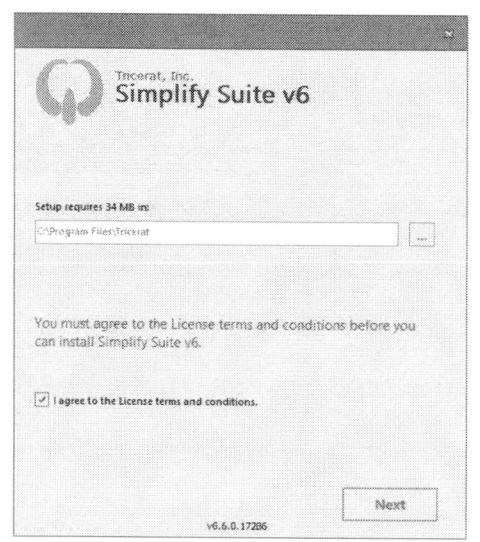

3. Select 'Simplify Console' only. Click 'Next'.

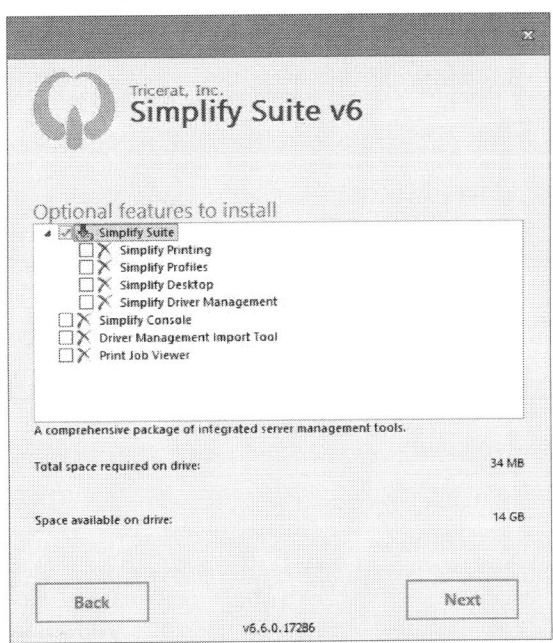

4. Enter the trial license you got from Tricerat (sent to the email you used to download the product) and click 'Next'.

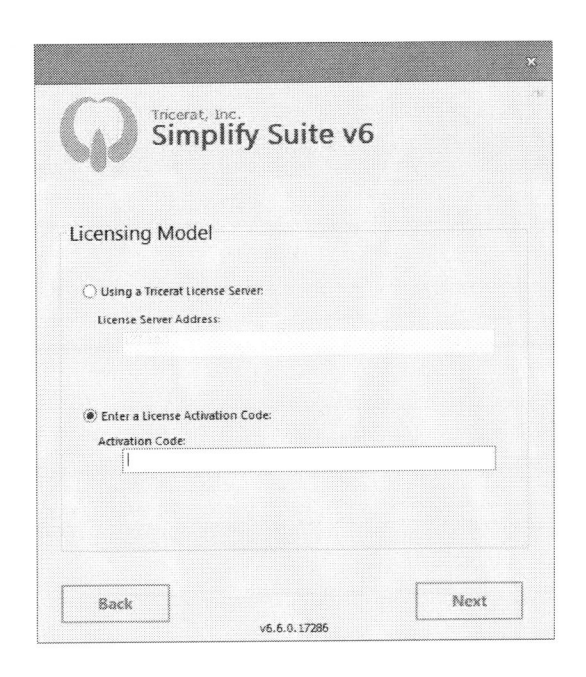

5. The installer will display some information about the SQL server setup procedure. Click 'Next'.

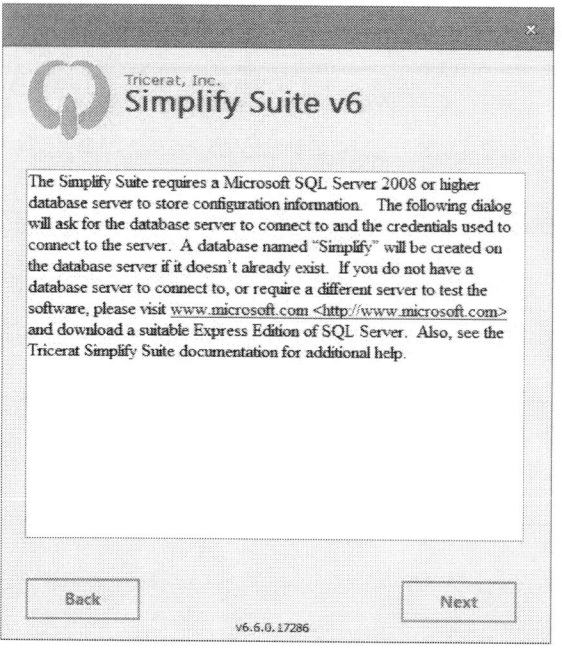

6. Select the SQL Server you will use (in our case, the same one we used for the RDCB HA, 'CRLAB-SQ01') and select the authentication method you want to use. The installer will show you the database name that will be created. Click 'Next'.

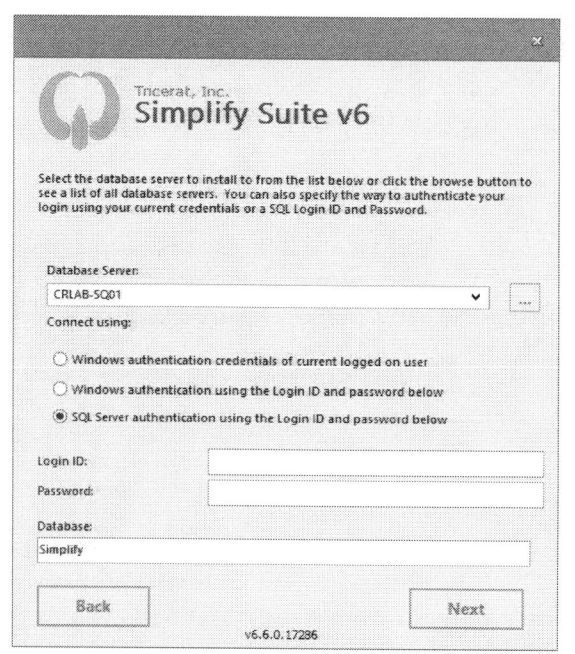

7. Click 'Install' to perform the installation.

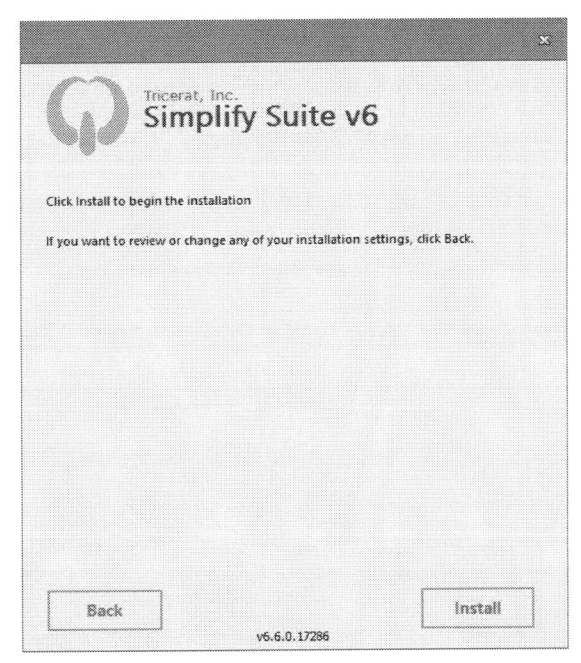

8. The setup procedure will start, showing you what is happening under the hood. Just wait...

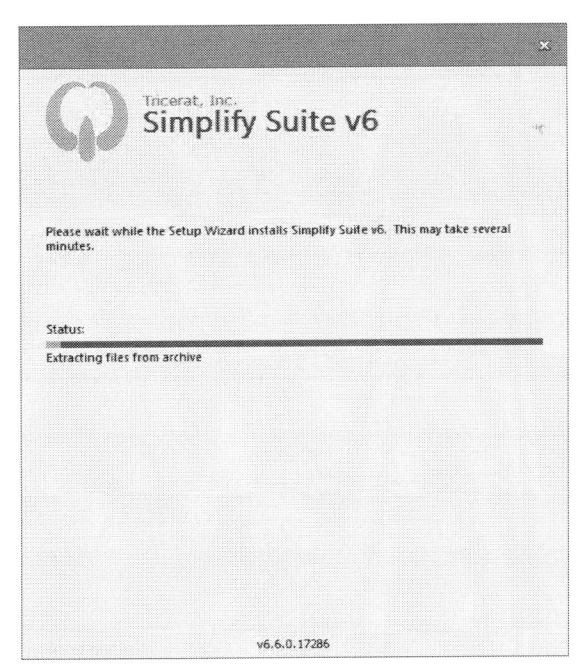

9. You are done. Click 'Finish'.

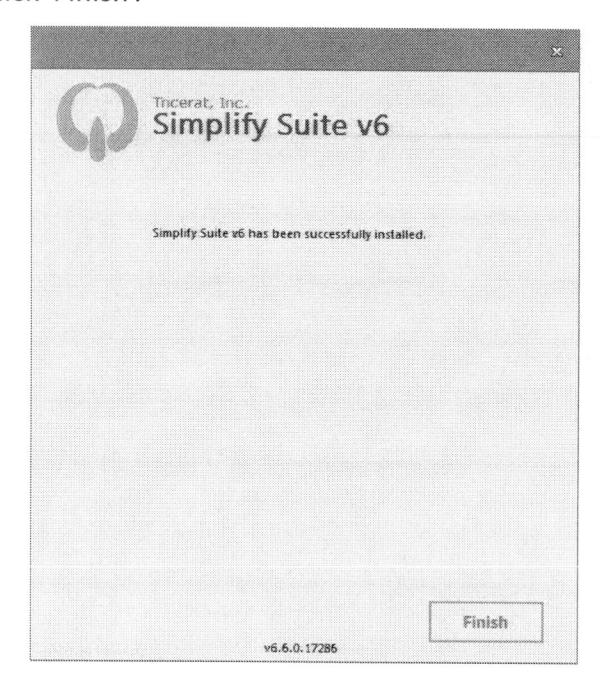

Installing the 'Simplify Printing' Server

Now that we have the console up and running, we need to install the required software on all our print servers. Again, we are going for the full-blown solution, the one that allows you to have seamless printing not only from redirected printers but also from network printers.

1. Logon to your print server (this has to be done on all print servers you may have) and launch the specific installer for print servers (named something like 'ScrewDriversPrintServer_Version' – make sure you run the proper one for the platform you are using – x86 or x64). Select the language you want to use and click 'Next'.

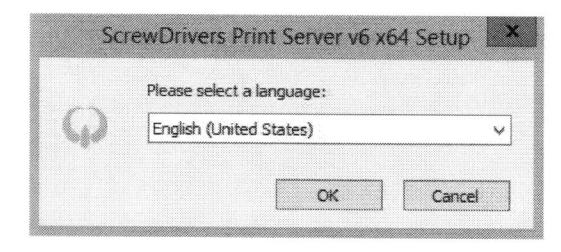

2. Agree to the licensing terms and click 'Install'.

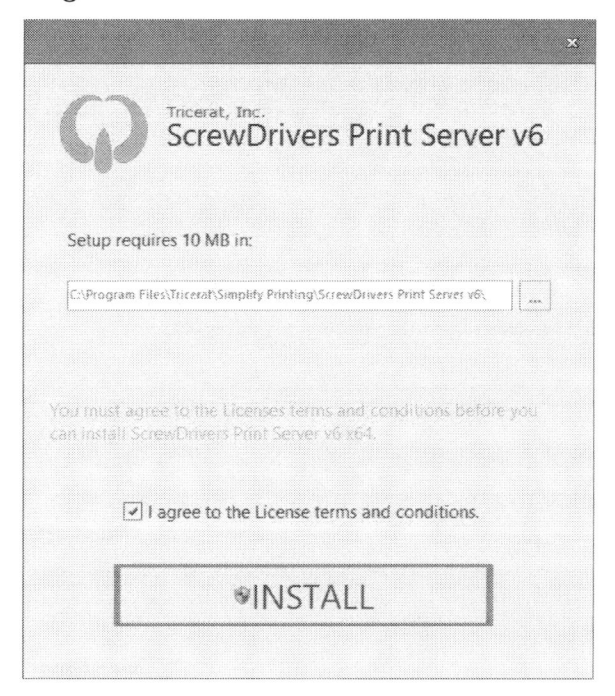

3. The installation will start, showing its progress.

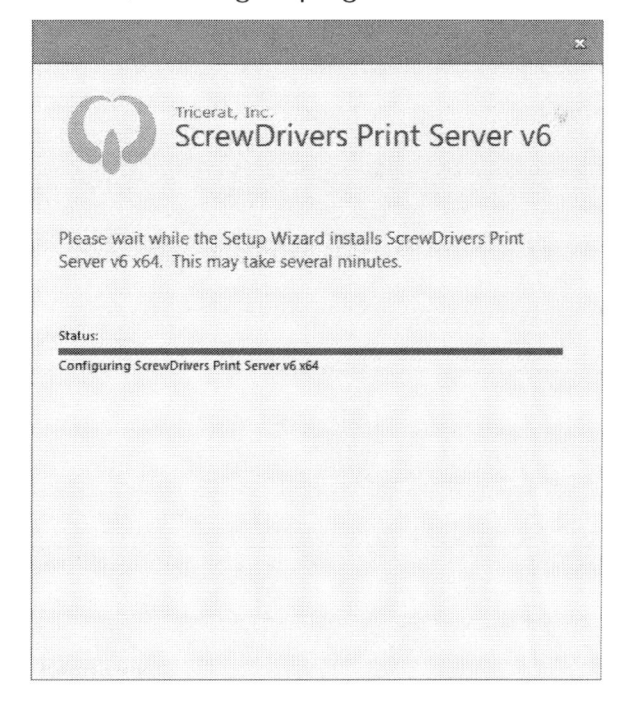

4. Once the installation ends, simply click 'Finish'.

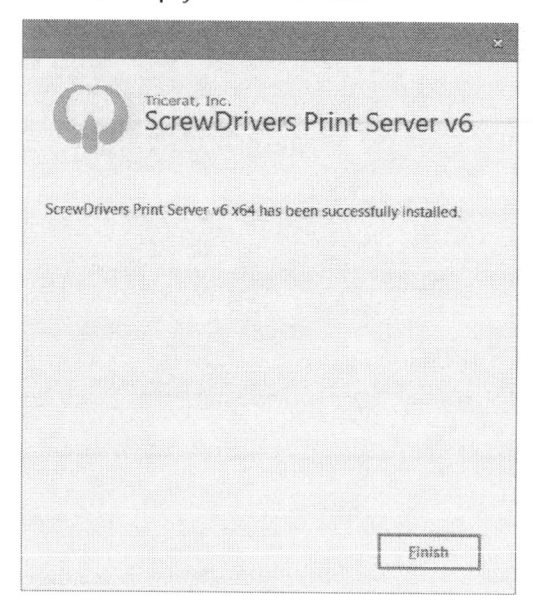

Installing the 'Simplify Printing' VDI/RDSH Agent

Now let's install the required agent on the servers (or VDI desktops for example) where the users will run their apps. In our case this means all our RDSHs (i.e. CRLAB-SH01, CRLAB-SH02).

1. Logon to every single RDSH and launch the installer. Select the desired language and click 'Next'.

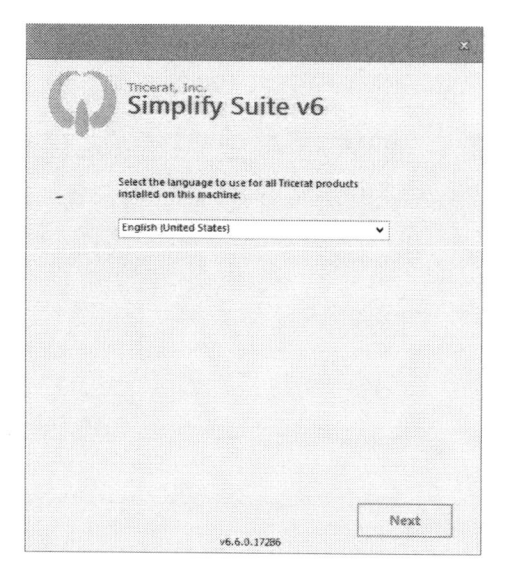

2. Agree to the licensing terms and click 'Next'.

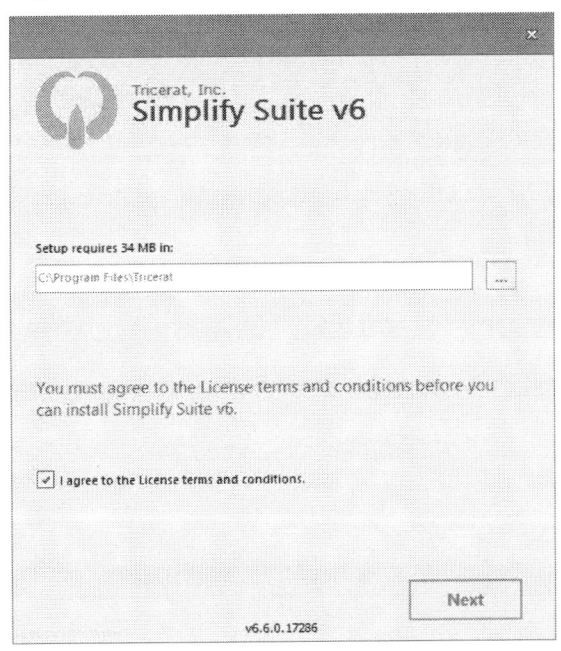

3. Select 'Simplify Printing', 'Simplify Driver Management', 'Driver Management Import Tool' and 'Print Job Viewer'. Click 'Next'.

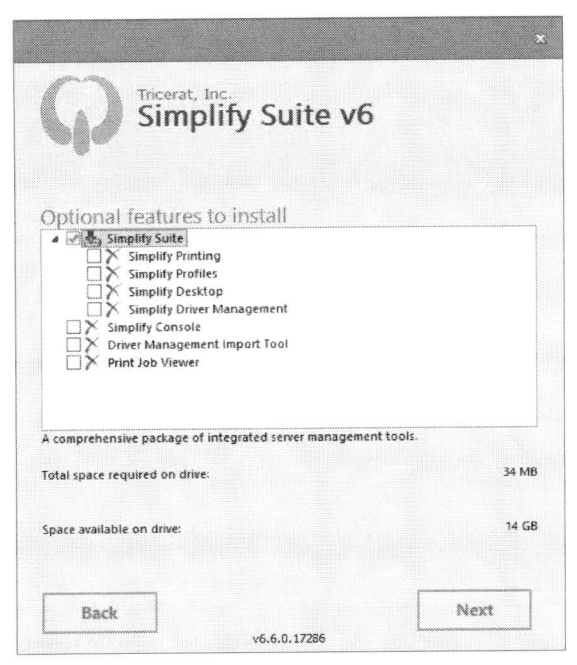

4. Enter the trial license you got from Tricerat (sent to the email you used to download the product) and click 'Next'.

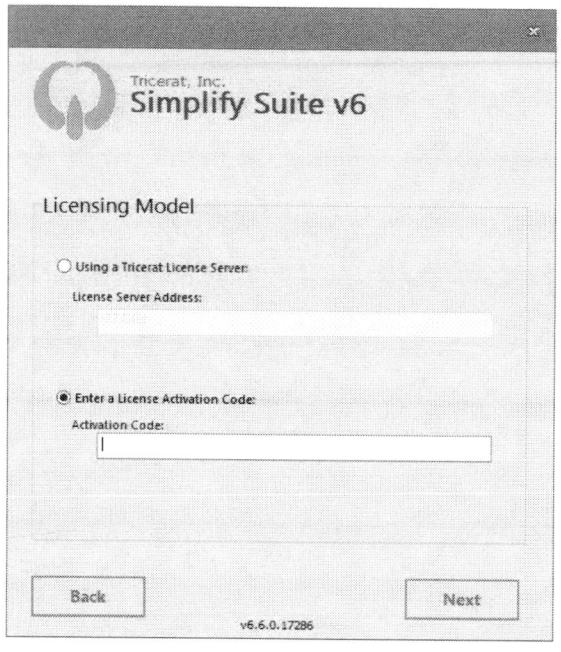

5. The installer will display some information about the SQL server setup procedure. Click 'Next'.

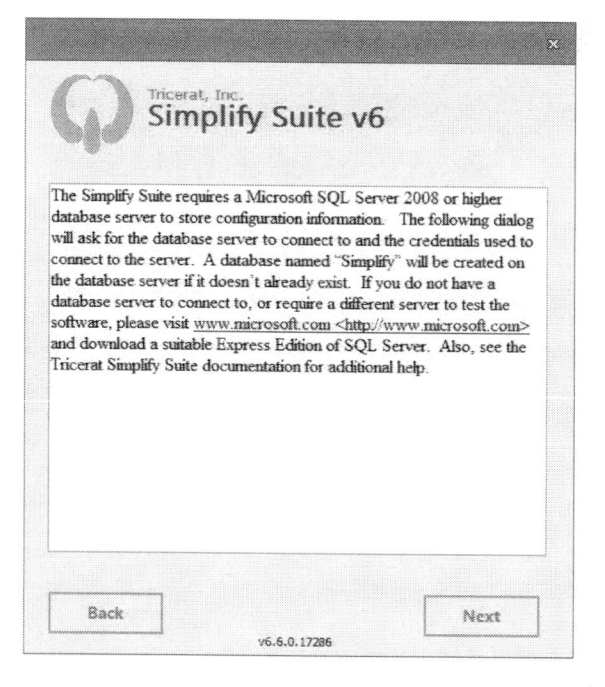

6. Select the same SQL Server and authentication method you used before. Click 'Next'.

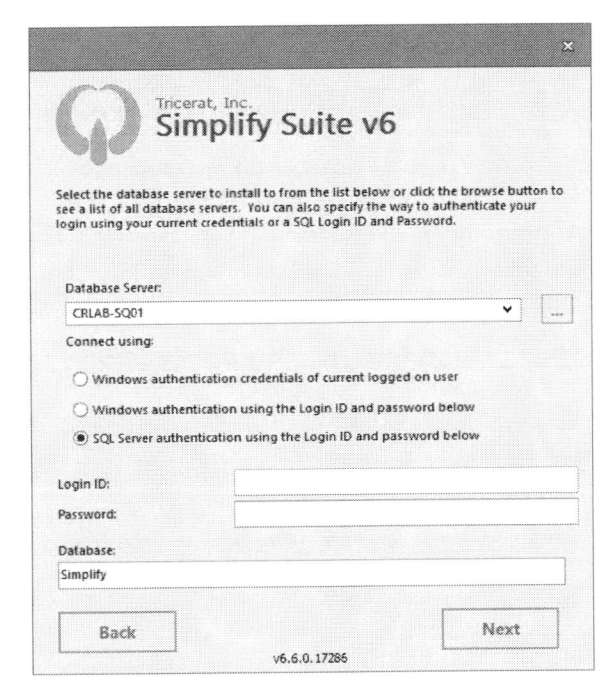

7. Click 'Install' to perform the installation.

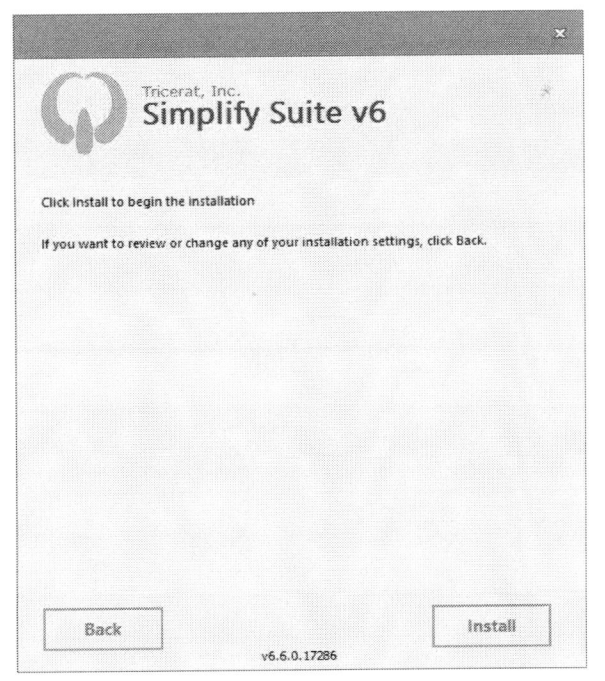

8. The setup procedure will start, showing you what is happening under the hood. Just wait...

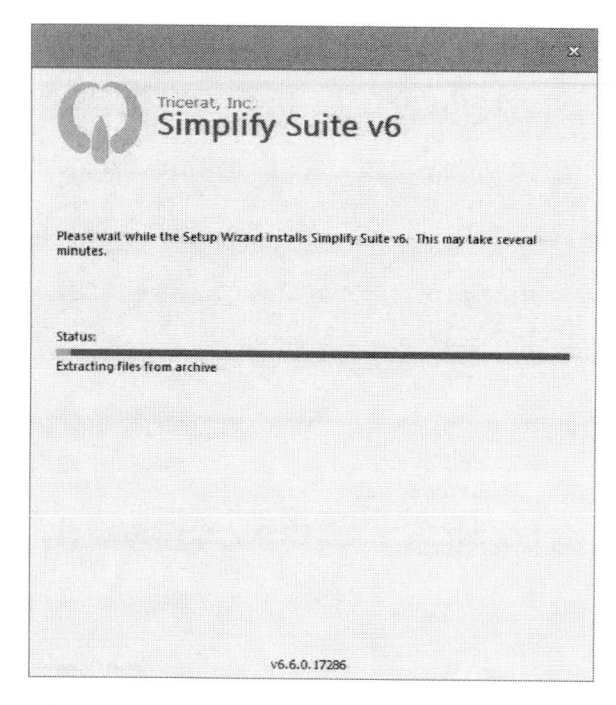

9. You are done. Click 'Finish'.

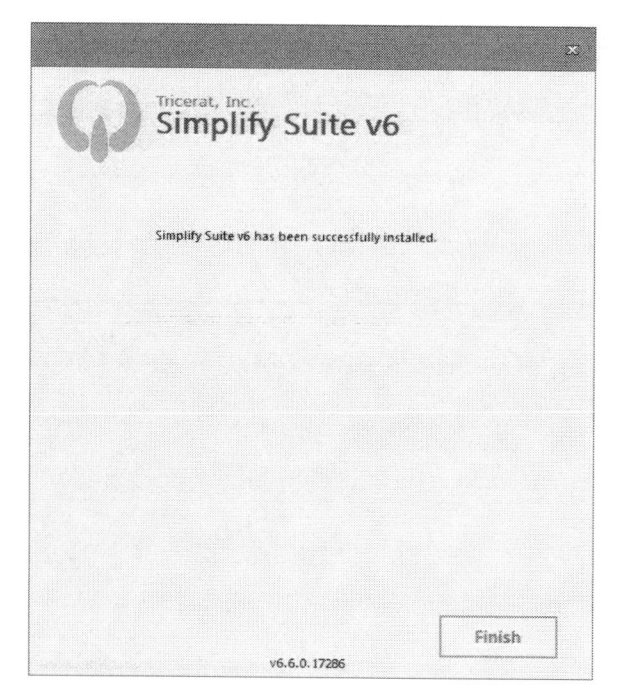

Importing printers to 'Simplify Printing'

Now that we have the console, the RDS agents and the print server installed, the next step is to add all the print servers running the 'Simplify Printing' solution in order to retrieve all the printers managed by such servers.

1. On the machine where you installed the 'Simplify Printing' console, launch it. The console will load.

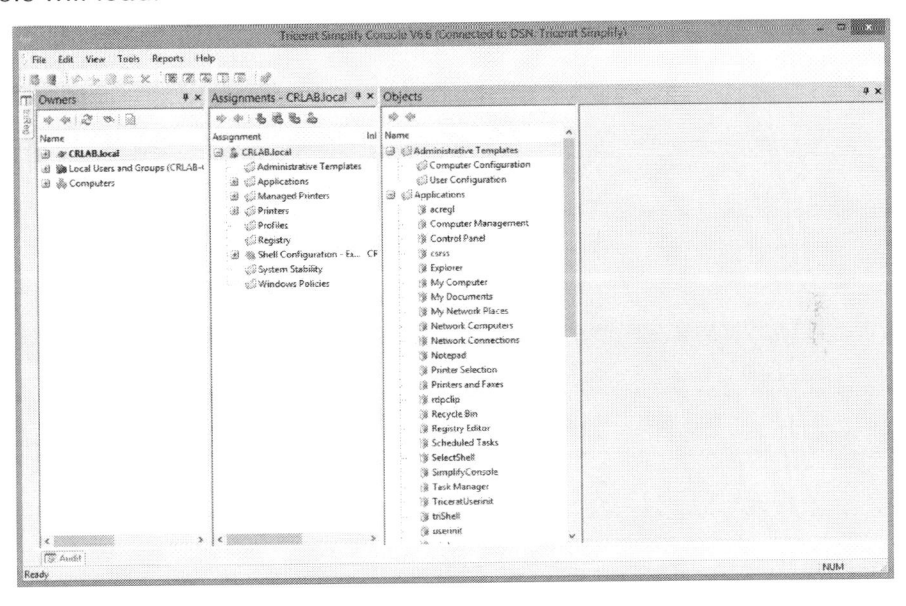

2. Under 'Objects' (pane on the right), expand 'Printers' | 'ScrewDrivers' and right-click 'v6 Print Servers'. Select 'New Object'.

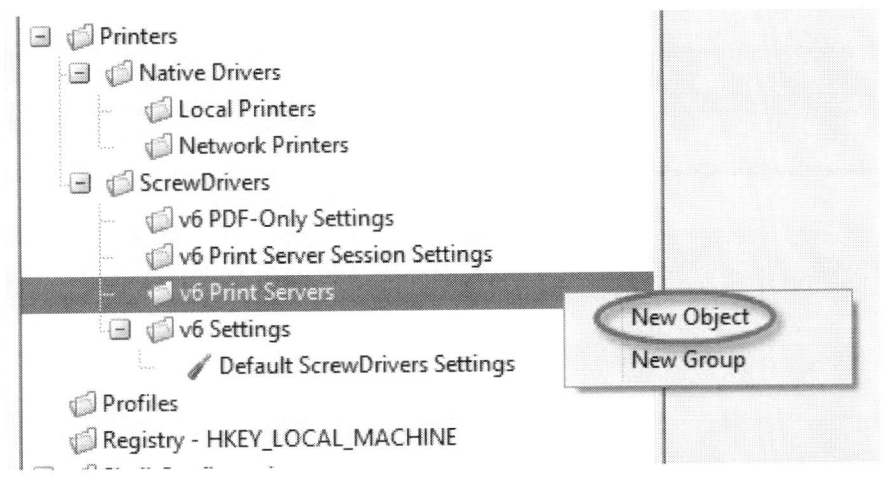

3. A new pane will open on the right, showing you basic information about the print server. Enter the print server hostname or IP address and click 'Test Connection' (make sure port TCP 3350 is open on the print server).

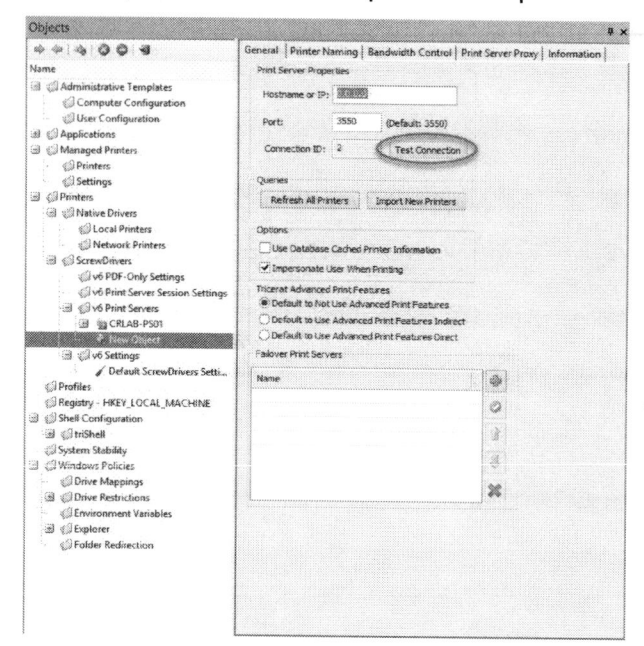

4. If the required port is open, you should see a message like this:

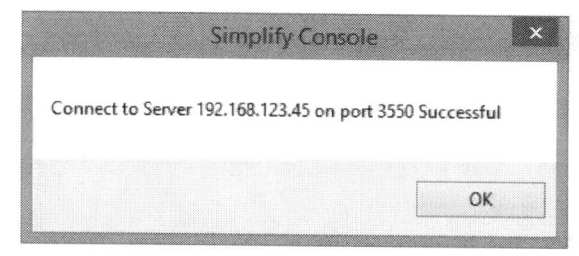

5. Leave all other settings as default and click 'Import New Printers'.

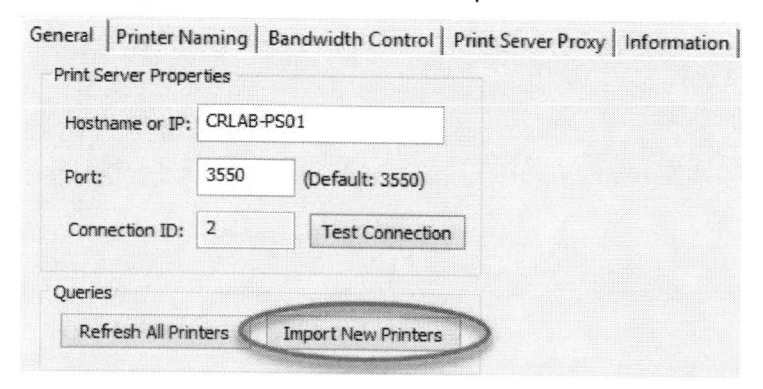

6. 'Simplify Printing' will show you a list of all the printers found on the print server. Click 'OK'.

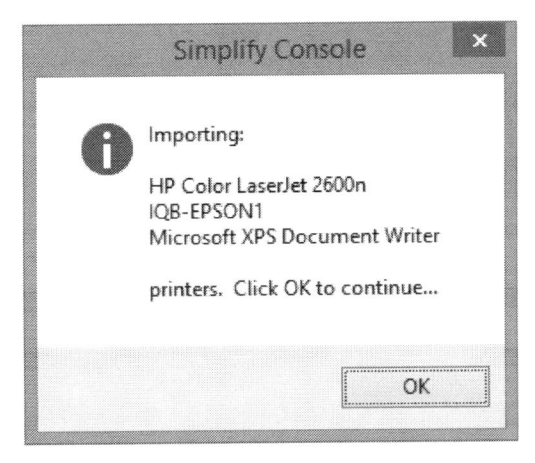

7. The console will go through all printers and import the required information (this may take time depending on how many printers you have on that print server). Once it is done, you will see your printers listed under a print server named 'New Object'.

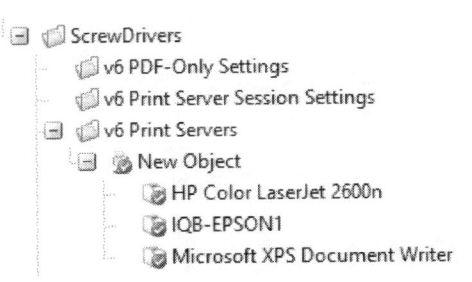

8. Before anything else, click on the 'Apply' button at the top.

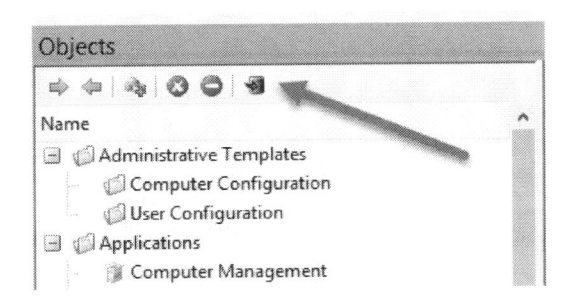

9. Simply right-click 'New Object' and select 'Rename'. The current name ('New Object') will be highlighted. Simply type the new name (we recommend the actual print server hostname) and press enter.

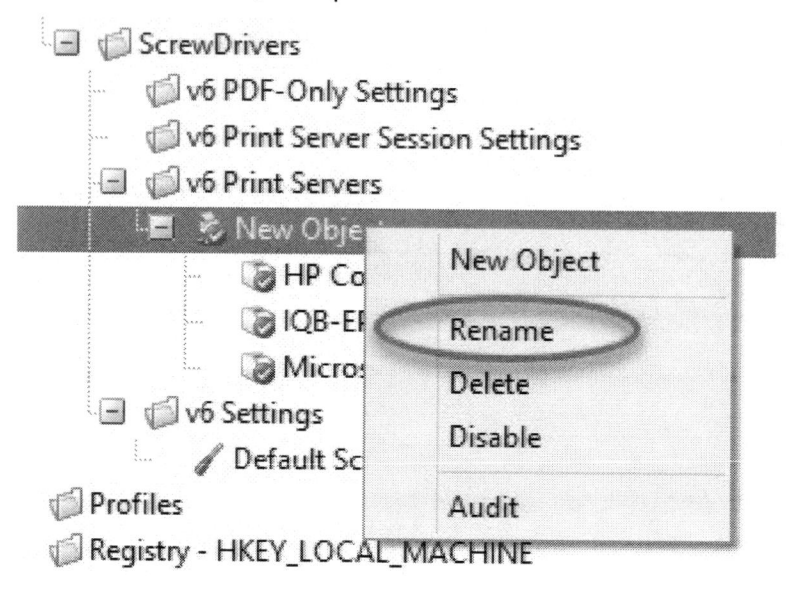

10. Your print server and all its printers are now ready to be assigned. If there are any printers you do not want to use with 'Simplify Printing', you can simply right click them and select 'Delete'.

11. Your end result should be similar to this:

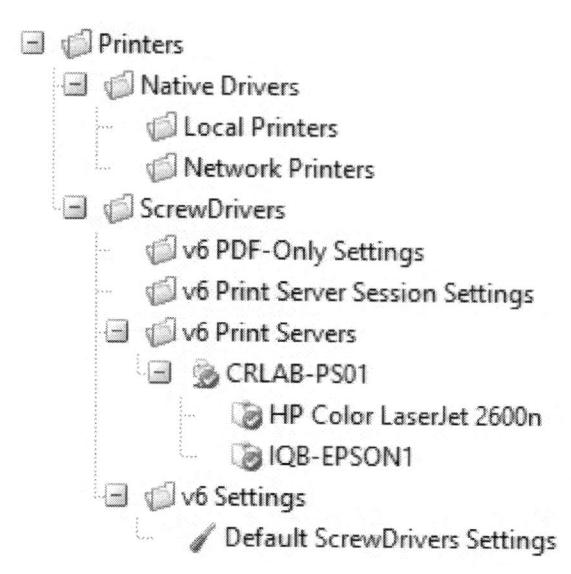

Assigning printers with 'Simplify Printing'

Once you import all your print servers and printers to the console, the final step is to assign such printers to what Tricerat define as an 'owner'. Before we do it, it is important to clarify what an owner means and the different assignments available.

As you have guessed, users and groups are of course possible owners. But Tricerat goes beyond that. Printers can be assigned based on IP address and even client name! This greatly simplifies managing printers in environments like hospitals for example, where doctors go from room to room, and want to be able to print to the closest printer to that particular device.

You may say that such scenario could be addressed by installing the printer locally on such device (i.e. as a TCP/IP port) and then mapping it within the session. That is correct. The problem with such approach is simple: first, you would have to install and manage such printers on all devices. Secondly, the printer would be redirected what means you would need the same drivers on the server for full functionality (as Easy Print may not work, the mapping trick may not get you a suitable driver, the device is non-Windows, etc). Not a simple thing to manage for sure.

'Simplify Printing' eliminates all that. No need to deal with drivers anywhere. Much cleaner and of course much more stable.

Now that you know what an 'owner' means, what about the assignment types available? It is actually simple:

- **Admin Assigned:** this is the most restrictive type. Once a printer is 'admin' assigned, it will always be displayed on the list of available printers and there is nothing the owner can do about it. The printer will be 'built' for the owner and will be ready to be used.
- **User Allowed:** in this case, the printer is listed as available but it is not 'built' automatically for the owner within the session. It is up to the owner to decide if he wants to use that printer or not.
- **User Assigned:** by default, a User Assigned printer is always built for the owner during a session, but the owner has the option of removing a User Assigned printer. You should make this assignment if the owner is to be able to remove a printer from a session.

With that in mind, let's create an assignment to a test account and check what the user sees when that is in place.

1. On the machine where you installed the 'Simplify Printing' console, launch it. The console will load.

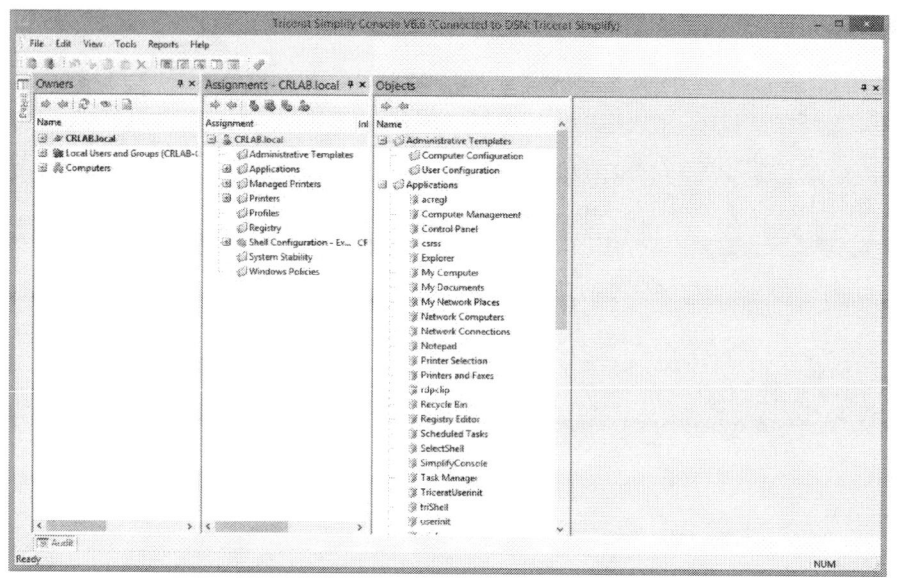

2. Under 'Owners' (pane on the left), expand your domain until you find the user you want to assign a printer to and click on the user name. In our case, we will use the 'TestUser1' account.

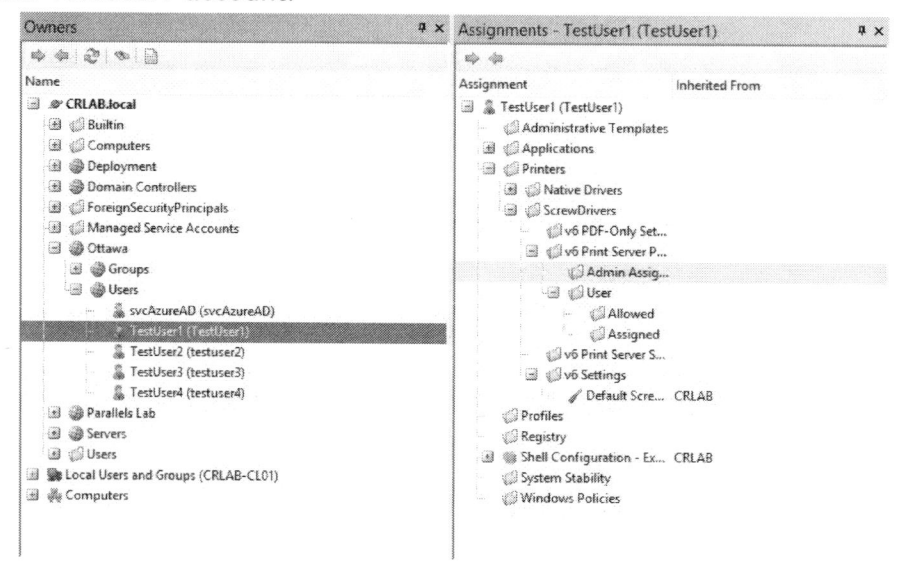

3. From the right panel, under 'Printers' | 'V6 Print Servers' | 'Your Print Server Name' (in our case, 'CRLAB-PS01') you should see the printers you previously imported. Simply drag-and-drop the printer you want to the 'Admin Assigned' folder under the 'Assignments' panel for that user (in our case, 'TestUser1'). The printer is now there and you will notice the username is now shown in bold on the left panel.

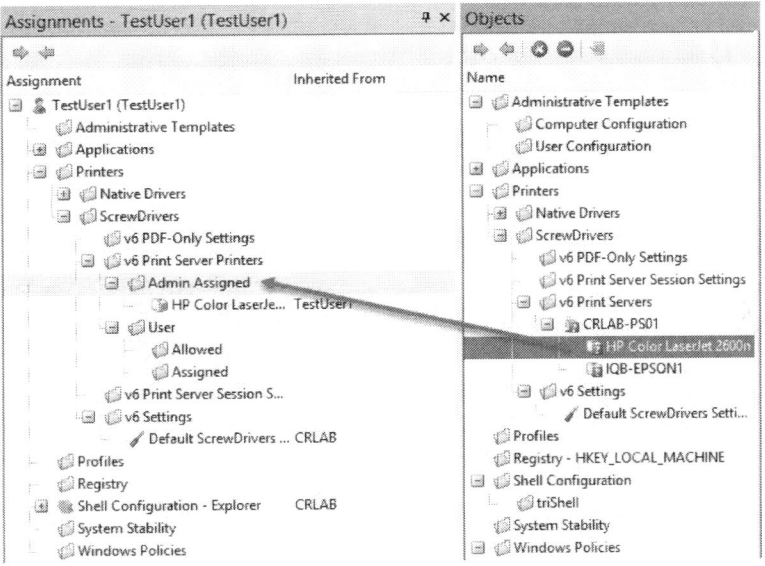

4. The final step is to simply right click the printer under 'Admin Assigned' and select 'Set as Default' (I am assuming you want that for testing purposes).

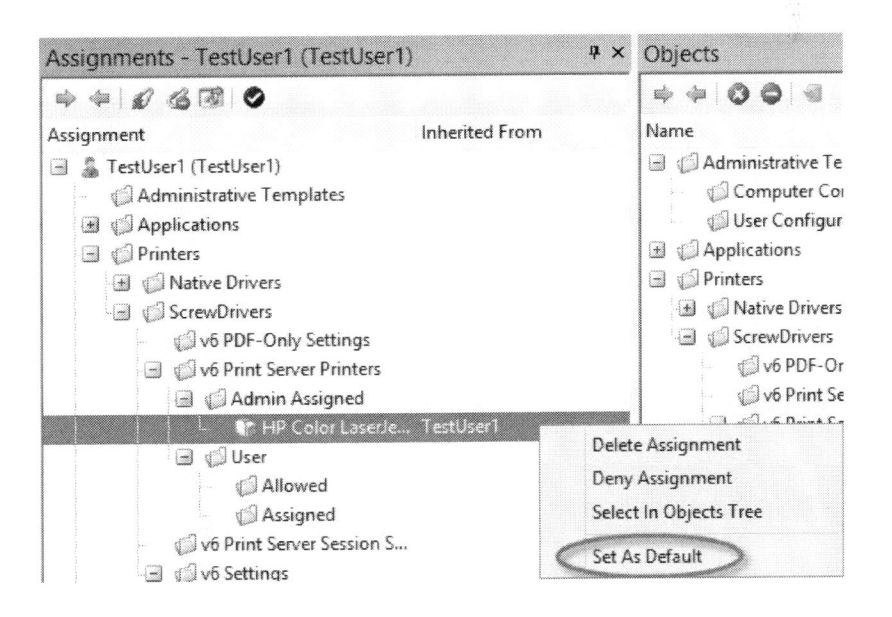

5. That is all you have to do. Really, it is that simple. They call it 'Simplify Printing' for a reason. Time to test.
6. Open your RDWA page and enter the credentials for the user we just assigned the printer to (again, in our case, 'TestUser1').
7. Launch an application (in our case, 'WordPad'). Type something and then try to print it. As you can see in the print dialog, the printer we assigned is there and set as the default printer!

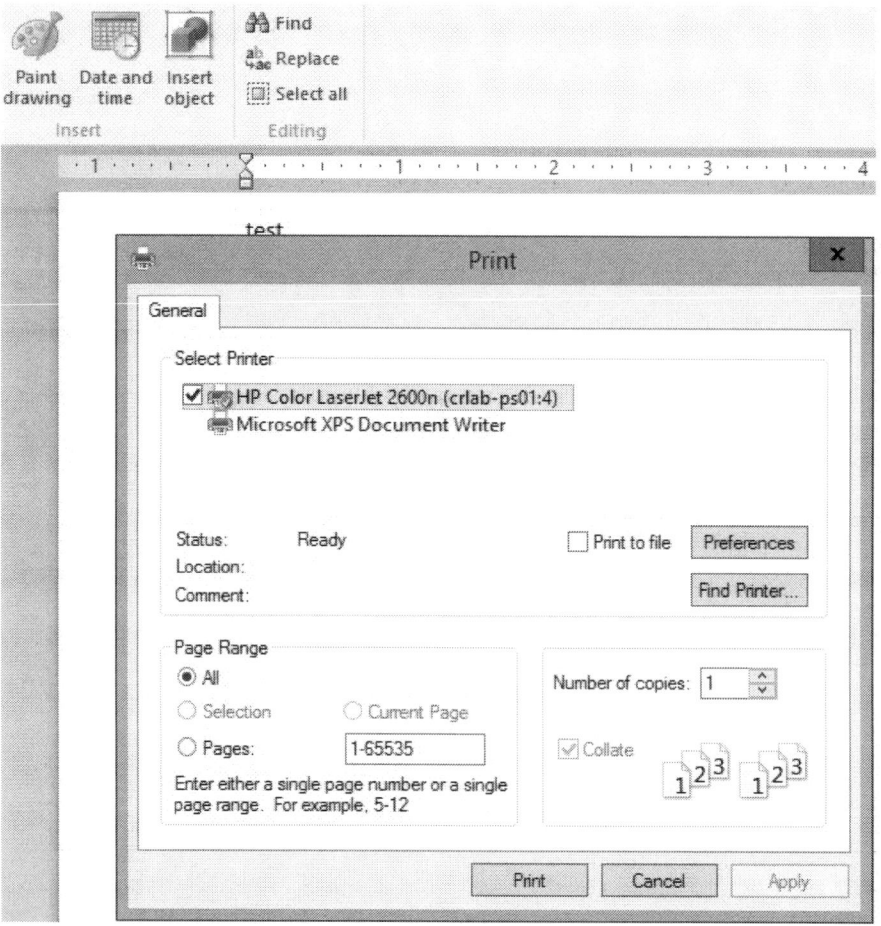

8. Success! You now have an environment that can deal with any printer, regardless of manufacturer and driver. No more driver installations or spooler crashes.

You may say this one was just too easy and that you have a more complex scenario in mind. For example, you may want your users being able to print to the closest printer to the thin client they will be logging in. Like doctors walking in a room, using the thin client that is available there and of course wanting to print to the printer that is close to that room. If he then goes to another floor and walks into another room, now he wants to print on that floor. Simplify Printing has you covered, using 'Proximity Based' printing. Let's make it happen then.

1. On the machine where you installed the 'Simplify Printing' console, launch it. The console will load.

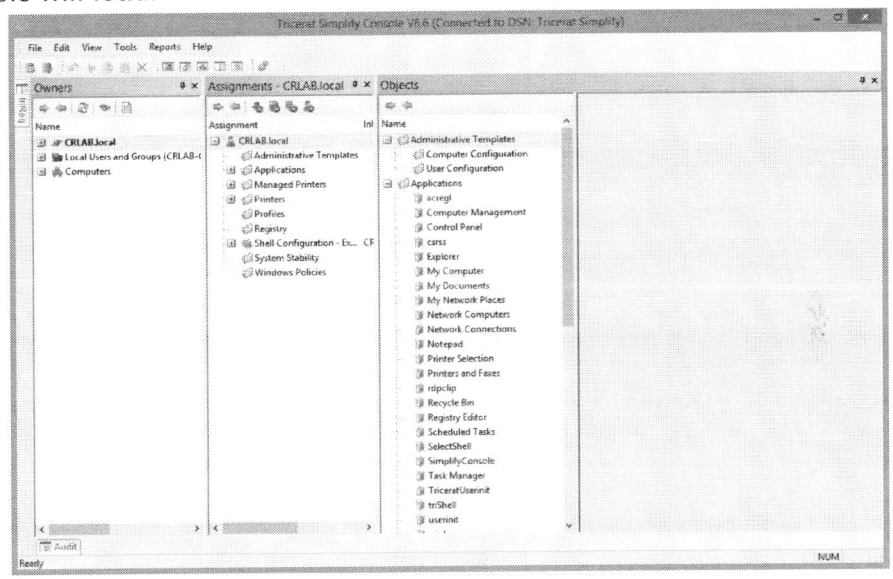

2. Under 'Owners' (pane on the left), right click the 'Computers' node at the bottom and select 'Add' | Computer.

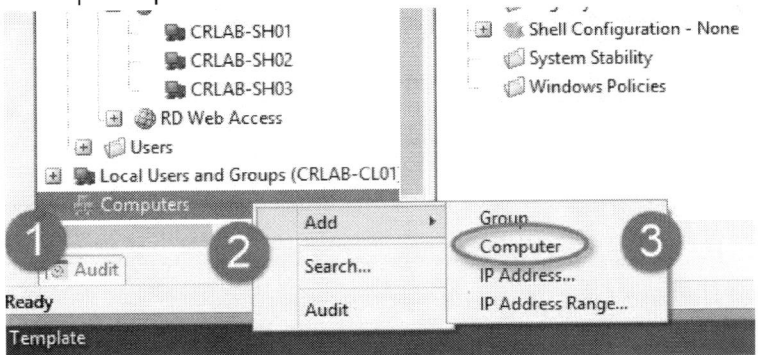

3. A blank computer object will be created. Simply type the name of the device the user will be using (i.e. the thin client terminal on waiting room #1, in our example, CRLAB-DC01). Repeat these exact same steps for the other devices (for this example we also added CRLAB-CL01 in our imaginary waiting room #2). Your final result should look similar to this:

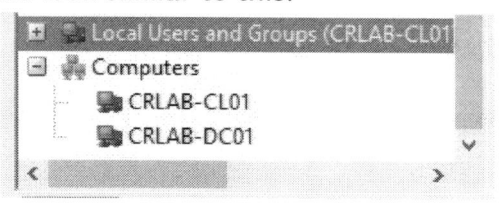

4. The final step is to assign the printers you want to these particular computers. Still on the left pane, click on one of the computers you just added. You will see it listed in the middle pane. Simply drag-and-drop the printer from the right pane to the 'Admin Assigned' folder (as you realize this is exactly what we did before, when assigning printers to users). Repeat for the second computer added (make sure you assign different printers so you can test and see the results). Make sure you right-click the assigned printer to set it as the default. Once you are done, you should have something like this:

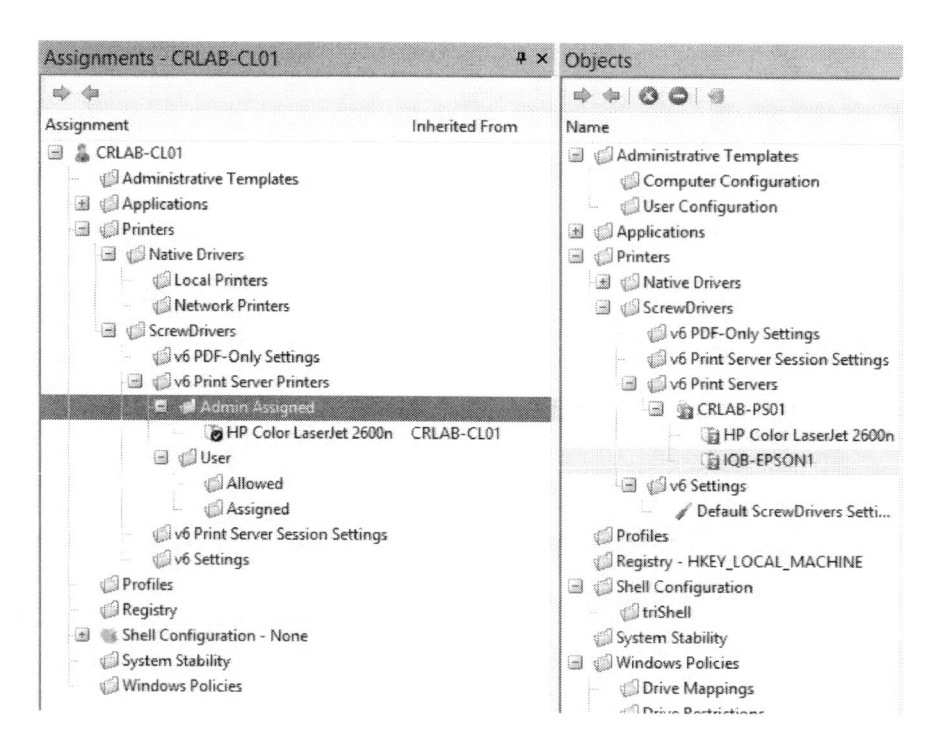

5. Time to test. Connect to your RDS environment from these two clients and try to print a document from any application. After logging in to our client VM (CRLAB-CL01) and launching 'Notepad', when trying to print, this is what we see, regardless of the user that is logged in (as again, this assignment is done at the client level, not the user):

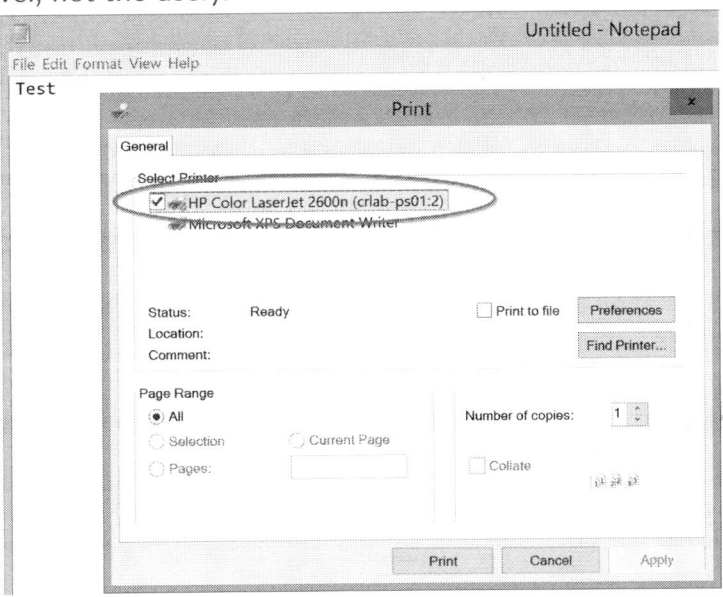

6. Likewise, when launching the session from the other computer we added as a client (CRLAB-DC01), after logging in as the same user and trying to print from another application, we can see this:

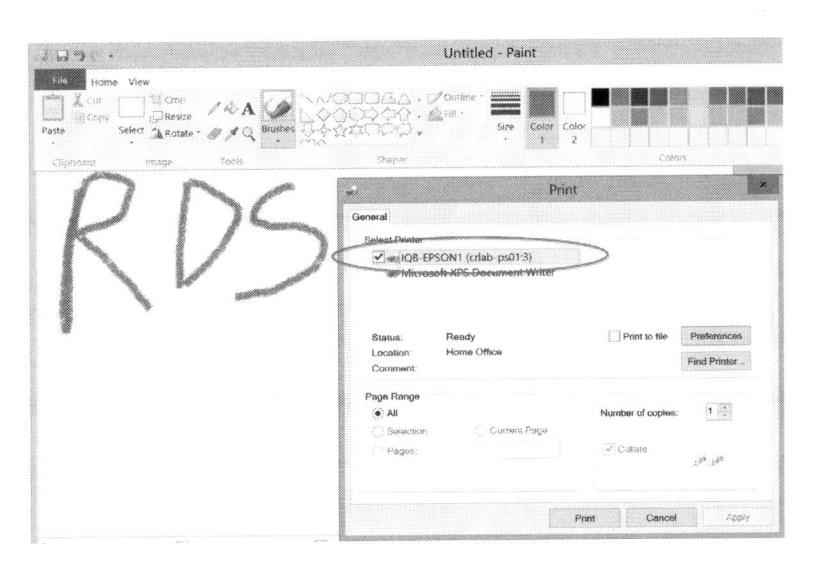

7. Working exactly as needed. Regardless of the user logging in on any of these endpoints, the printer closer to the device is assigned. Success!

So, what is next? Well, as we mentioned earlier, as of today, even with Windows Server 2016, there is no way to print from mobile clients like Android and iOS phones and tablets. Once again, Tricerat has you covered. The answer now is 'Simplify Printing TX' and that is exactly what we are covering next. This will give you an end-to-end printing solution, covering all, from driverless printing to mobile printing. Welcome to 2018. ☺

The icing on the cake: 'Simplify Printing TX'

Now we have a fully functional printing solution that allows our users to print to any of their local printers (from Mac and PCs, no matter what sort of printer they have) and without having to deal with any printer driver on the RDSHs. More than that we went above and beyond and even got network printers covered. Yes, your RDSHs can print to any network printer with no drivers at all. This was all part of 'Simplify Printing' (as we mentioned, if you do not need to deal with network printers, 'ScrewDrivers' is all you need).

But now, as this is the year 2018, users do have mobile devices like smartphones and tablets and I can bet, they want to print. That is where 'Simplify Printing TX' comes to the picture. It will cover that last mile and get us an end-to-end printing solution that covers all our needs. Let's get our hands dirty one more time.

Installing the 'Simplify Printing TX' server

The first step is to get the server software up and running (you can indeed have a highly available setup but this is beyond the scope of this book – for such advanced scenarios, please check http://www.tricerat.com), what is quite straight forward. That said, let's get it going:

1. Logon to the machine where you want the server installed (in our case, 'CRLAB-TX01' – a separate server created exclusively for this) and launch the installer (SPTXServer_x64.exe). Accept the EULA and click 'Next'.

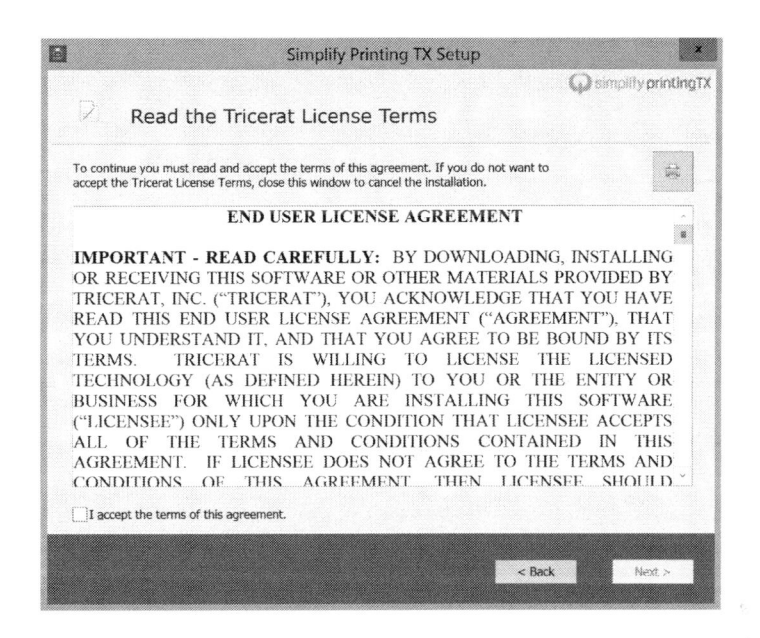

2. Select 'Request an evaluation license for Simplify Printing TX' and fill in your information (for evaluation purposes). Click 'Next'.

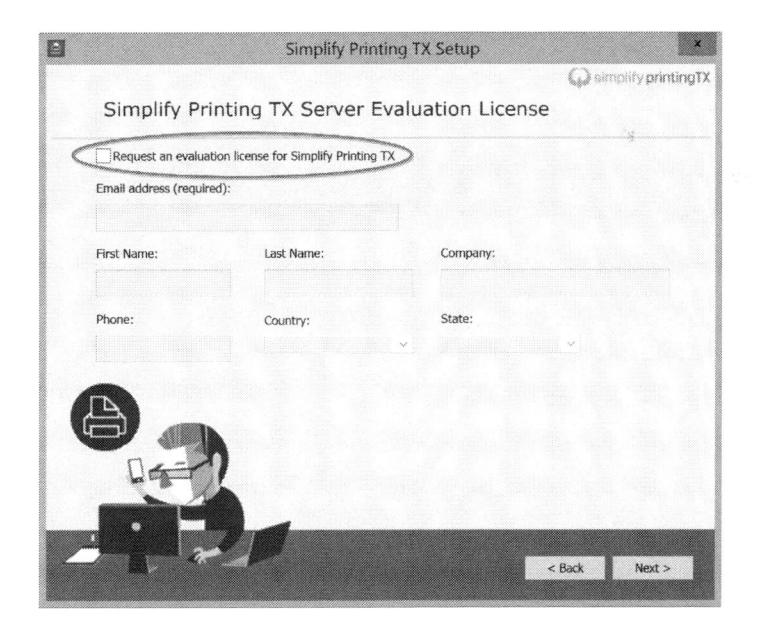

3. As our test machine is domain joined, the installer will automatically select 'Active Directory Domain Services'. Click 'Next'.

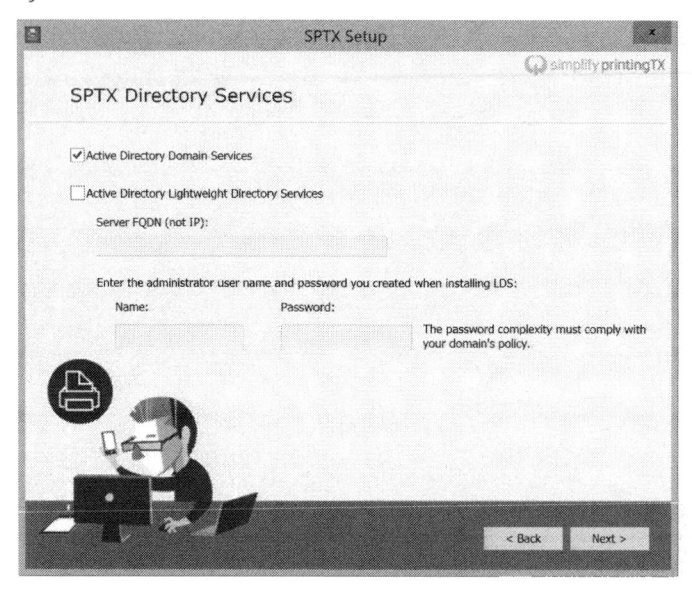

4. 'Simplify Printing TX' relies on a Mongo database and depending on the environment size, it is recommended you use a separate drive for it. Security wise, in our case as we used an account part of the 'Domain Admins' group, it will be used as the default group with administrative rights to the 'Simplify Printing TX' infrastructure. Finally, in case you want to use proper certificates for securing access to the server just click on 'Creating SSL Keys'.

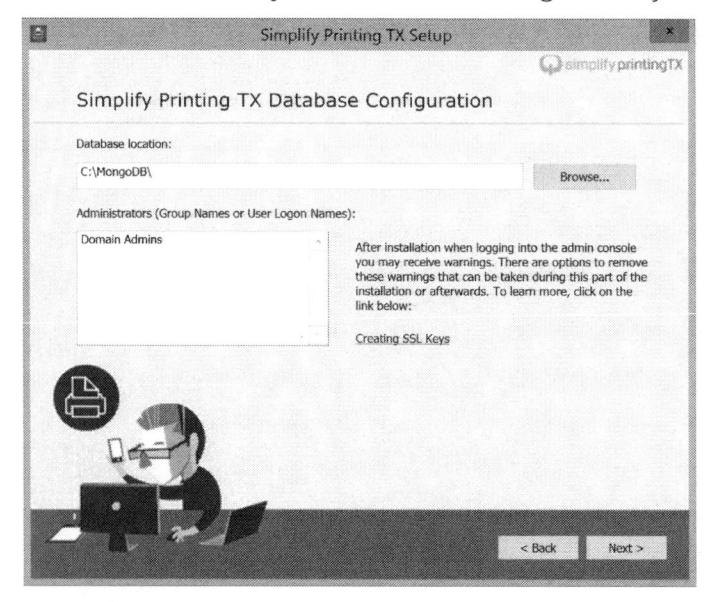

5. Accept the default location for the installation and click 'Install'.

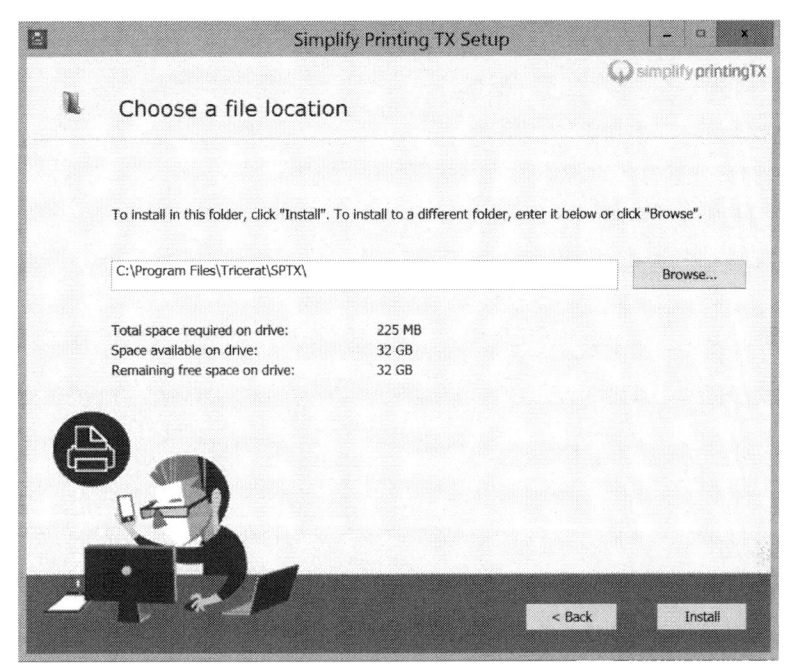

6. For iOS devices to work, 'Bonjour' is required. The installer will take care of this and you will see a separate installer launching. Click 'Next'.

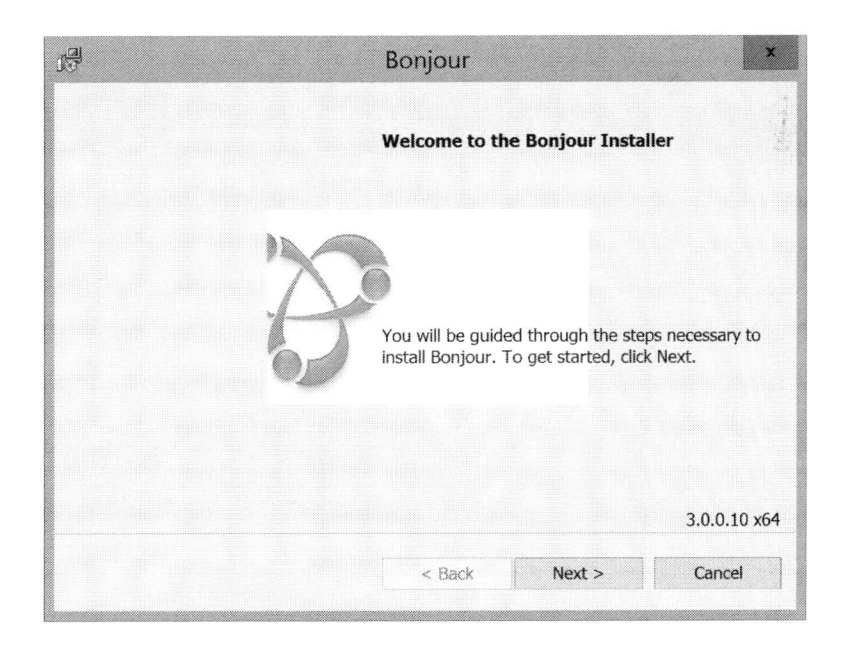

7. Accept the Apple EULA and click 'Next'.

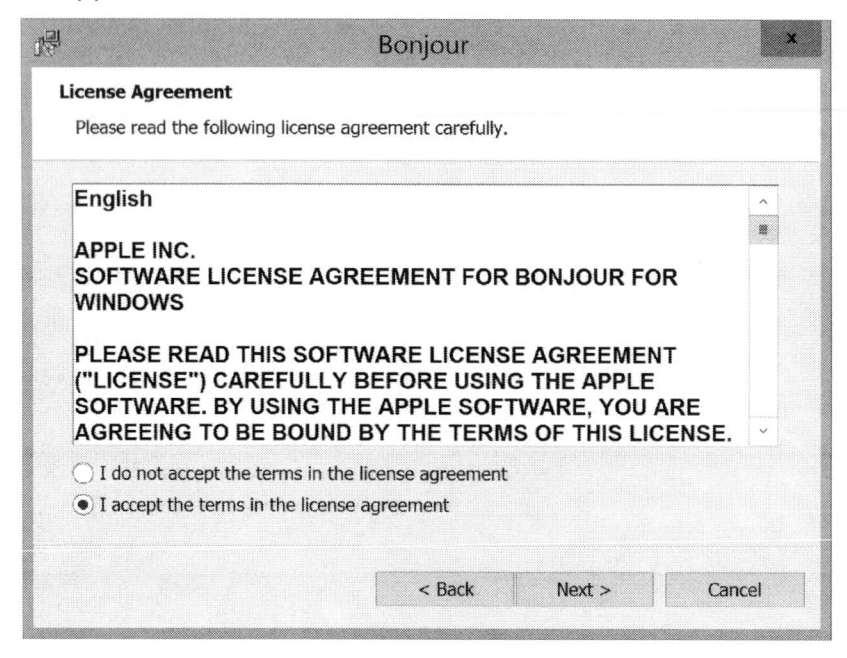

8. Click 'Install'.

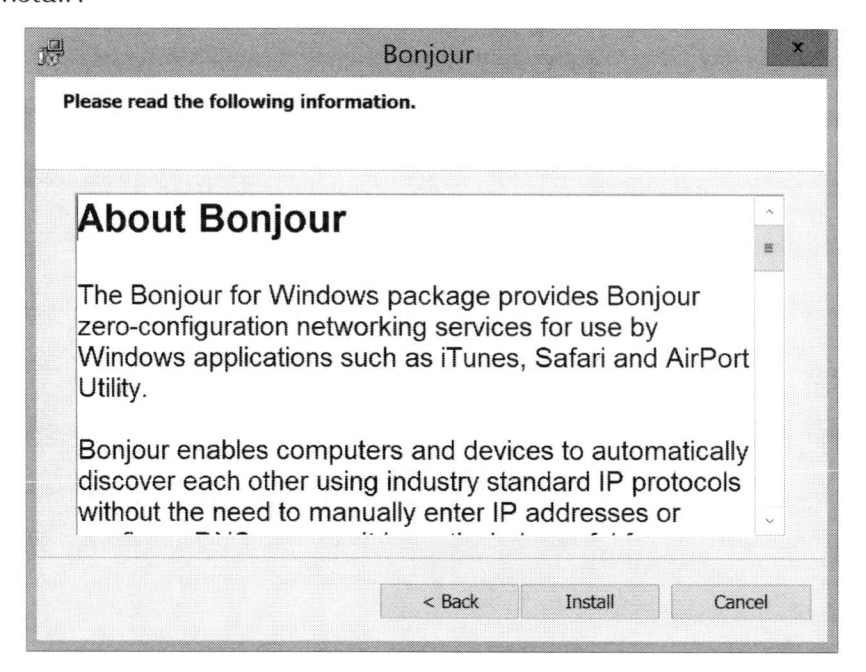

9. If everything works as expected, you will be greeted with a 'Congratulations' message. Go celebrate as this is a rare sight for Apple software on Windows devices ☺. Click 'Finish'.

10. The 'Simplify Printing TX' installer will resume and you may see some command prompt like windows popping up. This is normal. Once it is all finished just click 'Close'.

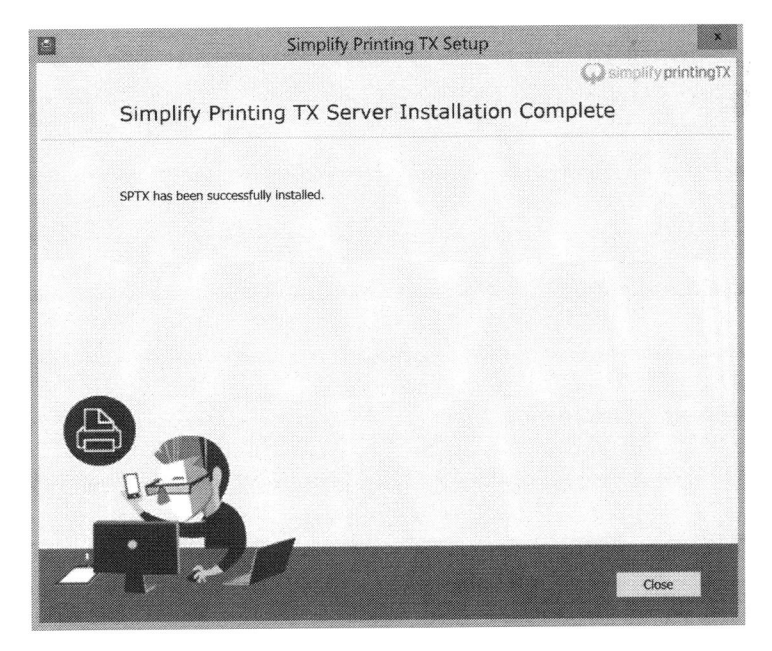

To make sure it is all well, launch a browser (i.e. Internet Explorer) and on the 'Simplify Printing TX' server go to https://localhost:8080. You should see the logon screen for the system. We are ready for the next step (getting printers on it).

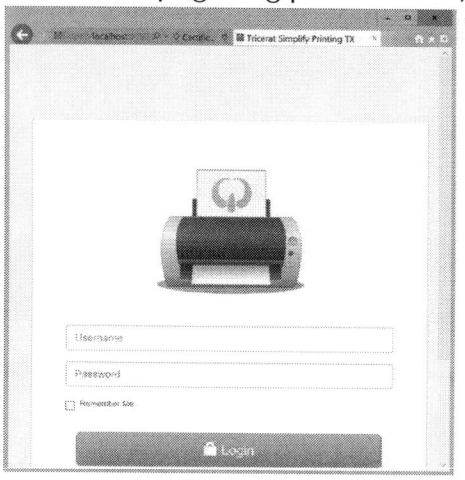

Installing the 'Simplify Printing TX' Server Agent

At this point we have the 'Simplify Printing TX' server installed along its web-based console. The next step is to load the 'Simplify Printing TX' Print Server agent on all your print servers.

1. Logon to one of your print servers (in our case 'CRLAB-PS01') and run the print server agent installer for your platform (x86 or x64). In our case we have a 64-bit server so we run 'SPTXPrintServer_x64.exe'. Accept the EULA and click 'Next'.

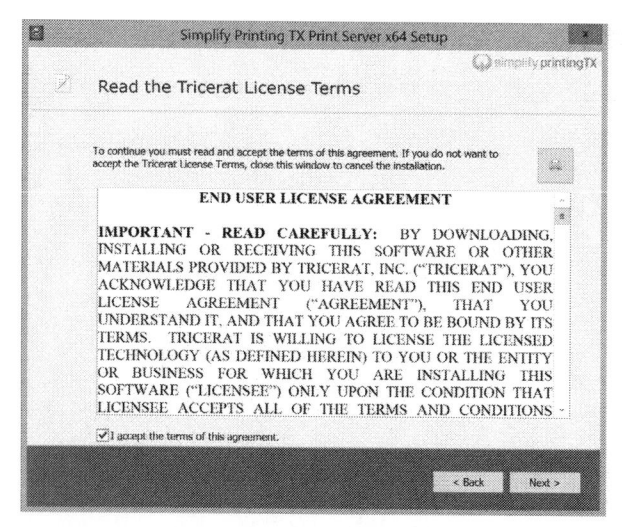

2. Accept the default location and click 'Next'.

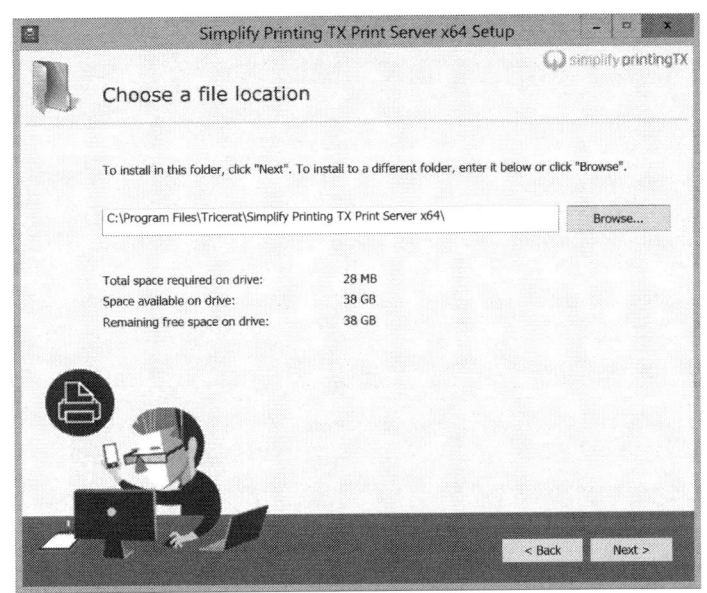

3. Enter the IP address or FQDN for the 'Simplify Printing TX' server (in our case 'CRLAB-TX01') and click 'Install'.

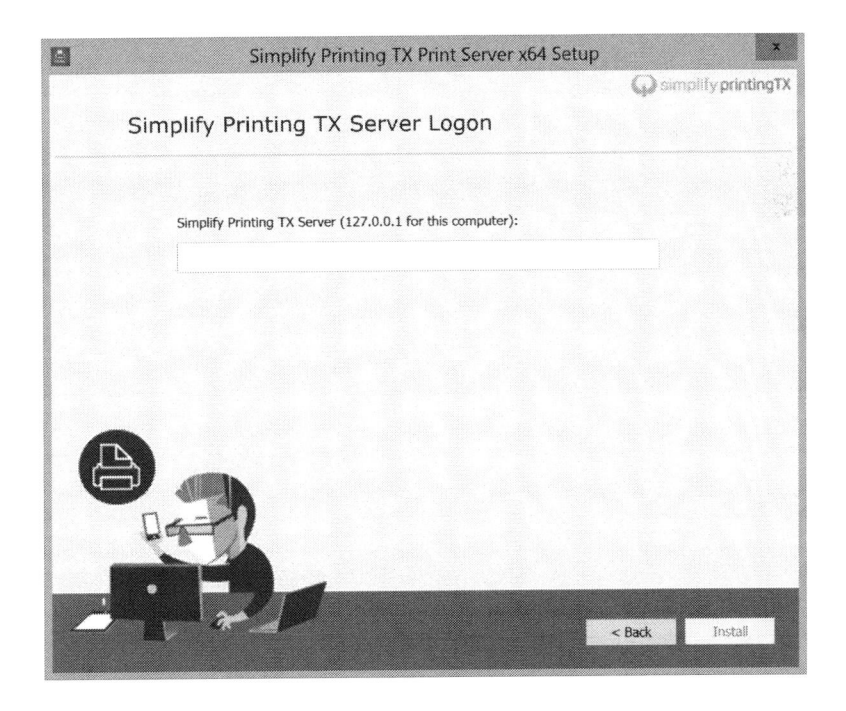

4. For iOS devices to work, 'Bonjour' is required. The installer will take care of this and you will see a separate installer launching. Click 'Next'.

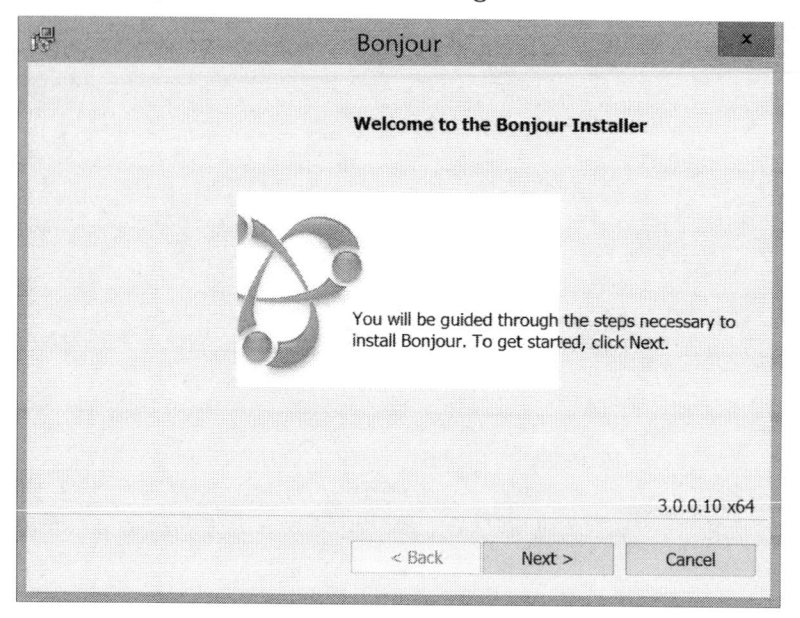

5. Accept the Apple EULA and click 'Next'.

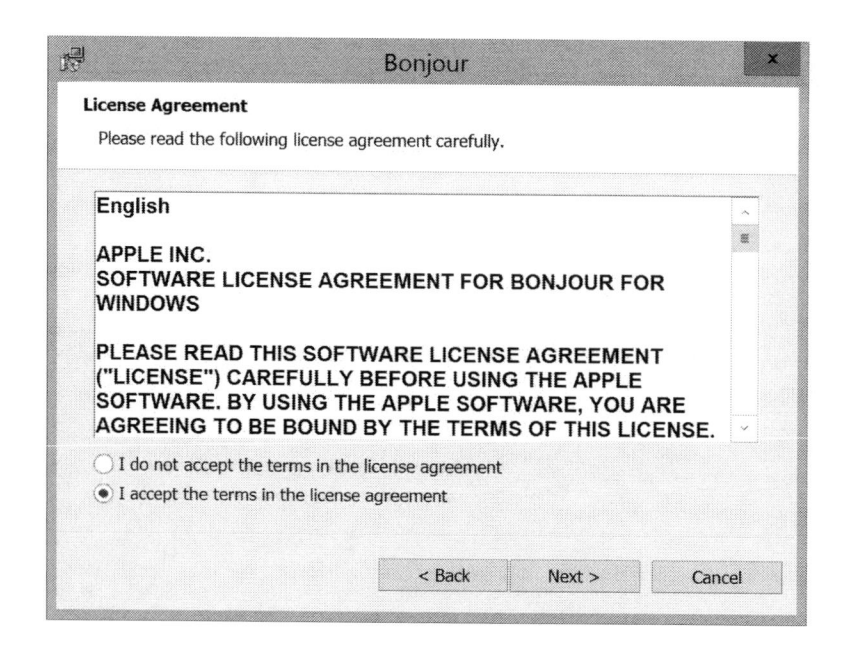

6. Click 'Install'.

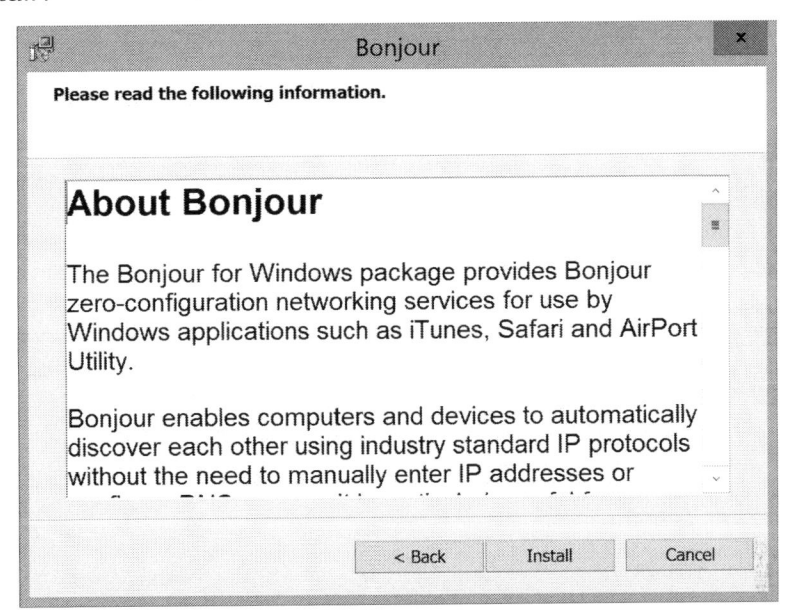

7. Assuming the Apple software managed to not crash, you are all done here (ok I promise no more Apple jokes ☺). Click 'Finish'.

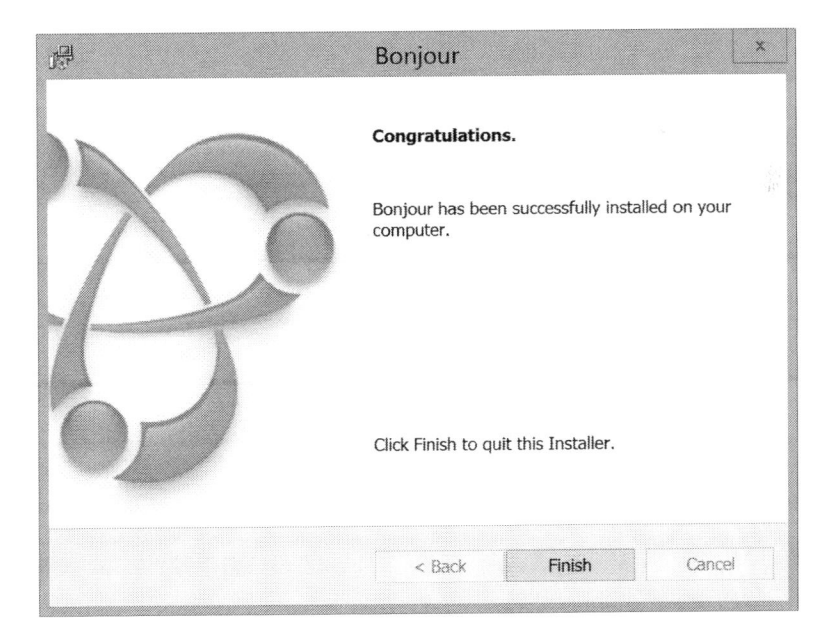

8. The installer will resume and finish. Just click 'Close'.

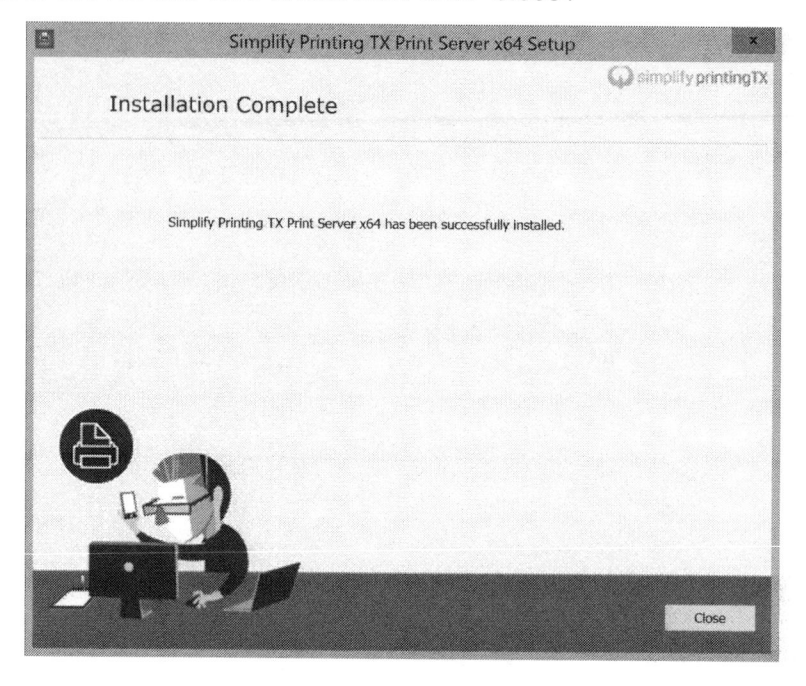

9. Restart your print server just to be on the safe side.
10. If everything worked as expected, if you logon to the 'Simplify Printing TX' console (in our case, https://crlab-tx01:8080) and click on the 'Printers' section on the left, you should see the printers that were installed on your print server now listed at the console. Sweet.

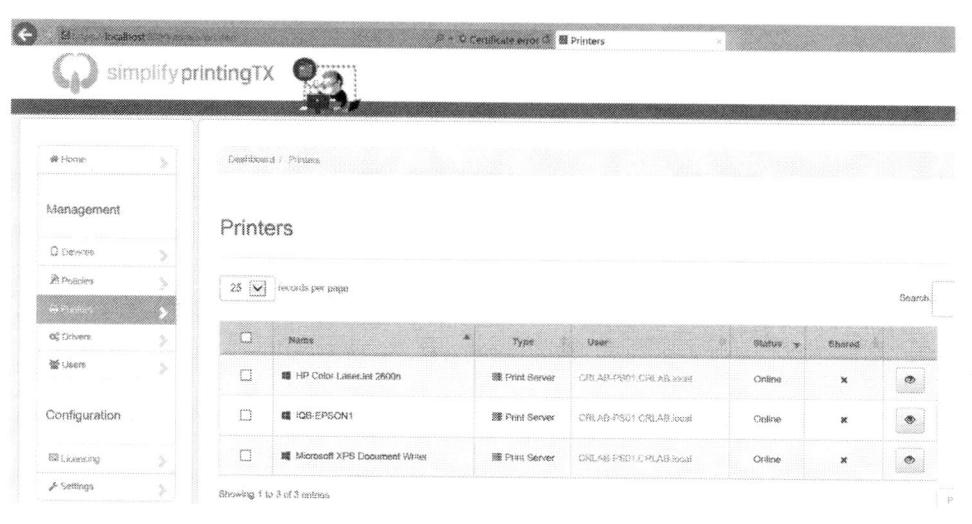

Installing the 'Simplify Printing TX' Agent

The final step of the puzzle, on the infrastructure side, is to have the RDSHs loaded with the 'Simplify Printing TX' agent. This will allow the session hosts where users connect to run their applications, to print to the 'Simplify Printing TX' printers.

1. On every single RDSH, logon to the console using an account with administrative privileges.
2. Locate the installer (in our case, 'SPTXClient_Win_x64.exe') and launch it. Accept the licensing terms and click 'Install'.

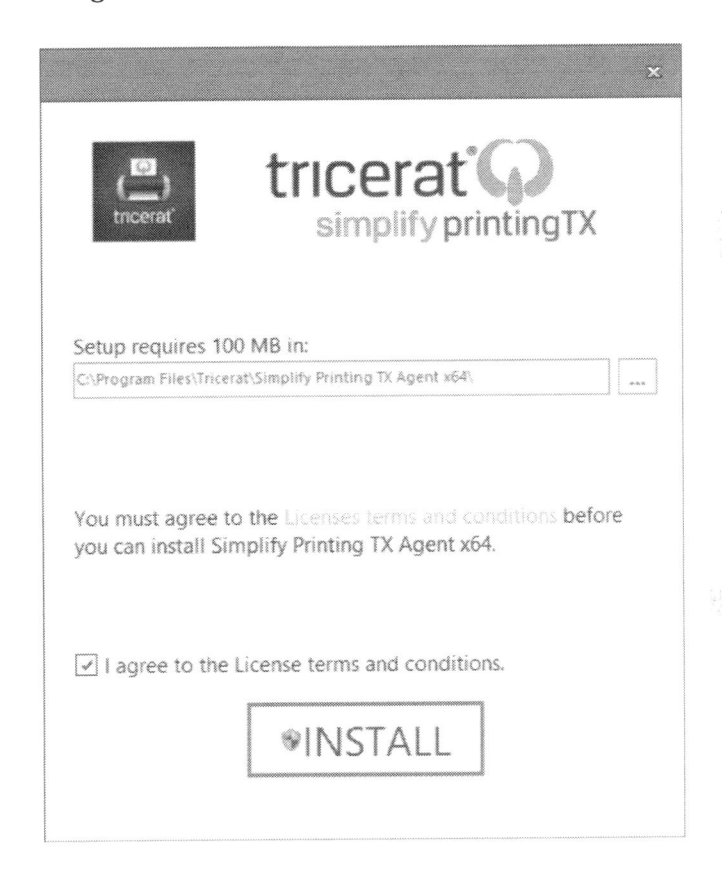

3. For iOS devices to work, 'Bonjour' is required. The installer will take care of this and you will see a separate installer launching. Click 'Next'.

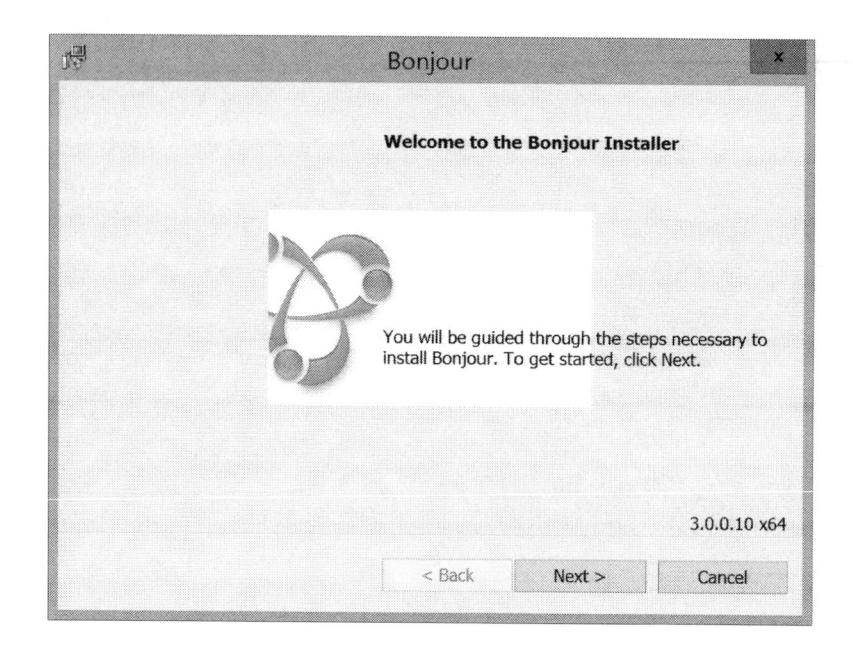

4. Accept the Apple EULA and click 'Next'.

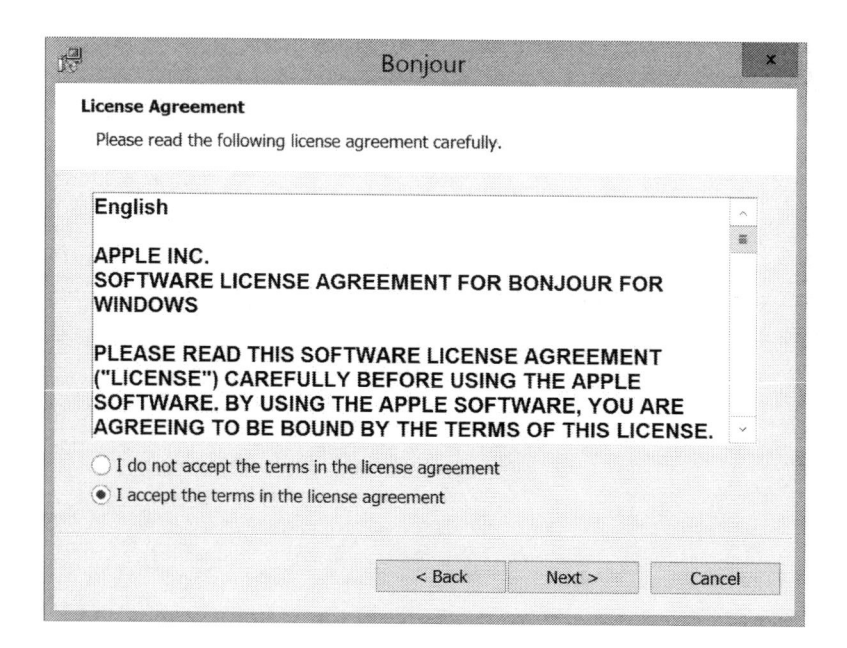

5. Click 'Install'.

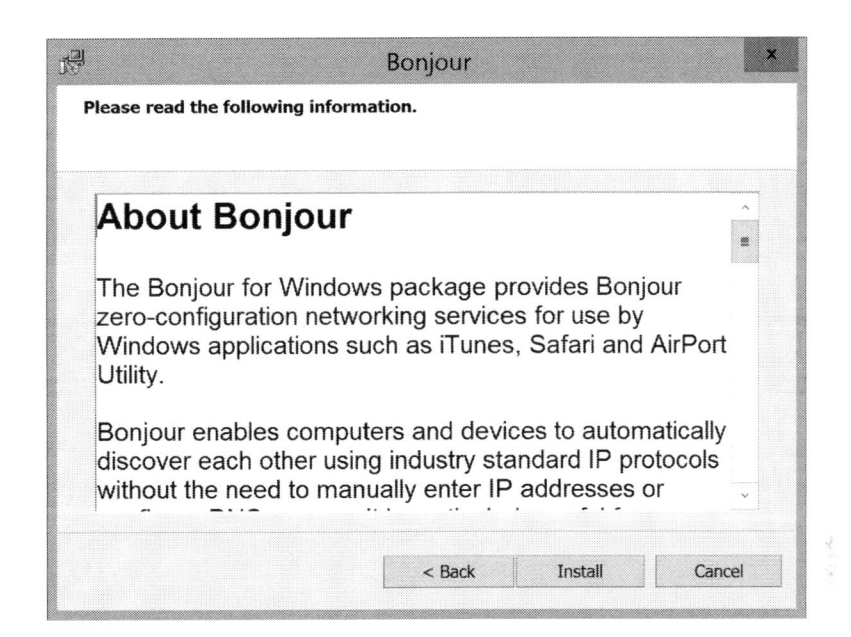

6. Click 'Finish'.

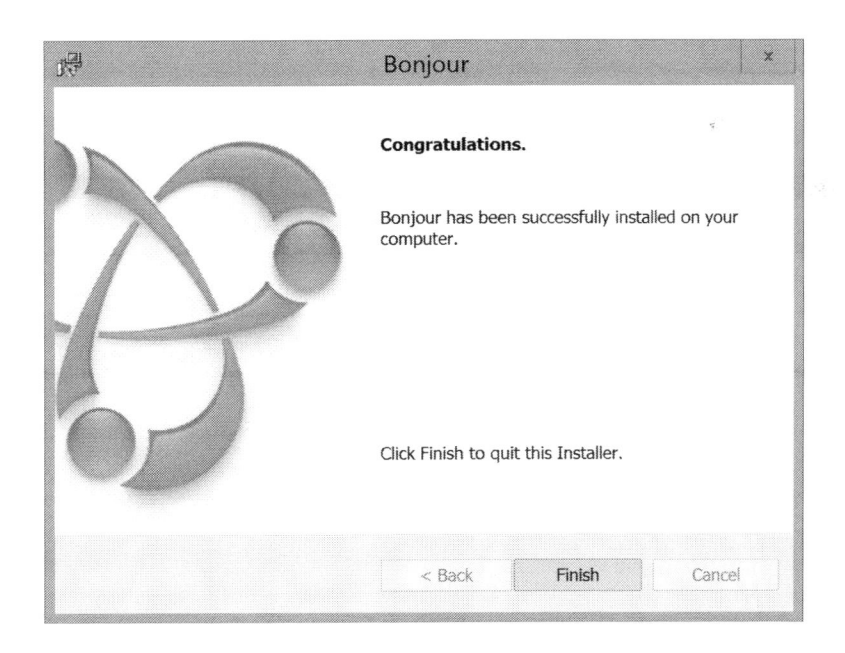

7. You may see a message about the installer having to close existing applications. Just select 'Automatically close applications and attempt to restart them after setup is complete' and click 'OK'.

8. We are done here. Click 'Finish'.

Note: the 'Simplify Printing TX' agent, if you did not realize it yet, can be installed on any machine where you have printers that you want to make available through your 'Simplify Printing TX' infrastructure. For example, your printers at home, setup on your home PC or Mac. Or even printers connected directly to your computer at work. As long as you install the agent on these machines and logon to the infrastructure with your username and password, all these printers could be made available to you or other clients. This means you would be able to print from your RDSHs to your printers at home for example, even if you are connected to them from a hotel in a completely different country!

Enabling Access to 'Simplify Printing TX'

Now that we are done with all the infrastructure installation, the final step is to change the built-in certificate (by default, issued to 'localhost') and set the proper FQDN that will be used by the clients (and administrators) to access and manage the 'Simplify Printing TX' environment.

In a nutshell, this is what has to be done:

- Define the FQDN you want to use. In the book, we decided to use tx.iqbridge.ca.
- From the outside, clients connect to the 'Simplify Printing TX' infrastructure on port TCP 40404 so it has to be opened on your firewall and pointing to the 'Simplify Printing TX' server.
- The correct certificate installed on the 'Simplify Printing TX' server.
- Internally, create the proper service location (SRV) record on your AD DNS so the client is able to launch and pass the credentials automatically, with no user intervention (will explain this in more details).

I am assuming you can tackle the first two items on your own ☺. For the certificate, which must be in PEM format, this has to be done:

1. If you are using a PFX (the most common format on Windows systems) you must export it with the private key and then convert it to PEM.
2. To convert it to PEM, you will need OpenSSL installed. You can download the Windows binaries directly from https://slproweb.com/products/Win32OpenSSL.html.

3. Once you install OpenSSL, simply open a command prompt and from the OpenSSL binaries directory (by default, C:\OpenSSL-Win32\bin), use the following command (you will be asked for the export password):
openssl pkcs12 -in C:\Temp\YOUR_CERT.pfx -out C:\Temp\YOUR_CERT.pem -nodes
4. Launch 'Notepad' and open the converted certificate (the .PEM file).
5. You should see something like this (private information erased for the purposes of this book):

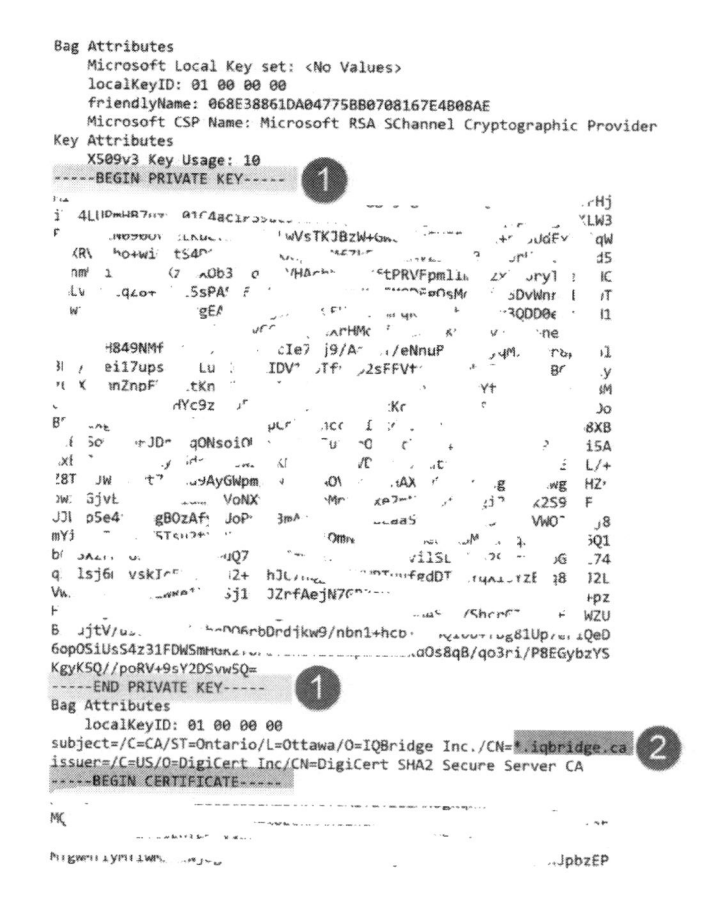

```
Bag Attributes
    Microsoft Local Key set: <No Values>
    localKeyID: 01 00 00 00
    friendlyName: 068E38861DA04775BB0708167E4B08AE
    Microsoft CSP Name: Microsoft RSA SChannel Cryptographic Provider
Key Attributes
    X509v3 Key Usage: 10
-----BEGIN PRIVATE KEY-----          ①

       [key data obscured]

-----END PRIVATE KEY-----            ①
Bag Attributes
    localKeyID: 01 00 00 00
subject=/C=CA/ST=Ontario/L=Ottawa/O=IQBridge Inc./CN=*.iqbridge.ca   ②
issuer=/C=US/O=DigiCert Inc/CN=DigiCert SHA2 Secure Server CA
-----BEGIN CERTIFICATE-----
```

6. Now you have to copy and paste the contents between '--- BEGIN PRIVATE KEY ---' and '--- END PRIVATE KEY --- ' (make sure you do include these two lines – marked with the number one), to a new Notepad document (blank). Save it as 'yourkey.pem'.
7. Repeat the same procedure but now for the contents between '--- BEGIN CERTIFICATE ---' and '--- END CERTIFICATE ---' (pay attention on this one. The 'BEGIN CERTIFICATE' line is the one right after the FQDN for this certificate, in

our case as you can see above, *.iqbridge.ca, marked with the number two). Save it as 'yourcert.pem'.

8. On the 'Simplify Printing TX' server (in our case this is the one, as it is where we installed the 'Simplify Printing TX' admin console), copy these two files to the folder 'C:\Program Files\Tricerat\SPTXAdmin' (you can see ours below).

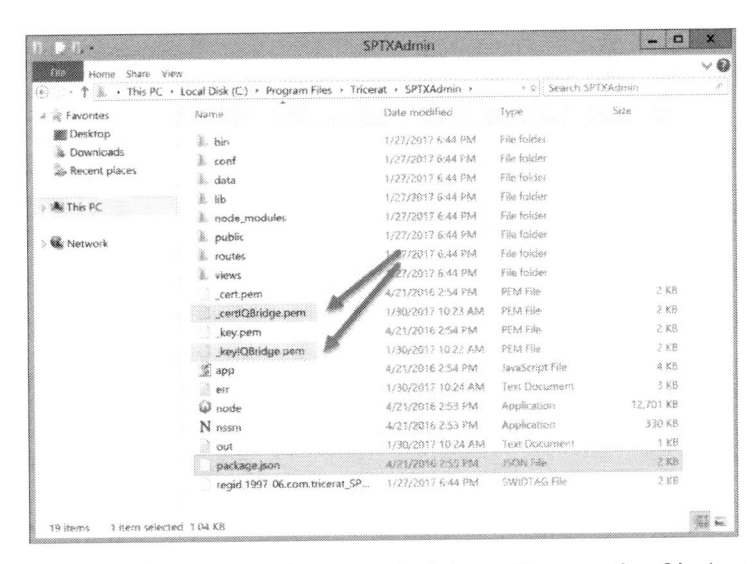

9. Under 'C:\Program Files\Tricerat\SPTXAdmin\conf' open the file 'sptx.json' with Notepad and under 'certificates' locate the names for the default certificates (_key.pem, _cert.pem) and replace these with the names of your two certificates you just created on Steps 6 and 7. Your 'sptx.json' file should now look similar to this:

10. Save the file and under 'Services', restart the 'SPTXAdmin' service. If you did create a DNS entry for your 'Simplify Printing TX' server (in our case we decided to use 'tx.iqbridge.ca' as already mentioned), you can now access the console directly at 'https://SPTXFQDN:8080' (https://tx.iqbridge.ca:8080 in our case).
11. The next step is to open port TCP 40404 on your firewall and point it to the internal IP address of your 'Simplify Printing TX' server.
12. The last step is to create the proper service location record. On your domain controller (we are assuming you do have DNS as part of your AD DCs) right-click your domain name (in our case 'CRLAB.local') and select 'Other New Records...'.

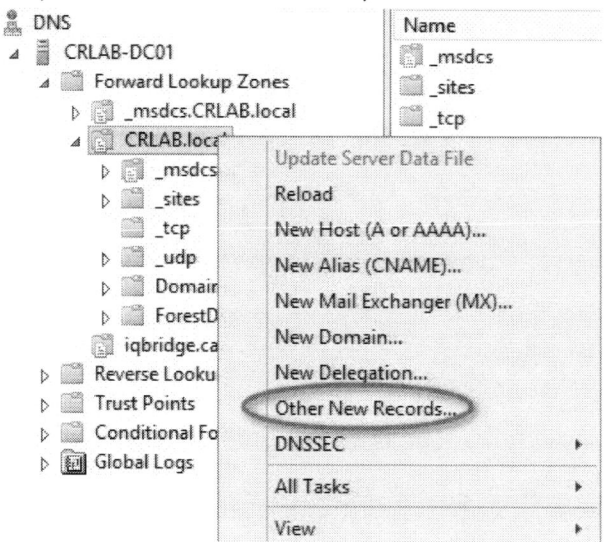

13. Select 'Service Location (SRV)' and click 'Create Record...'.

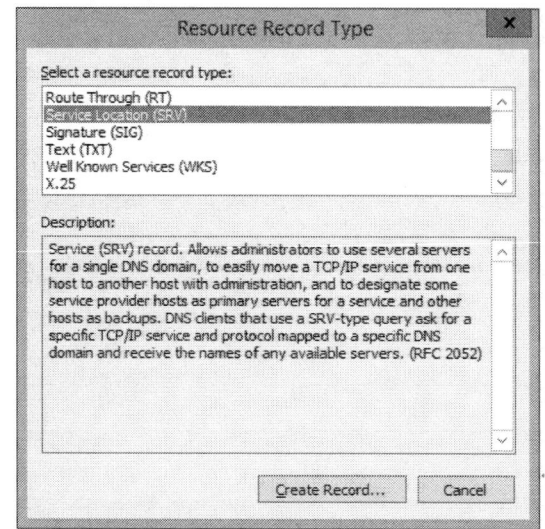

14. Enter the following under the appropriate fields and click 'OK':
    Service: _sptx
    Protocol: _tcp
    Port number: 40404
    Host offering this service: FQDN of your 'Simplify Printing TX' server. In our case, CRLAB-TX01.IQBRIDGE.local.

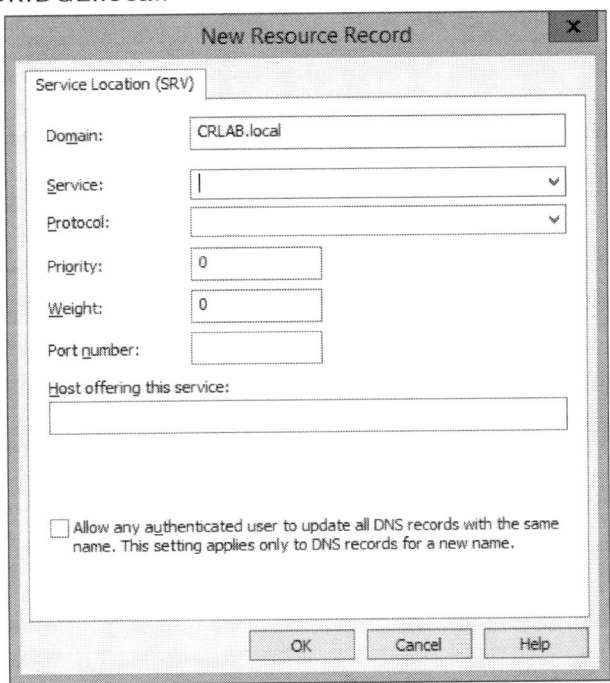

15. You should now see your SRV record.

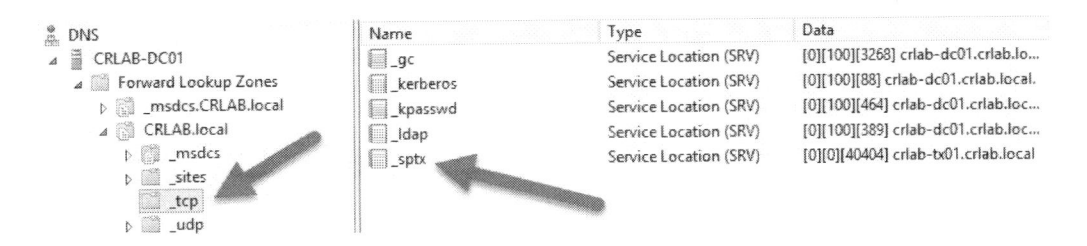

16. The reason you need this is simple. Once the 'Simplify Printing TX' agent is loaded on the RDSHs, by default it will run as soon as a user session starts and it will attempt to logon as that user, to the 'Simplify Printing TX' server. If this SRV record is not in place, the login will fail and the printers available will not be created under the user session. If users are connecting through a published desktop this may not be an issue as they would be able to launch the agent

GUI from the system tray and manually enter the server FQDN. Problem is, if only RemoteApps are in use, the GUI is not shown (this is a known issue on this release – Tricerat is working on a fix and should have it available soon) and the user cannot enter the required information to logon. Therefore, make sure the SRV record is in place.
17. You are now ready to start using this amazing product. Go grab a beer to celebrate.

Using 'Simplify Printing TX'

Now that your full 'Simplify Printing TX' infrastructure is up and running, how do we use it? How do I assign printers to users or to particular devices, exactly as we did using 'Simplify Printing'? Let's take a quick look at this and go over some simple scenarios.

The first one, let's assign a particular printer to a user, no matter where that user logs in. A follow-me scenario. For this we will use two test accounts ('testuser3' and 'testuser4') and the two printers we have on our print server, 'CRLAB-PS01'. As we did install the 'Simplify Printing TX' server agent on that machine, the two printers are now available under 'Simplify Printing TX'.

1. Logon to your 'Simplify Printing TX' server (in our case, 'CRLAB-TX01') and launch a browser (as the console is web based) and go to https://SPTX_FQDN_YOU_CHOSE:8080 (https://tx.iqbridge.ca:8080 in our case). You should see the web console. Enter your administrative credentials and click 'Login'.

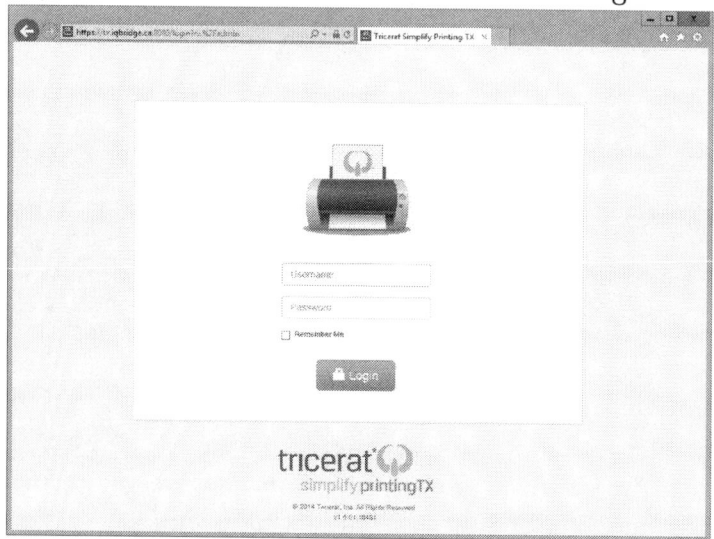

2. The home page should come up.

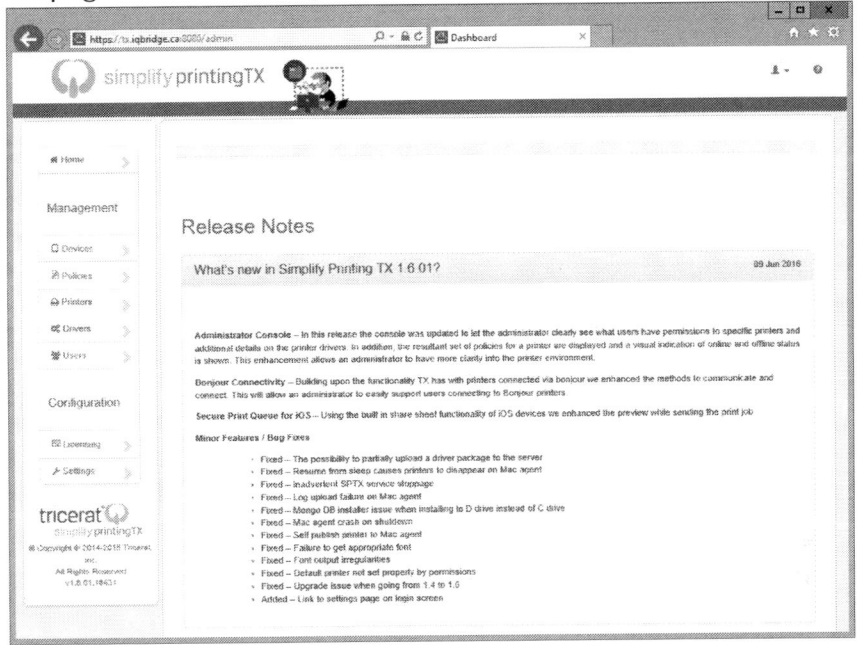

3. Before we go ahead and work on the scenario described, let's take a quick look at the web console GUI. On the left side, you can see the dashboard, showing us things like 'Devices', 'Policies', 'Printers' and so on. As we did install the 'Simplify Printing TX' server agent on our print server, we should see it listed under 'Devices'. It not only shows it but also which account is using that particular device (in the case of a print server, it will show the server FQDN)

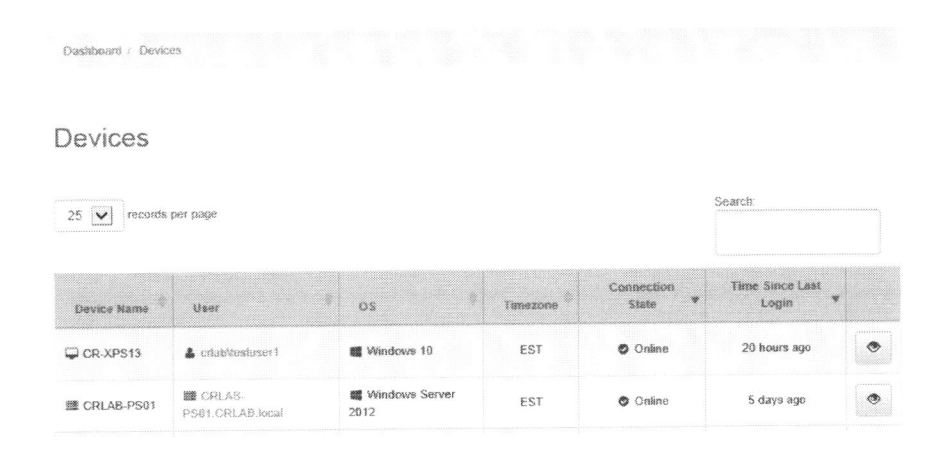

4. Now if we look at the 'Printers' section, it will show you all the printers available through the 'Simplify Printing TX' infrastructure. In this particular case, you can see the printers that came from my own laptop (listed as 'User Printer') and the ones from the actual print server (type shown as 'Print Server').

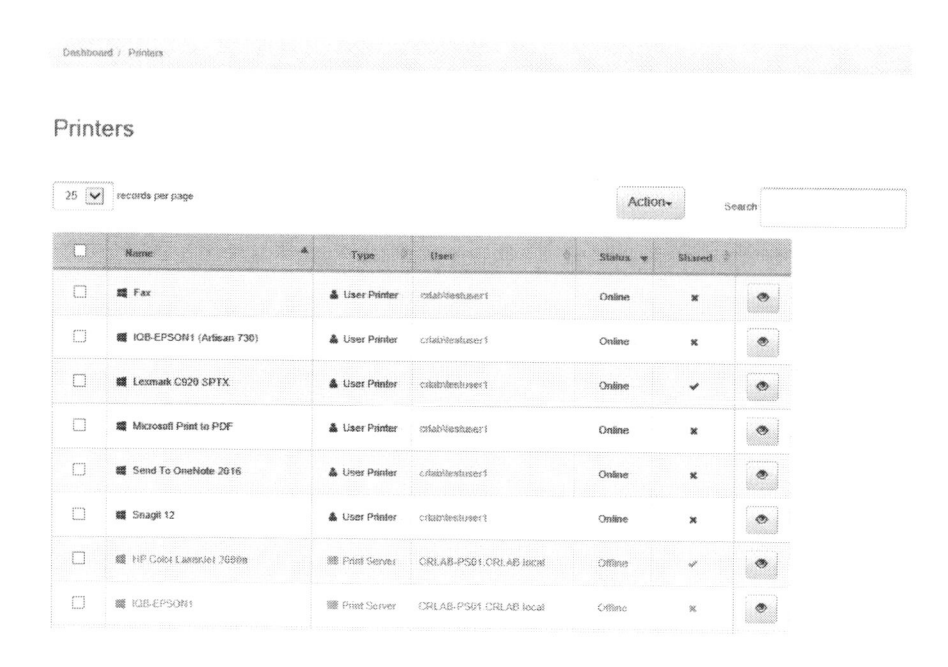

5. Under 'Drivers', as expected, it will list the drivers in use for the printers you have.

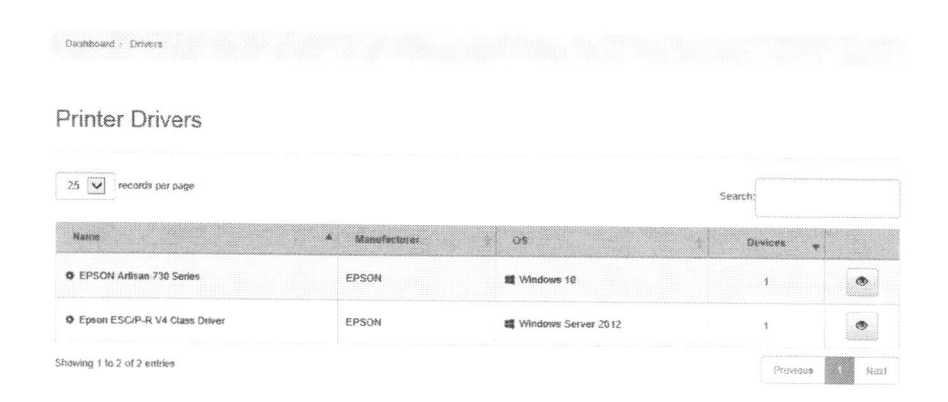

6. And as expected, under 'Users' you can see all the users that logged in to the 'Simplify Printing TX' infrastructure.

7. Ok this is great. But how do you actually assign printers to users? This is done under the 'Policies' section. Let's take a look at it and create our first policy, that will do the following:
    a. Assign the 'HP Color LaserJet 2600n' from our print server to the 'testuser3' account.
    b. Assign the 'IQB-EPSON1' from our print server to the 'testuser4' account.
8. To do it, under the 'Policies' section, click on '+New Policy'.

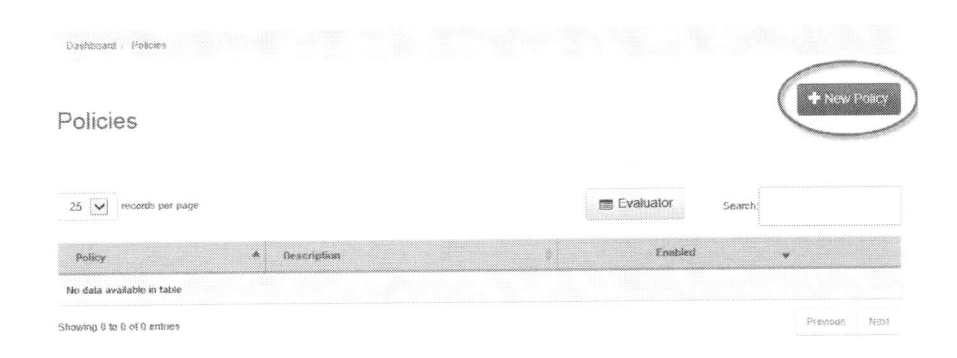

9. Give it a name and a description and click '+ Create'.

10. A blank policy, with the name entered, is created. As you can see these are divided into two different parts: 'actions' and 'conditions'. The first part controls what you actually want to perform (in this example, assign a printer). The second one controls when that action has to be performed (i.e. when logging in to a certain client). Let's do it for this particular case, assigning the HP printer to the 'testuser3' account. Click on '+Add Action'.

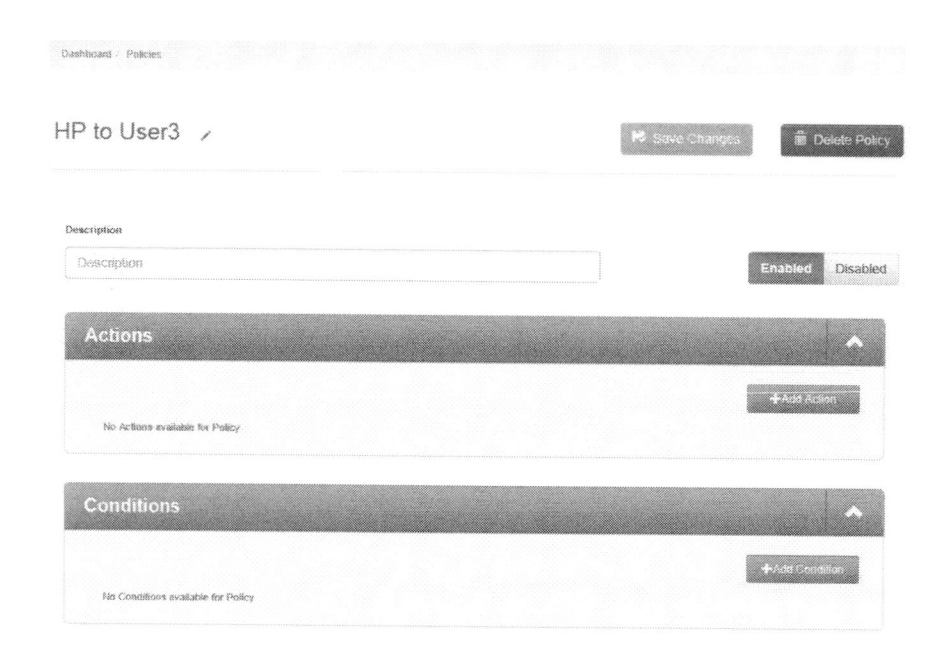

11. On the left list you select which action you want to perform, in our case, 'Assign Printer' and on the right one, the printer you want to assign. Finally, you click on the little checkbox mark to save that action.

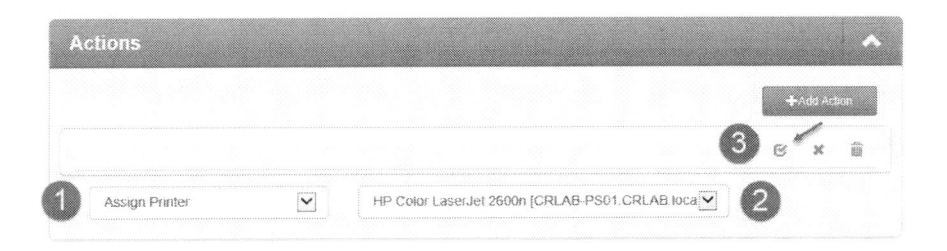

12. You should see it listed.

13. The thing is, as you may be wondering, you can indeed cascade multiple actions. In that case, the next logical step is to make sure that printer is set as the default one. One more time we click on '+Add Action' and select the appropriate options to make that happen.

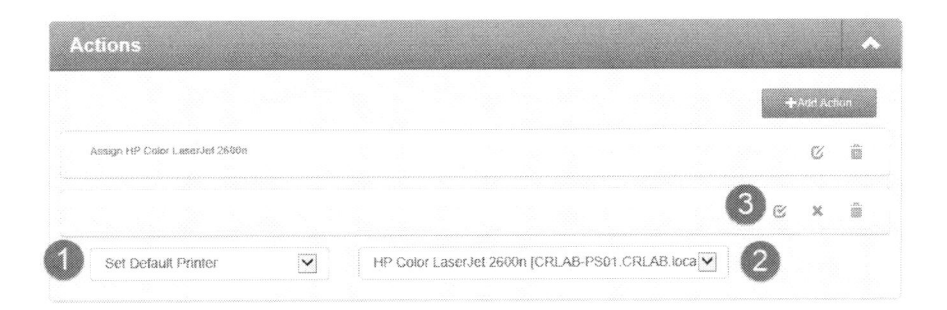

14. Perfect. This is exactly what we want to achieve.

15. The final step is to define the correct condition when the action we just created must be applied. Click on '+Add Condition'.

16. As before, we select the proper condition for this case (the user is our good old 'testuser3') and finally click on the little checkbox mark.

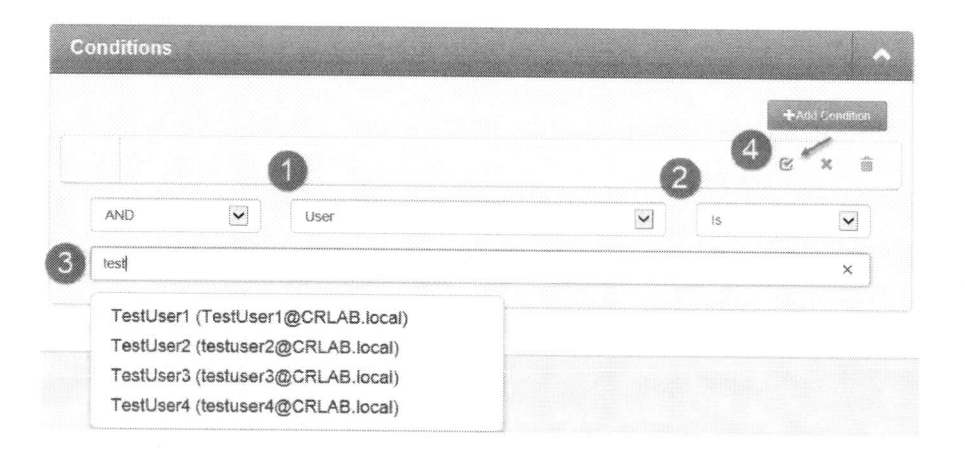

17. Perfect. Click on 'Save Changes'.

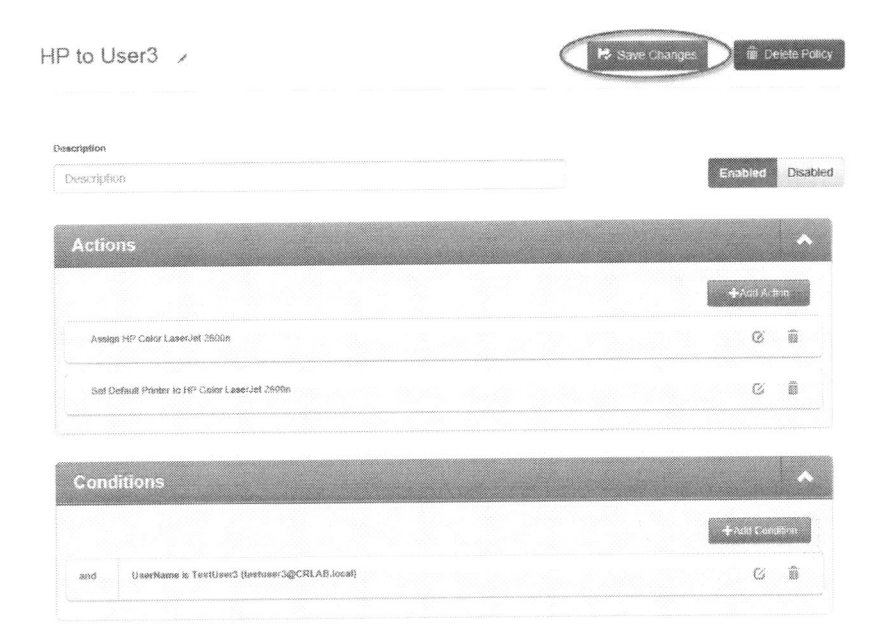

18. Time to test. Logon to your RDWA with the user account you selected under 'Conditions' and launch an application. Try to print and check which printers are available and which one is the default. Bingo! As expected, 'Simplify Printing TX' created the printer and set it as default for our 'testuser3' account.

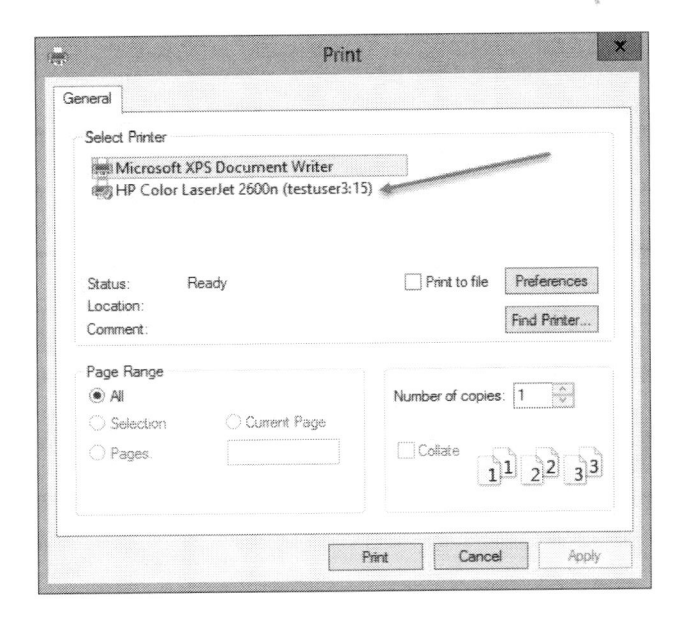

19. Now it is just a matter of repeating the exact same procedure but with a different action and condition. Once you are done, you should have something similar to this:

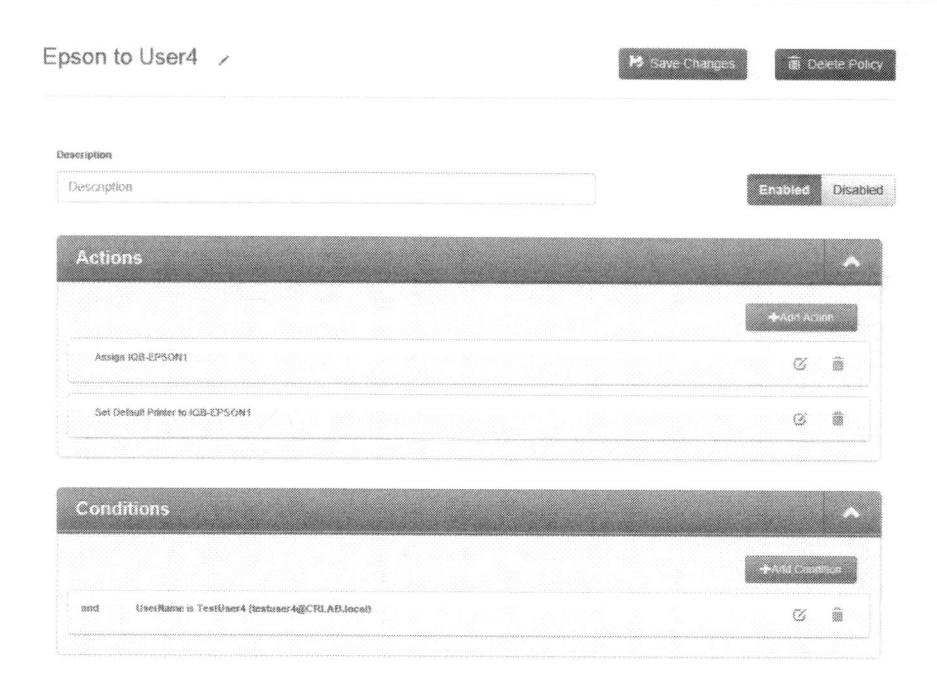

20. And as expected, listed under 'Policies', you should see the two policies we just created.

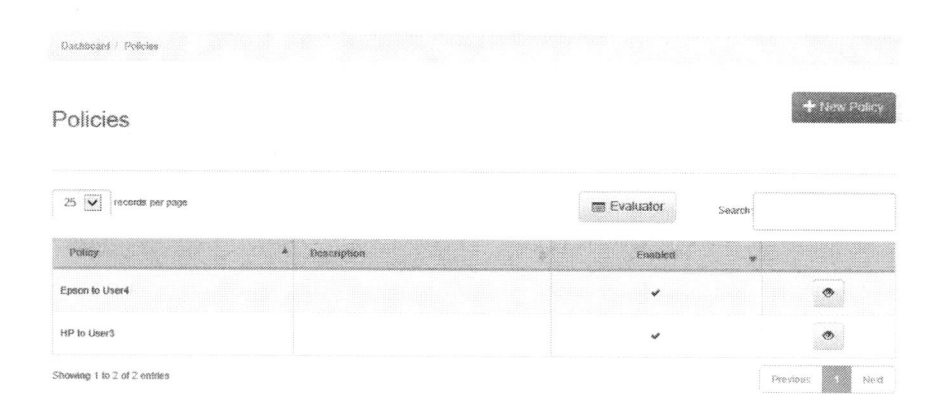

21. Of course, when testing with our 'testuser4', the results are exactly as expected.

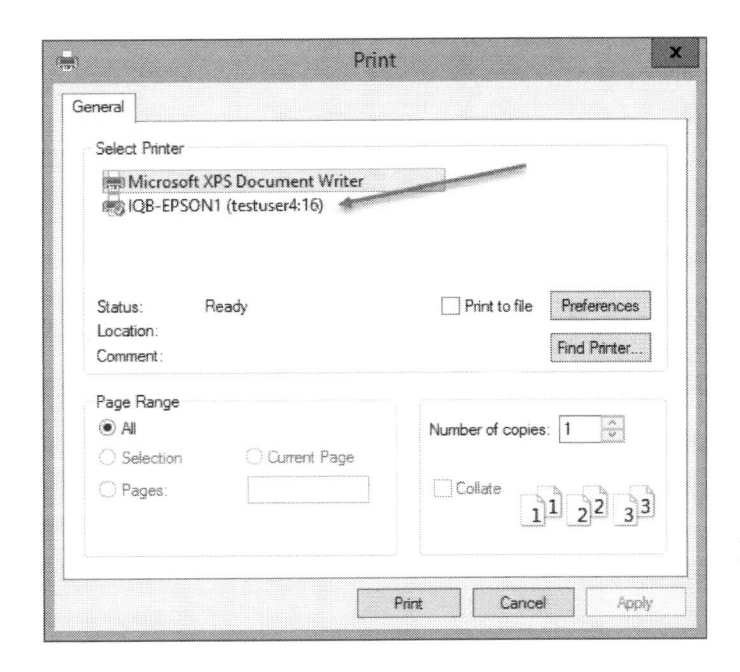

22. To wrap it up in grand style, let's get that other scenario going. The same one we used for 'Simplify Printing', where a doctor roams from room to room and always wants to print to the closest printer to the terminal he is currently logged in. One more time we will use our 'testuser3' and 'testuser4' accounts. When logging in to the thin client 'CRLAB-DC01' the printer assigned will always be the HP one. When using the 'CRLAB-CL01' endpoint, we will assign the Epson printer.

23. First step is to delete the policies we just created. That is simple. Simply go to the 'Policies' section on the dashboard, and click on the little 'eye' on the right (you will have to repeat these steps for both policies).

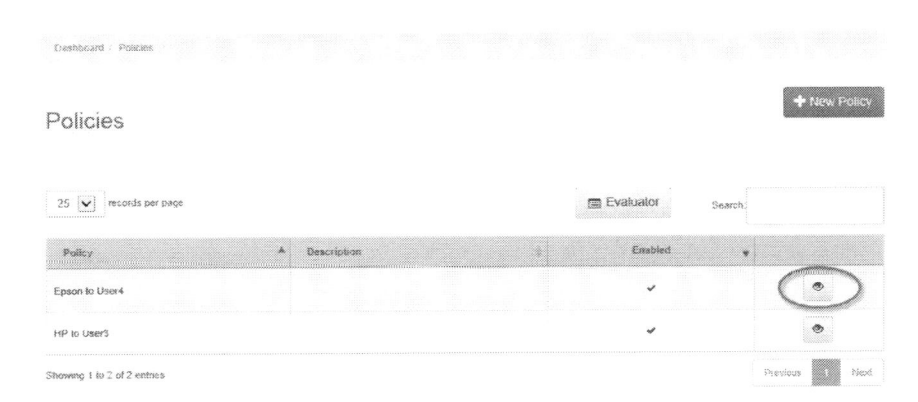

RDS - The Complete Guide | Page 377

24. Click on 'Delete Policy' and then 'OK' when prompted.

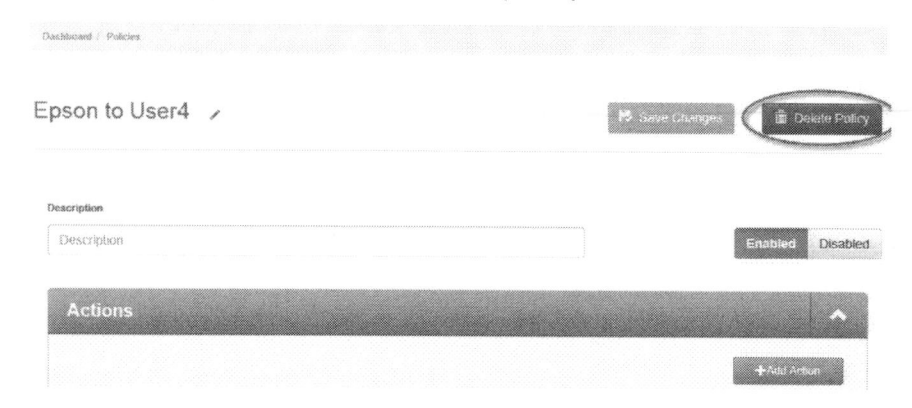

25. Time to create two new policies. The difference here is simply the conditions. If you did it correctly, you should have something similar to this on each policy:

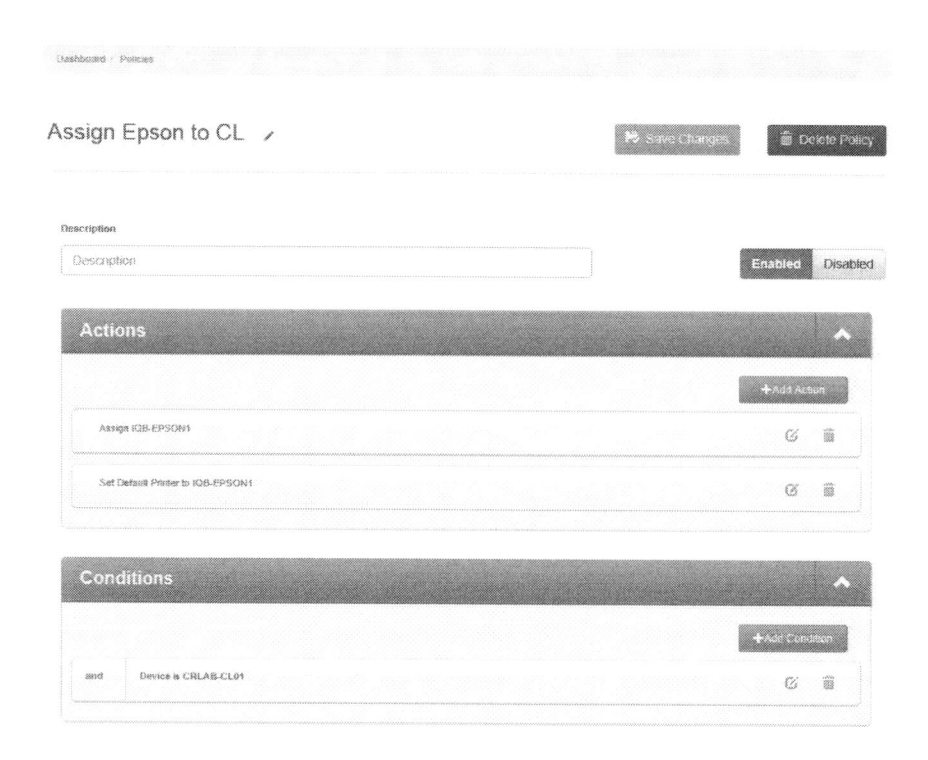

26. And you will then see both policies in the dashboard:

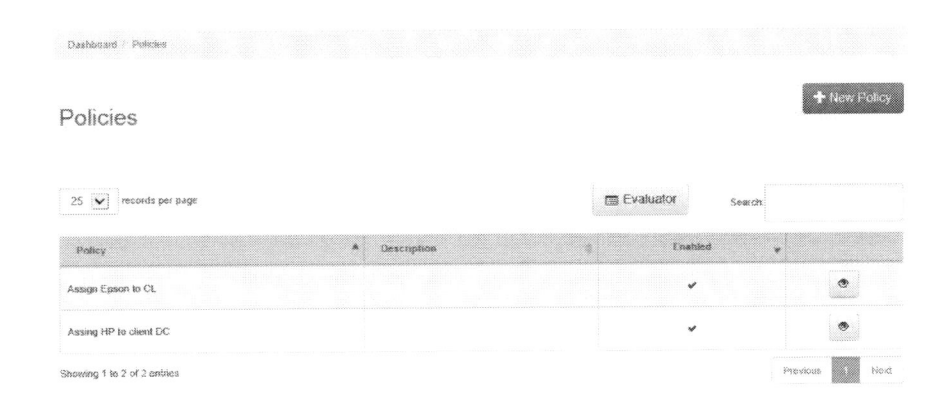

27. Time to test! If we log in using any account to any of these clients, we should see the correct printer assigned. When logging in from the 'CRLAB-DC01' machine, this is what we see, no matter which user is logged in:

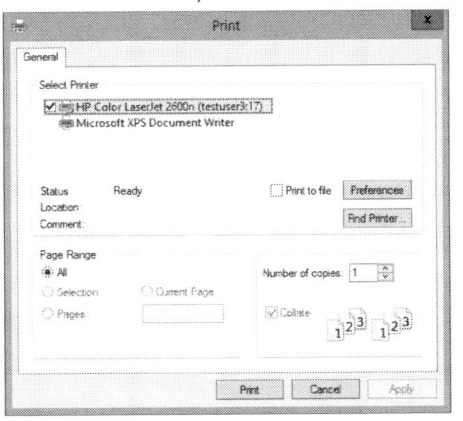

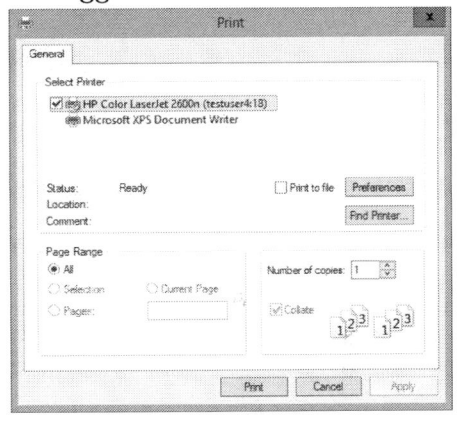

28. If we try to login from the 'CRLAB-CL01' client, this now changes:

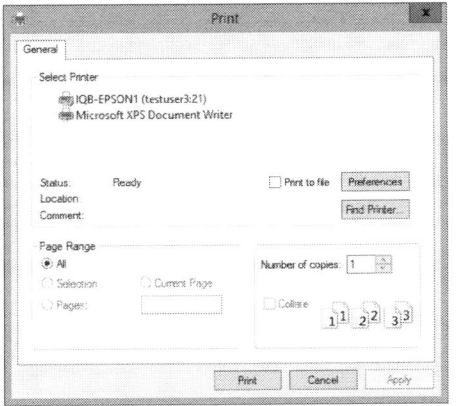

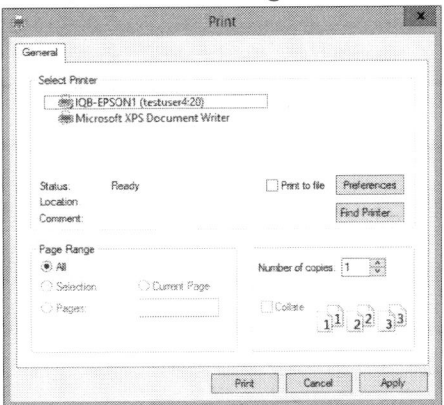

As you can see, the same scenario we simulated under 'Simplify Printing' is now working under 'Simplify Printing TX'. This may lead you to the question "In that case, can TX address all my printing needs?". The answer to that, as in many questions related to RDS in general, is "it depends". The reason is simple: it will get down to how many advanced features you do need for your network printers for example. Or if you do think 'Simplify Printing TX' is a more complex product to setup. Again, depending on needs and use cases, maybe 'Simplify Printing TX' will be able to deliver everything you required from 'Simplify Printing' while still handling all your mobile printing needs. I wish I could give you a more definite answer but that is not always possible. And more than that, this is a great reason to reach out to Tricerat directly! Now that you have everything up and running, I am sure they would love to hear from you.

Installing the 'Simplify Printing TX' Mobile Client

We got everything up and running. Everything working great when connecting to the RDS environment and with a single driver. Yes, you are not dreaming. Time to push 'Simplify Printing TX' to its limits.

In this final section, we will show you what can be achieved from mobile clients (in this case, Android but the same applies to iOS devices) and also from web applications (Google Apps). That is where 'Simplify Printing TX' shines in our humble opinion, opening up so many new use cases and scenarios. Therefore, time to get this done.

1. On your mobile device, go to the appropriate store and look for 'Simplify Printing TX'. It should show you the mobile client. Install it on your device.
2. On Android, it will add a new printing service under 'Settings' | 'Advanced' | 'Printing'. It should be listed and flagged as 'On'.

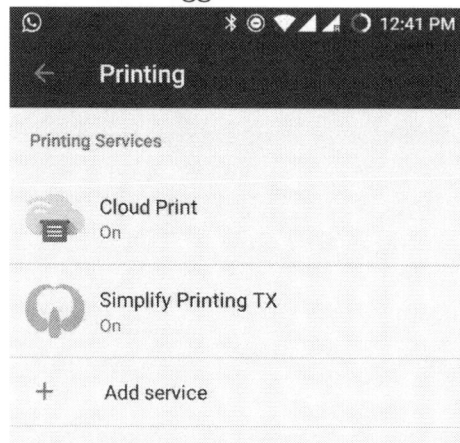

3. If you tap on 'Simplify Printing TX' it will prompt you for the login information (username, password and the server). As we installed the server as part of our domain, it will allow any of our users to authenticate but if no policies are in place they will see no printers. For the server name, make sure you use the FQDN you chose when issuing the certificate (as per everything we have showed you above – in our case, 'tx.iqbridge.ca') and also that you have the correct port opened at the firewall (TCP 40404).

4. Once you login, you should see all the printers available to you. These printers are coming from all the machines where you installed the 'Simplify Printing TX' agent (and logged in with the same account) or directly from print servers where the server agent was installed.

5. Now what? Well if you launch any mobile application that should have printing capabilities (i.e. 'Microsoft Word') you will be able to print directly from it. That means no matter where you are and from where you open your documents, these printers will always be available! The screenshot below shows 'Microsoft Word' running on Android, with a document ready to be printed to our 'HP Color LaserJet 2600n' we have been using in the book.

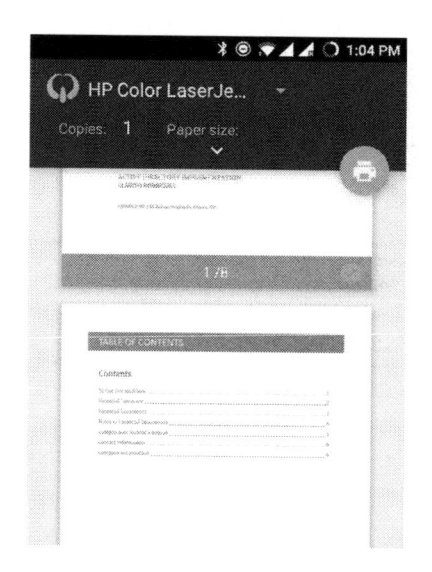

Again, this is what sets 'Simplify Printing TX' apart not only from its siblings but from the competition. This is an end-to-end printing solution that can not only simplify and stabilize your RDS printing environment (due to its single driver nature) but also take printing to all your mobile devices. But as expected, there is one final thing we want to show you.

Cloudifying your printers

On top of everything you have seen so far, there is one final feature I want to highlight: the built-in ability to share any printer that is part of your 'Simplify Printing TX' infrastructure with Google's Cloud Print service.

This allows you to logon to your Google account from anywhere in the world, on any device (owned by you or not, like an Internet kiosk) and print to all your 'Simplify Printing TX' printers. Yes, you read it correctly.

The craziest part about all this is how simple this integration is. In a nutshell, all you have to do is to select a printer and choose 'Register with Google Cloud Print' from the action menu. It will then prompt you for your Google credentials and you are all set! Let's see this in action.

1. Logon to your 'Simplify Printing TX' server console and on the dashboard, click 'Printers'. Click the printer you want to make available on Google Cloud Printing and then click the 'Action' button. Select 'Register with Google Cloud Print'.

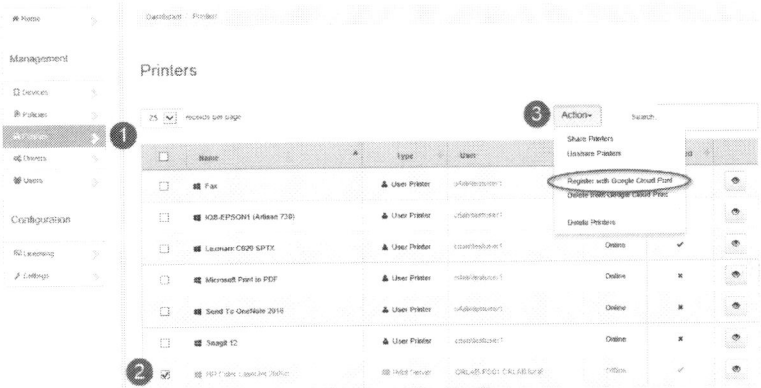

2. As this is the first time you are attempting this, you will be prompted with a message, asking you to click on it to finalize this operation. Just click where asked.

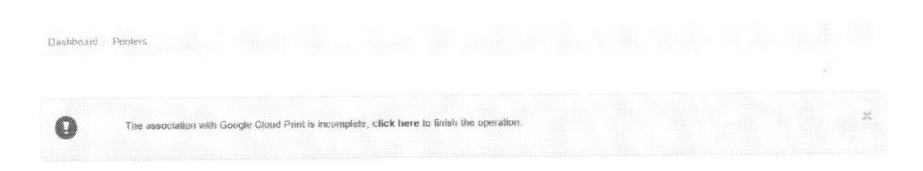

3. Your browser will launch and may prompt you to logon to your Google account. Once you login, you should see a similar message, asking for your authorization. Just click 'Finish printer registration'.

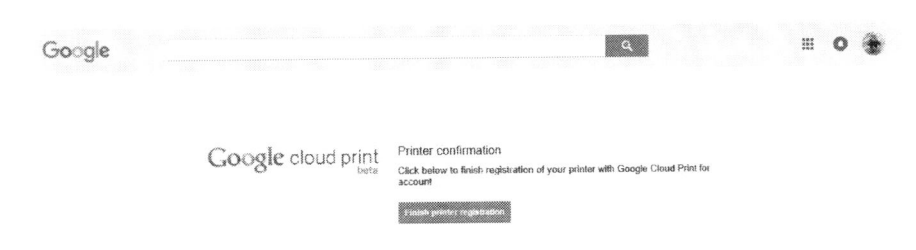

4. A message will show you the operation succeeded. That is all you need to do. This printer is now available from anywhere when you access your Google Apps.

> **Google cloud print** beta
>
> Thanks, you're ready to start!
> Your printer is now registered with Google Cloud Print.
>
> Manage your printers

5. If you did not notice, under your 'Printers', the printer you just enabled on Google Cloud Print now shows a little icon, to identify this was done.

6. The final step is to test this! From a completely different machine, located at a customer site in a far, far way land, I launched a web browser and logged in to my Google account. Guess what? The printer was there, ready to use!

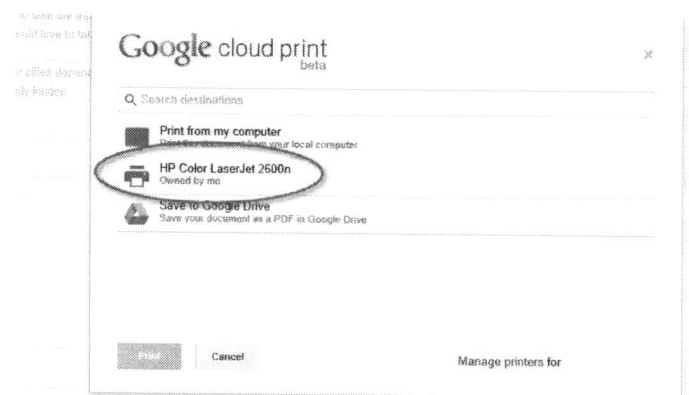

That is all we have for 'Simplify Printing TX'. Actually, that is all we have regarding printing. By now you should have a clear understanding of how printing works under RDS and the best practices around it. But more than that, we do hope you understand the limitations that come with the built-in printing mechanism and why products like 'Simplify Printing' and 'Simplify Printing TX' address all your printing needs and potentially more.

Connecting to the environment

So now you do have a fully functional RDS 2012 R2 environment. You know everything about PowerShell, how to deploy new RemoteApps and deal with UPDs. Great.

The thing is, to perform all these tasks, on your own or remote environments, of course you need to connect to these servers. This is done as you would expect, using the Microsoft Remote Desktop client.

The problem is, once you have several machines under your belt, and potentially several different environments, how do you manage all these connections? Trust me, a folder with '.rdp' files on it is not really efficient.

For that reason, several alternatives were created, including Microsoft's own 'Remote Desktop Connection Manager' that you can download here:

https://www.microsoft.com/en-ca/download/details.aspx?id=44989

Let's take a look at RDCMan and what it can do for you.

Setting up RDCMan

Once you download it from the link above, the next step is to install it. It can be installed on pretty much any OS (Desktop or Server). For the purposes of this book we will load it on our client machine, CRLAB-CL01.

1. Connect to the machine where you will install RDCMan and launch the installer (rdcman.msi).

2. The installer will launch. Click 'Next'.

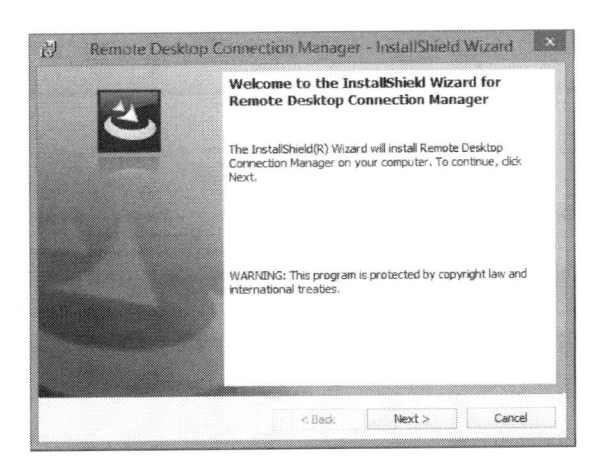

3. Accept the license agreement and click 'Next'.

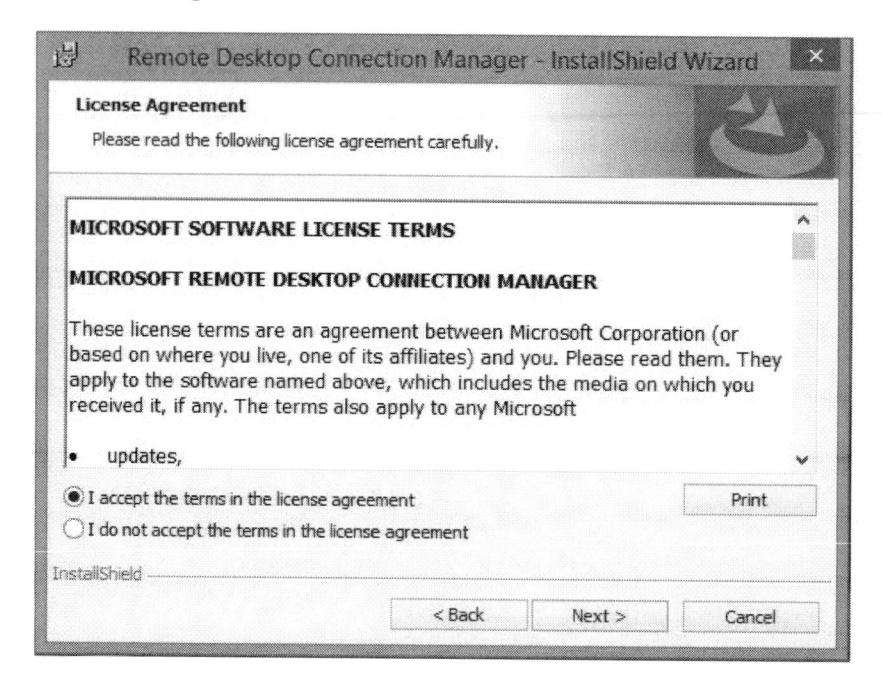

4. Choose a folder for the installation

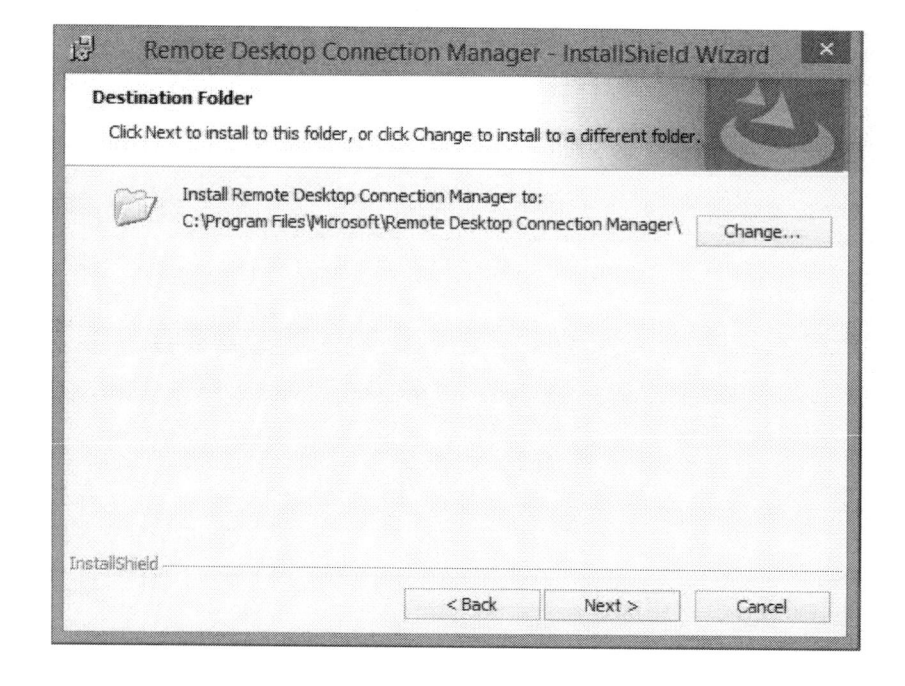

5. Review the selected settings and click 'Install'.

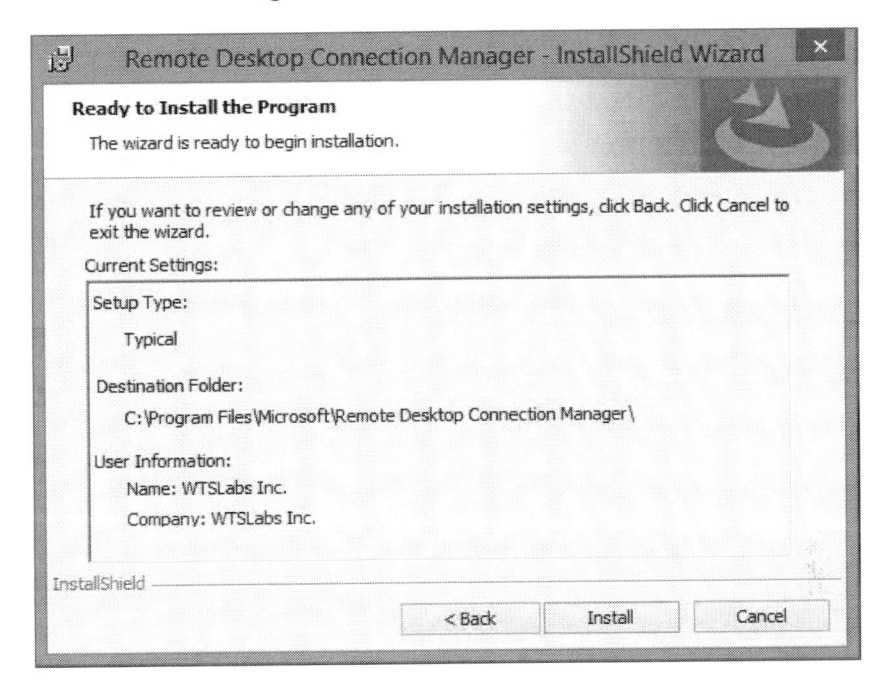

6. Click 'Finish'.

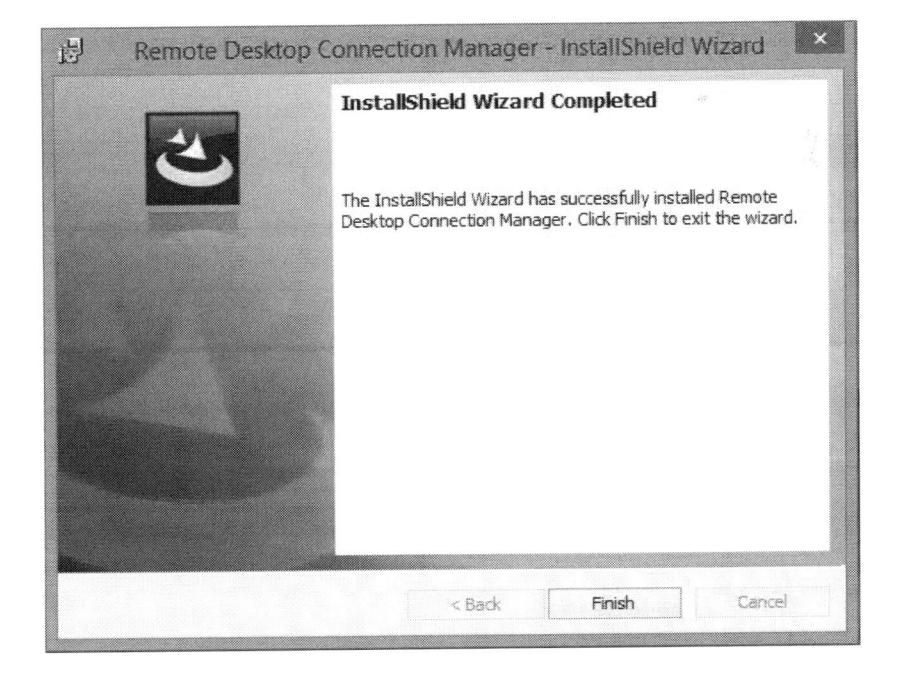

Using RDCMan

Just launch the shortcut created on the start menu, 'Remote Desktop Connection Manager' or create one on the desktop as shown below (it points to "C:\Program Files\Microsoft\Remote Desktop Connection Manager\RDCMan.exe").

The first step is to create a group, where all your connections will reside. Go to 'File' | 'New' and enter a name for the new group and click 'Save'.

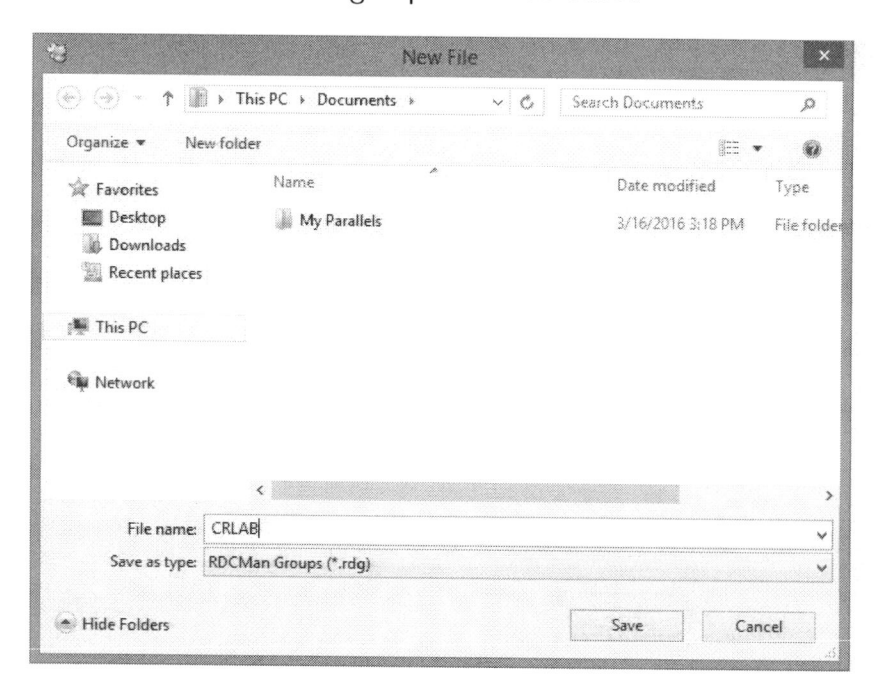

Once you have your group, under it you can have sub-groups (i.e. one group for your entire lab and sub-groups for each of the roles) and then under these the server connections. Credentials can be set for the group and be inherited by the sub-groups and servers. So for our lab we created sub-groups for the RDCBs, RDGWs, RDWAs and RDSHs.

To create a sub-group simply right-click the main group (in our case 'CRLAB') and select 'Add group...'.

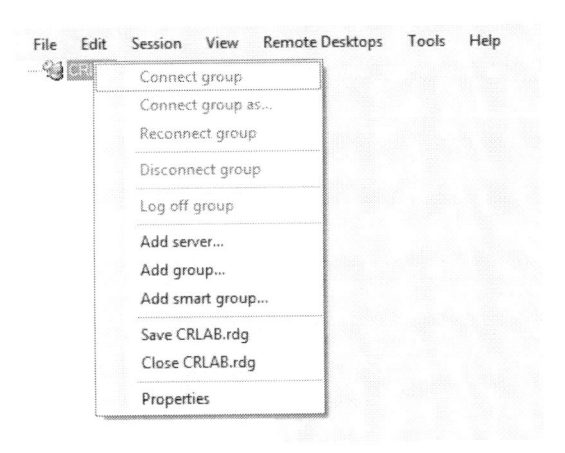

You should end up with something like this:

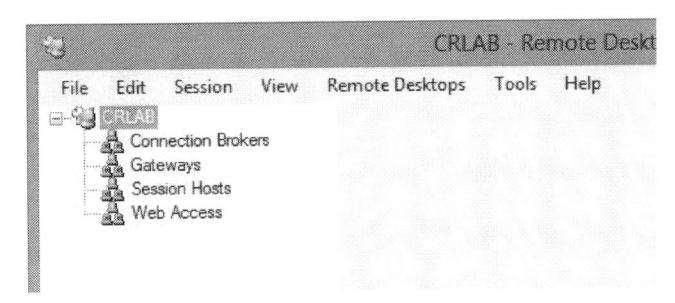

If you now right-click the top group ('CRLAB') and select 'Properties' you will be able to set the default credentials that will be inherited by all groups under it.

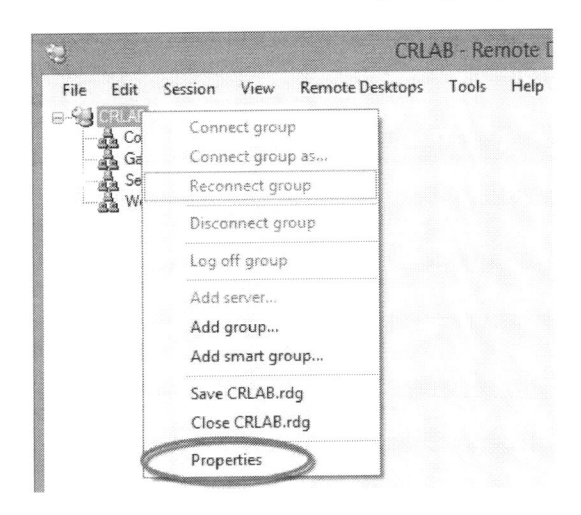

Select the 'Logon Credentials' tab and make sure you uncheck 'Inherit from parent' (as this will be the parent for all sub-groups under it). Enter the credentials for your environment and click 'OK'.

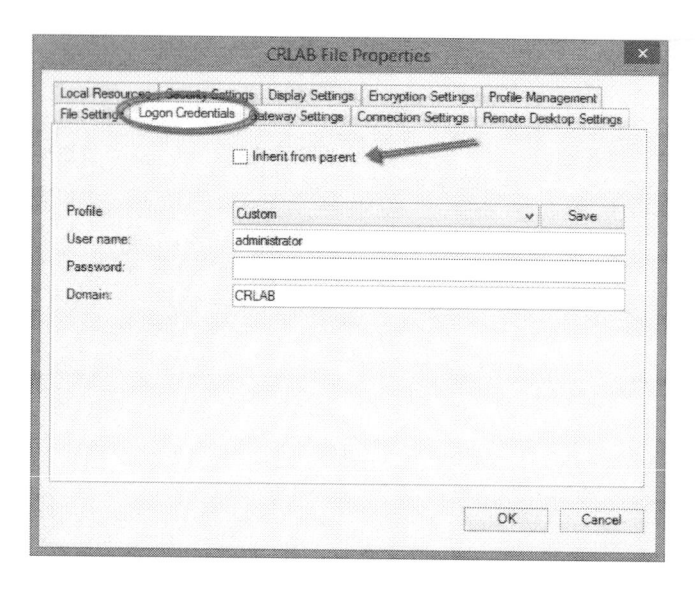

Now create a connection on the 'Connection Brokers' sub-group for your first RDCB. Simply right-click the sub-group and select 'Add server...'.

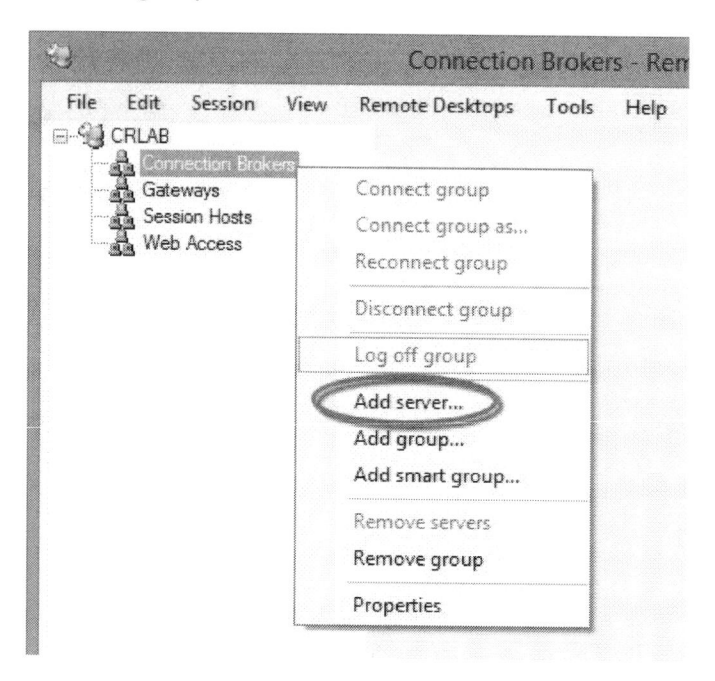

Enter the server name (or IP address) and click 'Add'.

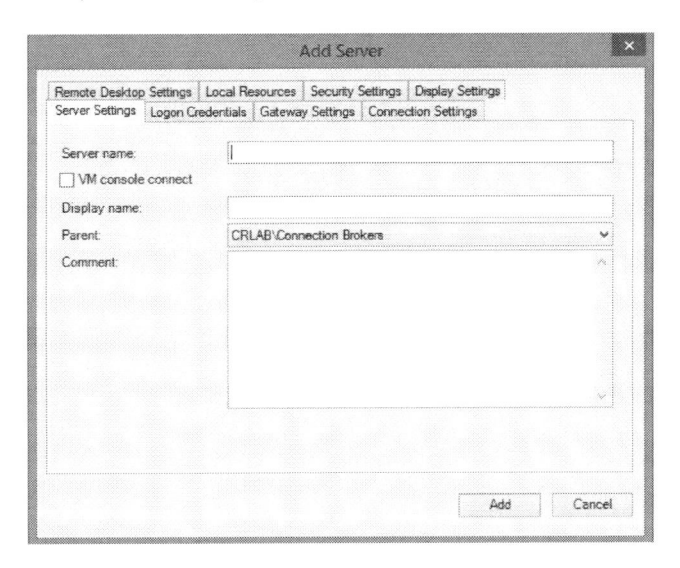

Repeat for all the servers on the environment and you should have something similar to this:

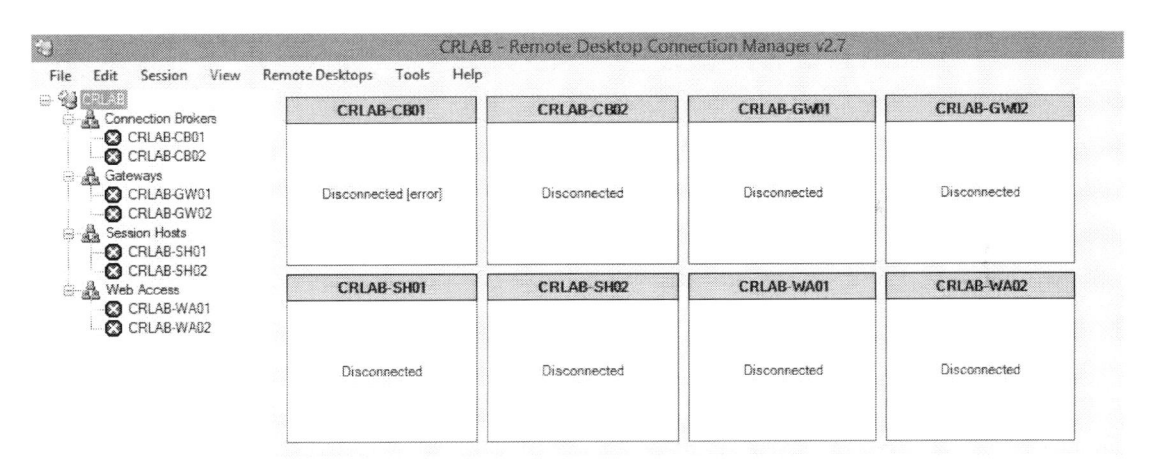

This is by far a much better alternative to simply creating '.rdp' files and storing these somewhere. With RDCMan you can organize your connections by groups (i.e. environments like PROD, TEST, UAT, etc) and define certain settings for each of these, that will be inherited by all servers in that particular group. Very neat, eh?

But that said, if you created the connections as we did above, you learned the hard way you cannot simply 'copy' and 'paste' servers or groups. More than that, what if you need to manage these from a different OS like OSX?

RDCMan provides the basic functionality and assumes you only need this on Windows. That is where better tools come to the picture and after testing and using many of these, we can certainly say the best of the breed out there as of today is for sure 'Remote Desktop Manager' from Devolutions. And that is exactly what we will show you next.

Devolutions Remote Desktop Manager

RDM for short, it was created to be way more than a simple 'RDP Manager' tool. Even after using it on a daily basis for over three years, we still find new capabilities within the tool. Before we jump on it and show you how to get it up and running and what it can do for you, it is worth mentioning the top features (according to us) on RDM:

- **Cross-platform.** This is a big one. Pretty much the same tool is available for Windows and OSX. You can easily export all the connections you created on one platform to the other. Very handy.

- **Location aware.** Ok you got all your connections to your environment created. They work great when you are at the office. Now you go home. If you are using RDCMan, you first need to somehow connect to your work environment (i.e. VPN) and then open the connections. RDM takes this to the next level. For each company under RDM, you can specify what type of VPN you need to use and the credentials for these. RDM will then detect if it can reach the servers directly or not and if not, will automatically open the correct VPN client, pass your credentials and establish the connection to the servers. Does not get easier than that.

- **Connects to anything.** Seriously. If you can think of one type of connection, RDM can handle it. RDP, ICA, SSH, FTP, anything really. All Cloud connectors are there (AWS, Azure, etc). It is that good. Some I do not even know people that actually use them like 'HP Remote Graphics Receiver'.

- **Centralized repository.** Depending on your needs you can store all your connections in the cloud (encrypted of course – and the best part, completely FREE for a single user) and for enterprise environments, a centralized database is supported. So different teams can share a common repository of connections and credentials. Of course these can be filtered by Active Directory groups/users.

- **Free Edition.** The icing on the cake is the fact there is a free edition available that is pretty good. Sure it may lack some of the features seen on the 'Enterprise' version but beats RDCMan hands down. Also if you are a Microsoft MVP, Citrix CTP or VMware vExpert, guess what? You can get a free license for the 'Enterprise' version, and we will show you how to do it.

So enough of talking how great RDM is. Let's get it up and running and show you how it is done by the PROs. ☺

Setting up Devolutions RDM

First, we need to get the tool. Devolutions created this special download page for you, readers of this amazing book. The QR code below gets you to the landing page with the download link and more than that, instructional videos in case you want to master RDM beyond the basics.

Once you download it from the code above (get the 'Enterprise' version, trial is good for thirty days), the next step is to install it. It can be installed on pretty much any OS (Desktop or Server). For the purposes of this book, as we did with RDCMan, we will load it on our client machine, CRLAB-CL01.

1. Download RDM from the link above and launch its installer. Click 'Next'.

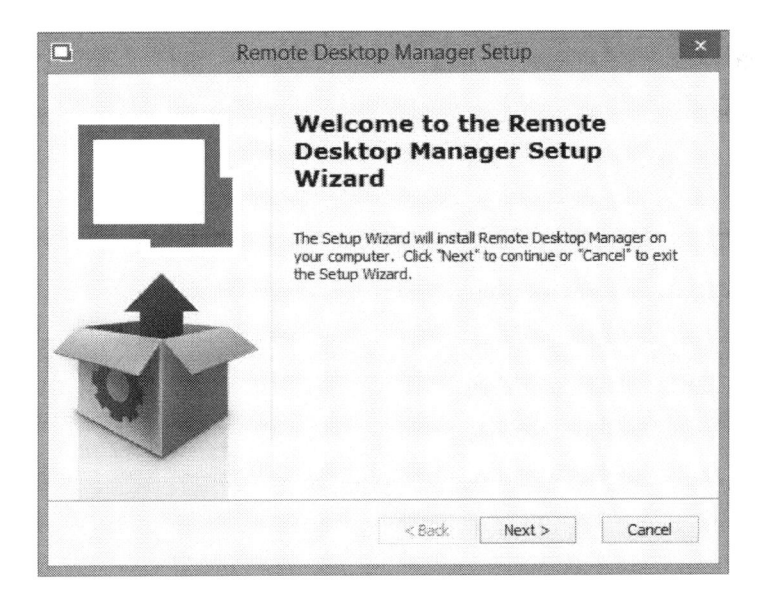

2. Click 'Typical'.

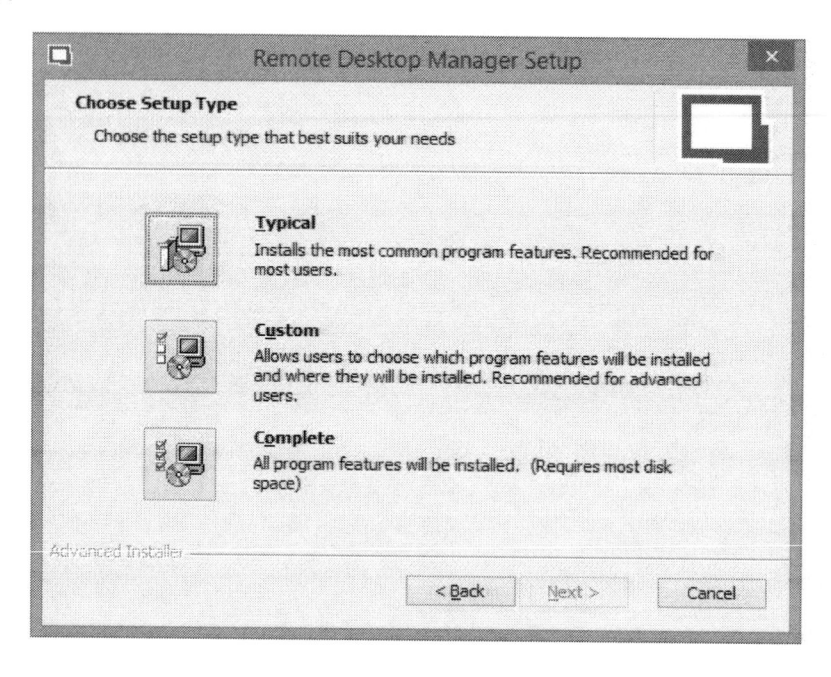

3. By default, the installer will create shortcuts on the desktop and on the start menu folder. If you are ok with that, click 'Next'.

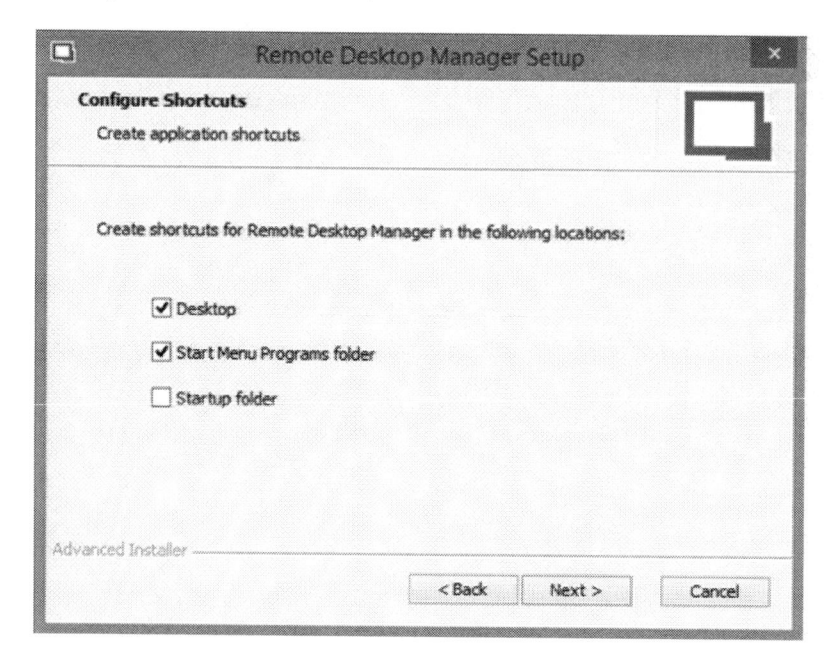

4. RDM can take over the '.rdp' file associations if you want, what we do recommend if this is a management machine. Click 'Next'.

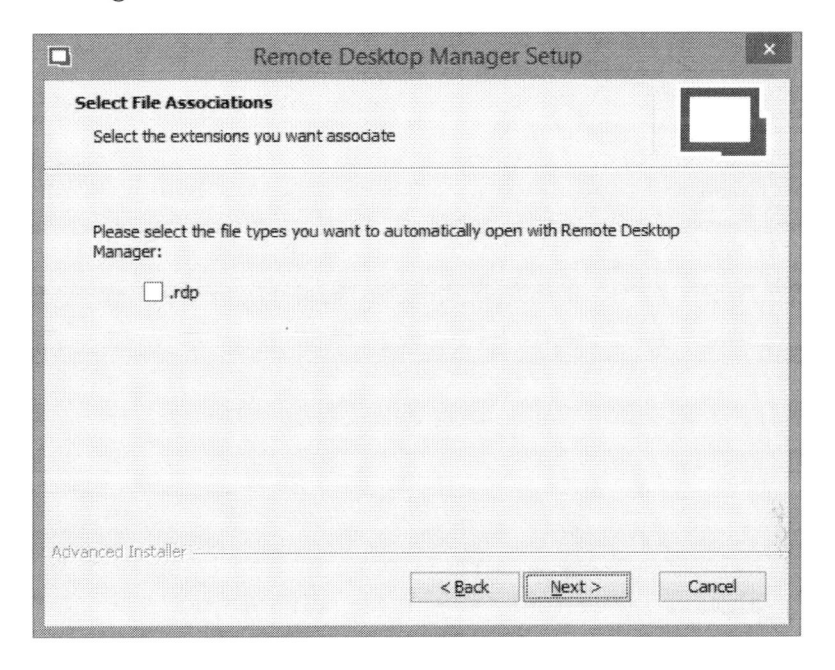

5. Accept the license agreement and click 'Next'.

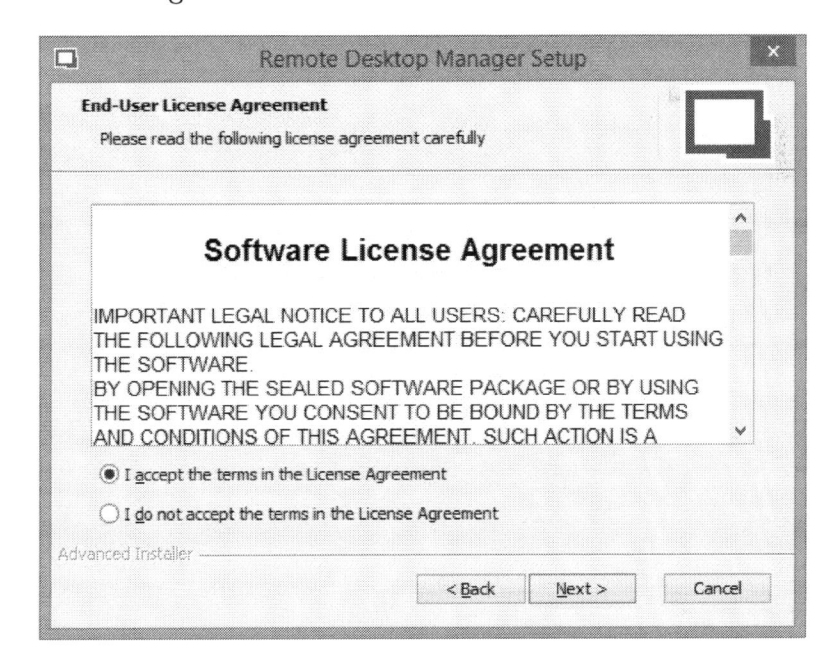

6. We are now ready for the installation. Click 'Install'. The installer will install any required pre-requisites and will prompt you to accept these accordingly.

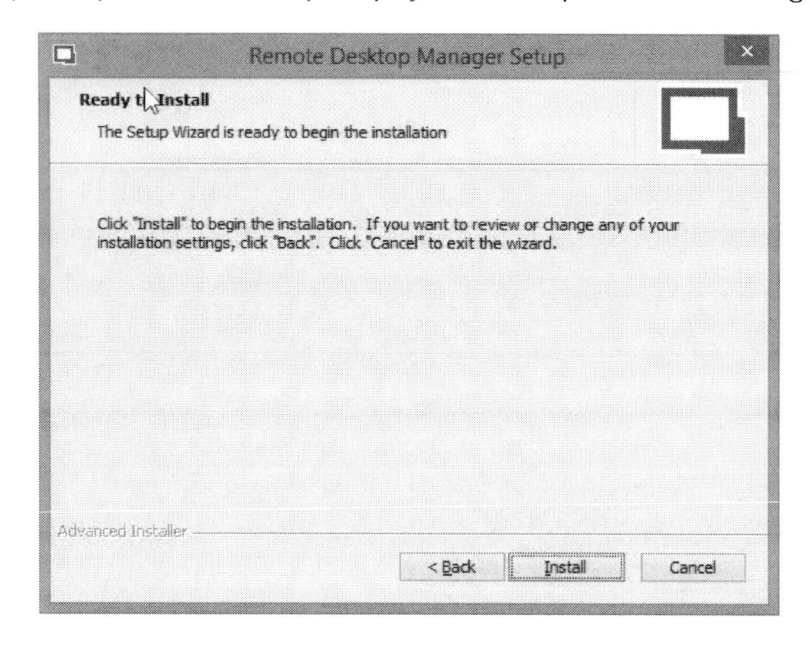

7. All done. Click 'Finish'.

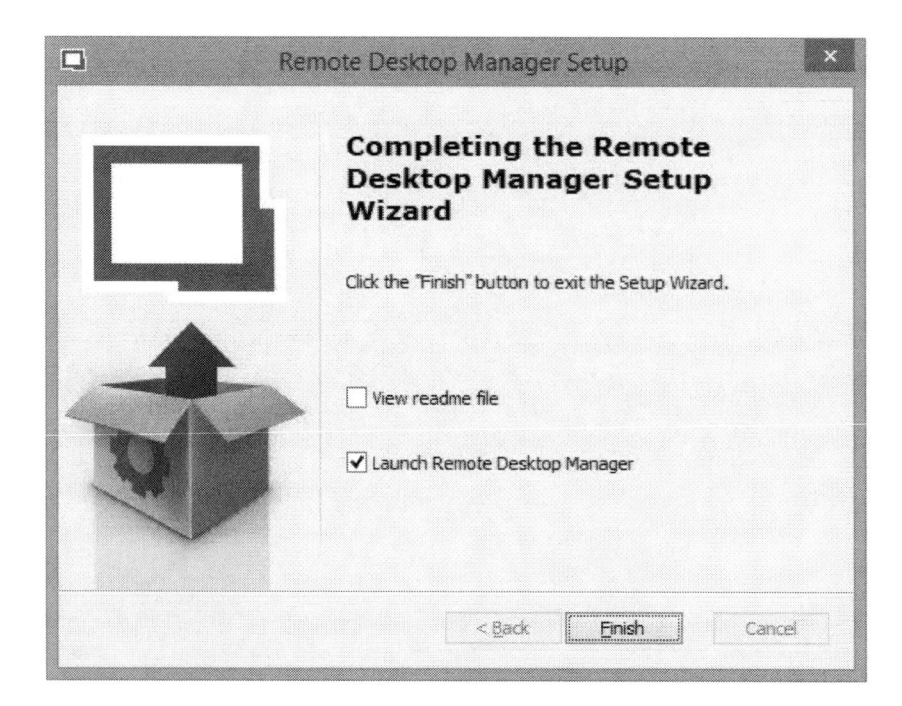

Using Devolutions RDM

Once the installation finishes, RDM will launch. As we mentioned before, RDM can store all your connections in the cloud (the 'Devolutions Cloud') and at no cost, when used in a single user mode (if you want to have a team of people, all working off the same connections, this requires a yearly fee). This allows you to seamlessly access all your connections from all devices you may have (even iOS and Android). So, the first step is to get your online account setup.

'Devolutions Cloud' account setup

1. Launch RDM and click 'File'.

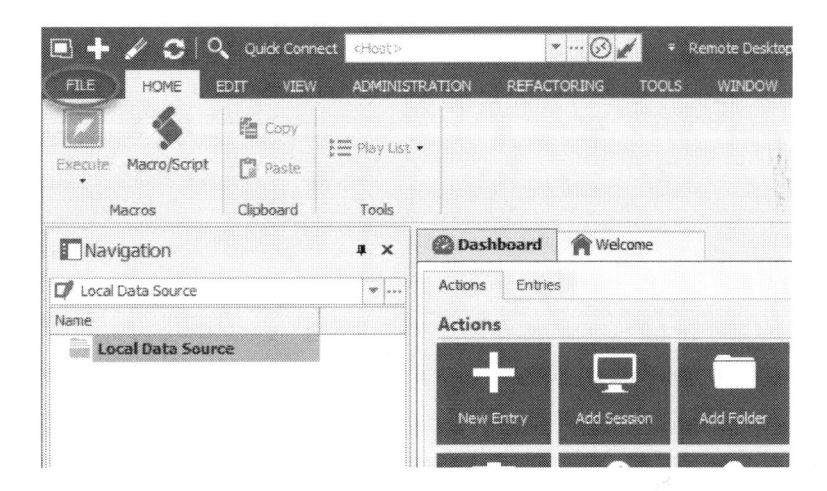

2. Now go to 'Cloud Account' and select 'Create a New Cloud Account'.

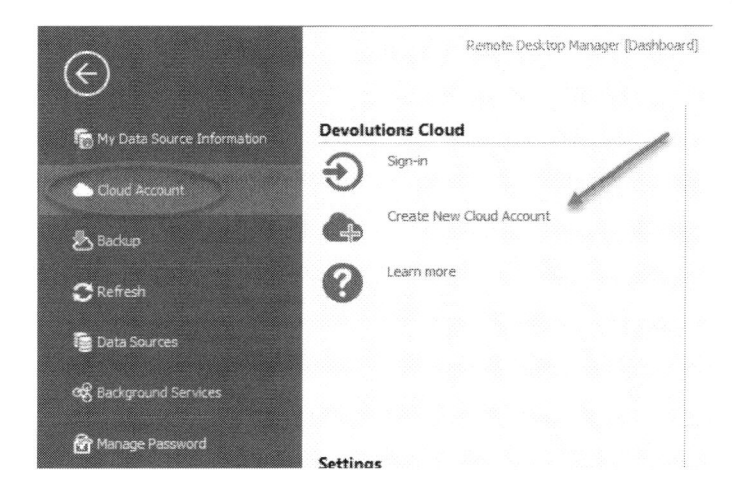

3. Enter all the required information and click 'OK'.

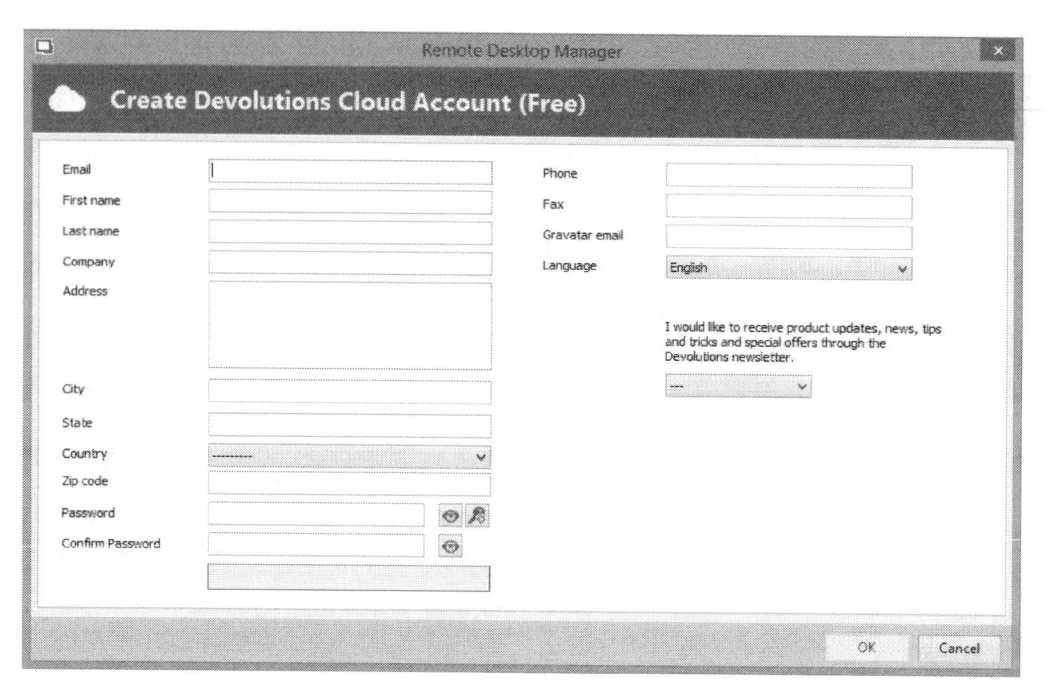

4. You should receive on-screen confirmation that everything worked as expected.

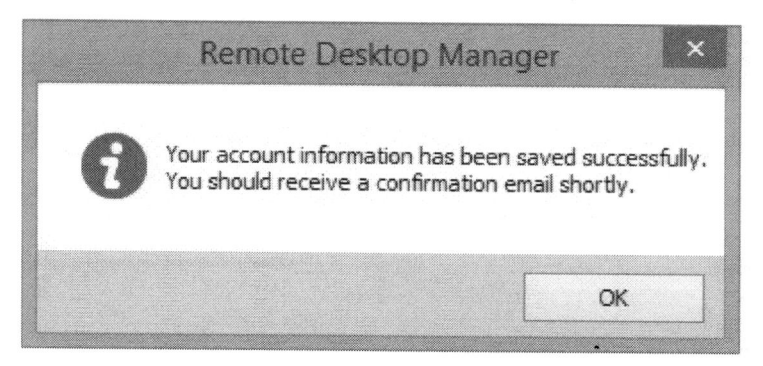

5. Make sure you confirm your email address (you should receive an email from infos@devolutions.net - if you do not see one, check your spam folder).

6. Now that you have your account on the 'Devolutions Cloud', click 'Sign-in'.

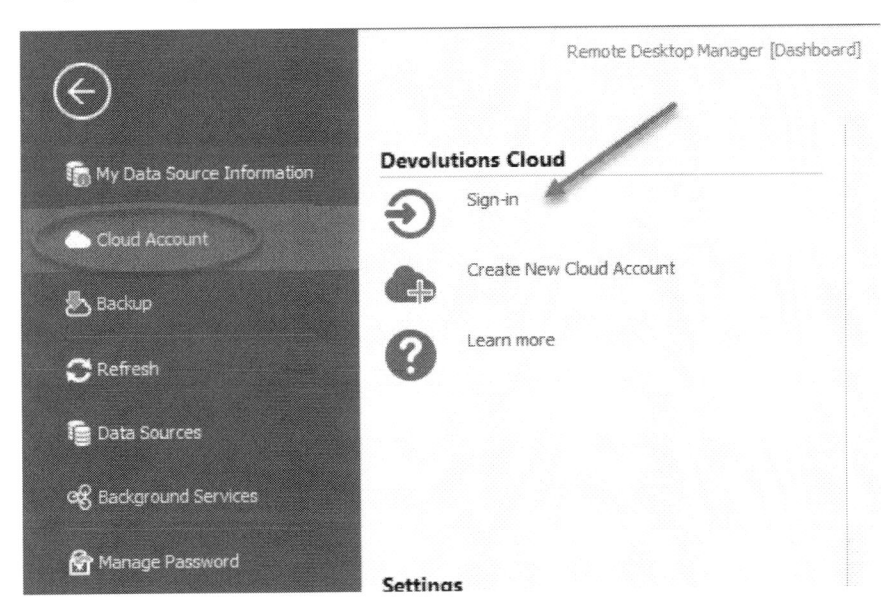

7. RDM will now show you are online and give you the option to sign-out.

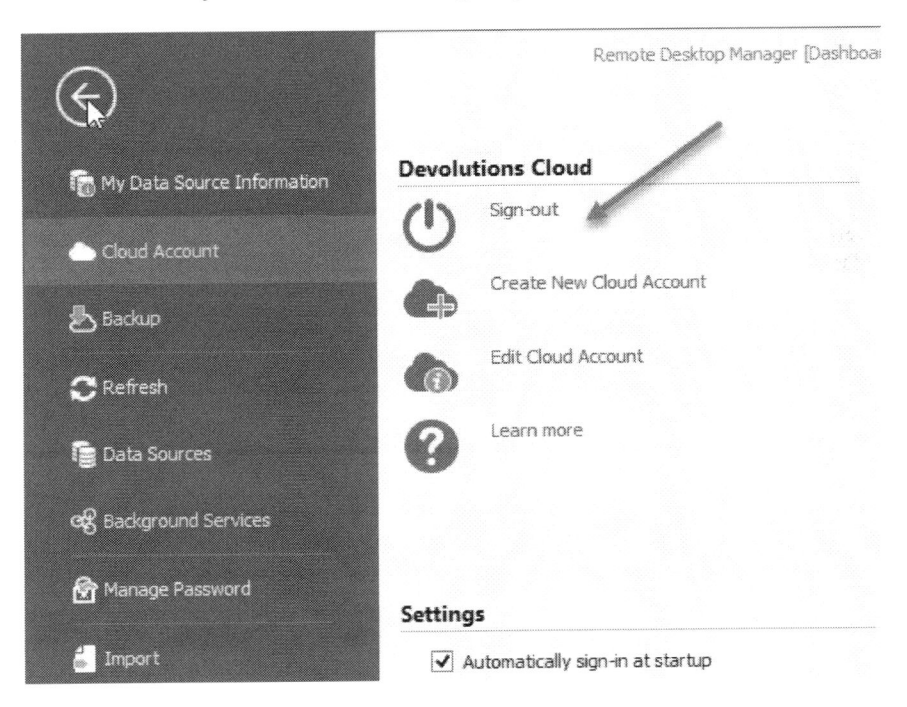

8. You are now done with the 'Devolutions Cloud' account.

Creating connections on Devolutions RDM

RDM is now installed and we do have an online account setup and verified. Great. The next natural step is to start creating your connections. As mentioned before, RDM can handle pretty much any known-to-man connection type (seriously) and the best part, can import these from several other applications, including the old-fashioned '.rdp' files.

But as we are not that old-fashioned, we will use one of the coolest features on RDM: the ability to scan a subnet and create the connections for us for the devices found on the network.

To perform this task, follow these steps:

1. Click on the 'File' menu.

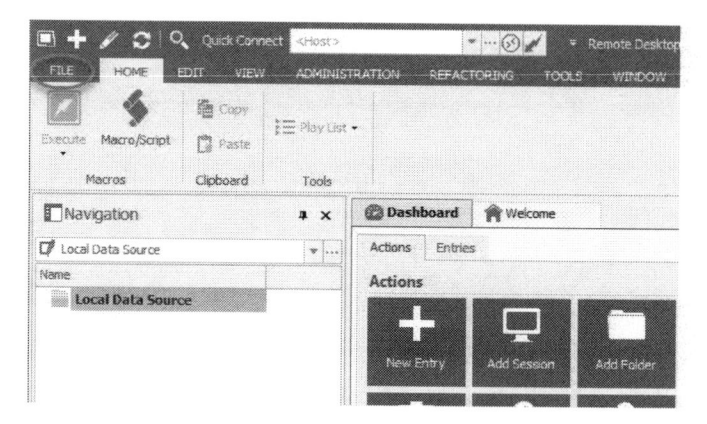

2. Select 'Import' and click on 'Import with Network Scan'.

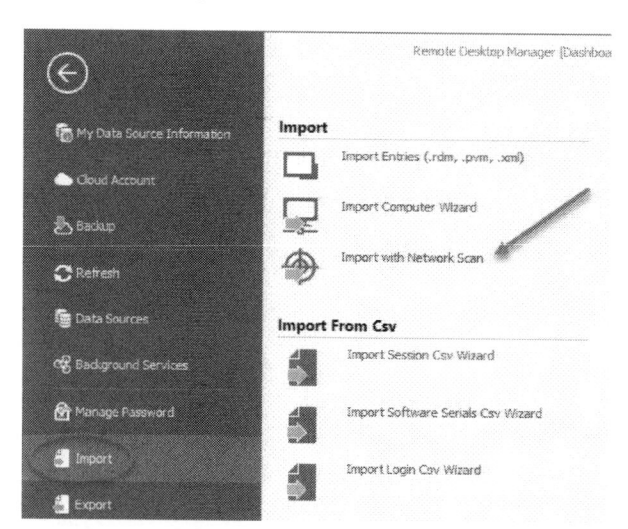

3. Enter the IP range for the RDS servers and make sure you uncheck 'Ping before scan' (unless you have ping enabled) and click 'Scan'.

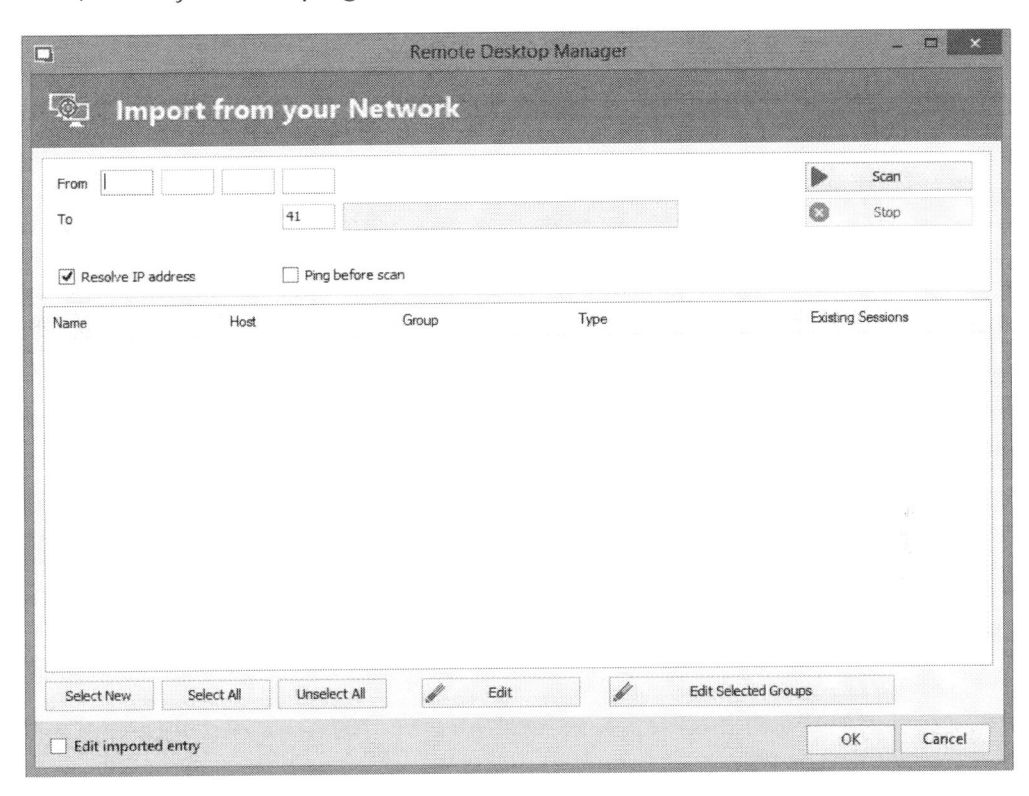

4. After a couple minutes RDM shows you the list of machines it found for that particular IP range.

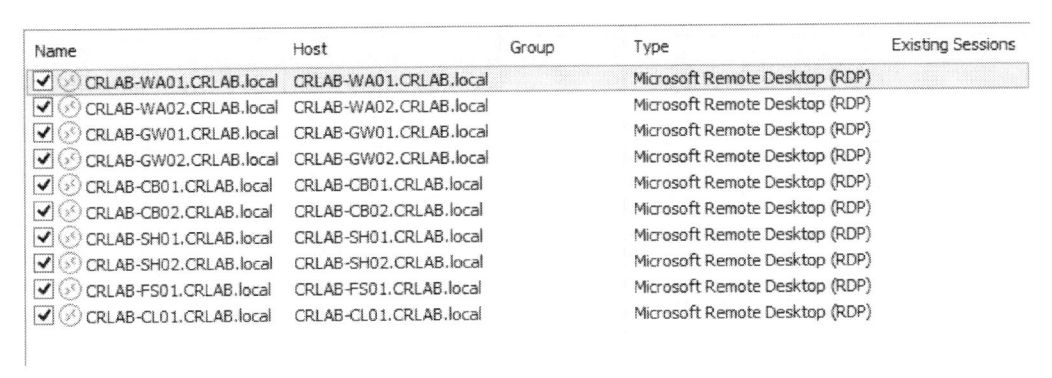

5. Click 'OK'. You now have all your connections under 'Sessions'.

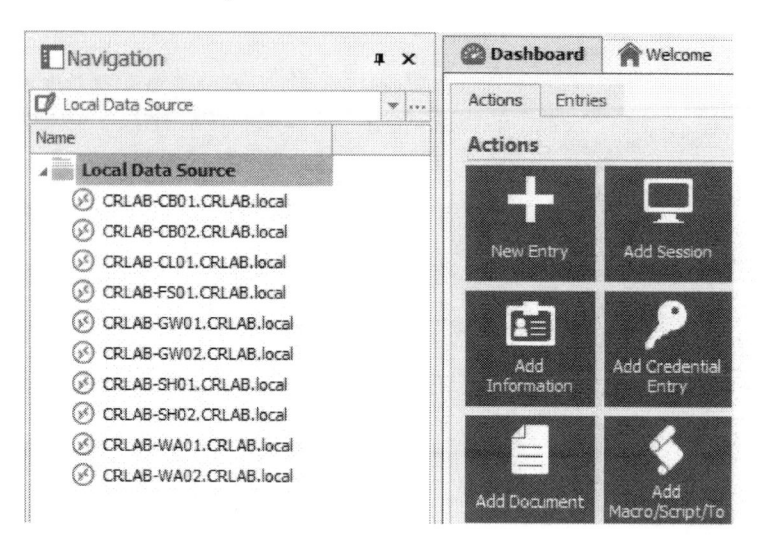

6. Now if you double click on any entry you will notice RDM will prompt you for credentials. That is why we do not have these connections that were just imported by the scanner, inheriting credentials from a parent object. Let's take care of this.

7. Right-click 'Local Data Source' and select 'New Entry'.

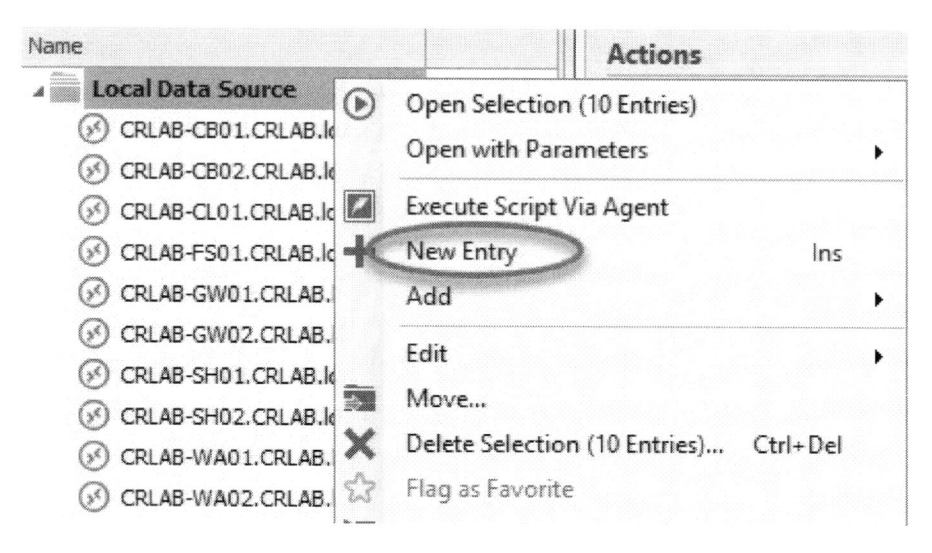

8. Under 'Folder', select 'Site' and click 'OK'.

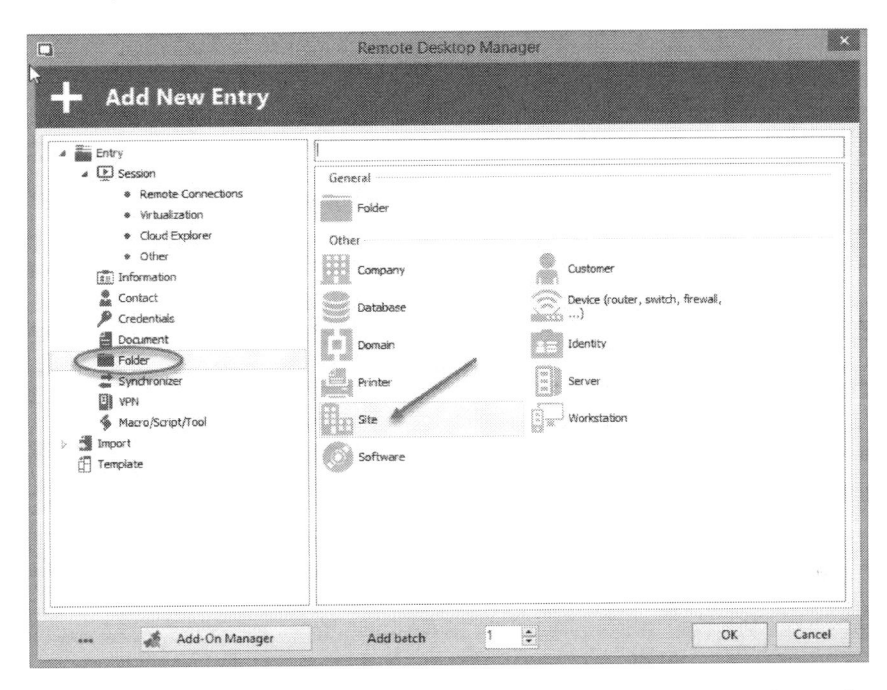

9. Enter a name for the site (in our case, 'CRLAB') and the credentials (under 'Details') that will be used for all the servers under this particular site. If you want, click on the icon to customize it. Click 'OK'.

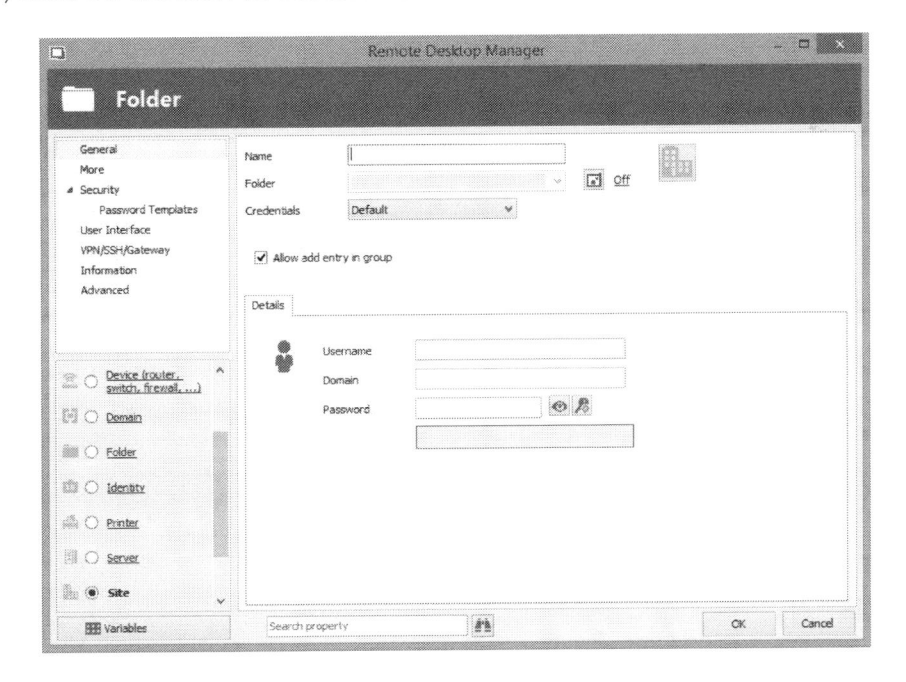

10. Now simply drag-and-drop all the connections we got when we did the network scan to the site you just created. It should look like this:

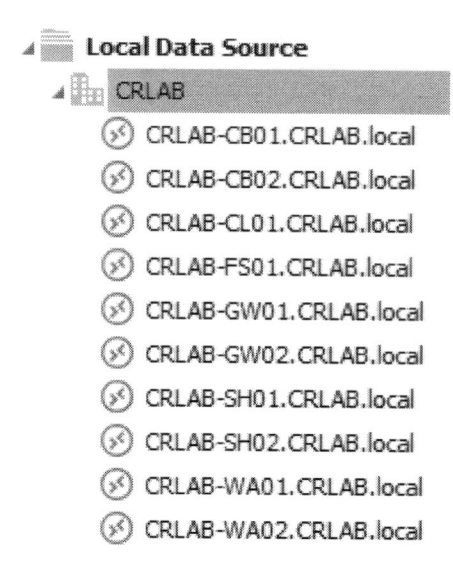

▲ Local Data Source
    ▲ CRLAB
        CRLAB-CB01.CRLAB.local
        CRLAB-CB02.CRLAB.local
        CRLAB-CL01.CRLAB.local
        CRLAB-FS01.CRLAB.local
        CRLAB-GW01.CRLAB.local
        CRLAB-GW02.CRLAB.local
        CRLAB-SH01.CRLAB.local
        CRLAB-SH02.CRLAB.local
        CRLAB-WA01.CRLAB.local
        CRLAB-WA02.CRLAB.local

11. Now we need to change all the entries to set them to inherit the credentials. Simply select all the entries and right-click on them. Select 'Edit' | 'Batch Edit' | 'Change Saved Credentials...'.

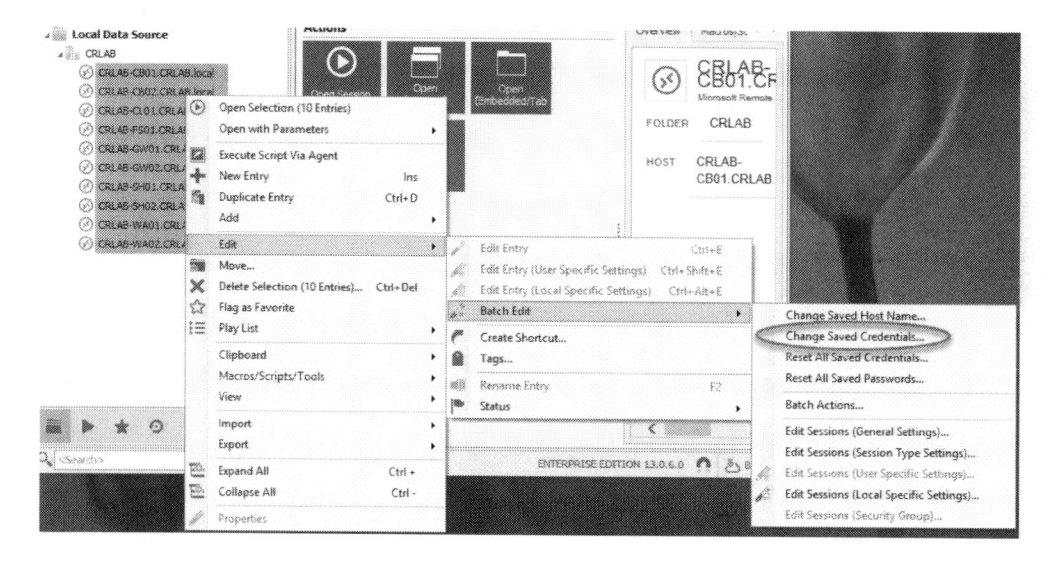

12. Select 'Use inherited' and click 'Save'. Now all your sessions under that particular site will inherit the credentials set at the parent level.

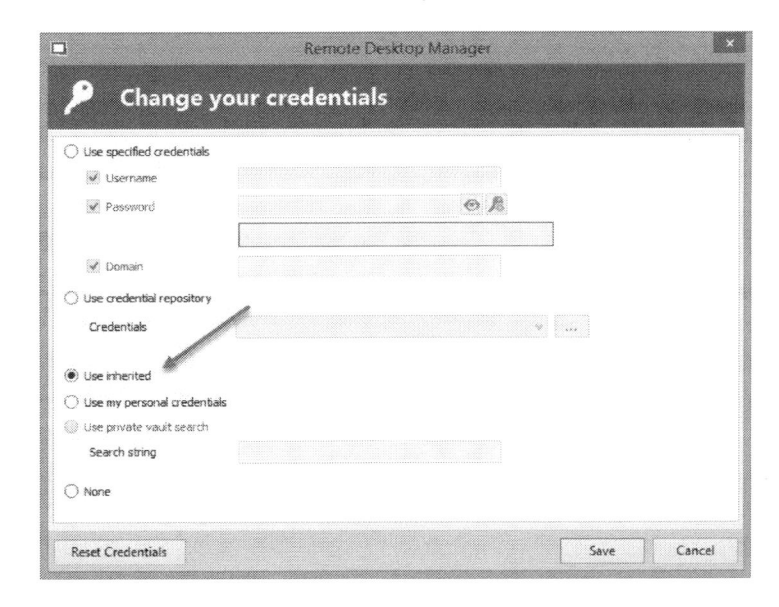

13. Now, if you try launching any of the connections discovered you will notice the RDP client will no longer ask for credentials.

If you noticed, RDM, by default, displays the connections inside its interface, in what is called 'tabbed' mode. You can easily change this. Simply right-click the connection you want to change and select 'Edit' | 'Edit Entry'. Under 'Display' select 'External' or 'Undocked'. And before you ask, yes, you can batch edit this too.

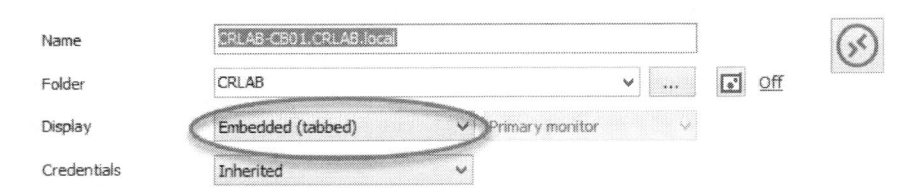

Note: The main difference here is when 'External' is used, Microsoft's own RDP client is called and the connection is established. 'Undocked' calls Devolutions' own RDP implementation.

Backing up and restoring your Devolutions RDM connections

Now that we have all the required connections in place, it is time to show you how the backup process works, where all your connections can be saved (and restored) to the cloud.

Assuming you are still logged in to your 'Devolutions Cloud' account, click on the 'File' menu and select 'Backup' | 'Execute Backup'.

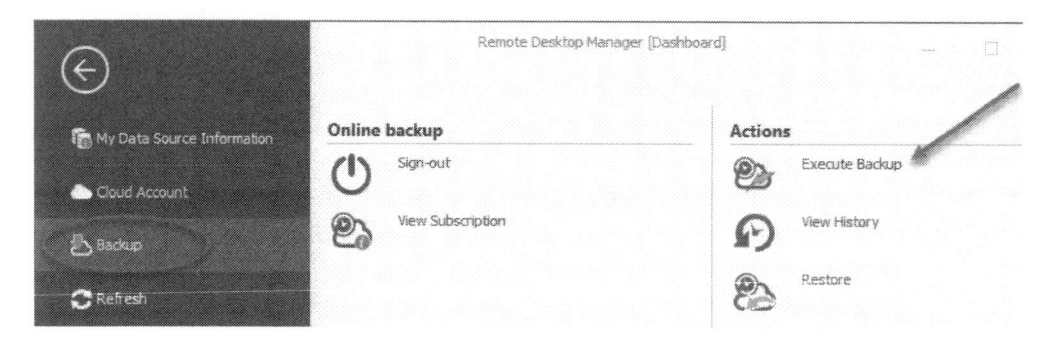

RDM creates the backup and displays a message saying it was successful.

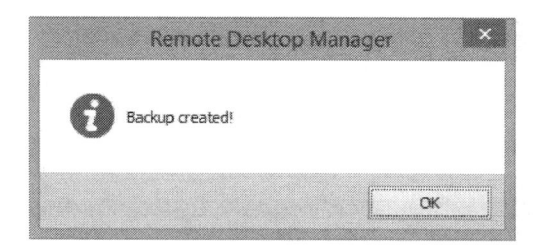

If you click on 'View History' RDM displays all the backups/restores performed:

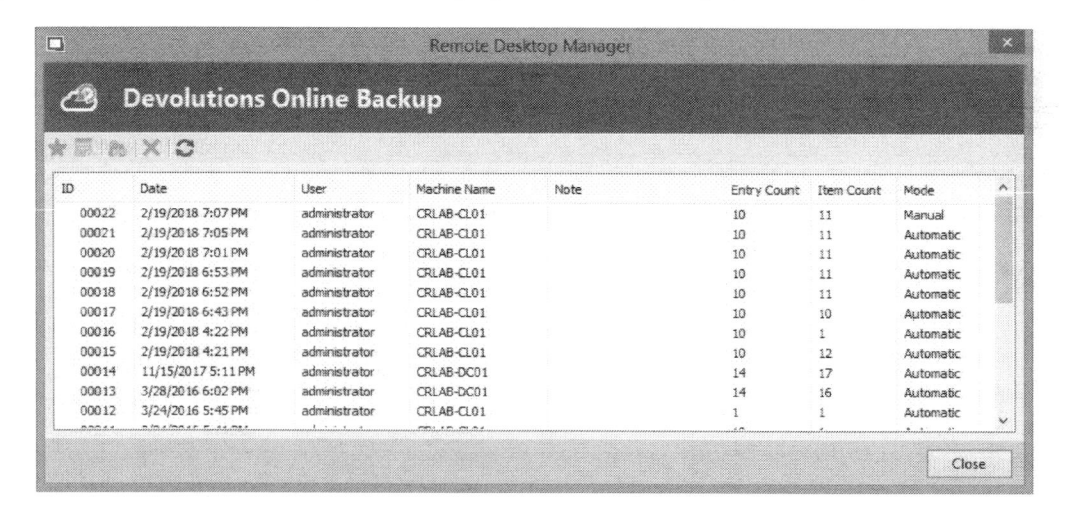

What is interesting here is, if you noticed, many of these are shown as 'Automatic' under 'Mode'. Yes, this is correct. As you add or change items on RDM, it creates a backup in the cloud for you, minimizing the risks of losing entries or changes implemented.

Now to fully try a restore, let's go ahead and delete the site where all our connections reside.

Click the site name (in our case, 'CRLAB'), then click on the 'Edit' menu and finally click 'Delete Entry' on the ribbon.

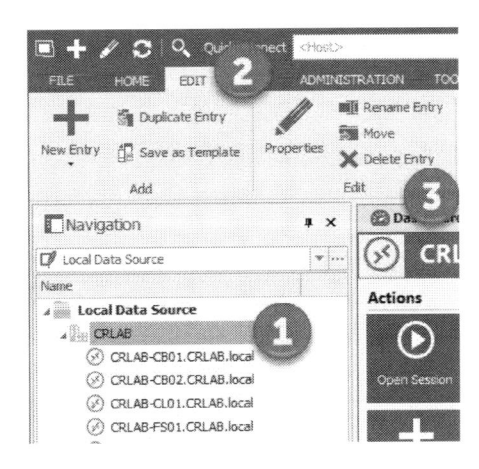

You will be prompted to confirm it. Click 'Yes'.

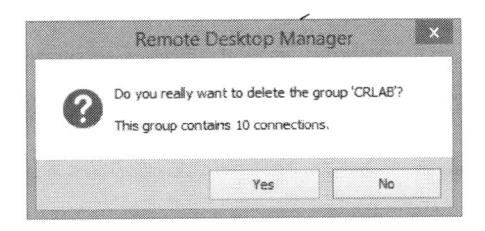

BAM! All your sessions gone.

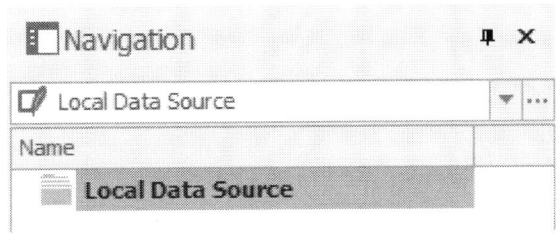

Time to check if the restore does work. ☺

Go to 'File' | 'Backup' and click 'Restore'.

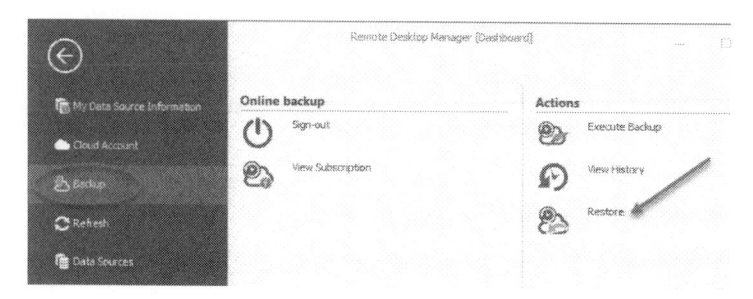

Select the entry that says 'Manual' (as this is the one we triggered manually) and click 'Select'.

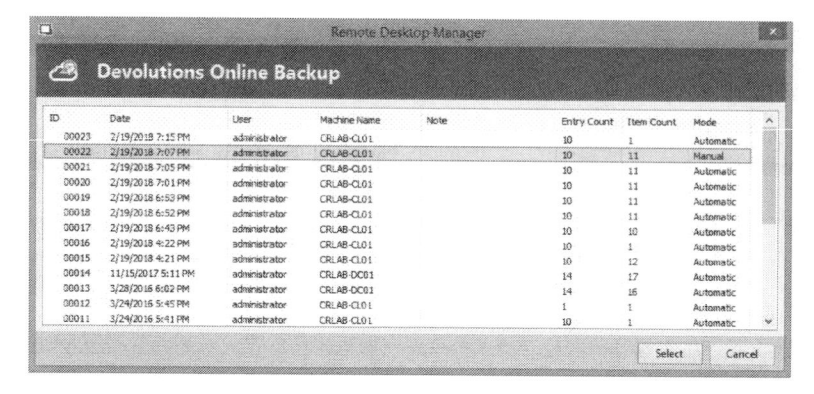

Review the information and click 'Next'.

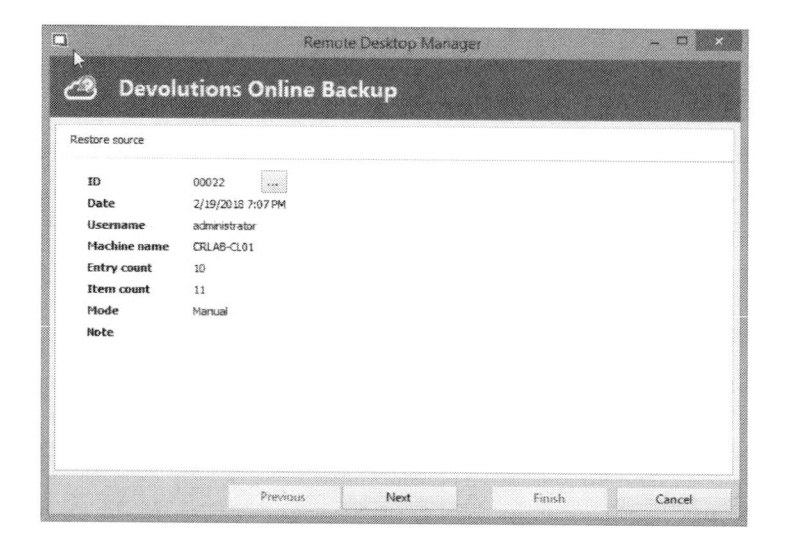

In our case, accept the default options and click 'Finish'.

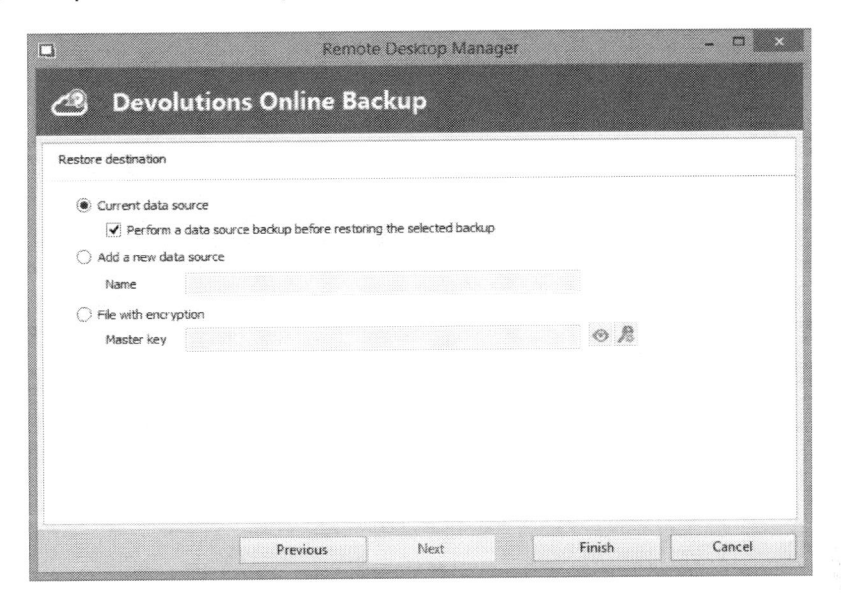

As you can see, all our connections are back. Success!

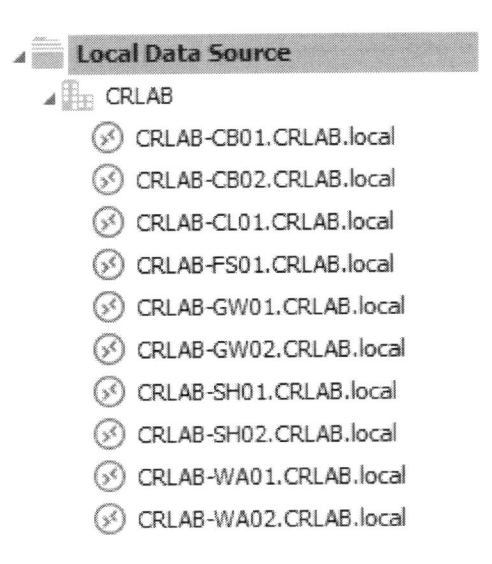

But as we mentioned, RDM is much more than this. All sorts of information are readily available for your entries. For example, you can get the 'Services' snap-in to launch for that particular machine by simply clicking on the entry and then, on the right pane, under the 'Macro/Scripts/Tools' tab, clicking on 'Services'.

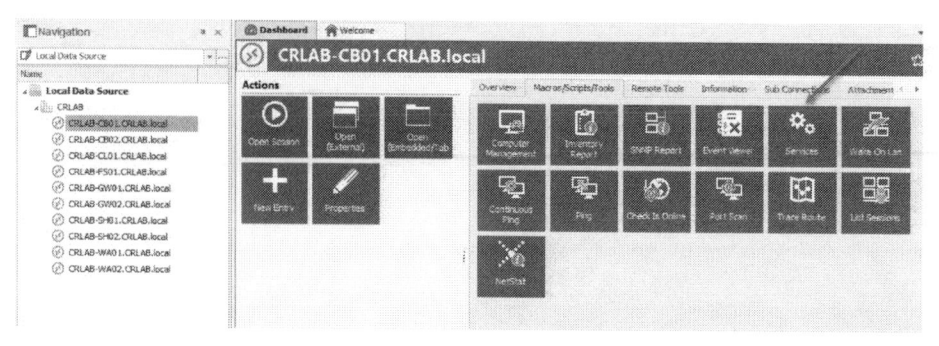

This is way more than what a simple tool like RDCMan can do. You can even automate commands or scripts that you can run against a particular site (i.e. a 'gpupdate /force').

And the fact you can have all these connections, credentials and automation tasks in a single repository, tied to Active Directory accounts for security (requires the 'Devolutions Server', a paid add-on), makes RDM a must have tool on any RDS environment. Talking about connections and security, is there a way to achieve that without 'Devolutions Server'? Yes, there is. And that is what we will tackle next.

Setting up Devolutions RDM for multiple users

So far you learned how to create, backup and restore your RDM connections. The next step is to understand how to setup RDM for multiple users with different rights (i.e., certain users may only see the RDSHs). To achieve this, we need to use a centralized database like SQL or the 'Devolutions Cloud' (in this case with a yearly cost). For the purposes of this book and given the fact RDS requires SQL for the RDCB HA, the easiest path here is to get RDM to use a SQL database. Let's do it.

1. Launch RDM and on the 'Navigation' pane, click on the three dots on the right side.

2. The data sources window will come up. Click on 'Add a New Data Source'.

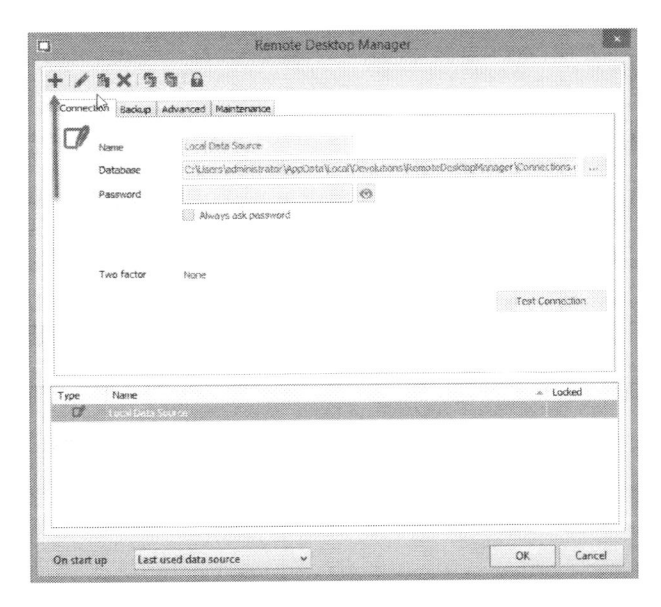

3. Select 'Microsoft SQL Server' and click 'OK'.

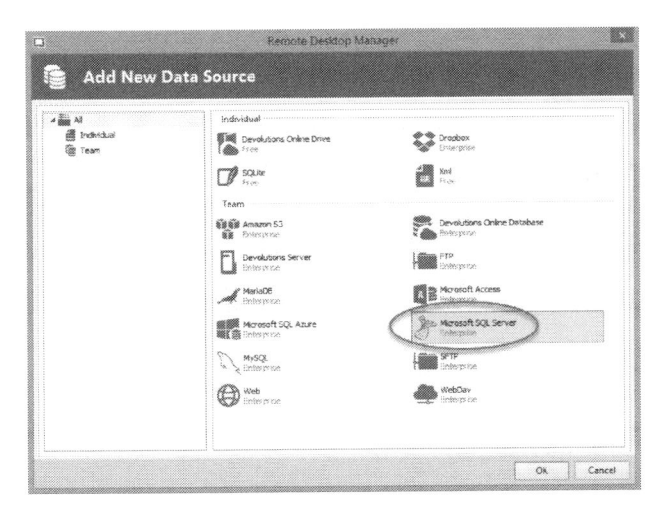

4. Enter the name you want for the data source, the correct server name or IP address, the required credentials and the database name. Click on 'Test Server' to make sure you can reach your SQL Server.

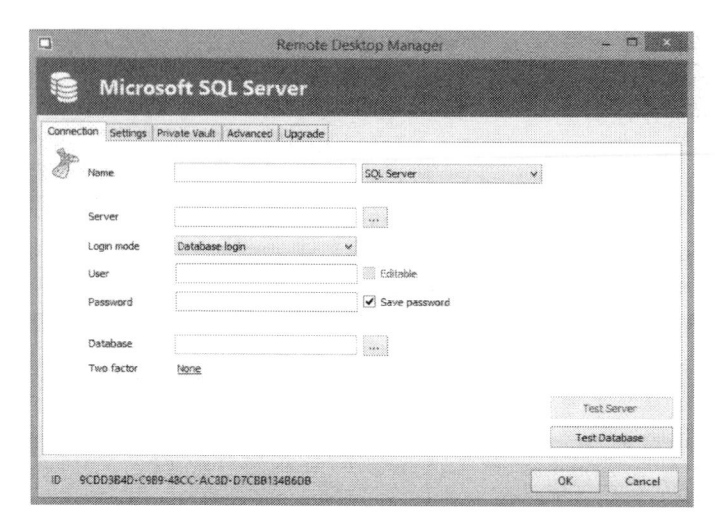

5. Now click on the 'Upgrade' tab and then on 'Create Database'.

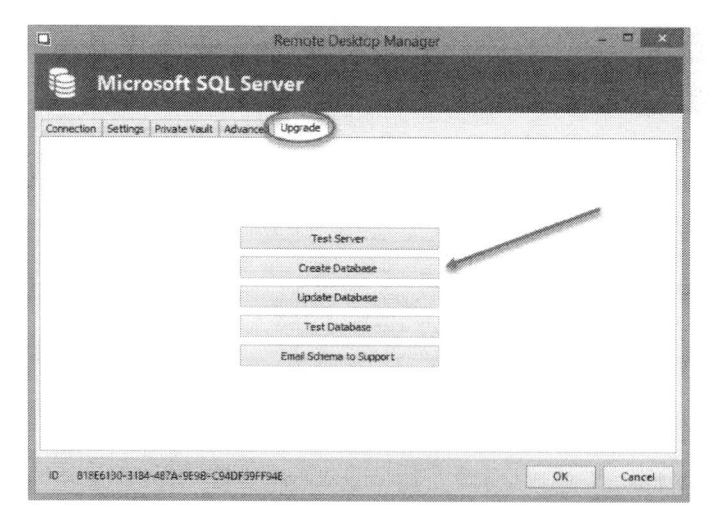

6. Accept the default and click 'OK'.

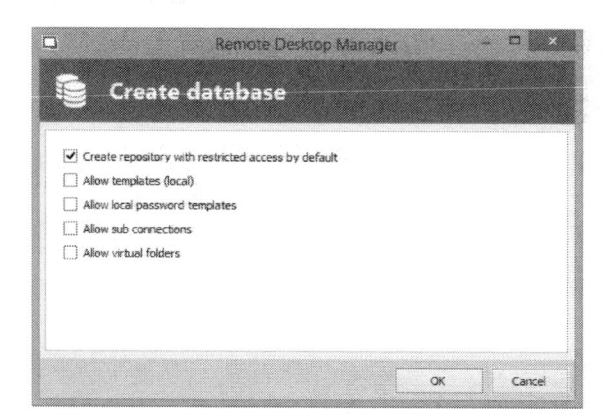

7. If the account used has the proper credentials on the SQL server, you should see a message stating the database was successfully created. Click 'OK' and then click 'OK' twice to close the main window.

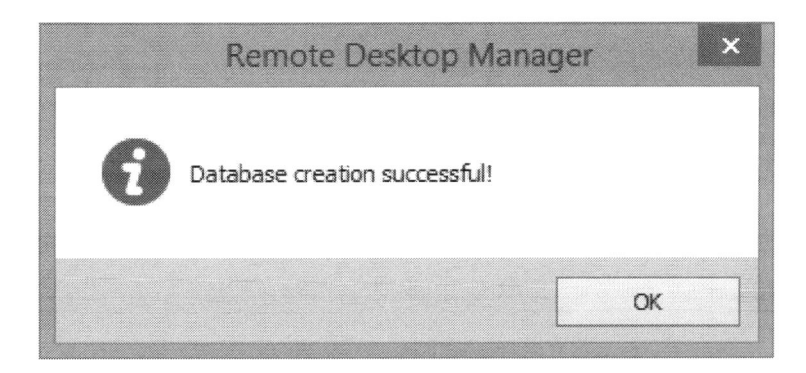

8. As part of this learning experience, and to get all your sessions saved to the new SQL database, let's export all the RDM session entries. Right-click 'Local Data Source' on the 'Navigation' pane and under 'Export', select 'Export All Entries (.rdm)...'.

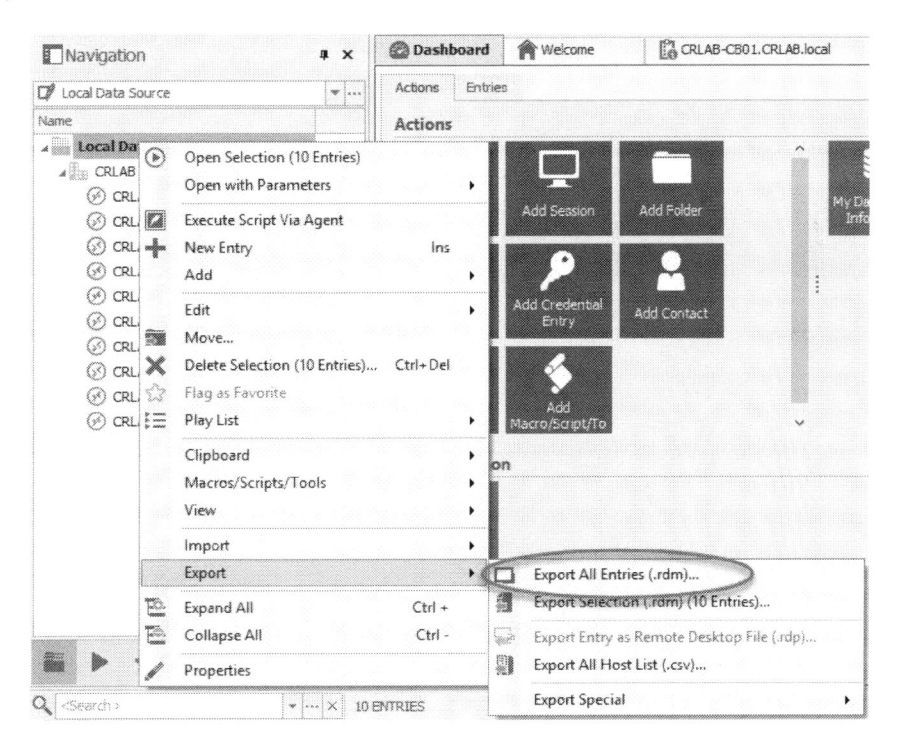

9. Make sure 'Include credentials' is checked and click 'OK'.

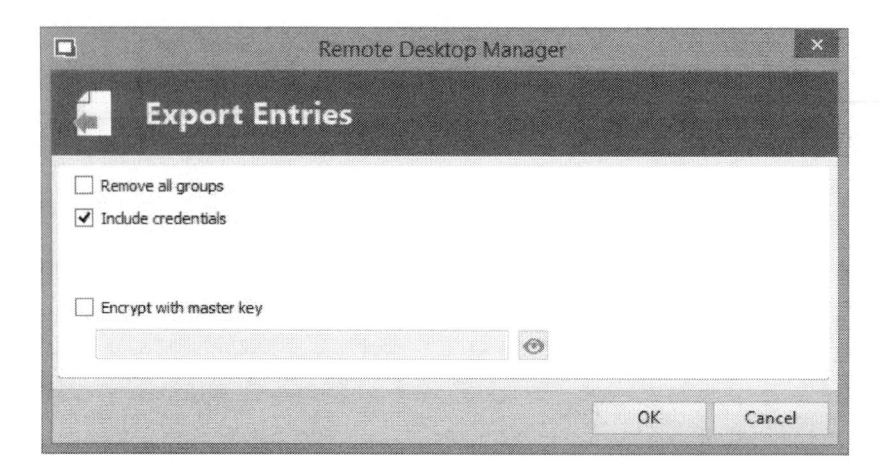

10. Browse to the folder where you want to save the exported file and enter a name for it. Click 'Save'.

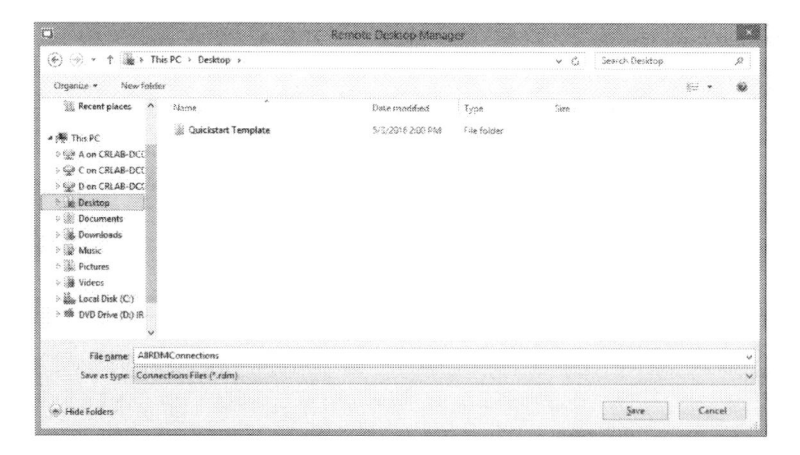

11. Back to the 'Navigation' pane, click on the arrow and select the SQL data source you just created.

12. You can now see your sessions for this particular data source and as expected, there are none listed. Time to import the sessions we exported previously. Right-click 'Sessions' and under 'Import', click 'Import Entries (.rdm, .pvm, .xml)...'.

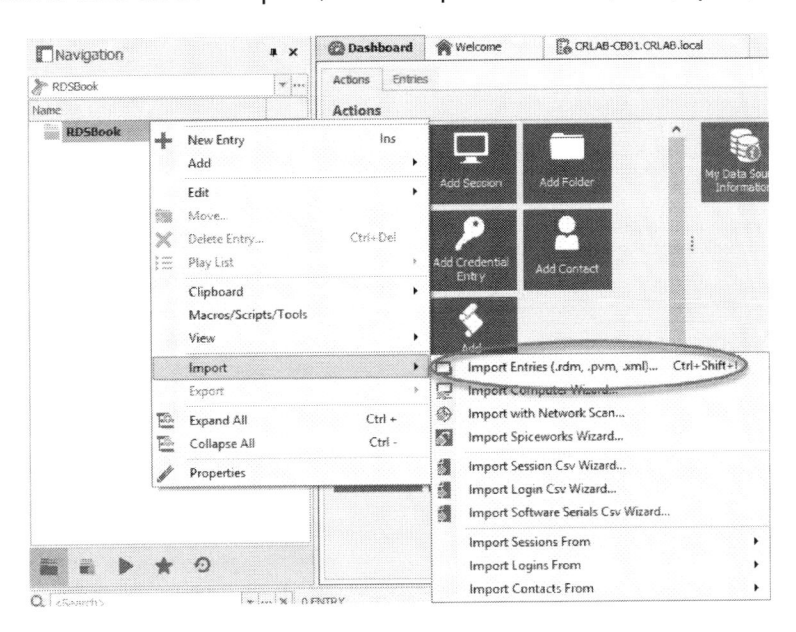

13. RDM will prompt you for the file to be imported. Once you select it, RDM will show you the file. Click 'OK'.

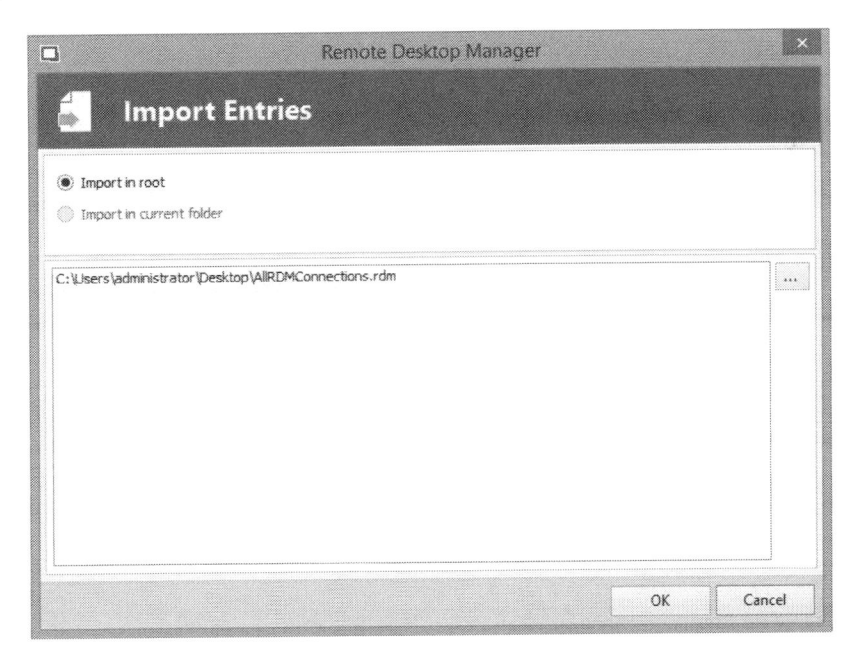

14. Click 'Select All' and then click 'OK'.

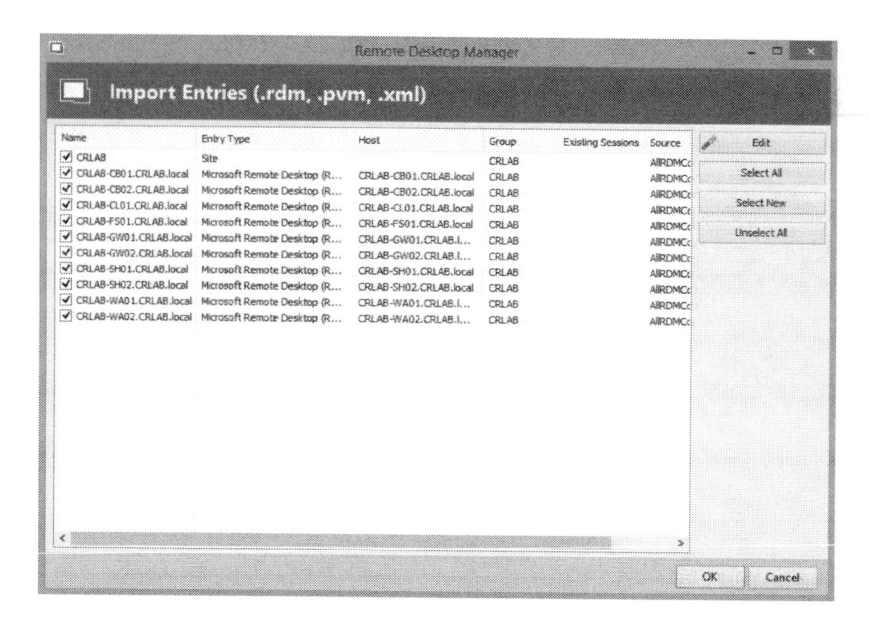

15. All your entries are now listed under the name you gave ('RDSBook' in our case). Great. We are now ready for the next step.

Creating users and security groups

RDM was developed with multi-user capabilities out of-the-box. It has everything you need to import your users from AD and then create security groups to control access to folders and entries. Before diving into it, as an exercise for this chapter, try organizing your sessions into groups as we did within our lab. It should look similar to this:

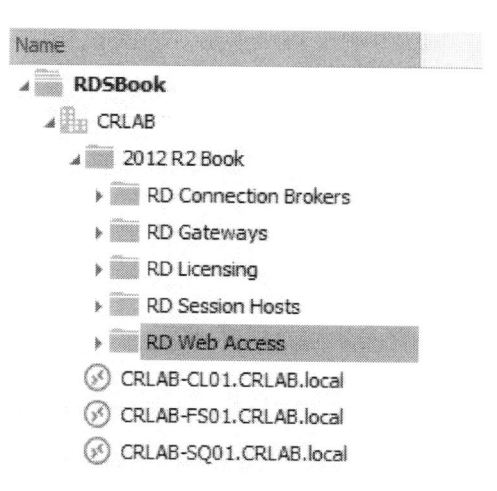

When dealing with multiple administrators and different access roles the main idea is to assign rights on certain objects (i.e. folders and connections) to certain groups so when users logon to RDM, they only see the objects they have rights to.

The RDM Enterprise version allows you to do this but not with AD groups directly. By that we mean, assigning rights directly to AD groups. For that, you will need the 'Devolutions Server', an extra, paid option for RDM, as we mentioned at the beginning of this chapter. Without 'Devolutions Server' you can still assign rights to groups but these groups must be created within RDM (they will be stored on the SQL) and users manually imported to these.

With all that in mind, let's go ahead and start tweaking the environment so certain users only see certain connections.

1. The first step is to add our users to RDM. As mentioned above, these we can import directly from AD. Launch RDM and on the ribbon, under the 'Administration' tab, click 'Users'.

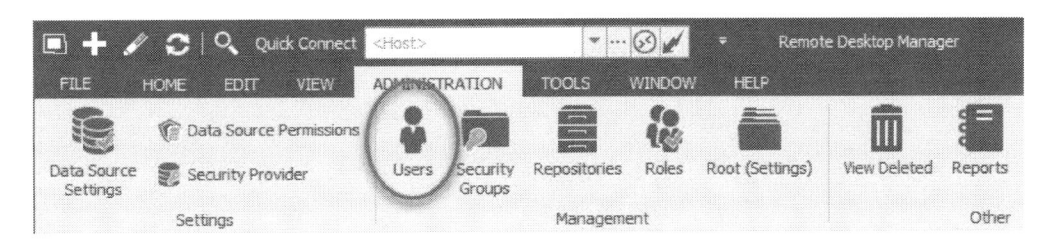

2. You should see the current list of users you have. Click on 'Add User'.

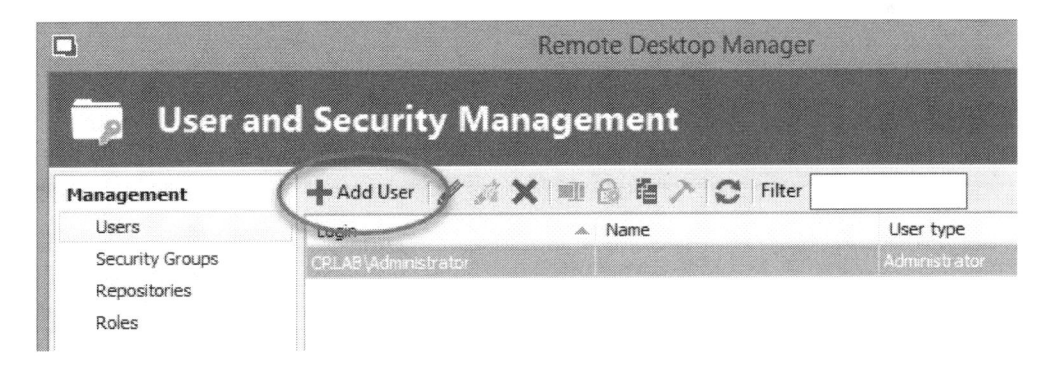

3. First make sure 'Integrated security (Active Directory)' is checked and then click on the little browse button (the three dots).

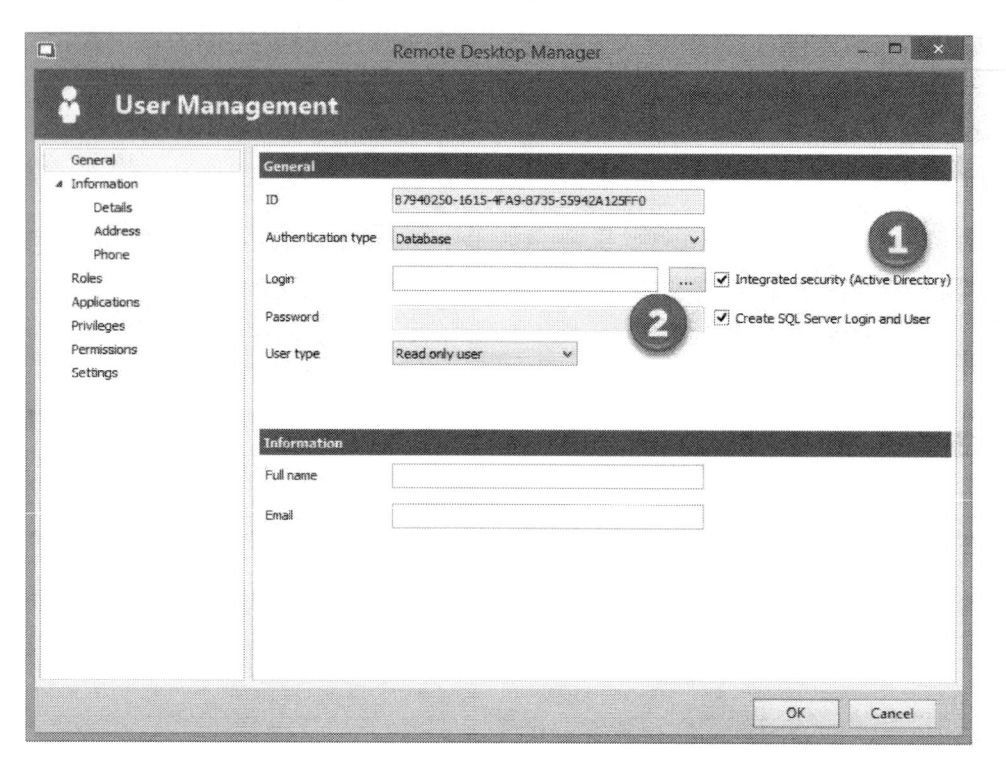

4. Select the user you want to add from your domain.

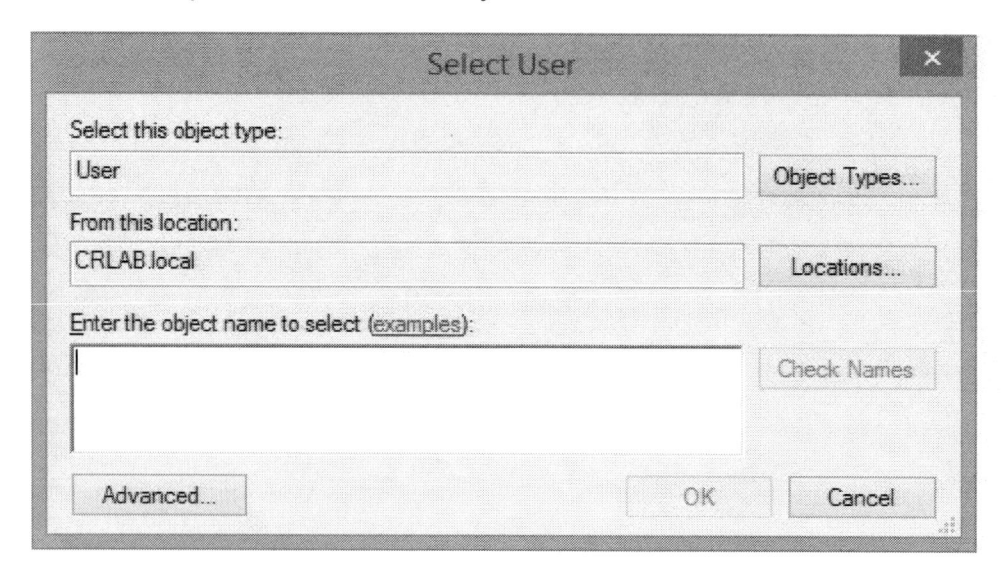

5. Click 'OK'.

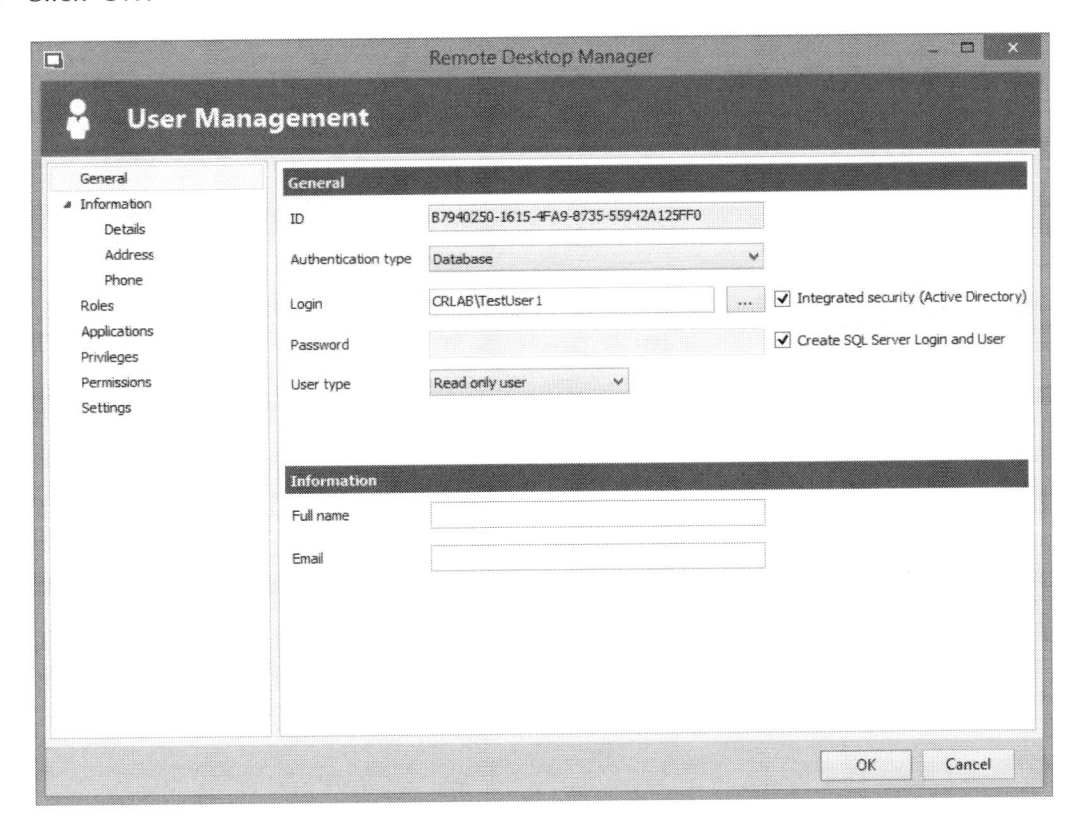

6. You should see a message regarding the password (as the account is being imported from AD). Just click 'OK'.

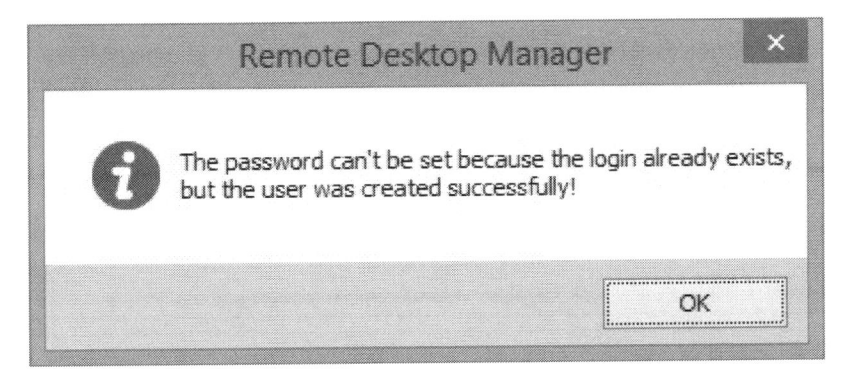

7. If you have more users to add, simply repeat the steps above. In our example, we added two users as we will be assigning different roles/views to each of them. Once all the users you want are added, just click 'Close'.

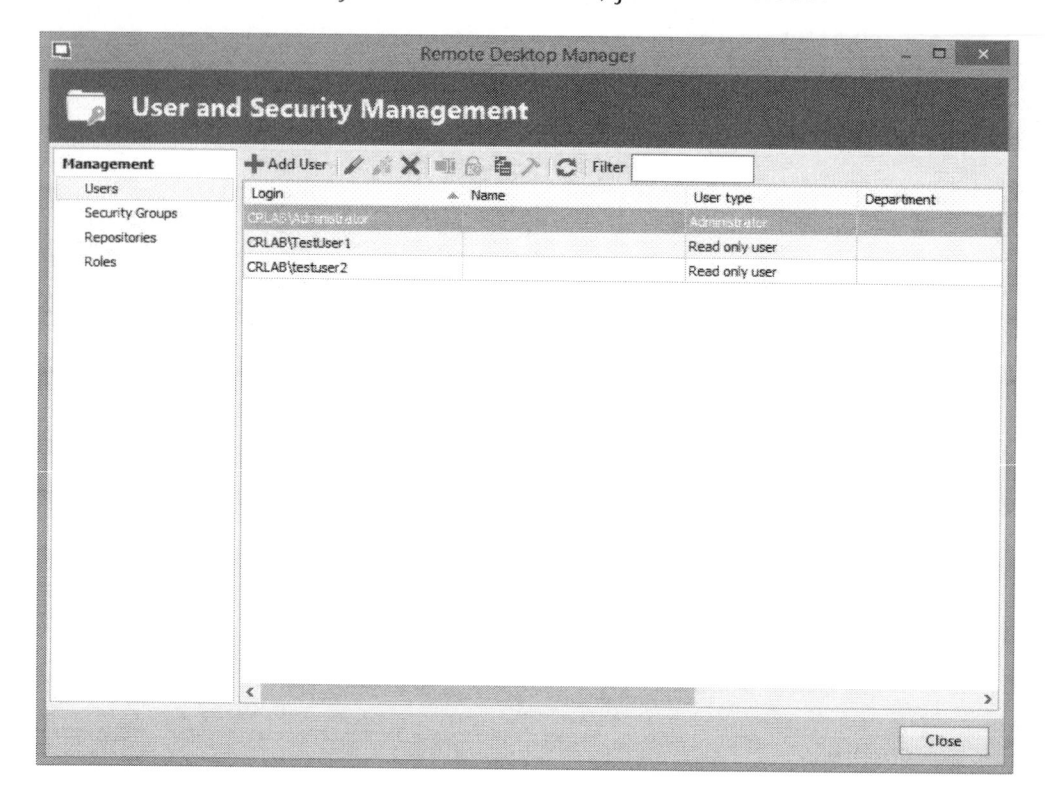

Next on the list is to create our security groups. Once we have these, we will them filter the connection objects using these groups. For this example, we will create two different groups, one with access to RDSHs only and one with access to the whole infrastructure. We will name these groups 'RDS Session Hosts' and 'RDS Infrastructure'. Let's keep moving.

1. Still under the 'Administration' tab, now click on 'Security Groups'.

2. Click on 'Add Security Group'.

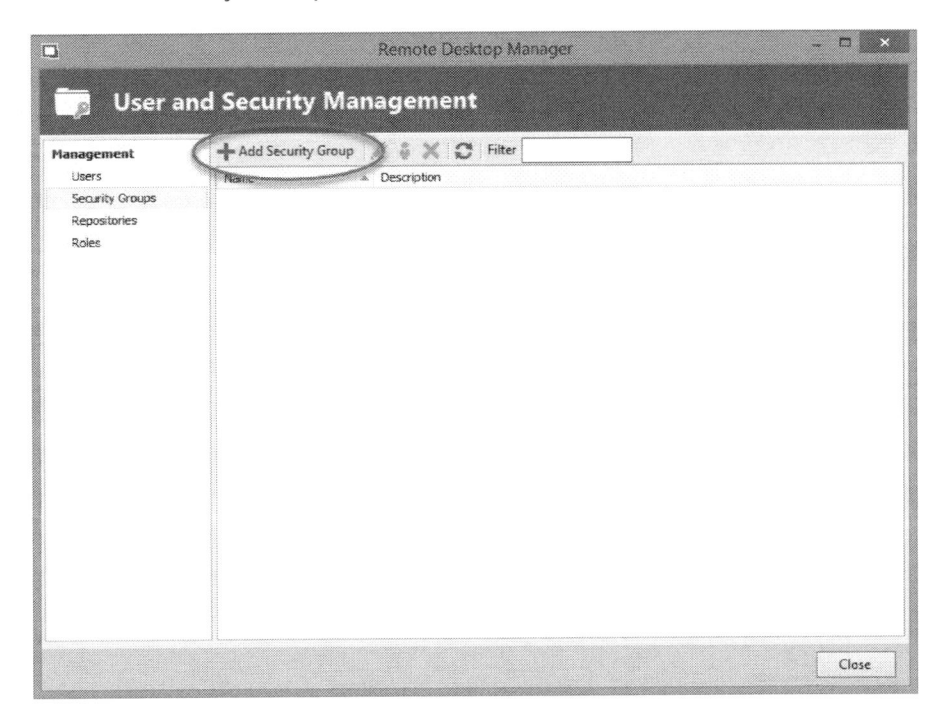

3. Enter a name and a description for the group and click 'OK'.

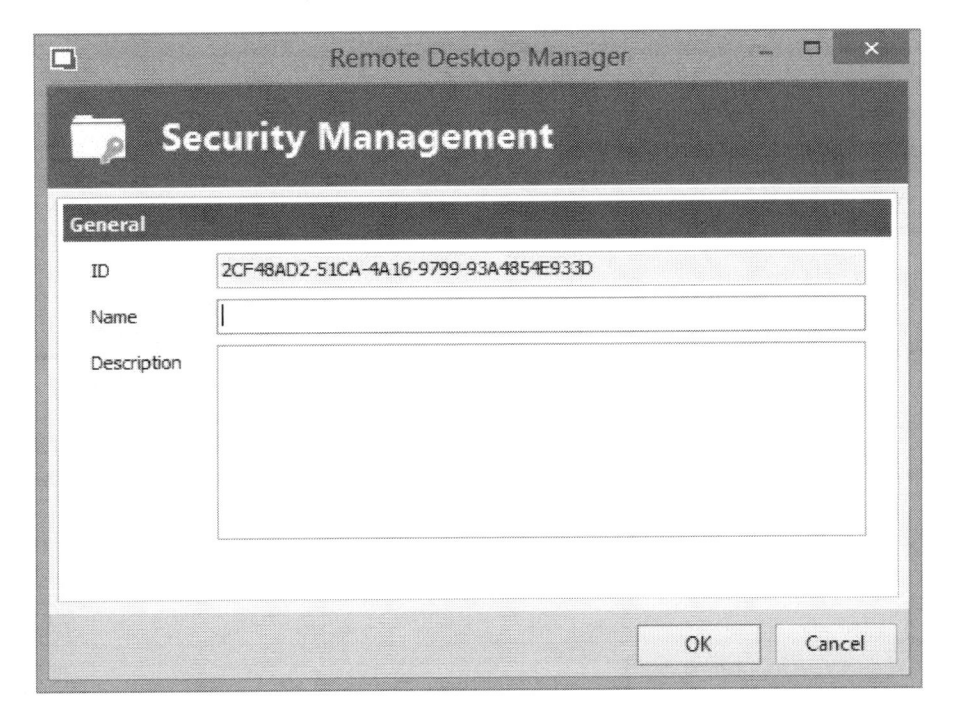

4. RDM will then allow you to select which users should be part of this group by selecting which particular rights they will have within the group. Click on what you need and once done, click 'Save'. Make sure for the users you will be adding you select 'View' only (so they cannot modify the connection).

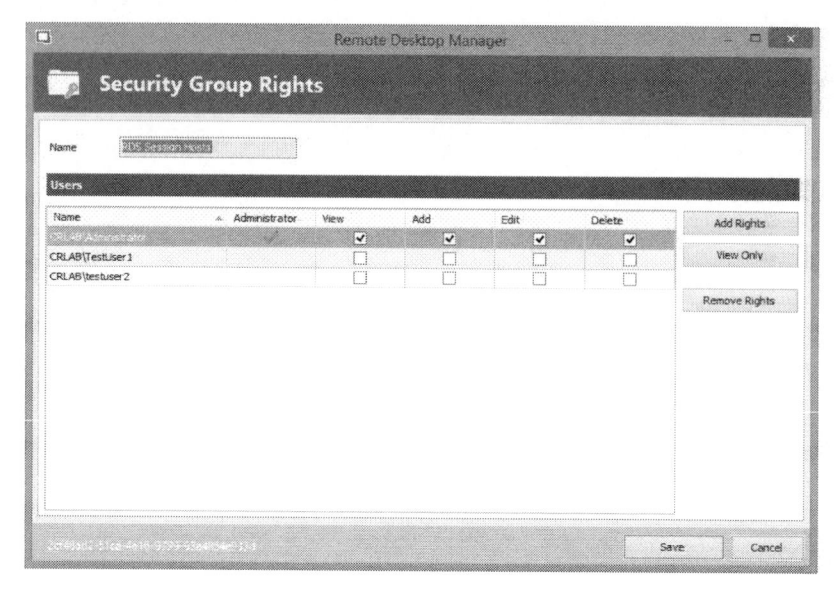

5. Repeat for all the groups you need on your environment. Once all groups are added, it should look similar to the screenshot below. Click 'Close'.

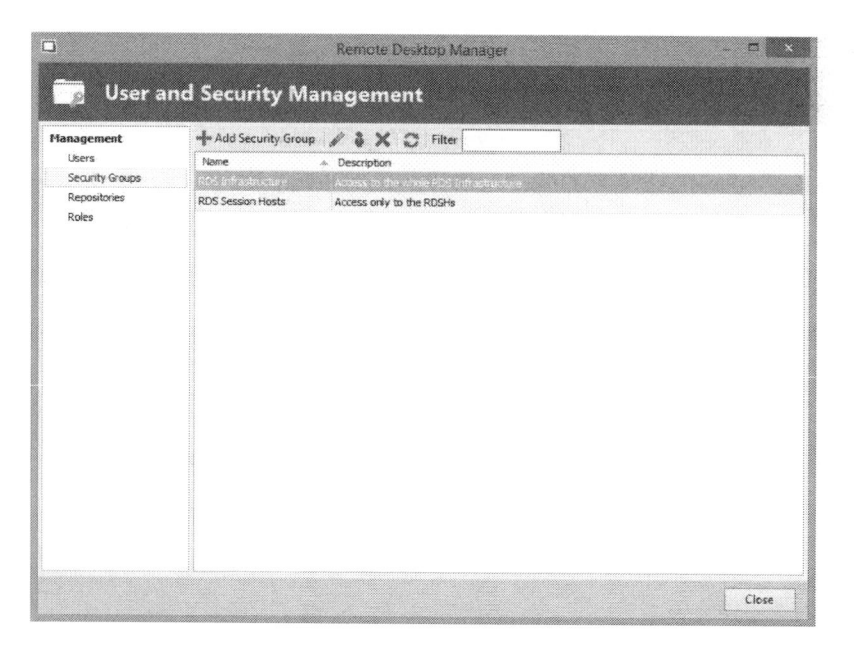

Note: one thing to keep in mind is, in our example, the 'RDS Session Hosts' group is more restrictive than the 'RDS Infrastructure' one and as the idea is to show only the RDSHs to members of the 'RDS Session Hosts' group, if a user that is added to 'RDS Infrastructure' is not added to 'RDS Session Hosts' as well, he will not see the RDSHs. Therefore, you must add that particular user to both groups if he is supposed to see the whole infrastructure. Another approach is to create individual groups for each role and add your users to the individual groups based on their needs, meaning if a user needs to see different servers, add him to each of the server roles groups.

The final step is to change the security on the folders holding the connections to be tied to the groups we just added to RDM. If you tidied up your connections and separated them into groups, as shown at the beginning of this chapter, this is quite easy. One more time, the connections should be similar to this:

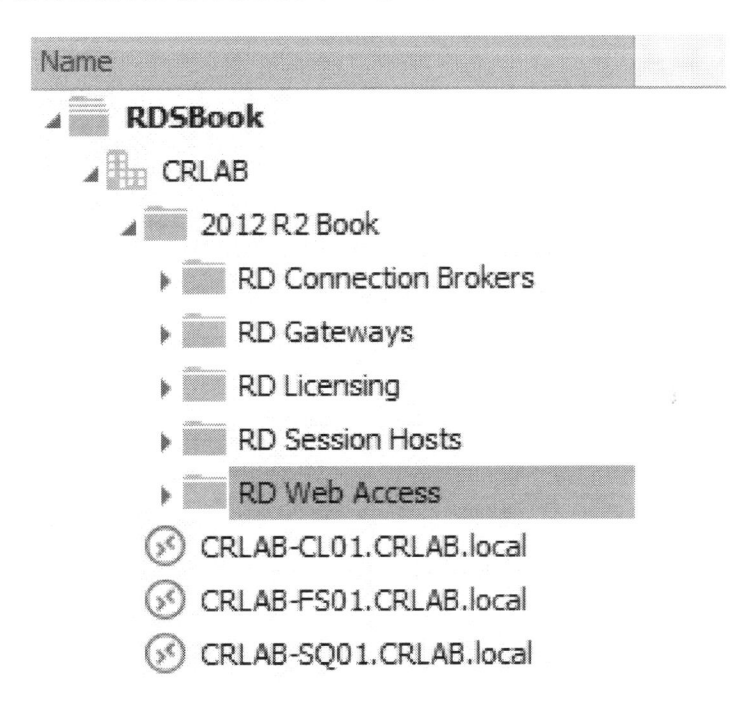

```
Name
▲ RDSBook
   ▲ CRLAB
      ▲ 2012 R2 Book
         ▶ RD Connection Brokers
         ▶ RD Gateways
         ▶ RD Licensing
         ▶ RD Session Hosts
         ▶ RD Web Access
      CRLAB-CL01.CRLAB.local
      CRLAB-FS01.CRLAB.local
      CRLAB-SQ01.CRLAB.local
```

To change the security for the folders holding connections:

1. Right-click the folder you want to change and select 'Properties'.

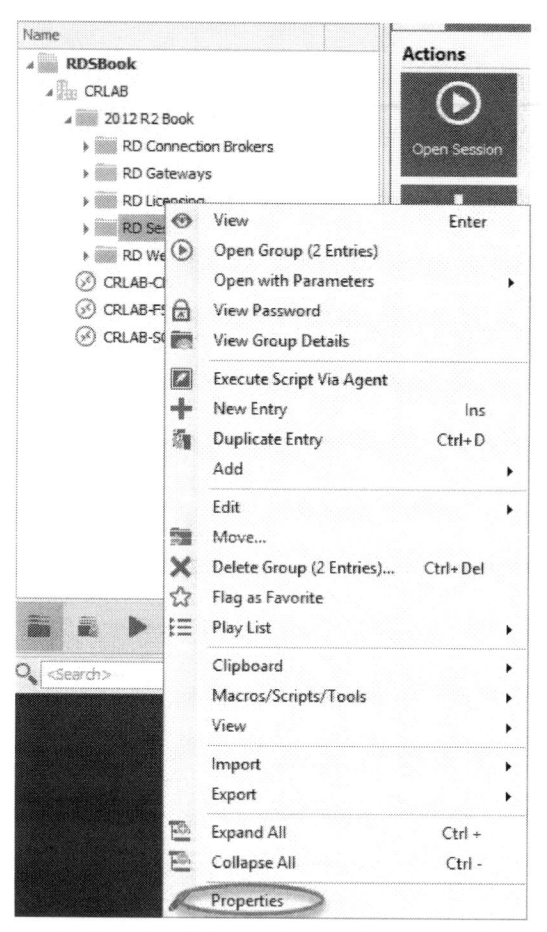

2. Under 'Security'| 'Permissions', click on 'Security group' and select the correct group that will have access to this folder. In our case, 'RDS Session Hosts'. Click 'OK'.

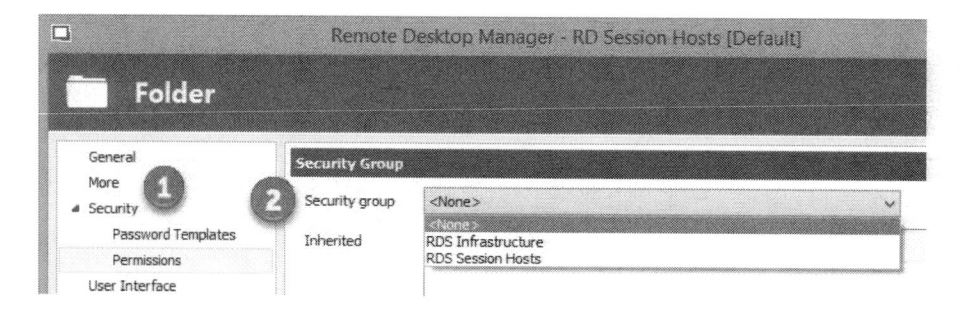

3. Now repeat for all the folders you want to control access to. Once finished you should have something similar to this (to see the 'Security' column, simply right-click the 'Name' column and select 'Column Chooser'; then double-click the item you want to see listed):

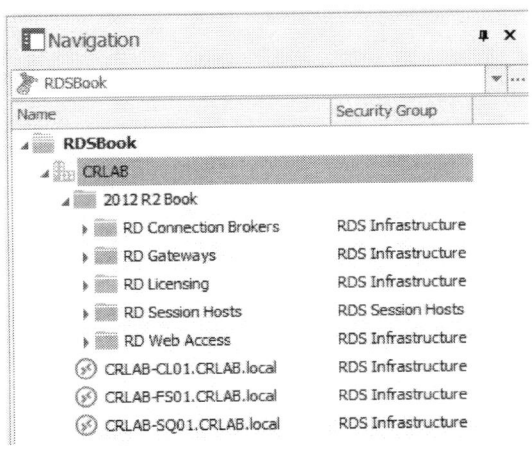

4. The final step is to make sure at the root folder, you change the permissions so by default all users are not denied access. To do that, go to the root folder (in our case 'CRLAB'), right-click it and select 'Properties'.

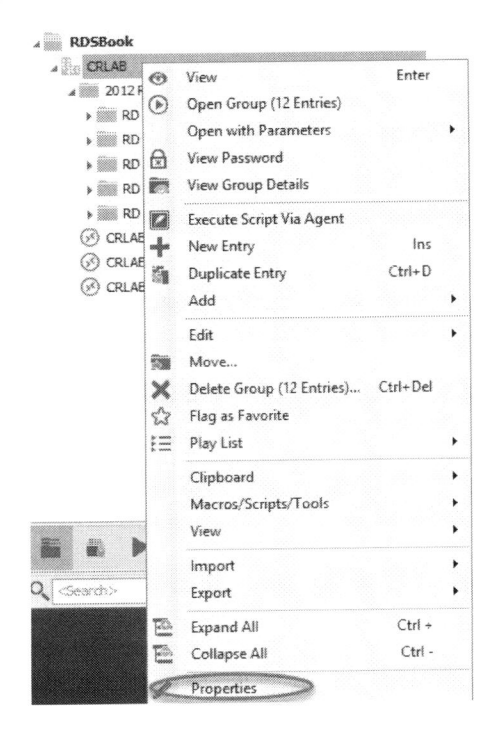

5. Make sure under 'Security' | 'Permissions', you set the 'Permission' to 'Default'. Click 'OK'.

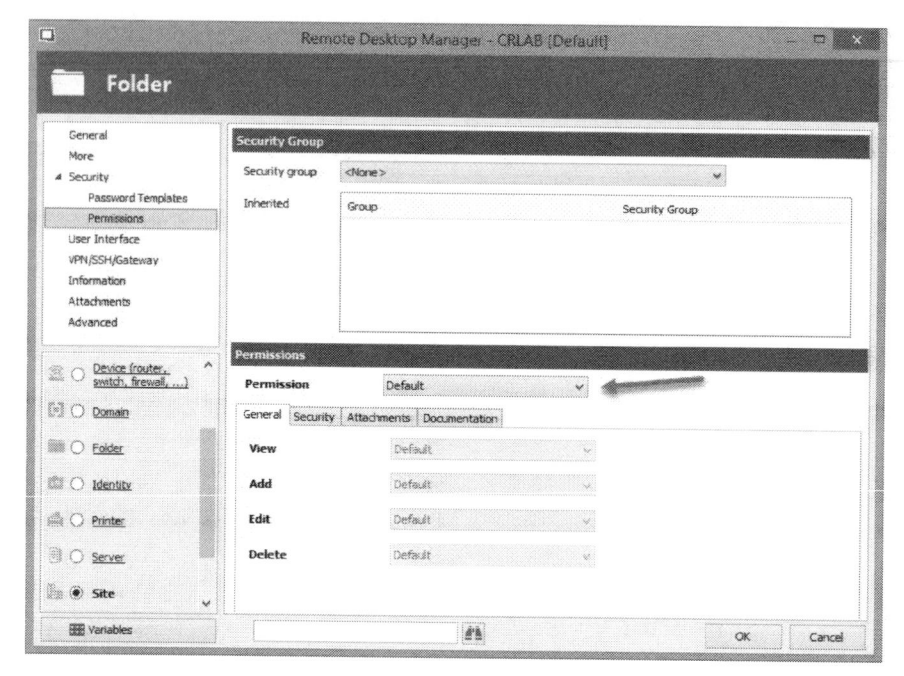

6. You are done. Seriously, that is all.

Now, how do we know it is working? Simple. On a machine that is domain joined and that has RDM installed, logon as one user you just gave access to RDM and to certain folders only. In our tests we will be doing this as two different users, one that is part of both the 'RDS Infrastructure' and 'RDS Session Hosts' groups and one that is part of 'RDS Session Hosts' only.

After logging in and launching RDM you will have to setup a data source connection to the SQL. Let's do it then.

1. After launching RDM, under 'Navigation', click on the 'Data Sources' detail button.

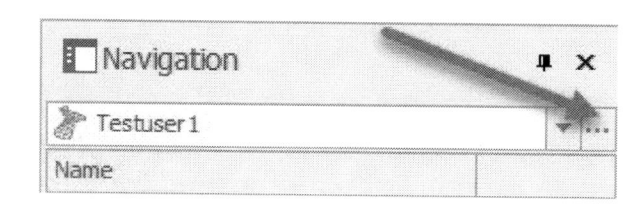

2. Click on the 'Add a New Data Source' button.

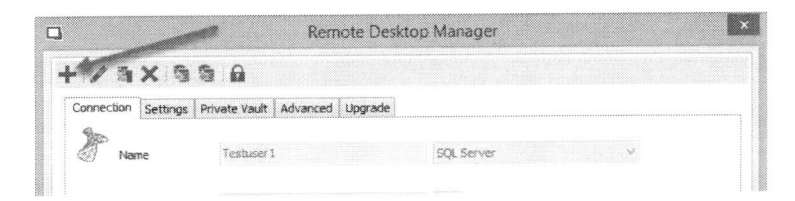

3. Select 'Microsoft SQL Server' and click 'OK'.

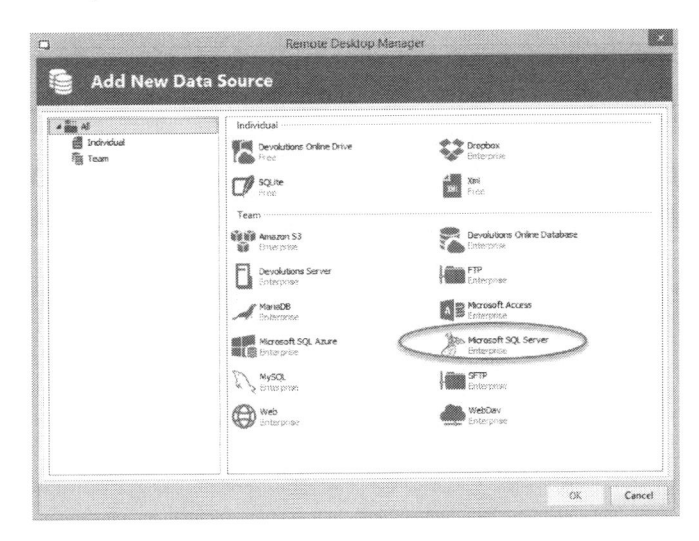

4. Enter the details for the SQL connection (description, the SQL Server and the actual RDM database). Make sure 'Integrated security' is selected for the 'Login mode'.

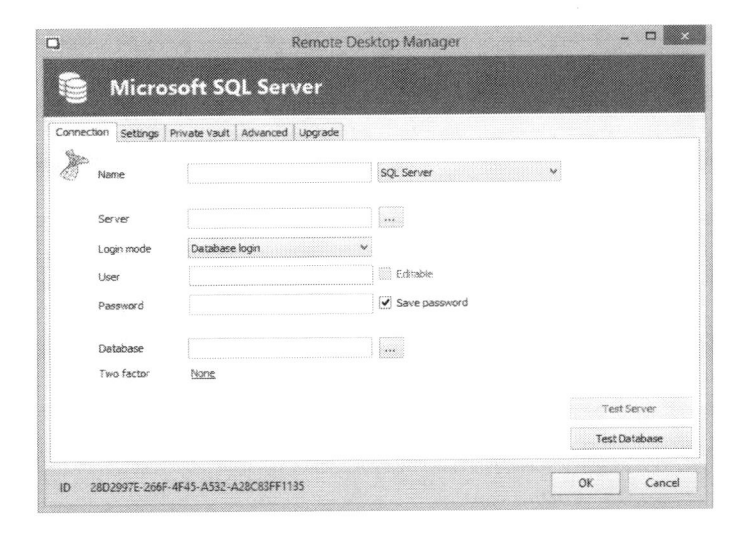

5. Your new SQL connection is now listed. Now we can remove the old local data source and set RDM to always use the SQL connection.

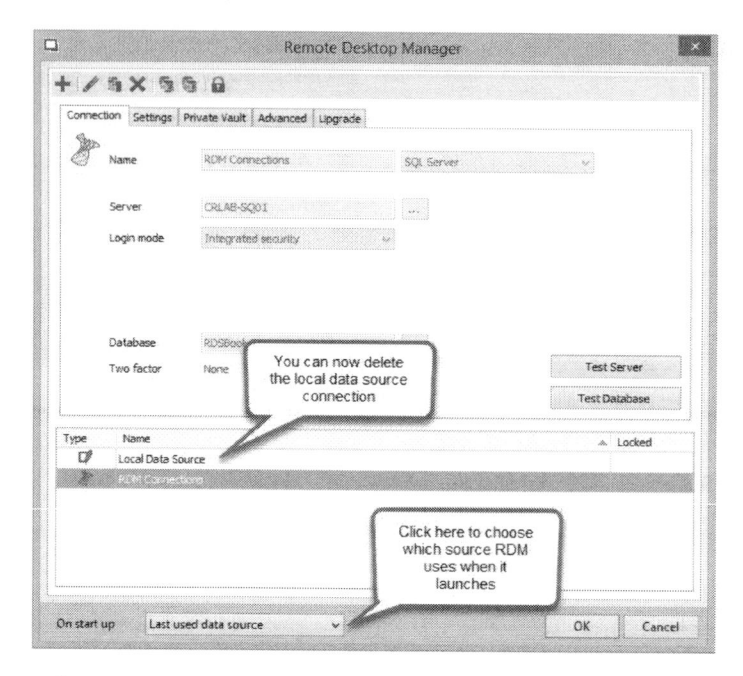

6. First click 'Local Data Source' and then click the 'Delete Data Source' button in the toolbar.

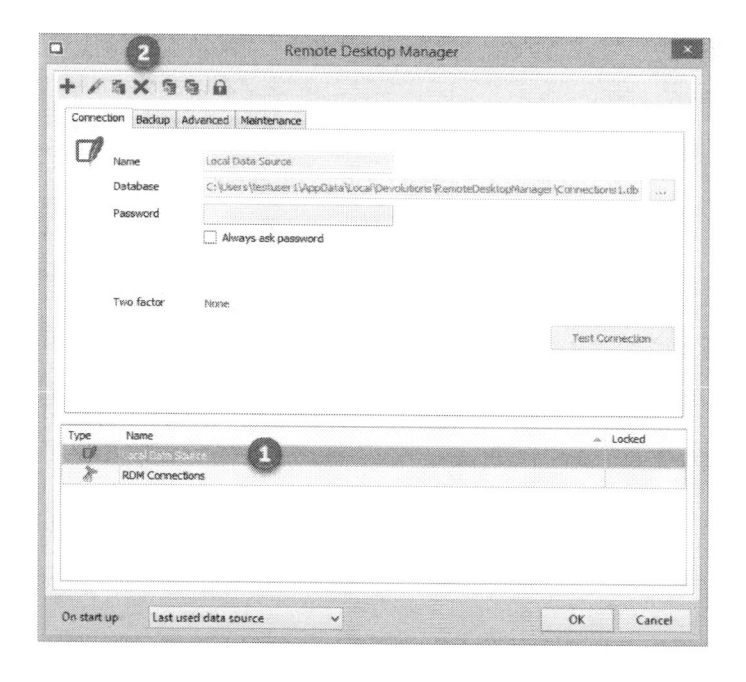

7. It will prompt you for confirmation. Click 'Yes.

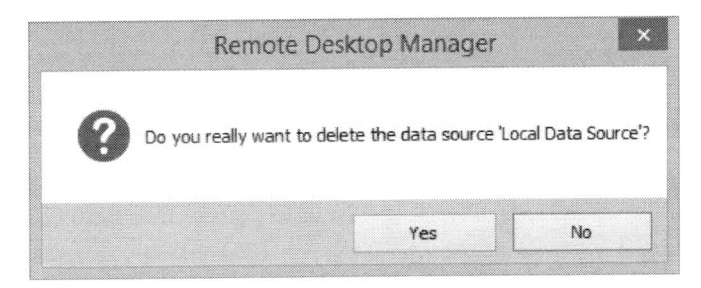

8. Now at the bottom, click on 'Last used data source'.

9. Select 'Use default data source' and then select the SQL data source you just created. Click 'OK'.

10. That is all. You should now see the connections you have rights to as that particular user.

In our case, with the two test accounts in use, this is what we see:

- TestUser1 (Part of 'RDS Session Hosts' only):

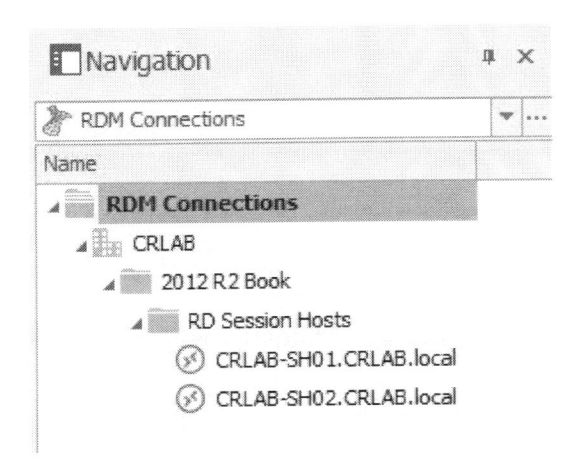

- TestUser2 (Part of both 'RDS Infrastructure' and 'RDS Session Hosts').

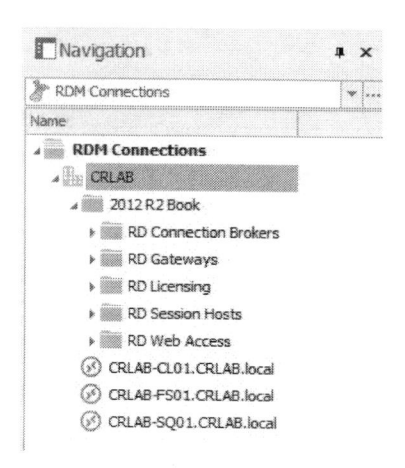

Working exactly as expected. If the user has access to that particular folder, he can then see all the connections under it. RDM gets granular to the point that you could even change the security for each connection individually. As you can see this is extremely powerful.

Now, as you remember, we gave these users 'View' rights to the connections. So, what happens when the user right-clicks a connection?

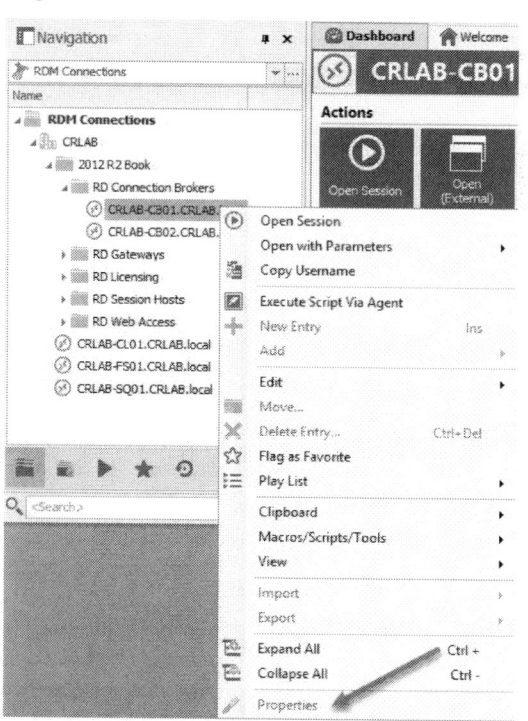

As expected, the user has no rights to edit the connection. All he can do is use it to launch a session to the server.

I know by now you are in love with RDM. And that is exactly what we felt after using it. It is a powerful solution that simplifies connecting to all sorts of platforms and environments. To cover all its features, we would need a whole book just about RDM.

Even though we did not cover the whole RDM solution, this section gave you a very good understanding of the product and how to make it work not only for standalone users but also in a corporate, team based, setup. That said, there is much more for you to discover about RDM! All that great information, with additional topics and videos is available directly at:

http://www.remotedesktopmanager.com/RDS2012R2Complete.

Monitoring the environment

Once everything is up and running and your users are happily using the RDS 2012 R2 deployment you just created, the next big step, and a critical one, is to keep an eye on everything, to make sure all components are available and performing as expected. This can be resumed into a single word: monitoring.

Like your car, where you have at least gauges for your coolant temperature and your fuel and you keep an eye on these when driving, your RDS environment is no different.

The main problem here is simple: Microsoft does provide several metrics relevant to RDS but not in a way that shows you the whole environment health in a single place. Unfortunately, you will have to monitor each server individually or go down the route of writing your own scripts if you do need something like a single pane of glass.

That said, we will show you the basic metrics you should monitor on your RDS deployment using the built-in Microsoft tools.

Creating an RDS dashboard with Performance Monitor

One of the most well-known tools in the Windows world is for sure 'Performance Monitor' or 'Perfmon' for short. I remember using it since the Windows NT days, a very long time ago. And now, in 2018, it is still the tool to use in case you want to keep an eye on your RDS environment.

Given all the RDS components (again, RDCB, RDLS, RDSHs, RDWAs and RDGWs), we need to know from each of these, which parameters to monitor. Let's take a look then at what we need, before adding these to the 'Perfmon' dashboard:

- RDSHs

    - Terminal Services | Active Sessions
    - Terminal Services | Inactive Sessions
    - Terminal Services | Total Sessions

- RDGWs

    - Terminal Service Gateway | Current connections
    - Terminal Service Gateway | Failed connections

- All Servers (RDSHs, RDGWs, RDLSs, RDCBs, RDWAs)
    - Processor | %Processor Time | _Total
    - Memory | Available Mbytes
    - Logical Disk | Disk Reads/sec | _Total
    - Logical Disk | Disk Writes/sec | _Total

The main goal here is to keep an eye on how many sessions you have on the environment (the 'Active Sessions', 'Inactive Sessions' and 'Total Sessions' on each RDSH you may have) and how the RDGWs are performing ('Current connections' and 'Failed connections' for each RDGW). To wrap it up, you then grab the most common counters that will show if something is obviously wrong (CPU, Memory and Disk Performance) with all the components (so, yes you will need to get these from all servers part of the deployment).

Once you add everything to your 'Perfmon' you should see something similar to this:

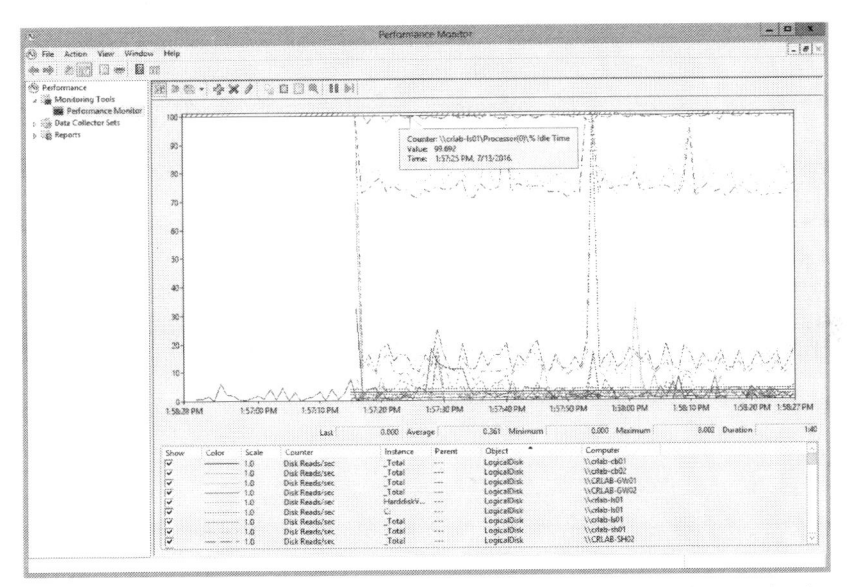

Unfortunately, and I will have to agree with you on it, this is far from ideal. It is not only a lot of information in a single graph but also, it does nothing regarding alerting you when something is wrong. However, it is a start.

The ideal solution is to get down to PowerShell. It will not only make things much simpler but you can also use it to make some pretty nice graphs ☺. Let's take a look at how we do it then.

Creating an RDS dashboard with PowerShell

As you learned a bit of RDS PowerShell in a previous chapter, it is time to make use of such amazing knowledge you now have. The idea is actually quite simple. We will retrieve the counters we discussed in the previous section and simply create some graphs from these. Once that is working, the next step is to create a simple web page to display these. Of course, you would then create scheduled tasks to retrieve these counters every couple minutes (depending how often you need that information refreshed) so the graphs are updated accordingly.

First step is to determine how to retrieve performance counters using PowerShell. This is quite easy actually. All you need is to use 'Get-Counter'.

SYNTAX

>   Get-Counter [[-Counter] <String[]>] [-ComputerName <String[]>] [-Continuous] [-MaxSamples <Int64>] [-SampleInterval <Int32>] [<CommonParameters>]

The counter is defined like this:

> $AllDiskReadsSec_Counter = '\PhysicalDisk(_Total)\Disk Reads/sec'

So in this case the variable '$AllDiskReadsSec_Counter' is set to '\PhysicalDisk(_Total)\Disk Reads/sec'. From the previous section, these are all the counters you need then:

- RDSHs

    - 'Terminal Services\Active Sessions'
    - 'Terminal Services\Inactive Sessions'
    - 'Terminal Services\Total Sessions'

- RDGWs

    - 'Terminal Service Gateway\Current connections'
    - 'Terminal Service Gateway\Failed connections'

- All Servers (RDSHs, RDGWs, RDLSs, RDCBs, RDWAs)

    - '\Memory\Available MBytes'
    - '\Processor(_Total)\% Processor Time'
    - '\PhysicalDisk(_Total)\Disk Reads/sec'
    - '\PhysicalDisk(_Total)\Disk Writes/sec'

Now that we know which counters to retrieve in PowerShell we just need to determine from which computers we will retrieve them. As per above, we do not need all counters from all computers that are part of our deployment. We need some counters from the RDSHs, some from the RDGWs and the remaining from all servers.

You can retrieve which computers are running certain roles in an RDS deployment by using the cmdlet 'Get-RDServer':

SYNTAX

    Get-RDServer [[-ConnectionBroker] <String>] [[-Role] <String[]>] [<CommonParameters>]

To retrieve RDSHs only, in our case we would run:

Get-RDServer –ConnectionBroker CRLAB-CB01.crlab.local –Role RDS-RD-SERVER

As expected, RDS-GATEWAY gets you only RDGWs. If you do not pass anything as a role, it retrieves all servers that are part of the deployment.

Now that we know what to get and from where, it is just a matter of using the Chart controls available with .NET to plot the graphs. The end results will be similar to this:

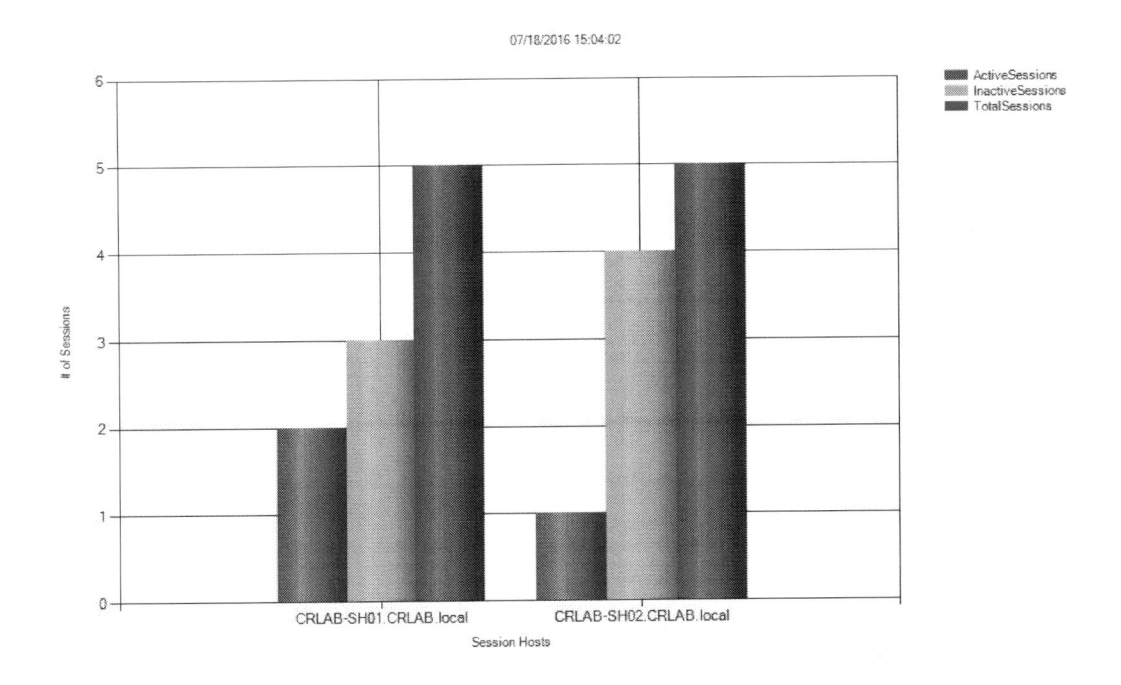

So here you have the final code (remember you must change the variables $ConnectionBroker and $SavePath on all scripts, to point to your own RDCB and the directory where you want the graph saved to)/

RDSH Active/Inactive/Total connections

```
Import-Module RemoteDesktop

# Sets your ACTIVE connection broker and the path where to save the image
$RDConnectionBroker = "CRLAB-CB01.crlab.local"
$SavePath = "C:\"

# Counters for the RD Session Hosts
$RDSHActiveSessions_Counter = 'Terminal Services\Active Sessions'
$RDSHInactiveSessions_Counter = 'Terminal Services\Inactive Sessions'
$RDSHTotalSessions_Counter = 'Terminal Services\Total Sessions'

# Retrieves which servers are in the deployment and running which roles
$RDSessionHosts = Get-RDServer -ConnectionBroker $RDConnectionBroker -Role RDS-RD-SERVER | Select-Object Server

# Gets the counters
$GetRDSHActiveSessions = Get-Counter –counter $RDSHActiveSessions_Counter -ComputerName $RDSessionHosts.Server
$GetRDSHInactiveSessions = Get-Counter -counter $RDSHInactiveSessions_Counter -ComputerName $RDSessionHosts.Server
$GetRDSHTotalSessions = Get-Counter -counter $RDSHTotalSessions_Counter -ComputerName $RDSessionHosts.Server

# Gets the data we need (CookedValue)
$RDSHActiveSessions_Data = $GetRDSHActiveSessions.CounterSamples | Select-Object CookedValue
$RDSHInactiveSessions_Data = $GetRDSHInactiveSessions.CounterSamples | Select-Object CookedValue
$RDSHTotalSessions_Data = $GetRDSHTotalSessions.CounterSamples | Select-Object CookedValue

# Loads the appropriate assemblies for the graphs
[void][Reflection.Assembly]::LoadWithPartialName("System.Windows.Forms")
```

```powershell
[void][Reflection.Assembly]::LoadWithPartialName("System.Windows.Forms.DataVisualization")

# Creates a chart object
$Chart = New-object System.Windows.Forms.DataVisualization.Charting.Chart
$Chart.Width = 1000
$Chart.Height = 600
$Chart.Left = 10
$Chart.Top = 10

# Creates a chartarea for the RD Session Hosts Data
$ChartArea = New-Object System.Windows.Forms.DataVisualization.Charting.ChartArea
$ChartArea.AxisX.Interval = 1
$ChartArea.AxisX.Title = "Session Hosts"
$ChartArea.AxisY.Interval = 1
$ChartArea.AxisY.Title = "# of Sessions"
$Chart.ChartAreas.Add($ChartArea)

[void]$Chart.Series.Add("ActiveSessions")
$Chart.Series["ActiveSessions"]["DrawingStyle"] = "Cylinder"
$Chart.Series["ActiveSessions"].color = "#FF0000"

[void]$Chart.Series.Add("InactiveSessions")
$Chart.Series["InactiveSessions"]["DrawingStyle"] = "Cylinder"
$Chart.Series["InactiveSessions"].color = "#00FF00"

[void]$Chart.Series.Add("TotalSessions")
$Chart.Series["TotalSessions"]["DrawingStyle"] = "Cylinder"
$Chart.Series["TotalSessions"].color = "#0000FF"

# Adds Legends
$Legend = New-Object system.Windows.Forms.DataVisualization.Charting.Legend
$Legend.name = "Legend1"
$Chart.Legends.Add($Legend)
$Chart.Series["ActiveSessions"].Legend = "Legend1"
$Chart.Series["InactiveSessions"].Legend = "Legend1"
$Chart.Series["TotalSessions"].Legend = "Legend1"
```

```
$Chart.Series["ActiveSessions"].Points.DataBindXY($RDSessionHosts.Server,
$RDSHActiveSessions_Data.CookedValue)
$Chart.Series["InactiveSessions"].Points.DataBindXY($RDSessionHosts.Server,
$RDSHInactiveSessions_Data.CookedValue)
$Chart.Series["TotalSessions"].Points.DataBindXY($RDSessionHosts.Server,
$RDSHTotalSessions_Data.CookedValue)

# Sets the title to the date and time
$title = new-object System.Windows.Forms.DataVisualization.Charting.Title
$Chart.Titles.Add( $title )
$Chart.Titles[0].Text = date

# Saves the chart to a file
$Chart.SaveImage("$SavePath" + "RDSHConnections.png","png")
```

RDGW Current/Failed connections

```
Import-Module RemoteDesktop

# Sets your ACTIVE connection broker and the path where to save the image
$RDConnectionBroker = "CRLAB-CB01.crlab.local"
$SavePath = "C:\"

# Counters for the RD Gateways
$RDGWCurrentConnections_Counter = 'Terminal Service Gateway\Current
connections'
$RDGWFailedConnections_Counter = 'Terminal Service Gateway\Failed connections'

# Retrieves which servers are in the deployment and running which roles
$RDGateways = Get-RDServer -ConnectionBroker $RDConnectionBroker -Role RDS-
GATEWAY | Select-Object Server

# Retrieves the counters we need
$GetRDGWCurrentConnections = Get-Counter -counter $RDGWCurrentConnections_
Counter -ComputerName $RDGateways.Server

$GetRDGWFailedConnections = Get-Counter -counter $RDGWFailedConnections_
Counter -ComputerName $RDGateways.Server
```

```
$RDGWCurrentConnections_Data = $GetRDGWCurrentConnections.CounterSamples | Select-Object CookedValue

$RDGWFailedConnections_Data = $GetRDGWFailedConnections.CounterSamples | Select-Object CookedValue

# Loads the appropriate assemblies for the graphs
[void][Reflection.Assembly]::LoadWithPartialName("System.Windows.Forms")
[void][Reflection.Assembly]::LoadWithPartialName("System.Windows.Forms.DataVisualization")

# Creates a chart object
$Chart = New-object System.Windows.Forms.DataVisualization.Charting.Chart
$Chart.Width = 1000
$Chart.Height = 600
$Chart.Left = 10
$Chart.Top = 10

# Sets the title to the date and time
$title = new-object System.Windows.Forms.DataVisualization.Charting.Title
$Chart.Titles.Add( $title )
$Chart.Titles[0].Text = date

# Creates a chartarea for the RD Gateway Data
$ChartArea = New-Object System.Windows.Forms.DataVisualization.Charting.ChartArea
$ChartArea.AxisX.Interval = 1
$ChartArea.AxisX.Title = "Gateways"
$ChartArea.AxisY.Interval = 1
$ChartArea.AxisY.Title = "# of Connections"
$Chart.ChartAreas.Add($ChartArea)

[void]$Chart.Series.Add("CurrentConnections")
$Chart.Series["CurrentConnections"]["DrawingStyle"] = "Cylinder"
$Chart.Series["CurrentConnections"].color = "#FF0000"

[void]$Chart.Series.Add("FailedConnections")
$Chart.Series["FailedConnections"]["DrawingStyle"] = "Cylinder"
$Chart.Series["FailedConnections"].color = "#00FF00"
```

```
# Adds Legends
$Legend = New-Object system.Windows.Forms.DataVisualization.Charting.Legend
$Legend.name = "Legend"
$Chart.Legends.Add($Legend)
$Chart.Series["CurrentConnections"].Legend = "Legend"
$Chart.Series["FailedConnections"].Legend = "Legend"

# Plots the data
$Chart.Series["CurrentConnections"].Points.DataBindXY($RDGateways.Server, $RDGWCurrentConnections_Data.CookedValue)
$Chart.Series["FailedConnections"].Points.DataBindXY($RDGateways.Server, $RDGWFailedConnections_Data.CookedValue)

# Saves the chart to a file
$Chart.SaveImage("$SavePath" + "RDGWConnections.png","png")
```

Deployment CPU

```
Import-Module RemoteDesktop

# Sets your ACTIVE connection broker and the path where to save the image
$RDConnectionBroker = "CRLAB-CB01.crlab.local"
$SavePath = "C:\"

# CPU Counter for all servers part of the RDS deployment
$AllProcessorTime_Counter = '\Processor(_Total)\% Processor Time'

# Retrieves which servers are in the deployment
$DeploymentComputers = Get-RDServer -ConnectionBroker $RDConnectionBroker | Select-Object Server

# Retrieves the counters we need
$GetAllProcessorTime = Get-Counter -counter $AllProcessorTime_Counter -ComputerName $DeploymentComputers.Server

$AllProcessorTime_Data = $GetAllProcessorTime.CounterSamples | Select-Object CookedValue

# Loads the appropriate assemblies for the graphs
[void][Reflection.Assembly]::LoadWithPartialName("System.Windows.Forms")
```

```powershell
[void][Reflection.Assembly]::LoadWithPartialName("System.Windows.Forms.DataVisualization")

# Creates a chart object
$Chart = New-object System.Windows.Forms.DataVisualization.Charting.Chart
$Chart.Width = 1000
$Chart.Height = 600
$Chart.Left = 10
$Chart.Top = 10

# Creates a chartarea for the Memory Data
$ChartArea = New-Object System.Windows.Forms.DataVisualization.Charting.ChartArea
$ChartArea.AxisX.Interval = 1
$ChartArea.AxisX.Title = "Deployment Hosts"
$ChartArea.AxisY.Interval = 10
$ChartArea.AxisY.Title = "% Processor Time"
$Chart.ChartAreas.Add($ChartArea)
[void]$Chart.Series.Add("CPU")
$Chart.Series["CPU"]["DrawingStyle"] = "Cylinder"
$Chart.Series["CPU"].color = "#00FF00"

# Adds Legends
$Legend = New-Object system.Windows.Forms.DataVisualization.Charting.Legend
$Legend.name = "Legend1"
$Chart.Legends.Add($Legend)
$Chart.Series["CPU"].Legend = "Legend1"

# Plots the data
$Chart.Series["CPU"].Points.DataBindXY($DeploymentComputers.Server, $AllProcessorTime_Data.CookedValue)

# Sets the title to the date and time
$title = new-object System.Windows.Forms.DataVisualization.Charting.Title
$Chart.Titles.Add( $title )
$Chart.Titles[0].Text = date

# Saves the chart to a file
$Chart.SaveImage("$SavePath" + "RDDeploymentCPU.png","png")
```

Deployment Memory

```
Import-Module RemoteDesktop

# Sets your ACTIVE connection broker and the path where to save the image
$RDConnectionBroker = "CRLAB-CB01.crlab.local"
$SavePath = "C:\"

# Memory counter for all servers part of the RDS deployment
$AllMemAvailableMB_Counter = '\Memory\Available MBytes'

# Retrieves which servers are in the deployment
$DeploymentComputers = Get-RDServer -ConnectionBroker $RDConnectionBroker | Select-Object Server

# Retrieves the counters
$GetAllMemAvailableMB = Get-Counter -counter $AllMemAvailableMB_Counter -ComputerName $DeploymentComputers.Server
$AllMemAvailableMB_Data = $GetAllMemAvailableMB.CounterSamples | Select-Object CookedValue

# Loads the appropriate assemblies for the graphs
[void][Reflection.Assembly]::LoadWithPartialName("System.Windows.Forms")
[void][Reflection.Assembly]::LoadWithPartialName("System.Windows.Forms.DataVisualization")

# Creates a chart object
$Chart = New-object System.Windows.Forms.DataVisualization.Charting.Chart
$Chart.Width = 1000
$Chart.Height = 600
$Chart.Left = 10
$Chart.Top = 10

# Creates a chartarea for the Memory Data
$ChartArea = New-Object System.Windows.Forms.DataVisualization.Charting.ChartArea
$ChartArea.AxisX.Interval = 1
$ChartArea.AxisX.Title = "Deployment Hosts"
$ChartArea.AxisY.Interval = 100
```

```powershell
$ChartArea.AxisY.Title = "Memory Used (MBytes)"
$Chart.ChartAreas.Add($ChartArea)

[void]$Chart.Series.Add("Memory")
$Chart.Series["Memory"]["DrawingStyle"] = "Cylinder"
$Chart.Series["Memory"].color = "#00FF00"

# Adds Legends
$Legend = New-Object system.Windows.Forms.DataVisualization.Charting.Legend
$Legend.name = "Legend1"
$Chart.Legends.Add($Legend)
$Chart.Series["Memory"].Legend = "Legend1"
$Chart.Series["Memory"].Points.DataBindXY($DeploymentComputers.Server, $AllMemAvailableMB_Data.CookedValue)

# Sets the title to the date and time
$title = new-object System.Windows.Forms.DataVisualization.Charting.Title
$Chart.Titles.Add( $title )
$Chart.Titles[0].Text = date

# Saves the chart to a file
$Chart.SaveImage("$SavePath" + "C:\RDDeploymentMem.png","png")
```

Deployment IO

```powershell
Import-Module RemoteDesktop

# Sets your ACTIVE connection broker and the path where to save the image
$RDConnectionBroker = "CRLAB-CB01.crlab.local"
$SavePath = "C:\"

# Disk Counters for all servers part of the RDS deployment
$AllDiskReadsSec_Counter = '\PhysicalDisk(_Total)\Disk Reads/sec'
$AllDiskWritesSec_Counter = '\PhysicalDisk(_Total)\Disk Writes/sec'

# Retrieves which servers are in the deployment
$DeploymentComputers = Get-RDServer -ConnectionBroker $RDConnectionBroker | Select-Object Server
```

```powershell
# Retrieves the counters
$GetAllDiskReadsSec = Get-Counter -counter $AllDiskReadsSec_Counter
-ComputerName $DeploymentComputers.Server
$GetAllDiskWritesSec = Get-Counter -counter $AllDiskWritesSec_Counter
-ComputerName $DeploymentComputers.Server

$AllDiskReadsSec_Data = $GetAllDiskReadsSec.CounterSamples | Select-Object
CookedValue
$AllDiskWritesSec_Data = $GetAllDiskWritesSec.CounterSamples | Select-Object
CookedValue

# Loads the appropriate assemblies for the graphs
[void][Reflection.Assembly]::LoadWithPartialName("System.Windows.Forms")
[void][Reflection.Assembly]::LoadWithPartialName("System.Windows.Forms.
DataVisualization")

# Creates a chart object
$Chart = New-object System.Windows.Forms.DataVisualization.Charting.Chart
$Chart.Width = 1000
$Chart.Height = 600
$Chart.Left = 10
$Chart.Top = 10

# Creates a chartarea for the Memory Data
$ChartArea = New-Object System.Windows.Forms.DataVisualization.Charting.
ChartArea
$ChartArea.AxisX.Interval = 1
$ChartArea.AxisX.Title = "Deployment Hosts"
$ChartArea.AxisY.Interval = 100
$ChartArea.AxisY.Title = "Disk Operations"
$Chart.ChartAreas.Add($ChartArea)


[void]$Chart.Series.Add("DiskReads")
$Chart.Series["DiskReads"]["DrawingStyle"] = "Cylinder"
$Chart.Series["DiskReads"].color = "#00FF00"
```

```
[void]$Chart.Series.Add("DiskWrites")
$Chart.Series["DiskWrites"]["DrawingStyle"] = "Cylinder"
$Chart.Series["DiskWrites"].color = "#0000FF"

# Adds Legends
$Legend = New-Object system.Windows.Forms.DataVisualization.Charting.Legend
$Legend.name = "Legend1"
$Chart.Legends.Add($Legend)
$Chart.Series["DiskReads"].Legend = "Legend1"
$Chart.Series["DiskWrites"].Legend = "Legend1"

# Plots the data
$Chart.Series["DiskReads"].Points.DataBindXY($DeploymentComputers.Server, $AllDiskReadsSec_Data.CookedValue)
$Chart.Series["DiskWrites"].Points.DataBindXY($DeploymentComputers.Server, $AllDiskWritesSec_Data.CookedValue)

# Sets the title to the date and time
$title = new-object System.Windows.Forms.DataVisualization.Charting.Title
$Chart.Titles.Add( $title )
$Chart.Titles[0].Text = date

# Saves the chart to a file
$Chart.SaveImage("$SavePath" + "C:\RDDeploymentDisk.png","png")
```

Now the final step is to create a simple web page that will show all five graphs created by the scripts above.

Launch 'Notepad' and copy and paste the following:

```
<html xmlns="http://www.w3.org/1999/xhtml">
    <head>
        <title>RDS Deployment</title>
        <meta http-equiv="refresh" content="60">
    </head>
    <body>
        <img src=".\RDDeploymentCPU.png">
        <img src=".\RDDeploymentMem.png">
```

```html
            <img src=".\RDDeploymentDisk.png">
            <img src=".\RDSHConnections.png">
            <img src=".\RDGWConnections.png">
        </body>
</html>
```

Save it to a file named RDS.html. Normally we copy this to a folder on a webserver and change the path on the scripts where the files will be saved to match the folder on the remote web server.

This will give you a nice and simple dashboard with full visibility on your RDS deployment. Is it perfect? Nope. But it is better than using 'Perfmon' in our opinion.

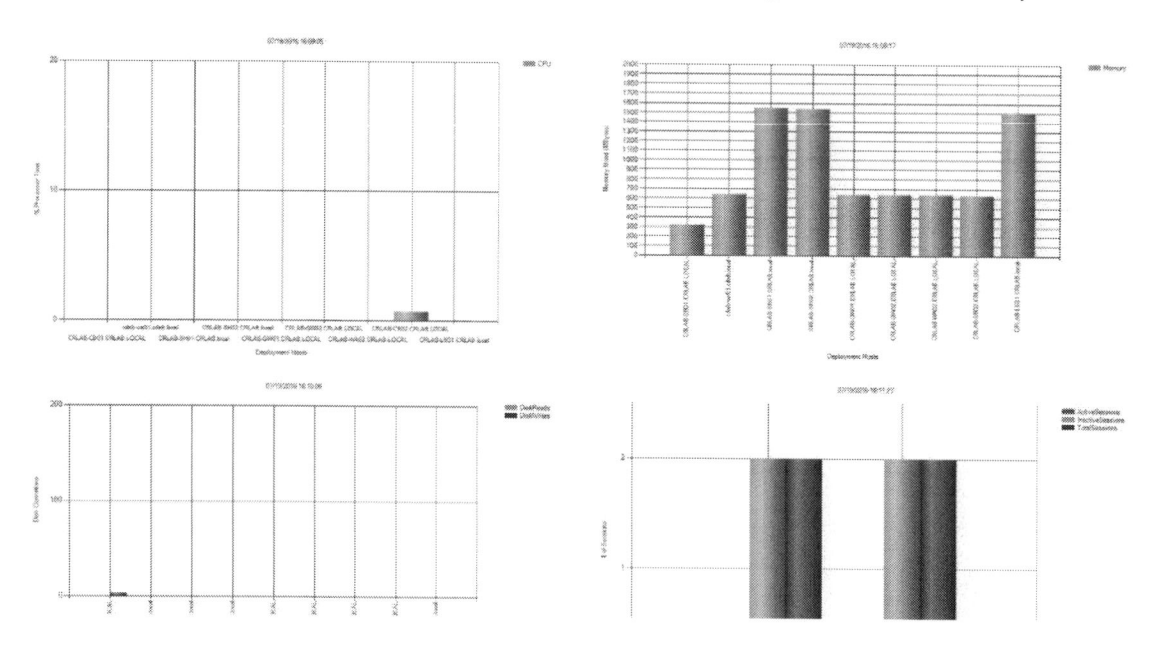

ControlUp Real-time

When dealing with multiple servers, managing an RDS environment becomes a major problem. And by multiple servers we do not mean medium or large environments with fifty (50) or more servers. As you realized by now, even a small RDS deployment, if done properly and with full HA on all components, does require a minimum of ten (10) servers. Why? A quick recap:

- Two RDCBs.
- Two RDGWs.
- Two RDLSs.
- Two RDWAs.
- Two RDSHs.

In addition, if we add the required backend servers to the picture, you are now dealing with at least fourteen (14) servers. Yes, two file servers (clustered) and two SQL servers (clustering, AlwaysOn, etc).

Using the built-in tools will be a major pain. Trust us. We had to go through this several times. Even though we were able to create a simple web-based dashboard using PowerShell (that can certainly be improved), the reality is once you reach a certain scale, you need more visibility about the environment and more than that, the ability to actually manage it instead of just keeping an eye on a dashboard.

What most people do not realize is the fact it takes time to build an in-house solution (i.e. with scripts) to monitor everything. Time is money so at the end of the day even a homegrown solution costs money. By doing the math you will realize it costs way more than initially thought and potentially more than something already developed by companies that specialize in that particular area. That is where ControlUp comes to the picture with their amazing ControlUp Real-time solution.

It not only gives you a complete overview of your environment, in an easy-to-read dashboard but it goes beyond that, allowing you to automate many tasks you have to perform on a daily basis.

After testing many tools in this market, tailored for RDS, we guarantee you, ControlUp Real-time is the way to go for its features and affordable pricing.

Installing ControlUp Real-time

Before you proceed, we highly recommend you dedicate a machine for management purposes. We mentioned that when we did our first RDS deployment ever. If you do not remember why, let's refresh your memory a bit.

Ideally, you want to have a server (two for redundancy) for management purposes only, where all your required consoles to manage the environment would be installed.

The managed components would then be configured to only allow changes if these were coming from the management servers. In addition, to top it off, a session recording solution would be installed and enabled on these, so every single change and action by administrators would be recorded for later playback. Does not get better than this.

So assuming you do have such server, connect to it and download ControlUp Real-time from here:

https://www.controlup.com/download-direct-controlup/?autodownload=true

The installation is quite simple as there is nothing to install ☺. All you need to do is to unzip the folder you downloaded and copy the only executable (ControlUpConsole.exe) to a folder (i.e. C:\Program Files\ControlUp) and create a shortcut to it on the server desktop or start menu.

1. After launching it you will be greeted by the signup screen. Click 'Create a new account'.

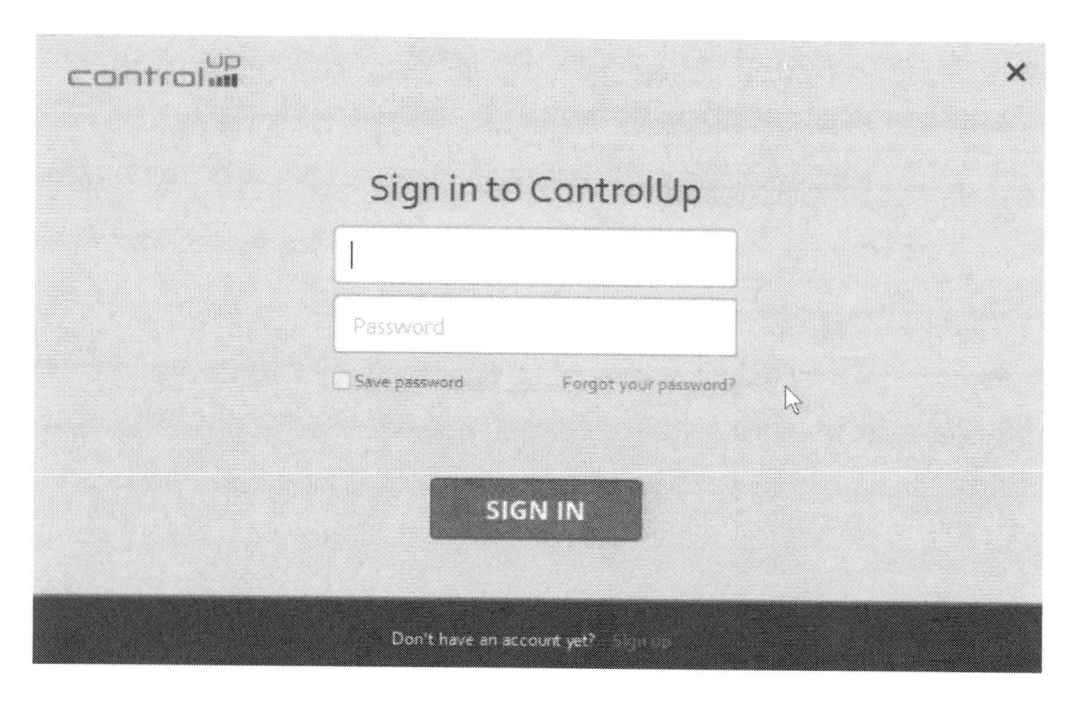

2. Enter your information and accept the terms of use.

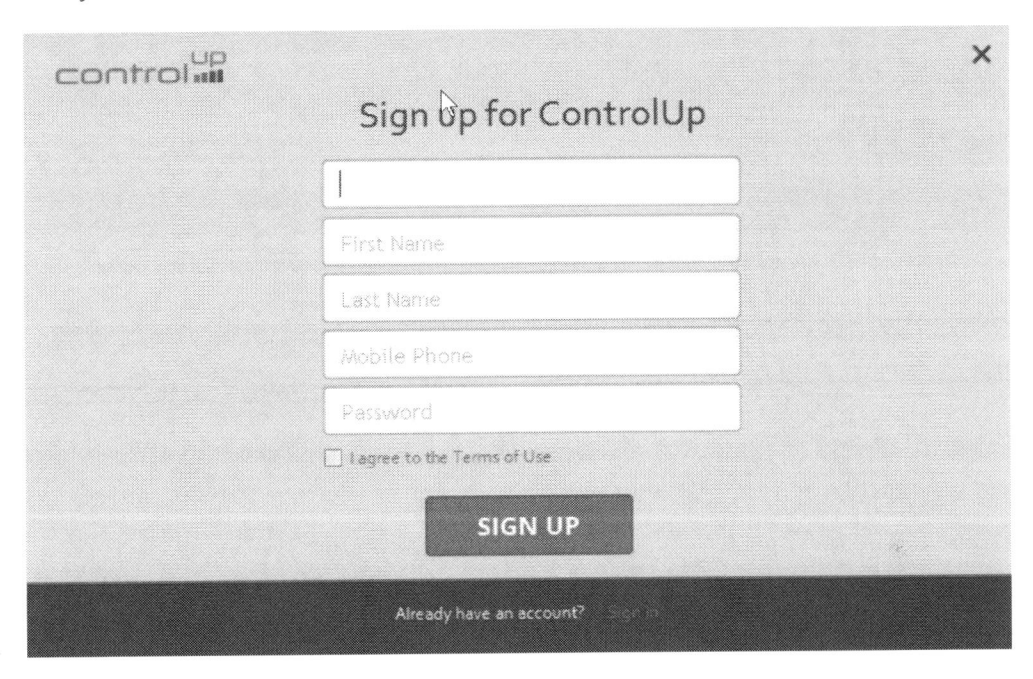

3. It will ask you to validate your email address. Click 'OK'.

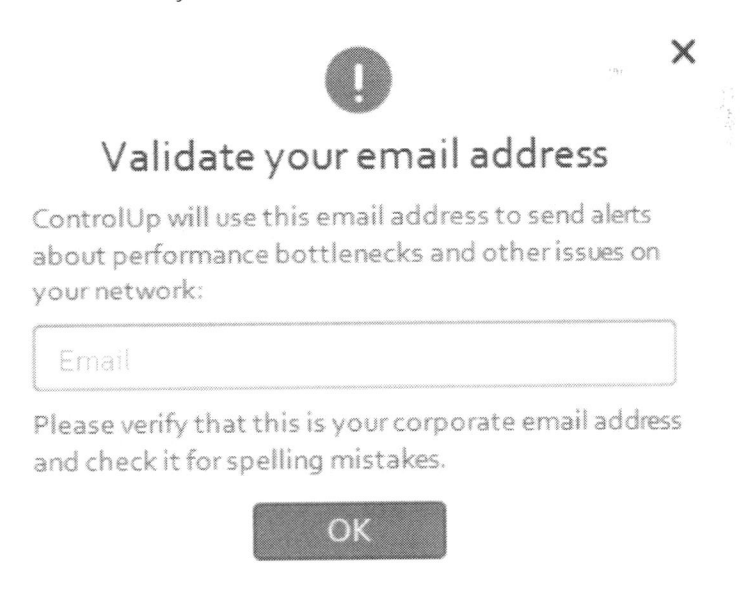

4. The first thing you need to do is to create a 'ControlUp Organization'. These entities represent groups of computers managed by the same administrative personnel. You can indeed have as many organizations as needed (i.e. to differentiate production and test environments). Enter a name and click 'Continue'.

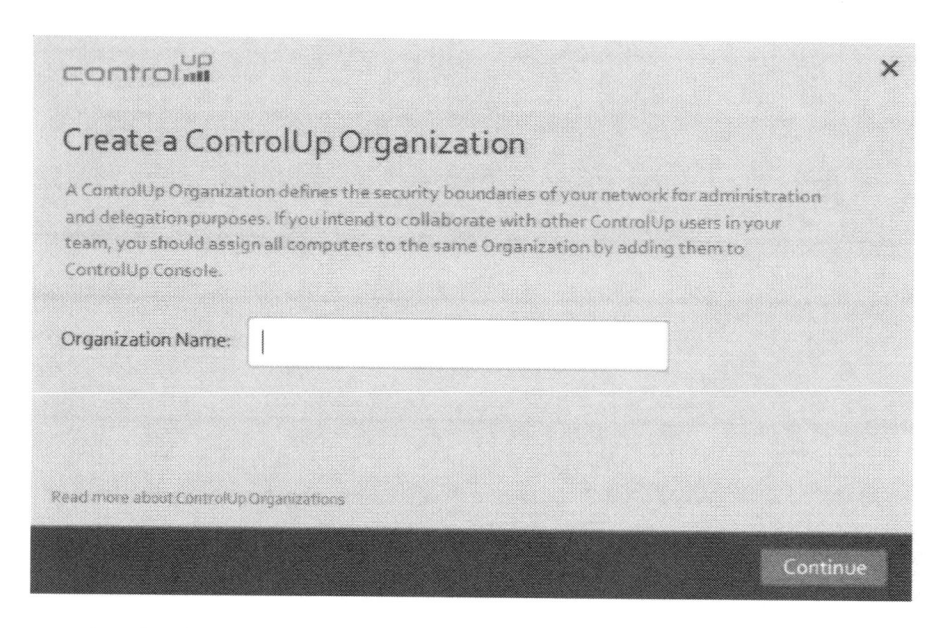

5. The wizard will take care of everything, setting up your first organization. Time to get a coffee.

6. The console is now ready. Time to start using 'ControlUp Real-time'.

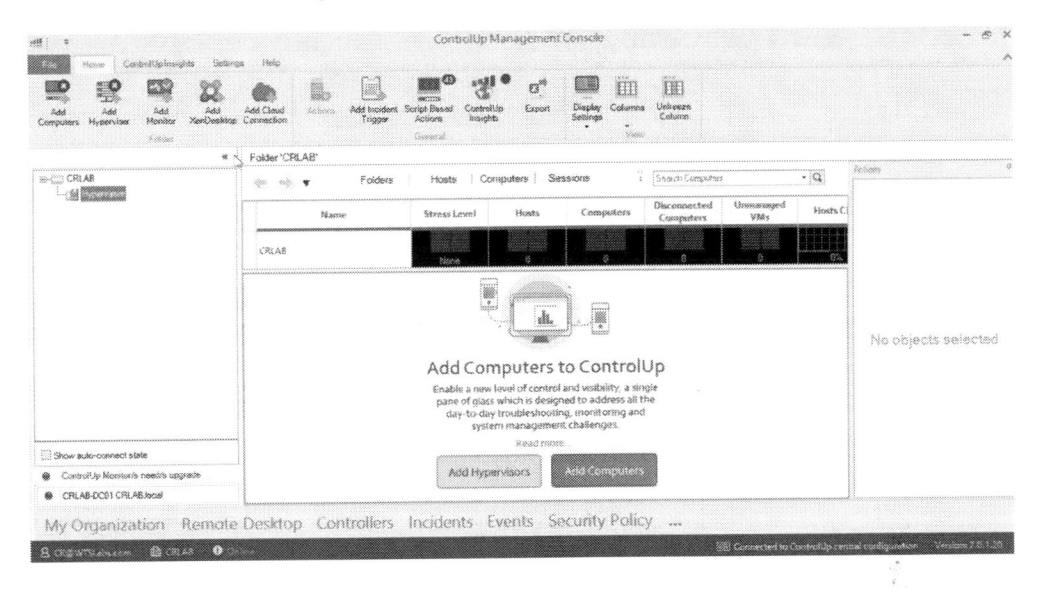

Configuring ControlUp Real-time

As you could see, installing the product could not be easier. Single executable copy. Nice. Now that we have it up and running, time to configure it, so we can have our entire RDS infrastructure loaded in the console.

1. On the main window, click 'Add Computers' (note you can indeed add your hypervisor in case the RDS environment is VM-based).

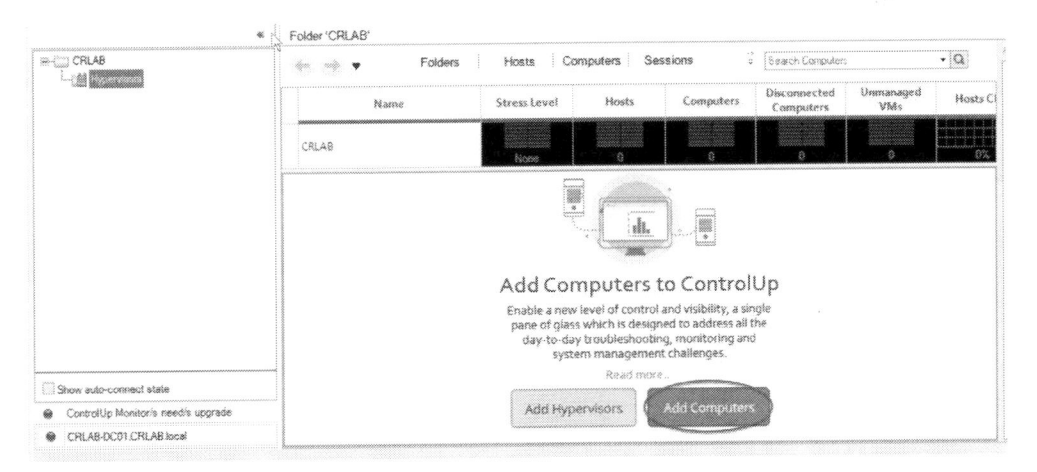

2. Assuming you do have rights to your domain (remember, you need that), you will see a list of computers, all retrieved from the domain by the console! Select all the RDS servers, click 'Add', and then click 'OK'.

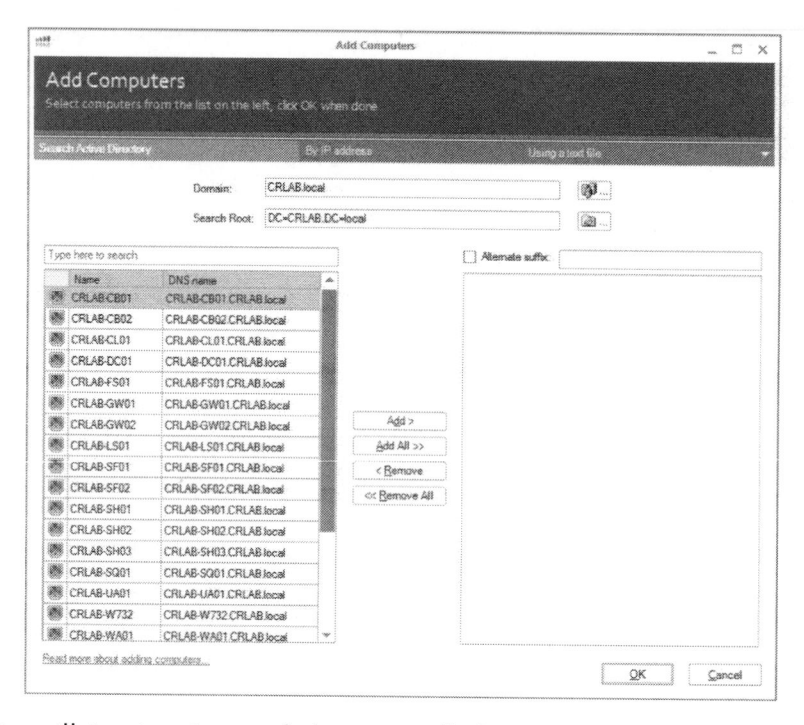

3. ControlUp will try to ping and then install the agent on all these computers remotely. In case RPC/WMI is blocked by the Windows Firewall, the easiest way to get the installation done is to temporarily disable the Windows Firewall on all these servers (i.e. using a group policy) and once the agent is installed, re-enable the firewall. You will also need to allow the ControlUp agent to communicate (cuAgent.exe, on port TCP 40705). This can be done by creating a firewall rule and enforcing it with a group policy as well.

Note: you can also download the agent directly from the ControlUp website and deploy it on all your computers using any Electronic Software Distribution (ESD) system you may have (i.e. SCCM, LanDesk) or a simple group policy. In this case, the MSI downloaded will also take care of opening the appropriate ports on the Windows Firewall. You can download it here:

https://www.controlup.com/products/controlup/agent/

4. Once the agent is installed and the appropriate ports opened at the firewall, you can now see your whole environment:

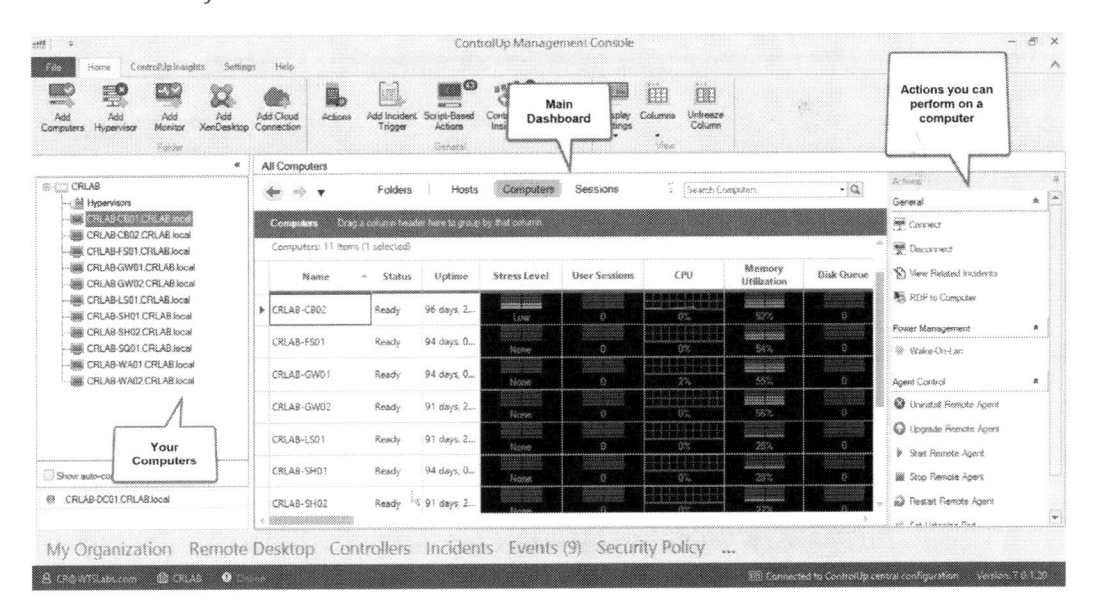

5. The next step, for total integration, is to add the hypervisor. On the ribbon, click 'Home' and then 'Add Hypervisor'.

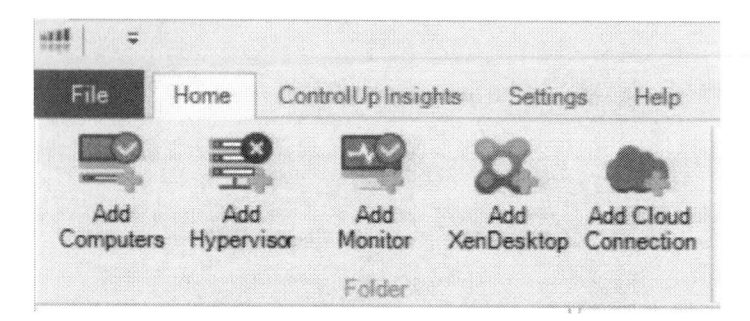

6. Select the hypervisor you have (VMware or XenServer) and enter the required information, as seen on the screen. Then click 'OK'.

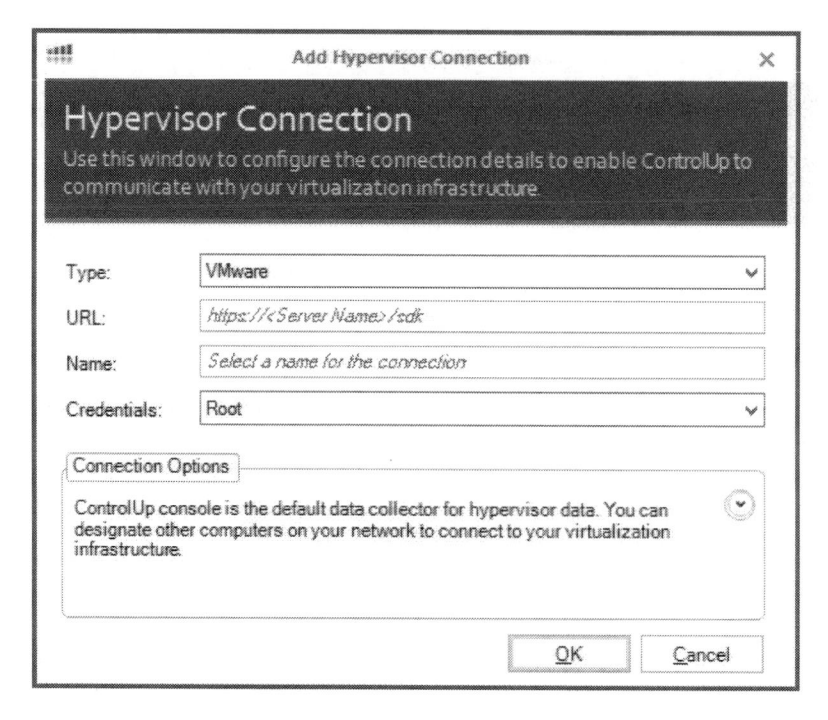

7. Your hypervisor should appear on the left pane.

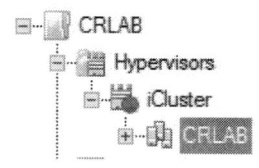

8. Before we dig into the important information about the RDS environment that ControlUp can give you, let's take a quick look at what is shown for the hypervisor, as it is not only extremely relevant information but also very cool. ☺ As you can see it shows the two hosts I have on my lab, both running ESXi 5.5. It then shows how many CPU cores, installed memory and how much work these servers are doing (the 'Stress Level'). Then you see it, the vCPU/pCPU ratio, something many people seem to ignore. This shows you how much CPU you are overcommitting. Right now on my lab, we can see I am using 12 cores in one host and 16 on the second one (therefore the vCPU/pCPU ratio of 3 and 4 respectively). This is something you cannot easily get using the out-of-the-box tools that come with Windows. Here? Easy.

Hosts: 2 Items

Name	Hypervisor Version	CPU Cores	Installed Memory	Stress Level	vCPU/pCPU Ratio
192.168.123.240	VMware ESXi 5.5.0 build-1623387	4	15.9 (GB)	Low	3
192.168.123.241	VMware ESXi 5.5.0 build-1623387	4	15.9 (GB)	Low	4

So far, as you can see, ControlUp provides a lot of information about pretty much everything on your RDS infrastructure, from the hypervisor layer all the way to the RDSHs users connect to run their applications.

Before we continue, it is important to clarify a couple things on how ControlUp works and its components. This will give you a much better understanding about the product, where the data goes and how to use it in a corporate environment.

The main components on ControlUp 7.X are:

- **Console.** That single executable you extracted and ran, to configure the product for the first time. Once it is up and running, if you added any hosts or computers to the console, it will then retrieve the metrics from all the managed objects. As you have guessed, if the console is off, nothing gets retrieved.

- **Monitor.** We will get to it in a second. The monitor is like the console but with a big difference: it runs as a service and therefore, runs all the time. It will use whatever credentials you want, collecting information about everything you entered at the console. So normally you will have multiple consoles (for let's say multiple administrators within your organization) and two monitors (for redundancy purposes). That is why the monitor can track things like machines being powered on and off (as it runs all the time) and the console cannot.

- **Agents.** We saw these already. Needed on all managed devices. Can be downloaded and deployed using any ESD as it is in MSI format. Needs port TCP 40705 (the MSI installer opens the required port). Console and monitor communicate with the agent over this port.

Now what about all the collected data? As you have guessed, once you sign up, all the data being collected is stored in the 'ControlUp Cloud'. This is the default way the product works. Of course, if due to regulations or any other reason you do want to use ControlUp fully on-premises, that is not a problem. The product can be installed and configured to work that way. Even offline if required. How to do it is beyond the scope of this book (hey this is an RDS 2012 R2 book, not a full hands-on guide for ControlUp after all ☺). All that information, including handy videos, is readily available on their website, on our special landing page!

http://www.controlup.com/RDS2012R2Complete.

The final piece of the puzzle, introduced with ControlUp 5.x is 'ControlUp Insights' and as you correctly guessed, we will be covering it. The main idea is, all the data collected is uploaded to the the 'ControlUp Cloud' (again, if using the default architecture) and once there, 'Insights' will analyze all the data and produce some excellent reports, correlating all the information collected. Amazing stuff.

Before we get all this going, time to get the 'ControlUp Monitor' going.

Configuring ControlUp Monitor

Now that everything is up and running, time to add a monitor to the environment.

1. Launch the 'ControlUp Console' and under 'Home', click 'Add Monitor'.

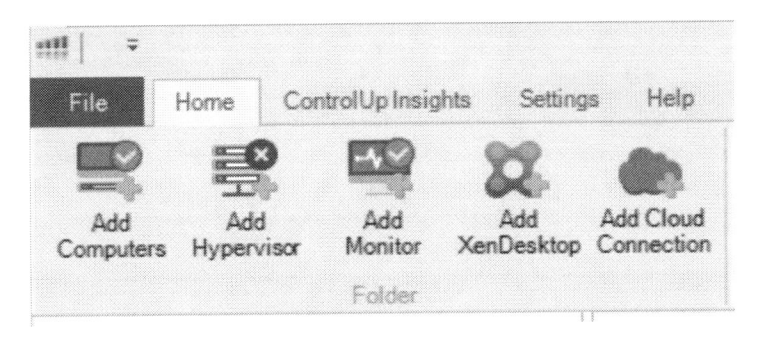

2. The wizard will launch. Click 'Next'.

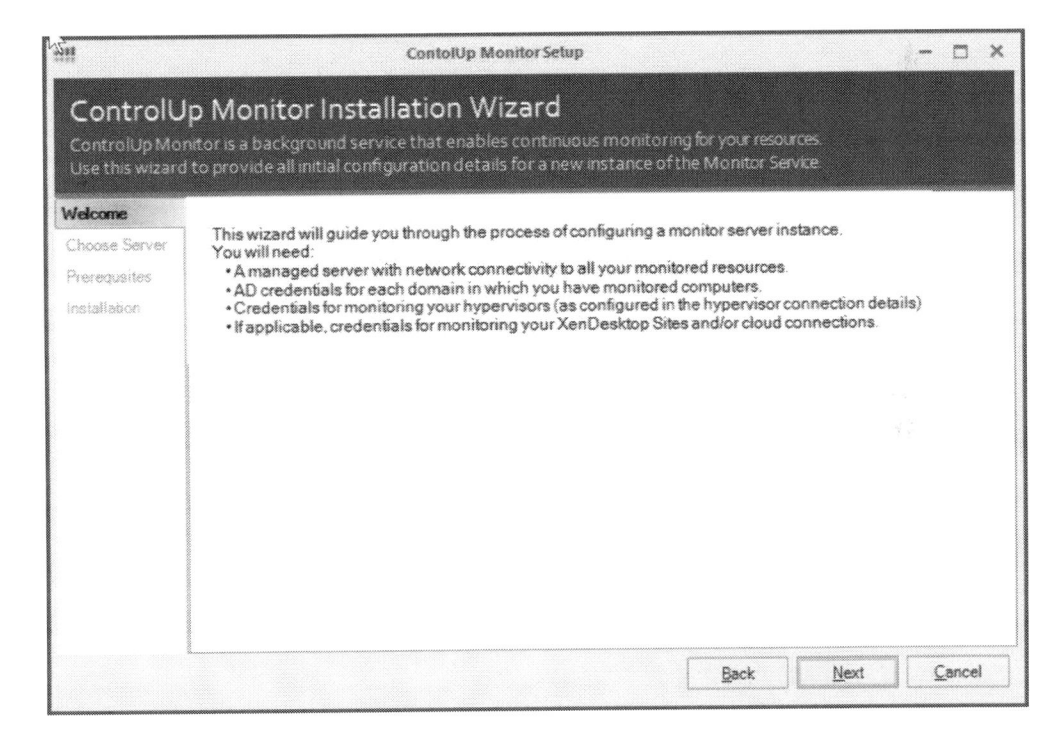

3. Select the computer you want to host the monitoring service. We do recommend a management server (as already explained). Click 'Next'.

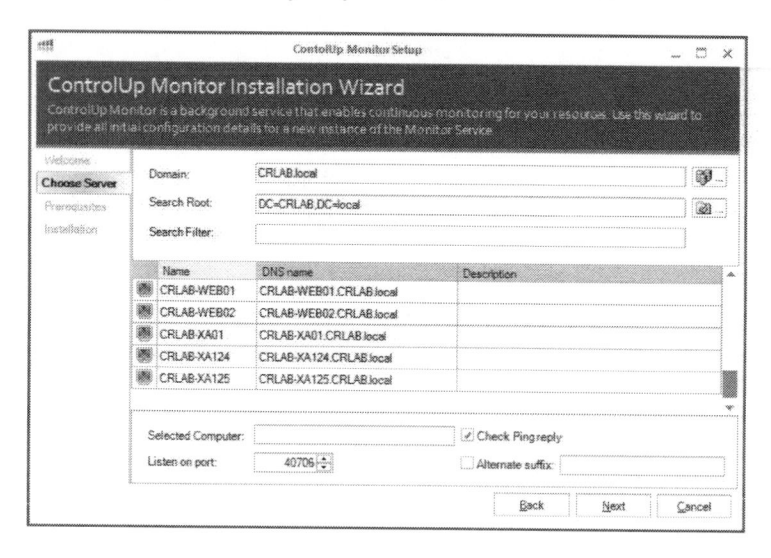

4. The wizard will run a couple tests to determine if all pre-requisites are met. Click 'Next'.

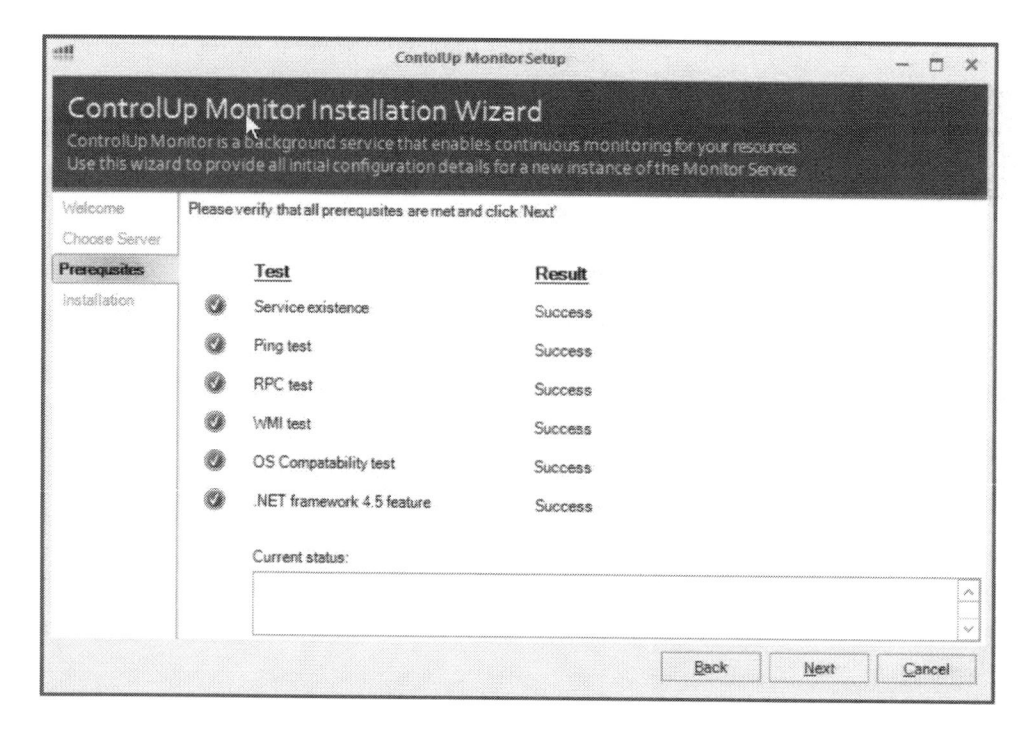

5. The installation will start.

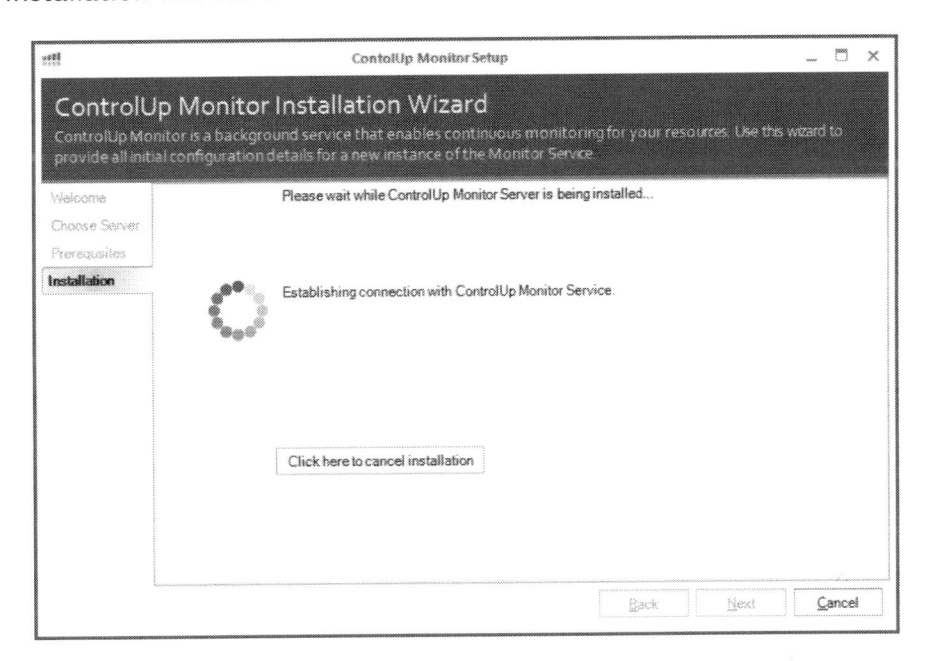

6. Once the install is done, the wizard will automatically go to the next step and will ask you to select or create new credentials that will be used by the monitoring service. Enter the required information (we do recommend a service account for this) and click 'OK'.

7. Review the information and click 'Next'. If you want to monitor the hypervisor as well, you will need to enter credentials for that (just click 'Add Credentials Set...' on the lower left corner).

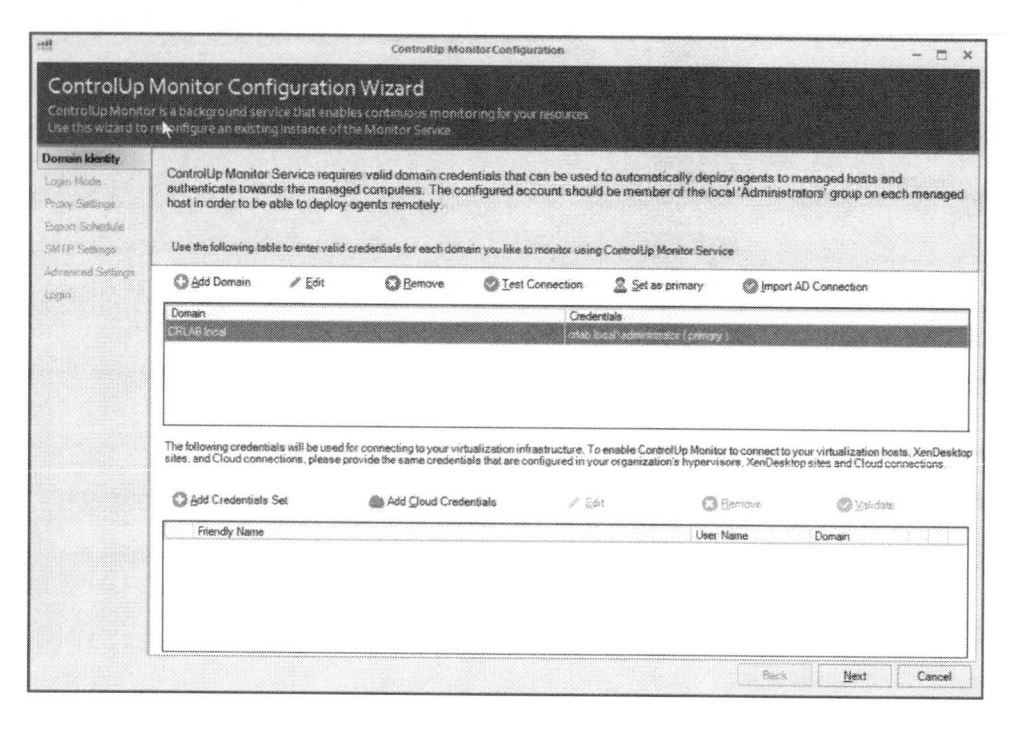

8. If you do not enter any credentials for the hypervisor, you may get a warning message. Simply click 'Yes'.

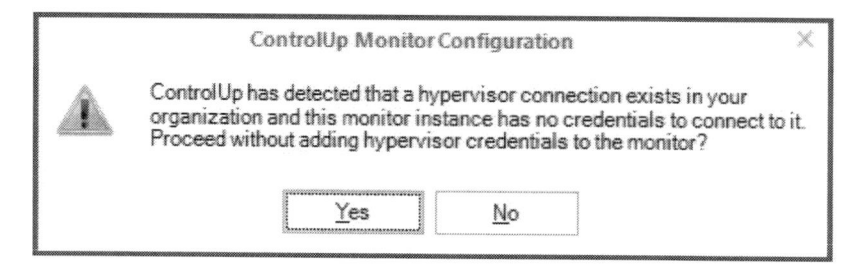

9. Select the authentication method you want to use and click 'Next'. This is how ControlUp determines the license you have. To use it in offline mode, you will need to request an offline license (simply select 'Offline' and then click 'Create a new Offline License Request' – note that in this case, email alerting and incident analysis will not be available).

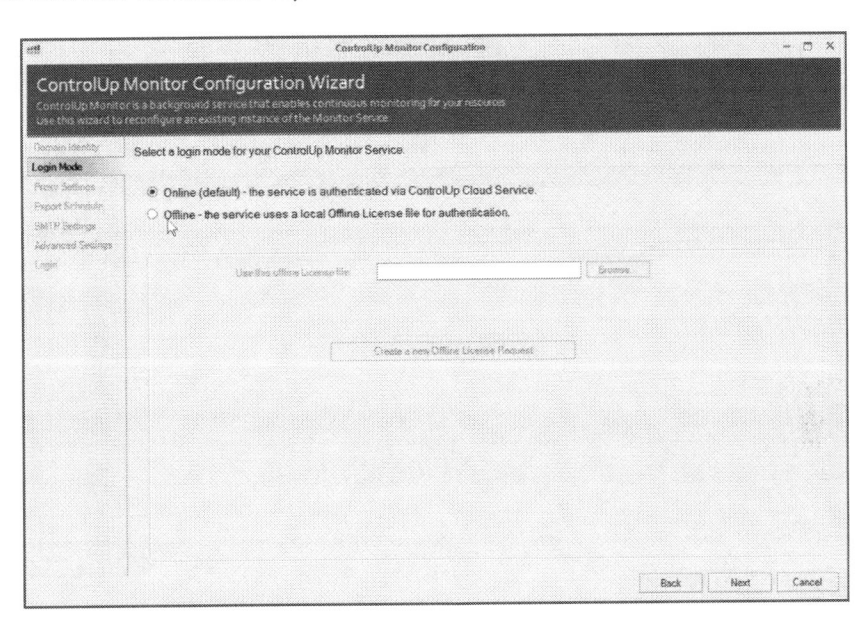

10. Choose your proxy settings and click 'Next'.

11. If you want, you can export the data collected by the monitor on a particular schedule, so you can analyze it using something like Excel. For the purposes of this book, simply click 'Next'.

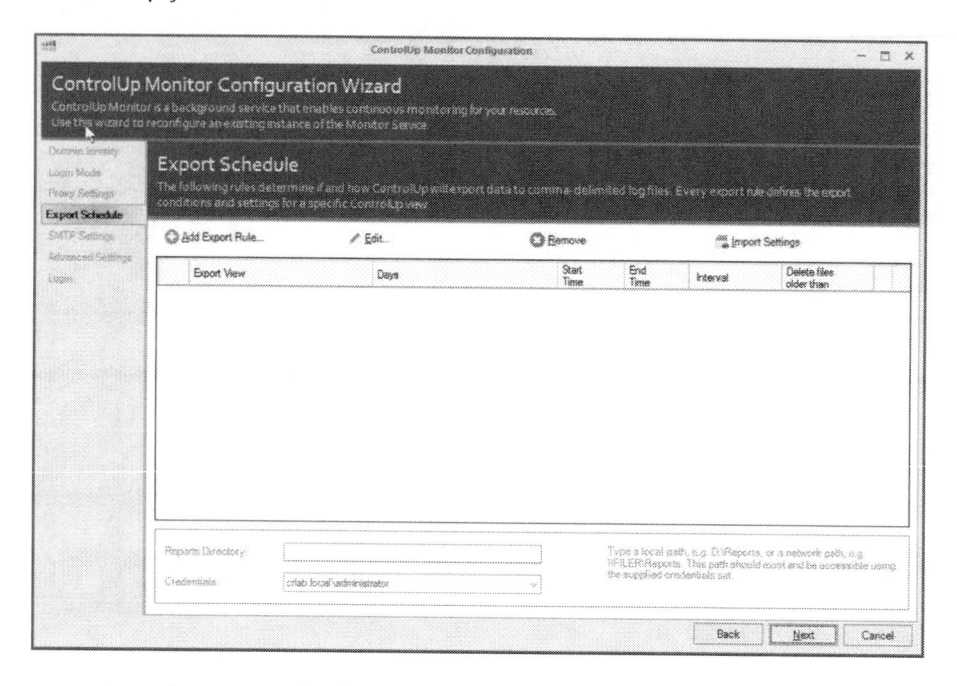

12. If you want to have email alerts, just click 'Add SMTP Server' to add all the required information (server, sender address, port, etc) and then click 'Next'.

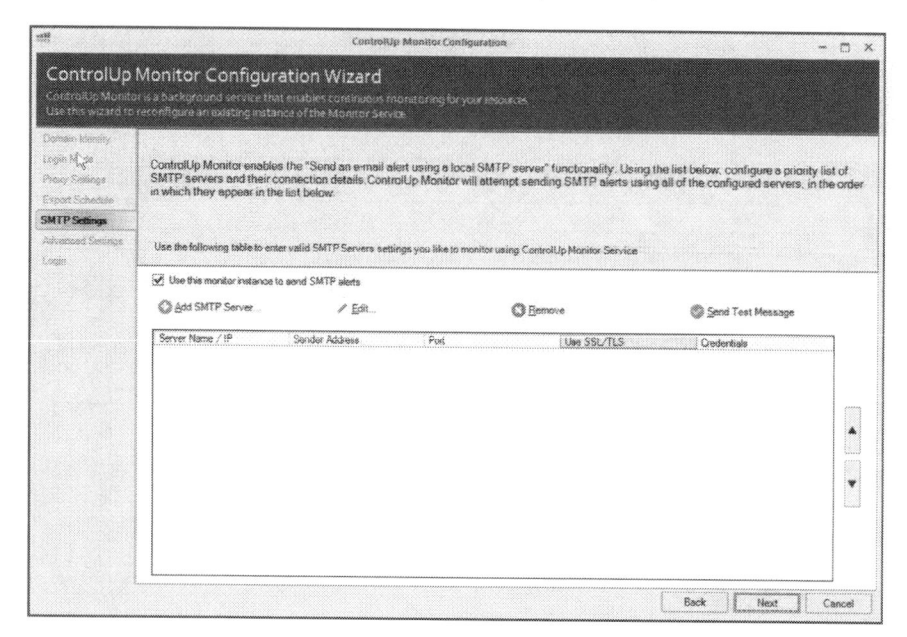

Page 462 | RDS - The Complete Guide

13. For the 'Advanced Settings' just accept the default and click 'Next'.

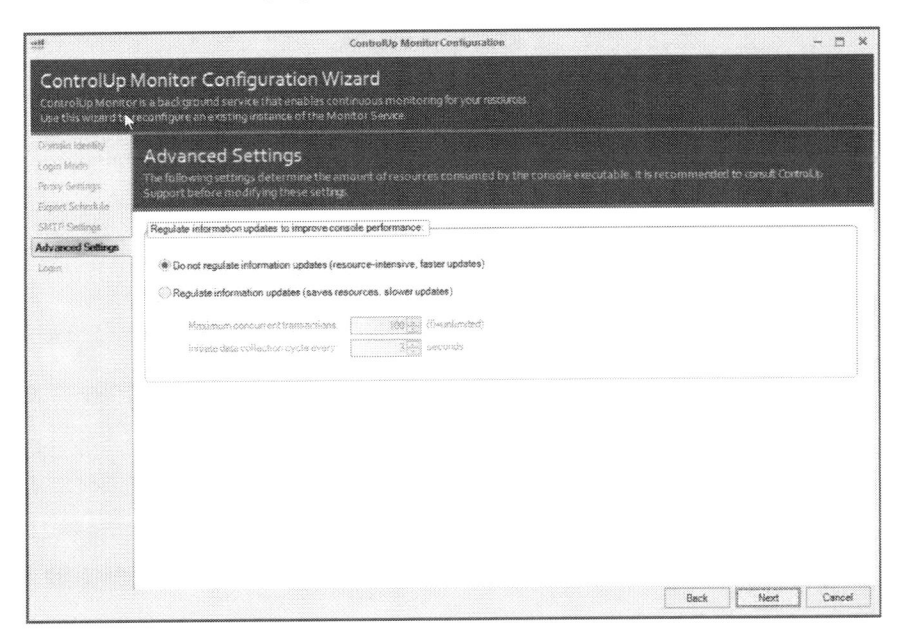

14. The wizard will attempt to login (assuming 'Online' mode). You are done. Click 'Finish'.

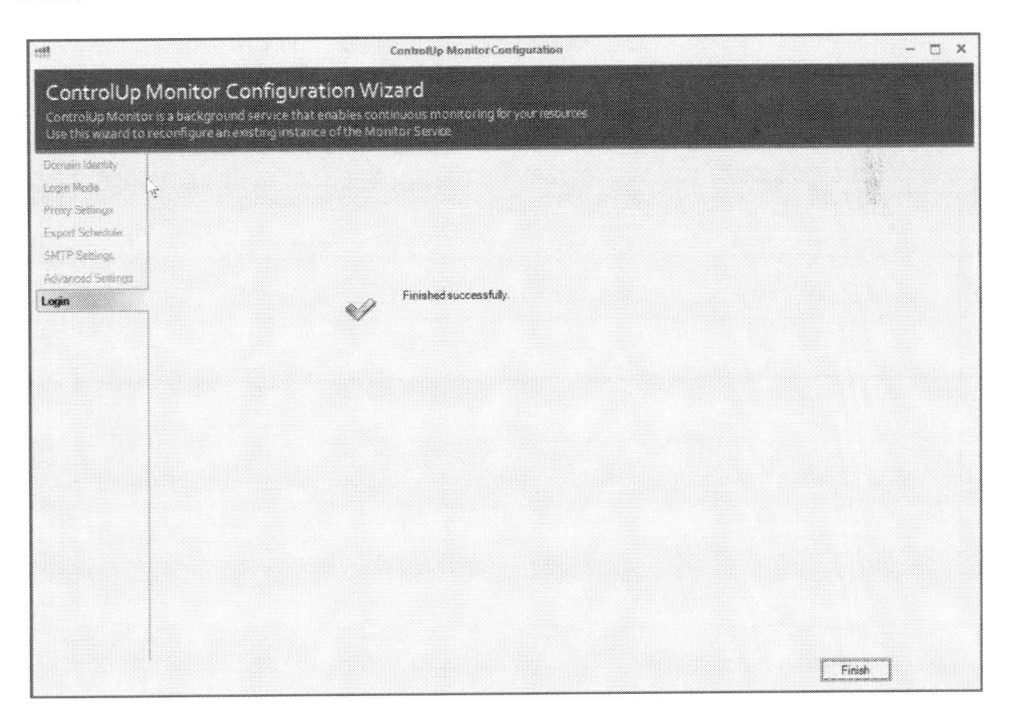

Ok, great. We do have a monitor up and running. Now what can we do with all that information? That is where 'ControlUp Insights' comes to the picture. Let's get it working and see what it is capable of.

ControlUp Insights

We are not only looking at the pretty dashboards in the 'ControlUp Console' but now we have our monitoring service collecting all this data for us about our environment. So what do we do with all this data? That is the job of 'ControlUp Insights'.

In its current form, it gives us a series of very important reports for any RDS environment. Everything is ready for us out-of-the-box. More than that, if there is a need for additional reports, ControlUp can add these easily!

However, the best part of all this is the fact all the metrics collected, from all ControlUp customers worldwide, are analyzed and the averages for all these, calculated. This allows you to determine how your own environment is performing compared to everyone else on the globe!

Note: it is worth mentioning this data does not contain any sensitive information about the environment where these were collected. It is important to clarify this in case your company asks. ControlUp can explain in details what is collected and for how long such data is stored. Of course, your own data, only accessible by your company, will have information about your domain, usernames, and computer names and so on. However, the data used for calculating the averages mentioned does not carry such sensitive information over.

The next step is to setup an account within your company to have access to the 'ControlUp Insights' platform.

Configuring ControlUp Insights

1. Launch the 'ControlUp Console' and under the 'ControlUp Insights' tab, click 'User Permissions'.

2. The account you created when installing the product should be listed. Select 'Permitted to use ControlUp Insights' on the right. Click 'Ok'.

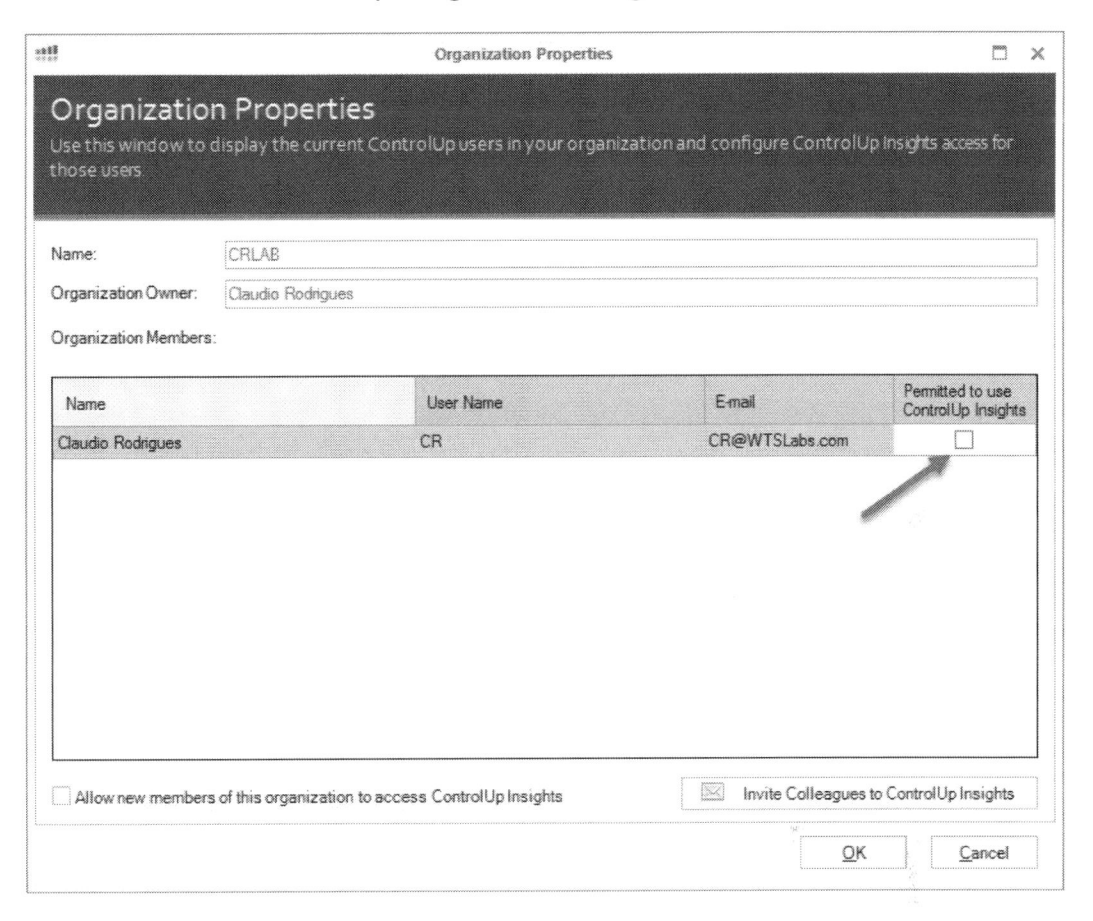

3. Now under 'ControlUp Insights' click on 'ControlUp Insights' (yes I know it sounds redundant but hey, I am not the developer).

4. If you did not check the checkbox mentioned above, you will see an error similar to this:

5. Assuming you did what we told you to do ☺ you should get connected to the 'ControlUp Insights' website, with no further credentials required (it will use the credentials you used to logon at the console) and the 'ControlUp Insights' dashboard will come up.

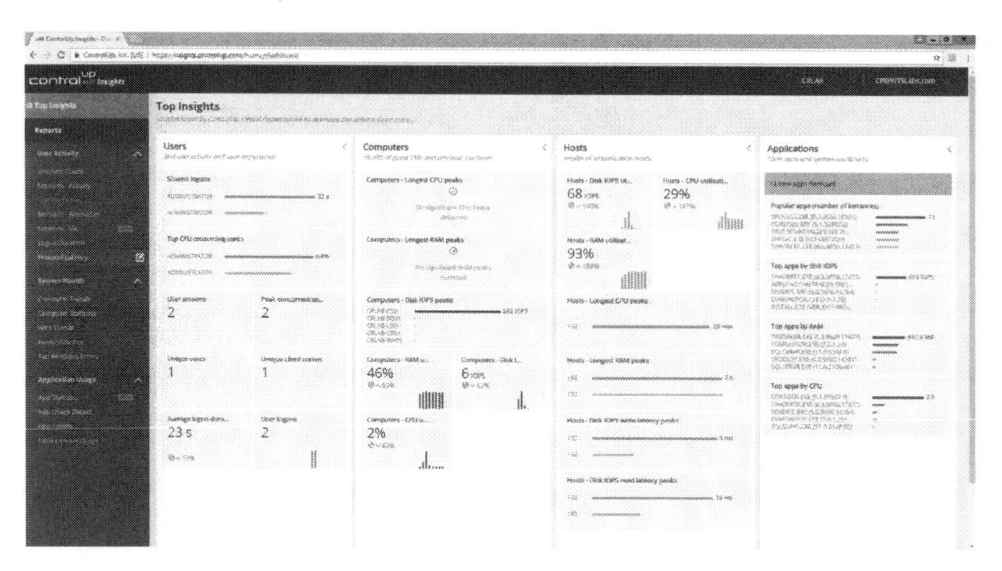

6. 'ControlUp Insights' is now working, with data collected and uploaded by the 'ControlUp Monitor' server we setup earlier. Keep in mind there is a delay until all the data is available for the reports.

ControlUp Insights reports

As we mentioned before, 'ControlUp Insights' is what I call a 'community fueled' reporting engine. The reason for that is the fact it compares your own environment performance to the average calculated from data collected around the globe, from existing ControlUp customers.

This not only gives you a good indication on how your own environment is performing but also how close (or far) you are to what is out there, performance wise.

Now that you have the whole ControlUp infrastructure up and running, let's take a look at some of the reports built-in to 'ControlUp Insights'.

- **Sessions Count:** this shows you all the computers monitored by ControlUp and all the sessions on them. If you have an RDS environment and you want to only see the sessions on your RDSHs, the best way to achieve this, is to create a folder under the 'ControlUp Console' for your RDSHs and move all the servers there. Once you do this, 'ControlUp Insights' can show you this information only for the hosts in that folder.

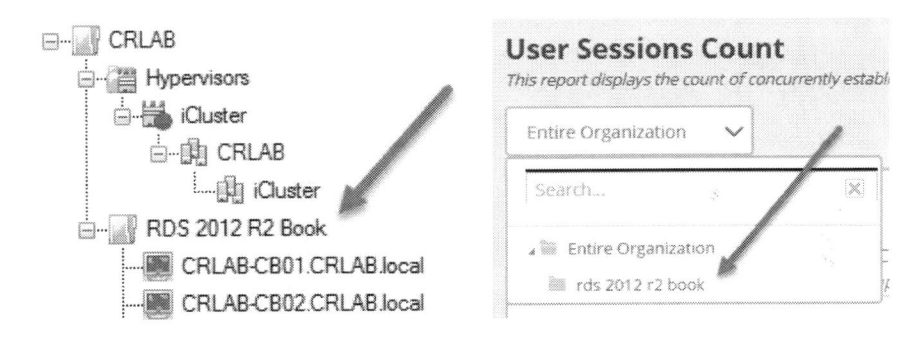

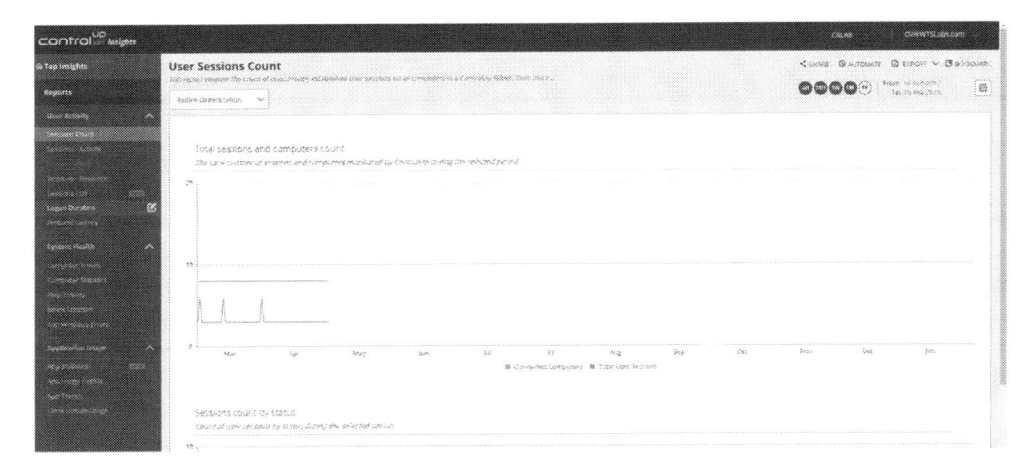

- **Sessions Activity:** shows all the sessions that were established to the computers within your ControlUp organization. As mentioned above, it can be filtered to show only sessions on your RDSHs. Here you get a general overview of the user session with some very useful metrics and information like logon duration, profile load time, client name and even which DC authenticated the user.

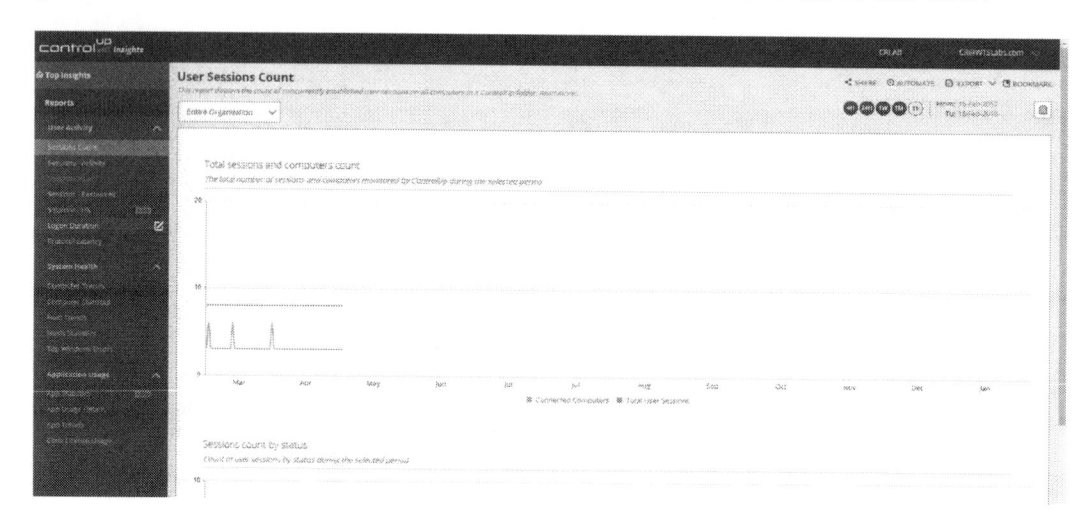

- **Session Details:** Once you click on a username within the 'Session Activity' report, it drills down to that particular user session, showing additional information. Extremely useful when troubleshooting slow session startup for example.

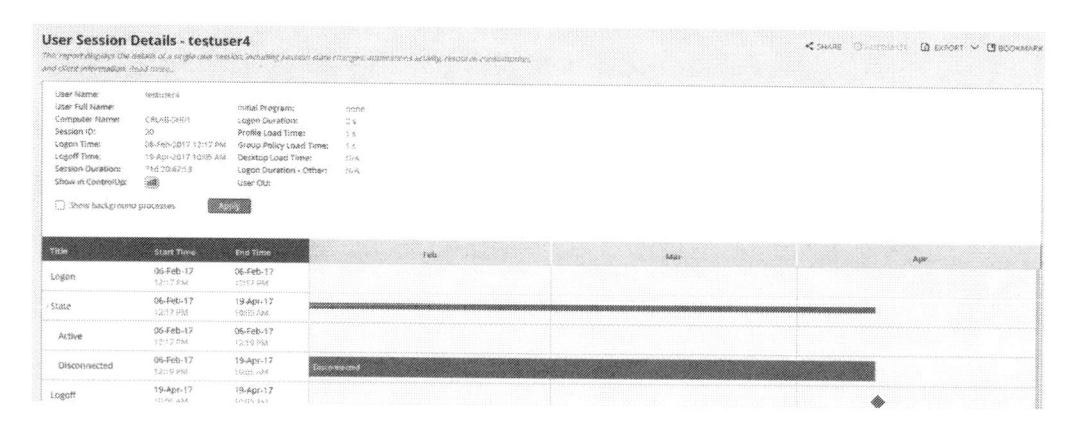

It displays every step taken until the user starts working on a particular application (just scroll down):

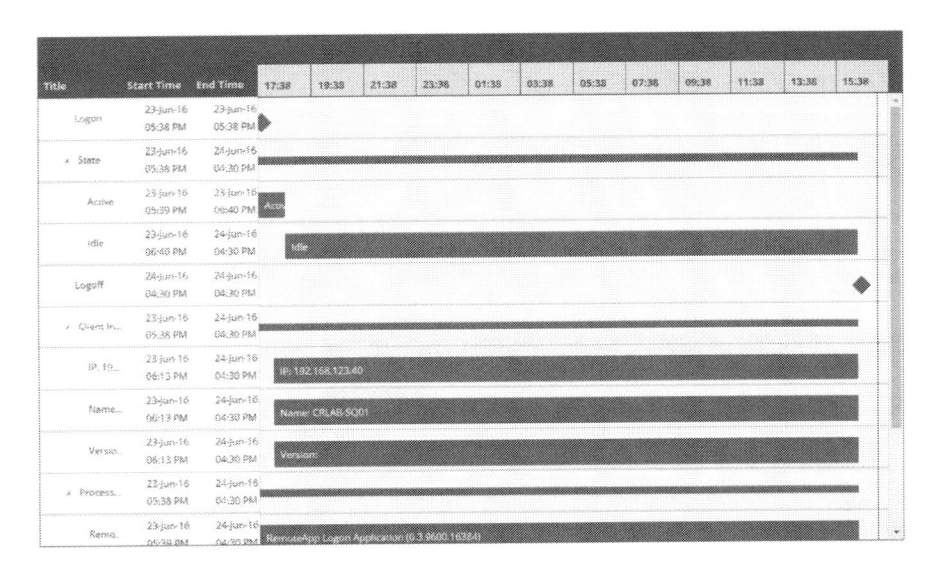

This is the level of detail that you cannot simply get out-of-the-box with RDS 2012 R2. By the way, ControlUp created a PowerShell script to help you troubleshooting slow logons and you can download it right here:

https://www.controlup.com/analyze-logon-duration/

- **Logon Duration:** the main purpose of this report is to show you how your environment is performing, comparing it to the community. As you can see on my lab, the average logon time for my test accounts is 3s, while the community average sits at 27s. The beauty of running all your systems off SSD drives. ☺

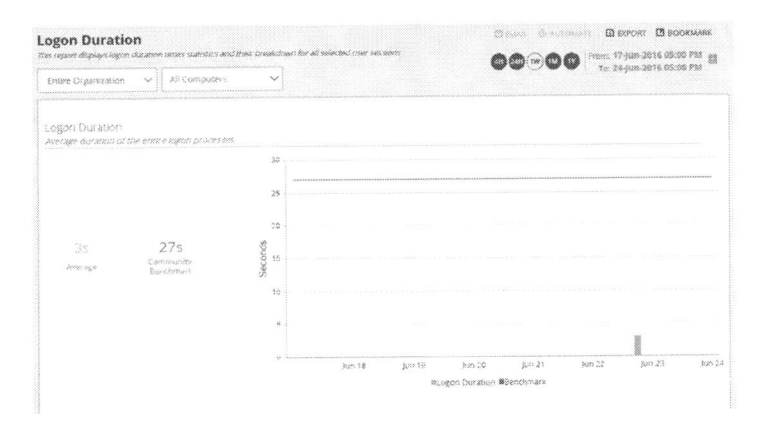

- **Host Trends:** this graph drills down into the hypervisors in use and retrieves all the relevant information that shows how your hosts are performing (CPU, RAM, I/O and Network). Very helpful as sometimes the slowness seen on RDS environments relates to overcommitting host resources like CPU and RAM (what you definitely want to avoid).

- **Top Windows Errors:** a very helpful one. It shows you the most common errors reported on your servers and how often these have been reported in the wild. This allows you to determine if you are experiencing a unique issue or something already seen in many customers. It even has links to the error seen and its causes (from EventID.NET).

- **Application Usage Details:** once you select an application listed on the right hand side, it displays a graph showing how many users have launched that particular application and its peak usage.

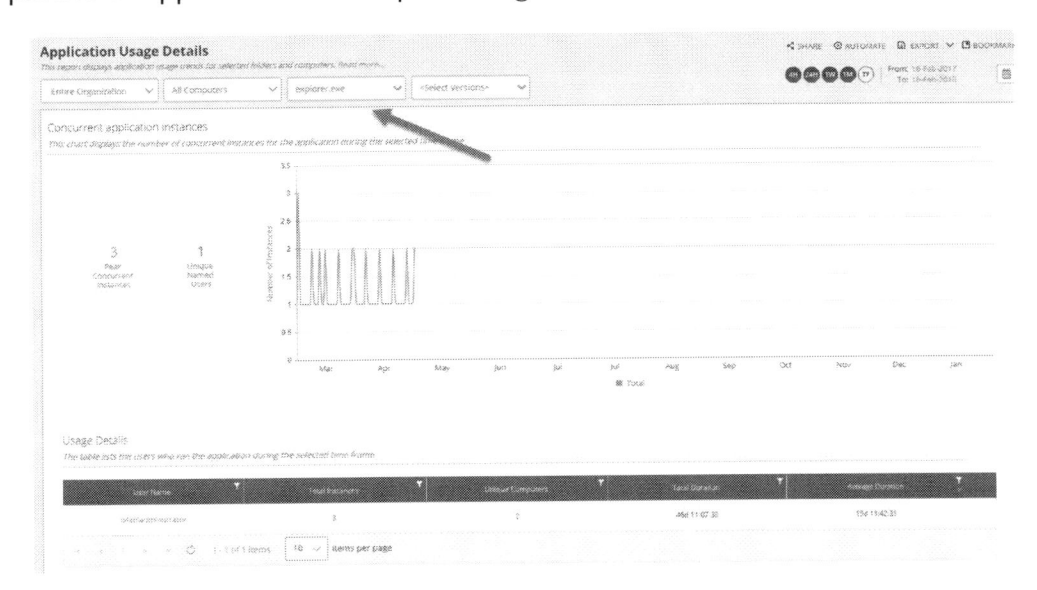

At the bottom, you can easily see from how many endpoints a particular user connected from and the total time spent on a particular application.

This is all regarding 'ControlUp Insights'. Keep in mind it is an evolving platform, where ControlUp keeps adding new reports often. In addition, as we discussed, being able to compare your own environment with what is out there, from thousands of real production environments is indeed extremely valuable.

Additional ControlUp Real-time Features

Even though this is a monitoring product, ControlUp Real-time offers much more. It greatly enhances how administrators interact with the users, in ways not possible with RDMS and the built-in Microsoft tools. Let's take a quick look at some of these amazing features.

Chat

As the name implies, 'Chat' allows you to establish a real-time, two-way chat with any user connected to any of the servers you see in your ControlUp dashboard. Once you double-click a server, you will see a list of all the sessions on that server. You can then right-click the username and select 'Chat' or click on it using the right side panel.

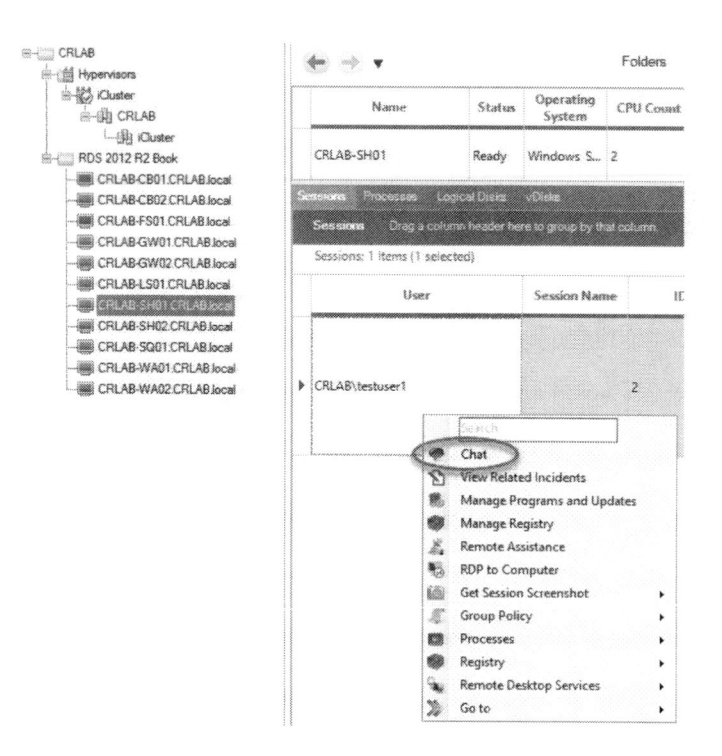

Once selected, the chat application starts on both sides (the administrator and the user session).

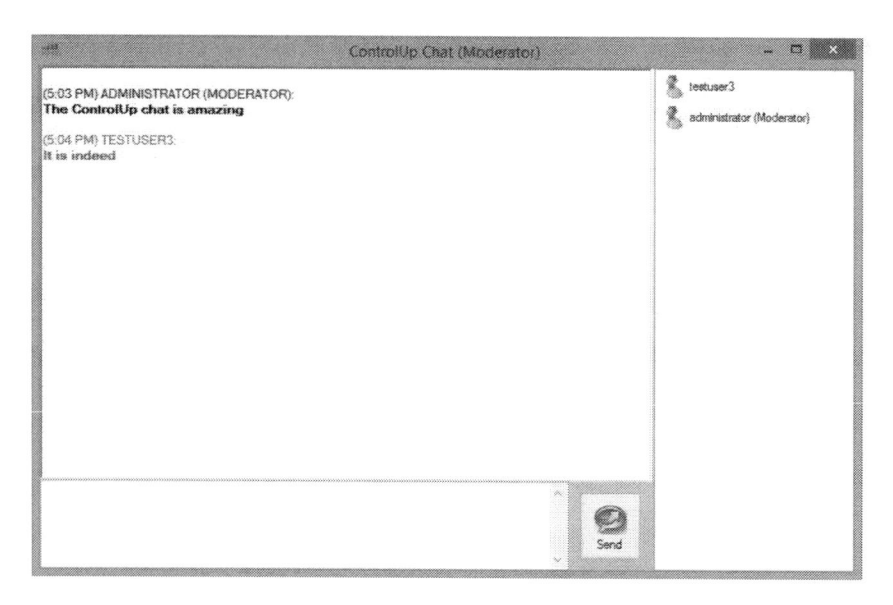

Even though RDMS does offer a way to message users, these are one-way. Users cannot reply to the message.

Session Screenshot

In most case, a picture is worth a thousand words. Exactly the case here. ControlUp allows you to take screenshots of any session running on the servers that are part of the ControlUp environment, with or without the user approval and notification. As with the 'Chat' tool, simply right-click a user and select 'Get Session Screenshot' and then if you want to notify the user (and ask for his approval).

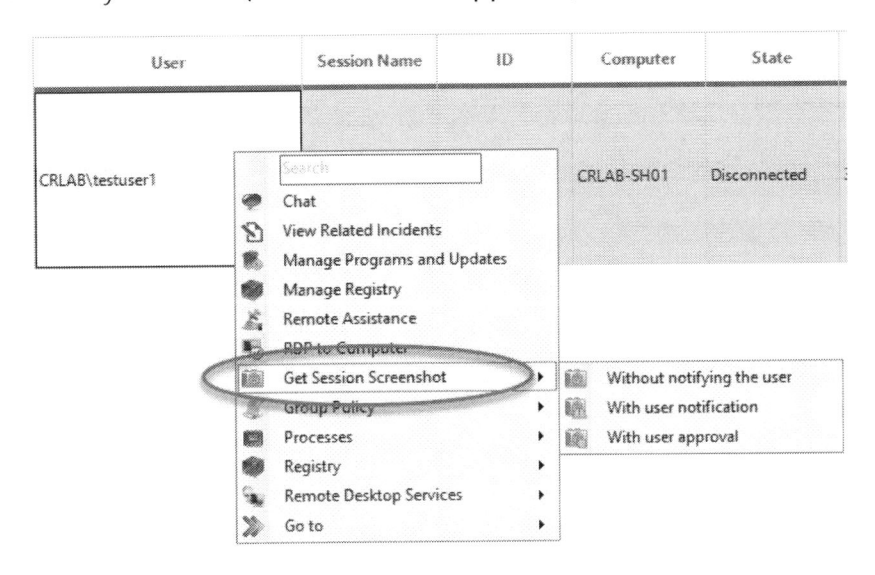

Once you select an option, you should see the session screenshot in a separate window, allowing you to save it.

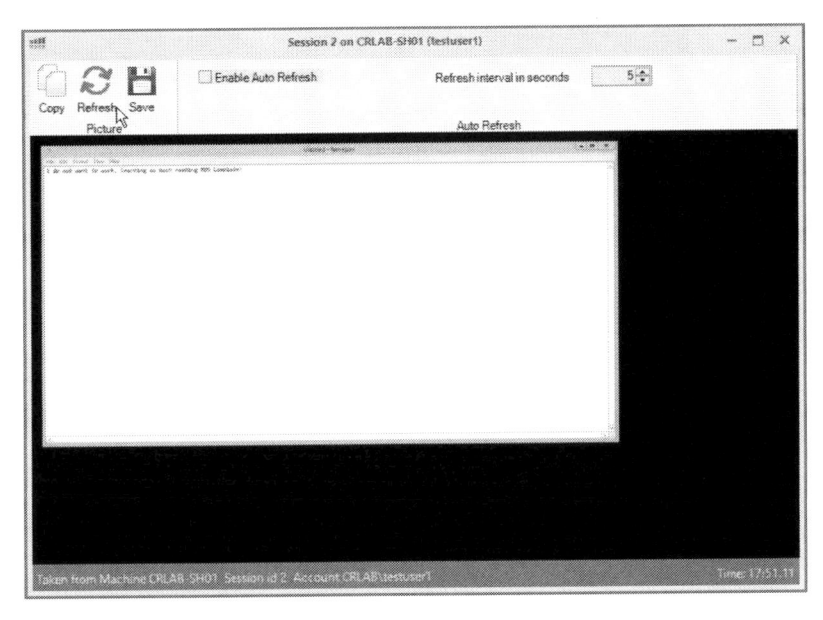

You may say you could do something similar by simply remote controlling the user and then taking a screenshot. Sure thing, you can. The difference is, it not only takes much longer to do it but also requires the user permission, what is not the case here. Faster and under cover. ☺

Note: keep in mind in certain countries, users must be aware that such mechanisms for session recording are in place and more than that, notified every single time this is actually happening. Therefore, be careful when using this feature, in order to comply with local privacy laws and regulations.

Super Message

Yes, plain RDS does allow you to send a message to your users. But as mentioned before, it is a one-way thing. ControlUp does have the 'Chat' option we have seen before but sometimes all you want is to get back from the user something as simple as a 'Yes' or 'No'. Super message does exactly that! As before, right-click a user and select 'Send Super Message'.

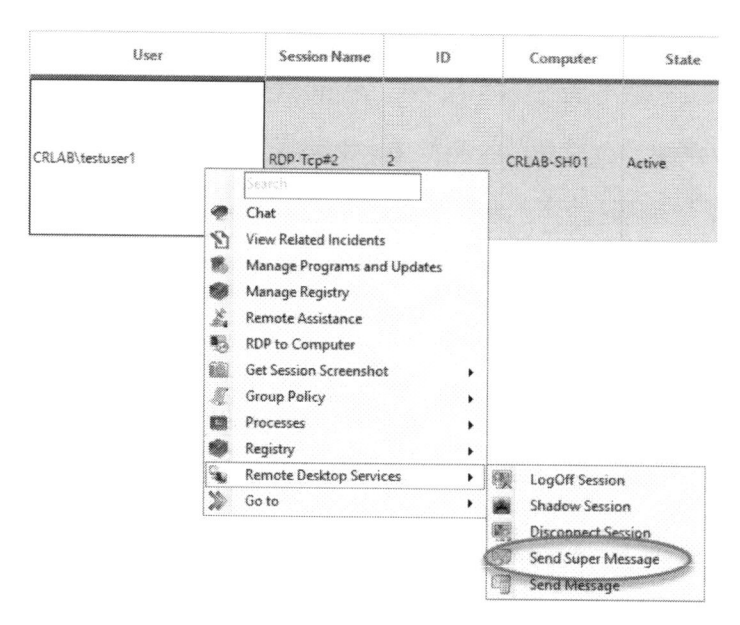

You can then select several different options for the message, including being always on top (so the user cannot tell you he did not see it) and get an actual answer from him (whatever you want on the buttons!). Extremely simple and handy.

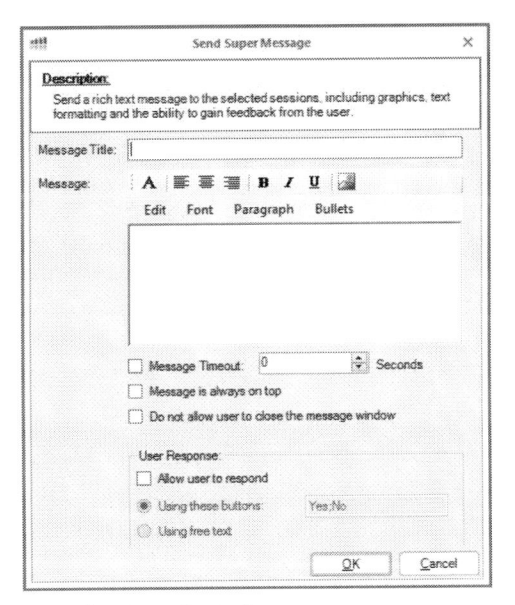

Once you send the message, this is what the user sees:

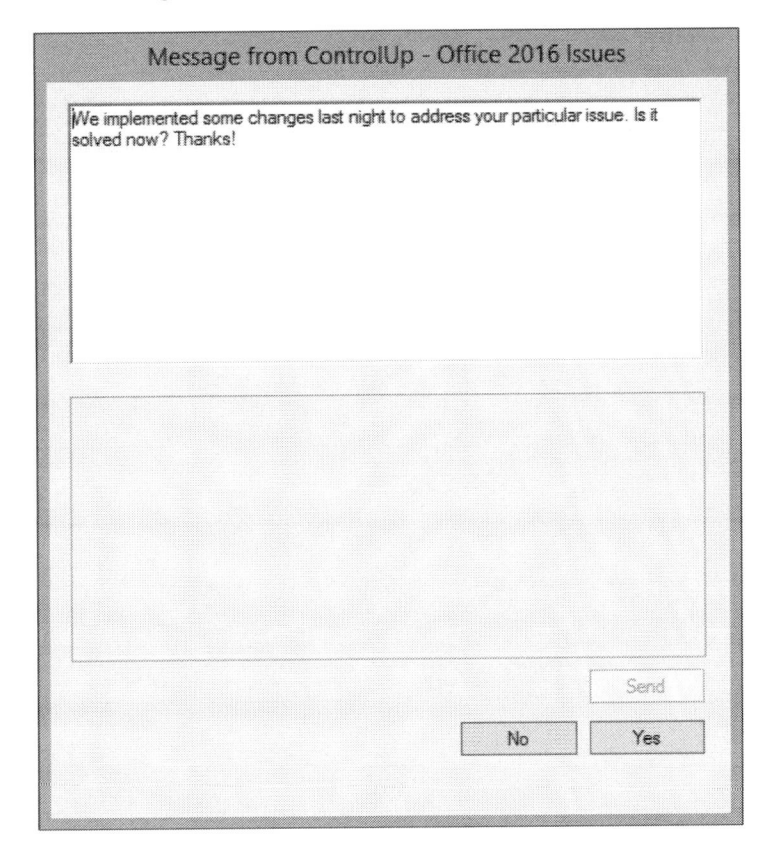

In addition, on the console itself, you can see what the user actually responded:

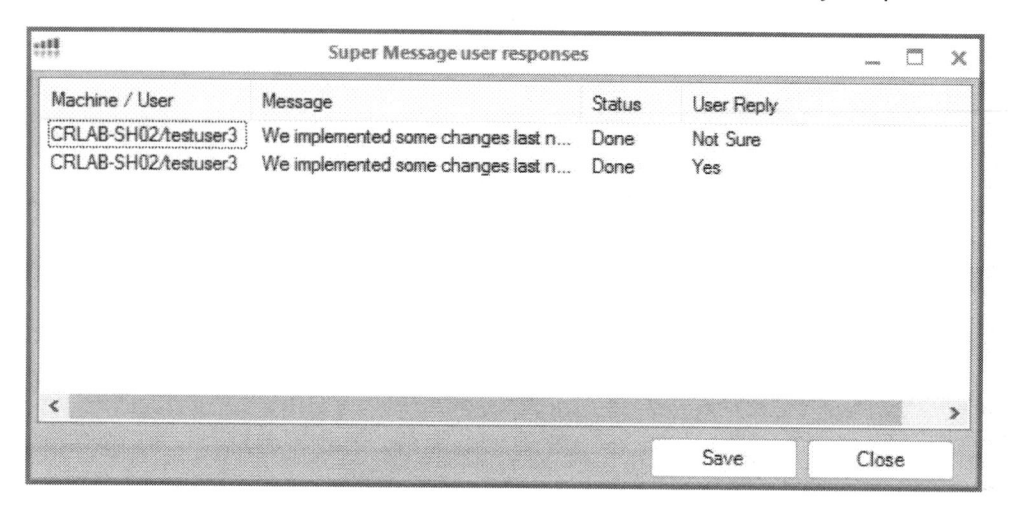

Machine / User	Message	Status	User Reply
CRLAB-SH02/testuser3	We implemented some changes last n...	Done	Not Sure
CRLAB-SH02/testuser3	We implemented some changes last n...	Done	Yes

The best part? You can save all the responses you got for that particular message, in CSV format. Ready for Excel. ☺ Nice!

We could go on and on about 'ControlUp Real-time'. It is that powerful. After all, this is a book about RDS 2012 R2 and not ControlUp. ☺

That said, we are sure you now have a very good understanding of 'ControlUp Real-time' and what it can do for you. So, head out to their website to learn even more about it.

http://www.controlup.com/RDS2012R2Complete

Printed in Great Britain
by Amazon